International
Psychology

International

Psychology

VIEWS FROM AROUND THE WORLD

EDITED BY VIRGINIA STAUDT SEXTON

AND JOHN D. HOGAN

UNIVERSITY OF NEBRASKA PRESS   LINCOLN & LONDON

© 1992 by the University of Nebraska Press
All rights reserved
Manufactured in the United States of America

The paper in this book meets the minimum
requirements of American National Standard
for Information Sciences—Permanence of
Paper for Printed Library Materials,
ANSI Z39.48–1984.

Library of Congress Cataloging-in-
Publication Data
International psychology : views from around
the world / edited by Virginia Staudt Sexton
and John D. Hogan.
    p. cm.
   Includes bibliographical references and
index.
    ISBN 0-8032-4184-4 (alk. paper)
    1. Psychology.   2. Psychology—History.
I. Sexton, Virginia Staudt.   II. Hogan,
John D., 1939–   .
B121.I5645   1992
150'.9—dc20   91-32299
                CIP

Contents

Preface

Psychology around the World (Sexton & Misiak, 1976) received many favorable reviews, and years later it was still being cited for the extent of its contribution. Over (1984), for example, identified the volume as the major source of information in the English language about national psychologies, and Gilgen and Gilgen (1987) called it "the most significant publication relative to the internationalizing of psychology."

In the years since that publication, interest in international psychology has grown, and many articles, chapters, and books have appeared. Much of the relevant work is scattered, however, with only a few broadly based references available. Moreover, the early volume is out of print. Clearly, it is time for an updated volume.

Henryk Misiak enthusiastically endorsed the project but was unable to participate. Instead, a new partnership was born which, among other advantages, had the coeditors located in the same building at the same university and with constant and easy access to one another.

Because all the chapters were to be new, we reviewed the criteria by which countries were included. The earlier edition used countries that were listed in the 1966 *International Directory of Psychologists* and that had reached a certain density of psychologists in the general population. Twenty-eight countries and three regions (Latin America; sub-Saharan Africa; and Armenia) were selected in that way. For this volume, we chose those countries that were member nations of the International Union of Psychological Science. This choice guaranteed a certain degree of structure and national development in psychology since the union (usually abbreviated IUPsyS) is an organization of national psychological societies, not of individuals. At the time of our selection (the fall of 1986), forty-eight countries were members of the IUPsyS. Countries that joined later were not included. Three other entries were carried over from the early edition for the sake of continuity (Armenia, Austria, and Greece).

Unfortunately, there were two countries, Panama and Nicaragua, from which we were unable to obtain a commitment. The political climate of the time undoubtedly was the major obstacle. Furthermore, although we had agreements signed by authors from four other countries (Bulgaria, China, Denmark, and Sweden) and we had extended their deadlines by more than 2 years, we never received their manuscripts. Finally, we had to proceed without them. If we have one regret about this volume, it is the omission of those countries.

There was never any doubt as to which authors we would ask to write the chapters. We simply wanted the most knowledgeable authors available, preferably native ones. We also wanted the manuscript in English. This last requirement was dictated by the experience of the early edition, in which translations were expensive, placed great demands on accuracy, and resulted in considerable lost time.

It was many months before we were able to identify and reach agreement with all the authors, but their participation was worth the effort. We are proud that our contributors, five of whom also wrote for the early edition, are among the most distinguished psychologists in their respective countries. In the few cases in which non-native authors were used, they came to us with the highest recommendations and with impeccable credentials.

Each author received a page allotment based on our estimate of the size and development of the discipline in the country. We were not rigid on page count, returning only two chapters for drastic cutting and retaining several others that went significantly beyond our requested length. In the latter case, a few authors made special requests to extend their chapters and we found it difficult to refuse. Most of the chapters, however, were the approximate length requested.

Each author also received a page of guidelines. These were more detailed than for the early edition because we hoped to compare some characteristics across all countries. At the same time, we did not expect total uniformity in presentation. Instead, we anticipated that the organization and content would be directed, at least to some extent, by national needs and circumstances. We were particularly interested in learning the degree to which national psychologies were largely translations of the psychologies of other, more developed nations. We also wished to know the extent to which truly indigenous psychologies were emerging, if any. This last item has become a matter of some debate. Some believe there is only one psychology, despite the happenstance of geography (e.g., Matarazzo, 1987; Kunkel, 1989). Others make a case for multiple psychologies (e.g., Moghaddam, 1987). Still others argue that the development of an indigenous psychology can be a sign of maturity in the discipline (e.g., Azuma, quoted in Rosenzweig, 1984, p. 880).

Some of the guideline questions explored specific aspects of the profession (e.g., the status of licensure); others involved broader questions aimed at the development of the science (e.g., the nature and extent of research support). Our intention was to generate a broad view of each country's psychology, as a general introduction for the interested reader. Among the many questions, there were nine core areas in which we hoped to make direct comparisons among all the countries: (1) the definition of a psychologist, (2) the number of psychologists and their growth or decline over the years, (3) male/female ratios in the discipline, (4) the state of licensure or certification, (5) the proportion of "science versus practice," (6) public image, (7) major influences, (8) national emphases, and (9) future directions.

We realized from the beginning that some problems were implicit in our approach. For instance, our viewpoint was that of psychologists from the USA. Whatever care was taken in developing the guidelines, they were bound to reflect our geographic and educational origins. Also, we hoped that information on national psychologies would be as available to others as it is to us in the USA. For some countries, that was true; for others, it was demonstrably not. A third item of difficulty was the matter of references. Authors in the early edition supplied the volume with long lists of references, many of them in foreign languages and not readily available to the reader. The publisher was reluctant to print them. Consequently, an agreement was reached to limit the references. With that history in mind, we limited the authors in this volume to 10 references. We soon saw the difficulty of holding to that number for the chapter on the United States. On the other hand, some authors chose to list fewer than 10 references.

Despite the difficulties, we are proud that we are able to present 45 countries from six continents in this volume. For that, we owe the greatest thanks to the 55 authors who contributed. This work would have been impossible without their generous and thoughtful participation.

There is a host of others to whom we also owe thanks. Richard Sexton, Catherine Casella, and Florence Staudt reviewed and corrected the manuscript each step of the way. The Chair of the St. John's University Department of Psychology, Louis H. Primavera; the Dean of Graduate Arts and Sciences, Paul T. Medici, and the Academic Vice-President, Barbara L. Morris, were continuously sensitive to our needs and helped lighten our load in many ways. Megan Missett, Aldo Tartaglini, Alicia Kaplan, and Wesley Brown, doctoral fellows in the Department of Psychology, assisted in compiling the indices and charts and handled much of the library work and related chores. Members of the University Word Processing Center typed and retyped what must have seemed an endless series of chapters, with more unfamiliar names and accent marks than most people see in a lifetime. Finally, the departmental secretaries, Helen Czanowicki and Jo Abrusci, handled many other details related to the publication of the volume, including nurturance and support for the editors.

Bibliography

Gilgen, A. R., & Gilgen, C. K. (1987). *International handbook of psychology*. New York: Greenwood Press.

Kunkel, J. H. (1989). How many psychologies are there? [Comment]. *American Psychologist, 44,* 573–574.

Matarazzo, J. D. (1987). There is only one psychology, no specialties, but many applications. *American Psychologist, 42,* 893–903.

Moghaddam, F. M. (1987). Psychology in the three worlds: As reflected by the crisis in social psychology and the move toward indigenous third-world psychology. *American Psychologist, 42,* 912–920.

Over, R. (1984). Psychology and psychologists in Europe: A bibliography of English language publications. *Psychological Documents, 14,* 19. (Ms. No. 2638).

Rosenzweig, M. R. (1984). U. S. psychology and world psychology. *American Psychologist, 39,* 877–884.

Sexton, V. S., & Misiak, H. (1976). *Psychology around the world*. Monterey, CA: Brooks/Cole.

A Panoramic View

The United States has been the principal guardian of psychology during a vital formative period. . . . But this custody cannot be expected to last forever, and it is no doubt a good thing that it cannot.—D. E. Berlyne

This volume is intended to serve several purposes. On the most basic level, it is an exposition on the state of psychology as it exists today in a group of diverse countries around the world. Included are descriptions of theoretical emphases, practical applications, the state of licensure—in short, a whole series of remarks meant to characterize the development of psychology, both as a science and as a profession, in the country under consideration. The emphasis is on the period from 1960 to the present, although some authors have chosen to provide a more historical view. If the information from each chapter does nothing more, it should serve as a vehicle of mutual introduction to a worldwide network of occupational kinfolk, many of whom have scant knowledge of one another.

On another level, this volume is meant to be a cross-national study of psychology itself, with all of the clarifying potential and inherent difficulty such a study implies. Just as early cross-cultural researchers investigated different styles of living, hoping to identify the essential nature of the human being, this anthology has the potential to shed some light on what may be essential to the discipline of psychology. But just as with those early researchers, the potential is limited. Psychology, as a social science, differs from other sciences. By its very nature, it is more likely to be involved in the context in which it develops. The form that psychology takes in different countries, the manner in which it gives evidence of a national flavor or fails to, should in itself serve as a kind of instruction.

Finally, this volume may succeed on a more subtle level, which may be the most exciting aspect of all—as a window to the future. The history of modern psychology, as it is usually described, has clear geographic underpinnings. Beginning in Europe, with its strongest development in Germany, the power base of psychology shifted to the United States by the 1930s, and there it has remained for more than half a century. But the power base in the USA has never been all-encompassing. Innovations have continued to emerge from Europe even in recent years (e.g., clinical neuropsychology, sport psychology), and questions have been raised about the potential contribution of other approaches to psychology (e.g., Asian psychology). It may be that significant changes for the future of worldwide psychology are spoken of quietly in the pages of some of the chapters that follow. In any case, the diverse voices of psychology from around the world are available if we wish to listen.

Psychologists in the USA: An Isolated Group

It has been estimated that most of the world's psychologists work in the United States, where most of the research and publication in psychology take place (e.g., Ardila, 1982a). But as a sad corollary, it must also be said that psychologists in the USA show little interest in psychological activities outside of their country.

It is not difficult to understand some of their reasons. So many journals are published in the USA that it is a formidable task to keep up with them, much less to consider reading journals of other countries. In addition, only a small number of psychologists in the USA can read any language other than English. Even the traditional foreign-language requirement, once generally imposed for the completion of the psychology doctoral degree, has been largely abandoned. That is the current state of affairs. But it is also true that "no society in today's world can long exist in isolation—nor can its sciences or its professions" (Russell, 1984, p. 1022).

Sexton (1983) described American psychology as xenophobic, noting that journals published abroad cite American publications far more frequently than vice versa. When *Time* magazine published a special issue in 1986 entitled "America's Best," it asked a group of noted individuals from five continents to present their views of the ways in which Americans excel. Carlos Fuentes, a Mexican writer, commented: "What the U.S. does *best* is to understand itself. What it does *worst*, is to understand others." Many feel that North American psychologists have contributed little to international understanding. In their pursuit of psychology as a science, the history and tradition of other cultures were considered irrelevant. And yet the benefits of such an understanding are already apparent and would seem to be increasing.

A survey conducted by Gilgen (1982) is instructive. He asked a random sample of the members of the American Psychological Association (among others) to rank the most influential psychologists in the USA in the post–World War II period. Persons included in the top 10 were Freud, Piaget, Erikson, Lewin, and Jung. Need it be emphasized that this half of the top 10 were neither born nor educated in the USA? Some of the names listed not far behind included Fisher, Adler, Fromm, Eysenck, Lorenz, and Köehler. Surely, all are contributors to be reckoned with and, again, all were born and educated outside of the USA. Perhaps it is too easily forgotten that "psychological statistics, intelligence testing, Pavlovian conditioning, psychoanalysis, Gestalt psychology, the Rorschach test, and many other theoretical approaches, methods, and tools came to America from Europe" (Sexton & Misiak, 1984, p. 1026).

Some of these contributions were the result of a historical aberration that led to the flight of European intellectuals to the USA in the period surrounding World War II. But many of the contributions emerged from completely different contexts: for example, the influence of Piaget or the British tradition in statistics and psychometrics. The fact is that European influence on USA psychology did not end when students from the USA stopped attending European universities or when the informal trading of ideas among academic psychologists began to wane in the early part of the century. It exists even now, and it appears to be expanding.

More than two decades ago Berlyne (1968) issued an eerie warning: "Most of the important advances in psychology of the next few decades will, it is safe to predict, grow out of American psychology. But many of these will take place outside of the United States" (p. 452). There is evidence that he was correct, but it may be some time before we can judge the extent of his accuracy. Just as it took decades for American psychologists to become acquainted with Piaget, it may take years for the typical psychologist to learn of other innovators. The likelihood that the discipline could open itself up to thinkers from even more unfamiliar cultures (e.g., Asia and Africa) seems that much more remote.

There is one other reason for psychologists to become acquainted with the psychologies of other nations—to gain a better understanding of their own psychology. To be immersed so totally in one national psychology is to be blind to the assumptions of that psychology. Psychologists in the USA are limited in direct proportion to their lack of historical and cross-national understanding. To be exposed to national psychologies that have not simply repeated the same research questions and methods but, instead, have tried to reformulate their disciplines to reflect local issues and needs should be an exhilarating experience. In such an environment lies the potential for constructing entirely new conceptions of the human experience and the opportunity to refocus old conceptions. In either case, it may be an occasion to question aspects of psychology which would go unchallenged without the benefit of cross-national comparison.

In their evaluation of psychology in the USA, representatives from other countries have sometimes found the discipline to be "alien" (Ardila, 1982b,

p. 120), infused with "feelings of general superiority" (Brandt, 1970, p. 1093), and even trivial (Schwendler, 1984, p. 14). It is surely worth investigating the sources of those remarks. Perhaps, in the process, psychologists in the USA can use these characterizations to expand their understanding of the strengths and limits of their own national discipline.

The Changing Face of International Psychology

The history of modern psychology, though brief, has described a discipline of remarkable change. Its lessons, when understood, promote an acceptance of change—that it is an error to think that the psychology of today will necessarily be the psychology of tomorrow. "Relatively rapid changes in social concerns during the past half century have been reflected in changes in the roles for psychologists that a society is willing to support. What has been acceptable during one decade has received highly emotional criticism in the next" (Russell, 1984, p. 1019). It seems inevitable that as the world changes, psychology around the world will also change and that, ultimately, some of these changes will become important points of interest, demanding our attention.

Rosenzweig (1984) has indicated not only that the formal discipline of psychology is spreading to countries in which it did not previously exist, but that its growth in many countries is more rapid than in the USA. As a consequence, American psychology will become a continually smaller part of the international psychological community. Presumably, its power will also decrease. That is not expected to happen soon. Through its size, the influence of its leaders, and the power of its journals and research centers, the USA will remain in the forefront for some time to come. But it is already in competition with other countries on some measures. For example, in density of psychologists (i.e., the number of psychologists per population), five other countries approximate the levels found in the USA (Rosenzweig, 1984).

Rosenzweig points to two additional items that will lead to further growth in international psychology. The first is the fact that in many psychological subfields there is considerable expertise found outside of the USA. Researchers and professionals who are on the "cutting edge" ignore national boundaries and the inconvenience of unfamiliar languages. They seek creative thinkers wherever they are found. Communication among these leaders will automatically result in an expansion in the international psychological community.

The second item mentioned by Rosenzweig is the need for international cooperation to conduct certain kinds of research. "There are important psychological endeavors that require international cooperation and that cannot be achieved by the psychological community of any single nation, however strong and well organized it may be" (Rosenzweig, 1984, p. 877). As one example, it is increasingly common for publications in cross-cultural psychology to have contributors who represent several different countries. In another area, the cooperation among international investigators in developmental psychology has become highly visible and seems to increase on a yearly basis. Members of other subfields could undoubtedly cite further examples of cross-national cooperation.

Yet another source of growth for international psychology must surely be due to the increased visibility and importance of international organizations of psychologists. They serve as a source of both personal and professional exchange. They include the International Association of Applied Psychology (IAAP), the oldest international society of psychologists; the International Council of Psychologists (ICP), originally an association of women psychologists organized as part of the World War II effort; and the International Union of Psychological Science. Other opportunities for information exchange include the World Congress for Mental Health, the Interamerican Congress of Psychology, the European Association of Experimental Psychology, the International Society of Comparative Psychology, l'Association de Psychologic Scientifique de Langue Française, the International Society for the Study of Behavioral Development, and with its start in 1989, the European Congress of Psychology.

The Future of International Psychology

It should be noted that some observers offer a less optimistic assessment of the state of international psychology. Ardila (1982a) has written persuasively on the negative effect of the dominance by the USA, arguing that the world view of psychology is limited to a specific culture in a specific moment in history. "Interest in psychology is worldwide, but as long as the discipline is so much influenced by one culture (and it does not matter which culture) there cannot be a truly international psychology" (p. 328).

Smith (1983) disagreed with Ardila's notion of American dominance and introduced another notion as well. He proposed that the "English-only" psychology may be the one that suffers the significant disadvantage. Psychologists from other countries often read English publications, but it is the "English-only" psychologists who are isolated from the significant publications of other countries.

Howard et al. (1986) documented the dramatic changes that have taken place in psychology in the USA in recent decades. Among the more note-worthy are the huge increase in the number of psychologists, the continuing gender shift to a more female profession, and the modification in special-ization from the research and academically oriented subfields to the health-service-provider specialties. If they continue, these changes predict a differ-ent form for psychology in the USA in the next century.

How is it around the world? Are the same forces working to influence psychology in other countries? Rosenzweig's data (1982) suggest that at least some of the trends in the USA may hold worldwide—for example, the tre-mendous growth in the number of psychologists (as seen by the 94 percent overall increase in his sample from 1969 to 1979). They also suggest that other USA trends may have limited generalizability, such as the increasing dominance of women in the discipline (Rosenzweig, 1982, p. 133). In a larger sense, what interests do psychologists have in common? Are there enough overlapping objectives to speak of an international psychology in one voice? Answers to these and other questions regarding status and change for psy-chology around the world should be found on the pages that follow.

Bibliography

America's best. (1986, June 16). *Time, 127*(24), 52.

Ardila, R. (1982a). International psychology. *American Psychologist, 37*, 323–329.

Ardila, R. (1982b). Psychology in Latin America. *Annual Review of Psychology, 33*, 103–122.

Berlyne, D. E. (1968). American and European psychology. *American Psychologist, 23*, 447–452.

Brandt, L. (1970). American psychology. *American Psychologist, 25*, 1091–1093.

Gilgen, A. R. (1982). *American psychology since World War II: A profile of the discipline.* Westport, CT: Greenwood Press.

Howard, A., Pion, G. M., Gottfredson, G. D., Plattau, P. E., Oskamp, S., Pfafflin, S., Bray, D. W., & Burstein, A. G. (1986). The changing face of American psychology. *American Psychologist, 41*, 1311–1327.

Kunkel, J. H. (1989). How many psychologies are there? [Comment]. *American Psychologist, 44*, 573–574.

Moghaddam, F. M. (1987). Psychology in the three worlds: As reflected by the crisis in social psychology and the move toward indigenous third-world psychology. *American Psychologist, 42*, 912–920.

Rosenzweig, M. R. (1982). Trends in development and status of psychology: An international perspective. *International Journal of Psychology, 17*, 117–140.

Rosenzweig, M. R. (1982). Trends in development and status of psychology: An international perspective. *International Journal of Psychology, 17,* 117–140.

Russell, R. W. (1984). Psychology in its world context. *American Psychologist, 39,* 1017–1025.

Schwendler, W. (1984). UNESCO's project on the exchange of knowledge for endogenous development. *International Journal of Psychology, 19,* 3–15.

Sexton, V. S. (1983). *Is American psychology xenophobic?* Presidential address presented at the annual meeting of the Eastern Psychological Association, Baltimore, MD.

Sexton, V. S., & Misiak, H. (1976). *Psychology around the world.* Monterey, CA: Brooks/Cole.

Sexton, V. S., & Misiak, H. (1984). American psychologists and psychology abroad. *American Psychologist, 39,* 1026–1031.

Smith, R. J. (1983). On Ardila's "International psychology" [Comment]. *American Psychologist, 38,* 122–123.

1 / Argentina

NURIA CORTADA DE KOHAN

Nuria Cortada de Kohan studied at the University N. de Cuyo in Argentina and at Ohio State University in the USA. Her primary areas of interest have been statistics, psychometric methods, and vocational guidance. The author of more than 70 articles for various journals in psychology and education, she is also the editor of such books as Estadística aplicada, *(Applied statistics),* Construcción de pruebas objectivas de rendimiento, *(Construction of objective proficiency tests), and* El professor y la orientación vocacional *(The professor and vocational orientation). A past president of the Argentine Society of Psychology and former director of the Department of Vocational Guidance at the University of Buenos Aires, she is now retired from her position as professor of statistics in psychology and education at the University of Buenos Aires.*

To become a psychologist in Argentina, it is necessary to obtain a degree approximately equivalent to an MA (*licenciado*), which is available from public and private universities. This degree requires 5 years of study and is preceded by 5 years of secondary school. A doctorate may be obtained after following the *licenciado* at the universities of Buenos Aires, Rosario, Córdoba, Tucumán, and San Luis, among others. The doctorate implies supervised graduate study for approximately 2 more years plus a dissertation that is approved by a panel of selected professors. Most of the psychologists now working in Argentina have been trained locally; only a few have degrees from foreign universities, mainly the USA and France.

It is difficult to estimate the total number of psychologists in the country, but lately it has become a popular vocational choice. Given the yearly increase in the number of students, one estimate places the number of *licenciados* in psychology at around 10,000, of which approximately 80 percent are women.

In the 1960s psychologists worked mostly in mental hospitals or private clinics. Now it is not unusual to find psychologists working in general hospitals, primary and secondary schools, research laboratories, educational institutions, government agencies, business organizations, and so on. Clinical psychologists predominate, however, and most of them are psychoanalytically oriented.

In 1974 the Bureau of Public Health granted a certification of license to those interested in the independent practice of psychology.

Psychology as an independent university career was started around 1957. Previously, psychological studies were offered in schools of philosophy. Since the turn of the century, many people have been interested in psychology, some of them quite prominent. Among them, for instance, were Victor Mercante, Horacio Piñero, Rodolfo Senet, Alfredo Calcagno, José Ingenieros, Enrique Mouchet, Anibal Ponce, and Telma Reca, all of whom pioneered studies in experimental psychology (Gottheld, 1969). Almost all of them came from the fields of medicine, psychiatry, neurology, or education. They made important contributions that are now mainly of historical interest.

Between 1950 and 1955 those interested in psychological research or in the treatment of problem children recognized the need for the development of psychology as a career (Rimoldi, 1957), and between 1957 and 1960 psychology was organized formally as an independent field, though usually as a subdepartment of the schools of humanities (Bertin, 1974). Now approximately 20 universities, some public and some private, have separate schools of psychology with their own housing, faculty, deans, and so on.

Education

The following list of subjects included in most psychology curricula at different universities provides an idea of the requirements needed to become a psychologist. The differences among universities are mostly in the emphasis placed in different areas. Usually, the studies have an introductory stage, a basic stage, and a specialized stage.

In the introductory cycle, which lasts about 2 years, the subjects are the following: (1) introduction to psychology, (2) introduction to sociology, (3) introduction to biology, (4) introduction to anthropology, (5) logic and epistemology, (6) anatomy and physiology of the nervous system, (7) elementary courses in mathematics, and (8) language courses chosen from English, French, Italian, or German.

In the basic cycle, which also lasts about 2 years, the subjects are (1) one or two courses in general psychology, (2) one or two courses in child and adolescent psychology, (3) social psychology, (4) personality, (5) history of psychology, (6) psychoanalysis, (7) one or two courses in statistics, (8) research in psychology, (9) theory and practice of mental tests, (10) projective techniques, and (11) mental health.

Four areas are usually included in the specialized cycle: clinical, educational, industrial, and social psychology. Six subjects are usually chosen among many courses, such as (1) clinical psychology for children, (2) clinical psychology for adults, (3) psychopathology and neurology, (4) vocational guidance, (5) Rorschach, (6) institutional psychology, (7) human relations, (8) market techniques, (9) juvenile delinquency, (10) school psychology, and (11) exceptional children.

Journals

A few specialized journals are published. The most well known are *Revista Argentina de Psicología* (Journal of Argentine psychology), which has appeared since 1969; *Revista Argentina de Psicoanálisis* (Journal of Argentine psychoanalysis), published by the Society of Psychoanalysis of Argentina since 1955; and *Interdisciplinaria* (a bilingual journal of psychology and related disciplines), published since 1980. At the universities and also at some research centers certain foreign journals of psychology may be received. Among the more common ones are the *Revista de Psicología General y Aplicad* (Madrid, Spain), the *Revista Latinoamericana de Psicología* (Bogotá, Colombia), and the *Revista Interamericana de Psicología*, the official journal of the Interamerican Society of Psychology (SIP).

Professional Associations

In Argentina there are two professional societies of psychology. The first one, founded in 1908, the Sociedad Argentina de Psicología (Argentine Society of Psychology), is predominantly academic. It was organized by Enrique Mouchet and now has little influence in the field. The second is the Sociedad de Psicólogos de Buenos Aires (Association of Buenos Aires Psychologists), which is very active in professional matters. Its membership is approximately 1,200. There are also some other small associations such as the Society for Social Psychologists, the Society for Vocational Guidance Counselors, and a society for experimental psychologists which is currently in formation.

Financial Support

There is no special governmental financial support for psychology. Now that psychology has attained the same status as other professions, however, many possibilities for funding exist in the form of scholarships given by the universities and also financial assistance by CONICET, the Consejo Nacional de Investigaciones Científicas y Técnicas (National Research Council of Argentina). This institution also provides financial support to some research centers in psychology.

Research

One of the most important centers for research is the Interdisciplinary Center of Research in Mathematical and Experimental Psychology, organized in 1971 and directed by H. Rimoldi. Its staff includes more than 30 full-time research scientists interested in different problems mainly in the cognitive area. The center has an excellent library and computational sections, receives foreign scientists, and sends investigators abroad. Several projects have been undertaken with foreign universities, and others are now in progress. Another research center is the Laboratory of Sensorial Research, directed by M. Guirao. There are also some centers for child clinical psychology, as well as a Center of Neurology and Psychology, directed by J. Azcoaga.

Universities have some limited financial resources for research. At the University of Buenos Aires, there is a Center for Vocational Guidance organized to help the students of the university in their vocational choices. Research problems pertaining to vocational choice, psychometrics, and standardization of intelligence tests, as well as evaluation of aptitudes and interests, have been conducted by its former director (Cortada de Kohan, 1978; Ardila, 1968).

Outside Buenos Aires the work by O. Oñativia, at the University of Salta; by P. Horas, at the University of San Luis; by A. Vilanova, at the University of Mar del Plata; by J. Bianchi, at the University of Tucumán; by H. Fogliatto, Arias de Miranda, and others, at the University of Córdoba, are noteworthy. Their fields of interest cover a wide range, including school psychology, projective techniques, juvenile delinquency, vocational guidance, psychometrics, and disabled children.

Public Acceptance

It must be emphasized that the role of the psychologist is now recognized and accepted by the layperson in Argentina. In this sense, much has improved. Today in Argentina psychologists appear often on radio and television, and public lectures on psychological issues always attract a large audience. It is not unusual for mothers to seek the advice of psychologists for their children, and vocational guidance at the end of secondary school is regarded as a real need by parents and teachers.

Future Trends

As stressed previously, psychology during the 1960s and 1970s was strongly influenced by psychoanalysis. It was as if the main goal of the psychologist was the practice of psychotherapy, but that is changing. Lately, more emphasis has been placed on social psychology. Many experimental psychologists have also found new areas of research interest. Psychology in Argentina appears to be growing in a positive direction, with the hope of attaining some higher scientific status.

Bibliography

Ardila, R. (1971). *Los pioneros de la psicología*. Buenos Aires: Paidos.

Bertin, M. A. (1974). *An overview of psychology in Latin America*. Chicago: Department

Bertin, M. A. (1974). *An overview of psychology in Latin America*. Chicago: Department of the Navy, Chicago Branch, Office of Naval Research, 35.

Cortada de Kohan, Nuria. (1978). La psicología en la Argentina. In R. Ardila (Ed.), *La profesión del psicólogo* (pp. 31–42). Mexico City: Trillas.

Gottheld, R. (1969). Historia de la psicología en la Argentina. *Revista Latinoamericana de Psicología, 1,* 13–33 and 183–198.

Rimoldi, H. J. A. (1957). El problema científico universitario argentino. *Ciencia e Investigación, 6,* 40–46.

2 / Armenia

HAGOP S. PAMBOOKIAN

Hagop S. Pambookian (born 1932) received his PhD from the University of Michigan in 1972. A specialist in educational and developmental psychology, he has written for various journals, including the Journal of Educational Psychology, Instructional Science, *the* Journal of School Psychology, *and the* Encyclopedia of Special Education. *He taught as a Senior Fulbright Fellow, lecturing in Armenian, his native language, at the Yerevan State University in the Armenian SSR and was the first US scholar to receive a 9-month Fulbright Fellowship in psychology for the USSR. Pambookian is associate professor of psychology at Shawnee State University in Portsmouth, Ohio.*

From the early years of their history, Armenians have shown an interest in theology, philosophy, the arts, education, and other humanities and sciences. But it was the creation of the Armenian alphabet by Mesrob Mashtotz in the year 405 that facilitated the opening of schools and centers of scholarship in the country; made possible the translation of the works of Plato, Aristotle, and lesser-known philosophers and writers; and gave rise to an intellectually stimulating environment in which Armenian philosophical and educational thinking could flourish.

Thus, from the 5th century on, Tavit Anhaght ("the Invincible"), Anania Shiragatzi, Hovhannes Yerzengatzi, Krikor Datevatzi, and Mekhitar Heratzi, among other intellectuals, tackled various issues in philosophy, metaphysics, mathematics, logic, anatomy, medicine, grammar, theology, and ethics. Anhaght, who lived during the 5th and 6th centuries, wrote about the psychological foundation of cognition, logical thinking, and ethical behavior. Datevatzi, who died in 1410, refuted the "innateness of ideas and morality" concept almost 300 years before John Locke's description of the mind as a *tabula rasa*. Scholarship and psychological thought were developed further during the Middle Ages at universities such as Klatzor, Datev, Ani, Sanaheen, and Haghpad.

Psychoeducational observations and analyses were made by writers, educators, and philosophers long before psychology became an established discipline. For example, in the 19th century Khachadoor Apovian, Mikayel

Nalbandian, Steppanos Nazaryantz, and Ghazaros Aghayan all wrote essays on psychological issues. In the early 1900s psychology was taught in several Armenian higher schools and institutes, including the Kevorkian Seminary in Echmiadzin.

Early Influences

Two important traditions, Wundtian and Pavlovian, played a decisive role in the development of psychology in Soviet Armenia in the 1930s. A student of Wilhelm Wundt, Koorken Edilian (1885–1942), who studied at the universities of Jena, Leipzig, and Berne and was influenced by Wundt, Hermann Ebbinghaus, and Hugo Münsterberg, had an indelible impact on the development of Soviet experimental psychology. It was Edilian who founded the first Armenian experimental laboratory in psychology, who was the first psychology lecturer at the Yerevan State University, and who developed the first psychology course in higher education. He was also a founder of the Yerevan State University in 1920. In recognition of his many contributions, the Armenian government named a school after him.

Two of Ivan P. Pavlov's talented students, Levon A. Orbeli (1882–1958) and Ezras A. Asratian (1903–1981), were instrumental in bringing the Pavlovian tradition to Armenia. They researched and further publicized their teacher's theories of conditioned reflex and higher nervous activity.

Orbeli went to St. Petersburg (Leningrad) in 1899 at age 17 and graduated, 5 years later, from its Military Medical Academy. Pavlov was his teacher there. Following the defense of his doctoral dissertation in 1908, Orbeli began a lifelong career at Petrograd's Institute of Experimental Medicine (1907–1920) and the First Institute of Medicine (1920–1931). After Pavlov's death in 1936, he became the director of the I. P. Pavlov Institute of Physiology (1936–1950) and, after its establishment in 1956, the director of the I. M. Sechenov Institute of Physiological Evolution, of the USSR Academy of Sciences.

Orbeli has written extensively on the conditioned reflex, higher nervous activity, and evolution in physiology and had a significant influence on physiology in Armenia and other Soviet republics. Prominent among his students were Asratian, Ardashess H. Karamian, and A. Aleksanian. Orbeli has been honored in his native country and in the USSR: the Armenian Academy of Sciences named the Scientific Research Institute of Physiology after him (in 1959), the USSR Academy of Sciences established the L. A. Orbeli Prize for the best scientific work in physiology, and the Yerevan Institute of Medicine instituted the L. A. Orbeli Scholarship program for students. Orbeli was named a member of the USSR Academy of Sciences (1935) and the Academy of Medical Sciences (1935), as well as of the Armenian Academy of Sciences (1943).

The other noted follower of Pavlovian tradition was Ezras A. Asratian. Although a student in the Faculty of Agriculture at the Yerevan State University, Asratian became interested in biology after reading Pavlov's writings on the higher nervous system. He went to Leningrad, where he met Levon Orbeli and Ivan Pavlov. It was Pavlov who advised the young man to enter the Institute of Medicine. Asratian returned to Armenia and studied medicine while lecturing at the Yerevan State University, where he established the first physiology laboratory in the Armenian Republic. After receiving his doctorate in Leningrad, he began a productive association as Pavlov's assistant and friend.

Returning to Armenia after World War II, Asratian directed the Research Institute of Physiology of the Academy of Sciences in Yerevan; 3 years later he moved to Moscow. There he established the Research Institute of Higher Nervous Activity and Neurophysiology of the Soviet Academy of Sciences and remained its director until his death. Asratian also directed the Laboratory for the Restoration of the Functions of the Nervous System and the Institute of Higher Nervous Activity.

Asratian developed and disseminated Pavlov's concepts and theories further, including an analysis of his teacher's writings and research. He discussed these and related matters in his 1979 book *Ivan Petrovich Pavlov*. Although written in Armenian, this book was not a precise translation of the 1974 Russian edition of the same-named volume. The book in Armenian differs from all publications on Pavlov and is likely to be the most authoritative and definitive work on the Russian physiologist/psychologist.

Asratian received the I. P. Pavlov Prize (in 1951) and the I. P. Pavlov Gold Medal (in 1963) for the best scientific work in physiology and research on Pavlov's concepts and theories. Asratian became a corresponding member of the USSR Academy of Sciences (1939) and a member of the Armenian Academy of Sciences (1947). The Armenian government named a street after him in Yerevan and issued a commemorative stamp bearing his portrait.

Several other psychologists contributed to the early development of psychology in Armenia, including Boris G. Ananiev (1907–1972), Yevgeni A. Millerian (1913–1983), and Megerdich A. Mazmanian (1910–1977).

Ananiev grew up in a family of an Armenian teacher but lived and worked in Leningrad. Graduating from the Gorskii Pedagogical Institute, he completed his postgraduate studies at the V. M. Bekhterev Institute for the Study of the Brain. In 1967 Ananiev became dean of the Faculty of Psychology at the Leningrad State University, where he conducted research and prepared students for various areas of Soviet psychology. He investigated sensation, sensory perception and thinking, and educational and applied psychology. In 1968 Ananiev became a member of the Academy of Sciences of the USSR.

Millerian lived and worked in Kiev, the capital of the Ukrainian SSR. A doctor of psychological sciences (1968) and full professor (1969), Millerian was associated for many years with the Research Institute of Psychology, of the Ukrainian Ministry of Education, in Kiev. He was employed there as a researcher before becoming the director of the institute's Psychology of Work sector. But in 1975 he came to Armenia and directed the Laboratory of the Psychology of Work and the Professional-Technical Training Division of the Khachadoor Apovian Pedagogical Institute in Yerevan.

Millerian did research on the psychology of work and on professional-technical training. He constructed several psychometric instruments that primarily measured attention and volition in the training of pilots and automobile drivers. He wrote more than 150 publications, including the following books in Russian: *The Psychology of Aviator Selection* (1966), *The Psychology of the Formation of Polytechnical Work Skill* (1973), and *An Outline of the Psychology of the Operator* (1974).

Another significant figure in the development of psychology and in the training of psychologists in Armenia was Mazmanian, who graduated from the Yerevan State University Faculty of Pedagogy in 1930. He lectured at the university (1933) and also served as dean and, later, pro-rector at the Valery Pruysov Institute of Russian and Foreign Languages in Yerevan.

In 1951 Mazmanian became the director of the Department of Psychology at the Kh. Apovian Pedagogical Institute and in 1957 became head of its Psychology Laboratory. Under his leadership, the department became an important center for training young psychologists for colleges and research institutes and for preparing textbooks for postsecondary students.

Academician Mazmanian investigated issues and problems in the history of Armenian psychology, theoretical psychology, and the psychology of creativity, especially the role of the unconscious. He provided a conceptual and methodological base for the study of the history of psychology. Mazmanian had a doctorate in psychological sciences (1965) and held the academic rank of full professor (1966). From 1948 to 1952 he edited *Sovedagan Mangavarj* (Soviet educator), the educational monthly of the Armenian Ministry of Education; his books include *Lectures from Psychology* (1959), *Temperament* (1969), and *Issues of Educational Psychology* (1975).

Characteristics of Psychology

Students usually study at one of the 13 institutes and the Yerevan State University in Armenia, but they may receive their college education in any of the 895 institutions of higher learning in the USSR. A student receives a diploma after a 4- or 5-year course of study at an institute or university. To receive the candidate of psychological sciences degree (similar to the PhD in the US), a student must study 3 additional years; take the qualifying examinations in dialectical materialism, a foreign language, and psychology; and write and defend a dissertation. The doctor of psychological sciences degree, a more advanced and highly respected degree, requires additional study, research, and another dissertation and/or relevant publication. Few Soviet psychologists ever receive this doctorate. In fact, only 105, or 10.6 percent, of the 993 Soviet Psychological Society members who had their training in psychology, as listed in the 1985 edition of the *International Directory of Psychologists*, had been awarded the doctorate of psychological sciences degree and had been approved by the Supreme Certifying Commission in Moscow.

Although Yerevan State University, Khachadoor Apovian Pedagogical Institute, the Institute of Physical Culture in Yerevan, and the Valery Pruysov Institute of Russian and Foreign Languages offer courses at the undergraduate level, only the Apovian Pedagogical Institute has a graduate program and is authorized to award the candidate of psychological sciences degree to those specializing in psychology.

Armenian psychology students can pursue their postgraduate studies at a handful of degree-granting universities, pedagogical institutes, or research institutes in the Soviet Union. Psychological education is rather general, and doctoral students get full training in psychology with no concern for overspecialization within the discipline.

Armenian- and Russian-language psychology and education journals publish articles on a wide range of specialties. Psychologists and students of psychology have access to the *Sovedagan Mangavarj* (Soviet educator), a monthly journal published since 1926 (its current editor is psychologist Mikayel H. Megerdchian, candidate of psychological sciences), and *Sovedagan Tebrotz* (Soviet school), published weekly since 1932. In addition, Armenian psychologists can use all the journals and periodicals published in the USSR by various academies. These journals include *Voprosy Psikhologii* (Problems of psychology), published since 1955; *Psikhologicheskii Zhurnal* (Psychological journal), since 1980; *Semya i Shkola* (Family and school), since 1946; and *Sovietskaya Pedagogika* (Soviet pedagogy), since 1937.

Psychology books and textbooks in Armenian (and Russian) are few but in great demand. There is a need for well-written and comprehensive psychology books in Armenian at all levels. The Armenian translations of several basic Russian textbooks are now used in psychology classes at the Yerevan State University, the Kh. Apovian Pedagogical Institute, and the Valery Pruysov Institute of Russian and Foreign Languages.

The Myasnikian State Library in Yerevan and the libraries of Yerevan State University and the Apovian Pedagogical Institute have a few English-language books in general psychology, child psychology, developmental psychology, learning, and motivation. But the best and most up-to-date collection of psychology books and journals in English can be found at the Armenian Academy of Sciences Library (Fundamentalnaya Biblioteka Akademii Nauk) in Yerevan. In recent years this author has sent more than 1,600 psychology books to this library. Among the journals sent thus far are *American Psychologist* (1946–87) and several volumes of other leading journals of the American Psychological Association.

The Armenian Psychological Society (APS), an affiliate/division of the USSR Psychological Society, was formed in 1957 through the efforts of Mazmanian and his colleagues at the Khachadoor Apovian Pedagogical Institute and the Psychology Laboratory. Within a short time, the society had brought together psychologists and other scientists interested in psychological issues and problems. It has had occasional local scientific meetings and organized several Transcaucasian conferences in Armenia, Georgia, and Azerbaijan. Its members participate in regional and all-union psychology conventions throughout the country.

Although listed incompletely in the 1,946-member Soviet Psychological Society's *International Directory of Psychologists,* more than 100 Armenian psychologists now teach at various institutions of higher education and conduct studies at scientific research institutes and psychology laboratories in Armenia and in major cities of the USSR. The APS members are primarily employed at the Kh. Apovian Pedagogical Institute, the Yerevan State University, the Institute of Physical Culture in Yerevan, the Valery Pruysov Institute of Russian and Foreign Languages, the Yerevan State Medical Institute, and the Research Institute of Pedagogy.

Close to 50 percent of the members have training and degrees in psychology, and the remainder are in pedagogy, medicine, and other disciplines. This figure is consistent with the most recent membership data of the Soviet Psychological Society (SPS): 66.4 percent of the SPS members were trained in psychological sciences, 15 percent in pedagogical sciences, and 9 percent in medical and biological sciences. Interestingly, more than half of the APS members are female, but only one of them has a doctor of psychological sciences degree.

There is renewed interest among Armenian psychologists to develop psychological services for the general public to help with personal problems, marital conflicts, and parent-child relationships. Weekly television programs on development, aggression, lying, and parenting, which began a few years ago, reach many segments of society. But psychology as a science and profession needs further strengthening and vitality. Reorganization and farsighted leadership are required to make psychology relevant and respectable.

Current Research

The philosophical concepts of dialectical materialism and the neurophysiological research findings of Pavlov, Orbeli, and Asratian provide the foundation of Armenian psychology.

The dialectical materialistic, or Marxist-Leninist, conception of human beings is essentially a social one. The personality, consciousness, or behavior of individuals, as social beings, is determined by social relationships in a social environment. This environment is indispensable to individual action, development, and change. There is unity between consciousness and behavior, and the individual in society is formed through activities that are basic to the acquisition of knowledge, cognitive development, and personality. Thus human consciousness is of social origin, is developed in society, and is social in its functioning. In Armenia, as well as in the other Soviet republics, the philosophy of dialectical materialism provides the methodological basis for all research and has influenced the nature of human development, childrearing, education, occupation, and work.

At one time or another the following Armenian psychologists have investigated psychoeducational issues and problems at the Psychological Research Laboratory of the Khachadoor Apovian Pedagogical Institute and at the psychology laboratories of the Yerevan State University and the Yerevan Institute of Physical Culture: Hovsep M. Tutunjian, Aleksander A. Lalayan, M. Yeritzian, Albert H. Kostanian, Emma A. Aleksandrian, and Albert A. Nalchajian.

The Laboratory at the Apovian Pedagogical Institute has been an important research center. Beginning in 1959, it has issued several volumes of scientific work and studies. Hovsep Tutunjian is currently head of the Psychology Department at the Yerevan State University, a position he has held since 1976. Receiving his doctor of psychological sciences degree in 1967, Tutunjian was elevated to professor in 1971. A prolific writer, he has authored more than 130 publications on child psychology, and the history of psychology, particularly French history. He introduced Henri Wallon to Armenian and Soviet psychologists. In fact, in his book *Problems of Child*

Psychology (1980), Tutunjian discusses several views on the characteristics of children postulated by French Marxist psychologists Henri Wallon, Rene Zazzo, Pierre Oleron, and Philip Malrieu. Among his other books are *The Principal Psychological Characteristics of the Younger School Child* (1962), *Doubt and Its Role in Logical Thought* (1965), *The Psychological Conception of Henri Wallon* (1966), and *From the History of French Psychology* (1967).

Aleksander Lalayan, who was associated with the Armenian Institute of Physical Culture until his death in 1983, was well known for his studies and publications on sport psychology. He was one of the first in the Soviet Union to investigate psychological training of athletes and to compile a manual, or handbook. Lalayan presented ideas and data on the problems of psychological preparation of athletic competition and the relationship of coach and athlete at congresses on sport psychology as early as 1956 at the First All-Union Conference on Psychology of Sport in Leningrad. Among his many publications are *Psychological Questions of Sports Competition* (1959), *Motivational Qualities of a Basketball Player* (1963), *Outline of the Psychology of Basketball* (1964, coauthored with K. Vartanian), *Psychology of Sport* (1966), *The Teacher of Physical Culture* (1969), and *Psychology: Some Problems* (1980, coauthored with Shavarsh S. Simonian).

Lalayan was also interested in vocational development. In his book *The School and Vocational Orientation* (1977), written in Armenian, he discusses the work done on adolescent vocational development in Armenian schools. He presents research data pertaining to vocational interests and their relationship to teachers, work training, and extracurricular activities, such as the Young Pioneers and the Komsomol (the Young Communist League). He points out the importance of cooperation among the schools and of the family in the youngsters' work interest and orientation. Moreover, he strongly advocates providing assistance not only to 7th, 8th, and 9th graders, but to others who need help in seeking meaningful occupations. (Earlier, in 1973, Lalayan had published a related book on the topic: *Professional Orientation*.)

M. Yeritzian is one of the founders of the Research Laboratory in Psychology at the Apovian Pedagogical Institute. A senior researcher in 1958, he became the director of the institute's educational psychology sector (in 1962) and the head of its Laboratory of Psychology Problems (in 1977). From 1967 to 1974 he was the president of the Armenian Psychological Society.

Yeritzian is interested in applied psychology, psychology of thinking, and work and engineering psychology. For years, with a group of associates, he studied the psychological problems of learning the Armenian and Russian languages, psychoeducational problems, and learning and deductive reasoning. In keeping with his doctoral dissertation on the psychology of reasoning, thought is the central theme in his research. His publications number more than 70 and include the book *The Psychological Characteristics of School Children's Deductive Conclusion* (1975).

Another Armenian psychologist interested in the psychology of sport and the psychological problems of movement is Albert Kostanian. He has more than 80 scientific publications, including *The Influence of Physical Exercises on Deaf School Children's Movement Reaction Speed* (1962) and *Swimming* (1975, coauthored with I. K. Safarian). Kostanian has been working since 1952 at the Armenian Institute of Physical Culture, where he became the head of the Department of Swimming in 1965. A doctor of psychological sciences (1970), he holds a professorship (since 1971). For his many accomplishments, Kostanian has been honored as a Distinguished Worker of Physical Culture and Sports in Soviet Armenia (1975).

Emma Aleksandrian, the first Armenian woman to receive a doctorate in psychological sciences (in 1970) and to become a professor (in 1971), is well known for her work in preschool development. Her interest in young children may have been stimulated by her mother, a teacher who knew and corresponded with Nadezhda K. Krupskaya, the wife of V. I. Lenin, regarding the establishment of preschools in Armenia.

As dean (since 1972) of the Faculty of Preschool Education and Psychology at the Kh. Apovian Pedagogical Institute, Aleksandrian has trained many psychologists and educators and has conducted research at the Psychology Laboratory and at the experimental kindergarten she organized in 1962. Aleksandrian's doctoral work in Moscow and her studies of I. M. Sechenov and I. P. Pavlov strengthened her interest in the application of physiological principles to child development. Based on her investigations, Aleksandrian pointed out that infants could differentiate between physical and social utterances in the environment and that the human voice played an important role in the activity of the brain for infants as young as 2 months. Therefore, she suggested starting work on the development of children's speech before they begin to understand words and sentences.

An energetic and creative scholar, with a background in mechanical engineering and mathematics, Albert Nalchajian completed his doctoral studies in psychology at the Kh. Apovian Pedagogical Institute. His dissertation dealt with intuition. He has since held several positions, including the presidency of the Armenian Psychological Society (1974–76). His academic positions include the directorship of the Education and Psychology Department, of the Psychology Department at the Valery Pruysov Russian and Foreign Languages Institute, and finally (since 1981), of the Psychology Section of the Institute of Philosophy and Law, of the Armenian Academy of

Sciences. Despite these responsibilities, Nalchajian has conducted research and written in many areas: personality, frustration and defense mechanisms, sleep and dreams, and intuition.

Nalchajian has several landmark publications, including *Intuition in the Process of Scientific Creativity* (1976), *Motive, Conflict, Frustration* (1978, coauthored with M. H. Megerdchian, psychologist and editor of the *Sovedagan Mangavarj*), *The Individual and His Dreams: Psychology of Sleep and Dreams* (1982), *Psychological Dictionary* (1984, a first in Armenia), and *The Psycho-Social Adaptation of the Individual* (published in Russian in Yerevan, 1988), which deals with forms, mechanisms, and strategies. In 1980 Nalchajian published *Personality, Psychic Adaptation, and Creativity* in Yerevan. Written in Russian, the book tackles the theoretical study of various psychological issues related to personality, psyche, and creativity in Soviet children. In this publication, Nalchajian uses the latest data from studies in psychogenetics, sleep and dreams, and perception and sensation to develop a theory on the level of human psychic activity. His study is the first published in the Soviet Union in which concepts of frustration and psychological defenses are discussed.

The investigations and writings of Armenian medical psychologists and psychiatrists are also of interest to psychology. Although trained in medicine and employed at the Institute of Medicine in Yerevan, Antranig H. Mehrabian and Vahan H. Hovhannisian have contributed to the understanding of abnormal and normal personality and psychopathology.

Mehrabian, a prominent psychiatrist, has been interested in alcoholism, schizophrenia, psychosis, narcomania, and the classification and treatment of psychopathology. He is the author of *On the Nature of Individual Consciousness* (1959), *Depersonalization* (1962), *Theoretical Problems of Psychopathology* (1967), *General Psychopathology* (1972), and *Personality and Consciousness* (1978). In these books he presents and discusses several levels of consciousness and psychic deterioration resulting from different mental illnesses, and he clarifies consciousness and personality (in normal and abnormal conditions), psychological alienation, illusion, and depersonalization problems. Mehrabian, a doctor of medical sciences (1941) and professor (1942), became the director of the Department of Psychiatry of the Institute of Medicine in Yerevan in 1944. That year he also assumed the presidency of the newly established Armenian Society of Psychiatrists and Neuropathologists. Mehrabian has been (since 1961) a corresponding member of the USSR Academy of Medical Sciences.

Psychiatrist Hovhannisian, a graduate of the Yerevan Institute of Medicine and a teacher and researcher (since 1964) at its Department of Psychiatry, is interested in drug addiction and alcoholism. He has conducted extensive studies regarding the understanding, treatment, and prevention of substance use/abuse. Before leading the Psychoneurology Clinic in Yerevan, Hovhannisian organized clinics in the Armenian cities of Leninagan and Girovagan. He is a doctor of medical sciences (1971) and professor (1972) and currently is the executive secretary of the Armenian Society of Psychiatrists and Neuropathologists.

It must be noted here that, earlier, Levon A. Hovhannisian (1885–1970) influenced the development not only of medical sciences but also of medical psychology in Armenia. His wide-ranging interests in psychopathological symptoms of somatic disorders and heart disease are discussed in his books: *On the Connection between Psychological and Somatic Spheres in the Clinic of Internal Diseases* (1961) and *On the Psychological Profile of the Heart Patient* (1963). Hovhannisian was a member of the Armenian Academy of Sciences (1943) and the USSR Academy of Medical Sciences (1944).

Future Directions

Obviously, the general policies of *glasnost* (openness) and *perestroika* (restructuring) in the USSR are bringing changes in every republic and sector of society. Armenian scholars in the social sciences, including psychology, will pursue areas of interest unhindered but within the constraints of the dialectical materialistic conception of human beings.

Armenian psychology will likely show advances in the near future as the socioideological environment becomes conducive to more innovative psychological research and practice. Furthermore, the availability of Western (especially North American) psychology books, journals, and tests and their frequent use are likely (a) to increase Armenian psychologists' exposure to diverse subjects, studies, up-to-date information and data, theoretical concepts, and viewpoints and (b) to contribute to Armenian psychology as a science and profession.

Moreover, Armenian psychologists will probably be more involved in collaborative research and the publishing of comprehensive psychology textbooks in Armenian. The establishment of a psychological council and working cooperatively will generate new interest and creativity in psychology, making it more relevant and respectable. (There is at present no council to oversee and guide the preparation and work of psychologists in the republic.)

Other developments in psychology in Armenia will likely include (a) an emphasis on the application of psychology to everyday life and on psychological practica in the psychology curriculum; (b) the organization of activities and seminars/workshops for psychology students, psychologists, and other interested scientists and individuals; (c) an expansion of informative and instructional psychology programs on television; (d) the translation, adaptation, and/or development of psychological tests for use with school-children and working men and women; (e) the easy availability of psycho-logical services to those in need; and (f) the reorganization of the Armenian Psychological Society.

Addendum

On December 7, 1988, after this chapter was completed, a devastating earthquake hit Armenia. It destroyed 40 percent of the republic in the northwest, including 199 educational institutions, and it killed more than 25,000 persons, of whom 6,000 were students, teachers, and other educational personnel.

Bibliography

Aleksanian, L. B. (1973). *Koorken Edilian*. Yerevan: Yerevan State University.

Asratian, E. A. (1979). *Ivan Petrovich Pavlov*. Yerevan: Hayasdan.

Hagopian, A. H. (1973). Social sciences: Psychology. In K. P. Bedrossian (Ed.), *Science in Armenia: Past fifty years* (pp. 180–187). Yerevan: Academy of Sciences, Armenian SSR.

Orbeli, L. A. (1982). *Memoirs* (R. H. Harootunian, Trans.). Yerevan: Hayasdan. (Original work in Russian published 1966)

Orbeli, L. A. (1982). *The problems of higher nervous activity* (R. H. Harootunian, Trans.). Yerevan: Armenian Academy of Sciences. (Original work in Russian published 1949)

Pambookian, H. S. (1982). Teachers and teaching in the Soviet Union. *International Psychologist, 23* (1), 18–19.

Pambookian, H. S. (1984). Soviet psychology: A book on "Personality and Creativity" by Albert A. Nalchajian. *International Psychologist, 25* (2), 19–20.

Pambookian, H. S., & Holowinsky, I. Z. (1987). School psychology in the USSR. *Journal of School Psychology, 25*, 209–221.

Pawlik, K. (Ed.). (1985). *International directory of psychologists* (4th ed., pp. 867–935). Amsterdam: Elsevier Science B. V.

3 / Australia

MARY CREIGHTON NIXON

Mary Creighton Nixon (born 1922) received her PhD from the University of Melbourne in 1968. Her publications have focused chiefly on developmental psychology, particularly cognition, and professional issues. Among the books she has authored or edited are Psychology in Australia: Achievements and Prospects, *with R. Taft, and* Issues in Psychological Practice.

She was a member of the Victorian Psychological Council, the statutory body that registers psychologists in the state of Victoria, and she has served in several offices of the Australian Psychological Society, including president. Nixon was senior lecturer in psychology, Faculty of Education at Monash University, until her retirement. She is now honorary research associate in the Psychology Department at the University of New England, Armidale, New South Wales.

In 1988 Australia celebrated 200 years of European settlement and more than 100 years of higher education. The first two universities were established in the 1850s, in Sydney and Melbourne. The first teaching of psychology began in 1890, but no full undergraduate program was available until the late 1920s. By 1940, six universities had been established, with two subsidiary university colleges. The University of Sydney, the University of Western Australia, and the University College of New England in Armidale had departments of psychology, while psychology was largely taught in philosophy departments of the other institutions. In the years following World War II, 1945 to 1960, increased demand for higher education led to a government inquiry. The outcome was the expansion of university facilities and establishment of new universities, with the existing university colleges becoming independent universities. In 1987 there were 19 universities to serve Australia's needs for university education, 18 of them with departments of psychology (although not all of them use that name). Other departments also carry out psychological research and teaching: psychiatry, education, social work, and management, for instance.

Of the 18 universities with departments of psychology, 13 are located in

I thank Ronald Taft and Ross Day for permitting me to read their paper before publication (Taft & Day, 1988).

capital cities. Australia has a large land mass and a relatively small population (16 million) in an area about the size of mainland United States. About two thirds of the population lives in the broad arc connecting Sydney, Canberra, and Melbourne, in the southeast of the continent. No fewer than nine universities serve that area, and three others are not far away. Each of them has a psychology department.

Colleges of advanced education (CAEs) form a second tier of tertiary education. These colleges were originally established as teacher training, agricultural, and technical colleges. During the 1960s and 1970s they became independent degree-granting institutions and expanded their functions. Nearly all of them teach psychology in some form, and 13 of them have psychology departments whose programs are accredited by the Australian Psychological Society for purposes of membership. The CAEs are located in capital and provincial cities; a high proportion of them are close to rural communities. Australian students usually seek higher education at an institution close to home; hence the colleges rather than the universities educate rural students.

Significant Research Emphases

According to a 1983 survey (Nixon, 1987), psychology in Australian universities is highly experimental, concentrates on humans rather than animals, and maintains a balance between social and biological components. Psychology in the CAEs emphasizes social and human components, and balances humanistic with experimental approaches. This perspective permits examination of a recent review of Australian psychology (Feather, 1985). Feather accepted an invitation from the Australian Academy of Social Sciences to edit a book, one of a series on the social sciences, that would describe and evaluate psychological research in Australia. Most of the reported work focuses on human behavior, most of the research is broadly experimental (although survey and clinical approaches are included where appropriate), and social correlates of behavior receive more attention than biological ones. While the chapters can be sorted in different ways, any sorting shows a strong emphasis on social psychology; 7 of the 15 contributions can be so described. Five reflect strongly experimental approaches, giving accounts of Australian research in perception, cognition, developmental psychology, psycholinguistics, and behavior modification (including behavior therapy and behavior analysis). The remaining chapters describe Australian research on neurological processes and behavior, psychometrics and mathematical psychology, imagery and hypnosis, and the adaptation of migrants to Australia. This sorting gives a broad indication of the emphases that are typical of Australian psychology.

Feather's book demonstrates a significant feature of Australian psychology: psychologists in Australia are closely linked with colleagues and co-workers in other research centers, especially in Britain, the United States, and Canada, but also in Switzerland, France, Scandinavia, Southeast Asia, South Africa, New Zealand, Papua New Guinea, and other countries. Feather's authors all come from university psychology departments (or schools or units) in 9 of the 19 universities: Flinders University in Adelaide; La Trobe, Melbourne, and Monash Universities in Melbourne; Macquarie University in Sydney; the University of Newcastle; the University of Queensland in Brisbane; the University of Tasmania in Hobart; and the University of Western Australia in Perth. Though most of the authors are Australian born and had at least part of their psychological education at Australian universities, about half of them obtained higher degrees from universities in Britain and North America. The remainder obtained higher degrees from Australian universities. Some of them have worked for long periods in foreign universities; most or all of them have spent appreciable periods of time at institutions outside Australia.

International Links

The practices of making overseas visits for work, study, or other professional purposes and of maintaining international contacts are typical of Australian psychologists, and not only of those employed in institutions of higher learning. They attend international conferences across the globe in significant numbers and contribute vigorously to both the intellectual and social sides of such gatherings. Their efforts led to the holding of the 1988 Congress of the International Union of Psychological Science (IUPsyS) in Sydney, the first time the congress was held in the Southern Hemisphere. Australian psychologists hold appointments in universities, colleges, and other institutions in Canada, the United States, and Britain, as well as in countries closer to home, such as New Zealand, Papua New Guinea, and Southeast Asia. These international links bring significant numbers of foreign born and trained psychologists to Australia on visits or to take appointments in Australian universities, colleges, and applied psychology organizations.

Psychological Institutions

The Australian Psychological Society (APS), established in 1966, replaced the Australian Branch of the British Psychological Society, which was founded in 1945. The APS is the principal learned and professional society for psychologists in Australia and has some 4,000 members.

Although there are a few other psychological societies, it is APS that is affiliated with IUPsyS, and it is largely through APS's influences that individuals join the International Association of Applied Psychology (IAAP). The APS publishes two refereed quarterly journals (the *Australian Journal of Psychology* and the *Australian Psychologist*) and the *Bulletin of the Australian Psychological Society*, which appears six times a year. Through APS's good relationships with other national psychological societies, members can subscribe to a wide range of journals at favorable rates; they use mainly English-language, British and North American publications.

When the APS was first formed in 1966, it adopted a draft code of professional conduct, which has since gone through two revisions. The code adopted in 1986 contains sections on assessment procedures, consulting relationships, the teaching of psychology, supervision and training, research, public statements, and professional relationships; it has guidelines on client/psychologist physical contact, blind test interpretation and report writing, and the use of aversive therapeutic procedures. The society places great importance on providing guidance to members and others on the proper practice of psychology, in research, teaching, and the provision of services.

Australian society is male-dominated; only slowly are women taking their place in the professions. The APS governing body, the Council, for 1986–87, had nine women among the 34 councillors, and since its establishment in 1966 only two women have become president of the society. In 1966 22 percent of the APS membership was female; in 1986 female membership had increased to 45 percent. Few women hold senior academic or administrative positions in Australian psychology, although more women than men enroll in psychology courses.

The Australian Behavior Modification Association is one of several bodies that serve the interests of specialist psychologists. In addition, informal groups arrange annual or biennial conferences on experimental, social, and developmental psychology, sometimes held in conjunction with the annual conference of APS, more often independently. Psychologists interested in exceptionality, hypnosis, psychology and law, pain management, ergonomics, and numerous other specialties associate themselves with multidisciplinary organizations with these specialist orientations.

Access to tests and psychometric instruments depends to a considerable extent on the Australian Council for Education Research (ACER). This body, established in the 1930s with the assistance of the Carnegie Corporation and located in Melbourne, is the principal agency for developing, publishing, importing, and distributing psychological measurement devices. In addition, ACER publishes a *Bulletin for Psychologists,* which reviews recent and revised instruments; editing the *Bulletin* is undertaken by the psychologists in ACER's Test Advisory Division. The network associated with ACER links psychologists across the entire country, including those engaged in psychometric research and teaching and those in educational and other applied fields that employ psychometric assessment procedures.

The Academy of Social Sciences has elected 25 psychologists as fellows. This is the academy within which psychology is accommodated, regardless of whether it is social, experimental, mathematical, or biological. The Academy of Science has recently addressed this anomaly by establishing a National Committee for Psychology (Taft & Day, 1988).

Psychologists participate in the proceedings of the Australian and New Zealand Association for the Advancement of Science (ANZAAS) and organize one section of the ANZAAS conference, which is held every 18 months. The extent of psychological participation depends largely on the location of the conference and the interest of local psychologists. ANZAAS provides one of the few ways in which Australian and New Zealand psychologists work together, although a recent joint conference of the Australian and New Zealand Psychological Societies was held in New Zealand and proved successful.

The Australian Psychological Society enjoys excellent relationships with similar societies in other countries. A fair number of Australian psychologists belong to societies outside Australia, especially the British Psychological Society and the American Psychological Association. Many others belong to specialist international organizations, both research and applied.

Facilities

Resources for psychological research, teaching, and service provisions range from fair to excellent. During the economic boom years of the 1960s and 1970s university psychology departments were well equipped with staff, space, and laboratory, teaching, and clinical resources. That investment remains but shows signs of decreasing as economic support is reduced. During the same period, university libraries established collections and reader facilities far superior to those previously available in Australia and comparable to those of good libraries in other developed countries. Since publishing in Australia is on a relatively small scale, most books, journals, and computer software are of foreign origin. Consequently, Australian psychologists are made aware of theoretical trends and controversies, research movements, and changing practices in applied psychology emanating from the principal international centers of psychological work. These resources for Australia are largely, but not exclusively, British and North American, but exceptions to this rule have already been mentioned. A negative aspect of dependence on foreign publications is that they do not address local issues. A recent increase in publication of Australian texts has therefore been warmly welcomed.

The computer revolution in Australia followed closely on the heels of that in Europe and North America, beginning in the late 1950s. Reflecting the economic prosperity of the period, computer installation and use developed rapidly, and as a result, psychological research, teaching, and applied psychometrics can call on sophisticated computing and word-processing support.

Provision of personal computers to the academic staff of universities and colleges currently proceeds with deliberate speed. Expansion of computer use is driven by the needs to maintain leadership in the field and to keep abreast of developments abroad, but it has been limited by the dwindling of financial resources in the wake of the boom years.

Australia's first private university was established so recently that any comment, save that it might herald a change in provision of higher education, is impossible. Otherwise, funds for buildings, equipment, staff, maintenance, and research for universities and CAEs come almost entirely from government resources. Psychology shares this support. Industry funds some research, and private foundations provide some support for specialist research and teaching—for work dealing with disability, for instance. The bulk of funding for psychological research comes from the Australian Research Grants System (ARGS) and the National Health and Medical Research Council (NH & MRC), both of which are instruments of the Commonwealth government. Universities and colleges allot part of their funding to support their own research. Thus most research funding derives, directly or indirectly, from the Commonwealth government, as does other funding. Some of the CAEs are affiliated with religious organizations and receive limited support from their churches, usually in the form of land and buildings, but they rely almost entirely on government funds. University and college departments differ markedly in the scale of research undertaken. Although good work is done in college psychology departments, the amount carried out is usually much smaller than in university psychology departments.

Education and Training

It is convenient to describe the education and training of psychologists in terms of APS membership. Undergraduate and graduate programs are examined and accredited by APS for purposes of membership. An Australian "pass degree" consists of 3 years of study during which one or two subjects are studied in depth for the full 3 years, and three or more additional subjects are studied for shorter periods of time. An honors degree may be taken by students who complete the first 3 years at a high level; it entails a 4th year of education concentrating on the single subject studied in depth during the previous 3 years. Students who complete a pass degree with a 3-year sequence of study may complete an accredited 4th year in the form of a graduate diploma or a "pass master's" degree. Completion of a degree with an accredited 4-year sequence in psychology renders an applicant eligible for associate membership in APS, a grade that may be described as an apprenticeship. The second grade, membership, may be attained after 2 years of graduate work, completion of a 2-year master's degree, or 2 years of approved supervised work in psychology.

Persons who have completed no more than a degree with a 3-year sequence in psychology may become affiliates of APS, a nonvoting grade of association. The APS offers fellowship and honorary fellowship as recognition of notable achievements in psychology.

To disseminate knowledge of the society and its objectives, APS enables students enrolled in accredited programs of study to become student subscribers and offers an annual prize at the 4th-year level for each institution that has an accredited undergraduate program. Education and training share features of both British and North American models; the structure of degrees is more similar to that of Britain, while the arrangement of graduate work is rather more like that of the United States. That is, in the undergraduate years students study more psychology than their American counterparts but less than those in Britain; in graduate programs they complete more coursework than their British counterparts but less than those in the United States. A "research higher degree" thesis in Australia is typically a substantial piece of work and the major part of the degree requirement. In graduate coursework programs the thesis carries less weight but is still an important component.

The provision that 2 years of approved supervised experience enables associate members to become full members of APS has proved unsatisfactory and difficult to administer. The quality of supervision varies considerably, and so does the experience itself. Unambiguous guidelines have proved elusive, and the provision relies too heavily on the goodwill and integrity of individual supervisors. The APS is attempting to phase out the present form of supervision and to phase in short-course and structured programs that will improve the quality of induction to professional psychology (Campbell, 1987).

Statutory Recognition of Psychologists

Five of the six states of Australia have enacted legislation for the registration of psychologists, the most populous state, New South Wales, being the exception. Elsewhere, psychologists must register before engaging in practice, but teachers of psychology are exempt. In broad terms, registration is based on qualifications obtained from recognized tertiary institutions, plus approved experience; registering bodies have the power to set examinations but seldom use this power. The first act to register psychologists was passed in 1965 and was not universally welcomed by the psychological community, but now the APS strongly endorses registration as an effective means of controlling psychological services and of reducing quackery. In 1984 the number of registered psychologists was estimated at about 2,300 (Smith, 1984). The APS has about 4,000 members, and not all psychologists belong to it. Probably between 5,000 and 6,000 persons work as psychologists and have qualifications that would permit them to become members of APS and to be registered. In a country with a population of 16 million, that gives a ratio of just under 1:3000, a figure suggesting that psychological services are fairly readily available to persons seeking them.

Employment

Psychologists work in a wide range of settings, and most are employed by an agency rather than being self-employed. Agencies that hire psychologists include universities; CAES; state and commonwealth departments of health, education, employment, youth affairs, social services, and veterans' affairs; hospitals; specialist health and welfare organizations; courts of law; the defense forces; public authorities such as Telecom, Australia Post, and road safety boards; and private clinical, management, and consulting firms. Colleges and universities employ psychologists in student counseling and welfare and in departments of psychology, psychiatry, social work, management, and education. Employers seek psychologists who are competent in broad fields such as educational, counseling and clinical, occupational, organizational, and industrial psychology. In some cases universities have designed coursework in master's programs specifically to meet these requirements. In other cases the universities have collaborated with employing organizations to design effective ways of delivering psychological services.

In a limited survey, Over, Parry, Geddes, and Levens (1985) found that 37 percent of their sample of 294 psychologists registered in Victoria reported that they engaged in some private practice, but only a small number did so full-time. The great majority were in salaried employment and engaged in private practice for a few hours each week. Private clinical practice has been limited by the fact that health benefit funds have not until recently included psychologists' fees in the schedule for which rebates are payable. Some health funds now include psychologists' fees, but the rebates are small and referral from medical practitioner to psychologist is required. In any case, only a few programs of graduate training at the master's or doctoral level equip psychology graduates to enter private clinical practice. Furthermore, the programs are far from standardized to the level that would persuade public health authorities that psychological services should be subsidized from the public purse. Nonetheless, graduate education programs are increasing in number and quality, and psychological services are improving.

Public Perception of Psychology

A recent survey (Sharpley, 1986) explored public perceptions of psychologists, compared with perceptions of psychiatrists, counselors, and social workers. The respondents, chosen as representative of Australian society, grouped psychologists with psychiatrists as private practitioners studying human behavior and thought. They acknowledged that psychologists could provide help and advice with problems but appeared to regard social workers and counselors as more caring people who would provide practical help. Although respondents did not know much about the training of psychologists, they were no better informed about the training of other professionals. Psychologists often maintain that the public is ignorant of the services they provide; Sharpley's survey suggests that while there are some misapprehensions about psychologists, the public knows as much about them as about other professionals with an orientation to human service.

Current and Emerging Trends

The history of Australian psychology began a century ago, and this chapter does not attempt to describe it, since other accounts are available (e.g., Bucklow, 1977; O'Neil, 1987). That history has produced a view of psychology as a systematic empirical discipline in search of independently verifiable explanations of behavior. This view underlies the education and training of Australian psychologists now as it has done since the teaching of psychology began in Australia. It strengthens the bond that has always existed between research and teaching and the application of psychology in practical service. Gilgen and Gilgen (1987) make the point that, worldwide, support for research in psychology depends largely on psychologists showing that their work is socially useful. That Australian research in psychology is supported as well as it is, compared with research in other disciplines, may indicate that its contribution to society is recognized and valued.

Bibliography

Bucklow, M. (1977). Applied psychology in Australia—The history. In M. C. Nixon & R. Taft (Eds.), *Psychology in Australia: Achievements and prospects* (pp. 23–34). Sydney: Pergamon Press.

Campbell, E. F. (1987). Brief on supervision. *Bulletin of the Australian Psychological Society, 9*, 17–19.

Feather, N. T. (Ed.). (1985). *Australian psychology: Review of research*. Sydney: Allen & Unwin.

Gilgen, A. R., & Gilgen, C. K. (1987). Introduction. In A. R. Gilgen & C. K. Gilgen (Eds.), *International handbook of psychology* (pp. 1–23). New York: Greenwood Press.

Nixon, M. C. (1987). Australia. In A. R. Gilgen & C. K. Gilgen (Eds.), *International handbook of psychology* (pp. 37–66). New York: Greenwood Press.

O'Neil, W. M. (1987). *A century of psychology in Australia*. Sydney: Sydney University Press.

Over, R., Parry, A., Geddes, J., & Levens, M. (1985). Psychologists in private practice in Victoria. *Australian Psychologist, 20*, 239–250.

Sharpley, C. E. (1986). Public perceptions of four mental health professions: A survey of knowledge and attitudes to psychologists, psychiatrists, social workers and counsellors. *Australian Psychologist, 21*, 57–67.

Smith, R. L. (1984). Registration of psychologists: Issues and implications. In M. C. Nixon (Ed.), *Issues in psychological practice* (pp. 234–251). Melbourne: Longman Cheshire.

Taft, R., & Day, R. H. (1988). Psychology in Australia. *Annual Review of Psychology, 39*, 375–400.

4 / Austria

GISELHER GUTTMANN & SUSAN C. ETLINGER

Giselher Guttmann (born 1934) received his PhD from the University of Vienna in 1963 and his habilitation degree from the same university in 1968. His specialties include DC-potentials, information processing, learning, sport psychology, diagnostics, and performance optimization. The editor of the International Journal of Psychophysiology, Archive of Psychology, *and* Zeitschrift für Psychologie, *he is also the author of a variety of publications, including the books* Einführung in die Neuropsychologie *(Introduction to neuropsychology), and* Lehrbuch der Neuropsychologie *(Textbook of neuropsychology). He is full professor and head of the Department of General, Experimental, and Neuropsychology at the University of Vienna.*

Susan C. Etlinger (born 1940) received her PhD from the University of Vienna in 1987. A specialist in psychophysiology, she has conducted research on attention, visual perception, and emotions, all at the electrophysiological level. A member of the Board of Directors of the International Organization for Psychophysiology, Etlinger has received three separate scholarships to study brain-electric phenomena at the Academy of Medical Sciences in Leningrad.

Characteristics of the Psychologist

Legal Definition and Unfortunate Loopholes

According to Austrian law, only those who have earned an academic degree with a major in psychology at one of the country's universities are allowed to call themselves "psychologist." Two such degrees are offered: the master's degree, entitling the recipient to be known as a "registered psychologist," and the PhD. The appellative is also granted those who have earned their degrees at foreign universities, providing that the equivalent degree has been awarded by an accredited institution (determined by international agreements with the corresponding country or university itself). It is, however, only on rare occasions that Austrians enroll outside of their own country, for the Austrian university system is public and tuition-free for any citizen qualifying for entrance. This qualification for academic studies, the so-called *Abitur* or *Matura,* is conferred on graduates of secondary schools whose curriculum is college-preparatory.

At present, the official Association of Professional Psychologists lists 850 registered members. It is estimated that there are probably an additional 400 to 500 qualified Austrians who have not sought membership. This can readily be explained. With a total of approximately 1,350 Austrian psychologists, the ratio to the entire population in Austria (approximately 7 million) is certainly awesome: nearly 1:5000. Further, it must be noted, psychological services, in contrast to psychiatric, are not included in the national health scheme. Thus a relatively small portion of the population is willing to pay for counseling over and above the mandatory contribution taken out of the paycheck. In general, Austrians are not accustomed to paying for health services out of pocket. Therefore, supply greatly exceeds demand, and a large proportion of the qualified psychologists in Austria cannot afford to practice this profession.

In contrast to the clear delineation of the title's usage, there is no impediment to using the term in its attributional form. Anyone can offer "psychological counseling" or any number of self-declared, self-defined "psychological" services. One domain, however, is indeed forbidden to either the registered or the brazenly self-declared psychologist—namely, "therapy." "Therapy," as stipulated by law, is solely the preserve of the physician, that is, the psychiatrist.

The group of practicing psychologists is fairly young, about four fifths being under 50 years of age and over 50 percent being 40 years old or younger. There are slightly more professionally active women than men (with a ratio of approximately 60:40), the best estimate being based on polls of this population. Disregarding professional activity, the ratio of graduated psychologists, female to male, would be even higher.

The university degree is equivalent to certification as a "psychologist" per se, but not necessarily to licensure as an expert practitioner of any particular therapeutic method. Such a license is issued solely after successful completion of appropriate courses held by licensed lectors and ensuing supervision. Participation in such seminars is limited to registered graduates of institutions of higher learning, including those whose diplomas are in the field of social work, theology, sociology, and medicine. According to their own registration, Austrian practitioners as a group are versed in administering counsel in one or more of the following psychohygienic methods: nondirective counseling (C. Rogers), group therapy (different psychoanalytic methods), psychodrama (J. Moreno), psychoanalysis (S. Freud), Gestalt therapy (F. Perls), behavior therapy (F. Kanfer), family therapy (e.g., S. Minuchin), marriage counseling, logotherapy (V. Frankl), neurolinguistic programming, autogenic training, schools emphasizing aspects of therapy according to Wilhelm Reich (e.g. bioenergetics, radix, core-energetics), kata-thymic image experiencing, analytical psychology (C. G. Jung), hypnosis, transactional analysis (E. Berne), communication therapy (P. Watzlawick, G. Bateson), and so on. From this list one can see that a great variety of therapy and counseling forms are available to the practitioner as well as, ultimately, to the public. Five of these pioneers—Moreno, Freud, Frankl, Reich, and Watzlawick—are Austrian or spent significant, formative years in the country.

Professional Reality

Statistics on Austrian psychologists' vocational activities are divided into three categories: full-time occupation, part-time, and preparing an expertise. In a recent survey (1987) of members of the Professional Association of Psychologists, 80 percent of the respondents reported that their main occupation is as a psychologist. Nevertheless, almost 85 percent of the same group are only working part-time as psychologists. One half of the professionally active psychologists have opened a practice. Usually, such a practice includes a team of psychologists, each practicing the methods learned in the special courses mentioned above. Finally, very few are occupied preparing an expertise (less than 7 percent), usually in the form of job qualification assessment. On the average, an Austrian psychologist holds 2.2 field-related jobs. There may be one position rated as main occupation, but it seldom pays well enough to provide an acceptable standard of living on its own.

Viewed in the light of the previous data, this subdivision (full-time vs. part-time) is not surprising for other reasons as well. Female psychologists predominate in the working population, and many are young, still within the age range of childbearing and rearing. Moreover, the age distribution reveals that the number of retiring psychologists does not in any way balance the number of newcomers to the field. Decades of active professional life still lie ahead of most colleagues.

Thus several factors conceivably contribute to the present situation of the job-collecting, job-sharing professional activity of Austria's psychologists. Many professional psychologists take on more than one job to make ends meet. An explanation for the opposite phenomenon (the part-time professional) is that the work load is spread thin to begin with. Another factor is that the work actually available is being shared by young females who are likely to be burdened with a double or triple role (professional, wife, mother) and may welcome a lighter work load considered as a source of supplemental income.

The Austrian population is served by approximately 700 psychosocial and/ or psychotherapeutic institutions. Nearly 500 offer ambulatory treatment and about 100 provide in-patient service. More than 175 other institutions have units for psychosocial/psychotherapeutic care but are closed to the general public (e.g., apprentices' dormitories, penal stations). Greater Vienna (Austria's capital) has by far the largest number of such institutions (more than 300), as well as the largest number of professionally practicing psychologists (close to 400). There are great differences in the quality of the services offered, if measured only by the differences in number of professionals employed and the hours the various institutions remain open. (Some are open around the clock and some only a few hours a month!)

If one lists the services according to their target group(s), the one all-pervasive fact of the Austrian psychologist's life is again confirmed: only slightly more than 1 in 10 of the institutions specialize in psychotherapy—still a problematic area of activity because of the legal limitations imposed on nonphysicians. Briefly, services aimed at problems related to youth (counseling of children themselves or their parents, dealing with school problems) are the raison d'être of more than half of all Austrian institutions. Other areas covered fall into the categories of addiction, the handicapped, psychosomatics, parolees, crisis intervention, rehabilitation, itinerates, sos telephone service, and a few others.

The largest employer of psychologists in Austria is the government; almost 60 percent have a position at an institution at some level of government (e.g., municipal, state, federal) or at an institution which receives substantial support from the state. Private institutions also offer psychosocial or psychotherapeutic services, but the governmental institutions predominate. Their activities can be subsumed under the following categories: counseling or evaluations related to the clinic, school/education, occupation/career, delinquent behavior, traffic safety, rehabilitation, and army—to name the most notable in descending order of representation.

Characteristics of Psychology

Academic Program

The program of study for psychology is stipulated by federal law and is generally valid throughout Austria. University training is divided into lower- and upper-division stages of equal duration (4–6 semesters each). The first emphasizes the acquisition of basic concepts and gaining practice in methodology (e.g., statistics, experimental design). Upper-division courses introduce and intensify knowledge in applied psychology, including clinical, developmental, social, biological, mathematical, and other areas of psychology.

This curriculum is offered at institutions in six of Austria's provincial capitals: University of Graz (Styria), University of Innsbruck (Tyrol), University of Salzburg (Salzburg), and at the University of Vienna (Vienna), as well as at the colleges in Klagenfurt (Carinthia) and Linz (Upper Austria). In three of Austria's provinces, the westernmost (Vorarlberg), the easternmost (Burgenland), and that surrounding Vienna (Lower Austria), there is no institution at which a diploma in psychology can be earned. The people of these areas are, however, well served by the institutions in the neighboring provinces in a country the size of the state of Maine in the USA.

References and Sources

There is only one Austrian journal devoted to psychology, *Psychologie in Oesterreich* (Psychology in Austria), published by the Austrian Association of Professional Psychologists. Austrian psychologists share several publications with German-speaking colleagues from other middle European states and are amply represented among their editors. Austrian research in psychology is reported regularly in the *Archiv für Psychologie* (Archive for psychology), *Zeitschrift für Klinische Psychologie* (Journal of clinical psychology), *Zeitschrift für Differentielle und Diagnostische Psychologie* (Journal of differential and diagnostic psychology), and *Zeitschrift für Experimentelle und Angewandte Psychologie* (Journal of experimental and applied psychology) and is summarized in English in the *German Journal of Psychology—A Quarterly of Abstracts and Review Articles*. Moreover, Austrian psychologists contribute routinely to well-known international scientific journals. The Austrian university libraries are well stocked with a great variety of foreign periodicals, most of the present-day publications in the field of psychology being American, but including a generous sampling of, for instance, English, German, French, Scandinavian, and Swiss—some dating back to the turn of the century. The main library of the University of Vienna subscribes to the international data bank Psyndex, through which it is connected to the Psycinfo data base. The library of the Institute for Psychology in Vienna alone counts 127 journals and periodicals as well as 26,000 publications and volumes among its current references. Its sister institutions at the capitals of other Austrian provinces enjoy similar endowments.

Technical Outfitting

The main computer centers of each university are freely accessible for all of its adjoining institutes. The largest installations are in Vienna (IBM 3081) and in Linz (IBM 4381-P2). The computer facilities at the University of Innsbruck are the Cyber system by Control Data; Salzburg, Graz, and Klagenfurt are serviced by Digital Equipment (VAX). At the level of personal computers (PCs), the institutes' faculty members themselves are furnished, as a rule of thumb, in a rather haphazard fashion. This description refers to the fact that personal computers are in almost every case left to the private initiative of the individual scientist. And his or her choice is mandated as much by the best offer of the moment (in financial terms) as it is by considerations of complete compatibility.

Happily, psychological parameters are frequently of interest to physicians. The schools of medicine are, as a rule, better outfitted than institutes of psychology with measurement devices and usually welcome collaboration with the country's psychologists; the one school's psychometric equipment is complementary to the other's. Between the two of them, psychology is adequately supplied with the usual repertory of instrumentation at all of the universities (e.g., Flimmer Frequency Device, Pauli Test, Breidt's Perseveration Device, Pursuit Rotor, Cambridge Clock Test, Dichotic Listening Device, Tachistoscope, Eye-Pupil Movement Tracking Device, and others). Some now-standard equipment was developed in Austria (e.g. motor performance series ["MLS": Schoppe, 1974], Cognitrone [Klemenjak, 1983], Viennese Determination Device II (Kisser, Krafack, & Vaughan, 1985]), although most devices in use have been imported. One private firm (Dr. G. Schuhfried) located near Vienna does manufacture psychometric instruments according to individual specifications.

Financing

Psychology as a science is formally the business and responsibility of the Austrian federal government, all universities being public. The institutes' budgets are, however, modest and leave room for creative initiative on the part of the individual. Large-scale research projects are commonly financed by one of the following private or semipublic institutions: any of the Ludwig Boltzmann Societies (linked to the Austrian Academy of Sciences), Austrian National Bank, Jubilaeumsfonds (Anniversary funds), Fonds zur Foerderung der wissenchaftlichen Forschung (Funds for the endowment of scientific research), and the Forschungsfoerderungsfonds für die gewerbliche Wirtschaft (Scientific endowment funds for industry and trade). Together, these reserves total several hundred million schillings per annum and represent significant contributions to psychological research among the beneficiaries.

"Psychology," defined from the standpoint of the practicing professional, also receives support in the form of employment from government agencies offering counseling within the various systems of social services.

Public Image

One can safely say that the average Austrian intermingles high respect with an aura of mystic, penetrating, omniscient forces attributed to those who call themselves psychologists. If one were to place a psychologist and a typical Austrian together at random, the former would almost inevitably meet with a straightforward frankness otherwise atypical of Austrians. It seems that concepts defining the image of the psychologist in this country also must include the terms "receiver," "counselor," and "empathizer" as synonyms.

Trends in Psychology

Background

The Thun-Hohenstein Reform of 1848 marked the advent of academic freedom at Austria's universities and the introduction to the free play of ideas and empirical procedures.

Franz Brentano, who delivered lectures at the University of Vienna in various capacities from 1874 to 1895, greatly influenced psychology in Austria through his own and his pupils' work. He himself founded a school of thought, act psychology, which addressed the mind/body problem by separating (extraverted) intentions ("acts": perceptions, sensations, judgments, desires, abstentions, etc.) from the (introverted) contents of the soul (objects of introspection). Alexius Meinong, one of Brentano's pupils and a professor at the University of Graz, brought these reflections into the Theory of Objects, his interpretation of experience as an object-directed process more complex than a naive addition of simple elements. Meinong, as professor for philosophy in Graz, set up the first psychological laboratory in Austria (1894). Christian M. von Ehrenfels, the first to speak of "*Gestalt*," was his pupil as well as Ernst Mach's pupil (see below).

Since the end of the last century, Austrian psychology has been forcefully influenced by a group of positivistic philosophers called the Vienna Circle, including Rudolf Carnap, Moritz Schlick, Ernst Mach, Ludwig Boltzmann, Victor Kraft, Hans Hahn, Herbert Feigl, Otto Neurath, Else Frenkel, Egon Brunswik, and, indirectly, Karl Popper and Ludwig Wittgenstein. They are the founders of logical empiricism, to whom thoughts basic to the theory of relativity—for example, the realization that the act of observation changes the observation itself—can be traced. The thinking of these physicists and philosophers has had a great influence on matters concerning space, sensation, reflexes, will, instinct, imagination, imagery, optical illusions, the acoustical experience, sense of time, rotation perception, and the ego, as well as other psychological phenomena.

Psychology as a separate field of study in Austria lies embedded in these roots: in the strict observance of empirical methods. The chair of psychology at the University of Vienna, the first in Austria, was established for one of the pioneers of experimental Gestalt and cognitive psychology, Karl Bühler, in 1922. Bühler, head of the institute until his forced emigration in 1938, had been Oswald Külpe's pupil in Würzburg, the teacher himself a student of Brentano. Bühler devoted the years in Vienna to research into the transient, *hic et nunc* cognitive experience, devising novel approaches to its quantification. For instance, by adapting the Müller-Pilzecker paired-associates' learning paradigm from cvc-trigram pairs to the study of pairs of sayings, adages, and aphorisms with similar meaning content in various experimental designs, he showed the primary status of meaning vs. association per se for recall. Bühler's interests centered on language and speech in general, the semantic aspects in particular. In his later years his philosophical orientation was semasiology, the study of philosophical and psychological meaning. Bühler's successor, Hubert Rohracher, headed the institute in Vienna for 30 years (1943–72). Rohracher's ties to the natural sciences gave psychology in Vienna its biological basis. Rohracher was one of the first to recognize the electroencephalograph (EEG) as an instrument for investigating psychological parameters, the earliest being stages of consciousness. Their colleague in Innsbruck, Theodore Erismann, full professor from 1925 to 1956, also had a background in the natural sciences (physics). It was Erismann who invented reversal and prisma glasses to study the contribution of learning processes to visual perception.

Austrians at Home and Abroad

If one is asked what product(s) Austria exports, the answer could very easily be "intellect." The list of prominent Austrians who received their educational background in Austria and later left, for political but also for occupational reasons, is long. The common denominator here is that their work is considered psychology, whether as basic research or as an applied science: Alfred Adler (individual psychology), August Aichhorn (psychoanalytic pedagogy), Ludwig von Bertalanffy (organismic psychology, society for the general study of systems), Bruno Bettelheim (pedagogical psychology), Egon Brunswik (Gestalt theory, "Purposivismus"), Charlotte and Karl Bühler (humanistic psychology), Ernest Dichter (motivational research, psychology of advertising), Rudolf Dreikurs (Adlerian social psychiatry, child guidance centers), Erik Erikson (psychoanalytical theory of development), Klaus Foppa (learning theory), Else Frenkel (the authoritarian personality, prejudice), Karl von Frisch (Nobel Prize, with K. Lorenz and N. Tinbergen, for studies in animal behavior, communication among bees), Friedrich Hacker (psychology of conflict), Paul Lazarsfeld (sociological psychology), Gustav

Lienert (biostatistics, pharmacopsychology), Marie Jahoda (with Lazarsfeld and H. Zeisel: the unemployed of Marienthal), Jakob Moreno (psychodrama), Kurt Pawlik (factor analysis, EEG studies), Karl H. Pribram (holonomic brain theory), Otto Rank (birth trauma), Wilhelm Reich (neurosis caused by sexual disturbances, "Bionen," "Orgon"), Rene Spitz (mother-child relationship), Wilhelm Stekel (Freud disciple, initiated short-term therapy), Walter Toman (personality psychology), Paul Watzlawick (communication therapy), Albert Wellek (theoretical psychology, music psychology, and characterology), to name just the better-known among them.

The highest-ranking Austrian body dedicated to intellectual pursuit, the Austrian Academy of Sciences, counts one psychologist (and one of this chapter's authors) among its present-day members, Giselher Guttmann, head of the Departments of General, Experimental, and Neuropsychology at the University of Vienna. Guttmann, biologist as well as psychologist, has continued the experimental tradition of his predecessors. Perhaps most notable are his studies of slow potential (DC) brainwave phenomena, indicators of stress, and self-control techniques directed toward optimizing performance—approaches aptly summarized by the phrases he has coined: "the brain trigger design," "ergopsychometry," and "the teachable moment." Other members of the academy also engage in psychological research, most prominent among them being the late Konrad Lorenz (Nobel Prize in Physiology, 1973; studies in, e.g., ethology/comparative behavior, aggression) and Hellmuth Petsche, head of the Institute of Neurophysiology at the School of Medicine in Vienna, who sees the best insights into the working mechanisms of the brain in the study of psychological functions (EEG investigations of diverse aptitudes: imagery, bilingualism, and the musical experience counted among them).

The leading present-day psychologists practicing in Austria exert substantial immediate influence not only among German-speaking colleagues but also among the members of the Danubian community to the east by virtue of their regular and close contacts, both formal (e.g., German Psychological Society, All-Danubian Conference) and informal. These psychologists are, in general, found at the various institutes of the country's universities. Only a few of those whose influence exceeds these boundaries are mentioned as representative of the types of work going on in Austria: B. Rollett (head of the Institute and the Department for Developmental Psychology in Vienna): performance-avoidance motivation; G. Fischer (head of the Department for Methodology, Vienna): linear logistic models for latent trait analysis and the measurement of change; and Erich Mittenecker (head of the Department of General Psychology, University of Graz): the search for laws postulated by learning theory which are able to explain psychophysiological phenomena. In Innsbruck, Erismann was succeeded by Ivo Kohler, also a physicist by initial training, who continued the innovative studies in visual perception. Kohler's position is now occupied by Dieter Klebelsberg, whose main interest is in applied psychology, traffic psychology, and pharmacopsychology in particular.

Erwin Roth (head of the Department of Organizational Psychology, University of Salzburg) is well known for his work in differential psychology and brainwave research. Urs Baumann has gained wide recognition for his work there as head of the Department for Clinical Psychology and Psychoanalysis.

Common Purpose
Scientifically, Austrian psychologists place high priority on bridging the gap between basic research and the application of its findings to everyday practice. In this sense, the country's institutes maintain excellent contacts with the public school authorities and systems, the clinics and hospitals of the national health system as well as private institutions, and such semipublic bodies as the Austrian Board for Traffic Safety, rehabilitation centers of insurance companies, and the like.

Being situated at a sensitive European crossroads, Austria has a unique role in being able to provide a mellow setting for mediating the international exchange of scientific experience between East and West, a role that proceeds naturally from its historical and present geopolitical position.

Bibliography

Bonin, W. F. (1983). *Hermes Handlexikon: Die grossen Psychologen*. Duesseldorf: Econ.

Deimann, P., Stumm, G., Weber, G., & Wirth, B. (1985). *Psychotherapie in Oesterreich: Teil II: Ausbildungsmoeglichkeiten—Ausbildungsinstitutionen*. Vienna: Verlag der Oesterreichischischen Hochschuelerschaft.

Guttmann, G. (1984). Psychology in Austria. In R. J. Corsini (Ed.), *Encyclopedia of psychology* (Vol. 3, pp. 115–117). New York: Wiley.

Guttmann, G. (1987). Austria. In A. R. Gilgen & C. K. Gilgen (Eds.), *International handbook of psychology* (pp. 67–78). New York: Greenwood Press.

Kisser, R., Krafack, A., & Vaughan, Ch. (1985). Determinationsgeraete. In R. Brickenkamp (Ed.), *Handbuch apparativer Testverfahren in der Psychologie*. Goettingen: Hogrefe.

Klemenjak, W. (1983). *Der Aufmerksamkeitsbegriff aus verkehrspsychologischer Sicht*. Unpublished doctoral dissertation, University of Vienna, Vienna.

Rohracher, H. (1976). *Einführung in die Psychologie* (1st ed.). Munich: Urban & Schwarzenberg.

Schoppe, K. J. (1974). Das MLS-Geraet: Ein neuer Testapparat zur Messung feinmotorischer Leistungen. *Diagnostica, 20,* 43–46.

Stumm, G. (Ed.). (1988). *Handbuch für Psychotherapie und psychologische Beratung.* Vienna: Falter Verlag.

5 / Belgium

GÉRY D'YDEWALLE

Géry d'Ydewalle (born 1946) received his PhD from the University of Leuven in 1974. A specialist in memory and perception, he has authored three books and several dozen articles, and frequently presents papers at professional meetings. D'Ydewalle has served as editor-in-chief of the International Journal of Psychology *(1979–87), deputy secretary-general of the International Union of Psychological Science (1987–), vice-president of the Belgian Psychological Society (1987–90), and president of the International Committee for Social Science Information and Documentation in* UNESCO *(1985–), and he is copresident of the International Congress of Psychology for Brussels, 1992.*

He is a member of the editorial board of the European Bulletin of Cognitive Psychology, Revista Portuguesa de Educacão *(Portuguese journal of education),* Tijdschrift voor Onderwijsresearch *(Journal of educational research),* Bulletin of European Cognitive Science, *and the* European Journal of Cognitive Psychology. *He is professor at the University of Leuven, where he has been director of the Laboratory of Experimental Psychology since 1980, and guest professor at both the University of London and the University of Liège.*

Characteristics of the Psychologist

Educational Background

In Belgium students who finish high school are entitled to enroll in universities. During the first year, however, all students are required to take examinations. As a result, it is not unusual to have a dropout rate of 50 percent by the end of the first year. Students then may choose another discipline or leave the university to enter a vocational school (called "higher non-university education").

All six universities are free to define the training program of psychologists for themselves, but the programs are quite similar. They all begin with 2 years of candidatures. These years involve classes in various topics, including philosophy, statistics, biology, anthropology, logic, neuropsychology and psychophysiology, sociology, and a few more introductory classes in general psychology, experimental psychology, developmental psychology, human assessment, personality psychology, and psychopathology. As a rule there are no optional classes in the candidatures. Optional classes are available only after these 2 years. ("Candidature" is an official diploma but is of no further use in professional life.) Students then begin their 3 years of "license." Very few students stop at the level of the candidature. In the license, they must choose between major orientations of psychology: industrial/organizational psychology, assessment and school psychology, clinical psychology, and basic research. Students must also complete an original piece of research, usually written in a thesis of approximately 120 pages (the license thesis). The last year of the license involves an internship in a clinical, school, industrial, or research setting, which could last up to 7 months. Most students (almost 95 percent) stop their training after obtaining the license.

The remaining 5 percent enter doctoral programs. In Belgium this does not imply attending classes. Preparation for a doctoral degree involves, on the whole, 5 to 6 years of research under the supervision of a professor. The final product, the doctoral thesis, must be an original piece of research with a substantial contribution in the field (it is more or less a monograph). There is a public defense of the doctoral thesis, and some universities require the publication of the thesis before officially bestowing the title "doctor in psychology."

At the level of candidature and license, there are few foreigners in the program. The bulk of foreigners can be found in doctoral level programs. At one time, many African and Indonesian students were studying at this level, but that trend is declining quickly, most likely because of the growth of indigenous programs in the Third World.

It is unusual to begin training at one university and to continue at another one; students generally complete all their training (candidature, license, and doctoral program) at the same university. The European Community launched the Erasmus Project, allowing students to obtain class credits at other universities. This program has started slowly in psychology but is expected to grow significantly. At this point, this exchange is limited mainly to third-license students. Although students get credit at a university in another country within the European Community, the final diploma comes from the university where their studies originated.

Outside the universities, some schools have created courses that prepare the student for the position of assistant psychologist. The function of an assistant psychologist consists mainly of testing subjects under the supervision of a university-trained psychologist or medical personnel.

Number of Psychologists

It is difficult to estimate the number of psychologists in the country, as there are no official records or lists of psychologists. However, the number of students who finish their license degrees every year is known. Using the criterion of license, the number of psychologists in the country must be above 6,000. (The population of Belgium is slightly below 10 million.) There have been more French-speaking psychologists in the past. Nevertheless, the number of Dutch-speaking psychologists has been increasing very rapidly, and they now exceed the number of French-speaking psychologists.

Male-to-Female Ratio in the Profession

In the area of sex differences a big difference exists between the two language communities. There have always been many more female than male French-speaking psychologists (approximately a 70:30 ratio) with a license degree. Up to the late 1970s, Dutch-speaking psychologists (with a license degree) were male by a clear majority. A shift to more female Dutch-speaking students began in the mid-1980s. In 1982 and 1985 49.4 percent male and 50.6 per cent female Dutch-speaking psychologists finished their studies (Lagrou & De Witte, 1988). In marked contrast, only a few female psychologists receive an academic position at a university. This is true in both language communities, and no change is expected in the near future.

Usual Work Settings and Specialties

Lagrou and De Witte (1988) conducted a survey regarding the employment and specialization of Dutch-speaking psychologists who completed their studies in 1982 and 1985. The pattern of findings is likely to be representative for the whole country (with slightly more unemployed French-speaking psychologists). They found the following distribution: jobs in industrial/organizational psychology, 15.7 percent; assessment/school psychology, 3.0 percent; clinical psychology, 68.3 percent; basic research, 3.4 percent; nonactive psychologists, 2.4 percent; and unemployed/job-seeking psychologists, 7.1 percent.

Recent trends indicate an increasing number of jobs available in industrial/organizational psychology and in research, with a clear decline in clinical jobs. Clinical employment is critically dependent on general governmental policies for health care; a single governmental decision may change at once the employment prospects in clinical psychology.

Status of Licensure

Although the university degree of license of psychology is legally protected, the title "psychologist" is not yet protected. For many years, the Belgian Psychological Society and the Federation of Belgian Psychologists have been actively seeking legal protection. Considerable progress has been made in recent years. A law has been submitted for approval in the Parliament and should be voted on in the near future. Since there are no basic objections, it is anticipated that the law will pass without problems.

Characteristics of Psychology

Universities Offering Study in Psychology

There are now six main universities in Belgium, and they all offer a full curriculum in psychology (candidature, license, and doctoral degree). The Catholic University of Louvain/Leuven was divided in 1968 into two new universities: one Dutch-speaking (Katholieke Universiteit Leuven), which stayed in Louvain/Leuven, and the other French-speaking (Université Catholique de Louvain), which moved to a new campus (20 miles farther south), Louvain-La-Neuve. They account for the largest number of students from the Dutch and French parts of the country, respectively. The same language split occurred at the Free University of Brussels, although in this case both universities (Université Libre de Bruxelles and Vrije Universiteit Brussel) remained in the same vicinity, near the center of Brussels. The two remaining universities, at Ghent (Dutch-speaking, Rijksuniversiteit Gent) and Liège (French-speaking, Université de Liège) are state universities, although all six of them are supported by the state at about the same level. The main difference between state and private universities is in the official body that is entitled to appoint new professors.

In response to the large increase in students at the end of the 1960s, regional universities were established. This decentralization, however, was not carried out for psychology, except in Mons, where a program in psychology also exists.

National Journals

The Belgian Psychological Society publishes a scientific journal, *Psychologica Belgica* (two issues a year). It contains articles in French, English, and Dutch (but always preceded by an English summary). In addition to the journal, the society has a newsletter (published four times a year), the *BVP/SBP Bulletin;* articles are in French, English, or Dutch. The Federation of Belgian Psychologists also publishes two newsletters, one in Dutch and the other in French. There are several smaller professional organizations, and most of them have their own newsletters.

Societies and Organizations

The Belgian Psychological Society was founded in 1947 to bring together all those who employ psychology (understood as a nonphilosophical discipline) as the object of their theoretical research or their practical and professional activity. Membership is open to university-trained people working in psychology (license or doctoral degree). Full members have a degree in psychology; others are associate members. Within the society different interest groups have been created to represent the different theoretical and applied fields: animal psychology, cognitive psychology, social psychology, developmental psychology, clinical psychology, industrial and organizational psychology, hermeneutics, data analysis, and instructional psychology. These groups have regular meetings and seminars. The society organizes an annual general meeting for all the members to provide the opportunity for presenting current research.

The Belgian Psychological Society is a member society of the International Union of Psychological Science. Several members have played an active role in the International Union, a striking achievement in view of the small size of the country. Two members (Michotte and Nuttin) have been presidents of the union, and d'Ydewalle is currently the deputy secretary-general.

The Belgian Federation of Psychologists, founded in 1979, is a professional psychological association made up of many different associations: Association des Conseillers-Directeur des Centres Psycho-Médico-Sociaux et Offices d'Orientations Libres Francophones (ADLF), Association Professionnelle des Psychologues en Centre Psycho-Médico-Sociaux (APMS), Associations de Psychologues Psychothérapeutes Francophones (APPF), Belgische Beroepsunie der Psychologues (BBP), Belgische Vereniging voor Psychologie/ Société Beige de Psychologie (BVP/SBP), Groupement des Psychologues Universitaires (GPU), Nationale Vereniging van Praktizerende Universitaire Psychologen/Association Nationale des Psychologues Practiciens Universitaires (NVPUP/ANPPU), Régionale de Psychologie du Hainaut Occidental (REPHO), Vereniging Antwerpse Psychologen (VAP), Vereniging voor Organizatie-, Consumenten- en Arbeidspsychologen (VOCAP), Vereniging voor Psychologen uit PMS-Centra (VPP), Vlaamse Vereniging van Klinische Psychologen (VVKP), and Vlaamse Vereniging van Psychologen-Psychotherapeuten (VVP-SOP). The major purpose of the federation in the immediate future is to obtain legal protection for the title "psychologist" and for the profession. To become a member of the federation, one must belong to at least one of the aforementioned federated associations.

The federation has almost 1,000 members; the Belgian Psychological Society has at least 1,000 members (although only 400 of them pay their dues regularly). Both the federation and the society have organizational structures that reflect the politicolinguistic situation in Belgium. For example, the Belgian Psychological Society has two secretaries-general and two deputy secretaries, one of each for the Dutch section of the country and one of each for the French-speaking part.

Availability of Textbooks and Psychometric Instruments

Scientific psychology is well established in the country and in the universities. All major international publications are available. The publisher Mardaga, based in Liège and directed by M. Richelle (professor in Liège), is particularly important for the francophone world of French publications in psychology: it has an influential series on human sciences, with most of them on psychology. A considerable number of psychometric instruments have been developed in the country for the two language communities. All modern research equipment, including various kinds of computer facilities, can be found in the research centers. Almost all university libraries are interconnected, and a large data base of publications is accessible by an elaborate electronic retrieval system. Virtually anyone can make a search through his or her computer terminal or personal computer. All research centers are also connected to EARN (European Academic Research Network). Belgian researchers, particularly in psychology, are heavy users of electronic mailing.

Governmental Financial Support for Psychology

Financial support for psychology hovers somewhere between the level of support given to the human sciences and to the medical sciences, that is, more than other disciplines of human sciences but less than the medical sciences. Governmental support is mainly provided through the Belgian National Fund for Scientific Research. A few other foundations in Belgium are able to support science (e.g., Francqui Foundation, IWONL/IRSEA). Some further support is now coming from the European Community.

Public Views of Psychology

Psychologists are no longer viewed suspiciously. They have penetrated into the public life of the country and into all major activities. In addition to their involvement in school psychology, psychologists have become active in many clinics and hospitals, banks, and major industries. Since health care is paid mainly by the government, the government supports the activities of many clinical psychologists. The position of the clinical psychologists vis-à-vis psychiatrists is an issue of major debate in the country. Recently, an intense discussion arose from a decision by the government to consider clinical psychologists a paramedical profession. There were strong negative reactions from psychologists, who prefer not to be dependent on psychiatrists.

Current Status of Psychology (1960–87)

Major Philosophical and Theoretical Influences
As is occurring all over the world, Belgian psychology has been heavily influenced by the recent upsurge in cognitive psychology. This influence is also apparent in almost all professional areas of psychology. Techniques of assessment have been revised to take into account recent developments in cognitive psychology; cognitive neuropsychology is flourishing; social psychology leans heavily in the direction of cognitive psychology; and so forth.

The main ideas of scientific psychology are in the tradition of American and major European forms of psychology. It is fair to say that there is no strong competition among schools of psychology in the country (with a few exceptions). Psychotherapy, for example, uses rather flexible ideas and techniques from psychoanalysis, humanistic psychology, and cognitive behavior therapy.

Leading Native Psychologists and Research Centers
The growth of psychology in Belgium into a full-fledged discipline and recognized profession is probably more intimately linked to the research work of a small number of individuals than may be the case in other countries. Nuttin (1961) provides comprehensive descriptions of the leading psychologists in the country. An abridged version can be found in d'Ydewalle (1984). Modern psychology in Belgium, however, can no longer be described by the work of a few individuals. As the field reached maturity, all subdisciplines were actively pursued in all the main universities. Although some topics of psychology receive more emphasis in some departments, all the main universities provide training and research in almost all parts of psychology. It is probably unfair to list here a few of the more outstanding psychologists.

A special issue of *Psychologica Belgica* was published in 1971 describing all research activities at the several universities. A new special issue is being prepared with updated information and will appear before the 25th International Congress of Psychology, to be held in Brussels in 1992.

The Future
The Belgian Psychological Society is organizing the 1992 International Congress of Psychology. Accepting the challenge of organizing such a large and complicated meeting requires many Belgian psychologists to work together to achieve a well-balanced scientific program. All psychologists will have the opportunity to learn about the most advanced ideas in psychol-

ogy. Moreover, the congress will help to improve the status of scientific psychology and of psychologists in the country.

This congress (July 19–24, 1992) will be a special event in several ways. First, it is the twenty-fifth of a long series of highly successful international congresses. Included in the program will be several items concerning the history of those congresses. Second, it offers the opportunity to commemorate the beginning of scientific psychology in Belgium, where some of the first laboratories were established around 1890. Finally, 1992 is the year when many barriers are to be abolished within the European Community, and the United States of Europe will be officially established. It is thus fitting that the congress will be held in the Belgian capital. At the crossroads of two language communities (representing the north and the south of Europe), Brussels is an appropriate place to represent the two official languages (English and French) of the International Union of Psychological Science.

Bibliography

d'Ydewalle, G. (1984). Psychology in Belgium. In R. J. Corsini (Ed.), *Encyclopedia of psychology* (Vol. 3, pp. 117–118). New York: Wiley.

Lagrou, L., & De Witte, H. (1988). Kenmerken van de loopbaan van recent afgestudeerden psychologen. *Informatiebulletin van de Belgische Federatie van Psychologen, 9,* 6–23.

Nuttin, J. R. (1961). *Psychology in Belgium.* Louvain: Publications Universitaires.

Richelle, M., Janssen, P. J., & Bredart, S. (1992). Psychology in Belgium. *Annual Review of Psychology, 43.*

6 / Brazil

ANGELA M. B. BIAGGIO & ROBERT E. GRINDER

Angela M. B. Biaggio (born 1940) received a PhD in educational psychology from the University of Wisconsin in 1967. A specialist in developmental psychology, she has written a developmental textbook, Psicologia do desenvolvimento *(Developmental psychology), and more than 40 articles. Biaggio has served on the editorial boards of six journals, as an officer of the Interamerican Society of Psychology, and as an adviser to the Brazilian National Research Council and to the Ministry of Education. She is professor of psychology and education at the Federal University, in Porto Alegre, Brazil, and a senior researcher of the Brazilian National Research Council.*

Robert E. Grinder (born 1929) received the EdD degree from Harvard University in 1960. His publications are largely in his two specialties, human development and the history of psychology, and include the books A History of Genetic Psychology *and* Adolescence. *Grinder has served as president of Division 15 (educational psychology) of the American Psychological Association and as a visiting Fulbright Professor at the Federal University, Rio Grande do Sul, Brazil (1987). He is professor in the Division of Psychology in Education at Arizona State University.*

Brazil is the most industrialized nation in Latin America. Rio de Janeiro is one of the most beautiful cosmopolitan communities in the world, and Sao Paulo is the third largest commercial hub. The country's population is 138 million, of whom 27.5 million live in cities having populations greater than 1 million, and 85 million in cities of more than 50,000 (*Almanaque Abril*, 1987).

Although the urban landscape in Brazil is growing in leaps and bounds, it spans a century of social and industrial change. For a great many Brazilians, a crude feudalism takes the place of the modern state. Volkswagens, Fords, and Chevrolets share suburban streets with two-wheeled, horse-drawn carts, laden with milk, old newspapers, vegetables, and fruit. Curb and sidewalk entrepreneurs compete vigorously with modern supermar-

This chapter was written during the spring of 1987, when Robert E. Grinder was a Visiting Fulbright Professor at Federal University, Rio Grande do Sul, Brazil.

kets. Banks, insurance companies, agricultural enterprises, and manufacturing companies participate in worldwide markets while a great many tenant farmers, domestics, and illiterate, unskilled workers are still not part of the money economy.

Brazil is a country of contradictions. Whereas nationwide participation in the industrial revolution has given rise to substantial middle-class affluence, many Brazilians who migrated from rural areas to the cities have attained neither employment nor adequate living conditions. To ameliorate their poverty, these citizens have created neighborhoods, or *favelas*, of shanties constructed of cardboard and tin amid shiny new apartments, condominiums, and architect-designed homes. Brazilians in general are preoccupied with fighting off the ravages of poverty, a circumstance that causes them to be somewhat insensitive to scores of abandoned children and adolescents (half of the population of Brazil is under 17 years of age) who live and sleep on the street. Most of these youngsters are doomed to a life of illiteracy, crime, alcohol, and drugs.

The Training of Psychologists

Comprehensive, formal education represents a relatively recent appendage to the Brazilian culture. Jesuit priests established a few isolated schools and seminaries during the 300 years that Brazil was a colony of Portugal. These schools functioned not for the purpose of enriching the culture but for proselytizing the natives. Following the country's emancipation in 1889 as a republic, a new government established nationwide programs in elementary and secondary education and, in keeping with the practice in Europe, also founded secular or normal schools for training prospective teachers. In about 1900 the government also organized learned faculties into separate schools of law, medicine, engineering, and philosophy. The revolution of 1930 brought to power Getulio Vargas, a dedicated social reformer. Under his leadership, the government established universities by bringing together in different localities the existing faculties in engineering, law, medicine, and philosophy. Each faculty governed itself for several years and, during this period, competed separately for funds. When the Brazilian Congress enacted administrative reforms in 1961, the four faculties and the humanities—a new, fifth faculty—were brought under the control of a central administration.

The Brazilian government formally acknowledged the discipline of psychology in 1962 when it passed a law setting forth a 5-year professional program leading to a "diploma of psychologist," that is, to a license to practice clinical, organizational, and/or educational (school) psychology. The program requires currently about 500 hours of supervised practicum in each of the three areas.

The 5-year professional program is somewhat comparable to an undergraduate degree in psychology in the United States. In Brazil, however, students obtain liberal arts training in high school and, on entering a university at age 18, study psychology intensively for 5 years. The program thus offers much more time for professional training than would a conventional liberal arts major in psychology in the United States. Graduates, as a consequence, are certified to work as clinicians, organizational psychologists, *and* school psychologists.

In 1968 the Brazilian government legislated that departments of psychology be created in the federal universities within the faculties in humanities. By 1971 28 departments of psychology were operational. With the recent growth of departments of psychology in the private sector, the number of departments functioning today exceeds 100. The proliferation is a result of private sector initiatives to meet the demands of Brazilians for professional training in psychology. Indeed, private schools are currently graduating 65 to 85 percent of the students in psychology. The programs are oriented entirely toward developing students' applied skills. Such programs are inexpensive compared to those in the natural and physical sciences, where laboratory instruction is required. Nonetheless, private-sector offerings in psychology, which survive mainly because demand exists for them, are often undercapitalized. Unfortunately, instruction and training in the marginal programs often are quite inferior.

Courses in psychology were available, of course, long before the creation of departments. Psychological laboratories for testing pupils and training teachers were founded in the early normal schools. University-level courses began to appear in the 1950s when the first programs in psychology were established by Hans Lippmann and Antonious Benko at the Pontificia Universidade Catolica (Catholic University), Rio de Janeiro, in 1955 and by Arrigo Angelini at the Universidade de Sao Paulo (University of Sao Paulo) in 1958.

The first master's program in psychology was created in 1966 and the first doctoral program in 1974. Fifteen MA and four PhD programs are now offered in Brazil. The PhD programs are located in Rio de Janeiro (Pontificia Universidade Catolica; Fundacao Getulio Vargas) and Sao Paulo (Pontificia Universidade Catolica; Universidade de Sao Paulo). Programs of study for both degrees include seminars and a thesis requirement. For the MA, a residency of 1 year and proficiency in one foreign language is required; for the PhD, 2 years' residency and two foreign languages are required.

As of May 1987, according to the Conselho Federal de Psicologia (Federal Council of Psychology), 61,213 psychologists—nearly all of whom graduated from the 5-year professional program—were registered in Brazil. Ninety percent are under 40 years of age. Nearly all are poorly paid. The ratio of females to males in the profession is about 3:1 (Rosemberg, 1984). Fifty percent of the men and 25 percent of the women work full-time as psychologists. One third are employed also as receptionists, cab drivers, and secretaries.

Sex-role differentiation in the Brazilian work force accounts for the relatively high number of females attracted to the profession. Women in Brazil have been directed traditionally toward the humanities and away from the sciences. Many of them accept it as destiny to be socialized to expressive rather than instrumental roles, and study in psychology allows them to adapt and compromise their aspirations for motherhood and work. It is thus popular among women, who see it as background for their roles as wives and mothers. A career in psychology enables them to supplement family income by working part-time as psychologists or as day-care teachers, kindergarten teachers, secretaries, journalists, receptionists, and opinion-poll researchers.

Since women apply in large numbers to the social sciences, particularly to psychology, rather than to male-dominated, high-status programs in engineering, medicine, and pure sciences, competition is intense for openings in the psychology programs in the federal universities. The circumstance leads admission standards in psychology to be as stringent as those in the "hard" sciences, in spite of the fact that the field is relatively less prestigious.

The overwhelming emphasis on applied activities in the 5-year professional programs makes it difficult to attract students to research-oriented graduate programs. When students begin work for either the MA or PhD degree, they are unacquainted with issues and opportunities in research. Moreover, to strengthen their position in the marketplace, they reject exposure to research in favor of enhancing practical skills. Since research is unappreciated, faculty who participate in graduate training face a dilemma as they address student expectations and seek simultaneously to uphold research standards for the MA and PhD degrees.

Although more than 100 institutions in Brazil offer programs in professional psychology, only 11 of them also conduct graduate programs. Faculty who participate in the graduate programs generally have earned a PhD degree from an American, European, or Brazilian university. Most of them are employed full-time by one institution. Some faculty members, however, work in two or more graduate programs. Dual appointments are most common in Rio de Janeiro, where several programs are in close proximity. Unfortunately, the practice limits time for research, publishing, and interaction with students.

Professors of psychology in the graduate programs began obtaining doctorates during the 1960s and 1970s. When the first university courses in psychology were established in the 1950s, professors tended to be drawn from the disciplines of philosophy, medicine, and education. These early professors obtained on their own a background in psychology through informal reading. Before the reform of university education in 1968, which established the graduate programs, individuals with faculty appointments could obtain a doctoral degree in psychology by writing a thesis. The few psychologists in the country who were qualified to examine them served on their committees. In the 1960s a European-trained psychologist teaching at Catholic University, Rio de Janeiro, Father Antonius Benko, recognized that graduate programs were about to burgeon in Brazil. He inspired six of his students to seek doctorates abroad. Father Benko and Julian C. Stanley, then at the University of Wisconsin, Madison, helped the students obtain scholarships and assistantships. Four joined Stanley at Wisconsin, one went to Belgium, and another to the University of California at Los Angeles. Subsequently, in the 1970s, the Brazilian Ministry of Education provided scholarships for faculty members who were teaching in federal universities to obtain doctoral degrees—primarily in the United States and secondarily in Europe.

Professional Journals and Books

The most widely read journal in Brazil is *Arquivos Brasileiros de Psicologia* (Brazilian archives of psychology). It has been published since 1948 and is the only Brazilian journal abstracted for *Psychological Abstracts*. *Revista de Psicologia* (Journal of psychology), another venerable journal, is published by the University of Sao Paulo. The *Interamerican Journal of Psychology*, sponsored by the Interamerican Society of Psychology, is also popular among Brazilian psychologists. The journal publishes articles in any one of the four major languages of the Americas: English, French, Portuguese, or Spanish. Three recent journals of good quality are *Psicologia: Teoria e Pesquisa* (Psychology: Theory and practice), started in 1985 by the Department of Psychology, University of Brasilia; *Psicologia: Ciencia e Profissao* (Psychology: Science and profession), initiated in 1979 by the Federal Council of Psychology; and *Psicologia: Reflexao e Critica* (Psychology: Thoughts and reviews), which had its beginning in 1986 in the Department of Psychology, Federal University, Rio Grande do Sul.

Before psychology was recognized as a profession in Brazil, most of the available resource materials and textbooks were translations into Portuguese from the works of such European psychologists as Claparède, Freud, and

Piaget. By the time the profession was officially established, texts of such distinguished American psychologists as Allport, Hilgard, Keller, Klineberg, Rogers, and Skinner had been translated into Portuguese. More recently, with the infusion of funds and the growth of graduate programs in the 1970s, translations have been made of textbooks in various fields of psychology: developmental (Bee; Mussen, Conger, & Kagan; Stone & Church), personality (Hall & Lindzey), educational (Klausmeier), social (Krech, Crutchfield & Ballachey; Klineberg), statistics (Siegel), general (Krech & Crutchfield; Morgan; Whittaker), and testing (Anastasi).

A great many Brazilian faculty members in psychology can read English fluently, but economic conditions limit severely the availability of current books dealing with theory and research. Burdensome import taxes, currency restrictions, postal delays, and delivery uncertainties deter Brazilian psychologists from importing books and journals. Fortunately, Brazilian textbook writers have augmented access to contemporary scholarship. For example, the textbooks of Biaggio (1975, 1983) in developmental psychology, Marques (1983) in educational psychology, Novaes (1970) in school psychology, Rodrigues (1973) in social psychology, and Van Kolck (1975) in psychological testing have been used extensively.

The relative paucity of textbooks, in both English and Portuguese, stems also from the fact that both faculty and students resist using them. Textbooks are said to provide one-sided perspectives that tend to force students into a single mode of thinking and to discourage library research and development of individual interests. Instead, faculty and students favor reading lists—of perhaps 20 books—from which students may elect to read whatever they are inclined to read. Since the students are seldom tested, those who are not strongly motivated often ignore the readings.

Financial Support for Research in Psychology

Virtually all of the financial support for research in psychology is provided by either the Ministry of Education or the Brazilian National Research Council. The ministry distributes support funds to universities mainly for research infrastructures, that is, basic supplies, space, secretarial services, faculty released time, and graduate student scholarships. The ministry also includes such divisions as the Instituto Nacional de Estudos Pedagogicos (INEP, National Institute of Pedagogical Studies), which sponsors individual and institutional research projects in education, many of which are in educational psychology. However, the Conselho Nacional de Desenvolvimento Cientifico e Tecnologico (CNPq; National Council of Scientific and Technological Development), a function of the National Research Council, is the major source of research funds in Brazil. The Conselho awards research grants to individuals in the form of salary supplements and graduate student scholarships. It also furnishes funds for purchasing equipment, employing research assistants, and sponsoring visiting research scholars and scientific meetings.

Professional Associations

Three types of associations in Brazil support professional activity in psychology. First, there are the councils, which were created by the Brazilian Congress in 1971 to monitor professional practices, uphold ethical standards, and regulate the functions and responsibilities of psychologists in Brazil. Brazil is divided into eight regional councils. Membership in one of them and payment of an annual fee is required of all practicing psychologists. The members of each council elect a regional governing board and delegates to serve on the Federal Council of Psychology, which, in turn, performs a consultative and mediational role for the regional councils.

Second, statewide and special interest associations are organized to foster substantive communication among psychologists via scientific meetings, including conferences, congresses, and seminars. The newest association is the Associacao Nacional de Pesquisa e Pos-Graduacao em Psicologia (ANPEPP, National Association for Graduate Study and Research in Psychology). It was founded in 1983 to stimulate research in psychology by encouraging the training of researchers, the financing of research, the publication of scientific papers, and the exchange of researchers among institutions. Membership is by graduate program, each of which pays dues to the association. A meeting is held biennially for representatives from each program.

Third, some psychologists in Brazil have organized regional *sindicatos*, which are analogous to labor unions. The *sindicatos*, supported from annual membership fees, make efforts to improve the salaries of employed psychologists.

No national organization in Brazil is equivalent to the American Psychological Association. In 1977, after considerable discussion, the Sociedade Brasileira de Psicologia (SBP), Sao Paulo, was chosen over the Associacao Brasileira de Psicologia Aplicada (ABPA), Rio de Janeiro, to represent the country in the International Union of Psychological Sciences. These prominent organizations notwithstanding, the most important, nationwide, scientific gathering of psychologists occurs when the Sociedade de Psicologia de Ribeirao-Preto holds its annual meeting.

Significant Areas of Research and Current Trends

Research in Brazil centers on graduate programs and distinguished psychologists. In the 1960s Fred Keller, Robert Berryman, and Carolina Bori developed programs in the Skinnerian tradition at the University of Brasilia and at the University of Sao Paulo (USP). Joao Claudio Todorov, Cesar Ades, Maria Amelia Mattos, and Dora Ventura currently support the strong traditions in experimental psychology at their universities. The University of Sao Paulo is also known for its Piagetian studies, directed by Zelia Chiarottino and Lino de Macedo, and for the work of Arrigo Angelini, the late Nelson Rosmilha, and Dante Moreira Leite in, respectively, educational, developmental, and personality psychology. At the University of Sao Paulo at Ribeirao-Preto (USPRP), Luis M. de Oliveira and Jose Lino Bueno conduct research in psychobiology; also at (USPRP), Maria Cotilde Ferreira studies the physical ecology of day-care centers and promotes mother-child interaction research. Further, Aroldo Rodrigues of Rio de Janeiro, with studies in balance, attribution, and equity theory, has established an international reputation in social psychology. He has also contributed to the study of the Brazilian national character in collaboration with J. Dela Coleta (Uberlandia) and Maria Alice D'Amorim. At the Federal University of Pernambuco (Recife), Terezinha Carraher, David Carraher, and Analucia Schliemann lead a strong program in cognitive-developmental psychology. At the Federal University, Rio Grande do Sul, Juracy Marques has developed attractive programs in applied learning, and Angela Biaggio has established an active research program in moral development.

Given the European roots of the discipline of psychology in Brazil and the migration in the 1960s and 1970s of young Brazilian psychologists to the United States for PhDs, a lively pluralism of theoretical orientations has arisen. The current dialectical tension centers primarily on the experimental-quantitative versus phenomenological-qualitative approaches. In addition, stimulating dialogue between Piagetians and behaviorists, psychoanalysts and behaviorists, and basic and action researchers occurs in the journals, at scientific meetings, and during discussions about research in the graduate programs. The discipline of psychology became a formal reality only in 1962, yet today in Brazil there are more than 60,000 registered psychologists! As research traditions develop and as relevant theory and findings influence the practicing professionals, prospects for the future of psychology in Brazil are indeed promising.

Bibliography

Almanaque Abril. (1987). Sao Paulo: Editora Abril, S.A.

Biaggio, A. M. B. (1975). *Psicologia do desenvolvimento.* Petropolis, RJ: Editora Vozes Ltda.

Biaggio, A. M. B. (1983). *Pesquisas em psicologia do desenvolvimento e da personalidade.* Porto Alegre: Editora da Universidade Federal do Rio Grande do Sul.

Marques, J. C. (1983). *Ensinando para o desenvolvimento pessoal: Psicologia das relacoes interpessoais.* Petropolis, RJ: Editora Vozes Ltda.

Novaes, M. H. (1970). *Psicologia escolar.* Petropolis, RJ: Editora Vozes Ltda.

Rodrigues, A. S. S. (1973). *Psicologia social.* Petropolis, RJ: Editora Vozes Ltda.

Rosemberg, F. (1984). Afinal, por que somos tantas psicologas? *Psicologia: Ciencia e Profissao, 4,* 6–12.

Van Kolck, O. (1975). *Tecnicas de exame psicologico* (Vols. 1–2). Petropolis, RJ: Editora Vozes Ltda.

7 / Canada

TERRENCE P. HOGAN &

MICHEL PIERRE JANISSE

Terrence P. Hogan (born 1937) received his PhD from Catholic University in the USA in 1963. A clinical psychologist, he has edited four books and published several dozen articles on such diverse topics as family therapy, decision making, psychology and the law, and training issues in psychology. He also serves on the editorial board for Canadian Psychology *and* Canada's Mental Health. *Hogan was elected president of the Canadian Psychological Association for 1982–83 and was five times president of the Psychological Association of Manitoba between 1978 and 1983. In 1984 he received an award from the Canadian Psychological Association for distinguished contributions to psychology as a profession. He is currently associate vice-president (academic development), professor of psychology, and special lecturer of psychiatry at the University of Manitoba, Winnipeg.*

Michel Pierre Janisse (born 1943) received a PhD in psychology from the University of Waterloo in 1970. A fellow of the Canadian Psychological Association, he has published several dozen articles in the areas of personality, stress and anxiety, and psychophysiology. He has authored The Psychology of the Pupillary Response *(1977) and edited two other books,* Pupillary Dynamics and Behavior *(1974) and* Individual Differences, Stress, and Health Psychology *(1988). Janisse has reviewed for major Canadian and USA research councils and has chaired the Doctoral Fellowship Panel of the Social Sciences and Humanities Research Council of Canada. He is professor at the University of Manitoba, where he has also held the positions of associate dean of graduate studies (1982–84) and head of the Department of Psychology (1985–88). Since 1988 he has been dean of the Continuing Education Division.*

Psychology in Canada is a well-established and mature discipline. The discipline is part of the mainstream of modern psychological research and practice and, as such, includes most major orientations and theoretical approaches.

The development of the discipline of psychology in Canada has been affected both by the geography of the country and its history. Canada geographically is the world's second largest country but has a relatively small population of 26 million. Because Canada is an immigrant nation, its population is highly multicultural. The effect on psychology in having two founding nations and cultures is clear. The academic and professional traditions associated with the English and French cultures are seen in the differences between universities and professions in the anglophone and francophone regions of the country.

The most distinctive aspect of Canadian psychology (and one of the few characteristics that differentiates it from psychology in the USA) is the large body of research, thought, and clinical and applied practice in the French language. The fortuitous happenstance of Canada's bilingual nature has added a richness to the discipline of psychology in Canada that is rarely found elsewhere. As a result, the world has benefited from research both splendid and zealous. A significant example is the investigation into cross-cultural psychology, using what some consider to be the natural laboratory of Quebec, as well as the many other "pockets" of French-speaking citizens in various locations in Canada. More fundamentally, inquiries into the nature of second language acquisition, as well as bilingual language development itself, have broken new ground and have attracted psychologists from around the world to examine this uniquely Canadian area of study.

In recent years large numbers of immigrants have entered the country from southern Europe, South Asia, and East Asia. The effects of these new cultural additions are currently being experienced not only by Canada as a country, but by Canadian psychology as well. Moreover, Canadian psychologists are now beginning to recognize the importance of the native or aboriginal peoples of Canada (North American Indians and the Inuit) as an important part of the Canadian mosaic of cultures.

Canada's geography and its small population have produced widely spaced population centers spread in a narrow band across the 10,000-kilometer border with the United States. The major political result has been the development of 10 relatively independent provinces, which under the Canadian Constitution are responsible entirely for education and health care, among other areas. Considerable variation has developed between provinces in the development of their educational and health care systems, two areas of immense interest to psychologists and with a clear impact on psychology as a profession. One common element among the provinces is that university education is almost totally funded by the public purse. Private university education as it is known elsewhere in the world, particularly in the United States, does not exist in Canada.

As noted later, research funding traditionally has been a federal responsibility in Canada, even though provinces are not precluded constitutionally from funding research. In fact, some provinces have begun to contribute significant amounts of money to the support of research.

Characteristics of the Psychologist

There are approximately 8,000 psychologists in Canada, all of whom hold either a master's or PhD degree. Although the PhD is considered the preferred terminal degree for all psychologists, a large number of psychologists who hold the master's degree work in applied settings.

Most Canadian psychologists have been educated in Canadian universities, although a significant minority have been educated in American, British, or Western European institutions. Approximately 20 percent of Canadian psychologists work in university or college settings, with their primary responsibilities being teaching and research. Of those psychologists in universities, the great majority, probably more than 90 percent, hold the PhD degree. Approximately 60 percent of Canadian psychologists working in applied settings hold doctoral degrees, and 40 percent master's degrees. Approximately 62 percent are male and 38 percent are female.

In 1984 a detailed survey of Canadian psychologists by the Canadian Psychological Association indicated that they are employed in a wide variety of work settings. Table 7.1 lists the types of position respondents to the survey noted in regard to their primary work area. The majority indicated that they were involved in providing direct human services, with the remainder noting faculty positions at a university or college, research positions, administration, or other. Table 7.2 from the same survey indicates the main area of specialization of the respondents. These data came from a survey

TABLE 7.1
Type of Positions Held by Canadian Psychologists (N = 1,085)

Type of Position	%
Faculty	18.0
Research	6.4
Direct human services	56.4
Administration	8.8
Other	10.4
Total	100.0

TABLE 7.2

Main Areas of Specialization of Canadian Psychologists (N = 1,085)

Field	%
Psychological evaluation	48.2
Psychotherapy	57.7
Vocational guidance	14.2
Education	15.9
Forensic	5.2
Community	8.0
Neuropsychology	5.4
Industrial	3.5
Organizational development	5.8
Health	6.8
Program evaluation	6.6
Gerontology	2.0
Engineering	2.0
Sport	0.2
Learning disabilities	6.3
Drug abuse	2.9
Teaching	16.5
Applied research	11.1
Pure research	3.7
Rehabilitation	3.0
Environmental	0.5

Note. Since many respondents answered more than once, the percentage value was computed using the total sample, i.e., 1,085, as a reference point.

of all Canadian psychologists (which at the time of the survey numbered approximately 7,000), with 1,085 responding. As can be seen in Table 7.2, the dominant activities of psychologists working in applied settings were psychological evaluation and psychotherapy.

Licensure or registration of psychologists is required in most Canadian jurisdictions. Because the control and registration of professional activities in Canada is a provincial responsibility, the requirements for licensure or registration vary from province to province. At the present time only Prince Edward Island, of Canada's 10 provinces, does not require certification. Most of the other provinces require the doctoral degree, some period of supervised experience, and the passing of examinations for a psychologist to become licensed or registered. In addition to provincial registration and licensing acts, a nationwide register of psychologists offering health services has been established on a voluntary basis. It is hoped that this voluntary national registry will lead to a greater consistency of licensing and registration requirements across the country.

Characteristics of Psychology

Nearly every university and college in Canada, in all 10 provinces, offers psychology at the undergraduate level. The wide breadth of the discipline of psychology is shown in the diversity of program emphases and of courses offered at the different institutions.

The structure and content of both graduate and undergraduate degree programs in Canada reflect the traditional mixture of American and British university traditions and practices. Psychology programs are typically offered at the undergraduate level within both general degree programs and honors programs. Students planning to attend graduate schools have traditionally chosen to pursue an undergraduate honors degree, but increasing numbers of students currently are preparing themselves for graduate study in general degree programs. Most undergraduate programs require their students to take a minimum of 33 percent or, more typically, 50 percent or more of their education in psychology.

By and large there tends to be an emphasis on experimental psychology —including perception, psychobiology, psychophysiology, cognition, and comparative psychology—at the larger institutions. The "softer" side of psychology—including clinical, developmental, personality, and social psychology—tends to be emphasized at the smaller institutions. As with all generalizations, there are many exceptions to this image of Canadian undergraduate offerings, but on the whole it is a fairly accurate characterization.

Required courses typically include general psychology, research methods, and statistics, with a wide variety of courses in subdisciplinary areas making up the rest of the undergraduate program. Most graduate education in Canada generally includes distinct master's and PhD programs. Virtually all graduate programs in Canada at both the master's and PhD levels are research-oriented, although coursework and examinations are typically required of the students as well. Students in applied areas, in addition, have to complete lengthy periods of supervised applied work experience.

With regard to graduate education, 9 of the 10 provinces in Canada have at least one university offering doctoral-level programs (Table 7.3). The Univer-

TABLE 7.3

Canadian Universities Offering Doctoral Programs in Psychology

Province	University
British Columbia	Simon Fraser University
	University of British Columbia
	University of Victoria
Alberta	University of Alberta
	University of Calgary
Saskatchewan	University of Regina
	University of Saskatchewan
Manitoba	University of Manitoba
Ontario	Carleton University
	Guelph University
	McMaster University
	Queen's University
	University of Ottawa
	University of Toronto
	University of Waterloo
	University of Western Ontario
	University of Windsor
	York University
Quebec	Concordia University
	Université Laval
	McGill University
	Université de Montréal
	Université de Sherbrooke
	Université du Québec
New Brunswick	University of New Brunswick
Nova Scotia	Dalhousie University
Newfoundland	Memorial University of Newfoundland

sity of Prince Edward Island in the province of Prince Edward Island is the only major provincial university that does not offer doctoral-level training in psychology in Canada. In addition to those listed, many colleges in Canada offer master's-level training in psychology, educational psychology, and applied psychology. Likewise, several universities offer doctorates in educational psychology or in counseling psychology, and the Ontario Institute for Studies in Education offers a PhD in applied psychology.

Three national journals are published quarterly by the Canadian Psychological Association. (1) *Canadian Psychology,* formerly known as the *Canadian Psychologist* and as the *Canadian Psychological Review,* is a generalist journal that appeals broadly to psychologists in Canada. In recent years it has moved away from publishing mainly scientific review articles to papers of more concern to professional psychologists. It also includes many book reviews. Another function of the journal is to serve as the official record of the Canadian Psychological Association, publishing most of the archival data of that organization. (2) The *Canadian Journal of Behavioural Science* publishes articles in several applied areas and in abnormal, aging, child and adolescent, cross-cultural, personality, and social psychology. It is noteworthy that more than 40 percent of the articles published here are submitted from nonacademic settings, and a substantial minority come from smaller colleges. This journal is partially supported by grants from the Social Sciences and Humanities Research Council. (3) The *Canadian Journal of Psychology* is in many ways the flagship journal of the association. It is recognized as a journal of consequence around the world in that, unlike the other journals, it regularly publishes articles by non-Canadian authors. It is noted for publishing both theoretical and empirical articles in many areas of experimental psychology, with its major focus on animal and human learning, memory, perception, and the like. The journal is partially supported by the Natural Sciences and Engineering Research Council.

Other Canadian journals of particular interest to psychologists include the *Canadian Journal of Community Psychology* and *Canada's Mental Health.* Most of the provincial organizations also publish their own journals that deal largely with local professional matters. In addition, psychologists in Canada have relatively easy access to most of the journals published in the world today.

The main national society is the Canadian Psychological Association (CPA). Its approximately 4,500 members represent all branches of psychology in Canada. While the major components of the organization are the research-academic and applied-clinical wings, the association has many special interest groups that represent everything from women's issues to military psychology. The association is bilingual and provides for the needs of the two major language groups in Canada, publishing all of its informational texts in both English and French. It organizes a major conference each year in different parts of Canada, as well as several instructional institutes offered more frequently but on an irregular basis. Another aspect of the association's mandate is to represent the interests of Canadian psychology to the federal government. This is done through constant direct contact with the major funding councils, through unremitting lobbying of appropriate federal bodies, and through membership in such umbrella lobby groups as the

Social Science Federation of Canada. The association also maintains contacts and memberships in international psychological societies.

Each province has its own association, which primarily regulates or licenses the professional practice of psychology, since the regulation of professions, as noted earlier, is a provincial matter under the Canadian Constitution. These provincial associations also provide an occasion for fraternal gatherings, continuing education opportunities, a forum for research and communications, or simply the possibility for the exchange of information. Some provinces (e.g., Manitoba, Nova Scotia, Ontario, and Saskatchewan) have two organizations, one serving professional regulation, needs, and interests, and the other serving research and scholarly needs.

Two other national psychological organizations should be mentioned. The Council of Provincial Associations of Psychology is made up of representatives of all the provincial associations and CPA. It is an umbrella group whose major goal is to represent the concerns of provincial psychological associations, especially in regard to policies and plans of the federal government that affect professional psychology as it is practiced in the provinces. The second national organization is the Canadian Registry of Health Service Providers in Psychology. This group, which is the analogue of the Register in the USA, provides a list of professional psychologists who meet national and provincial standards related to the provision of health services. Although these organizations are not part of CPA, they use the address of the national organization.

Generally speaking, library and computer services in Canada are among the best in the world, and even those that are not still meet minimum standards. Textbooks, psychometric instruments, and laboratory equipment are readily available, either because they are produced in this country or because of the proximity and easy access to the United States.

Government support of psychology comes to universities through the provincial governments and is determined by the relative wealth of each province and by the priorities of each university. Approximately 50 percent of the provincial government funds are received by the province as transfer payments from the federal government, given on a complicated formula basis. Financial support of universities has generally been declining in real money terms since the mid-1970s, necessitating a great deal of belt-tightening and a reduction in the size of the professorial staff with, of course, a consequent reduction in the size of many programs, including those in psychology.

With regard to research, here too there have been severe cuts, reflected primarily in reduced government funding of the budgets of the major Canadian granting agencies. Psychologists have traditionally received support from the following three agencies. (1) The Social Sciences and Humanities Research Council of Canada supports several areas of research related to problems in such areas as social psychology, personality, development, aging, applied psychology, and the like. This council also provides funds for the publication of journals and books on a competitive basis and has a program to support promising young researchers for up to 5 years. (2) The Natural Sciences and Engineering Research Council supports those areas of psychology that are generally grouped under the rubric of experimental psychology (i.e., memory, human and animal learning, sensation and perception, physiological, psychophysiology, and the like). (3) The Medical Research Council generally sponsors research related to health issues and tends to support psychologists working in medical settings. Such areas as health psychology, behavioral medicine, and stress have been funded in the recent past.

In addition, research funds may also be available from a variety of other government sources and programs. The most prominent are the National Health Research and Development Program of Health and Welfare of Canada, and Sports Canada.

Current Status of Psychology (1960–89)

Psychology in Canada since 1960 is most accurately portrayed as a mirror reflecting the theoretical and philosophical influences and trends that affected North American psychology, particularly in the United States, during this period. The dominant influence has been the application of the hypothetico-deductive method to a broad array of psychological research topics in all of the major subdisciplinary areas. Although there have been critics within Canada of the dominance of this approach, most research laboratories in all areas of the country believe it is the most fruitful approach, both for the discipline and for their research.

In addition to this dominant influence, some Canadian psychologists have been affected by and have even become adherents to approaches originating from different philosophical bases. These other major influences include the behavioral approaches based on the work of B. F. Skinner, phenomenology, and—in the area of developmental psychology—Piagetian approaches to the study of child development. Though the effects of phenomenological and Piagetian approaches have been particularly evident in French Canada, they have also influenced psychologists elsewhere in the country.

A large number of Canadian psychologists in various subdisciplinary areas are internationally recognized. There is little doubt, however, that D. O. Hebb was the most influential psychologist within Canada and was Canadian psychology's best-known figure internationally from the mid-1960s to his death in 1985. Hebb, who did most of his work at McGill University, made major contributions in the neurosciences, perception, learning, motivation, and thinking. His work influenced a generation of psychologists in Canada, and during his most active years he had an immense impact on the development of the science in other areas of the world. In addition to his effect on psychology as a science, his leadership and influence greatly stimulated the overall development of psychology in Canada.

Many other psychologists in Canada have had a major impact on psychology as a science and as a profession. The Canadian Psychological Association established two major awards in 1979 to acknowledge distinguished contributions of Canadian psychologists (Table 7.4). The significant areas of research in Canada since the mid-1960s have been many and varied. Thus, it is necessary to be selective. A sense of the research accomplishments of the 1970s may be obtained by reading the two special issues of the *Canadian Psychologist* edited by Janisse (1981). Here prominent psychologists reviewed in depth the research in their own specialty areas and commented on the achievements of the previous 10 years. Another source that is current to 1984, and covers all aspects of psychology in Canada, is a book produced by the Canadian Psychological Association, entitled *The State of the Discipline, 1984* (Ritchie, Hogan, & Hogan, 1988).

Of major interest in the recent history of Canadian psychology has been work on bilingualism. These studies have been carried on mainly in the province of Quebec (e.g., at McGill University, Laval University, and the University of Quebec) but with pockets of interest in English-speaking areas of Canada also (e.g., the University of Western Ontario). Research into sensory deprivation or reduced environmental stimulation has been conducted at the University of Manitoba and the University of British Columbia. Although Canada is an arctic nation, remarkably little widespread psychological interest has been shown by psychologists in polar research. The exception has been the work done at the University of British Columbia in connection with the above-mentioned sensory research. In addition, the University of Montreal has produced excellent investigations on the related topic of stress. Noted studies on aggression have been conducted at the University of Alberta; on personality, at the University of British Columbia, the University of Western Ontario, and York University; on behavior modification and social psychology, at the University of Manitoba and the University of Waterloo; on memory, at Queen's University and the University of Toronto; on neuropsychology, at McGill University and the University of Windsor; on animal learning, at several centers, but in particular at Dalhousie Univer-

TABLE 7.4
Recipients of Awards for Distinguished Contributions to Canadian Psychology

For contributions to the science of psychology

1980	Donald Hebb	Neuropsychology
1981	Brenda Milner	Neuropsychology
1982	Allan Paivio	Cognition
1983	Endel Tulving	Memory
1984	Wallace Lambert	Bilingualism
1985	Doreen Kimura	Neuropsychology
1986	Ronald Melzack	Pain
1987	Fergus I. M. Craik	Memory and learning
1988	Phil Bryden	Neuropsychology
1989	No award made	

For contributions to the profession of psychology

1980	Virginia Douglas	Clinical psychology
1981	Park Davidson	Clinical/Community psychology
1982	Edward Webster	Industrial/Organizational
1983	Terrence Hogan	Professional practice
1984	C. Roger Myers	Organization of Canadian Psychology
1985	David Belanger	Development of psychology (esp. in French Canada)
1986	Raymond Berry	Professional psychology
1987	Stephanie Z. Dudek	Clinical psychology
1988	Wesley Coons	Professional psychology
1989	Donald Meichenbaum	Cognitive behavior modification

sity and the University of Alberta; and on hypnosis, at Carleton University. In the area of memory and cognition there is the "Southern Ontario Axis," consisting of many researchers from such universities as Brock, McMaster, Queen's, Trent, Toronto, Waterloo, Western Ontario, and York. Developmental processes in general have been studied at many sites, having been given their early impetus by the work at the University of Waterloo in the 1960s.

Major emerging trends appear in several areas. Research on aging, especially with regard to memory and other cognitive functions, is being studied at the University of Manitoba and the University of Toronto. Related to this work are the outstanding studies being done at the University of Alberta on Alzheimer's disease. Cognitive behavior modification continues to grow as a field of both research and clinical practice, being led by the group at the University of Waterloo, while influential research into a theory of cognitive functioning continues at the University of Western Ontario. The study of individual differences with regard to human behavior is an area that is rapidly gaining momentum, particularly at the University of British Columbia, the University of Ottawa, and York University. As is the case in much of the world, research in the broad areas of health psychology and behavioral medicine has been burgeoning, especially at such universities as Carleton, Manitoba, McMaster, Montreal, Saskatchewan, and York. Work in the area of women's issues and feminism continues to gain prominence, particularly with the research emerging from the Ontario Institute for Studies in Education, the University of Regina, and York University.

Bibliography

Ferguson, G. A. (1977). *Report of the Vancouver Conference on the Organization and Representation in Canada*. Toronto: Canadian Psychological Association.

MacLeod, R. B. (1955). *Psychology in Canadian universities and colleges*. Ottawa: Canadian Social Science Research Council.

Janisse, M. P. (Ed.). (1981). Canadian psychology, 1970–1980: A decade review. *Canadian Psychology, 22*, (1 & 2).

Ritchie, P. L.-J., Hogan, T. P., & Hogan, T. V. (Eds.). (1988). *Psychology in Canada: The state of the discipline, 1984*. Ottawa: Canadian Psychological Association.

Webster, E. C. (Ed.). (1967). *The Couchiching Conference on Professional Psychology*. Montreal: Industrial Relations Centre, McGill University.

Wright, M. J., & Myers, C. R. (Eds.). (1982). *History of academic psychology in Canada*. Toronto: Hogrefe.

8 / Colombia

RUBÉN ARDILA

Rubén Ardila (born 1942) received a PhD from the University of Nebraska in 1970. A specialist in both experimental psychology and the history of psychology, he has authored 20 books and more than 130 articles, in six languages. He is past president of the Interamerican Society of Psychology, the Latin American Association for the Analysis and Modification of Behavior, and the Colombian Federation of Psychology. Ardila has also been editor of the Latin American Journal of Psychology *since its founding in 1969.*

One of the most active Latin American psychologists, he has received the Interamerican Psychology Award, the Spanish Psychological Award, and the Colombian Psychological Award (1986). He is currently professor of psychology at the National University of Colombia in Bogotá.

Psychology and Psychologists

When I present psychology in Colombia to an international audience, I emphasize the need to place it in the context of Latin America. The countries of this area have common origins and probably face similar futures, in spite of the large differences that are found at the present time.

The basic information necessary to understand the development of psychology in this part of the world is presented in previous publications (see Ardila, 1970–87). Here I want to point out that Latin America has approximately 430 million inhabitants that speak Spanish, Portuguese, French, English, or "native" languages. The Latin American culture is a mixture of native American, European, and African traditions. In some cases, the native American aspect is most prominent (Mexico, Peru, Paraguay). In others, European culture is predominant (Argentina, Uruguay, Chile). In still other cases, African culture has priority (Haiti). The large majority of nations are a mixture of native American, European, and African groups. There are also countries in which different geographical areas emphasize different cultural aspects: African on the coast, native American in the mountains, European in the large cities. Heterogeneity is the most obvious characteristic of Latin American culture.

Colombia is a *mestizo* country, with different racial proportions: 20 percent Caucasian, 50 percent *mestizos* (Indian-white), 4 percent black, 14 percent *mulatos* (black-white), and 3 percent *Zambos* (black-Indian). The groups usually live in different geographical areas but with a large measure of overlap (see Ardila, 1986b). Colombia has a democratic government, good relations with the USA and the USSR, freedom of the press, and an important tradition in education. Emphasis is given to a literary and humanistic education, including poetry, history, and art. Science is not strongly developed in Colombia nor is it given the importance that humanistic education receives. Colombians are proud to speak "the best" possible Spanish, to be well informed about literature and politics, and to have the oldest democracy in Latin America.

Psychology as a profession started in Colombia in 1947, being the second psychology training program in Latin America (the first began in Guatemala in 1946). It began at the National University of Colombia through the efforts of Mercedes Rodrigo, a Spanish psychologist who had fled her country during the Spanish Civil War and had come to Colombia in 1938, invited by the National University to help in the selection of students. Rodrigo organized the Section of Psychotecnics in 1939, and in 1947 she established the Institute of Applied Psychology, which began to train psychologists in 1948. A subsequent visit to training institutions in the United States, at the invitation of American Psychological Association, was one of her main sources of ideas for the organization of training of psychologists in Colombia.

Rodrigo lived in Colombia until 1950. She was especially interested in psychological measurement, including test construction and evaluation. She had studied with Claparède in Switzerland and was an active member of the International Association of Applied Psychology. But her work extended beyond psychometrics to vocational orientation and professional aspects of psychology. Her impact on Colombian psychology was felt during all the time she lived in the country.

Educational Background

Psychologists in Colombia are educated according to what is called the Latin American training model. It consists of 5 years of study that includes theoretical and practical courses and a thesis. The degree obtained is that of "psychologist," similar to the degree of engineer, architect, physician, and so forth. It is a professional degree that allows the recipient to work in any area of psychology.

The courses that the student should take are very broad: general psychology; history of psychology; developmental, social, physiological, experimental, comparative, clinical, industrial, educational, school, and philosophical psychology; as well as courses in related topics such as sociology, anthropology, mathematics, statistics, measurement, biology, physiology, and neuroanatomy. In comparison to training at the undergraduate level in the USA, Colombian training is more professionally oriented and more scientific. A person who receives the degree of psychologist in Colombia can work in clinical, educational, industrial, social, experimental psychology, and so on. In other words, the training of psychologists in Colombia is terminal and does not require additional (graduate) work.

The problem with this kind of training is that many people do not have the maturity when they finish high school (at 17 or 18 years of age) to decide on a major or a career. In all of Latin America, this professional model implies that the student has to remain in the chosen career; to change majors means that one must go back to the first semester of study. People do not have the flexibility to move to another department, to change majors, and, in general, to correct their errors.

The positive point with this training model is that it is professionally oriented. A psychology student receives information and practice in all areas of psychology. The student must also write a thesis, which usually is a high-level empirical work. The thesis is considered an original contribution to psychology. Practical training is also demanding and requires many hours of supervised work.

Number of Psychologists

A realistic estimation of the number of psychologists in Colombia, based on the registration of diplomas, is 4,000. There are approximately 8,000 psychology students. These numbers are growing; psychology is a popular major in the country. Many people want to study psychology, although the admission requirements are strict.

Male-to-Female Ratio

At the beginning (1948), psychology was basically a "feminine" career. With the passage of time, the opening of new work areas, and improvement in the prestige of psychology, the number of male students has increased. At the present time probably 60 percent of professional psychologists are women and 40 percent are men.

It is important to point out that in general the status of professional women is high in Colombia. There are women politicians, physicians, educators, scientists, writers, and artists who have no problem finding a place in society. The status of professional women in Colombia has improved considerably since 1960, in spite of the traditional "machism" of Latin America, especially in certain countries, among them Colombia.

As noted, psychology in Colombia is a profession studied and practiced more by women than by men. But men accept this situation, do not feel threatened by the larger proportion of women psychologists, and consider status in society to depend on qualifications, intelligence, and motivation, not gender. Nevertheless, the number of male psychologists is growing. In some universities there are more men than women studying psychology. This increase is related to the professionalization of psychology in the last few years. Men consider psychology to be an appropriate field in which to earn a livelihood and to pursue as a professional career. As psychology becomes more competitive professionally, the ratio of men and women may become more equal.

Work Settings

In previous publications I have indicated that the government is the main employer of psychologists in Colombia, as in many other countries. In fact, in Colombia the government is the main employer of professionals in general, not only of psychologists. The work setting that has increased most rapidly in psychology in the last few years is private practice.

In private practice a psychologist in Colombia may work as a clinician, engaging in diagnosis, psychotherapy, research, and prevention (more psychotherapy and diagnosis than anything else). The psychologist could also be an industrial psychologist who does consulting work for large firms and organizations. For those with an interest in educational/school psychology, the work setting could be in the schools, colleges, and universities and would include work in guidance and counseling and learning disabilities.

The role of psychologists is accepted, psychological services are sought, and in general, private practice is one of the most promising areas of psychological activity in Colombia. Table 8.1 presents the main work settings of psychologists in the country.

It must be pointed out that this information is approximate. Many psychologists combine several settings—for example, university and private practice—or they work part-time. The table's final category, "Do not work as psychologists," includes psychologists who are abroad doing graduate work, are unemployed, or have a nonpsychological activity.

Certification of Psychologists

Psychology as a profession was legalized by the Colombian government in 1983 (Law 58, December 28, 1983). The law was presented to the Congress much earlier, as part of the 5-year plan to develop Colombian psychology (1970–75). The certification is considered one of the primary achievements of the profession in this decade.

The main functions of psychologists, according to the law, are the use

TABLE 8.1

Work Settings of Psychologists in Colombia

Setting	%
Government offices	24
Industries	14
Hospitals and clinics	12
Nonclinical institutions	10
Universities	10
Schools	9
Private practice	6
Do not work as psychologists	15
TOTAL	100

of psychological methods and techniques for basic and applied research; teaching; psychological diagnosis; psychotherapy; guidance, vocational, and professional selection and orientation; analysis and modification of behavior, in individuals and in groups; and psychological prophylaxis (Article 11, Law 58 of 1983). Guidelines are also provided for the training of psychologists, ethics, relations with other disciplines, and so forth.

General Characteristics

University Education in Psychology

Psychology as a profession began in Latin America in 1946 (Guatemala), 1947 (Colombia), and 1948 (Chile). The profession of psychology in Colombia has grown steadily in the last decades. The universities offering professional training are presented in Table 8.2. It is important to indicate that a professional degree is *not* equivalent to the BA or the BS in the USA; psychology in Colombia follows the Latin American training model (see Ardila, 1978), more similar to the training obtained in Germany and some other European countries. This kind of professional training probably resembles the training of engineers or architects in the USA.

Table 8.3 lists the universities that offer graduate work in psychology. It must be remembered that graduate work is *not* required for the practice of psychology at the professional level. It is additional training, a kind of "specialization" very different from the MA, MS, or PhD in the United States. As a matter of fact, to obtain a master's or a PhD degree in Colombia is consid-

TABLE 8.2
Professional Training Sites in Psychology in Colombia

1. National University of Colombia (Bogotá)
2. Javeriana University (Bogotá)
3. University of the Andes (Bogotá)
4. University of St. Thomas (Bogotá)
5. Incca University (Bogotá)
6. University of the Savanna (Bogotá)
7. Catholic University (Bogotá)
8. Konrad Lorenz Institute (Bogotá)
9. University of San Buenaventura (Medellín)
10. University of Antioquia (Medellín)
11. University of Valle (Cali)
12. Javeriana University (Cali)
13. University of the North (Barranquilla)
14. Metropolitan University (Barranquilla)
15. University of Manizales (Manizales)

TABLE 8.3
Graduate Training in Psychology & Areas of Specialization

1. National University of Colombia: health psychology
2. Javeriana University: community psychology
3. University of the Andes: clinical psychology
4. University of St. Thomas: clinical and family psychology
5. University of San Buenaventura: clinical psychology
6. University of the North: clinical psychology

ered a "luxury" and is not necessary in order to work as a psychologist. The majority of psychologists who have done graduate work studied in the USA, Canada, Belgium, the USSR, Mexico, France, and Poland.

Journals

Several psychology journals are published in Colombia. The most widely read are *Revista Latinoamericana de Psicología* (Latin American journal of psychology, founded in 1969), and *Avances en Psicología Clínica Latinoamericana* (Advances in Latin American clinical psychology, founded in 1982). Other

Columbian journals are *Cuadernos Psicología* (Psychology notebooks, founded in 1977), *Revista de Psicología* (Journal of psychology, published irregularly since 1956), and *Revista Interamericana de Psicología Ocupacional* (Interamerican journal of occupational psychology, founded in 1982). Other journals commonly used are *Revista Interamericana de Psicología* (Interamerican journal of psychology, usa), *Acta* (Argentina), *Revista de Psicología General y Aplicada* (Journal of general and applied psychology, Spain). Journals in English are generally read and, to a lesser extent, so are journals in French.

Professional Societies

A large number of psychological societies have been organized in Colombia. Two of them are devoted to psychology as a whole: the Colombian Federation of Psychology, founded in 1955, and the Colombian Society of Psychology, founded in 1978. Many other societies are devoted to specific aspects of psychology: clinical, educational, industrial, sport, occupational, and social psychology, neuropsychology, analysis and modification of behavior, and gerontology.

The Foundation for the Advancement of Psychology was created in 1977. It is an active forum for psychology and publishes the main psychological journals issued in the country. It also organizes seminars and congresses and takes part in the majority of the psychological events held in Latin America.

Textbooks, Tests, Laboratories, and Computer Facilities

A few decades ago Colombian psychology was isolated. Today the situation has greatly improved. Major textbooks are translated into Spanish in Mexico, Argentina, or Spain and arrive quickly in this country. The information level is appropriate in Colombia.

A short time ago I carried out a survey of test usage in Colombia and found that the most widely used psychological tests are Wechsler (both the wisc and the wais), revised; Rorschach; Kuder Preference Record (occupational, personal, vocational); Thematic Apperception Test (tat); and Raven Progressive Matrices.

Some of them have been validated in this country, and norms exist for different populations (children, adults, special groups, mentally retarded, gifted groups, and so on). Some are just translated. The list does not exhaust the number of tests used by Colombian psychologists, of course. A large majority of us tests, and also many European and Latin American tests, are known here. Among the most widely used Latin American tests are Mira y Lópe's p.m.k., Filho's abc, and Angelini's test. Some Colombian psychologists have also produced original tests; they cover aptitudes, achievement, personality, interests, and study habits, to name just a few topics. However, these "native" tests are not as widely used as the "foreign" (mainly North American) tests.

Colombia's psychological laboratories are relatively good. They usually belong to universities, particularly to those more experimentally oriented. All the universities and research institutes have psychological laboratories, relatively well endowed with the main instruments to carry out basic experiments in perception, learning, cognition, and social psychological processes.

Computer facilities are good. Usually, psychologists are relatively well informed about programming, simulation, and so on. Engineers and technicians collaborate with psychologists in the use of computers for data analysis.

Financial Support

There is government support for psychology, for both training and research. Some of the psychology programs are located at public universities. Scholarships and fellowships exist but are very limited.

For research, the main source of financial support is Colciencias, the government organization that finances science in general (its equivalent in the USA is the National Science Foundation). Research projects in psychology are supported every year. Private sources of financial aid also exist. Universities, foundations, private firms, and other organizations support different areas of scholarship, among them psychology.

Public Image of Psychology

As is the case in many countries, the general public in Colombia still does not have a correct image of psychology. Probably the discipline is identified in the mass media with clinical work in private practice and with personnel selection in industry. In the last few years, with the impact of behaviorism and behavior therapy, the general public has been concerned with the danger of "control" by behavioral psychologists.

Nevertheless, in the 1970s and 1980s the public image of psychology improved considerably in Colombia. Psychology has become an "important" career, an area of science that has many relevant things to contribute to society. Also, people have become better informed about the field, and it is common to find that the general public is able to differentiate among experimental psychology, psychoanalysis, and social psychology, for example. People look for psychological aid when they are having difficulty with their children, when they want to retire, when they want to choose a career, and for similar problems.

Current Status

Philosophical and Theoretical Influences

The history of psychology in Colombia can be divided into three main periods: psychometric (1948–60), psychoanalytic (1960–70), and experimental (1970–today). To a certain extent, the periods refer to differences in emphasis. Psychology in the earliest period was centered on measurement and evaluation because of the influence of Mercedes Rodrigo and the psychologists she trained at the Institute of Applied Psychology. From 1960 to 1970 psychoanalysis was predominant because of the influence of medical people, followers of Freud. Since 1970 the discipline has been clearly experimental, because of the training of young psychologists and the interest in laboratory work (i.e., operant conditioning, experimental social psychology) and its applications (behavior therapy, community psychology).

Centers and Areas of Research

The major areas and their centers include experimental psychology (Foundation for the Advancement of Psychology, Catholic University, Colciencias, K. Lorenz Institute), physiological psychology (Colombian Institute of Neurology), experimental analysis of behavior (University of the Andes, Skinner Center, Alamoc, Catholic University, K. Lorenz Institute, University of the North), perception, motivation, and cognition (K. Lorenz Institute, Javeriana University), developmental psychology (Foundation for the Advancement of Psychology, Colombian Institute for Family Welfare, University of Valle), clinical psychology (University of the Andes, Javeriana University, Metropolitan University, Secretary of Health, Division of Mental Health, University of the Savanna), educational psychology (Pedagogical University), industrial and organizational psychology (Sena, Civil Service, University of the Andes), health psychology (National University of Colombia, K. Lorenz Institute), social psychology (University of Valle, Javeriana University, University of Manizales, Foundation for the Advancement of Psychology, Incca University), gerontological psychology (Colombian Center for Gerontology), family psychology (University of St. Thomas), sexology (University of Valle, University of San Buenaventura, University of Manizales), community psychology (National University of Colombia, Javeriana University, University of the North).

Current Trends

The main trends in Colombian psychology are related to the international panorama and to the social conditions of the country. The experimental emphasis of psychology in Colombia will likely continue, and the interest in social issues (violence, crime, poverty, divorce, child abuse and neglect) will increase.

Multidisciplinary problems must be studied from a multidisciplinary point of view, and the current problems of Colombia are no exception. The interest in community psychology and in social problems becomes more salient every day. Nevertheless, the basic scientific approach to behavioral problems which has characterized Colombian psychology since 1970 is here to stay.

Bibliography

Ardila, R. (1970). Applied psychology in Colombia. *International Review of Applied Psychology, 19,* 155–160.

Ardila, R. (1973). *La psicología en Colombia, desarrollo histórico.* Mexico City: Trillas.

Ardila, R. (1976). Latin America. In V. S. Sexton & H. Misiak (Eds.), *Psychology around the world* (pp. 259–279). Monterey, CA: Brooks/Cole.

Ardila, R. (1978). *La profesión del psicólogo.* Mexico City: Trillas.

Ardila, R. (1982a). International psychology. *American Psychologist, 37,* 323–329.

Ardila, R. (1982b). Psychology in Latin America today. *Annual Review of Psychology, 33,* 103–122.

Ardila, R. (1985). El análisis experimental del comportamiento en Colombia. *Revista Latinoamericana de Psicología, 17,* 351–370.

Ardila, R. (1986a). *La psicología en América Latina, pasado, presente y futuro.* Mexico City: Siglo XXI.

Ardila, R. (1986b). *Psiocología del hombre colombiano.* Bogotá: Planeta.

Ardila, R. (1987). Colombia. In A. R. Gilgen & C. K. Gilgen (Eds.), *International handbook of psychology* (pp. 125–136). New York: Greenwood Press.

9 / Cuba

GUILLERMO BERNAL & WANDA RODRÍGUEZ

Guillermo Bernal (born 1949) received his PhD in clinical psychology from the University of Massachusetts in 1978. His interest areas include family therapy, community psychology, Latino mental health, drug rehabilitation, and Latin American psychology. The author of more than 30 articles and book chapters, he has also written the book A Family Like Yours: Breaking the Patterns of Drug Abuse, *with J. L. Sorensen. He has served on the editorial board of several publications and as a consultant to the National Institute of Mental Health. Bernal is associate professor in the Department of Psychology and director of the Psychological Services and Research University Center at the University of Puerto Rico, Río Piedras.*

Wanda Rodríguez (born 1952) received an MEd degree in 1977 and an MA degree in psychology in 1985, both from the University of Puerto Rico, Río Piedras. The author of several articles on professional issues, she is a part-time instructor in psychology at the university and a full-time graduate student in the doctoral program. Her areas of specialization are counseling psychology and human development. In 1985 she received the Graduate Student of the Year Award given by the Puerto Rico Psychological Association.

Psychology in Cuba must be understood within the broader context of the social, historical, and economic forces that have conditioned its development. Cuba is a small, Third World country struggling to overcome a legacy of underdevelopment, poverty, neocolonialism, and dependency. The success of the Cuban Revolution in 1959 marked a new phase of development

The curricular model for education and training of psychology was made public and discussed by the Facultad de Psicología at the University of Havana in a Pre-Congress Seminar, held as part of the 21st Interamerican Congress of Psychology, attended by both authors in the summer of 1987. The information presented on these pages is partially based on presentations made at that seminar and on interviews conducted with psychologists working in different settings in Cuba. The authors are particularly grateful to Eduardo Cairo, Alberto Edreira, Georgina Fariñas, Lourdes García-Averasturi, Eduardo González Rey, Juan José Guevara, Albertina Mitjans, Isabela Louro, Noemí Pérez-Valdez, and Marcelo-Vazquez.

that was to change the structure of society and, with it, the demographic, health, and educational profile. For example, in the 28 years since the revolution, the health-care delivery system has been transformed into one that approximates that of a developed country (Pérez-Stable, 1985).

The shift from capitalism to socialism transformed all aspects of everyday life. Technology and science were now viewed as tools created to improve life and as having tremendous social value. Thus, psychology, as both a science and a profession, experienced a surge of development. This view is contrary to the attitude held before 1959, when psychology was seen as an esoteric field limited to the elite (Bernal, 1985).

The few academic psychologists during the prerevolutionary period of Cuban society were employed mainly as professors in educational institutions or in private practice. Psychological services were limited to a privileged minority. Indeed, before 1959 psychology was not part of any organized system of health care or education.

Education and Training

In 1961, as part of extensive educational reform, a psychology program was established at the Universidad de las Villas (University of las Villas). In 1962 an analogous program was instituted at the Universidad de la Habana (University of Havana). Both programs were under the Faculty of Science and remained so until 1976, when psychology was recognized as an independent faculty, or school. Since then, the two institutions have worked together to develop a curricular model for the education and training of professional psychologists.

The curriculum for professional psychology, as with all other curricula that affect human resources, is developed in coordination with, and with the advice of, a special commission of experts. The commission is responsible for guaranteeing that academic and training programs correspond to the broader plans of the nation. Concerning the training of psychologists, the commission has the mandate to study "the perspectives for working positions in which psychologists can be placed, as well as the perspectives for the development of psychology at a worldwide level, which is complemented with rigorous study of the achievements, deficiencies, and insufficiencies of previous plans of study, and a detailed analysis of the efficiency of our graduates in the practice of the profession" (Mitjans-Martínez, Cairo-Valárcel, Morenza-Padilla, Rodríguez-Pérez & Moros-Fernández, 1987, p. 8).

Once a professional profile was finished by the commission and the final objectives for the training of psychologists were established, the curricular model was submitted to prospective employers and practicing psychologists for their review. Their recommendations were integrated into the final study plan.

The main characteristic of the training program for psychologists in Cuba is the integration of theoretical knowledge, training in research, and the practice of professional skills. The curriculum is conceptualized as three interdependent subsystems: (1) general and specific academic subject matters, which constitute the core knowledge base of the training; (2) student scientific work, which emphasizes the development of skills required for research, as well as the development of scientific thinking, initiative, and creativity; and (3) "production practice work," which offers the opportunity to demonstrate motivation, independence, understanding, and commitment in the use of psychological knowledge and derived techniques in particular professional activities (Mitjans-Martínez et al., 1987).

The training program lasts 5 years. Admission to the program is based on the centralized planning of the economy. Openings for students depend on 5-year projections that, in part, guarantee employment on graduation. University admissions are highly competitive and are based on high school grades and entrance exams. Once a student is admitted, the government pays all expenses, including housing, food, books, supplies, and transportation.

Graduates are awarded the university degree of *licenciado en psicología*, a degree more or less equivalent to a combined bachelor's and master's degree in the United States (Marín, 1987). The presentation of an original research project (similar to a master's thesis) called *tesina* is required for the degree. The project must reflect the integration of the knowledge base, research skills, and practical competencies developed in the previous years of study.

The first 3 years of training constitute an introduction to the study of basic theoretical and methodological issues in psychology. During this period emphasis is placed on the contributions of Cuban psychologists toward solutions of the country's problems. Students are also exposed to the original works of well-known theorists and philosophers (Marín, 1987; Mitjans-Martínez et al., 1987). The last 2 years are devoted to examining in greater detail the application of psychology among four well-defined areas of specialization.

Specialty areas correspond to the four departments that comprise the Facultad de Psicología, which, like a School of Psychology, has its own dean, associate deans, and department chairs. The departments are clinical psychology, general psychology, social and work psychology, and educational and child psychology. Graduates are employed mainly in health and educational systems, as well as in labor organizations and work centers.

Since 1966 between 1,800 and 2,000 psychologists and psychometricians have been graduated from universities (Guevara, personal communication, 1987). All of the graduates are employed, because state-level planning of human resources places psychologists at different work sites around the country. Little information is available on the male-female ratio of psychologists. However, female enrollment in higher education has increased, reaching 54.9 percent of the total population of 290,262 students during the academic year 1986–87. The increasing participation of women in all fields of work outside the home is claimed as one of the principal achievements of the revolutionary government.

The professional competence of psychologists is guaranteed by a continuous process of supervision during the training years. The *licenciatura* degree awarded after 5 years of training with the Facultad de Psicología enables graduates to assume a professional role and to function as psychologists. There is no special process for obtaining certification or a license to practice because the degree in itself is a license.

Education after the 5-year program is considered important. There are two forms of postgraduate education: professional development (continuing education) and the acquisition of a scientific degree (equivalent to a PhD or a doctorate in research). The doctorate in research is considered a necessary degree for professors, researchers, and other specialists involved in scientific inquiry, and it follows a European model of mentorship. Advancement to candidacy requires demonstrated competence in a specialty area, philosophy, a foreign language, and a detailed plan for graduate study. The faculty reviews the plan and appoints a committee to evaluate it. The committee also evaluates the dissertation with an oral examination and defense. Generally, all requirements for the doctorate are completed within 5 or 6 years of full-time study (Bernal, 1985).

Work Settings

Health, education, and production have been the main concerns of the revolutionary government. In each area, psychologists have played an increasingly important role, as demonstrated by the growing number of psychologists who have been placed in these settings. Although it is difficult to estimate how many psychologists were working in Cuba before 1959, there were few who were well trained. Most left the country at the time of the revolution. The first group of psychologists trained in revolutionary Cuba graduated in 1966 from the newly developed psychology program at the University of Havana. By 1968, in sharp contrast to their predecessors, academic psychologists were working full-time at commensurate rates of pay and were carrying out useful social activities within the universities (Sommers, 1969).

Many of the first psychologists to graduate were employed by the Ministry of Public Health (MINSAP), which remains a major employment source. Also in 1968 the Grupo Nacional de Psicología (National Group of Psychology) was formed within MINSAP to coordinate and organize the activities of psychologists in the health sector. A network was soon established between the national group and 14 provincial groups to implement nationwide plans. The Grupo Nacional de Psicología, under the visionary leadership of Lourdes García-Averasturi from its formation until 1986,[1] firmly established the independent nature of psychology. As an integral part of health care, psychology moved beyond its traditional role toward the new service-oriented community and health psychology.

García-Averasturi (1985) states that in 1980 MINSAP alone employed 310 psychologists and 350 psychometricians. Psychometricians have the equivalent of an associate degree in psychology and perform technical functions that parallel the role of a nurse or psychiatric technician. They work under the supervision of a licensed psychologist. Marín (1987) notes that by 1984 the number of psychologists working in MINSAP had increased to 500.

In the area of health, psychologists have important functions in community medicine programs (García-Averasturi, 1985; Pérez-Stable, 1985). Psychologists work in primary, secondary, and tertiary prevention in settings such as local community health clinics, general hospitals, provincial hospitals, and rural hospitals. Professional functions include guidance in physical and mental health, and research and consultation in the psychological components of physical illness. With the new family doctor program (Morales-Calatayud et al., 1987) established in 1984, the prevention, promotion, and rehabilitative efforts for the health of a specified number of families became the responsibility of a family physician. Psychologists working alongside the family doctor are likely to make new advances as part of this unique and ambitious program of health care.

In educational settings, the thrust of psychology is in developmental psychology. One of the most important functions of psychologists employed by the Ministry of Education is the study of moral development, the processes and mechanisms underlying the formation of attitudes, beliefs, ideas, and other qualities of moral regulation and learning (González-Rey, 1985). This study is translated into specific programs aimed at improving the teaching-learning process and promoting the educational development of students. The research and theoretical writings of Fernando González-Rey (1985) are one example of the creative investigations conducted on problems of personality and moral development. Since the development of ethical principles is of critical importance for the construction of socialism, investigators have made particular efforts in the study of moral regulation, self-consciousness, and personality. The writings of these authors have been briefly reviewed elsewhere (Bernal, 1985).

Hospital settings in general and psychiatric units in particular are another context in which psychologists have significant responsibilities. In clinical psychology, programs developed for the treatment of chronic mental patients stand out as exemplary (Pérez-Valdez & Calvo-Montalvo, 1985). The wide range of therapeutic and diagnostic innovations has been the focus of extensive study. A five-volume work published in 1985 by the Havana Psychiatric Hospital (*Memorias del II Congreso Nacional de Psicología de la Salud*/Proceedings of the II National Congress of Health Psychology) records the most recent advances in research, practice, and training. One of the more original contributions has been the therapeutic modality of *psicoballet* (Fariñas, 1984). The treatment program integrates classical ballet with child psychotherapy. Clinical outcome studies have shown this modality to be remarkably effective.

Social and work psychologists provide consultation, conduct research, and develop preventive programs in factories, cultural and recreational organizations, sport organizations, and centers for the study of labor relations (Casaña, Fuentes, Sorín & Ojalvo, 1984). On the one hand, psychologists in these centers aim to promote productivity, discipline, and motivation. On the other hand, they are charged with the task of protecting workers from environmental stresses. As early as 1964, social psychologists investigated topics such as working relations and motivation at new sugar mills. The attitudes of fishermen and construction workers in the city of Nuevitas were the focus of another study. In general, these early studies illustrate the vital function of psychologists working toward the economic, social, and political development of the country.

An important setting that employs primarily research psychologists is the Academia de Ciencias Cubana (Cuban Academy of Sciences). Within the academy there are institutes for research and training such as the Enrique José Varona Pedagogic Institute. This institute offers a *licenciatura* in learning and physical disabilities (*defectología*). The Instituto de Investigaciones Fundamentales del Cerebro (Institute of Basic Research on the Brain) has several research centers each with major research programs. For example, the Psychological and Sociological Research Center (directed by Angela Casaña) has three departments: psychology, sociology, and philosophy. Each department uses an interdisciplinary team approach. Some of the current research projects are focused on family, youth, the characteristics of women in leadership positions, stress, aging, and neuropsychophysiological processes of laterality.

In summary, current and prospective psychology is being oriented to the study of development in a Vygotskian perspective. The new emphasis is on the mechanism of change in the development of personality which is rooted in society and culture. Thus, the socialization processes in personality formation and the study of cognitive and language development in children are areas of research with important priorities at the University of Havana. Neuropsychology (Cairo-Valcárcel, 1987) is another emerging field that will probably continue to make important contributions. Indeed, the subject matter of neuropsychology—the psychophysiological functions of brain activity—is at the core of Marxist philosophy, that is, the material basis of all phenomena.

Current Status

The development of psychology in Cuba since 1959 is characterized by status, growth, innovation, and a search for pragmatic models to satisfy social and community needs. Psychologists may be found in nontraditional settings such as day-care centers, factories, schools, and political, cultural, and recreational organizations, as well as the more traditional sites such as psychiatric institutions, hospitals, community health centers, universities, and research institutes.

Several psychological journals are published in Cuba. Among them are the *Revista del Hospital Psiquiátrico de la Habana* (Journal of the Havana Psychiatric Hospital), recently the focus of an extensive review (Marín, 1985); the *Boletín de Psicología* (Psychology bulletin), published by the Department of Psychology of the Havana Psychiatric Hospital; and the *Revista Cubana de Psicología* (Cuban journal of psychology), published by the Facultad de Psicología at the University of Havana. This journal publishes articles from both Cuban and foreign psychologists; recent issues include translations of the writings of important European authors. The Grupo Nacional de Psicología publishes *Actualidades en Psicología* (Current developments in psychology), which is oriented toward psychologists working in the field and also publishes translations of important developments.

The professionalization of psychology in Cuba is evident in the participation of psychologists in organizations dedicated to professional concerns. The two main professional organizations are the Sociedad Cubana de Psicólogos de la Salud (Cuban Society of Health Psychologists) and the Sociedad de Psicólogos de Cuba (Society of Cuban Psychologists). The former was founded in 1978 and is composed of psychologists with common interests in the health area. The latter, established in 1964, is a more general type of organization and is subdivided into scientific sections that correspond to specific professional concerns, such as neurophysiology and education.

Both professional organizations in Cuba work toward intellectual exchange with psychologists of other countries. For example, since 1980 there have been four international conventions, seminars, or congresses held in Cuba. Most recently, the 21st Interamerican Congress of Psychology was held in Havana in 1987 with the participation of more than 2,000 psychologists from North, South, and Central America, the Caribbean, and Europe. Both psychological associations, the MINSAP, the Facultad de Psycología of the University of Havana, and the Interamerican Society of Psychology cosponsored the event.

Cuban psychologists share ideas from other countries through a program of educational development abroad, mainly in the Soviet Union and, until recently, the German Democratic Republic (Marín, 1987). In addition, the University of Havana receives extensive technical assistance from experts of various socialist countries. Nevertheless, psychologists in Cuba are quick to point out that the economic and informational blockade by the United States has interrupted the intellectual influence of North American psychology in Cuba. The extreme difficulty of obtaining books, journals, psychological tests, and diagnostic instruments produced in the United States has made it difficult to keep up with recent developments. In spite of the current US government policy discouraging professional contact and scientific exchange between psychologists in Cuba and the United States, the work and writings of leading US psychologists are known in Cuba. The individual efforts of progressive psychologists and other health professionals from the United States (as well as from other countries such as Canada and Mexico) have contributed to cracking the informational blockade.

Perspectives for Future Development

Psychology in Cuba will continue to develop along the principles of Marxist philosophy. The theoretical influence of dialectical materialism in Cuban psychology has helped to define psychology as the study of the formation and transformation of cognitive, behavioral, affective, and other human processes in a particular social context. All forms of human behavior are examined in their sociohistorical determinants. Psychological phenomena are studied as active processes, in which motion and change are central to a possible explanation.

Psychology and psychologists within the individual-societal dialectic are part of the active process of change: the construction of a socialist society. The problems that psychology is confronting are those specific to a Third World developing society. Therefore, the contribution of psychologists to the health of the population, epidemiologic preventive hygiene, education, and orientation of the masses on issues of health and education, and primary health care at the most basic community level represent the initial but firm steps toward the establishment of a new model of psychology.

Psychologists in Cuba are working at developing research strategies that can be applied to the study of specific social problems. Psychological research has a strong participatory emphasis linking the search for knowledge to action-oriented programs. The development and implementation of preventive strategies in health, education, and work are central to the Third World paradigm for psychology emerging in Cuba.

Note

1. Lourdes García-Averasturi, who now works as a research psychologist at MIN-SAP's Instituto Nacional de Higiene y Epidemiología, was succeeded by Jorge Grau Abalo, who works at the Hermanos Ameijeiras Hospital in Havana.

Bibliography

Bernal, G. (1985). A history of psychology in Cuba. *Journal of Community Psychology, 13*, 222–235.

Cairo-Valcárcel, E. (1987). *Neuropsicología*. Havana: Universidad de la Habana, Ministerio de Educación Superior.

Casaña, A., Fuentes, M., Sorín, M., & Ojalvo, V. (1984). Estado actual y perspectivas de desarrollo de la psicología en Cuba. *Revista Cubana de Psicología, 1*, 17–53.

Fariñas, G. (1984). El psicoballet, una experiencia cubana. *Revista del Hospital Psiquiátrico de la Habana, 25*, 603–621.

García-Averasturi, L. (1985). Community health psychology in Cuba. *Journal of Community Psychology, 13*, 117–124.

González-Rey, F. (1985). *Psicología de la personalidad*. Havana: Editorial Pueblo y Educación.

Marín, B. V. (1985). Community psychology in Cuba: A literature review. *Journal of Community Psychology, 13*, 138–154.

Marín, G. (1987). Cuba. In A. R. Gilgen & C. K. Gilgen (Eds.), *International handbook of psychology* (pp. 137–144). New York: Greenwood Press.

Mitjans-Martínez, A., Cairo-Valárcel, E., Morenza-Padilla, L., Rodríguez-Pérez, M. E., & Moros-Fernández, H. (1987). *La formación del psicólogo en Cuba: Diseño curricular.* Havana: Facultad de Psicología.

Morales-Calatayud, F., Ordoñez-Carceller, C., Ruiz-Rodríguez, G., Casal-Sosa, A., Edreira-López, A., Díaz-González, J., Infante Pedreira, O., & Azcaño Rodríguez, R. (1987). *La psicología de la salud en la atención primaria.* Havana: XXI Congreso Interamericano de Psicología.

Pérez-Stable, E. J. (1985). Community medicine in Cuba. *Journal of Community Psychology, 13,* 124–137.

Pérez-Valdez, N., & Calvo-Montalvo, N. (1985). Psychology in the rehabilitation of the chronic mental patient. *Journal of Community Psychology, 13,* 155–161.

Sommers, B. J. (1969). Psychology education and mental health services in Cuba in 1968. *American Psychologist, 24,* 941–946.

10 / Czechoslovakia

DAMÍÁN KOVÁČ

Damián Kováč (born 1929) received his PhD from Comenius University in 1953 and the DSc degree from the Slovak Academy of Sciences in 1969. He has written more than 375 articles for professional journals, both native and international, on such topics as general psychology, methodology, cognitive functions in personality, and laterality. His books include Visuelles Wahrnemen *(Visual perception) in German, and* Psychologickápropedeutika *(Psychological propedeutics) and* Teória Všeobecnej Psychológie *(Theory of general psychology), both in Slovak.*

Kováč is the founder and editor-in-chief of Studia Psychologica, *an international journal for basic research in the psychological sciences. A former president of the Czechoslovak Psychological Society (1978–85) and the Slovak Psychological Society (1978–83), he is currently director of the Institute of Experimental Psychology, of the Slovak Academy of Sciences (1960–).*

It is difficult to present accurately the development and growth of a branch of science in which one has been engaged for a long time. In the case of Czechoslovakia, however, one must note Heisenberger's statement that science is, as a matter of fact, made by people. In Czechoslovakia in the period under review, various social changes have been reflected more in psychology than, for example, in physics. There were also marked manifestations of an old handicap, namely, that we can be blind to the history of our own psychology. Apart from bibliographic surveys in certain areas and a few historical probes, no systematic work has been carried out in this sphere in Czechoslovakia. There are available, however, various addresses at anniversaries of psychological institutions as well as addresses by distinguished personalities which, by themselves, are a matter of historical interest. Nonetheless, there is a lack of empirical analyses such as we attempted to present in the Slovak Psychological Society in 1979.

In short, a self-reflection based on historical fact has not yet fully begun in Czechoslovak psychology. This report on the development and state of psy-

Translated by Eva Salnerová.

chology for the years between 1960 and 1988 should be understood within that context.

Characteristics of the Psychologist

Psychology as an independent university subject began to be studied by 1948. Before then, psychologists were those graduates of teacher's study in philosophy who had defended a doctor's dissertation (the PhD) in psychology. The specialized study of psychology has passed through several reforms. In the 1950s psychology graduates obtained a diploma in psychology and in some related subject such as sociology or pedagogics. In 1950 there was only a single-subject, 5-year study of psychology, which bestowed the title "graduated psychologist." Later, in the years 1965–81, in Bratislava there was a teacher's study of pedagogical psychology that was combined with language study.

Currently, professional psychologists are graduates of a 4-year independent study at the philosophical faculty. Reducing the time of study from 5 to 4 years was due to a new university law passed in 1978. Psychology can be studied in both the Czech and Slovak languages. Two foreign languages are compulsory subjects of graduate study: Russian and another world language of one's own choice.

By the end of 1980 there were approximately 3,500 professional psychologists in Czechoslovakia. These data are approximate for two reasons: not all psychologists are members of the Czechoslovak Psychological Society, and they are not all listed as psychologists in the yearbook because some of them choose to practice other professions.

In the profession of psychology women outnumber men; in 1978 this ratio was 63 percent to 37 percent in Slovakia, and the feminization continues to increase. The mean age is relatively low. In 1978 34 percent of the psychologists in Bohemia and almost 44 percent of those in Slovakia were less than 29 years old.

Most psychologists are engaged in educational consulting centers. In every district town of the ČSSR there is a pedagogical-psychological consulting center. The second largest group is composed of clinical psychologists who work in psychiatric and other health establishments. Recently, there has been a decline rather than an increase in the number of industrial psychologists and specialists in the psychology of work, previously a well-established tradition in Czechoslovakia. Almost 30 percent of psychologists deal with teaching and research activities. Approximately half of them are professional researchers.

There is no federal law in Czechoslovakia governing psychology. Efforts to create such a law in Slovakia resulted in a nonauthorized version at the beginning of the 1980s. In some departments the activity of professional psychologists is regulated and protected by their own agencies—for example, the health service or law courts.

Characteristics of Psychology

In Czechoslovakia there are five university establishments for professional psychologists. Psychology is studied in departments of psychology at philosophical faculties of the following universities: (1) Department of Psychology at the Philosophical Faculty of Charles University, Prague (J. Janoušek, head), O. Mikšík, J. Čáp, J. Srnec, J. Hoskovec, J. Štikar, R. Oliverius, E. Urban. (See also the Psychological Institute of Charles University.) (2) Department of Psychology at the Philosophical Faculty of the University of J. E. Purkyně, Brno (J. Kuric, head), J. Švancara, B. Chalupa, J. Sedlák, V. Smékal, L. Míček, M. Svoboda, L. Vasina. (3) Department of Psychology at the Philosophical Faculty of Palacký University, Olomouc (Ch. Valoušek, head), D. Osladilová, P. Mohapl, M. Homola, Zd. Ftípil. (4) Department of Psychological Sciences at the Philosophical Faculty of the Comenius University in Bratislava (T. Kollárik, head), O. Kondáš, J. Boroš, L. Ďurič, L. Kačáni, M. Bandžejova, O. Blaškovič, J. Štefanovič, J. Grác, J. Čulen, M. Brožiková, I. Brezina, and emeritus professor T. Pardel. (5) Department of Psychology of the University of P. J. Šafárik, Prešov, previously Košice (V. Kubáni, head), Ľ. Fábryová, E. Šímova, Š. Tatranský, F. Olejár, and founder emeritus professor J. Hvozdík.

Postgraduate study of psychology is consistent with the Law of Universities and includes certificates in consulting, clinical psychology, and the psychology of work. The system has been legally established for some time. In scientific education it consists of research student posts lasting 3 to 5 years, during which graduates, under their supervisors' charge, extend their knowledge and work on their dissertations. After defending the dissertation before a commission, the candidate attains the scientific degree of candidate of psychological sciences (CSc). The highest scientific degree in this field, doctor of psychological sciences (DrSc), is conferred on mature scientists who have defended their dissertations, published, contributed markedly to theory and practice, and established an international reputation.

Journals and Societies

Four professional periodicals are currently published in Czechoslovakia. *Československá Psychologie* (Czechoslovak psychology) is a journal for psychological theory and practice. Issued by the Psychological Institute of the Czechoslovak Academy of Sciences through its publishing arm, the House of Academia, since 1956, it is published six times a year; articles are written in Czech and Slovak with summaries in Russian and English. *Studia Psychologica*, an international quarterly for basic research in the psychological sciences, has been published by the Institute of Experimental Psychology of the Slovak Academy of Sciences since 1957 through the academy's Veda Publishing House. It includes a bibliographic supplement of the socialist community countries; articles come from Czechoslovakia as well as from abroad in the congress languages of psychology. It is approximately 80 percent in English. *Psychológia a Patopsychológia Dieťaťa* (Psychology and pathopsychology of the child) is published by the Research Institute of Child Psychology and Pathopsychology through the Slovak Pedagogical Publishing House six times a year (since 1964). Articles appear both in Slovak and Czech with summaries in Russian and English. *Psychológie v Ekonomické Praxi* (Psychology in economic practice), a quarterly, has been published since 1964 by Charles University. Articles appear both in Czech and Slovak with summaries in English, Russian, and German. In addition, psychological articles are regularly published in journals such as *Activitas Nevrosa Superior*, *Výchovný Poradca* (Educational counselor), *Jednotná Škola* (Unified school), and *Ekonomika Práce* (Economics of labor).

In 1958 the Czechoslovak Psychological Society and the Slovak Psychological Society were founded; both societies, as well as some other scientific societies, have joined the Czechoslovak or Slovak Academy of Science. The societies represent a voluntary association of psychologists who are particularly concerned with the development of psychology as a science. They are mainly involved in organizing congresses as professional scientific conferences. They have also been striving to protect psychological service through legislation, and they work toward a better social functioning of psychology in Czechoslovakia. The individual components of the society—sections and commissions—organize various specific professional events, seminars, and training experiences. Groups from the particular regions of the republic have also become active. The greatest activity is characteristic of the Bratislava regional group of the Slovak Psychological Society.

The societies issue a common publication, a bulletin called *Psychológ v Československu* (Psychologist in Czechoslovakia), twice a year for members. Apart from questions concerned with the strategic development of psychology and internal problems of its optimal development, it contains a chronology of psychological life in Czechoslovakia.

Books, Tests, and Funding

The information available for pregraduate psychology in the ČSSR has been gathered from both foreign and home sources. In experimental psychology, for example, after translations of R. S. Woodworth and H. Schlosberg (1959), R. Meili and H. Rohracher (1967), and P. Fraisse (1967, 1968) were used for many years, an indigenous text finally appeared in 1987. At present, an effort is being made to prepare indigenous textbooks in all basic areas, as well as specialty areas of pregraduate study, and to make them uniform for all Czech and Slovak universities. The postgraduate education of psychologists is particularly enhanced by integrative works by domestic authors from the fields of history, theory, and methodology of psychology, and by monographs from different topical fields such as cognitive processes, creativity, social communication, psychotherapy, and guidance.

Czechoslovakia ranks among the first countries of the socialist community to establish (in 1968) an independently functioning psychology-based enterprise, Psychodiagnostické a Didaktické Testy (Psychodiagnostic and didactic tests), directed by V. Černý. As of 1988 this organization had published 131 psychodiagnostic devices both foreign and local, 14 other instruments, and 51 titles in the professional psychological literature.

Research in the psychological sciences has been undertaken primarily by workplaces of basic research in the Czechoslovak or Slovak Academy of Sciences. In the state plan of basic research, designed for a 5-year period, educational and scientific activity is ensured by university centers of the departments of the Ministry of Education in Bohemia and Slovakia; other professional activity of psychologists is financed from national or republic budgets. In Czechoslovakia, so far, psychological service has been neither cooperatively nor privately provided for. It is estimated that more than 300,000 subjects undergo yearly psychodiagnostic examination in such areas as school-related skills, occupational ability, and forensic reviews.

After some stagnation in the 1970s, psychology in the ČSSR has been gaining in popularity among both professionals and the general public. This trend can be seen mainly in the greater number of psychological articles in the mass media, particularly radio, television, and magazines; the growing demands on psychological expertise in social development, education, health services, and the political sphere; and the growing interest in the study of psychology in professional areas, extension courses, and postgraduate study.

Present State of Psychology (1960–88)

In the 1950s psychology was established after considerable difficulty, under the new sociopolitical conditions in Czechoslovakia. Seen as a branch of science, a subject of both specific and general education, and a professional and practical activity, it developed rapidly in the 1960s. The number of students of psychology multiplied, new psychological workplaces appeared, a system of professional and practical activity was established in educational-psychological consultancy, and so forth. Several anniversary addresses expressed the view that psychology in the Czechoslovak Socialist Republic had in a short time achieved substantial progress in comparison to the world average. In the 1970s, however, the accelerated stage of the progress of psychology in Czechoslovakia was halted. Instead, various inhibitory phenomena could be observed: canceling or integrating workplaces, restricting the growth of psychology undergraduates, and the inability to satisfy several demands (e.g., legislation on psychology, the regulation of school psychologists, the construction of central bodies for the coordination of psychological activity in practice). Only in the second half of the 1980s can one see some signs of a turnaround. With the 1990s comes hope for a new chance to establish a program for complex human research.

As for general methodological starting points, psychology in Czechoslovakia, like other scientific branches, is based on the premises of materialistic dialectics. Some differences among theoretical psychologists are reflected in their concern with philosophical concepts underlying methodology. These differences are manifested in distinct labeling; some call it Marx-Leninist psychology, others refer to it as psychology with Marxian methodology, and still another group refers to it as psychological science. Following tradition, psychology is understood as a part of the social sciences. Only in one psychological workplace, the Institute of Psychology of the Philosophical Faculty at the Comenius University in Bratislava, is research carried out on animals. Just a few psychologists are engaged in this activity, in which they cooperate with other specialists from biological and medical centers. Since the 1960s a so-called hominist conception of psychology has been developing in Slovakia which continues to gain supporters. More and more, one reads and hears about psychology as a science of humanity, though for initiators of this change, human sciences are related to a new interdisciplinary integration macrosphere of scientific knowledge. For others, the sciences of humanity still represent a part of social sciences.

As for the methodological approaches used in the overall production of Czechoslovak psychology, the empirical approach dominates, though one can still see the retreating remnants of speculative thinking. After a period of building psychological laboratories early in the 1960s, only one workplace continued to carry out experimental laboratory research: the Institute of Experimental Psychology of the Slovak Academy of Sciences in Bratislava. The so-called mathematization of psychology, whose bases in Czechoslovak psychology were due mainly to the development of experimental psychology and later psychometric demands put on psychodiagnostic methods, is the basis for significant psychological production. The institutes of basic research already offer computer-aided methods.

Though the theoretico-methodological reorientation of psychology after World War II showed some inclination toward conceptions developed in the USSR, neither of the Soviet schools has been fully adopted in Czechoslovak psychology. The authors of textbooks frequently refer to the theory of activity, or rather to the activity principle in psychology. However, one can speak about the rise and development of schools in Czechoslovak psychology only to a limited degree.

Leading Personalities

This section names those prominent Czechoslovak psychologists who have died within the time interval covered. From among Czech psychologists we should note Jan Doležal (1902–65), the postwar strategist of developing psychology in the ČSSR; Václav Příhoda (1889–1979), the author of four volumes on psychological ontogenesis; Josef Stavél (1901–85), an expert in psychotechnics and author of a remarkable monograph on the psychology of hunger; F. Hyhlík (1905–81), an enthusiastic propagator of psychology; and Vladimír Tardy (1906–87), an outstanding general theoretician.

Of psychologists working in Moravia, we can name the nestor of experimental psychology, Vilém Chmelař (1892–1988); a fine theoretician and practitioner in psychopathology, Robert Konečný (1906–81); and a distinctive developer of the psychology of thinking, Emil Holas (1917–86).

The first Slovak psychologists were educated by the generally proficient and prolific "father of Slovak psychology," Anton Jurovský (1908–86), and by the interdisciplinarily oriented Juraj Čečetka (1907–83). Among other prominent researchers who have passed away are the pioneer of programmed instruction, M. Milan (1915–76); Martin Jurčo (1926–83), who introduced psychological approaches in education; and Ivan Šípoš (1927–88), an inventive experimenter of cognitive processes.

Trends and Centers of Research

The Czechoslovak Academy of Sciences is not only a scholarly society but also a system of scientific and research institutes. Psychology has been represented in it in Bratislava from the very beginning of its existence in 1953. Soon there were two independent psychological institutes and specialized psychological sections in several other institutes.

The Institute of Psychology of the Czechoslovak Academy of Sciences in Prague (1967–) has been active in general and social psychology and in the psychology of personality. Its particular themes are the development of personality, human activity and consciousness, personality and collectivism, and the application of computer techniques to psychological investigation. The institute is the main organizer of the international Prague conferences, the first of which was held in 1969, the fifth in 1986. Among the leading personalities of the institute are M. Kodým (director), J. Khol, J. Kotásková, A. Velehradský, J. Hlavsa, L. Sedláková, M. Langová, V. Kebza, and numerous younger research workers. The former director, J. Linhart, continues to work there as a consultant.

The Institute of Experimental Psychology of the Slovak Academy of Sciences in Bratislava (1955–) works in the areas of psychophysiology, general and engineering psychology, psychology of personality, and methodology of psychology. It is oriented monothematically to research of cognitive functions of personality. In the 1960s problems of perception were in the foreground. In the 1970s it was memory; in the 1980s it was thinking. Within these topics, special attention is paid to the study of lateral interaction, load and stress, creativity, shift work, risk factors in disease, and social communication. The institute initiated the first meetings of psychologists from the Danubian countries (the first in 1967 in the ČSSR, the eighth in 1987 in the FRG) and organizes international conferences in cognitive processes and personality (the first in 1978, the fourth in 1989).

The institute is a sponsoring workplace for the human research of the Slovak Academy of Sciences. Its long-term research workers include D. Kováč (director), J. Daniel, M. Stríženec, A. Uherík, O. Halmiová, and O. Árochová. The middle generation of psychologists is represented particularly by I. Ruisel, A. Potašová, K. Jariabková, F. Šebej, M. Jurčová, and M. Hrabovsky, as well as by several specialists from other scientific spheres.

Within other institutes of the Czechoslovak and Slovak academies of sciences are the following psychological institutions. The Psychological Department at the Institute of the Research of Social Consciousness in Brno was, from 1964 to 1987, an independent workplace known as the Psychological Laboratory of the Czechoslovak Academy of Sciences. It is oriented to research in personality and its structure, value orientations, and artistic creativity. J. Hudeček is the head, and other researchers include D. Kolařiková and J. Viewegh. The Department of Pedagogical Psychology of the Pedagogical Institute of J. A. Comenius in Prague concentrates on research in student learning, the socialization of personality, and understanding the teaching process. Its staff includes Zd. Helus (head), V. Kulič, I. Pavelková, K. Bláha, J. Pstružinová, Zd. Novák, and A. Pohlová. The Department of Social Psychology of the Socioscientific Institute of SASC in Košice has done research on attitudes, particularly among the youth of different ethnic groups, ethnopsychology and social cognition, and the social psychology of personality. J. Výrost is the director, and other researchers include L. Lovaš, A. Zelová, and V. Bačová. Within the framework of the Institute of Theory and Prognosis of Science in Bratislava a group of young psychologists dealing with topical questions of psychology, among them M. Kubeš and P. Benkovič, have generated public attention.

In the period under consideration the scientific and research base of the universities in Bohemia became weaker institutionally. The Institute of Psychology of Charles University in Prague, founded in 1960, was in 1972 integrated with the university's Department of Psychology, in the Philosophical Faculty. The study of psychophysiological mechanisms of stress, reliability of achievement, will regulation, training by means of training machines, and the methodology of psychology is being partially continued with a new staff. M. Machač is the director. The staff includes Zd. Bureš, V. Břicháček, and M. Brichcín.

The Institute of Psychology of the Philosophical Faculty at the Comenius University in Bratislava, founded in 1957, integrated the Laboratory of Comparative Psychology and the Institute of Psychological Professional Development and Guidance in the early 1970s. Special areas of research include a broad orientation to general psychology, methodology and prehistory of psychology, and the problems of biodromal development in shaping a personality. Recently, attention has turned to questions of motivation, behavior, and the fundamental dimensions of the life course. T. Kollárik is the director, and the research staff includes J. Koščo, L. Maršalová, V. Hlavenka, and M. Czako.

The Research Institute of Child Psychology and Pathopsychology of the Child in Bratislava, founded in 1964, studies cognitive, personality, and social development in normal children and adolescents, in mentally and sensory retarded children and adolescents, and in children with learning disorders. The institute is also oriented to educational guidance and has undertaken the role of the methods center in Slovakia. Within this framework the institute investigates problems concerning the development of creativity, the identification of gifted children, prosocial behavior, school success, and criminality and its prevention, among other topics. It provides supporting materials and expertise for the Department of Education of the Slovak Socialist Republic. L. Páleník is the director. The staff includes V. Kováliková, K. Adamovič, L. Košč, I. Učeň, D. Kopasová, M. Zelina, J. Šípošová, and V. Diešková. The former director is M. Pavlovkin.

Research activity is also carried out by the departments of psychology at philosophical faculties of universities. In Prague the center of these activities has shifted toward psychological regulation of common activity, active protection of mental health, the integrity of personality, stress and relaxation techniques, and the development of the younger generation, particularly motivation and interests. In Bratislava research focuses on the problems of shaping the personality in a socialist society and the prevention of certain inadequate behaviors. In Brno attention has turned to research on the psychological characteristics of students and to the psychology of art. In Olomouc research workers in the psychology department concentrate on the development of personality and on special questions of work psychology. In Prešov (as previously in Košice) school psychology is the area of greatest research and theoretical development.

Several other departmental institutions are made up of independent psychological or interdisciplinary psychological sections. Several of these psychological posts are occupied by distinguished psychologists. Listed below are the members of various departments. The Department of Education includes J. Růžička, D. Tollingerová, K. Pavlica, H. Pešinová, Z. Rymeš, E. Bedrnová, J. Koluchová, F. Man, I. Šmahel, J. Taxová, Ľ. Klindová, L. Požár, A. Gronský, E. Harineková, I. Glázerová, I. Perlaky, and H. Florek. Educational Guidance includes L. Kamenčík, E. Kolényi, J. Ihnacík, M. Šulek, J. Danko, J. Moc, R. Kohoutek, V. Caponi, and T. Novák. The Department of Health Service employs J. Křivohlavý, Zd. Matějček, J. Langmeier, S. Fraňková, J. Čepelák, K. Balcar, P. Říčan, St. Kratochvíl, G. Dobrotka, O. Stančák, and I. Štúr. In the Department of Industry, Work, and Social Affairs are M. Kubalák, J. Ch. Raiskup, F. Bury, O. Matoušek, A. Hladký, and M. Šolc. Sports Organization, including education, employs M. Vaňek, I. Macák, V. Hlošek, J. Bezák, and E. Komárik.

New Research Goals

Social movement in the second half of the 1980s has been affected by the spirit of *perestroika*. The life of society allows for considerable contribution from psychology in all its variations. Without the participation of psychology, the new dialectics of the relationship between people and society would be impossible. Its effective fulfillment at the research level, for the time being, is presumed to be ensured by employing scientific and research capacities to the maximum degree. The possibility of greater development exists through interdisciplinary cooperation.

In this respect, one can expect increased interest in professional and practical activity, not only for the correction of problem individuals but also for the efficient intervention and optimization of social groups. Moreover, psychologists in Czechoslovakia expect to see substantial growth in contacts with psychologically developed countries.

Bibliography

Chmelař, V., Lukavský, C., Helus, Zd., & Kováč, D. (1977). Pětadvacet let ČSAV a psychologie. *Československa Psychologie, 21*, 524–547.

Kodým, M., & Špaček, M. (1985). Aufgaben und Ergebnisse der tschechoslowakischen Psychologie. *Psychologie für die Praxis*, 266–275.

Koščo, J. (1976). Czechoslovakia: The development and current status of psychology in Czechoslovakia. In V. S. Sexton & H. Misiak (Eds.), *Psychology around the world* (pp. 91–103). Monterey, CA: Brooks Cole.

Kováč, D. (1981). Psychology in Czechoslovakia: 1976–1980. *Studia Psychologica, 23*, 171–182.

Kováč, D. (1986). Psikhologiya v Chekhoslovakii: 1981–1985. *Studia Psychologica, 28*, 99–112.

Lingart, J., Kováč, D., Kodým, M., & Pardel, T. (1981). Psikhologiya v Chekhoslovakii. In B. F. Lomov (Ed.), *Psikhologischeskaya nauka v socialistecheskich stranach* (pp. 159–180). Moscow: Nauka.

Pardel, T., & Kováč, D. (1976). Psychology in Slovakia on the 30th anniversary of the foundation of ČSSR. *Studia Psychologica, 18*, 5–17.

Rapoš, I. (Ed.). (1988). 30 rokov Psychologického ústavu University Komenského. *Psychologica XXXIV*, Univ. Komenského, Bratislava.

11 / Dominican Republic

ANGEL ENRIQUE PACHECO

Angel Enrique Pacheco (born 1947) received his licenciatura en psicología *from the Universidad Nacional Pedro Henríquez Ureña, Santo Domingo, in 1972, and his PhD from the California School of Professional Psychology in 1976. A founding member and president of the Asociación Conductista Dominicana (1978–1982), he was also a founding member of the Bi-cultural Association of Spanish-Speaking Therapists and Advocates, San Francisco, CA. The recipient of a Benito Juárez/Fulbright-Hays Fellowship and of a fellowship from the Organization of American States, he serves as area coordinator for the International Council of Psychologists and for the Asociación Latinoamericana de Análisis y Modificación del Comportamiento. Pacheco is a behavioral clinical psychologist in private practice in Santo Domingo and president of PSILAB, s.a.*

Hispaniola, the island shared by the Dominican Republic and Haiti in the middle of the Caribbean, has been called "the land Columbus loved best." The Dominican Republic occupies the eastern two thirds of the second largest island in the Caribbean. With a geographic area of 48,442 square kilometers (about the size of Vermont and New Hampshire together), the population is 6 million, with more than 1.5 million living in the capital city of Santo Domingo de Guzmán. The second largest group of Dominicans lives in New York City, where they have become one of the biggest minority groups. For the past quarter century the government has been democratic, with a bicameral congress and presidential elections every 4 years. Civil liberties are respected in general and freedom of speech and of the press in particular. The Spanish language reflects the nation's Hispanic ancestry, although the proximity to the United States, the influence of USA cable television networks, and the growing influx of tourism is causing a slow but steady loss in old traditions. In their place stand the new mores imposed by technology-based societies.

I wish to acknowledge the kind collaboration of Dr. Huberto Bogaert, Clara Benedicto, and Roselín de los Santos, directors of the Maestrías en Psicología, Universidad APEC; Departamento de Psicología, UASD; and Departamento de Psicología y Orientación, UNPHU, respectively, in the preparation of this chapter.

Education

Psychology in the Dominican Republic was born as a discipline in the fall of 1967, when two departments of psychology were created simultaneously, one at the Universidad Autónoma de Santo Domingo (UASD) and at the Universidad Nacional Pedro Henríquez Ureña (UNPHU).

Psychology is an independent profession in the Dominican Republic, with growing respectability as it matures and as more psychologists offer their services at clinics, hospitals, schools, and industry. The estimated number of professional psychologists in the country is 900 (C. Benedicto, personal communication, January 20, 1988). The standard level of education for a professional psychologist is the *licenciatura*, a rather flexible academic degree (which follows the high school diploma). At UASD it is a 4-year degree, at the Instituto Tecnológico de Santo Domingo (INTEC) it takes 3½ years, and at UNPHU it is a 5-year degree. UASD will soon follow UNPHU's lead and have a 5-year degree program, with majors in specialty areas and the requirement of a scholarly thesis.

After graduation from an accredited university, the *licenciado* is required by law to obtain an *exequatur*, the permission given by the government to practice the profession. Although this is just a bureaucratic formality requiring no qualifying examination, it is estimated that only 20 percent of the *licenciados* actually apply for the *exequatur* (C. Benedicto, personal communication, January 20, 1988). Neither government authorities nor the psychological association attempt to enforce this regulation.

Currently, of the 25 officially recognized universities, 3 major ones offer degree programs at the *licenciatura* level (UASD, UNPHU, and INTEC) and only 2 at the master's level (UASD and Universidad APEC). The master's level specialty areas offered at UASD are in human development and social and community psychology. Forty students are active in the program. Ten have already graduated from the Social and Community Psychology Program. Universidad APEC offers two master's-level programs in psychology: clinical and industrial. The clinical program has 27 active students (7 men and 20 women) and 18 students (7 men and 11 women) who have finished the coursework but have not yet graduated. The industrial program has 13 active students (2 men and 11 women) and 11 students (3 men and 8 women) who have finished the coursework but still have not graduated. No doctoral programs in psychology have yet been established in the country.

The master's programs in psychology at Universidad APEC were established in the fall of 1985 and offered within the Faculty of Humanities and Sciences. The requirement is 46 and 48 quarter hours, respectively, for the clinical and industrial programs. A final paper is required in both programs, but not a thesis. Ten faculty members have doctorates, and two are doctoral candidates. Ten of the faculty are men; two are women.

UASD, founded in 1538, is the oldest university in the New World. It is the only university that is totally state-supported (but autonomous), whereas the others are private, with minimal or no state funding. UASD's Department of Psychology, located in the Faculty of Humanities, was established in October 1967 and has a faculty of 60 professors and 10 teaching assistants. The distribution of the educational level of the faculty is as follows: 1 holds a doctorate in psychology, 3 hold doctorates in other fields, 20 are at the master's level, and the rest are at the *licenciatura* level. There are 6 full-time professors, with the rest working part-time; academic loads range from 3 to 21 credit hours per semester. Of the faculty, 34 are women and 26 are men. The *licenciatura* program currently has 1,100 students and has graduated 500. Additionally, 300 have completed all requirements but the thesis. Of the graduates, 95 percent are women and only 5 percent are men.

The Departamento de Psicología y Orientación at UNPHU opened in October 1967, within the Faculty of Education, as a psychological guidance program, but it soon became a *licenciatura* in psychology. In 1969 specialties were offered for the first time in clinical and school psychology. Later industrial psychology was added. These *licenciaturas* have a requirement of 185 semester hours of training, whereas the one in school guidance requires only 73 semester credits. However, a prerequisite for the latter is a diploma as *licenciado* in the sciences of education. The faculty consists of 36 professors, of which 2 are full-time, 5 half-time, and the remainder part-time. Of the faculty, 3 have doctorates and 12 hold master's degrees; 17 are men and 19 are women. Statistics available for the period 1968–84 (Universidad Nacional Pedro Henríquez Ureña, 1986) show that a total of 329 students have graduated from the program, with a distribution by sex of 57 men (17.3 percent) and 272 women (82.7 percent). The distribution of graduates by specialty area is as follows: 40 (24 women and 16 men) in psychology (former generalist degree); 112 (100 women and 12 men) in clinical psychology; 44 (38 women and 6 men) in school psychology; 34 (30 women and 4 men) in industrial psychology; and 99 (80 women and 19 men) in school guidance.

Associations

The Asociación Dominicana de Psicologiá, Inc. (Dominican Association of Psychology) (ADOPSI), founded in 1975, is at present the only active association in psychology in the Dominican Republic. Typical activities are business meetings, and annual meetings with the presentation of scholarly papers and invited addresses. The association's major accomplishments include the publication of a bulletin, of a code of ethics, and of a directory, and the establishment of April 6 for the commemoration of the Day of the Psychologist.

The Asociación Conductista Dominicana, Inc. (Dominican Behaviorist Association) (ACD), a group for the advancement of behaviorism, was founded in 1978. ACD led a most fruitful—but short—institutional life until it became inactive in 1982. In its 4 years of existence, it offered 19 scientific events, with a total attendance of 2,162 participants and a mean score on the quality of the events reported at 3.83, out of a maximum of 5.0 (Pacheco, 1981a). Another major contribution was the creation in 1980 of the Inter-Institutional Committee for the Advancement of Psychology in the Dominican Republic (CIAP-RD). Members included the chief executives of the Departments of Psychology at UNPHU and UASD, of the State Mental Health Division, and of the two professional associations, ADOPSI and ACD (Pacheco, 1981b). Unfortunately for Dominican psychology, this committee disappeared soon after its creation.

Research

The advancement of research is difficult when basic needs have not been met. Further, although universities require the presentation of a thesis or a formal paper, in many instances these products are primarily exercises in futility, if ever completed. Data banks, computers, computer-assisted data search and retrieval, and large and up-to-date libraries are practically nonexistent or not available. Another major shortcoming in research is the lack of a professional journal for the dissemination of scientific findings.

Areas of significant research parallel the principal philosophical and theoretical influences in the country and are best exemplified by the work of investigators in fields such as behaviorism: Pacheco (1986) in family therapy, Almonte and Jiménez (1982) in progressive muscular relaxation, Paniagua and Baer (1985) in the correspondence of verbal and nonverbal behavior, and Escala and Sánchez (1977) on behavioral analysis applied to education; psychoanalysis: Bogaert (1986) in hermeneutics; family systems: Alma de Ruiz and Valdez de Nova (1986) on the prevalence of child abuse; and social psychology: Silvestre (1980) on the prevention of alcoholism and neurosis.

Outlook for the Future

A revision of the role of the departments of psychology is urgently needed, for it is critical that they assume their leadership in directing psychology as a discipline and as a force for good in the country. These departments must stimulate applied research, promote professional associations and publications, and defend the welfare of the general public as the ultimate recipients of psychological services. If these goals are accomplished, and no doubt they will be, the future will be bright.

Bibliography

Alma de Ruiz, Z., & Valdez de Nova, L. (1986). Prevalencia del abuso infantil en la prolación universitaria de Santo Domingo. *Revista Dominicana de Psiquiatría, 3*(1), 57–64.

Almonte, M. M., & Jiménez, N. F. (1982). *Entrenamiento en relajación muscular progresiva a operadores telefónicos: Un estudio experimental.* Unpublished *licenciatura* thesis, Universidad Autónoma de Santo Domingo, Santo Domingo, Dominican Republic.

Bogaert, H. (1986). Psicoanálisis y hermenéutica. *Revista Dominicana de Psiquiatría, 3*(1), 65–68.

Escala, M. J., & Sánchez, J. C. (1977). Análisis conductual aplicado a la educación: ¿Liberación o domesticación? *Revista Latinoamericana de Psicología, 9*(3), 397–407.

Pacheco, A. E. (1981a, June). *Psicología en la República Dominicana: Asociación Conductista Dominicana, Inc., Grupo para el Avance del Conductismo.* Paper presented at the meeting of the Sociedad Interamericana de Psicología, Santo Domingo, Dominican Republic.

Pacheco, A. E. (1981b, June). *Psicología en la República Dominicana: Comité Inter-Institucional para el Avance de la Psicología en la República Dominicana (CIAP-RD).* Paper presented at the meeting of the Sociedad Interamericana de Psicología, Santo Domingo, Dominican Republic.

Pacheco, A. E. (1986). Terapia de la interacción: Aproximación conductual a la psicoterapia familiar. *Revista Dominicana de Psiquiatría, 3*(1), 69–73.

Paniagua, F. A., & Baer, D. M. (1985). Correspondencia entre conducta verbal y conducta no verbal: Un análisis secuencial y funcional. *Revista de Análisis del Comportamiento, 3*(1), 3–20.

Silvestre, E. (1980). Evaluación de un programa integral de prevención del alcoholismo y la neurosis. *Revista Latinoamericana de Psicología, 12*(1), 127–144.

Universidad Nacional Pedro Henríquez Ureña. (1986). *Boletín Estadístico, 1*(1 & 2), 55–80.

12 / Egypt

FOUAD A-L. H. ABOU-HATAB

Fouad A-L. H. Abou-Hatab (born 1935) received a PhD from the University of London in 1967. A specialist in educational psychology, assessment, cognitive processes, and experimental psychology, he is the author of 5 books and more than 30 journal articles. His book Mental Abilities, *now in its fourth edition, won the Egyptian State Prize in Psychology.*

Abou-Hatab is editor-in-chief of the Egyptian Yearbook of Psychology *and holds two other editorial positions for international journals. He has served as a* UNESCO *consultant for the gifted and talented, as chief consultant in personnel selection for Islamic Banks, and as chief researcher for a study of psychological and educational research in Egypt. Abou-Hatab has also been president of the Egyptian Association for Psychological Studies since 1984 and was awarded the Medal of Science and Arts by the president of Egypt. He is professor of educational psychology in the College of Education, Ain-Shams University, Cairo.*

Historical Background

When Egypt became part of the Muslim world in the 7th century, classical institutions for Islamic general education were introduced. The small, one-teacher, multilevel school called *Kottab* was used for children; mosques were used for adolescents and adults. In some of these mosques sophisticated Islamic and Arabic knowledge was taught. With the establishment of formal colleges, philosophy, the womb of psychology and other human sciences, was introduced. Eventually, philosophy became a great Islamic endeavor. Throughout the period from the 9th to the 12th centuries, great names such as Al-Kindi (796–873), Al-Razi (865–925), Al-Farabi (878–950), Ibn Sina (Avicenna, 980–1037), Al-Ghazali (1058–1111), and Ibn Rushd (Averroes, 1126–98) dominated the scene. Although most of them were from parts of the Muslim world other than Egypt, they influenced Egyptian Islamic culture. Their impact on the Western Middle Ages and the Renaissance is well documented, although their contribution to modern scientific psychology has not been recognized by historians of psychology, with the exception of Brett (1921).

The Al-Azhar mosque was founded in Cairo in the 10th century but was soon transformed into a great Muslim university. In the 12th and 13th centuries Egypt witnessed the establishment of many "collegiate mosques" with major changes in content. Philosophy, history, geography, science, engineering, medicine, and music were introduced. Furthermore, medicine, including some form of psychiatry, was taught and practiced in hospitals. Al-Azhar University was affected by such developments. A further major change occurred in the 14th century when Ibn-Khaldun (1332–1406) arrived in Egypt to teach at the Al-Azhar. His lectures in *al-omarn* (sociology) included many references of a sociopsychological nature. However, these developments were not permanent. Before long, Al-Azhar returned to its theological function (from the 15th to 19th centuries). One major shortcoming of this change was that Egypt missed the scientific-industrial-cultural revolution emerging in Europe during this period.

The first modern confrontation between Egypt and the Western world occurred with the French occupation from 1798 to 1801. However, it was also an opportunity to form a modern society and a new state. This mission was carried out by Mohammed Ali, who ruled Egypt from 1805 to 1848. Education was his major strategy. Through him the modern educational system, influenced by the French, was introduced.

Institutionalization of Psychology

In the second half of the 19th century educational interest in Egypt was directed to colleges for teacher training. The first of such colleges was Dar Al-Ulum (House of Sciences), established in 1872 for Arabic-language teachers. Two more comprehensive colleges for teachers of science, mathematics, languages, and arts were founded, one for men in 1880 and another for women in 1890. Psychology appeared in the teacher-training college curriculum in 1906 as a minor part of educational science. Among 4-year programs, only 1 hour per week in the last 2 years was allotted to psychology. Nevertheless, it was the first appearance of psychology in the Egyptian educational system.

In 1906 an Egyptian university was proposed by some Egyptian national leaders. It was officially opened in 1908 as a non-governmental institution, with study limited to literature, history, philosophy, mathematics, and physics. Some lectures in psychology were also offered. In 1919 the American University in Cairo (AUC) was established. Then, in 1925, the Egyptian University came under government control (now the University of Cairo). The College of Arts was one of its foundational three colleges. Psychology became a major component of the Department of Philosophy curriculum, and qualified French professors were appointed to teach the subject. At the same time, qualified Egyptian professors were teaching psychology at the teacher-training colleges. In 1928 it was proposed to the Ministry of Education to abolish the teacher-training colleges and to establish a Higher Institute for Education.

The year 1929 is significant for the development of psychology in Egypt. The first group of philosophy students graduated from the University of Cairo in the College of Arts. The Higher Institute of Education (HIE) was also founded. Both institutes sent their best graduates to study psychology in Europe. At the same time, the first Department of Educational Psychology was established in HIE. Nevertheless, psychology in the HIE College of Arts was part of the Department of Philosophy. This tradition was extended to the second College of Arts, founded in the University of Alexandria in 1942. With the establishment of Ain-Shams University in 1950, psychology became a section of the larger Department of Sociology and Psychological Studies. However, the structure of the new university included 2 higher institutes of education: the College of Education and the College of Women, each with an independent Department of Educational Psychology. After a few years a Department of Mental Hygiene was added to the College of Education, and a Department of Childhood Studies was added to the College of Women. Furthermore, psychology in the Ain-Shams University College of Arts became fully independent in 1956. This status was achieved in the colleges of arts of Cairo and Alexandria universities in the early 1970s.

In 1957 the fourth modern Egyptian university was established, and in 1961 the most ancient Islamic University, Al-Azhar, was modernized, and new colleges were added. By 1987 Egypt had 13 universities. The distribution of departments of psychology in the colleges and institutes of these universities is shown in Table 12.1. Currently, Egypt has 30 departments of psychology in 27 colleges and institutes.

Education and Training

Egyptian psychologists are educated in colleges of arts or of education in the 13 universities. The courses offered at the college of education undergraduate level are primarily for teacher training and include introduction to psychology, developmental psychology, educational psychology, social psychology, mental health, testing and measurement, and evaluation. Colleges of education are responsible for training teachers of psychology at

TABLE 12.1

Distribution of Departments of Psychology in Egyptian Universities

University	College or Institute	No. of Depts.	Founding Date	Notes
Al-Azhar	a. Education	2	1970	
	b. Human Studies	1	1970	For women only
Cairo	a. Arts	1	1971	
	b. Education	1	1980	In Fayoum City
	c. Educational Studies	1	1987	Graduate Institute
Alexandria	a. Arts	1	1975	
	b. Education	1	1966	
Ain-Shams	a. Education	2	1929	1 for Mental Hygiene in 1956
	b. Women	2	1934	1 for Childhood Studies founded
	c. Arts	1	1956	in 1977
	d. Childhood Studies	1	1979	Graduate Institute
Asiut	a. Education	1	1975	
	b. Education	1	1977	In Sohaj City
Mansoura	a. Education	1	1972	
	b. Arts	1	1980	
Zagazig	a. Education	1	1972	
	b. Education	1	1978	In Benha City
	c. Arts	1	1982	
	d. Arts	1	1983	In Benha City
Tanta	a. Education	1	1973	
	b. Arts	1	1984	
Menia	a. Education	1	1975	
	b. Arts	1	1979	
Suez Canal	a. Education	1	1979	
Manoufya	a. Education	1	1971	
Helwan	a. Education	1	1975	
American University		1	1971	Unit of larger department

the secondary school level. The training of the general practitioner psychologist is the responsibility of departments of psychology in the colleges of arts. After a 4-year, full-time program the student is awarded a BA in psychology.

The graduate training of psychologists takes two major forms. In colleges of education a special diploma in education, with major emphasis on psychology, is required to pursue the master's degree, and the MA is a basic requirement for the PhD. Both degrees are based on a thesis and may be awarded in either educational psychology or mental health. A similar system operates in the colleges of arts. After 1 year of advanced courses in psychological theory and methodology the student progresses to a master's degree. In the colleges of arts, in both Cairo and Menia universities, there is a 1-year program for a diploma in applied psychology.

Work Settings and Licensing

Most graduates of psychology departments work in civil service, including teaching in Egyptian schools. Some work as general practitioners with a BA in psychology as a minimum requirement. The general practitioner is limited to nonclinical psychological activities, such as testing, personnel selection, and training in the Ministries of Health, Social Work, Human Resources, Defense, Interior, and Education. The practitioner works with a team that includes a physician, psychiatrist, social worker, and psychologist. Some graduates with a special diploma in education serve as general practitioner psychologists in special education, especially with the handicapped and mentally retarded. The practice of clinical psychology, however, whether in private clinics or in state mental hospitals, is restricted to licensed psychologists.

Licensing in Egypt has an interesting history. As Beshai (1960) stated, the first psychologist to practice psychotherapy along with psychiatrists and neurologists was Marcus Gregory in 1939, followed shortly by Mohammed Fathy, the late professor of criminology at Cairo University. In the late 1940s Egypt witnessed abuse and violation of practice. Some hypnotists, astrologists, and charlatans represented themselves as psychotherapists. As a result, Law No. 198 was promulgated in May 1956 to regulate the clinical practice of psychologists. By law, a license could be issued only to the holders of one of the following degrees: (1) diploma in neurology and psychiatry from a college of medicine; (2) certificate of specialization in psychotherapy and/or active membership in a recognized local or foreign association or organization of psychotherapy; (3) graduate degree in psychology with a minimum of 2 years of practice in a recognized and authorized clinic.

The committee on the Approval of Candidates for the Practice of Psychotherapy consists of an under-secretary of the Ministry of Public Health, the director general of the Department of Mental Health, a representative of the Council of State (jurisprudence body), the professor of neurology at the College of Medicine of Cairo University, and five experts in the field of psychotherapy chosen by the Ministry of Public Health. In some cases, tests are given and an oath is taken before the license is issued. However, the licensure system is rather lenient. There is a growing demand to restrict clinical psychological practice to a PhD degree in psychology, with a 1-year internship in an authorized clinic or mental hospital.

Most MAs and PhDs in psychology work in academia, whether in universities or research centers. Faculty membership is restricted to PhD holders. According to Law No. 49, which reorganized Egyptian universities in 1972, "lecturer" is the lowest University academic post. Promotion to assistant and full professorship in all specializations, including psychology, is based on research examined by committees established by the Supreme Council of Universities. Equivalent procedures are followed for psychologists in the two major research centers in Egypt: the National Centre for Social and Criminological Research (NCSCR), established in 1956, and the National Centre for Educational Research (NCER), founded in 1972.

From the early 20th century to the late 1930s the education and training of Egyptian psychologists was in either British or French universities. The majority of the first generation returned with either a BA or diploma in education. Some returned with an MA or MSc, and only 4 with doctorate degrees: El-Kousy from Britain; and Ragih, Mourad, and Ziwar from France. After World War II approximately 20 psychologists were sent for doctoral study to Britain, France, the USA, and Switzerland. Although a few remained in their host countries, the gain from the late 1940s to the late 1950s was rewarding. During the same period the University of Cairo, followed by Ain-Shams and Alexandria universities, awarded more than 20 MA and PhD degrees in psychology and educational psychology. By then the human resources base for Egyptian psychology was established, with approximately 40 psychologists forming the second generation.

The "third wave" began in the early 1960s, when there was a major shift toward the USA. Britain became the second preference, and other West European universities were third. A major change occurred in the mid-1960s, however, when some of the psychology scholars were sent to the Soviet Union and other East European universities. At the same time, the three major Egyptian universities produced more MAs and PhDs. In the early 1970s the estimated number of qualified high-level psychologists (MA at least) was 100.

After 1970 Egypt witnessed radical educational changes. Perhaps the most significant was the rapid increase of universities and departments of psychology offering a BA in psychology or a special diploma in education. Between 1956 and 1986 there were approximately 15,000 such graduates. Nevertheless, most of them were not granted full membership in the Egyptian Association for Psychological Studies (EAPS), only affiliate membership.

The percentages of male and female Egyptian psychologists are, according to EAPS statistics, 65 and 35, respectively. Among female psychologists, 12 are professors and most are deans, vice-deans, or heads of departments. The male psychologists serve throughout the national Egyptian administration. Two professors became ministers of education (the late El-Kabbani and Abdel-Ghaffar), one held a high-level post in UNESCO for several years (El-Kousy), and many were, for a time, under-secretaries for the Ministries of Education, Social Affairs, and Culture.

University teaching is the usual work setting, as in other Arab countries, with their great expansion into higher education since the early 1970s. For example, by 1970 there were only three universities in the oil-producing gulf states: Riyadh University in Saudi Arabia (1957), Baghdad University in Iraq (1958), and Kuwait University in Kuwait (1966). Since 1970 12 other universities have been established in Saudi Arabia, Qatar, the United Arab Emirates, Bahrain, Iraq, and the Sultanate of Oman. Still other universities were founded in Jordan, Lebanon, Yemen, Sudan, Libya, Tunisia, Algeria, and Morocco. In all cases, Egyptian specialists, including psychologists, have been in demand. This has been the most serious "brain drain" in Egyptian history.

Although most psychology graduates (BA or diploma) are employed in civil service agencies, a few work in the psychological profession proper. Some work in special education, crime, juvenile delinquency, and family planning. Others serve in various departments of the Ministries of Defense, Interior, Industry, Health, Human Resources, and Social Affairs. In the Ministry of Education most work as teachers in preparatory and secondary schools. Their teaching includes philosophy, sociology, and other social sciences in addition to psychology.

Characteristics of Psychology

Periodicals

Although the 1930s and 1940s were the formative decades, Egyptian psychology was known much earlier. The publication of *Al-Muktataf* (a general cultural periodical, first published in Beirut in 1878 and transferred to Cairo in 1885) was a milestone. Its editors were scientifically oriented with a special interest in empirical sciences, including psychology. For example, in 1916 a complete account of E. L. Thorndike's experiments on animal learning was published (Mourad, 1964). Until its discontinuance in 1953, the journal supplied general literacy in various areas of psychology.

The second periodical concerned with psychology was the *Journal of Modern Education*, published from 1928 to 1973 by the American University in Cairo (AUC). Its editor was the great Egyptian educator and psychologist Amir Boktor. The forty volumes of the journal are a psychological and educational treasure. The early volumes included mostly translations from original American materials; from the 1950s the journal published theoretical studies and empirical research by Egyptian psychologists.

In 1945 the first issue of the *Egyptian Journal of Psychology* was published, edited by two pioneer psychologists: Yousif Mourad and Mustapha Ziwar. Eight volumes were issued until the journal ceased publication in 1953. Some materials were translated into Arabic from French, English, and German. Other papers were especially written for the journal by leading French, British, and American psychologists and published in their original languages. Among the eminent psychologists who wrote for the journal were Henri Wallon and Paul Fraisse (from France); Cyril Burt, C. W. Valentine, and L. L. Wynn Jones (from Britain); and H. B. English (from the USA). Most papers were theoretical; a few were empirical, written in Arabic by Egyptian psychologists, with a summary in either English or French. These summaries were included in *Psychological Abstracts*.

In 1948 the *Journal of Education* was founded, and it was edited for the first 5 years by an eminent Egyptian psychologist, Ismail El-Kabbani. He was succeeded by another renowned psychologist, Abdel-Aziz El-Kousy, for another 5 years. From 1958 until the present, consecutive editors were exclusively educators. From the beginning, however, the editorial board included leading psychologists, and psychological material with an educational orientation was published.

In 1954 Yousif Mourad attempted to revise the *Egyptian Journal of Psychology* as the *Egyptian Yearbook of Psychology*. Unfortunately, only one issue was published. No specialized periodical was available until 1974, when EAPS published its first volume of the *Egyptian Yearbook of Psychology*, followed by another two volumes in 1975 and 1976. The three volumes were edited by the female president of the association, Somaya Fahmy. In 1984 the association was reorganized, and the *Yearbook* was published more regularly. Two volumes appeared in 1985 and 1987 under the editorship of this author, the current president of the association. In 1987 the government publishing agency began the first issue of the *Journal of Psychology*, a quarterly.

Since about 1950, Egyptian psychologists have published in other relevant journals, especially the following three. The first is the *Egyptian Journal of Mental Health,* published by the Egyptian Association for Mental Health since 1959. (The first editor of this journal was Mostapha Ziwar.) The other two are the *National Criminological Review* and the *National Social Review,* published by the NCSCR from 1958 and 1964, respectively. Furthermore, in 1973 a group of professors of psychology and education launched the *Yearbook of Psychology and Education.* Twelve volumes have been published to date. The early volumes were more "psychological," whereas the more recent ones have become more "educational."

The annals issued by most Egyptian colleges of arts and education are other available channels for publishing psychological research, as are those issued by universities in other Arab countries. The most distinguished of the latter are the *Arab Journal of Social Sciences,* the *Arab Journal of Human Sciences,* and the *Educational Journal,* all published by Kuwait University. Some Egyptian psychologists also publish in American, British, and continental periodicals.

Textbooks

It is common practice in Egypt to teach all branches of knowledge, except medicine, in Arabic—a practice initiated for the human sciences in the late 19th century. In the early 20th century some Arabic psychology textbooks were written for teacher-training college students by graduates educated in Britain.

Teaching psychology in Egyptian universities during the 1920s and 1930s was done by professors of philosophy. The language and textbooks used were French. The 1940s witnessed the first edition of two major Arabic textbooks: El-Kousy's *Fundamentals of Mental Health* in 1945 and Yousif Mourad's *Principles of General Psychology* in 1948. These two books soon became primary references. Four new editions and numerous reprints of both have appeared since then.

Since 1950 the number of Arabic textbooks has gradually increased. Among the most significant from the 1950s are El-Kousy's *Psychology and Its Educational Applications* (1950), A. Z. Saleh's *Educational Psychology* (first published in 1950), M. O. Nagaty's *Military Psychology* (1952), A. E. Rageh's *Foundations of Psychology* (1953), M. K. Barakat's *Mental Tests and Measurements* (1954), S. M. Khairy's *Statistics in Psychological, Educational, and Social Research* (1959), F. E. El-Sayed's *Developmental Psychology* and *Social Psychology* (1955 and 1956, respectively), and M. Hamza's *Psychology of the Handicapped* (1956).

In the 1950s psychology textbooks and monographs were increasingly translated. Major works of Sigmund Freud, Anna Freud, Susan Isaacs,

Henri Wallon, Jean Piaget, Cyril Burt, Arnold Gesell, Ernest Jones, Robert Woodworth, J. P. Guilford, Anne Anastasi, and J. Deese became available in Arabic.

The writing of psychology books in Arabic and translations of foreign works into Arabic were both facilitated by the availability of equivalent Arabic scientific terms. Efforts in this regard were begun in the 1940s by El-Kousy and Mourad. In the early 1950s the Academy of Arabic Language became more involved. I compiled and edited a dictionary of psychological terms approved by the academy in 1982.

During the period from 1960 to 1987 the Arabic Library of Psychology covered nearly every aspect of the discipline. In general, Egyptian library facilities are good, with a large national library in Cairo and several libraries in major cities. Furthermore, every university has one central library, supplemented by specialized libraries for colleges and departments. Computer facilities are available in Cairo and Ain-Shams universities, AUC, and the Academy for Science and Technology. Table 12.2 shows the main Egyptian authors in different areas, classified in general terms using the recent index of *Psychological Abstracts*.

Tests and Equipment

The first Egyptian empirical psychological research was conducted in 1928 in test standardization. El-Kabbani used Ballard's test of intelligence and Goodenough's Draw-a-Man Test on more than 4,000 school children from 7 to 15 years of age. Both tests were widely used in the psychological clinic established in 1934 in HIE.

El-Kabbani's efforts in testing were extensive. One of his major achievements was the Egyptian form of the 1916 American edition of the Stanford-Binet Test of Intelligence in the 1930s. The test was completely revised, using the 1937 American edition, by M. A. Ahmed and L. K. Melika, and the new form appeared in 1956. Although there have been several US revisions during the 30 intervening years, the Egyptian published form remains in its 1956 edition. However, various parts of the test were revised in research for MA and PhD degrees at Ain-Shams University in the 1980s.

In 1956 the Egyptian form of the Wechsler-Bellevue Intelligence Scale for Adults was standardized and published by M. E. Ismail and L. K. Melika. In 1961 they published the children's scale. The Draw-a-Man Test and Raven's Progressive Matrices have also been studied. The most comprehensive standardization was carried out in Saudi Arabia in 1976 by an Egyptian and Saudi team led by F. Abou-Hatab and Amal A. M. Sadek.

Two intelligence tests by S. M. Khairy have enjoyed wide use since 1958 for research and clinical purposes: the Preparatory Intelligence Test and the

TABLE 12.2

Main Egyptian Authors in Psychology, 1960–87, by Area

Area	Authors
Behavior therapy	M. Souif
Childhood studies	S. Fahmy, K. Abdel-Fattah, S. Bahader
Cognitive processes & cognitive psychology	F. Abou-Hatab, S. A. Osman, S. E. El-Saikh
Counseling and mental health	A. M. Hana, S. Galal, S. Magharious, A. Abdel-Ghaffar, H. Zahran, O. Farrag, R. A. Khalil, T. M. Ghebrial, M. Helmi
Cross-cultural studies	M. O. Nagaty, G. Abdel-Hamid, S. E. El-Sheikh, F. A. Taha, M. S. Aboul-Nil
Developmental psychology	F. E. El-Sayed, E. Ismail, H. Zahran, H. El-Melegi, H. El-Fiqi, I. Qashqush, F. Abou-Hatab, Amal A. M. Sadek
Drug psychology	M. Souif, S. El-Maghraly, Abdel-Halim M. El-Sayed
Educational psychology	G. A. Gaber, H. El-Abd, S. A. Houter, S. Khairalla, F. Abou-Hatab, Amal A. M. Sadek
Experimental psychology	A. Z. Saleh, A. Abdel-Khalik
Handicapped & mental retardation	H. Barrada, Farouk M. Sadek
Learning	A. Z. Saleh, R. El-Gharib, I. W. Mohmoud, A. El-Sharkawy
Music psychology and teaching	Amal A. M. Sadek
Occupational, industrial, and applied psychology	S. M. Khairy, M. O. Nagaty, K. Donsouki, G. A. Gaber, Farag A. Taha, M. S. Aboul-Nil, A. M. Awad, S. A. Morsi, M. El-Sharkawy
Personality	E. Ismail, R. F. Mansour, N. I. Ibrahim, L. K. Melika, M. Souif, A. A. Salama, A. Abdel-Khalik, S. El-Aasar, E. Z. Mohammed, K. Abdel-Fattah, S. M. Ghonaim, S. M. Ali, A. M. Awad
Physiological psychology	A. Okasha
Political psychology	Q. M. Hefni

TABLE 12.2
(*Continued*)

Area	Authors
Psychoanalysis	S. H. Mokhaimer, A. Fayeq, F. A. Farag, Q. M. Hefni, S. El-Qattan
Psychometrics	M. A. Ahmed, R. El-Gharib, F. E. El-Sayed, F. Abou-Hatab, Amal A. M. Sadek, S. E. Farag
Social psychology	M. Souif, A. Abdel-Ghaffar, S. A. Osman, H. Zahran, M. Abdel-Kader, M. Aboul-Nil, Abdel-Halim M. El-Sayed
Speech therapy	M. Fahmy, H. Barrada
Statistics	F. E. El-Sayed, M. S. R. El-Gharib, M. S. Aboul-Nil, S. Allam

High Intelligence Test, both based on Spearman's concept of "g." Similarly familiar are the Pictorial Test of Intelligence by A. Z. Saleh and the Nonverbal Intelligence Test by A. M. Hana, although the published forms need further revision. Most of the well-known multiple-aptitude batteries have been standardized for the Egyptian culture, including the SRA Primary Abilities Tests by A. Z. Saleh, the Differential Aptitude Tests (DAT) by S. M. Khairy and L. K. Melika, the General Aptitude Test Battery (GATB) by M. Abdel-Kader, and the Kit of Factor-Referenced Cognitive Tests by S. E. El-Sheikh, A. El-Sharkawy, and N. Abdel-Salam.

Major tests for specialized abilities have been "Egyptianized." Since 1968 Amal A. M. Sadek has engaged in an ambitious project for musical abilities. The Seashore Measures of Musical Talent, the Bently Musical Tests for Children, and the Wing Tests of Musical Intelligence were all standardized in Egypt. Sadek also created five other tests of Arab music: Musical Closure, Melody Identification, Rhythmic Identification, Interval Recognition, and Interval Estimation. The two major batteries of creative thinking were also adopted for Egyptian culture: Guilford's Battery of Creative Thinking by A. Abdel-Ghaffar, and Torrance's Battery by A. M. Soliman and F. Abou-Hatab. The Watson-Glaser Battery for Critical Thinking was adapted by G. A. Gaber and Y. Hindam. Other batteries are available for motor, mechanical, and clerical abilities.

Major personality tests were also adapted. The first to be adapted in the early 1950s was the Woodworth Personal Data Sheet by A. Z. Saleh, followed in the 1960s by the Bernreuter Personality Inventory by M. O. Nagaty and the Edward Personal Preference Schedule by G. A. Gaber. The standardization of the Minnesota Multiphasic Personality Inventory (MMPI) was a major project of A. M. Hana, M. E. Ismail, and L. K. Melika. Furthermore, the Minnesota Counseling Inventory was prepared by M. E. Ismail and S. M. Morsi, the California Personality Inventory by A. M. Hana, the Kuder Occupational Interest Survey by A. Z. Saleh, Strong's test by A. M. Hana, the Mooney Problem Check List by M. Fahmy, Bell's Adjustment Inventory by M. O. Nagaty, Cattell's 16 PF batteries by S. Ghonaim and A. Abdel-Ghaffar, Eysenck's Personality Inventory by G. A. Gaber and M. Al-Islam, and the Gordon Personnel Profile and Gordon Personal Inventory by G. A. Gaber and F. Abou-Hatab. The Bender-Gestalt, Rorschach Inkblots, and the Thematic Apperception Test (TAT) are also available for research and clinical uses. For the documentation of test-standardization research, a two-volume handbook was edited by Abou-Hatab (1977, 1979).

The first psychological laboratory was established in 1930 in HIE. Other laboratories were subsequently created in other departments of psychology. During the 1934–80 period, most equipment available was that found in classical references for the study of psychophysics, reaction time, attention, memory, perception, and learning. In 1980, however, a radical modernization of the laboratory of Ain-Shams University, College of Education, occurred, and more sophisticated and up-to-date equipment was introduced, permitting graduate students to investigate newer problems in areas such as information processing.

Clinical Movement

The first psychological clinic was founded in 1934, annexed to the HIE. It was modeled after child guidance clinics in Europe and the USA, to introduce psychological services to the pupils of the institute's experimental schools. Later the demand for clinical services exceeded its capacity. Only 15 to 25 pupils were seen annually throughout the first 10 years, with a total number of 220 cases by 1945. The clinic became more active afterward, with a full-time staff. In 1987 four professors, an associate professor, three lecturers, an assistant lecturer, seven instructors, a neurologist, a psychiatrist, a speech therapy specialist, and a social worker were available on either a full-time or a part-time basis. The total number of cases was 150 in the 1986–87 academic year, which is more than half the number studied from 1934 to 1944.

From the beginning the clinic was based on the collaboration of psychological, medical, and social efforts in both diagnosis and therapy, and this strategy is still in force. The clinic's immediate clients are schoolchildren, adolescents, and youth, although it is also concerned with the psychological problems of teachers. Various therapeutic techniques are used, including psychoanalysis, behavior therapy, client-centered therapy, and play therapy.

The second major development in the Egyptian clinical movement was the establishment, in 1954, of the School Social Services Office of the Cairo Department of Education. Its original plan was to introduce medical, social, and psychological services in the manner of clinics. Because of the lack of qualified psychologists, the major emphasis was on social services.

Since the 1930s the clinical movement has achieved many successes. The one clinic of the former HIE became three in Ain-Shams University. The Ministry of Health extended its services to the establishment of school psychological clinics, although the principal services in these clinics are psychiatric and neurological. School psychological services are provided for the Egyptian school population through various agencies, but such services are not offered in the schools by qualified school psychologists.

Egypt has schools for the mentally retarded and centers for the physically and sensory handicapped, sponsored by either the Ministry of Education or the Ministry of Social Affairs. The Ministry of Health oversees five mental hospitals. In addition, there are many private mental hospitals and psychological clinics. In most cases, the psychologist's role is limited to diagnosis.

Professional Organizations

The only professional organization is the Egyptian Association for Psychological Studies (EAPS), established in 1948 to promote psychological research and the profession. Full membership is restricted to graduates with degrees in psychology higher than the BA and BS. Other membership categories include honorary membership granted to distinguished psychologists, affiliates who do not fulfill the requirements for full membership, and student subscribers. Only full members may vote in elections.

Until 1984 the EAPS's activities were limited to casual general lectures and publications. In that year the association was reorganized and became more active. Four annual conferences were held from 1985 to 1988, and their proceedings were published. The *Yearbook of Psychology* became more regular. Egypt's petition for membership in the International Union of Psychological Science was approved, and in 1987 EAPS became the 47th member of IUPsyS.

Egyptian psychologists are granted membership in other professional and academic organizations. The Union of Teaching Professions and the Union of Social Services Professions are examples of the former, and the Egyptian Psychiatric Association and the Egyptian Association for Mental Health are examples of the latter. However, the academic status of psychology in Egypt is higher than its professional status. Current psychological services in social institutions, such as schools and industry, are provided through agencies that are not an immediate part of the system. This state of affairs poses many difficulties, the most serious of which are the lack of psychological services and the introduction of such services by nonqualified persons such as neurologists, psychiatrists, or social workers. Psychology in Egypt, as in other developing nations, has low status (although Egypt is probably the most advanced country, in this regard, in North Africa and among the Middle Eastern countries belonging to the Arab League). Paradoxically, the popular image of psychology is rather inflated, although it is often confused with psychiatry. More paradoxically, psychiatrists played an active role in this confusion.

Current Major Psychologies

Most psychological materials published in Egypt during the first quarter of the 20th century were philosophical-religious. The experience of the Leipzig Laboratory, the experiments of the Würzburg School, of Francis Galton, and of James McKeen Cattell, and the writings of Sigmund Freud and William James were all out of reach. McDougall's theory of instincts was familiar, however.

In HIE the first professor of psychology, Mohammed M. Said (MS in psychology and education, Birmingham University, 1925), was appointed in 1929. In the same year another psychologist, Ismail El-Kabbani (BA in psychology, University of London, 1917), was appointed professor of experimental education. Said concentrated on widening horizons for teaching psychology in Al-Azhar University, the Higher Institute for Drama, the Higher Health Institute, and the Police Academy. He also succeeded in introducing psychology into the secondary school curriculum in 1933. In contrast, El-Kabbani, a pioneer of the psychological testing movement in Egypt, was significant as an educational reformer. He was the first psychologist and educator to be appointed Minister of Education, in 1952.

The first Egyptian psychologist, in the academic sense, was Abdel-Aziz El-Kousy. Immediately after his graduation from Teacher Training College in 1928, he was sent to Britain to study psychology. On his return to Egypt in 1934, with a PhD in psychology from the University of London, University College, he was appointed to teach psychology in HIE. As a psychometrician, he collaborated with many associates and students in HIE in conducting factor-analytic research and standardizing psychological tests. He founded the first psychological laboratory and the first psychological clinic for schoolchildren and adolescents. It is apparent that by 1934 Egypt had a comprehensive psychology (psychometric, experimental, and clinical). The major practice was in what is now known as school psychology.

Three other contemporaries of El-Kousy were sent to France between 1929 and 1930 for higher degrees in psychology. The first, Ahmed E. Rageh, obtained his University of Paris doctorate in 1938. When he returned to Egypt, he initiated a comprehensive psychological movement, first in Alexandria HIE and later in Alexandria University, College of Arts. The second, Yousif Mourad, obtained his doctorat d'état from the Sorbonne in 1940. He pioneered an experimental-comparative-developmental movement in the University of Cairo, College of Arts. The third, Mustapha Ziwar, obtained his degree in medicine from France in 1941 with extensive training in psychoanalysis. He led the psychoanalytic-phenomenological orientation in Ain-Shams University, College of Arts.

A fifth pioneer of Egyptian modern psychology is Somaya A. Fahmy. Her undergraduate training in psychology was at the University of London (1930–34). From 1935 to 1937 she studied in Geneva under Piaget, and in 1955 she obtained her PhD in psychology from Indiana University. She spent all her academic life in the Higher Institute for Women Teachers (now Ain-Shams University, College of Women), with major interests in the psychology of learning and in clinical psychology.

The pioneers formed the first generation of Egyptian psychologists and laid the foundation for psychological science and practice during the first half of the 20th century. The second generation carried the mission further. Factor analysis of cognitive abilities was widened under the influence of Cyril Burt's model by S. M. Khairy and M. K. Barakat. P. E. Vernon's influence is strong in the research of F. E. El-Sayed. A. Z. Saleh was interested in cognitive factors involved in school learning. In 1969 he proposed a model for human learning largely influenced by C. E. Osgood. R. El-Gharib was the first to introduce the cybernetic model of learning. Cross-cultural studies were pioneered by M. O. Nagaty and L. K. Melika. The latter edited a major, four-volume handbook on social psychology in the Arab world. Parental attitudes, socialization, values, and superstition were the major research interests of N. I. Ibrahim, R. F. Mansour, and M. E. Ismail. Although social integration was an early interest of M. Souif, his primary contributions were in creativity and personality research.

Psychoanalysis was represented in the second generation by S. H. Mekhaimer. Other achievements of the same generation are A. M. Hana's research in personality and values, S. Magharious's studies on mental health in developing nations and his indigenous classification of adolescent behavior, and S. M. Ghonaim's research on the Rorschach.

The achievements of the contemporary third generation are still in a formative stage, but some distinguished examples can be mentioned. A. Abdel-Ghaffar and S. Khairalla are interested in creativity research. Recently, the research of Abdel-Ghaffar and his students has shifted to the psychology of alienation. His major theoretical orientation is humanistic psychology. S. A. Osman introduced the area of educational social psychology. His model of conformity and deviation as well as his concept of social responsibility have been studied since the early 1970s. His major research interests now focus on two principal topics: the Islamic personality and psychological enrichment in childhood.

Interest in "Islamic psychology," which began in the late 1970s, has become more widespread. Most writings are mere "translations" of psychological concepts into the terms of the teachings of the Holy Koran and Prophet Muhammad or the terms of major ideas of the great Muslim thinkers. I have criticized these attitudes and have expressed the need for a paradigm shift toward a new philosophy for scientific psychology.

My main theoretical and empirical interests have been in the domain of cognitive psychology and information processing since 1966. In 1972 I proposed a four-dimensional model for cognitive processes whose major contribution is the definition of *cognitive process* in terms of a detailed list of variables in each dimension. The model was presented internationally for the first time at the 23rd International Congress of Psychology, held in Mexico in 1984.

Other research interests of the present generation are diversified. H. A. Barrada is interested in Piaget's formulations and theories. Some of her studies involved graduate research on "psychometricized" Piagetian psychology. H. Zahran followed up his early (1966) research on self-concept. Amal A. M. Sadek has conducted research on the psychology of music since 1968. She has participated in conferences and seminars held in Britain, Canada, the USA, Austria, and the Federal Republic of Germany by the International Society for Music Education (ISME). Her research is mainly on musical testing, learning, perception, and education.

Psychoanalysis is advocated by Ziwar's students in Ain-Shams University, College of Arts, especially F. A. Farag and Q. Hefni. Hefni's efforts also extend to political psychology. F. A. Taha and M. Aboul-Nil are more interested in applied psychology. A. Abdel-Khalik has pursued Souif's and Eysenck's leads in research on personality. Souif's interest in creativity is followed more extensively by A. M. Sayed, with emphasis on family and childhood creativity.

Most research carried out by Egyptian psychologists of the last three generations has been self-financed, with the researcher paying all costs. Governmental financial support for psychological research is minimal. Few research projects are sponsored by the two primary research centers, NCSCR and NCER. However, these two centers have funded two major projects. The first is the NCSCR's program for drug research, supervised by Souif since 1960. Many psychologists have participated in the program, and many reports have been issued. The most recent was presented at the 3rd Annual Conference of EAPS in 1987 by M. Souif and A. M. Sayed. The other major project is the NCER's program on nutrition and school achievement, supervised since 1977 by S. Osman and F. Abou-Hatab.

Bibliography

Abou-Hatab, F. A-L. H. (1977, 1979). (Ed.). *Research in standardization of psychological tests* (Vols. 1, 2). Cairo: Anglo-Egyptian Bookshop.

Abou-Hatab, F. A-L. H. (1984). Towards a future for school psychology in Egypt. *School Psychology International, 5,* 9–13.

Abou-Hatab, F. A-L. H. (1987, September). *Egyptian psychology: A case history.* Paper presented at the 95th annual convention, American Psychological Association, New York.

Beshai, J. A. (1960). Current developments in the training and practice of psychology in Egypt. In D. Zoides & G. Zoides (Eds.), *Egypt today* (pp. 137–141). Cairo: Dar Al-Maarif.

Brett, G. S. A. (1921). *History of psychology.* London: Allen & Unwin.

El-Kousy, A. H. (1985). Fifty years with psychology in Egypt. In F. A-L. H. Abou-Hatab (Ed.), *Proceeding of 1st Conference of Egyptian Association for Psychological Studies.* Cairo: Anglo-Egyptian Bookshop.

Farag, S. E. (1987). Egypt. In A. R. Gilgen & C. K. Gilgen (Eds.), *International handbook of psychology* (pp. 172–183). New York: Greenwood Press.

King, D. W. (1984). Psychology in the Arab Republic of Egypt. *International Psychologist, 25,* 7–8.

Mourad, Y. (1964). Psychological studies in contemporary Egypt. *Al-Adib Magazine,* no. 2, 16–37.

Prothro, E. T., & Melikian, L. H. (1955). Psychology in the Arab Near East. *Psychological Bulletin, 52,* 301–310.

13 / Finland

PEKKA NIEMI

Pekka Niemi (born 1948) received his doctor of psychology degree from the University of Turku, Finland, in 1982. A specialist in cognitive processes, human learning, and reading acquisition, he coedited the book Psychology in the 1990s *with K. Lagerspetz. Niemi has published more than 60 articles, most recently in the areas of reading diagnostics and language processing. He was awarded a Fulbright grant for graduate study at the University of Oregon in 1974–75, is a member of the Experimental Psychology Society (UK), and currently is professor in the Department of Psychology of Åbo Akademi (the Swedish University of Turku).*

Characteristics of the Psychologist

Finnish psychologists are invariably trained in the universities. The programs are based on a statute concerning degrees in psychology, and the degree awarded is candidate of psychology. Six university departments offer a psychology program, and the total intake is about 140 majors each year. Completing the studies takes 5.5 to 6 years on the average. The most demanding part is at the end of the studies and consists of two items: one semester's practical training under the supervision of an experienced psychologist, and a scientific thesis, with the research usually done in a project led by a senior scientist.

During the 1980s the educational programs in psychology became increasingly structured. The benefit of this development has been that a high proportion, about 80 percent, of the students finish their studies successfully. The cost is a certain lack of flexibility in the programs, a feature often criticized by the students. Each of the six university programs leads to an equivalent formal competence, and the newly graduated psychologist can, in principle, apply for any open post. The only exceptions are the family and child guidance centers, which arrange a 1-year in-service study program for prospective psychological staff.

Two or 3 years of postgraduate studies at a university lead to the degree of licentiate. Doctoral programs do not exist in the usual sense of the word, and thus the students are mostly individually responsible for organizing their curricula. As a consequence, doctorates are usually earned at the age of 32 to 36 years. According to government statistics, 2,646 candidate degrees had been earned by 1985.

Because the profession of psychologist is relatively new in Finland, most graduates are actively engaged in work, 1,900 of them belonging to the Union of Finnish Psychologists. In addition, some 200 members are professionally inactive because of unemployment and maternity leave. The disparity between degrees earned and union statistics is largely due to the fact that psychologists working as teachers, researchers, and in the private sector rarely belong to the union. Given its population of 5 million, Finland displays one of the highest proportional densities of psychologists in the world (Rosenzweig, 1982). There is a preponderance of women in the profession, according to union statistics of 1986. The large number of graduated psychologists is not paralleled by the number of postgraduate degrees. By 1985 licentiate degrees totaled 143, while the number of doctorates was 83.

A comparison of Union of Finnish Psychologists membership statistics from 1986 and 1972 (Pitkänen, 1976) reveals that there have been some notable changes in the distribution of work settings (Pitkänen's 1972 data are in parentheses): clinical psychology, 33 percent (45 percent); vocational guidance, 13 percent (20 percent); educational guidance, 25 percent (13 percent); industrial psychology, 5 percent (9 percent); teaching and research, 8 percent (12 percent); and public health, 15 percent (0 percent). The relative increases are explained by legislation: the law on child guidance centers was passed in 1971 and the national health act in 1972. Not surprisingly, the public sector is the main employer of psychologists. Out of the 1,900 union members professionally active in 1986, 1,100 worked for the municipalities, 500 for the national government, and 300 in the private sector. This state of affairs results in a feature typical of relatively few countries, namely, that psychological services are fairly evenly distributed regionally and socially, since they are included in a broad system of social services to which the population has access (Nupponen, 1980).

The status of the psychological profession still remains unprotected by the law, as already reported by Pitkänen (1976). In principle, any private entrepreneur can claim to offer psychological services to the public. In practice, this phenomenon is fairly rare, because the main employers, that is, municipalities and the government, require the applicant to present a university diploma as a prerequisite for employment as a psychologist. Nevertheless, one of the major goals of the Union of Finnish Psychologists is to achieve legal protection for the title and work of the psychologist.

Characteristics of Psychology

The six university departments offering a curriculum in psychology are typically Finnish in their small size. In 1985 the number of staff members ranged from 4 to 24, the average being 13. In addition to permanent staff, there is an equivalent number of temporary researchers whose work is financed by the Academy of Finland or directly by the government. The total number of those engaged in teaching and research varies from 150 to 200. Each curriculum displays a similar structure and leads to the same formal competence. This feature is due to a government policy adopted in the 1960s, which sought to guarantee an access to higher education in all parts of the country. As a consequence, Finland now has 18 universities and other institutes of higher education. In the following sections, departments offering a curriculum are briefly described in alphabetical order. Emphasis is on their research orientation, which in practice affects the content of educational programs.

At the University of Helsinki the research interests of the Division of Applied Psychology include cognitive psychology, psychosomatics, comparison of cognitive and emotional development, human response to stress, and clinical neuropsychology. The Institute of General Psychology specializes in psychophysiology, experimental neuropsychology, vision research, and traffic behavior. Both departments have extensive international contacts. In the education of psychologists, the departments offer a joint curriculum.

The University of Joensuu, Department of Psychology, conducts research on career choice, creativity, personality, and the interplay between regional problems and developing local communities. The major orientation is toward the interaction of the individual and society.

The University of Jyväskylä, Department of Psychology, emphasizes the developmental approach in its research. Hence most of the studies deal with childrearing, upbringing, and schooling. Special topics are the way of life in the family, young families with children, life circumstances of the elderly, health education in nursery schools, early social development, family education, neuropsychology and learning difficulties, clinical psychology, family therapy, and psychophysiology.

At the University of Tampere, Department of Psychology, a significant part of the research deals with developmental psychology and the applications of psychology in public health and social service systems. Additional themes are environmental psychology, traffic behavior, and therapeutic communities.

The University of Turku, Department of Psychology, has a research tradition in human learning and memory. Specific topics are learning from texts and learning of skills, learning difficulties, and traffic behavior. Other research areas include experiences of divorce, abortion, and pregnancy; human aggression; bodily expression in psychotherapy; and social psychology of work groups.

Åbo Akademi (the Swedish University of Turku), Department of Psychology, focuses on two major themes: human and animal aggression and the psychological effects of alcohol.

There are also two departments of social psychology, one at the University of Helsinki and the other at the University of Tampere. The former has been directly involved in the activities of the Finnish Psychological Society, while the latter has contributed to national debates concerning the subject matter of psychology.

All departments also offer postgraduate training. However, the organization of these programs is less than satisfactory and there is little collaboration among the departments. This state of affairs was critically commented on during a national evaluation of psychological research recently organized by the Finnish Psychological Society (see Niemi, 1987). The society is a joint platform for scientific exchange within psychology and organizes general national meetings as well as seminars on specific topics. It also publishes the journal *Psykologia*, which is issued six times a year with a distribution of 3,500. Other publications of the society include the periodical *Acta Psychologica Fennica*, which appears on an irregular basis, usually as a themed issue or as congress proceedings. A monograph series under the same title was recently started to promote the exchange between research and application.

The professional organization is the Union of Finnish Psychologists, which has developed from a modest beginning in 1957 to a resourceful union of 2,100 full members (not including student members). The union publishes a newspaper, *Psykologiuutiset* (News for psychologists), 10 times a year with a distribution of 2,700. It can be said that the union graduated in 1984 when it organized a successful nationwide strike in the municipal sector to achieve goals set forth by its general assembly meeting. For the earlier history of the union, the interested reader is referred to Nupponen (1980).

Lack of adequate resources in both research and professional work was felt until the 1980s. Then the situation began improving markedly, a trend that culminated in 1986 with the governmental decision to double the expenditure on all research during the period 1987–91. It might be added, though, that the start was fairly low. In 1986 the entire expenditure was about 1.2 percent of the GNP, of which less than half came from the public sector. The effects of this policy are already being felt in the departments of psychology. Some are in a position for the first time to purchase the books, computers, and laboratory equipment they need. It is understandable that the advantageous financial situation has brought about an optimism that is reflected in new initiatives and international collaboration, the scarcity of which has been felt to prevent progress in the field.

In addition to hiring some 500 psychologists directly, the government financially supports the efforts by municipalities to establish psychological services. The criterion is that the type of work is specified by law. Typical organizations are family counseling and health centers. Efforts have been made to guarantee satisfactory access to services even in the most remote parts of the country. This has made a distinct contribution to the favorable public image of psychology. Because the majority of psychological services involve no immediate cost to the client, they are widely used and their existence is nowadays mostly taken for granted. Nevertheless, a culturally mediated factor somewhat counteracts this advantageous development. The image of psychology and of psychologists is often colored by associations with mental disorders, which have traditionally been met with caution and prejudice in Finland. Until recently, this bias has been reinforced by the psychologists' keen interest in clinical work. A newly emerging opinion is that significant areas awaiting the contributions of psychologists are job consultation and collaboration with other professionals devoted to human relations, such as teachers, medical personnel, and social workers.

Current Status of Psychology

After its modest start in Finland in the first half of the 19th century, psychology remained largely a hobby of philosophers influenced by the German school of philosophy and psychology. It is characteristic of this period that the first independent chair of psychology was founded as late as 1936 (for more details, see Pitkänen, 1976). The breakthrough of psychology in Finnish society had to wait until a demand was created because of the restructuring of the entire society after World War II. The country had to build new branches of industry, a large number of refugees from the surrendered areas had to be resettled, and the birth rate increased. These factors created a dynamic situation in the society which favored new ideas and initiatives. As a consequence, cultural and political values were reformed. Not surprisingly, the influence was immediately felt in psychology. The predominant German-inspired academic psychology was challenged by an American-born differential approach to personality and development. Factor-analytic treatment of extensive data sets replaced speculative typologies. It is worth noting that the new "exact front" in psychology, as it was called by some, also held new liberal values and did not hesitate to make them heard. A growing need for psychological expertise was felt in vocational counseling and social services, particularly in child guidance. This situation led to an expansion of academic training during the 1950s and 1960s (see Pitkänen, 1976). Departments of psychology were established and fresh orientations introduced. There was also a new feature, namely, that many chairs were defined to cover some subfield of psychology.

International contacts of Finnish psychology increased, although those with Germany collapsed. Through the century, Sweden has occupied a stable position. This is not surprising, given the cultural similarities between Sweden and Finland. Swedish psychology has never had a strong impact in Finland, however, and the contacts have characteristically taken the form of mutual collaboration. Profound foreign influences have come from Germany and more recently from the United States. It might be added, though, that behaviorism never attained a firm footing in Finland. Since 1975 the scope of international collaboration has been widening. In the years 1981–83 an approximately equal number of Finnish researchers visited the German Democratic Republic, the Federal Republic of Germany, the Soviet Union, Sweden, the United Kingdom, and the United States. Foreign scholars visiting Finland came from the same countries, but their number was dominated by the Americans and the Soviets.

One way to characterize the state of psychology is to outline its relationship to prevalent schools. In the present Finnish psychology one can easily observe the influence of Anglo-Saxon cognitive psychology, European developmental psychology, Soviet and Continental variations of Marxist psychology, and modern psychoanalysis. The last-named has a dominant role in Finnish psychiatry. The present picture is not one of separate schools but, instead, an attempt to reach a dynamic synthesis of ideas. Thus orthodox positions are rare, although departments admittedly differ in general approach. Moreover, many research projects carry a distinctive national flavor.

The most successful Finnish research groups work in the areas of psychophysiology (e.g., R. Näätänen), human and animal aggression (e.g., K. M. J. Lagerspetz), and cognitive processes (e.g., J. von Wright). The largest integrated department is at the University of Jyväskylä (M. Takala). Areas of considerable promise are traffic psychology, the need for which is daily demonstrated on Finnish roads, and neuropsychology, which reflects the growing concern with rehabilitation. It is also expected that educational psychology in general, and psychological theories of work and adult learning in particular, will occupy significant roles in the 1990s in view of the diminishing and aging labor force.

Bibliography

Acta Psychologica Fennica VII. Supplement to *Psykologia* 1980. Helsinki: Finnish Psychological Society.

Acta Psychologica Fennica VIII. Supplement to *Psykologia* 1981. Helsinki: Finnish Psychological Society.

Niemi, P. (1987). Evaluation of psychological research: The Finnish experience. *International Journal of Psychology, 22*, 387–393.

Nupponen, R. (1980). Professional psychology in Finland. *Acta Psychologica Fennica.* Supplement to *Psykologia* 1980, 9–21.

Pitkänen, L. (1976). Finland. In V. S. Sexton & H. Misiak (Eds.), *Psychology around the world* (pp. 118–130). Monterey, CA: Brooks/Cole.

Rosenzweig, M. R. (1982). Trends in development and status of psychology: An international perspective. *International Journal of Psychology, 17*, 117–140.

14 / France

ADÉRITO ALAIN SANCHES

Adérito Alain Sanches (born 1945) received his doctorat d'état *from Nice University in 1981. A specialist in the history of psychology and in research methodology, he has also published in social psychology, psychophysiology, economic psychology, and applied psychology. His works include* Heurs et malheurs de la science de l'ame *and the three-volume* Essai d'une définition mathématique de quelques variables fondamentales en psychologie. *The editor of two collections,* DN *(Didactique Nouvelle) in French and* Biblioteca de ciências humanas *in Portuguese, Sanches is joint director of the Laboratory of General, Differential, and Applied Psychology at Nice University.*

The Early Years: A Brief Overview

Modern French psychology emerged in the late 19th century, closely related to psychiatry and physiology. Early pioneers were the world-famous neurologist J. M. Charcot (1825–93) and the philosopher T. Ribot (1839–1916). Charcot headed the ephemeral Society of Physiological Psychology (1885–93), which in 1889 organized in Paris the first International Congress of Psychology. Ribot had been trying since 1870 to establish psychology as a field of investigation separate from philosophy. In 1876 he began the *Revue Philosophique de la France et de l'Etranger*, whose early issues encouraged the new psychology.

At the beginning of the 20th century two of Ribot's disciples, P. Janet (1859–1947) and G. Dumas (1866–1946), founded the French Psychological Society (1901) and the *Journal de Psychologie Normale et Pathologique* (1904). By that time two additional journals were available: the medically oriented *A. Médico-Psychologiques*, created in 1843 by J. Baillarger (1809–90), and *L'Année*

I am indebted to the colleagues who kindly answered my questionnaire. Special thanks to Profs. Albou, Anzieu, Brés, Ghiglione, Reuchlin, and Vexliard, as well as to Mr. Sillamy and Mr. Voutsinas, for their helpful comments.

Readers interested in contemporary French psychology can obtain additional references and information by writing to the Laboratoire de Psychologie Générale, Différentielle et Appliquée, 98, Bd. Ed. Herriot, 06007 Nice Cedex, France.

Psychologique, founded in 1895 by A. Binet (1857–1911). In this early period the works of Binet, Janet, and Dumas were influential. Other prominent contributions were those of J. M. Lahy, H. Wallon, and H. Piéron.

Lahy (1872–1943) was interested in applied psychology and conducted research to improve methods of job selection. Wallon (1879–1962) was influential in establishing French genetic psychology. He wrote several authoritative books on child mental development and in 1925 founded the Laboratory of Child Psychobiology at the Ecole Pratique des Hautes Etudes (School of Higher Learning). Piéron (1881–1964), Binet's successor at the Sorbonne, is generally acknowledged to be one of the most distinguished French psychologists of this period. In 1921 he became director of the newly created Institut de Psychologie de Paris (Psychology Institute of Paris), and in 1928 he founded the National Institute for the Study of Work and Vocational Guidance. For more than 50 years (1913–64) he edited *L'Année Psychologique,* one of the leading national journals devoted to psychology.

During these early decades of the 20th century the first professional non-medical applications of psychology began. By the end of World War II official diplomas and the professional use of the title "psychologist" had appeared. In 1945 Wallon recruited the first school psychologist. In 1947 a university degree in psychology (the *licence de psychologie*) was established. In 1955 the main teaching centers apart from Paris were Strasbourg, Lyons, Bordeaux, Montpellier, and Aix-Marseilles. In 1958 a doctorate with an option in psychology was offered. This degree allowed the universities to recruit instructors among advanced students trained in psychology, and not in philosophy or medicine.

The problem of organizing and defending the profession was an early concern of the practitioners. In 1950 the National Syndicate of Graduate Practicing Psychologists (which later became the Syndicat National des Psychologistes [National Syndicate of Psychologists]) was created. Other unions and professional associations were also formed during this period.

Psychology in the 1960s

Teaching

Normally, teaching and the awarding of degrees in psychology are the domain of the faculties of arts and humanities. Before 1967 it took 3 or 4 years to obtain a degree in psychology. The student had to pass five "certificates," each involving about one semester of coursework.

In 1967 as a result of educational reform, the situation was modified. Autonomous departments of psychology were established in the universities, and the course of study was divided into three levels: (1) the DUEL (*diplôme universitaire d'études littéraires*), (2) an intermediate level including the license and the *maîtrise,* and (3) the *doctorat de 3éme cycle* (a doctorate requiring a minimum of 2 years of research and the presentation of a thesis). Another doctorate—the *doctorat d'état*—prepared by candidates seeking a position as university professor and usually obtained after many years of research, was the highest diploma that could be earned.

In the mid-1960s psychology and psychoanalysis were popular among students, and enrollment increased considerably, with a gain of over 50 percent in the 1966–70 period compared to the early 1960s. In 1968 15 universities (out of a total of 23) offered degrees in psychology.

Among the lecturers were several prestigious figures: J. Favez-Boutonier, D. Anzieu, and C. Chiland, in clinical psychology (an area that had been significantly developed by D. Lagache); J. Piaget, M. Debesse, and R. Zazzo, in child psychology; J. Stoetzel and R. Daval, in social psychology; P. Fraisse, in experimental psychology; P. Pichot, in methodology, psychometrics, and psychopathology; M. Reuchlin, in differential and applied psychology; and R. Chauvin and P. Ropartz, in ethology and psychophysiology.

The teaching of psychology was no longer confined to the faculties of arts, science, or medicine. In 1965 P. Albou (later a professor of psychology at René Descartes University) gave the first course in economic psychology at the Faculty of Economics at Clermont-Ferrand.

Trends of Thought and Areas of Research
Three major ideological forces dominated postwar French psychology: phenomenological-existentialist philosophy, the psychoanalytical approach, and the objectivist movement of the behaviorists and experimentalists.

In the 1960s, while psychoanalysis and behaviorism continued to deserve attention, the previous attraction to existentialism and phenomenology began to fade. Instead, the "structuralist" movement, derived from Jakobson's linguistics, which inspired Lévy-Strauss's anthropology and Lacan's psychoanalytic conceptions, gained monentum. Lacan's nonconformist ideas were successful in psychopathology and in clinical psychology, where nondirective therapy also aroused much interest.

The trace of structuralism—even outside of Lacanian circles—was strongly felt within psychology. There was a deep concern for language and psycholinguistics. This new curiosity grew along with a renewed focus in diachronic and genetic approaches. The ideas of Wallon and Piaget, in particular, were widely discussed.

Social psychology, too, was popular: group dynamics, psychodrama (its first international conference was held in Paris in 1964), and the conceptions of the "human relations" school gained attention.

In the experimental areas of animal psychology and psychophysiology, investigations were carried out on conditioning, memory and learning, sleep and dreams, nutrition, and sexual behavior. Other significant fields of interest were human psychobiology, the study of cognitive functions, and psychopharmacology. In the previous edition of this book M. Huteau and P. Roubertoux (1976) gave a clear account of the research conducted during this decade.

Professional Practice

The number of practitioners increased significantly in the 1960s. A survey carried out in 1967–68 by the Institut National de la Santé et de la Recherche Médicale (National Institute of Health and Medical Research, INSERM) attests to this progress in the health sector. At the beginning of 1968 the number of psychologists in hospitals and medical psychology departments was approximately 1,000. About two thirds (663) of them participated in the survey. Their average age was 33, most (82 percent) were women, and a little over half (52 percent) had been working less than 4 years. Psychologists with more than 20 years of experience represented less than 3 percent of the total (Minivielle, Polge, & Maujol, 1968). In 1968 health psychologists felt sufficiently strong in numbers to contest the traditional dominant position of physicians. Clinical psychology has, since then, continued its fight to throw off the yoke of medicine, just as academic psychology had done previously in relation to philosophy.

Educational psychology also developed significantly. The recruiting of school psychologists had been severely restricted in 1954, except in the Grenoble region, but from 1960 on expansion was nationwide. Two other important areas of applied psychology—family and child aid, and industrial psychology—experienced a similar increase.

In an attempt to codify professional responsibilities, the Société Française de Psychologie (French Society of Psychology, SFP) had established in 1961 a professional code of ethics. Demands had followed for legal recognition. However, practitioners, even within the public sector, had diverse specialties and different levels of qualifications, and it was not easy to reach an agreement. The change of government in the late 1960s led to an unsatisfactory outcome. A project for a professional status prepared by D. Anzieu in 1968, at the request of the minister of education, was never followed up, and the position of psychologists remained unclear.

The Recent Years (1970–87)

Teaching and Training

Student protests in 1968 led to the modification of higher education through the Faure Law. This law established three principles that still form the basis of university life: (a) university autonomy (administrative, financial, and pedagogical), (b) student and staff participation in the running of the university through special committees, and (c) multidisciplinarity (new degrees were created, and the universities were deeply restructured). In 1971 another law upheld the right of wage earners to continuing education and job retraining. More recently, in 1984, the Savary Law was passed to promote research and adapt university education to the job market.

As a result of these new regulations, university education was changed. The old certificate system was replaced by a system of credits, similar to that found in American universities. The lower division (1st cycle) was modified in 1973; postgraduate studies (the 3rd cycle), in 1974; and the upper division (the 2nd cycle), in 1976. In the 1st cycle the old DUEL of the art faculties was replaced by a more multidisciplinary DEUG (diploma of general university studies). Changes in the 2nd cycle were minor, but in the 3rd cycle two new degrees appeared: the DESS (*diplôme d'études supérieures spécialisées*) and the DEA (*diplôme d'études approfondies*). Both require a year of study, but they are designed for different purposes. The DESS prepares students for their future professional activity and includes practical training outside the university. The DEA involves advanced research work. It constitutes the first year of the doctorate (more or less equivalent to a PhD), during which the student must prepare a thesis project.

Organization of Studies

Any secondary school graduate with the *baccalauréat* may enroll in psychology. Contrary to practice in medical schools, in schools of pharmacology, and in some other prestigious educational institutes, there is no selection process for admission or competitive examination at the end of the first year of study. The drop-out rate is nevertheless very high, with only one of three students continuing into the third year. This high drop-out rate, which is also observed in other university departments, was one of the reasons the government promulgated the Savary Law.

The organization of the 1st cycle was rethought with a view to improving the efficiency of the universities. A compulsory orientation period has been added, and various new diplomas (some of which correspond to short, vocationally oriented courses of study) have been created. In psychology the normal course of study still consists of (a) a 1st cycle of 700 teaching hours, with required courses in fundamental psychology, mathematics, statistics, and biology; (b) the *licence* (3rd year); (c) the *maîtrise* (4th year); and (d) a DESS for future practitioners or a DEA and a doctorate for future researchers and lecturers. Enrollment for the DESS and the DEA is restricted. Consequently, many *maîtrise* graduates are prevented from pursuing postgraduate degrees.

Universities Offering Psychology Degrees

Following passage of the Faure Law, the number of universities and related facilities more than doubled. In 1968 there were 23 universities in France, 1 per educational district. In 1971 there were 56 universities and an additional 14 institutes of higher education. By 1986–87 there were 70 universities and 7 other institutes of higher education. Among the 70 universities, 30 offer degrees in psychology. Of these, 27 offer honors degrees, 24 offer at least a DESS, and 23 offer at least a DEA.

In the 1986–87 period there were 35,000 to 40,000 psychology students in those 30 universities. The staff consists of approximately 850 permanent lecturers, assisted by outside practitioners and part-time lecturers. These figures represent about 4 percent of the student population (total = 1 million) and a little less than 2 percent of university staff (total = 45,000).

Distribution of students throughout the country is uneven. The six Paris universities offering psychology degrees account for one third of the total. Females outnumber males by three or four to one. The percentage of women teachers in psychology is about 35, which is small in relation to the number of female students or practitioners. Yet it is significantly greater than the overall total of 25 percent observed in the French university teaching body.

Libraries, Data Banks, and Specialized Works

Libraries are generally well organized and well endowed in the Paris region. The National Library, the main place where works published in France are stocked, is also an active research center in the human sciences. The university libraries (particularly that of the Sorbonne, with 2,200,000 volumes, and that of the School of Medicine, with about 500,000 books), together with those of the major cultural institutes, offer fine possibilities for research. More specialized libraries also exist.

Outside Paris, the main university libraries are those of Strasbourg, Bordeaux, Toulouse, Montpellier, Rennes, Caen, Lille, and Lyons. An interlibrary loan service, currently being computerized, allows students and researchers to consult books available in distant libraries, including foreign ones. Access to national or foreign bibliographic data banks is also possible.

There are at present three important French bibliographic data banks useful to psychologists: Pascal, Francis, and Bird. Pascal is most complete, with a list of more than 220,000 bibliographic references in psychology, psychopathology, and psychiatry. Most references are to medical psychology (about 50 percent), social psychology (8 percent), and human experimental psychology (8 percent). Francis has a section in educational science, with some 90,000 titles published since 1972. Finally, Bird is a more medically oriented bibliographic data bank with some 70,000 post-1980 references concerning child health problems.

New book titles are published at a reasonably high rate. Currently, manuals and reference books are available in all branches of psychology. The leading psychological journals usually review the most important of these new titles.

Several large companies publish collections of psychological works under the direction of distinguished editors. "Connaissance de l'Inconscient," "Le Fil Rouge," "Bibliothèque de Psychanalyse," "Le Champ Freudien," "Inconscient et Culture," "Psychismes," "BS: Science de l'Homme," and "Psychiatrie-Psychanalyse" are successful collections in clinical psychology; "Psychologie d'Aujourd'hui," in general psychology; and "Croissance de l'Enfant" and "L'Educateur," in developmental and educational psychology.

One of the poorly represented areas in publications remains the history of psychology. There are, however, excellent histories of medicine, psychiatry, and psychoanalysis recently written by French authors.

Among the most useful current reference books are the two-volume *Dictionnaire de la psychologie* (1980), edited by N. Sillamy, and the recent editions of several other specialized dictionaries: Piéron's *Vocabulaire de psychologie*, Laplanche and Pontalis's *Vocabulaire de la psychanalyse*, R. Lafon's *Dictionnaire de psychopédogogie et de psychiatrie de l'enfant*, Porot's *Manuel alphabétique de psychiatrie*, and G. Mialaret's *Vocabulaire de l'education*.

Research and Teaching Journals

Many periodicals are currently available. The 1987 edition of the *Catalogue des publications périodiques en psychologie*, prepared by D. Malrieu and A. Bastide, lists 140 French reviews of psychology. Summaries of the most important are usually available for English-speaking readers. Some 30 French periodicals are regularly analyzed by PsycINFO.

Among the main, less specialized, journals are the *Bulletin de Psychologie*, the review *Psychologie Française* of the French Psychological Society, the *Journal de Psychologie Normale et Pathologique*, and *L'Année Psychologique*.

Professional Journals

Information for practitioners appears regularly in certain scientific reviews, such as *Psychologie Française* or the *Bulletin de Psychologie*. Some publications are specifically aimed at the practicing psychologist, among them *Le Journal des Psychologues* and *Psychologues et Psychologies*. The former is published 10 times a year. Its team organizes forums for practitioners and the public and also publishes conference reports and practical books, including a directory and guide to psychology. The last-named is a review of the Syndicat National des Psychologues (SNP), which also prints a national directory of psychologists in private practice.

Significant Centers and Fields of Research

Centers and Institutes

A great part of the research effort is coordinated and organized on a national scale. A large, specialized group founded in 1939, the Centre National de la Recherche Scientifique (National Center of Scientific Research, CNRS), whose general aim is to promote scientific investigation, determines national research policy. The CNRS has its own units and helps to coordinate the action of many autonomous research centers and laboratories with which it is associated. It also launches and finances cooperative research programs.

Laboratories working in association with the CNRS are regularly catalogued by its documentation services. Most of the research units in psychology are listed by the Centre de Documentation Sciences Humaines, in Paris. Another important role of the CNRS is the evaluation of research in progress. In recent years, however, psychological research has often been evaluated according to criteria that some investigators have found irrelevant, because these criteria appear to be borrowed from molecular biology. This stance tended to reinforce a reductionist position that, in the 1980s, led to a protest from many researchers.

Dominant Trends and Main Fields

Laboratory research, particularly in psychophysiology, psychopharmacology, and experimental psychology, has regularly received support from the CNRS. Specific topics of investigation in these areas include sensory functions, perception, memory, language disorders, fatigue, sleep, hypnosis, psychotropic drugs, neurotransmitters, and behavior genetics.

Developments in computer science have reactivated research in artificial intelligence and human cognition. Models inspired by information theory, as well as the study of codes and, more generally, psycholinguistics, have aroused much interest.

In clinical psychology, Freud's ideas (in vogue again largely because of

Lacan) have been attentively reexamined. Since the early 1970s, however, psychoanalysis has lost much of its prestige, and in psychopathology, the psychoanalytical approach has met with competition from the systemic approach and theories of communication. Psychiatry as a whole also had to face up to controversy. This was related to the disclosure, in France, of the Anglo-Italian antipsychiatric views of the 1960s. In this context, interest in schizophrenia decreased a little. It is especially borderline cases, drug addiction, psychopathic conditions, and mental disorders related to acculturation that have most attracted researchers' attention over the last years.

Group observation and institution analysis have constituted other important topics of research. New concepts, such as Anzieu's "group illusion" or Anzieu and Kaës's "group psychic apparatus," were designed to permit psychoanalytical interpretations of the functioning of small groups. Systemic approaches have also met with some success.

Differential psychology is now oriented toward the establishment of a general psychological science based on individual differences. The principal architect of this renewal is M. Reuchlin.

In child psychology, much attention has been devoted to infant aptitude, to precocious mother-child interaction, and to the development of communication strategies during the first 2 years of life. Other significant areas of investigation emphasized since 1980 include the study of communication, the analysis of social representation of ideologies, the psychology of organizations, ergonomics, body therapies, and marital and family analytical psychotherapy.

Leading Psychologists and Research Teams

Three leading figures were particularly influential in the 1970s and in the early 1980s: P. Fraisse, the Geneva psychologist J. Piaget, and J. Lacan. Other distinguished names include D. Anzieu, P. Pichot, R. Zazzo, J. Stoetzel, M. Reuchlin, P. Albou, P. Ropartz, and R. Chauvin (already mentioned), as well as J. Paillard (psychophysiology); J. Laplanche, J. B. Pontalis, and J. Gagey (clinical psychology); G. Mialaret (psychopedagogics); C. Lévy Leboyer (environmental psychology); R. Francès, J. F. Le Ny, J. F. Richard, and R. Ghiglione (experimental psychology); and P. Goguelin (industrial psychology).

Generally speaking, it is in the Paris teaching centers that the most prominent teachers and research teams are still to be found. René Descartes University, which accounts for approximately 10 percent of all French psychology students, is particularly notable. Elsewhere, only the University of Aix-Marseilles can compete with the Paris teaching centers.

Comparisons to the Medical Profession

At the end of 1986 the number of psychologists practicing in France was between 16,000 and 18,000. This is a relatively low figure, especially when compared to that of physicians, whose total was about nine times higher (approximately 170,000, of whom more than 154,000 were actually practicing). In terms of relative density, there are now 2,800 physicians per 1 million inhabitants, one of the highest densities in the world, compared to 320 psychologists per 1 million inhabitants, a relatively modest density. Yet the differences between the professions are more than numerical. They also relate to training.

Medical schools are mostly attended by scientifically oriented graduates, for whom a strict selection process takes place at the end of the first year. University departments of psychology attract a majority of arts students and usually establish an official selection only at the beginning of the fifth year. Moreover, while physicians have long had an organized and powerful national association, in which every practitioner must normally enroll, psychologists have often been split. That was especially true up to 1980. Disagreements existed among many segments of the profession, resulting in the formation of more than 100 associations of psychologists, both local and national.

Professional Societies and Associations

The membership and influence of these associations are uneven. Only a few carry recognized weight in the country. Among these, the oldest is the Société Française de Psychologie, with more than 1,200 members. Created in 1901 and reorganized in 1920, the SFP has six specialized sections: experimental, clinical, child, social, and occupational psychology, and psychophysiology. An academic society, the SFP has also recently become greatly concerned with professional problems.

The Association des Educateurs Universitaires de Psychologie (University Psychology Teachers' Association, AEPU), created in 1966, has approximately 300 members, a little over a third of the total number of university psychology teachers. The AEPU plays an important role in the organization of teaching at the national level. In 1979 the SFP and the AEPU constituted a joint commission to examine the professional status of psychologists. A month later a dozen other organizations joined them. Based on this response, the decision was made to continue regular meetings. In 1983 the coordinating committee became the Association Nationale des Organisations de Psychologues (National Association of Psychologists' Organizations, ANOP). The ANOP is now by far the most representative association of psychologists. As it continues to evolve, it has brought together a diverse group of organizations, so that its latest yearbook lists some 8,000 members.

Current Status of Professional Practice

Distribution of Psychologists

At the end of 1987 there were approximately 18,000 psychologists in France. From the point of view of employment, four categories of psychologists can be distinguished: (a) civil servants and equivalent categories, 12,000 (67 percent); (b) employees of state administrations and companies, 1,000 (5 percent); (c) employees in private companies, 2,500 (14 percent); and (d) self-employed psychologists, also approximately 2,500 (14 percent).

Specialties include six major categories: (a) education, (b) health, (c) social services, especially child and family aid, (d) industrial and organizational psychology, (e) teaching and research, and (f) justice. A total of 7,000 psychologists work in the educational field: 3,300 as school psychologists, 3,500 as vocational guidance counselors, and 150 as employees of private schools. Approximately 5,000 psychologists work in hospitals and medico-psychopedagogical centers. Teaching and research employ another 1,000 psychologists. Industrial psychologists are also numerous, although for this and the remaining categories it is difficult to obtain accurate statistics. A more precise census of psychologists is planned by the ANOP.

Evolution of Regulations

The activities of professional psychologists working in the public sector are subject to regulations. However, that has not prevented the existence of a certain fuzziness at the level of the administrative status of the practitioner. Moreover, the different levels and types of training required have helped to delay the promulgation of a general law protecting the title of "psychologist."

Before 1985 anyone in France could use the title "psychologist." Since 1985 the title has been protected by law, but the decrees implementing this law have still not been passed. In conformity with the laws in other European countries, it is expected that proper use of the "psychologist" title will require a compulsory 5-year training period, with a DESS or DEA degree at the conclusion.

The Public Image of Psychology

In the 1940s and 1950s the public tended to regard psychology as a branch of philosophy, medicine, or educational science. The outlines and domains of the profession were not clearly drawn. Toward the mid-1960s psychology and psychoanalysis began to acquire a clearer and more favorable image, a change that coincided with an increase in the number of students and practitioners. This image was tarnished somewhat by the student protests of 1968, in which students of psychology were involved.

During the 1970s, because of the relatively small number of psychologists, their apparent limited effectiveness, the absence of legal protection for the title, and internal division, the image of psychology became less positive. Opposition to psychoanalysis and psychiatry spread to medical psychology as a whole. The lack of precision in diagnosis and the diversity of therapeutic practices were both criticized. Industrial psychology also aroused some suspicion. The use of tests and psychological interviews for recruitment or staff selection was strongly opposed. However, the work of psychologists in the field of education continued to be, in general, valued.

Since 1980 the situation has improved. Industrial psychologists have succeeded in having the value and diversity of their contributions recognized. Psychologists in the health sector have been more assertive in their relations with physicians. Further, the creation of the ANOP, together with regulations for title protection, have contributed to rehabilitating the profession in the eyes of many. These are some of the positive elements that should allow psychology to be more widely appreciated by all of French society in the years to come.

Bibliography

Huteau, M., & Roubertoux, P. (1976). France. In V. S. Sexton & H. Misiak (Eds.), *Psychology around the world* (pp. 131–153). Monterey, CA: Brooks/Cole.

Lecuyer, R., LeMarc, M., Pétard, J. P., Pithon, G., Ricateau, M., & Weil-Barais, A. (1985). Enquéte nationale sur les étudiants en psychologie. *Bulletin de Psychologie, 39* (1–2), 7–88.

Minivielle, D., Polge, M., & Maujol, L. (1968). Les psychologues dans les établissements hospitaliers et les services publics et semi-publics concourant à l'action sanitaire et sociale. *Bulletin de l'INSERM, 23*(3), 771–836.

Selosse, J. (1983). Quelques jalons à propos de la formation professionnelle des psychologues à l'education surveillée. *Psychologie Française, 28*(1), 77–81.

Voutsinas, D. (1957). *Dix années de psychologie française (1947–1956).* Paris: Groupe d'Etudes de Psychologie de l'Université de Paris.

Voutsinas, D. (1958–63). *Documentation sur la psychologie française* (Vols. 2–6). Paris: Groupe d'Etudes de Psychologie de l'Université de Paris.

15 / German Democratic Republic

ADOLF KOSSAKOWSKI

Adolf Kossakowski (born 1928) received the Dr. phil. degree from Karl Marx University of Leipzig in 1960 and the Dr. phil. habil. degree from the same university in 1964. A specialist in educational psychology and developmental psychology, he has published five books, the most recent being Psychische Entwicklung der Persönlichkeit in der Ontogenese. *In addition, he has written more than 80 articles in journals of various countries. A member of several editorial boards, Kossakowski has been president of the Psychological Society of the German Democratic Republic and the recipient of an honorary doctorate from the Teacher Training College at Erfurt,* GDR. *He is director of the Psychological Institute of the Academy of Pedagogical Science in Berlin.*

After World War II conditions for the development of psychology in Germany were very difficult. Scientific facilities had been destroyed or severely damaged, and the means for their reconstruction were badly restricted. Any serious scientific work in psychology was impossible. The practical work of psychologists was constrained as well.

Psychology received a definite stimulus at the beginning of the 1950s with the initial construction of a socialist society in the GDR. Together with the fundamental economic, political, and social transformations in the country, the duties of science in general rose to a new level. At that time psychologists were active chiefly in the training of teachers, doctors, lawyers, and so on; that is, above all they served as teachers. However, they were also involved in practical, clinical-psychological diagnosis and consultation and, to a limited extent, in research, which up to the beginning of the 1960s was still only sporadically conducted. At the same time, a systematic training of university psychology students (with a diploma certificate) was introduced. This event, as well as an intensive working through of the theoretical and methodological problems of psychology on the basis of dialectical and historical

This chapter was completed before the reunification of Germany and is being retained largely for historical purposes.

materialism, was an important precondition for the further development of psychology in the GDR.

The growing importance of psychology in the GDR was expressed by the founding in 1962 of the Society of Psychology of the GDR. The society has as its goal promoting the development of psychology in theory and practice, increasing its efficiency, and supporting international cooperation for the purpose of developing a humanist psychology.

One important step toward closer international cooperation was achieved on the occasion of the 18th International Congress of Psychology in Moscow, in 1966, through the admission of the Society of Psychology of the GDR to the International Union of Psychological Science. Another highlight was the 22nd International Congress of Psychology, held in Leipzig in 1980 and organized by the Society of Psychology of the GDR.

General Characteristics (1960–87)

In the GDR, psychologists have legal status. *Diplom-Psychologe* is the official title of a professional. Approximately 2,500 psychologists (about 60 percent females and 40 percent males) work in various practical areas as well as in scientific research centers at universities, science academies, and other governmental and public institutions. Elevation of the professional status of psychologists in the GDR, especially during the 1970s and 1980s, is closely linked to their contributions in several areas, including (a) the raising of work productivity through the creation of working conditions that simultaneously support the successful development of personality; (b) the preservation of the mental and psychical health of the population; (c) the development of psychologically based, long-term aims and techniques for the improvement of education; and (d) the support of increased efficiency in competitive sports.

Psychologists have wide-ranging duties in the training and further education of personnel in the traditional qualifications of teachers, educators, doctors, and other medical specialists, as well as in the psychological qualification for engineers, economists, sociologists, lawyers, and journalists among others. (About 20 percent of psychologists in the GDR are so engaged. [Percentages in this section surpass 100, because some psychologists are engaged simultaneously in work on various tasks of research, teaching, and practice.]) In just a short time, the need for psychological qualifications has spread, for example, to management personnel active in general social production and in state and public institutions. In such areas, training courses in psychology have proved successful in raising the efficiency of managerial work.

About 40 percent of GDR psychologists deal with extensive, immediately practical tasks in varied forms of diagnostic and therapeutic work in the health service system. In the 1980s, using various forms of educational counseling (including general health and sex counseling), not only the therapeutic but also the preventive aspects of their work have been strengthened. Also, within the framework of the health service system and alongside the existing extensive network of psychology departments in outpatient centers and hospitals, various advisory centers have been established where clinical psychology has an important role.

About 20 percent of psychologists work in the field of education in advising centers, especially in diagnostic and ambulatory therapy, along with individual counseling of teachers and parents who deal with children with difficulties in achievement and behavior. Psychologists are also active in the psychological education of teachers and in helping school officials, heads of schools, teachers, and educators deal with daily problems encountered in the schools, in before-and-after-school centers for schoolchildren, and in kindergartens. Along with general advisory work, psychologists also help teachers to overcome the learning and teaching difficulties of individual pupils as well as those of entire classes.

Not only industrial and engineering psychologists but, increasingly, social, educational, and clinical psychologists work directly in industrial production, the building industry, and the transport system (about 20 per cent). Their activities extend from participation in the construction of industrial plants and the means of work, through the creation of effective communication and management processes within the firm, the analysis of and solution to problems retarding the flow of production and contributing to strain and fatigue, right up to advising management personnel on selection and qualification of staff.

GDR sports psychologists contribute to the international successes of athletes, not only through the introduction of psychological knowledge to coaches, trainers, or sports teachers, but also through the participation of psychologists in training and in the direct preparation of men and women athletes for competitions.

Psychologists also work in the field of criminal justice. Their activities extend from psychological assessments of criminal offenses and offenders, through participation in the reeducation of offenders serving sentences, to the integration of previous offenders back into normal employment.

Recently, the direct participation of psychologists has been sought in many different areas of society—for example, in mass political work, in increasing the efficiency of the mass media in art and literature, in advertising, and in town planning. To widen psychology's range of social effectiveness, since about 1970 many practice-oriented publications for parents, teachers, medical workers, technicians, and leaders in economic and political organizations have been produced. The number of psychologists and the use of psychology, by the general public as well as by governmental and social institutions, have been increasing.

An important condition for satisfactory professional status is a well-organized, professional training program. The overall goal for psychology students is to provide them with training in the theoretical, methodological, and basic foundations of psychology and, at the same time, to enable them to be active either in specialized scientific research institutions or in special areas of social practice on completion of their studies. For this reason, after approximately 3 years of basic training in general psychology, personality and developmental psychology, social psychology, biological foundations of psychology, psychological research methods, mathematical psychology, and psychological statistics, as well as philosophy, students also receive 2 years of specialized training. Both general and specialized training are given at various institutions: in Berlin (Humboldt University: clinical, industrial/engineering psychology), in Leipzig (Karl Marx University: educational, clinical psychology), in Dresden (Technical University: industrial/engineering psychology), and in Jena (Friedrich Schiller University: social psychology). The tuition-free university study, lasting 5 years, ends with the students' defense of their diploma theses. The theses are usually in the research specialty of the university and connected with future professional work. Students receive their practical training, if possible, at the same location where they will work after graduation. Thus, in most cases, the newly trained psychologists know the special demands of their jobs. They also know their tasks and official status and thus can start work quite efficiently.

A further way to qualify psychologists for work in different areas is postgraduate study, organized by the Society of Psychology with the Ministry of Higher Education. In 1981 postgraduate study for psychologists employed in the health services was introduced. This program gives psychologists cooperating with medical staff the opportunity to undertake specialized study after university training, in order to gain professional status equivalent to that of medical specialists and to be designated by the professional title of "medical psychologist." In 1985 systematic postgraduate study was introduced for industrial and social psychologists.

The staff of scientific institutions, who are, as a rule, engaged in both research and teaching, qualify for their work by completing two doctoral degrees, degree A and degree B. They must first complete a theoretical and/or empirical (experimental) study and summarize it in a thesis (A or B, respectively) for defense. On completing the A thesis, a researcher acquires the degree of doctor (Dr.), and for the B thesis that of doctor of science (Dr. sc.). The latter is a precondition for appointment as a university lecturer or professor. These degrees can be acquired at universities, colleges, and academies of science.

Most psychologists are members of the Society of Psychology of the GDR. This society, according to its statutes, has the following objectives: It promotes the development of psychology in theory and practice and encourages cooperation with other scientific disciplines in the GDR and with psychologists from other countries and international psychological bodies. It represents the interests of psychologists in various social sectors and gives special attention to the exchange of experience among psychologists working in various institutions and to the professional qualifications of its members.

Every 4 years national congresses of the Society of Psychology are held for the presentation and discussion of research results in all fields of psychological science as well as the experience of psychologists working in practical fields. Specialized problems of different branches of psychology are dealt with in special sections and in central working groups. Within the scope of the Society of Psychology of the GDR, there are sections for general psychology (including personality psychology), industrial and engineering psychology, educational psychology, clinical psychology and social psychology, and central working groups for developmental psychology and forensic psychology. These sections and working groups hold annual conferences on specialized subjects and also sponsor an average of four annual regional work groups.

The results of scientific studies and experiences of psychologists in different areas are published in a journal of the Society of Psychology, *Psychologie für die Gesellschaftliche Praxis* (Psychology for social practice), as well as in a regular series called *Psychologie-Information*. Both are published quarterly. As part of *Psychologie-Information*, a supplementary volume is published annually which summarizes and reviews all publications by GDR psychologists in the preceding year. In addition, a *Zeitschrift für Psychologie* (Journal of psychology) is published, which is among the oldest journals in the world. Moreover, a large number of books publicize scientific research findings and practical experience. Particularly noteworthy are the manuals and special compendiums for the training of psychology students, the advanced training of psychologists, and the training and advanced education of teachers, medical workers, lawyers, and other professionals. Many publications are translations of studies by psychologists from other countries, notably socialist countries.

Current Trends and Areas of Research

One important principle of psychological research in the GDR is the close connection between applied research, oriented toward the essential social problems mentioned above, and basic research. Applied investigations are constructed and conducted so as to relate to fundamental theoretical concepts in psychology and thereby contribute to the solution of theoretical questions. Conversely, a significant part of fundamental research is constructed so that it not only improves general knowledge concerning the structure and function of mental processes but at the same time produces findings of use to applied research.

Based on the philosophical background of dialectical and historical materialism, the main principle of recent research is the following: Whatever is being investigated in a concrete situation, the psychological phenomenon in question is seen to have been generated by an actively exploring, controlling person, within an interactive system that includes influencing the environment and processing the effects of action with the goal of adapting environmental conditions to individual needs. This interaction results in changes of individual aptitude and competence in a lifelong process. The interaction includes, on the side of individual abilities, predispositions acquired phylogenetically and ontogenetically and, on the environmental side, natural as well as social and cultural conditions, reflecting the human being as an active biosocial unit, originating from a dialectical socialization and acculturation process. Therefore, research in the GDR cannot be reduced to s-r or s-o-r models. The main problem of experimental design, then, is to focus on the biosocial unit of human behavior in the generalization of microanalytical data (ecological validity). Further, the design must concentrate on semantic aspects of cognition more than on structural ones, and on the unity of cognition and motivational evaluation of objects and events in human behavior (H.-D. Schmidt). The elaboration of these theoretical and methodological assumptions can be seen as a collective work of many psychologists in the GDR, as well as of psychologists in other socialist countries, especially the Soviet Union. An important contribution to the working out of such generally agreed-on assumptions was the work, also done collectively by many GDR psychologists, on the *Wörterbuch der Psychologie* (Dictionary of psychology) (Clauss, 1976).

Basic Research

In the area of general psychology, research is undertaken to analyze perception, concept formation, classification, and problem-solving processes, particularly as they relate to the psychology of memory. This research is important not only for gaining new theoretical knowledge, but also for understanding mental processes in human-machine interaction, understanding the process of diagnosis, and raising efficiency in teaching processes (F. Klix, J. Hofmann, B. Krause). Cognitive processes (perception, concept formation, classification, problem-solving, and memory) are considered not only in their individual contexts but also in their relationship to motivation (F. Klix). Also interesting are investigations on complex visual pattern discrimination (H. G. Geissler). Other subjects of basic research are the analysis of the structure and functions of internal representation of the aims, conditions, and strategies of activity (internal models of activity), which make possible an effective regulation of activity (W. Hacker). Knowledge of these models constitutes an important precondition for applied research into engineering psychology.

Research into physiological psychology involves physiological analysis of cognitive operations, activation processes, and stress reaction of operators, among other subjects. Psychophysiological research, analyzing physiological parameters in problem solving as well as recording individual levels of attention and strain during mental activity, has provided important basic elements for research in work and engineering psychology, educational psychology, and clinical psychology. Research into the psychophysiological parameters of hypertension is also being carried out to determine valid variables for diagnosis.

Studies of personality and developmental psychology in the GDR have been closely linked, sometimes including social psychology. At the center of each of these three separate disciplines are problems of the process and determinants of mental development from an ontogenetic aspect and questions concerning the relationship of mental characteristics and social conditions present in a person's history (H. Hiebsch, A. Kossakowski et al.).

Recently, in personality psychology, psychic mechanisms that facilitate socially competent action were investigated using a theoretical model of the psychic regulation of human action. These studies serve both the further development of theoretical positions of personality psychology and the elaboration of effective training methods for people holding major social responsibility, such as work managers, teachers, and therapists (M. Vorwerg, H. Schröder).

In developmental psychology, comprehensive studies on theoretical problems of psychic development have been made (H.-D. Schmidt), centered mainly on psychic ontogenesis and the development of independent action regulation in children and adolescents (A. Kossakowski).

Research in social psychology has focused on the study of social perception and its significance for the development of personality and interpersonal relationships (H. Hiebsch, P. Pätzold). Further studies are directed toward achievement, social factors in cooperation, and personality development and social interaction in cooperation (H. Hiebsch, M. Vorwerg).

Research into the history of psychology was strongly stimulated by the celebration of the centenary of the foundation of the first psychological institute, by Wilhelm Wundt in Leipzig in 1879, and of anniversaries of outstanding German psychologists such as H. Ebbinghaus, G. Fechner, and W. Koehler (W. Meischner, G. Eckhardt, L. Sprung et al.).

Applied Research

Investigations in industrial and engineering psychology are aimed at raising the efficiency and productivity of work by creating working conditions that develop personality. Above all, research is carried out on the foundation of internal representations (the internal image system) of work activities, which include the precise aims of action, the representations of external and internal conditions of action, and the consequences of action. It was shown that work effectiveness is to a large extent determined by the precision of the internal representation of the most important elements in the actions of work (W. Hacker, B. Matern). An important part of such research is directed to the optimization of information processing within human-machine systems concerning the control and surveillance of modern production plants. Such research is particularly helpful in designing rational operating instruments and panels (F. Klix, K.-P. Timpe).

Clinical-psychological research is used to develop wide-ranging state measures to preserve the population's health and to return to society those people who have suffered physical and mental disorders. Since the main emphasis of clinical psychology has shifted from a primarily diagnostic orientation to a more therapeutic and preventive activity, research concerning the causes of neuropsychological disorders and physically or socially conditioned deficiencies of development has taken on greater significance.

Extensive comparative longitudinal research has been carried out with brain-damaged children on motor activities, intelligence, concentration, emotional stability, and performance in school (Gollnitz, H.-D. Rösler, H. Teichmann). On the basis of a scientifically based classification of neurotic disorders, tests have been devised to establish differential diagnosis of neuroses, in addition to techniques for successful therapy (J. Helm, Kasielke, J. Mehl). Further methods have been developed to help patients overcome conflicts independently and to change their social and material living conditions (Helm, Rösler, Szewczyk). Research in educational psychology is oriented toward the development of people capable of independent and socially responsible activity. The main investigations are therefore concerned with mental components of self-regulation in different activities (playing, learning, social activities), with productive thinking, and with problem solving and its systematic development (A. Kossakowski, J. Lompscher). Specific research has been done on the development of moral attitudes, on positive motives for learning (G. Rosenfeld), and on overcoming achievement and behavioral difficulties. Other research has dealt with the creation of group-related behavioral norms and collective activities, especially concerning the role of social-integrative leading styles of teachers and teacher-pupil relations (W. Kessel, Knauer). In recent years medical workers, psychologists, and educators, working closely together, have started a research project on enhancing the effectiveness of the work of teachers and on preserving the health of teachers (Kessel, Scheuch, Schröder, Rudow).

Significant attention in the GDR has focused on psychodiagnosis, serving mainly the elaboration of diagnostic methods for various applications, especially on school achievement and behavior, and on the development of methods to diagnose learning ability, the ability for creative thought, and the analysis of special achievement difficulties. In the last-named, there has been a marked shift recently from a status-oriented diagnosis to development-oriented and correction, or therapy-oriented, ones (J. Guthke, W. Gutjahr, G. Mathes, U. Schaarschmidt, G. Witzlack). In industrial and engineering psychology a series of tests has been developed to measure the effects of work strain produced by varying job requirements (Plath, J. Richter) and for the early diagnosis of noxious effects on mental functions, which can be prevented by the timely introduction of preventive measures. In clinical psychology a series of investigations has focused on the development of tests measuring therapeutically induced changes (I. Frohburg, J. Helm, Kasielke, Mehl).

In 1982 a psychodiagnosis center was established at Humboldt University which coordinates the development of psychodiagnostic methods and the publication of diagnostic procedures for most fields of practice (Schaarschmidt). Research in the GDR is coordinated by a Scientific Council for Psychology composed of leading GDR psychologists. Since the 1960s psychological research has been coordinated through the formation of scientific centers for the treatment of particular psychological problems. For example, problems of general psychology and of psychophysiology are studied especially at Humboldt University in Berlin, in work groups at the Academy of Sciences, and at the Karl Marx University in Leipzig. Research on the psychology of personality is done at Leipzig University and at the Academy of Pedagogical Sciences, and social psychological research is conducted primarily at Friedrich Schiller University in Jena. Investigations into problems of industrial and engineering psychology are concentrated at the Technical University of Dresden, Berlin's Humboldt University, and in several work groups in industrial centers. Research in educational psychology and developmental psychology is conducted at the Academy of Pedagogical Sciences, at Leipzig's Karl Marx University, and in several work groups in other educational institutions (universities and teacher training colleges). Groups working on clinical psychology study at the Wilhelm Pieck University in Rostock, at Humboldt University, and in major clinical centers. Research is predominantly financed by state funds from research institutes. Sometimes research contracts are made with industrial organizations or public institutions. The equipment of research institutes with necessary apparatus and scientific literature (mainly scientific periodicals) is generally in line with international standards.

Bibliography

Clauss, G. (Ed.). (1976). *Wörterbuch der Psychologie*. Leipzig: VEB Bibliogr. Inst.

Guthke, J., & Witzlack, G. (1981). *Zur Psychodiagnostik von Persönlichkeitsqualitäten bei Schülern*. vwv.

Hacker, W. (1973). *Allgemeine Arbeits- und Ingenieurpsychologie*. Berlin: Deutscher Verlag der Wissenschaften.

Helm, J., Rösler, H.-D., & Szewczyk, H. (1979). *Klinische Psychologie—theoretische und ideologische Probleme*. Berlin: Deutscher Verlag der Wissenschaften.

Hiebsch, H., & Vorwerg, M. (Eds.). (1979). *Sozialpsychologie*. Berlin: Deutscher Verlag der Wissenschaften.

Hoffmann, J. (1982). *Das aktive Gedächtnis: Psychologische Experimente und Theorien der menschlichen Gedächtnistätigkeit*. Berlin: Deutscher Verlag der Wissenschaften.

Klix, F. (1971). *Information und Verhalten*. Berlin: Deutscher Verlag der Wissenschaften.

Kossakowski, A. (Ed.). (1987). *Psychische Entwicklung der Persönlichkeit in der Ontogenese*. Berlin: Deutscher Verlag der Wissenschaften.

Schmidt, H.-D. (1970). *Allgemeine Entwicklungspsychologie*. Berlin: Deutscher Verlag der Wissenschaften.

Sydow, H., & Pätzold, P. (1981). *Mathematische Psychologie*. Berlin: Deutscher Verlag der Wissenschaften.

16 / Germany

JO GROEBEL

Jo Groebel (born 1950) received the Diplom-Psychologe *(1974) and the PhD (1981) from the Technical University of Aachen. His specialties include social psychology, media psychology, and research in aggression and terrorism. Among his publications are* Aggression and War: Their Biological and Social Bases *(with Robert Hinde),* Terrorism *(with Jeffrey Goldstein), and* Fernsehen und Angst *(Television and anxiety).*

Groebel is the editor of Medienpsychologie: Zeitschrift für Individual und Massenkommunikation *and serves on the editorial boards of* Aggressive Behavior *and* School Psychology International. *Groebel is currently Akademischer Oberrat at the University of Rheinland-Pfalz, Landau, Germany and chair of the Department of Social Psychology, University of Utrecht, the Netherlands.*

History

The Origins

Germany has played an important role in the development of psychology as an independent science. Wilhelm Wundt (1832–1920) founded the first department of psychology, at the University of Leipzig in 1879. In his works *Beiträge zur Theorie der Sinneswahrnehmung* (Contributions to the theory of sensory perception) (1862) and *Vorlesungen über die Menschen- und Tierseele* (Lectures on the psyche of man and animal) (1863), Wundt created the bases of experimental psychology. He defined psychology as the science of inner experience and consciousness, to be measured through experiment and self-observation. Among other achievements, he systematically described the connection between psychological and physiological processes, noting the interaction among external physical stimuli, nerve stimulation, and perception.

In addition to conducting his own experiments, Wundt integrated the findings of previous researchers such as J. Müller, H. L. F. von Helmholtz, E. H.

This chapter was originally prepared to represent the Federal Republic of Germany and has been modified slightly to represent unified Germany.

Weber, and G. T. Fechner in the fields of physiology and psychophysics; delineated the principles of the new science in the textbook *Grundzüge der physiologischen Psychologie* (Principles of physiological psychology) (1874); and edited what was, despite its original title, the first academic psychological journal, published as *Philosophische Studien* (Philosophical studies) from 1883 to 1903 and continued as *Psychologische Studien* (Psychological studies) from 1905 on. While Wundt regarded sensory processes as open to experimental analysis, he believed that higher mental processes could be understood only through historical observation of language and myth, as described in his *Völkerpsychologie* (Folk psychology) (1900–1920).

Many historians regard Wundt as the father of modern psychology, but others argue that the development of the science is better described in terms of historical and social processes than as a product of individual research activities (Ash & Geuter, 1985; Lück, Grünwald, Geuter, Miller & Rechtien, 1987). Despite the persuasiveness of the historically more complex view, the present description is confined to individual events, persons, and institutions. Nonetheless, as the German psychologist Hermann Ebbinghaus noted during the Fourth International Congress of Psychology in Paris in 1900, psychology and psychological thinking have a history extending far beyond their brief period as a scientific discipline following Wilhelm Wundt.

This tradition and its roots in philosophy were characterized not only by different concepts of human nature (e.g., pre- and post-Enlightenment), but by discussions on the existence of a material soul and the relationship between observable psychological processes and a possible underlying entity. With his work *De anima*, Phillip Melanchthon (1497–1560) was the first German to write a book on the mind. In the title of his book *Psychologia*, Rudolf Goclenius (1574–1628) was the first German author to use the Latin word, and the German term *Psychologie* was introduced by Christian Wolff (1676–1754). Another German, the former Heidelberg professor Friedrich August Rausch (1806–41), created the English term *psychology* in 1840, following his emigration to the USA. It was, however, the creator of the integral and differential calculus, Gottfried Wilhelm Leibniz (1646–1715), who developed a complex theory of the human mind, centered on the indivisible, immaterial "elements of things," or "monads." Leibniz is a forerunner of nonempirical, non-Lockean cultural science psychology rather than of experimental psychology. "Apperception" and "perception" were main terms in his theory, delimiting opposed areas on a continuum from clearest consciousness to darkest unconsciousness. He thus assumed the existence of areas of the psyche not accessible to mental control, a notion that later became one of the bases of psychoanalytical thinking (see below) and is related to the analysis of subliminal perception in cognitive psychology. The famous German philosopher Immanuel Kant (1724–1804) contradicted the view that logical conclusions on nonobserved phenomena could be inferred from actual perceived events, stating that scientific experiments are possible only within the limits of actual experience. It was this Kantian view that influenced psychological concepts in Germany during the 19th century, making consciousness the primary subject of psychology: that is, we perceive phenomena not as they really are, but as they appear on the basis of our consciousness.

J. F. Herbart (1776–1841), another pioneer of modern psychology (and of educational science), still assumed the existence of a metaphysical soul. In *Psychologie als Wissenschaft* (Psychology as science) (1824–25), he combined the principles of experience, metaphysics, and mathematics in a study of the development of children's abilities as a process of creating associations between what he saw as mental elements.

Herbart's principles of measurement, F. E. Beneke's (1798–1857) *Lehrbuch der Psychologie als Naturwissenschaft* (Textbook of psychology as a natural science), H. Lotze's (1817–81) *Medizinische Psychologie oder Physiologie der Seele* (Medical psychology or physiology of the psyche), and J. Müller's (1801–1858) "law of specific sensory energy" all contributed to the development of psychology as an "objective" natural science relating external stimuli to psychological/physiological reactions.

The work of three eminent researchers preceded the actual establishment of psychology as an official academic discipline. H. L. F. von Helmholtz (1821–94) measured the speed of nerve impulses and conducted seminal experiments in the areas of psychology, optics, and acoustics (see his *Handbuch der physiologischen Optik*) (Manual of physiological optics). E. H. Weber (1795–1878) determined the thresholds for the psychological perception of differences in the level of intensity of physical stimuli. This approach was perfected by G. T. Fechner (1801–87), another German pioneer of psychology, who in his work *Elemente der Psychophysik* (Elements of psychophysics) (1860) described methods of determining the relationship between psychological and physical variables, where the psychological estimation of the magnitude of a physical stimulus is a logarithmic function of that magnitude. In view of this final refutation of Kant's assumptions (that psychology cannot be a science since it is not accessible to measurement), many students of the history of psychology regard 1860 as a date equally important to 1879, the foundation date of the Psychological Institute in Leipzig.

Wundt considered the measurement of higher psychological processes impossible, but H. Ebbinghaus (1850–1909) showed that curves of forgetting or retention can be described as laws (see his *Über das Gedächtnis* [On memory], 1885). In 1890 Ebbinghaus and König founded the *Zeitschrift für Psychologie und Physiologie der Sinnesorgane* (Journal of the psychology and physiology of sense modalities), providing yet another basis for the establishment of psychology as an independent scientific discipline. The work of Ebbinghaus was continued by G. E. Müller (1850–1939) and N. Ach (1871–1946), who added will processes to learning.

Leipzig had become a widely recognized center of the new discipline, with such followers and supporters as Emil Kraepelin, Oswald Külpe, and, from the USA, G. S. Hall, James McKeen Cattell, and Hugo Münsterberg, the last-named originally from Germany and regarded as one of the founders of German applied psychology.

Some partially incompatible directions soon developed, characterized in 1900 by W. Stern, one of the founders of differential psychology, as a conflict between two psychologies, a "subject" and a "subject-less" psychology. H. Ebbinghaus and G. E. Müller denied the existence of a nonobservable soul or mind and concentrated on the empirical analysis of high-level cognitive processes such as learning. A second group, composed of Wundt's students and known as the Würzburg School, formed a group around Wundt's former assistant O. Külpe (1862–1915) and began, on an equally empirical basis, the experimental analysis of thinking.

The followers of "understanding" psychology took up a position opposed to the nomothetic view. Among their major representatives was W. Dilthey (1833–1911), who proposed the idiographic method by which the individual could be understood only as a whole person, in the context of his or her total cultural and societal environment. In this view, analytical methods should resemble those used by literature and history. Dilthey's pupil, E. Spranger (1882–1962), offered a typology based on the ethics of personality and human values. The understanding approach was supported by K. Jaspers (1883–1969), who regarded it as a subfield of phenomenological analysis. In addition to its influence on humanistic psychology, the idiographic method is perceived by some German psychologists as a better means of describing individuals in their natural context.

The Würzburg School, with its experimental orientation, had a much greater impact on modern German psychology. Its founder, O. Külpe, however, regarded thinking as a total process that should not be dissected into single associations. Here Külpe concurred with F. Brentano in his *Psychologie vom empirischen Standpunkt* (Psychology from an empirical standpoint) (1874) and C. Stumpf, together with Brentano the cofounder of act psychology. Unlike these two scientists, however, the Würzburg School used the experiment as one of its most important tools. Through introspection, subjects described their mental processes after exposure to different experimental conditions, e.g., solving a complex task. The analysis of these processes, applying the so-called *Fragemethode* (question method) created by K. Bühler (1879–1963), showed that, contrary to previous assumptions, thinking also involves abstract elements. Another finding was that people can themselves initiate a mental process determining a task which stimulates its solution ("determining tendencies"). Despite Wundt's rejection of aspects of the Würzburg methodology, it laid the foundation for research into cognitive processes which remains relevant today.

Another influential approach was the Berlin *Gestalttheorie*. Its finding that single film images create the illusion of movement if presented with sufficient rapidity (M. Wertheimer's "phi-phenomenon") led to the development of a holistic view in which the whole is more than the sum of its parts. Prominent representatives of this school, apart from Wertheimer (1880–1943), were K. Koffka (1886–1941), W. Köhler (1887–1967), K. Lewin (1890–1947), to a certain extent D. Katz (1884–1953), and somewhat later, W. Metzger (1899–1979); they influenced developmental, cognitive, and social psychology, as well as psychophysics.

Although these schools appeared to move away from Wundtian thinking, the *Ganzheitspsychologie* (genetic totality) school of Leipzig, founded by F. Krueger (1874–1948), may be regarded as continuing Wundt's approach by combining experimental and theoretical work. Mental processes form an organized total "structure" that can be described only in terms of their development. This development is linked to the cultural and societal environment. Representatives of this school were K. Dürckheim, P. Lersch, F. Sander, U. Undeutsch, E. Wartegg, and A. Wellek.

J. F. Herbart, referred to previously, may also be regarded as one of the founders of modern social psychology. Herbart was Kant's successor in the Königsberg chair of philosophy. For him, the individual could be understood only in his or her social context; new impressions, like "social attitudes" in modern social psychology, were selected and shaped on the basis of previous experience. Herbart's notions reappeared in Lazarus and Steinthal's *Völkerpsychologie* (see *Zeitschrift für Völkerpsychologie und Sprachwissenschaft* [Journal of folk psychology and language science], founded by these two scientists in 1860).

The term *Völkerpsychologie* originated with W. von Humboldt (1767–1835), who assumed a connection between different languages and different structures of thinking. Although Wundt wrote the 10-volume *Völkerpsychologie* dealing with the relationship of language, myth, and custom, and representing a genuine social psychological approach, this line of research, unlike his experimental work, inspired no immediate successors.

The roots of modern social psychological thinking are to be found rather in G. Lindner's *Ideen zur Psychologie der Gesellschaft als Grundlage der Sozialwissenschaft* (Ideas on the psychology of society as the basis of the social sciences) (1871), in which the future task of *Socialpsychologie* was defined as the description and explanation of the individual on the basis of his or her interaction with others in society. The first German institute of social psychology was founded in 1920 by Willy Hellpach (1877–1955), who 2 years later became the state of Baden's secretary of cultural and educational affairs. He represented a cultural science concept of social psychology, and in his *Psychologie der Umwelt* (Psychology of the environment) he systematized principles of environmental psychology. A strong empirical impact on social psychology, especially on the analysis of communication processes, came from Paul F. Lazarsfeld in Vienna.

Two other prominent, originally German scientists who influenced social psychology were Hugo Münsterberg (1863–1916), also regarded by many as the cofounder (with Karl Marbe, 1869–1953) of applied, media, and economic psychology, and Kurt Lewin (1890–1947), well known for his *Feldtheorie* (field theory) and, in association with E. Brunswik, for his basic considerations on ecological psychology. Lewin, also notable in private life as one of the first patrons of the Bauhaus style of interior decoration, and director of a film "The Child and Its World" (1937), emphasized the dynamics between elements in different reference systems. Elements might be different factors in the environment, members of a group, or perception units in social situations (as in the cognitive dissonance theory developed by Festinger, who was one of Lewin's students). Like many other German psychologists, Lewin emigrated to the USA when the Nazis took power in 1933. Lewinian thinking is apparent today in systems theory, group dynamics, environmental psychology, formal theories, multivariate approaches, and the like. In 1981 C. F. Graumann began publishing a complete edition of the works of Lewin.

The importance of social networks for the development of psychology becomes apparent in the following facts: Fritz Heider, another pioneer of social psychology born in Graz, lived in Berlin after World War I until 1933. There he met and worked with Köhler, Koffka, and especially Lewin, who, as Heider was without work for a while, suggested to him that he make lamps. Nevertheless, Heider became one of the major influences in the field of interpersonal relations (W. Stern helped him to attain his first American job). Paul F. Lazarsfeld, the eminent sociologist and social psychologist, "father" of survey research and empirical communication science, conducted major media analyses in Vienna and Germany and worked with the Bühlers before emigrating to the United States.

Although the majority of German psychologists outside universities still work in the clinical field, the history of clinical psychology is often neglected or viewed in a different context. Psychoanalysis plays a specific role in this respect. Regarded by many psychologists as nonscientific—a tendency reinforced by the strong emphasis on behaviorism in post–World War II German psychology—it is more often practiced by doctors of medicine than by psychologists. Yet with the increasing tendency to abandon "schools," and an approach often oriented toward practical tasks rather than orthodox theory, the strict borderline between the different fields tends to blur. That is especially true in cases in which phenomena, though described in different terms, are structurally identical. Therefore, a brief survey of post-Wundtian clinical psychology and psychoanalysis is provided.

The first psychological clinic (1896) and the first journal of clinical psychology (1907) were founded in the usa by Lightner Witmer, a student of Wundt. The first German to apply experimental psychological thinking to the clinical field was another of Wundt's students, E. Kraepelin (1856–1926). In his *Der psychologische Versuch in der Psychiatrie* (The psychological experiment in psychiatry) (1896), he proclaimed the importance of psychological taxonomies in psychodiagnosis. He was also one of the first researchers to study the effects of drugs on the psyche, thus counting as a pioneer psychopharmacologist. Until the 1970s, however, the psychologist in the German clinic was primarily responsible for psychometrics; pharmacological and psychoanalytical therapy were the province of the physician. Within the field of psychodiagnostics, projective tests played a major role until test theory cast doubt on their reliability and validity. Other clinical measures included the description of body structure associated with differing temperaments and mental disorders (e.g., Kretschmer).

Another clinical area associated with psychology is the field of psychosomatics. Gustav von Bergmann (1878–1955), Viktor von Weizsäcker (1886–1957), and Jacob von Uexküll (1864–1944) described the connection between the body and emotional processes as an originating factor in illnesses. The Baden-Baden physician Georg Groddeck (1866–1934) combined psychosomatics and psychoanalysis. Groddeck was first a student of Chancellor Bismarck's personal physician, E. Schweninger, and then of S. Freud in Vienna, with whom he conducted a long correspondence; some authors assume that Freud was actually indebted to Groddeck for the term *es* (id) (see his *Das Buch von Es* [The book of id], 1921–23). Groddeck's career underlines the strong bonds within the German-language academic community, linking universities in Germany, Austria, Switzerland, and (in those days) Prague.

Austria was an especially strong base for developments in the field of therapy, including ties with social psychology, as in the case of J. L. Moreno, active for a long period in Vienna. Another example of such cultural links is found in Freud's correspondence with the German writers Arnold Zweig and Thomas Mann, with the composer Gustav Mahler, who had briefly been his patient, and with Albert Einstein. Freud and Einstein shared a common concern about growing anti-Semitism and the movement toward war, factors that eventually led to the emigration of many German-speaking intellectuals. A brief discussion of psychoanalysis in Germany before 1933 follows.

Sigmund Freud, born in 1856 in Moravia (now Czechoslovakia), lived briefly in Leipzig before his family moved to Vienna. His conception of the individual includes the distinction between the "conscious" and the "unconscious," a distinction already formulated, using different terms, by Leibniz. Other crucial ideas contained in his theory include the existence and power of drives such as eros and death, defense mechanisms, the conflict among ego, superego, and id, and between nature and culture. These assumptions were formulated in a closed theory and applied to the therapy of neuroses as well as to the explanation of "normal" human behavior. Although psychoanalysis was not a primary element in the education in psychology offered by most universities—and was even the object of sharp criticism (e.g., by Wundt and Stern)—the German public often identified (and sometimes still identifies) psychology with psychoanalytical thinking. Among the many German-language authors influenced by Freud were his colleagues and students: Wilhelm Stekel, Karl Abraham, Ludwig Binswanger, Otto Rank, Karen Horney, Erich Fromm, Wilhelm Reich, and Magnus Hirschfeld (one of the founders of sexology), and their respective students. Anna Freud (1895–1982), Sigmund's daughter, became the founder of child psychoanalysis. Alfred Adler and C. G. Jung had also begun as followers of Freud but had split from him and developed their *Individualpsychologie* (individual psychology) and *Analytische Psychologie* (analytical psychology), respectively. Both also influenced empirical psychology to some extent—for example, the German-born Eysenck's concepts of extroversion and introversion, which developed from Jung's ideas on these traits. Adlerian psychotherapy, which stresses the importance of the social environment and pursues a self-realization concept of individual development, is often used by psychologists in conjunction with other forms of therapy. Another original follower of Freud, Fritz Perls (1893–1970), born in Berlin, turned to Gestalt theory as assistant to the Frankfurt professor, Kurt Goldstein, and developed basic ideas for Gestalt therapy. Today academic psychology takes a more "relaxed" view of psychoanalysis. The lack of empirical verification is still criticized, but the influence of many Freudian, Adlerian, and Jungian concepts is acknowledged.

It should be noted here that the historical roots and the development of psychology overlap with those of other academic disciplines such as biology, philosophy, sociology, and educational science. All of them have had eminent scholars who have also influenced psychology to a certain extent. Although it is tempting to consider the work of pioneers like Friedrich

Nietzsche, Georg Simmel, Emile Durkheim, Max Weber, Aby M. Warburg, Ludwig Wittgenstein, Karl Mannheim, Norbert Elias, Max Horkheimer, and Th. W. Adorno in this context, the interested reader can refer to history books of their respective disciplines for further information.

The Period 1933–45

The Nazi takeover marked a sharp caesura in the development of German psychology. Many of the "best minds" in psychology emigrated or were persecuted because they were Jewish or failed to identify with the political system. The list of those who lost their positions included (see Graumann, 1985) Rudolf Arnheim, Curt Bondy, Egon Brunswik (the eminent developmental psychologist and cofounder of humanistic psychology), Charlotte Bühler (1893–1974) and her husband Karl, Heinrich Düker, Karl Duncker, Kurt Goldstein, Fritz Heider, David Katz, Wolfgang Köhler, Paul Lazarsfeld, Kurt Lewin, Otto Selz, Erich Stern, Wilhelm Stern, and Max Wertheimer. Major representatives of psychoanalysis and individual psychology, such as Adler and Freud, also emigrated.

Ironically, at the same time, psychology finally became established as an independent academic discipline. Previously, it had usually been assigned to university departments of philosophy because very few psychologists worked in applied fields. Some psychological approaches reflected (not necessarily intentionally) the racist, political, and militarist ideas and needs of the Nazi government. That was particularly true of psychodiagnostics, military psychology, and personality psychology. Theories that supported the regime's ideology were further developed.

Seven of the 20 scientists holding psychology chairs at German universities before 1933 were among those who emigrated. Of the remaining professors, or those who took over the vacated chairs, some representatives of *Ganzheitspsychologie* and *Gestaltpsychologie* saw a positive parallel between developments in psychology and in German society. F. Krueger, his student F. Sander, and the Gestalt psychologist W. Metzger ranked the societal whole above the individual. Hitler's leadership and racism were explained (and partly legitimized) in this theoretical context. This does not, however, permit the conclusion that *Ganzheitspsychologie* and *Gestaltpsychologie* formed logical bases for Nazi ideology per se. Some authors used their terminology to lend analogous support to the political system, while *Gestaltpsychologie* was developed separately in the USA (see discussion of Lewin, above).

An especially doubtful role was played by psychologists who developed typologies directly serving racism. For example, E. Jaensch and G. Pfahler categorized individuals as "integrated" and "disintegrated," that is, as more "valuable" or less "valuable." Yet psychology was not sufficiently powerful to have a real influence on events. Even Jaensch's or Pfahler's categories were probably more a posteriori or parallel legitimations of racist attitudes. This, of course, in no sense reduces the extent of personal responsibility. Other German scientists of the period, whose work does not seem to be associated with Nazi ideology, were the characterologists P. Lersch, R. Heiss, and E. Rothacker, each of whom offered strata models of personality.

For the younger generation of German psychologists and for the scientific community as a whole, the question remains: To what extent were psychologists and psychology actively involved in or used for the goals of the system? Under what circumstances may similar developments be possible?

Characterology, the psychology of expressions and psychodiagnosis, based on the *Psychotechnik* (psycho technique) of industrial psychology, was used for the selection and classification of army and air force personnel, as part of a systematically established military psychology. This "practical application" of psychology was one of the factors that finally led to the official institution of specific regulations for examinations in psychology, thus establishing psychology as an independent academic discipline. The academic degree earned by successful examinees was (and still is) that of *Diplom-Psychologe* (ranking between the MA and the PhD level). After the army and air force psychology services were disbanded in 1942 (selection no longer being necessary), these regulations continued in force and served for the education of psychologists as consultants in the pedagogical field. With the active campaign of the Berlin psychology department under O. Kroh for the establishment of the diploma, German psychology became an "applied" science.

This is also the place to honor those psychologists who actively resisted the Nazi regime and were either imprisoned in concentration camps, like Heinrich Düker (1898–1986) (a psychopharmacologist and will psychologist), or executed, like Kurt Huber (a music psychologist sentenced to death as a member of the *Weisse Rose* [White Rose] resistance group). Emigrants like Wertheimer, Köhler, Lewin, and W. Stern continued their work in the USA at institutions such as the New School for Social Research, and Duke and Harvard universities.

Psychology after 1945
In the years following World War II some emigrants returned to Germany, such as C. Bondy. Some who had taken over professorial chairs between 1933 and 1945 were not accused of actively supporting the goals of the Nazi regime and retained their posts, among them P. Lersch (1898–1972) in Munich and R. Heiss (1903–74) in Freiburg. Politically, two independent German states were established in 1949: the German Democratic Republic

(GDR) in the east and the Federal Republic of Germany (FRG) in the west. In line with the political orientations of these two states, psychology in the GDR was influenced by Soviet science, especially by Pavlov, Luria, and Leontiev. Psychology in the FRG, after a period of pre- and post-1933 traditions such as *Ganzheitspsychologie,* characterology, and the psychology of expressions, was stimulated by approaches in the English-speaking world, particularly in the USA and especially by behaviorism.

Recent decades have seen increasing developments in German approaches, partly involving elements of traditional German and Anglo-American research, partly of a genuinely innovative nature. A high proportion of current German psychological research is linked with international activities, and more systematic cooperation between psychologists in the GDR and FRG has recently intensified. The political unification of Germany will, no doubt, lead to a common German psychology.

It is impossible to mention all significant projects. However, the following sections should provide some examples of important research trends in Germany.

In the mid-1950s 17 university chairs of psychology were in existence. The majority stemmed from the *Ganzheitspsychologie*/characterology tradition (e.g., Kroh, Wellek, Lersch, Undeutsch) or the *Gestalt* tradition (e.g., Metzger, Rausch). Some could not simply be categorized as belonging to either of these schools. W. Arnold, for example, combined personality psychology and experimental approaches.

Although quantitative empirical approaches were initially in a minority, the situation changed during the 1960s. Experimental studies became increasingly important, and scientists such as J. V. Allesch, Arnold, H. Bartenwerfer, J. Brengelmann, H. Düker, E. Duhm, K. Eyferth, K. Foppa, H. Heckhausen, O. Heller, H. Hörmann, H. J. Kornadt, G. A. Lienert, K. Mierke, M. Sader, F. Süllwold, W. Traxel, A. Vukovich, and W. Witte (to name some of the participants in the First Workshop for Experimental Psychologists, in Marburg, 1959) have conducted and supported quantitative studies in different areas of psychology. This development could be regarded as a continuation of the German experimental tradition before the early or mid-1930s and as a reimportation from the USA.

In the 1970s new approaches criticized "isolated," "often theory-less, method-centered," "ecologically relatively invalid" experiments. They postulated either multivariate testing of complex models or—from another, less well represented paradigmatic point of view—a return to qualitative and idiographic analyses. With the further development of methodological procedures such as LISREL, MDS, KFA, INFORM, and HYPAG, several "contradictions" among differing approaches disappeared.

In the 1980s some areas of psychology became more pragmatic in their choice of methods and developed a logic systematically combining single-case studies, experimental structural analyses, and longitudinal field analyses, without sacrificing the criteria of reliability and validity. Another approach has been the use of meta-analyses and quantitative literature reviews to systematize the existing body of knowledge. Analyses and taxonomies often appear more valuable than a series of new studies.

One can hardly speak of rival schools in the 1980s. The field is too broad and too differentiated (with more than 350 full and associate professors at more than 50 universities) to allow a homogeneous paradigm. It is true that one may speak of a certain dominance of "cognitive" approaches in different areas. Other recent focal points have included studies in emotion, situationalism, interactionism, communication, ecology, new technologies, organizational psychology, psychobiology, and psychopharmacology.

Specific Areas of Psychology

The following sections briefly describe recent developments in a few areas of German psychology.

Personality and Differential Psychology

Although personality psychology and characterology played a major role in Germany from the 1930s to the 1950s, there has been a quantitative decline of theory and research in this area in recent years. Still influential, however, are H. Thomae, with his cognitively oriented *Das Individuum und seine Welt* (The individual and his world) (2nd edition, 1972), and Eysenck's personality theory. In the context of psychological testing, personality theory has been applied by, among others, H. Selg and J. Fahrenberg (*Freiburger Persönlichkeitsinventar*—FPI—one of the most widely used German tests); M. Amelang (testing Eysenck's extraversion concept); D. Bartussek and A. Angleitner (Zuckermann's sensation seeking and Strelau's temperament); and W. D. Fröhlich, H. W. Krohne, and R. Schwarzer (coping behavior and anxiety). Situationalism and interactionism (see the pioneering approaches of Mischel and Magnusson, respectively) have dominated the debate since 1970, but with a growing interest in psychophysiology, psychobiology, and the field of genetics and twin research, there may be a less ideologically loaded renaissance of personality research in this area.

Developmental Psychology

Developmental analyses were attempted in ancient times by Plato and Aristotle, and 18th-century studies relied on systematic observation (by the German Dietrich Tiedemann in 1787) and on a wider age range (by F. A. Carus, 1770–1808). For a time, interest centered on child studies, probably because of their use in education. Several German investigations extended the age range under analysis. Perhaps the most famous is the longitudinal study led by H. Thomae. In this context, a special role is played by gerontology. One of its major representatives, U. Lehr, recently took over a chair in this subject at Heidelberg University (in late 1988 she was appointed German secretary of health, family, and youth). Other areas of German developmental research include methodological issues such as sophisticated time-series analyses (see P. Baltes), meta-analyses (see H. Nickel & R. Oerter), social interaction (K. Grossmann), and special problems such as drug abuse (see R. K. Silbereisen).

Pedagogical and Educational Psychology

General introductions to this field, with its strong link to the long history of educational science, have been provided by F. Weinert, G. Mietzel, and R. and A. M. Tausch. Typical problem-solving areas are educational styles and socialization (A. and K. H. Stapf, H. Lukesch), the relationship of family to school (H. D. Dann), general school education (E. Höhn), and problem children (K. Eyferth). Educational psychology has a long tradition in Germany and a standing that has led to the establishment of several research centers focusing on training and education, such as the Max Planck institutes in Munich and Berlin.

Special problems recently considered by researchers include talent (P. Orlik) and gifted children (B. Feger) and the link with other fields of psychology, such as ecology (K. Schneewind), mass communication (L. J. Issing, K. Strittmatter, H. Lukesch), and protection of the young (F. Fippinger).

Testing and Diagnostics

The history of pedagogical testing has been analyzed by K. H. Ingenkamp, who has also developed several school achievement tests. Tests and measurement procedures have been developed in Germany for virtually all fields of psychology. Most can be found in the two-volume compendium on psychological tests (*Handbuch psychologischer und pädagogischer Tests*, 1975) collated by R. Brickenkamp. Though certain areas of measurement have more or less vanished (e.g., projective tests or graphology—see the works of R. Heiss), all facets of test theory have been refined to allow construction of superior, more reliable, and more valid tests. In this context, diagnostics itself becomes the subject of diagnosis (*Diagnose der Diagnostik*, K. Pawlik, 1976). Naive measures like Lavater's, Gall's, and others' 18th- and 19th-century analogies between human and animal physiognomy are no longer possible. To avoid biases in less obvious cases, authors such as H. Wottawa, K. J. Klauer, G. A. Lienert, R. S. Jäger, and A. F. Vukovich have developed sophisticated tests or established criteria for test construction. Recent areas of interest are intelligence measures (e.g., the inclusion of noncognitive factors in problem solving), measures of traits, state and change, probability theory, and the relationship between testing and measurement theory.

Clinical Psychology

Most nonuniversity psychologists work in clinical or related fields (approximately 60 percent). However, they face difficult legal problems. Unlike medical therapy, independent clinical intervention by psychologists is not officially acknowledged. Thus a psychologist cannot charge fees to social security or insurance programs without having first called in a physician. This fact may also account for the increasing unemployment rate for clinical psychologists, who are dependent on private clients. The BDP (professional association of psychologists) has been trying to change the law for some years. It is hoped that new legislation, incorporating slight improvements, will be passed.

Some tendencies in psychotherapy and its research have already been referred to in the historical survey. Other aspects are outlined briefly here. After a period in which psychiatry and psychoanalysis were the predominant forms of mental health intervention, behavior therapy (J. C. Brengelmann, later R. Bastine, W. Butollo) and client-centered therapy (R. and A. M. Tausch) were introduced in Germany in the 1950s and 1960s. Gestalt and family therapy followed a little later. Although many doubtful developments were associated with the fashionable "psycho-boom" of the 1970s, clinical psychological research has developed methods for preparing the most adequate possible intervention techniques and testing their effects. Hence, greater objectivity in appraising therapies and therapists seemed at least attainable, though perhaps not altogether desirable in the view of many involved in the therapeutic process.

The original claim to exclusiveness posed by the different forms of therapy often gave way to a stance of more mutual acceptance or even integration (including the combination of occidental and oriental forms of dealing with life, such as in the work of K. Graf Dürckheim). Some recent projects have even begun to develop different taxonomies and diagnostic systems to determine the most satisfactory form of intervention. These often include treatment within the natural social environment.

In recent years areas of special interest for intervention by psychologists, either as sole or as cotherapists, have been drug addiction, cancer, AIDS, child abuse, anorexia nervosa, bulimia, partnership problems, and bullying—often as a result of the higher incidence of these problems or of greater public awareness. Nonetheless, many of these disorders are still regarded as taboo or are not officially recognized as requiring professional help. Other fields of cooperation have been neurology (aphasia research, K. Poeck and K. Willmes), psychosomatics (D. Beckmann and J. W. Scheer), and child psychiatry.

General Psychology: Cognition, Knowledge, and Language
The analysis of thinking and cognitive processes has traditionally formed one of the strongest areas of German psychological research. Publications and studies are both numerous and influential, and they overlap with many other areas of psychology. Following the work of O. Selz, K. Duncker, and Max Wertheimer, with their analyses of "productive thinking" between the 1920s and 1940s, C. F. Graumann and T. Herrmann continued research into thought processes in the 1960s. Between 1970 and the late 1980s, G. Lüer and D. Dörner conducted several studies on problem solving in complex situations. Using data collection techniques influenced by early German thought psychologists but acquired and processed with computer aid, they simulated various problem situations and measured thinking patterns and reactions (see D. Dörner et al.; Lohausen, 1981). In Göttingen a large, well-funded project was established in which psychologists and economists analyzed problem solving in complex decision-making processes (see Lüer). This undertaking marks a trend toward combined fundamental and applied research, offering new opportunities for training psychology students (cf. similar approaches in Aachen).

Sophisticated theories of language and psycholinguistics have been developed by H. Hörmann (*Psychologie der Sprache* [Psychology of language], 1967) and T. Herrmann (*Sprache* [Language], 1972), both of whom have stimulated additional research by others. The cognitive representation of knowledge has become another major area of research in Germany. In *Wissenspsychologie* (Psychology of knowledge) the editors, H. Mandl and H. Spada, have provided an overview of the status of knowledge about knowledge in 1988. There had also been increasing contact between the GDR and the FRG in the fields of cybernetics and information processing, in which theories were extensively studied in the GDR by F. Klix (*Information und Verhalten* [Information and behavior], 1971) and others. This research stimulated similar approaches in the FRG.

Learning and perception are now often integrated in the context of cognitive theories, especially since the recognition of cognition as a crucial element in adult human learning. In the field of perception, psychophysics still plays an important role, allowing as it does a precise quantitative determination of psychological reactions to physical features of the environment (see J. Drösler and others), providing perhaps the closest approximation to the ideal of psychology as a natural science. This aspect is also of importance for measurement theory.

Motivation and Emotion

Here again the psychology of volition (Ach), affect (Lewin), and motivation looks back on a long tradition, explicitly continued in the work of J. Kuhl (will psychology) and H. Heckhausen, who died in 1988 (*Motivation und Handeln* [Motivation and action], 1980). Both subscribe to an action theory explaining human behavior in terms of intended goal- and subgoal-oriented activities. These goals and activities can be represented formally, permitting a numerical prognosis of behavior. Other researchers have applied motivation and action theory to specific fields—for example, to aggression research (H. J. Kornadt) and environmental psychology (G. Kaminski). Motivation research (together with social psychology) also provides a broad field for other studies on aggression—for example, those by H. Selg and U. Mees, and by J. Groebel and R. Hinde, who integrate approaches on different levels from genetics via physiology, ethology, psychology, and history to political science in their edited volume *Aggression and War: Their Biological and Social Bases* (1989)—and on need achievement (H. Heckhausen) and intraindividual conflict (H. Feger).

After a certain interval, emotion research returned to German psychology in the 1980s (see, among others, N. Bischof). Again, it overlaps with cognition, social psychology, and physiological psychology. The relationship between cognition and emotion has yet to be clarified, and the problem sometimes seems to stem more from confusion in terminology than from methodological difficulties. K. Scheerer and H. Wallbott have conducted a long series of studies on the social perception of nonverbal expressions of emotion. Alternative explorations of the structure of emotions have recently been undertaken by E. D. Lantermann. Other promising approaches can probably be found in a combination of physiological and self-descriptive mood measures (G. Debus).

Social Psychology

As noted above, the term "social psychology" was already in use in Germany before 1900. Today it is one of the fields attracting the greatest research effort. After World War II P. R. Hofstätter, with his *Einführung in die Sozial-*

psychologie (Introduction to social psychology) (1959), and, perhaps to a lesser extent, K. S. Sodhi were primarily responsible for reintroducing social psychology. It must be remembered that by the 1930s many eminent social psychologists had emigrated (H. Münsterberg, K. Koffka, F. Heider, K. Lewin). Hofstätter took over from C. Bondy the Hamburg chair originally founded by W. Stern. His research fields were stereotyping, group dynamics, and public opinion.

Hofstätter himself was succeeded by H. Feger, who, besides performing analyses of intraindividual conflict, carried out studies in Berlin on attitudes and attitude measurement, quantitative sociometry, and, more recently, small group communication. Another center of social psychology has continued to be the University of Mannheim, where M. Irle (who also wrote the textbook *Lehrbuch der Sozialpsychologie* [Textbook on social psychology], 1975) chaired a long-term program on "decision research," actually covering many different topics such as interpersonal justice, risk perception, consumer behavior, cognitive dissonance, and game theory, and created a substantial "output" of junior social psychologists (such as D. Frey, V. Möntmann, and G. Trommsdorff). These "juniors" started new programs, and some now hold professorial posts of their own.

Fundamental theoretical work has come from C. F. Graumann and some methodological criticism from K. Holzkamp. A. Mummendey has provided a critical reconsideration of the concept of aggression, stressing the dependence on social content and norms in denoting acts as aggressive. Prosocial behavior has been analyzed by H. W. Bierhoff and L. Montada, partnership interaction by W. Stroebe, and the relationship between attitudes and behavior by B. Six. B. Krahé suggested a relatively new approach when she incorporated "naive" theories in social psychology concepts. The GDR has produced historical social psychology studies (Hiebsch & Vorwerg). Again, studies and authors in this field are too numerous for me to mention more than a small selection.

Applied Psychology

The term "applied psychology" implies that the findings of fundamental research have been applied to a specific practical field, such as learning theory to industrial psychology. This concept requires the psychologist to think in terms of analogies, that is, the fundamental experimental situation has a direct parallel in the everyday life context. Since many features of the current environment create new stimulus constellations and interactions, however, it is doubtful whether a strict distinction between fundamental and applied psychology always makes sense. The attempt should rather be to establish whether a transfer of fundamental findings is appropriate in a particular field or whether the assumption that analogous conditions exist is misleading.

Against this background, much current German "applied" research also provides new paradigms for fundamental science as a whole as soon as it passes beyond the bounds of mere routine investigation. Examples are research activities in the context of new technologies. Computers, mass media, and problem solving in real computer situations are all increasing areas of activity for modern German psychology, providing solutions not offered by any other scientific discipline.

Industrial and Organizational Psychology

Offering new job opportunities for psychologists, industrial and organizational psychology is on the rise in Germany. Its roots lie not so much in Taylorism but in the more humane German "psychotechniques" of Stern, Münsterberg, and Moede. Diagnosis is used to place the most suitable personnel in the most appropriate and convenient posts. This serves both professional efficiency and personal satisfaction, if interaction processes between the individual and the situation are taken into account (C. Graf Hoyos and R. Wakenhuth).

Another goal of this field is the creation of a more satisfying and less stressful work environment in addition to an "optimum" organizational structure (L. von Rosenstiel directs a Munich institute dealing with these and related problems). The GDR in particular originated sophisticated approaches to ergonomics (see W. Hacker). Recently, psychologists in the FRG worked in conjunction with computer engineers to develop "software ergonomics," adapting software language and configuration to human needs (N. Streitz and others).

Market and Media Psychology

Though psychologists have contributed to market research for some time, such as in developing product and advertisement tests (see H. Haase), media psychology constitutes a more recent field. Hugo Münsterberg published a volume on cinema in 1916, but it was not until the 1960s that German psychology turned to analyzing media (especially television) in a more systematic way. The work of Hertha Sturm, originally a television journalist, greatly influenced the debate. Recently, P. Winterhoff-Spurk, P. Vitouch, and J. Groebel, among others, have conducted relevant studies and published a series of journal articles and books in this field.

Forensic Psychology

Problems similar to those encountered in other branches of psychology also appear in forensic psychology: the quality, reliability, and validity of diagnosis and the social interaction between the individual involved and the situation. After a long period in which characterological approaches were predominant (stemming from the *Ganzheits* school), the difficulty of having to allow simultaneously for juridical and psychological criteria now forms the main focus of discussion (see W. Hommers and H. Wegener). In general, German psychologists play an important role as expert court witnesses and have an acknowledged impact on the decisions of the jury.

Other Applied Areas

The increasing job prospects in the field have led to the creation of some additional (sometimes postgraduate) courses offering a combination of basic psychology with training in practical problem solving. Examples are sex education (N. Kluge, K. Daumenlang), traffic psychology (W. Böcher), and thanatopsychology (R. Ochsmann), all of which are important areas for psychological support or intervention.

Methodology and Measurement

Training in quantitative methods is a necessary preparation for every student of psychology in Germany. All facets of methodology and measurement are covered by research activities, which have actually dominated the discussion in psychology for a certain period. A philosophy of science approach to methodology has been published by N. Groeben. New techniques have also been further developed, for qualitative data (G. Rudinger, G. A. Lienert, H. Wottawa) and in the fields of scaling (I. Borg, H. Feger) and probability theory (W. Tack).

Cross-Cultural Psychology

E. E. Boesch and L. Eckensberger have both proposed solutions for conceptual and methodological problems in the area of cross-cultural psychology. A major recent undertaking has been a complex comparison between Germany and Japan by H. J. Kornadt, G. Trommsdorff, and T. Herrmann.

Biopsychology, Physiological Psychology, and Psychopharmacology

Analysis of the link between psychological and bodily processes is a necessary element in psychology. Otherwise, as some studies on assumed centers in the brain have shown, artifacts may be created. As a solid research base develops, more scientists have turned to this field, and some have already earned international recognition (such as K. Pawlik, M. Pritzel, H. Marko-witsch).

Environmental Psychology

References to environmental psychology are given in the historical survey and in the section above on social psychology. Authors currently conducting research in this area include G. Kaminski and L. Kruse. The field has a greater impact in Germany than this brief description might suggest.

History of Psychology

Those who want to know more about German psychology are referred to the list of references. Scientists particularly active in this field are L. J. Pongratz, H. E. Lück, W. Traxel (Institute for the History of Psychology in Passau), M. Ash, and U. Geuter.

Basic Information

Education

There are more than 50 universities in the Federal Republic of Germany where one could study psychology. Enrollment in psychology courses is limited to high school/college students with grades not lower than approximately B+. There is an average of 2.4 applicants for every place. All universities are public; no fees are charged for attendance. There is also no official ranking system for different universities or psychology departments. In 1987/88 there were about 3,000 freshmen in psychology, with an estimated 30,000 psychology students in all. The population of the FRG was roughly 62 million. After at least 4 years (8 semesters) of study, students who have successfully passed their examinations are awarded the degree of *Diplom-Psychologe*. The average student might then be about 25 years old. The diploma entitles the graduate to work as an independent professional. However, at this stage they do not usually work as certified clinical psychologists, for which additional courses and examinations are required. Even after these additional qualifications have been obtained, the status problem for clinical psychologists is difficult, as previously noted.

For the academically inclined, there is the opportunity to read for a postgraduate degree (usually Dr. phil. or Dr. rer. nat.). Between 1986 and 1988, 292 psychology students received doctorates, and 56 more received their *Venia Legendi* (habilitation)—an advanced postgraduate degree unfamiliar in most other countries. There is an increasing tendency toward the establishment of intra- and interuniversity postgraduate programs offering a better professional basis. Examples are media psychology (see Sturm, Groebel, or Winterhoff-Spurk) and organizational and company development (see Sanders or Drumenlang).

Research

Most research is carried out in universities. Some special centers are devoted exclusively to psychological research—for example, the Max Planck institutes in Berlin and Munich. Most of the funding is from public sector sources (Deutsche Forschungsgemeinschaft [German Research Association]), with a smaller percentage from private or "semiprivate" foundations (e.g., the *Stiftung* Volkswagenwerk [Volkswagen Foundation]). By international comparison, German psychological research is quite well funded.

Psychology in Practice

In 1988 there were about 30,000 psychologists with recognized university diplomas (Schorr, 1988). In 1984 there were 34 psychologists per 100,000 of the population, as compared to 314 physicians. Slightly more than 50 percent of psychologists are women. The proportion of female psychologists actually working in the field is probably about 50 percent. Many psychologists are unemployed or choose to take up other careers. Of the 16,000 psychologists currently estimated to be active in the field, some 70 percent are employed in the clinical (60 percent) or consultancy (10 percent) sectors. Some believe the figure to be much higher. Fifteen percent are employed in science and research, and 15 percent in companies or public institutions.

Psychological Societies and Congresses

Apart from specialized psychological societies and associations, there are two more broadly based societies, the Berufsverband Deutscher Psychologen (Professional Association of German Psychologists, BDP), founded in 1947 primarily for practicing psychologists, and the Deutsche Gesellschaft für Psychologie (German Society for Psychology, DGfPS), founded in 1904 as the Gesellschaft für experimentelle Psychologie (Society for Experimental Psychology), exclusively for psychologists engaged in research or scientific work and holding a doctorate. The two organizations are associated through the Föderation Deutscher Psychologievereinigungen (Federation of German Psychological Associations) and in this capacity are members of the International Union of Psychological Science.

Every 2 years the BDP hosts the Kongress für angewandte Psychologie (Congress for Applied Psychology), and in the intervening years the DGfPS stages its congress. The BDP (president in 1988, A. Schorr) deals with legal matters related to the profession of psychology, while the DGfPS's major concerns are with university education and scientific research. During its biennial congress the officiating DGfPs president presents a policy speech often regarded as reflecting the current state of psychological science in Germany (president in 1988, G. Lüer). Previous presidents have included K. Foppa, F. E. Weinert, H. J. Kornadt, H. Heckhausen, K. Pawlik, H. Feger, and M. Irle.

Psychological Publications

Countless books on psychology in the German language appear each year. At least 16 different publishers (not all of them major) specialize exclusively in the field or have a psychology program. Perhaps the most ambitious project in psychology publishing is the 88-volume *Enzyklopädie der Psychologie* (Encyclopaedia of psychology) (see under Graumann et al. in bibliography), covering virtually every imaginable aspect of the subject (for example, two volumes alone are devoted to the psychology of sport). Nearly every major psychology publisher runs special series (e.g., introductory courses) and review volumes for different areas.

About 30 major quarterly journals of psychology are published, covering most fields within the discipline. They include the classic, the solidly established, and the more innovative journals, such as the *Zeitschrift für experimentelle und angewandte Psychologie* (Journal of experimental and applied psychology), *Zeitschrift für Sozialpsychologie* (Journal for social psychology), and *Medienpsychologie* (Media psychology). The English-language *German Journal of Psychology*, which since 1977 has published reviews and summaries covering German research at approximately 3-month intervals and which also lists all important journals, is of particular interest to the international psychological community.

Bibliography

Ash, M. G., & Geuter, U. (Eds.). (1985). *Geschichte der deutschen Psychologie im 20. Jahrhundert*. Opladen: Westdeutscher Verlag.

Brozek, J., & Pongratz, L. J. (1980). *Historiography of modern psychology*. Toronto: Hogrefe.

Dorsch, F. (1987). *Psychologisches Wösterbuch* (11th ed.). Bern: Huber.

German Journal of Psychology. A Quarterly. Reviews, Reports, and Comprehensive Abstracts. (1977–). Toronto: Hogrefe.

Geschichte der Psychologie. Nachrichtenblatt der Fachgruppe Geschichte der Psychologie DGFPs. (1984–).

Geuter, U. (1986). *Daten zur Geschichte der deutschen Psychologie. Vol. 1.* Göttingen: Hogrefe.

Graumann, C. F. (Ed.). (1981, and following). *Kurt Lewin Werkausgabe.* Bern, Stuttgart: Huber & Klett-Cotta.

Graumann, C. F. (Ed.). (1985). *Psychologie im Nationalsoztialismus.* Berlin: Springer.

Graumann, C. F., Hörmann, J., Irle, M., Thomae, H., & Weinert, F. E. (Eds.). *Enzyklopädie der Psychologie.* (1980s). 88 vols. Göttingen: Hogrefe.

Haas, R. (1980, 1988). *Wörterbuch der Psychologie und Psychiatrie: Vol. 1. Englisch-Deutsch. Vol. 2. Deutsch-Englisch.* Göttingen: Hogrefe.

Jütteman, G. (Ed.). (1988). *Wegbereiter der historischen Psychologie.* Munich: PVU.

Lück, H. E., Grünwald, H., Geuter, U., Miller, R., & Rechtien, W. (1987). *Sozialgeschichte der Psychologie.* Opladen: Leske & Budrich.

Lück, H. E., Miller, R., & Rechtien, W. (Eds.). (1984). *Geschichte der Psychologie: Ein Handbuch im Schlüsselbegriffen.* Munich: Urban & Schwarzenberg.

Passauer Schriften für Psychologiegeschichte (Vols. 1–9). (1988). Passau: Passavia.

Pongratz, L. J. (1967, 2nd ed. 1984). *Problemgeschichte der Psychologie.* Munich: Francke.

Psychologie und Geschichte. (Quarterly, 1989–). Heidelberg: Asanger.

Psychologische Rundschau. (1949–).

Report Psychologie. (1976–).

Schorr, A. (1988). *Angewandte Psychologie heute—Professionalisierung und Selbstverständnis im beruflichen Handeln.* Bonn: BDP.

17 / Greece

LAMBROS HOUSSIADAS

Lambros Houssiadas (born 1925) earned his PhD from the University of Leeds in 1958. A specialist in perception, cognitive development, and aging, he has published books and articles in these areas, including Perception of Changes of Form *and* The Perception of Causality. *A former vice-president of the British Psychological Society, South Australian Branch, he has also served as dean of the Faculty of Philosophy, member of the Senate, and chairman of the Psychology Section in the Department of Philosophy, Education, and Psychology at the University of Thessaloniki, Greece. He is currently professor of psychology at the University of Thessaloniki.*

The history of psychology in Greece is short. Its beginnings can be traced to the year 1926, when the subject was formally introduced into the curriculum of the School of Philosophy at the University of Athens. It was taught as part of a philosophy course by Theophilos Voréas (1873–1954), a student of Wundt at the psychological laboratory in Leipzig. In the same year, a psychological laboratory was established at the University of Athens and was attached to the chair of philosophy held by Voréas. It remained tied to that chair until 1977, when it was moved to the newly established chair of psychology at the School of Philosophy in the University of Athens. In 1926 a psychology chair was established in the School of Philosophy at the University of Thessaloniki in northern Greece, and the subject was taught independently of philosophy until 1941, when the chair was abolished. Thereafter until 1964 psychology was taught as part of a philosophy course.

The second psychological laboratory in Greece was founded in the School of Philosophy at the University of Thessaloniki in 1937. It was attached to the chair of psychology until 1941 and then to that of philosophy until 1964. A third psychological laboratory was established in the School of Philosophy at the newly founded University of Ioannina in northwestern Greece. It should be noted that in the Greek educational system a school of philosophy is a collection of departments like a faculty of arts in the Anglo-Saxon universities or the schools of philosophy in the German or East European universities. In 1982, following a governmental law, all chairs were abolished in Greek universities and other institutions of higher learning.

Since 1926 psychology has been suffering from an identity crisis. For some, including university teachers of the subject, it was identified with philosophy. For others, it was identified with psychiatry. The situation was finally resolved in 1964 with the establishment of three independent psychology chairs, one of general psychology at the University of Thessaloniki, and two at the University of Ioannina, in general psychology and child psychology, respectively. The existing psychological laboratories were attached to these chairs. In spite of some weak objections by philosophers, psychology was formally recognized at last as an independent science. The person credited with initiating these developments was Vassilios Tatakis (1896–1986), a professor of philosophy in the School of Philosophy at the University of Thessaloniki. The first professors elected to two of the chairs were myself (1966) and J. Paraskevopoulos, who took his appointment to the chair of child psychology at Ioannina in 1970. In 1978 Paraskevopoulos resigned from his Ioannina chair to assume the newly established chair of general psychology at the School of Philosophy in the University of Athens.

Following these appointments, Paraskevopoulos and I organized the laboratories and chairs as research and teaching centers. As part of that effort, we selected suitable staff, established psychology as an independent science, conducted research reflecting quantitative trends, and tried to bring Greek psychology in touch with that of the international community.

Psychology as a Profession

After the establishment of the scientific status of psychology in Greece, issues were raised by the Greek Psychological Society concerning certification and licensing procedures, especially for psychologists working outside of teaching institutions. After prolonged negotiations between representatives of the society and the Ministry of Social Welfare, which is responsible for professional licensing, a law was passed by the Greek Parliament in 1979 specifying the qualifications for the profession of psychology. According to the law, holders of a master's degree in psychology or its equivalent, such as the French *maîtrise* or the German *Magister Artium*, are entitled to practice psychology as a profession after certification from the Ministry of Social Welfare. Provision is also made for licensing specialists in psychology, such as those in school, clinical, and industrial psychology, and others. For such specialists, qualifications were to be stated, in due course, by the ministry, following recommendations from a committee operating within the ministry. Thus, the professional status of psychology and of psychologists was clarified. Although more than 8 years have elapsed since the law was passed, however, it has never been implemented because of the strong objections of the Greek Psychological Society.

The explanation for this development is related to changes within the society itself. Many members held psychology degrees not recognized by the appropriate agency of the Ministry of Education, known as DIKATSA (i.e., Interuniversity Center for Recognition of Degrees from Foreign Institutions). These degrees were granted by foreign universities to individuals who completed psychology courses in private centers in Greece not recognized by the Greek government. These individuals then proceeded to obtain first, and often postgraduate, degrees or diplomas in psychology. These degree holders have exercised great pressure, through the Greek Psychological Society, on DIKATSA, the Ministry of Education, and the Ministry of Social Welfare. At present no changes have occurred in the policies of the government. Nevertheless, licensing procedures, although established by law, are not being enforced. It should be noted that most psychologists in Greece are members of the Greek Psychological Society, although some, including university staff members, are not.

Estimating the number of individuals qualified as psychologists in Greece is not possible until the problem of the nonrecognized degrees is settled and the law concerning certification is implemented. Certainly, the number is not easily estimated from the membership of the Greek Psychological Society, for reasons indicated earlier. Yet it is actually the only basis for an estimate. Thus, in 1963, when the society was first established, there were 33 registered members (7 male, 26 female); by 1976 the number had increased to 81 (20 male, 61 female); in 1986 it rose to 596 (153 male, 443 female).

At present all psychologists in Greece have studied at foreign universities, since no recognized Greek institutions provide independent psychology degrees. Psychologists are employed in teaching positions at universities and other institutions of higher learning, in general or psychiatric hospitals, in governmental departments, in state health centers, in private and public schools, in industry, and in private practice. The highest proportion of professionals work as clinical psychologists in state or private psychiatric hospitals, health centers, and similar institutions, or in private practice. An unspecified number are employed by the secondary school system, both public and private, as school psychologists or counselors, and a small number are employed by industrial firms. Unemployment, however, is high, with rather pessimistic prospects for the near future. As a consequence of legal inactivity, professional psychologists in Greece have no official certification, since it is not required by employing agencies. Private practice is not subject to any legal restrictions.

Training and Research Facilities in Universities

Significant developments have taken place over the past few years, especially since 1982, in the structure of Greek universities. New schools and departments have been established, old schools have been departmentalized (for example, medical schools are now departments of the schools of health sciences), and smaller departments have been integrated into larger ones. Psychology was clearly affected by these developments. The Department of Psychology and Education at the University of Thessaloniki was abolished in 1983 and replaced by the Department of Philosophy, Education, and Psychology in the same year. The department belongs, as before, to the School of Philosophy. Such departments were also established within the Schools of Philosophy at the Universities of Athens and Ioannina in the same year. The intake of first-year students for the academic year 1987–88 was 270 for the University of Athens, 204 for the University of Thessaloniki, and 160 for Ioannina. Similar numbers of students were accepted in each of the previous four academic years.

In the departments of philosophy, education, and psychology of the three universities, psychology is taught along with philosophy and education and some electives from the human sciences, such as history, Latin, and classic and modern Greek literature. For interested students, the departments provide majors in the three subjects. Although there are some differences in the structure of courses from each department, the psychology major, the favorite among students, typically includes lectures, tutorials, and practical exercises in introductory, experimental, social, clinical, and developmental psychology. Also included are psycholinguistics and the history of psychology, along with more specific electives, such as psychology of motivation, aging, moral development, and psychometrics. Courses are distributed over the 4 years, or 8 semesters, required for the degree of bachelor in philosophy, education, and psychology. Needless to say, such degrees, even with psychology as a major subject, are not regarded as psychology degrees. Their holders are employed mainly as teachers in secondary education.

Graduates with psychology majors interested in pursuing further studies have the option of entering a postgraduate diploma course in psychology at the Department of Philosophy, Education, and Psychology at the University of Thessaloniki, the only postgraduate course available. Alternatively, they may apply for positions in foreign universities, especially in the USA, the UK, or France. Most applicants are accepted for postgraduate degrees, though some are required to complete their psychology studies by taking undergraduate courses and thus obtain a basic degree (the bachelor's of Anglo-Saxon universities, *maîtrise* in French universities, or the equivalent in other countries). In Greece, postgraduate studies in psychology are planned in the near future for other departments of philosophy, education, and psychology.

The psychological laboratories in all three departments are equipped with the necessary apparatus for practical exercises of students. Standard intelligence tests (such as the WAIS and the WISC, the Stanford-Binet Scales, and Raven's Progressive Matrices), personality tests (such as the Rorschach, TAT, CAT, and MMPI), and tests of specific abilities are also available. Most psychology books in central university libraries or in departmental libraries are in English, with some in French and some in German. Periodicals, again most of them in English, are well represented. Thus, the library of the University of Thessaloniki subscribes to more than 35 international journals, while those of Athens and Ioannina receive more than 30. Limited computer facilities are available in the psychological laboratories, and additional facilities are provided to researchers by the central computer of the universities.

A major development that may become a landmark for Greek psychology was the establishment of a psychology department within the School of Social Sciences at the University of Crete in September 1987. The number of students admitted for the academic year 1987–88 was 54. The following teaching positions were advertised in April 1987: clinical psychology (two positions), developmental psychology (one position), experimental psychology (one position), educational psychology (one position), social psychology (one position), neuropsychology (one position), psychology of work (one position), and psycholinguistics (one position). At present there are no suitable facilities in the new department for training psychology students. In addition, it is not known whether positions will be filled properly. Such points were raised by academics who suggested that the first psychology department should be established either at the University of Thessaloniki or the University of Athens, both of which could have provided experienced staff and fine facilities. However, the Ministry of Education, for political rather than academic reasons, decided to establish the department at the small town of Rethymnon in Crete. The first graduates of psychology in Greece are expected to receive their degrees in 1991.

Publications

At present no scientific or professional journal of psychology is published in Greece. The Greek Psychological Society plans to sponsor a journal in the near future. The form, policies, and other details of the journal are not yet known. Psychological publications in Greek usually take the form of general books on various topics addressed to psychology and education students, professional psychologists, teachers, and the interested public. Research findings or theoretical contributions, mainly by university staff, are published in international psychological journals; in the scientific annals of the schools of philosophy or departments of philosophy, education, and psychology; in periodicals publishing papers from other sciences; or in periodicals addressed to "informed readers."

Current State of Psychology

In the first edition of Sexton and Misiak's *Psychology around the World* I expressed some views in the chapter on Greek psychology concerning future prospects of psychology in Greece. It seems now that the developments since 1976 were in the general direction of those predictions. Psychology is accepted as an independent science, taught at universities or other institutions as an independent subject. The various governmental agencies have a clearer picture of the uses and potential of psychology. As stated above, positions for psychologists have been established in government, in higher learning institutions, in hospitals, and within the private and public sector of the secondary educational system. The first psychology department has been founded. The general public seems better informed about the applied aspects of psychology, and there are more psychologists working for private businesses or in private practice than in the mid-1970s. Certainly, the fact that psychology now appears in the title of university departments is one indication of the general public acceptance of its scientific status. The Greek Psychological Society, with its scientific activities, has also contributed to the clarification of psychology's image, although its views concerning the qualifications of a psychologist are sometimes regarded as detrimental to the profession. It is hoped that when the problem of the nonrecognized degrees has been settled, more people will assume a positive view of the profession. Psychological conferences in Greece are held more often than in the past, and visits of Greek psychologists to universities or other institutions of higher learning abroad are common. Visits of established psychologists to Greece and the Greek universities are also frequent. Cooperation in international projects between Greeks and psychologists abroad are not uncommon. In short, Greek psychology has moved out of its isolation and is becoming part of the international mainstream.

One of the weak features of Greek psychology is the loose communication among staff members of psychology departments. Members of one department are hardly aware of the activities of colleagues in other departments.

The Greek Psychological Society, which might have contributed to cooperation between departments, is preoccupied with its own internal problems and acts more as a professional syndicate than a scientific society. This lack of communication and cooperation at the national level may help to explain the lack of major philosophical or theoretical influences. The staff of each psychology department follows its own research interests, a fact that is reflected in the personal research they are conducting (see bibliography). One common characteristic is that they tend to carry out quantitative studies in whatever area of psychology they happen to work. Their interests are almost equally divided between basic and applied research. However, because of the limited funds provided by the government and the absence of funds from industry or other sources, research is usually limited in scope. Psychologists tend to deal with problems requiring "paper and pencil" facilities and/or apparatus of simple sophistication. Psychological research in Greece is conducted almost exclusively in the psychological laboratories of the Universities of Thessaloniki, Athens, and Ioannina, in that order. At present, emphasis seems to be on cognitive development, social psychology, psychological aspects of education, and clinical work. Research findings and writings of Greek psychologists have attracted the attention of psychologists from other parts of the world, such as the USA, Europe, and Australia. This trend is a recent hopeful development, and available signs suggest that it will continue into the future.

Bibliography

Besevengis, E., & Lore, R. K. (1983). The effects of an adult's presence on the social behavior of preschool children. *Aggressive Behavior, 9,* 243–252.

Demetriou, A., & Efklides, A. (1979). Formal operational thinking in young adults as a function of education and sex. *International Journal of Psychology, 14,* 241–253.

Demetriou, A., & Efklides, A. (1985). Structure and sequence of formal and post-formal thought. *Child Development, 56,* 1062–1091.

Houssiadas, L., & Brown, L. B. (1980). Egocentrism in language and space perception: An examination of the concept. *Genetic Psychology Monographs, 101,* 183–214.

Markoulis, D. (1979). The effects of language practice and familiarity with deductive modes of thinking on the reasoning ability of children. *Views on Language and Language Teaching, 5,* 115–126.

Natsopoulos, D. (1987). Processing implications and presuppositions by schoolchildren and adults: A developmental cross-linguistic comparison. *Journal of Psycholinguistic Research, 16,* 133–164.

Natsopoulos, D., & Abadzi, H. (1986). Understanding linguistic time sequence and simultaneity: A literature review and some new data. *Journal of Psycholinguistic Research, 15*, 243–273.

Papadopoulou, D. (1982). Interpersonal perception and reduction of cognitive conflict. In H. Brandstatter and H. H. Kelly (Eds.), *Social psychology*, (pp. 151–156). Berlin: VEB Deutsher Verlag der Wissenschaften.

Paraskevopoulos, J., & Kirk, S. A. (1969). *The development and psychometric characteristics of the revised ITPA*. Champaign: University of Illinois Press.

Vakali, M. (1985). Children's thinking in arithmetic word problem solving. *Journal of Experimental Education, 53*, 106–113.

18 / Hong Kong

DAVID YAU-FAI HO

David Yau-fai Ho (born 1939) received his PhD from the Illinois Institute of Psychology in 1967. A specialist in clinical psychology, social psychology, and cross-cultural psychology, with more than 60 papers to his credit, he has also published in psychiatry, sociology, linguistics, and education and was one of the editors of the book Asian Contributions to Psychology *(1988).*

In addition to several editorial positions, Ho has held office in the International Association for Cross-Cultural Psychology and the Hong Kong Psychological Society and served as president of the International Council of Psychologists, 1988–89. He is a reader in psychology in the Department of Psychology at the University of Hong Kong.

Various authors have already written on psychology in Hong Kong, focusing on research (Dawson, 1970), the role of psychologists in mental health (Ho, 1971), clinical psychology (Ho, 1969, 1985), educational psychology (Ripple, 1987), the development of psychology from a historical perspective (Blowers, 1987), factual information (Wolman, 1979, pp. 87–94), and problems and issues (Ho, 1980). This review provides an integrated account of the current status of psychology in Hong Kong and discusses its future directions.

Western psychology has had only a brief history in Hong Kong. Psychology courses were taught at the University of Hong Kong, the older of the only two universities in the territory, as early as 1939 (see Harrison, 1962, p. 130), but the formal inauguration of psychology as a separate academic discipline did not take place until 1968, when the Department of Psychology was established at the university. The growth of psychology in the 1970s and 1980s, however, has been considerable, in both the academic and the professional spheres.

The Hong Kong Psychological Society

A milestone in the development of organized scientific and professional psychology was the establishment of the Hong Kong Psychological Society in 1968. The society is a member of the International Union of Psychological Science and has reciprocal membership rights with the British Psychological Society. Currently, it has about 230 members and affiliates. Four classes of membership are defined: graduate, associate, fellow, and honorary fellow. In general, graduate membership requires a first degree or postgraduate qualification in psychology; associate status requires a first degree or postgraduate qualification in psychology and at least 5 years of postgraduate experience as a psychologist, including postgraduate training, or 6 years without postgraduate training; fellow status is awarded to members who have at least 10 years of experience as a psychologist, possess an advanced knowledge of psychology in at least one of its fields, and have made a substantial contribution to psychological knowledge or practice; and honorary fellows are distinguished psychologists who have contributed to the advancement of psychology. In addition, persons with a long-standing interest in psychology or a closely allied profession may apply to become affiliates. A Division of Clinical Psychology was formed in 1982 and is thus far the only division within the society. It has a current membership of about 60. Postgraduate training in clinical psychology is a requirement for membership in the division.

The society holds an annual conference and sponsors scientific meetings, seminars, and workshops throughout the year, conducted by local and visiting professionals. It also publishes the *Bulletin of the Hong Kong Psychological Society*, which appears twice a year and is devoted to academic and professional concerns relevant to Hong Kong. A code of professional conduct, to which all members of the society are bound, has been developed. The definition of a psychologist has also been formulated and specifies who may call or present himself or herself as a psychologist and offer psychological services. Generally speaking, the requirements are more stringent than those for graduate membership, in that appropriate work experience, or membership in other psychological bodies, is required of those who do not have postgraduate qualification in psychology.

Current Status

The size of the psychological establishment in Hong Kong pales into insignificance when measured against its gigantic North American counterpart, but the activity level of the psychologists is considerable. Academic psychologists are actively engaged in research and publication in international journals. Participation in international organizations is extensive; a few Hong Kong psychologists have served in leadership positions in the International Association for Cross-Cultural Psychology (IACCP) or the International Council of Psychologists (ICP). In recent years Hong Kong psychologists have hosted international conferences and symposia. Close ties are maintained with psychologists in Mainland China, Taiwan, the Philippines, the United States, and the United Kingdom. Psychologists in Hong Kong also enjoy the benefit of their geographical location, which allows them both formal and informal contacts with innumerable visiting psychologists from other countries.

Psychologists are recognized as experts on human behavior by the community and are frequently invited to give talks, participate in seminars, and express opinions through the mass media on a wide range of topics. They have become fairly influential molders of public opinion, out of proportion to their small number. In the courts, too, they are called on to serve as expert witnesses with increasing frequency.

Psychology is now firmly established as an academic discipline in Hong Kong's institutions of higher learning. A limited number of research-oriented psychologists are being trained at the master's or doctoral level. Professionally, psychology has begun to take shape, with clinical psychology taking the lead and educational psychology making its presence increasingly felt. Clinical and educational psychologists are being trained locally at the master's level. One indication of success can be seen in the excellent employment opportunities for professionally trained graduates, all of whom have been employed, locally or overseas. In terms of employment, at least, the community seems to have accepted psychologists remarkably well. One major problem remains, however. There is as yet no legislation concerning the psychology profession in general and no legal registration or licensing of psychological practitioners in particular.

Education and Professional Training

The introduction of modern psychology into Hong Kong society represents the transplantation of a science onto foreign soil that differs radically in cultural ethos from that which gave it birth. From its inception the teaching of psychology has followed Western models, conceptually and organizationally. Until recently, most teachers of psychology were Westerners. Textbooks and reference materials are almost exclusively in English, which is also the medium of instruction usually employed. It is hardly surprising that many students find themselves caught in a schism between two worlds: the English-language milieu of the academic institution and the Chinese-language experience of everyday life. The exposure to values embodied in Western psychology, almost wholesale, leaves students quite unsettled when they discover that their own beliefs, attitudes, and values are seriously challenged. I have discussed these problems in relation to the teaching of psychology in general (1980) and clinical psychology in particular (1985).

Training Institutions and Curricula

Departments of psychology have been established only in the two universities, and graduate training is available in only one of them. In addition to its undergraduate curricula, the Department of Psychology at the University of Hong Kong now offers graduate programs leading to the MPhil (master of philosophy) and PhD degrees by research and to the MSocSc (master of social science) degree by coursework in clinical psychology (introduced in 1971) and educational psychology (introduced in 1981). At the other university, the Chinese University of Hong Kong, a Psychology Section was formed within the Sociology Department in 1973, offering a minor in psychology. A separate Department of Psychology was established in 1982.

At other tertiary institutions, numbering about 10, psychology is being taught on a small, but growing, scale. Also, introductory psychology is taught as one of the advanced-level subjects in some secondary schools and is one of the subjects in the entrance (matriculation) examination of the University of Hong Kong.

Practice

Approximately 50 psychologists are employed by tertiary institutions, attached to departments (or schools) of psychology, education, social work, psychiatry, and business administration. Of these, more than half hold a doctoral degree and the rest hold a master's degree. The trend is toward requiring a doctoral degree for academic appointments, especially at the two universities. As yet, psychologists are rarely, if ever, engaged exclusively in research.

The majority of the practitioners hold a master's degree. Females tend to outnumber males. At present, about 70 clinical psychologists (inclusive of a few foreigners) are employed in academic institutions (counseling units), social service and rehabilitation agencies, hospitals and clinics (psychiatric and general), and government departments (medical and health, social welfare, police force, and correctional services). The diverse settings in which they find employment reflects the dynamic nature of their roles and functions and the growth of the profession. Private practice is limited to a handful, on a full-time or part-time basis. Educational psychologists in practice number about 40, of whom more than half were locally trained. Only a few psychologists work in forensic-correctional and industrial psychology.

Research

Hong Kong itself is an unprecedented sociopolitical experiment as well as a natural laboratory of cross-cultural interaction. Psychologists in Hong Kong are thus strategically well situated to conduct research in areas such as the effects of extreme crowding, cultural interchange and identity, and psychological consequences of colonialism and prolonged political uncertainty. It is small wonder that their research "tradition" has been characterized by a sensitivity to cross-cultural issues, both conceptual and methodological. Two additional factors may account for this sensitivity. The first is a matter of necessity—to be concerned with the question of how and to what extent Western psychological principles and techniques may be applied in the local context. The second is historical: Hong Kong psychologists were instrumental in creating the International Association for Cross-Cultural Psychology, in the process of which they acquired a taste for conducting cross-cultural research. Understandably, most psychological studies done locally pertain in one way or another to Hong Kong society or Chinese culture.

It may be said that the level of research activity is remarkably high. But some issues need to be addressed if psychology is to take root as a scientific enterprise in Hong Kong society. First, much basic work remains to be done—for example, the construction of psychometric instruments for use in a Chinese community and the investigation of socially relevant and urgent topics. Second, psychologists in Hong Kong need to work toward a creative synthesis of Eastern and Western learning (see Ho, 1980, p. 39; 1985).

Future Directions

No discussion of future directions for psychology—or any other intellectual discipline—in Hong Kong can avoid confronting the question of the territory's political future. The year 1997, when Hong Kong will be returned to Chinese sovereignty, looms large. For psychologists, the vital questions must be: How will psychology continue to be of service to Hong Kong (and to China)? How can conflicting ideologies be reconciled within psychology? Will a new psychology emerge, distinctively a product of Hong Kong's unique sociopolitical reality beyond 1997? If so, what would this new psychology be like? What role will the psychologist play? What changes in the education and training of psychologists will be needed? Psychology in Hong Kong beyond 1997 promises to be as exciting as Hong Kong itself will be.

Bibliography

Blowers, G. H. (1987). To know the heart: Psychology in Hong Kong. In G. H. Blowers & A. M. Turtle (Eds.), *Psychology moving East: The status of Western psychology in Asia and Oceania* (pp. 139–161). Boulder, CO: Westview Press; Sydney: Sydney University Press.

Dawson, J. L. M. (1970). Psychological research in Hong Kong. *International Journal of Psychology, 5,* 63–70. (Published also in *Australian Psychologist, 5,* 59–68.)

Harrison, B. (1962). The Faculty of Arts. In B. Harrison (Ed.), *University of Hong Kong: The first 50 years (1911–1961)* (pp. 127–134). Hong Kong: Hong Kong University Press.

Ho, D. Y. F. (1969, December). *The development of clinical psychology in Hong Kong.* Paper presented at the First Annual Conference of the Hong Kong Psychological Society, Hong Kong.

Ho, D. Y. F. (1971). The role of psychologists in mental health in Hong Kong. In W. H. Lo (Ed.), *Aspects of mental health in Hong Kong.* Hong Kong: Mental Health Association of Hong Kong.

Ho, D. Y. F. (1980). Reflections on the development of psychology in Hong Kong society: Students, teachers, and academic institutions. *Philippine Journal of Psychology, 13,* 34–39.

Ho, D. Y. F. (1985). Cultural values and professional issues in clinical psychology. *American Psychologist, 40,* 1212–1218.

Ripple, R. E. (1987). The many faces of educational psychology revisited: Reflections from afar. *Bulletin of the Hong Kong Psychological Society,* No. 18, 33–38.

Wolman, B. B. (1979). *International directory of psychology: A guide to people, places, and policies.* New York: Plenum.

19 / Hungary

JÁNOS LÁSZLÓ & CSABA PLÉH

János László (born 1948) received his PhD from Eötvös Lóránd University, Budapest, in 1974. A specialist in social psychology, he is the author of two books: Dráma és elóadás *(Drama and performance) and* Beszéd a szavak mögött*(Nonverbal communication), the latter with Béla Buda. Other publications have focused on cognitive and social psychological approaches to behavior. A recipient of the Youth Award of the Hungarian Academy of Science and an associate editor of* Pszichológia *(Psychology) since 1981, László is head of the Research Group in Cognitive Social Psychology of the Hungarian Academy of Science.*

Csaba Pléh (born 1945) received his PhD from Eötvös University in 1970. His books include A psyzicholingvisztika horizontga *(A psycholinguistic overview) and* A történetszerkezet és az emlékezeti sémák*(A history of patterns of the mind). He has also published, in English, research on the development of sentence interpretation in Hungarian. A section editor of* Magyar Pszichológiai Szemle *(Journal of Hungarian psychology), Pléh is head and associate professor of psychology in the Department of General Psychology at Eötvös University in Budapest.*

Psychology in Hungary has a long tradition both as a scientific enterprise and as a profession, although it has been interrupted several times. The roots of Hungarian psychology can be found in the progressive intellectual movement around the turn of the century. Experimental psychology started in the laboratory of Paul Ranschburg, who excelled as an experimentalist in the German tradition and as a founder of the child counseling movement in Hungary. The early involvement of Hungarian psychologists in the psychoanalytic movement dates from the same period. Between the two wars, development of psychology was gradual but slow and not well received officially. Political and racial discrimination was present that resulted in the emigration of many psychoanalysts and academics, such as Géza Révész, who became well known in the Netherlands. After the liberation in 1945, psychology, as a natural ally of progressive social and educational movements, flourished for a few years. This intellectually varied and open period was followed by a politically forced reduction of psychological activities and by an intellectually narrow-minded Pavlovianization of psychology during the Stalinist period. Since the early 1960s psychology has again become a respected science and profession. Regular training was reestablished, research activity and informational connections reactivated, and different institutions and professional organizations formed.

As a result of this discontinuous history, psychology is treated as a rather young and ambitious area in Hungary. The general outlook of Hungarian psychologists is cosmopolitan. They usually read both Western and Soviet literature, with many basic books available in Hungarian translations.

Psychologists in Hungary are trained at two universities: Lóránd Eötvös University in Budapest and Lajos Kossuth University at Debrecen. Both offer a 5-year comprehensive graduate program. Besides the 200 students enrolled in the regular program, about 200 other students are involved in "night classes," that is, in classes offered for people who already have a degree in some other field and are working in areas related to psychology (e.g., in medicine, human engineering, or special education).

The 5-year program leads to an MA degree in psychology. Recently, about 80 students have graduated per year. Basic training is supplemented by two year-long postgraduate courses in three practical areas: clinical, industrial, and educational psychology. These programs are offered for those who already have the MA degree and are working in the given area. The postgraduate training ends with a special license for that area. Licensing and employment of psychologists are regulated by laws issued by the different ministries involved in training and employment.

PhD degrees are awarded by the two universities providing basic training. No separate doctoral program is offered. The doctoral degree is given on the basis of comprehensive exams and the submission and defense of a dissertation based on independent research. This system is supplemented by two higher-level academic scientific degrees given by the Hungarian Academy of Sciences: the degree of candidate and the degree of doctor of sciences. They are usually given after the successful defense of a thesis.

Roughly 1,200 people are employed as full-time psychologists. About two thirds of them are female. Basic employers are various state-owned companies and institutions, although the law allows for private practice. About 15 percent of psychologists work in research and higher education. The Hungarian Academy of Sciences has a central Institute for Psychology employing 70 full-time researchers. The two universities giving degrees in psychology employ about 60 psychologists. Research-oriented people also have positions at other research institutes in medicine, education, and sociology and at other universities.

In practical areas the most visible employer is the medical field. Hospitals and outpatient centers employ the largest number of psychologists. For child psychologists, a nationwide system of educational guidance centers is the largest employer. In the last few years a new system has been designed in which school psychologists are employed directly by schools. Industrial psychologists work in state-owned companies, but quite a few of them are employed in nationwide screening centers (e.g., those concerning traffic safety) or management consulting firms.

The Hungarian Psychological Association, the professional society of psychologists, was founded in 1928. Its activity has been continuous since its reestablishment in 1962. Besides representing the professional interests of its 1,400 members, its sections (more than a dozen) organize scientific and professional meetings and conferences. Many psychologists are members of the Hungarian Psychiatric Association as well.

There are two professional journals for psychologists in Hungary, both published in Hungarian with detailed English abstracts. *Magyar Pszichológiai Szemle* (Journal of Hungarian psychology), the older of the two, appears six times a year and has recently begun specializing in clinical psychology. *Pszichológia* (Psychology) has four issues a year and is more theoretical.

The largest specialty library for psychology is in the Institute of Psychology of the Hungarian Academy of Sciences, with more than 10,000 volumes. Many university and public libraries also have large collections on psychology. Compared to those of American universities, modern collections are relatively weak. This is compensated for, however, by rather rich classic collections.

In the main research centers and larger applied psychology units, laboratory instrumentation is rather sophisticated. Hungarian-made biomedical equipment is used along with imported technology. Computerization is a relative newcomer in Hungarian psychology. Recently, however, computers have assumed a primary role in data processing, statistical analysis, stimulus presentation, and text processing. Hungarian and Western personal computers, as well as mainframes, are used together with major software systems like BMDP or SPSS. Most tests used in applied psychology are administered using a Hungarian national standard, and serious efforts have been made to improve them psychometrically.

Governmental support of psychological research comes in three basic forms. First, the research establishments and medical and educational units belong to different state-run institutional systems. The basic budget of these institutions is one form of state funding. During recent years, however, two other sources have become more important. Psychological research units take part in several nationwide governmental projects (e.g., on the cause and prevention of deviant behavior). The third form is through grants obtained through competitive grant systems administered by the Hungarian Academy of Sciences and other ministries.

Psychology as a profession has become visible and accepted by the general public mainly during the 1970s and 1980s. Mass communication, in which leading researchers and practitioners promote the science and profession, and the activity of the practice-oriented guidance centers have contributed to a positive public image. It is one of a helping profession that is mainly concerned with the well-being of the individual. To the general public, the prototypical psychologist is a clinician dealing with minor behavioral and adaptation problems.

General and Personality Psychology

General psychology is one of the leading fields of psychological research in Hungary. Three basic features of this research should be emphasized: a reliance on comparative and physiological models, the rise of cognitive psychology, and the combination of personality theory with general psychology.

Though cognitive psychology is the strongest single part of Hungarian general psychology, for most researchers it does not lead to a sterile cognitivism. In the comparative domain, the work of the late Lajos Kardos (1899–1985) stands out as the most relevant contribution. Kardos, a long-term doyen of experimental psychology in Hungary, developed a general theory on the origin of mental life (Kardos, 1986). In his experimental research he dealt with the issue of animal memory and its structural differences compared to human memory. Using sophisticated versions of maze learning and discrimination tasks, he proved that the memory image of animals is a concrete one with specific local signs to support spatial orientation. This is radically different from the more schematic human memory organization. In this sense, his research belongs to the Tolmanian cognitive-map tradition.

In the area of psychophysiology of cognitive phenomena, some studies also touch on evolutionary issues. Endre Grastyán of the Medical School at Pécs, on the basis of his research on mechanisms of conditioning and reinforcement in animals, has developed a cognitive theory of elementary learning phenomena. According to his view, the most crucial moment in any learning is learning how to orient in the environment. The executive phases of learning are preceded by an orientational-cognitive phase. In this theory the classic orienting response known from the studies on Pavlovian conditioning takes on a new significance: that of relating classical learning theory to contemporary cognitive views.

Most of the psychophysiological research done at the Section for General Psychology at the Institute for Psychology of the Hungarian Academy of Sciences deals with human cognitive phenomena. Several people work on electrophysiological correlates of visual processing, semantic processes, and word recognition (see Kardos, Pléh, & Marton, 1978). At the Department of General Psychology of Lóránd Eötvös University, creativity research has been one of the basic topics (Kardos, Pléh, & Barkóczi, 1987). Lately, this line of research has been related to the study of interhemispheric differences in cognitive processing and the mechanisms of intuition. Other psychophysiologically related research at the two universities deals with the psychophysiology of hypnosis, visceral conditioning, and the regulation of single motor-unit activity.

Some clearly cognitive work is done at Eötvös University. Work on sentence processing is done in a comparative psycholinguistic perspective—for example, comparison of sentence processing in Hungarian with that in other languages (see MacWhinney, Pléh, & Bates, 1985). The study of memory development and its relationship to semantic development, problem solving, heuristics, and cognitive-neurolinguistics supplement the picture.

One further feature of general psychology in Hungary is the close relationship between research on personality and individual differences on the one hand and the framework provided by contemporary general psychology on the other. Specifically, there is a strong tradition of studying the biological bases of personality and their relationship to cognitive styles. The framework is provided by the extraversion-introversion theories of Hans Eysenck and his followers and, more recently, by the framework of sensation seeking, as proposed by Zuckermann.

Social Psychology

Social psychology research reemerged in Hungary in the early 1960s after a 15-year interruption. Earlier research traditions concerned mostly the study of interpersonal relations and group processes, but during the 1960s Hungarian psychologists started working on the thematic repertoire of virtually the entire field. The different research groups active today represent varied points of view. Currently, social psychological research is based in six institutions. In the Institute for Psychology of the Hungarian Academy of Sciences three groups are engaged in social psychological research.

The Research Group for Cognitive Social Psychology works in a social information-processing framework. The major topics investigated by this group are structure and functions of social schemata, cognitive organization of the self, future orientation, and value orientation. From this perspective it explores the problems of dialogic organization and text processing, including literary text processing (see Halász, 1987). Several projects have been carried out in cooperation with international scholars from the USA, the USSR, and West Germany.

The main concern of the Group for Decision Research is risk perception. The group conducts comparative studies on factors influencing risk perception in different cultures. Another leading topic is the cascadic character of group decision making.

The Research Group for Social Issues deals mainly with social identity problems. Recently, the group launched a project on the consequences of the Holocaust for the second-generation Jewish population in Hungary.

The Research Group for Educational Social Psychology pursues a program aimed at discovering the implicit power relations in school and within classes. Members of this group have developed a new method of sociometry based on a theory that treats social psychological processes as analogous to economic processes, that is, it concerns the allocation of the resources of social psychological variables as they infiltrate a group. A similar project, based on a "hidden curriculum" theoretical background, is pursued at the Institute for Education and Instruction Research of the Ministry of Education.

Social psychological research at Lóránd Eötvös University, Budapest, is based in two departments. The Department of Social, Developmental, and Educational Psychology also follows a cognitive orientation. Besides the applied aspects of studying social psychological processes in the school, the major research emphasis is on social categorization. One specific aspect of this research is the investigation of the perception and evaluation of history. This project is carried out in cooperation with American researchers. The department also takes part in international risk-perception studies.

The Group of Social Psychology at the Department of Sociology studies problems of national identity and national stereotypes. It focuses on the relation of the Hungarian population to the present social system and the surrounding countries.

There is a long research tradition in social psychology in the Mass Communication Research Center, Budapest. The studies deal with the effects of mass media in a wide range from political attitudes to rumors and from implicit messages to family life.

Three relatively new units of social psychological research are at different universities. The Group of Social Psychology at the Lajos Kossuth University, Debrecen, deals with social psychological factors in the etiology of social deviance. Communication studies, particularly concerning literary communication, are conducted at the Institute for Communication of the Janus Pannonius University, Pécs. Finally, a unit of political psychology has been established at the University of the Hungarian Socialist Workers Party, Budapest.

Developmental and Educational Psychology

Rich traditions arose in developmental and educational psychology between the two world wars. Since the 1960s these traditions have developed further and new research areas have opened. Research on children's thinking has been done in all three institutions dealing with developmental studies. At the Institute for Psychology of the Hungarian Academy of Sciences the Research Group for Educational Psychology has extended this research into learning strategies. The Department of Social, Developmental, and Educational Psychology of the Lóránd Eötvös University, Budapest, is concerned with the relationship between the development of thinking and the development of creativity and with the integration of studies on thinking and communication. The Department of Developmental and Educational Psychology of the Lajos Kossuth University, Debrecen, is engaged in applying research on the development of thought to educational practice.

Beyond these cognitive developmental studies, each institution has specific orientations. At the Institute of Psychology of the Hungarian Academy of Sciences leading topics are aggression research and childrearing practices. Studies are also in progress concerning the problems of gifted children and of children in disadvantaged situations (e.g., deviant families, divorced parents). One longitudinal study has used several developmental measures on a representative sample over a 10-year period. At Lóránd Eötvös University some researchers study early cognitive development in terms of the specifics of mental representations and transformations, while others focus on the development of social competence. At Lajos Kossuth University a strong educational psychological orientation prevails with particular stress on the problems of instruction.

Psychologists in several institutions work with the original developmental psychological theory of Ferenc Mérei, which is based on the Wallonian genetic social psychology and focuses on children's interpersonal relations. Mérei (1909–86) was one of the leading figures of contemporary Hungarian psychology. Between 1928 and 1934 he was a student of Henri Wallon in Paris. After returning home, he worked with Leopold Szondi and began his theory of social determinants of child development. During the Second World War, as a Jew, he was forced to work in a labor camp. His foremost known work on shared experience was published in 1947 in Hungary and translated in 1949 into English (Mérei, 1949). This article was republished in several anthologies of social psychology. After an interruption of his activity for political reasons, he continued to publish significant contributions in social psychology, developmental psychology, and clinical psychology.

Clinical Psychology

Clinical psychology in Hungary has a relatively long history. Its recent developments can be traced to two distinct traditions. The first is the Hungarian tradition of psychoanalysis. Through the works of Sándor Ferenczi, one of the founders of the psychoanalytic movement, Hungarian psychiatrists and psychologists became involved very early in the psychoanalytic movement. This tradition has produced internationally known figures such as Géza Róheim, who was among the first to apply psychoanalytic thought to cultural anthropology; Franz Alexander, foremost representative of the psychoanalytic approach to psychosomatic medicine; and David Rapoport, one of the first figures in the psychoanalytic movement who tried to approach psychoanalytic thought as an experimental psychology. The list of Hungarian psychoanalysts who became famous in the West is rather long. Nevertheless, despite the official neglect between the wars and the active ideological opposition toward psychoanalysis in the 1950s, the Hungarian version of psychoanalysis managed to survive within Hungary itself. The foremost representative of the so-called Budapest school was the late Imre Hermann (1889–1984). His main contributions to psychoanalytic theory were his conceptualization of the psychoanalytic method (Hermann, 1933), his theory of human instincts with an emphasis on clinging as a separate instinct, and the use of data from comparative psychology to support psychoanalytic theory. He also contributed to the psychoanalytic literature on scientific creativity with his studies on Fechner, the Hungarian mathematician Bólyai, and Darwin (Hermann, 1980).

Recently, internationally accredited psychoanalysts have numbered in the dozens in Hungary. Psychoanalytic thought, however, is much more prevalent than the number of trained psychoanalysts would suggest. "Dynamic psychological aspects" prevail in most of Hungarian clinical psychology.

The second tradition of clinical psychology can be traced to the work of Paul Ranschburg, a pioneer of experimental psychology in Hungary. His laboratory started a tradition at the turn of the century in which experimental, clinical, and psychometric work was combined in the study of children, with a special emphasis on developmental problems and their correction.

Today a clinical psychologist in Hungary has an MA degree and frequently a special clinical license as well and has participated in several extracurricular courses on different therapies, from autogenic training to psychodrama and various group therapies. The prototypical clinical practitioner still works in a psychiatry ward or a mental institution. Everyday work there is partly diagnostic in nature. Different performance and projective methods are used for this task. There is much more reliance on projective methods than in the Anglo-Saxon world (the Rorschach is the most frequently used personality test), although recently, questionnaires (e.g., MMPI, Eyseneck) have been added to the repertory. Because of this fact, considerable psychometric research is conducted on projective methods. Psychologists usually participate in psychotherapy in these institutions, often with psychiatrists. Various types of group therapy are employed.

Recently, the clinical approach has spread to nonpsychiatric medical fields and to guidance centers as well. In child guidance centers psychologists work with pediatricians and teachers, combining a clinical-therapeutic and an adviser attitude in treating problem children (see Kardos, Pléh, & Popper, 1987).

Industrial Psychology

The second major employer of applied psychologists is industry. The introduction of industrial psychology into Hungary began with Taylorism during the 1930s. Psychotechnics and the human relations orientation emerged only in the early 1960s. Recently, the leading orientations have been ergonomics and organizational psychology. In the last few years several manager training schools have been established which have adopted various programs developed in industrialized countries. Psychologists' expertise has also been used in traditional fields such as the selection of labor and management personnel and the improvement of working conditions.

Bibliography

Halász, L. (Ed.). (1987). *Literary discourse: Aspects of cognitive and social psychological approaches*. Berlin: Walter de Gruyter.

Hermann, I. (1933). *Die Psychoanalyse als methode*. Vienna: Internationaler Psychoanalytischer Verlag.

Hermann, I. (1980). *Parallélismes*. Paris: Denoel.

Kardos, L. (1986). *The origin of neuropsychological information*. Budapest: Akadémiai.

Kardos, L., Pléh, Cs., & Barkóczi, I. (Eds.). (1987). *Studies in creativity*. Budapest: Akadémiai.

Kardos, L., Pléh, Cs., & Hunyadi, Gy. (Eds.). (1980). *Attitudes, interaction and personality*. Budapest: Akadémiai.

Kardos, L., Pléh, Cs., & Marton, M. L. (Eds.). (1978). *Problems of information processing and perceptual organization*. Budapest: Akadémiai.

Kardos, L., Pléh, Cs., & Popper, P. (Eds.). (1987). *Studies in clinical psychodiagnostics and psychotherapy*. Budapest: Akadémiai.

MacWhinney, B., Pléh, Cs., & Bates, E. (1985). The development of sentence interpretation in Hungarian. *Cognitive Psychology, 17*, 178–200.

Mérei, F. (1949). Group leadership and institutionalisation. *Human Relations, 2*, 23–39.

20 / India

MOHAN C. JOSHI

Mohan C. Joshi (born 1933) received his PhD from Banaras Hindu University in 1960. A specialist in psychological testing and clinical psychology, he authored Neo-Freudism *(1964) in Hindi and has constructed, standardized, and supervised research on general mental ability, the Multiphasic Personality Inventory, problem checklists, study habits, home and school environment scales, dynamic misperception tests, mental health potentialities, and quality of life scales.*

Joshi was the founding editor of the Indian Psychological Review *and president of the Indian Psychological Association (1984). He is professor at the University of Jodhpur, where he was also dean of the Faculty of Arts, Education, and Social Sciences, 1975–78 and 1982–85.*

The educational systems of Third World countries are a reflection of colonial interests. These systems do not emphasize a rural orientation (although the bulk of their population is rural), nor do they emphasize indigenous culture. Even after 40 years of independence India has not developed an effective educational system. The system remains academic, formalistic, and urban-oriented in addition to being merely reproductive and conforming. A Western type of education was reinforced because it was instrumental in acquiring positions of power in politics and administration. The leaders or freedom fighters were educated in the West, and similarly educated natives received higher positions in the administration on the departure of the colonial administrators.

In the areas of basic science technology, and, to a great extent, medicine, there are few cultural differentials. But in the social sciences in general and psychology in particular, there is a multitude of differences. There cannot be one cross-cultural theory, because each culture designs personality in a unique way. Third World psychologists have not been able yet to recognize their unique identity in their respective cultures. Instead, what goes on in the universities is a formal routine following in the footprints of Western

M. L. Mathur, vice-chancellor of the University of Jodhpur, generously sanctioned financial help for resource collection. L. K. Pathak, R. P. Singh, and A. K. Malik helped in the analysis of data. I am grateful to them all.

psychologists. Little consideration is given to the relevance of problems investigated. The focus of many Indian psychologists is to work on problems that are not yet out-of-date for the Western journals of psychology. The need for recognition at the international level is the main motivation of Indian psychologists who wish to acquire the mantle of leadership. They have not bothered to promote the professional growth of the discipline by making it indigenous and healthy, breathing in its own ethos. Individual attainments alone have been the goal of such psychologists.

Because of the history of this discipline in India, psychology has had little impact on society, policy planning, or even educational institutions, despite its immense potential for application in many fields. Yet it continues to be a popular undergraduate and postgraduate subject.

The work of the majority of Indian psychologists appears to be insensitive to the basic issues. Can contemporary Western theories, problems, and approaches be applied to Indian social matrices that are at the border between tradition and technological and economic progress? How is psychology to understand the changing social structure, the enforced and inevitable adaptation to modern times, the implications of newer values, the adoption of newer values, and the extent of resistance to the exploding alienation? Development and progress in the West have been sensitive to social needs, particularly throughout the history of modern psychology. It is disturbing to note that Indian psychologists have not recognized this reality. Instead, a scarecrow type of development of the discipline seems to have taken place. I am not advocating an unscientific or parochial discipline. Rather, scientific methodology must be applied to solve rampant problems rather than wasting efforts in providing supplementary data to affluent Western co-workers. I cannot agree with the four-phase development of psychology in India as Sinha (1986) explains it.

Education

Educationally, nearly 50 percent of the teacher-psychologists in a university department possess PhD degrees; the others hold master's degrees. In college departments the ratios lean more toward master's degrees rather than PhDs. In most of the progressive departments (i.e., those that have a particular emphasis on teaching quality and/or research contribution) there are usually foreign PhD teachers, mostly from the USA, Canada, and the UK. A smaller number of foreign-trained psychologists are scattered in other departments. The best ones are at the Utkal University (Orrisa) and Allahabad University (Uttar Pradesh). The departments of humanities and social sciences at the institutes of Bombay, Kanpur, Delhi, and Kharagpur also have strong faculties of foreign-trained psychologists, as do the organizational behavior faculties of the Indian Institutes of Management (Ahmedabad, Bangalore, and Calcutta). However, most psychologists possess a native education only.

A review of the *Universities Handbook*, published by the Association of Indian Universities (1985–86), and the *Commonwealth Universities Yearbook* published by the Association of Commonwealth Universities, London (1986), indicates that at present there are 160 institutions of higher education in India (including professional institutions of technology and engineering, medical, veterinary, and agricultural sciences). Among them are 81 universities or institutes that award degrees up to the PhD or DLitt in pyschology. These institutions are of three types: affiliating universities, residential-cum-affiliating universities, and residential universities. There are 20 affiliating universities. They have colleges under their jurisdictions which are governed by the state or under private management. Many of them do undergraduate and graduate teaching and supervision of PhD work. The university awards the degrees, but no department is run by the university itself. Residential-cum-affiliating universities have their own departments and set the syllabi for the colleges under their jurisdiction. The university has academic control over these colleges. There are 36 such universities. Finally, there are 25 residential universities. They have their own departments and may give academic affiliation to the colleges located in the same city only.

In terms of student strength, the affiliating universities cater to the largest number, followed by the residential-cum-affiliating ones. The residential universities have the smallest number of students. The exception is Delhi University, which has 65 constituent and 2 affiliated colleges in addition to its own departments.

Research and Practice

I sought firsthand information about faculty positions and research contributions from all the concerned universities by approaching the chairs of departments, the registrars (academic), and the vice-chancellors. Because the response was incomplete, however, the following account is based on secondary sources only. In a count of all the colleges, universities, and institutes offering psychology courses, it appears that there are about 5,000 psychologists in the country. In a few women's colleges females alone are employed, but in general the male:female ratio in the departments is about 5:2. One exception is Lucknow University, where the department has been composed of females only for approximately 15 years; the male senior teachers retired, and males could not compete with females among the new entrants. In general, in all university departments, female students have overtaken the males at the postgraduate level both in number and achievement, but most of them do not opt for a career.

The bulk of the psychological work in India emanates from the universities. Of course, psychologists also work in the institutes of agriculture, technology, management, and mental health and in the ministry of defense of the government of India. However, the typical work setting is academic and institutional. Provisions are available for different specialties, depending on the teachers' specialization. Among the current specialties are clinical, educational, guidance, industrial, organizational, personality, child, developmental, comparative, physiological, and criminal. The compulsory courses required, regardless of specialty, are experimental, social, and abnormal psychology, and history, contemporary systems, research methods and statistics, and testing.

Despite sporadic attempts made by practicing clinical psychologists, no legislation regarding licensure or certification has been instituted so far.

Many journals have been published by departments from time to time, but regular publication of the following alone has been able to stand the high cost of publication: *Indian Journal of Psychology, Psychological Studies, Indian Psychological Review, Indian Journal of Applied Psychology, Journal of Psychological Researches, Journal of Education and Psychology, Indian Journal of Clinical Psychology, Personality Study and Group Behavior, Manas, Psycholingua, Managerial Psychology, Asian Journal of Psychology, Advances in Psychology, Indian Journal of Current Psychological Research, Disabilities and Impairments,* and *The Mind.* In addition, most university departments subscribe to a few journals from the USA, Canada, the UK, and Japan, depending on their budgets.

Master's and research studies use mostly American books, followed by books from the UK. Teaching at the BA and MA level is done in regional languages in most universities. Though books in local languages are adequate for undergraduate teaching, there is a great scarcity of the same for MA studies. Except in universities and colleges in cosmopolitan cities, this situation has worsened.

Psychometric and laboratory instruments for conducting practical work are available, and resourceful departments import them. Library materials, laboratory equipment, and test quality and quantity vary with budgetary provisions, which are unequally distributed. The condition of the majority of the departments of colleges is far from satisfactory. Only at Allahabad, Bhubaneswar, Delhi, and Jodhpur are there microcomputers in the departments. But researchers have started using computer facilities available elsewhere. Only a few universities have centralized computer centers.

The University Grants Commission, the Indian Council of Medical Research, and the Indian Council of Social Science Research are the main agencies sponsoring research projects. These organizations are totally financed by the government and are autonomous in their workings, but their priorities are influenced by governmental perspectives.

The research work of Indian psychologists has been mostly of an academic orientation or of an orientation that uses problems, models, and concepts from contemporary Western work. Thus, the ordinary citizen is totally unaware of psychology. Even the elite class is blind to the immense potential of the subject. The blame falls on the shoulders of Indian psychologists who have so far avoided their professional responsibility to develop the discipline by nourishing it with the problems and solutions of their own society.

About 200 psychologists work in the various selection boards of the Ministry of Defense. They recruit cadets for training for commissions in the three wings of the defense forces. Their work is considered confidential and classified.

Some 35 to 40 clinical psychologists work in hospital or institute settings where psychiatrists and medical people dominate. There are no school psychologists in the schools, where nearly 50 percent of 10th- and 12th-grade students fail every year at their annual examination. Psychologists are employed in a few jails in the capital cities of the different states, yet their task and scope remain mostly unclear. Psychologists working in the Institutes of Management do undertake financially attractive and rewarding consultancy. They apply Western-based models to Indian conditions, in which trade unions (rather than the principles of scientific management) dictate practices.

There are three professional organizations, with members from different parts of the country: the Indian Psychological Association, the Indian Academy of Applied Psychology, and the Indian Association of Clinical Psychologists. These bodies were founded in 1925, 1963, and 1973, respectively. The Madras Psychological Society, founded in 1956, is an active, predominantly state-level body. But none of these has any control over professional problems or ethics. These vital professional responsibilities have been continuously overlooked. Publishing a journal and holding an annual conference have been the associations' only activities.

Contributions of Psychologists

In the work of Indian psychologists there is little indigenous philosophical and theoretical source of influence. As has been previously stressed, Indian psychology reacts to the lead from the West, although Hindu philosophy is richly interwoven with multiphasic psychological concepts and explanations. But a search for these concepts and investigations of the same are rare. A few scattered papers on Hindu psychological concepts such as types of personality, constitution, mental health, and abnormalities can be found. Recently, at Jodhpur University eight experimental studies were completed on TM (transcendental meditation). But there is no perceptible philosophical or theoretical wave of ideas flowing over this subcontinent. The Indian psychologist has yet to reach the maturity of being proactive.

During the period under review the following psychologists have been among those responsible for stimulating research work. S. Jalota, working in psychological testing, studied the general mental ability and multidimensional personality in Hindi, Nepali, Panjabi, Assamese, and Malayalam languages. His students have expanded on his research. This has led to preparation of general mental ability tests from primary to college levels in the respective languages and to a series of personality tests, all with proper standardization. This work was conducted at the Banaras Hindu University, Gorakhpur University, G. N. Dev University, Jodhpur University, R. S. University, and Gauhati University. Some of the researchers diversified the movement to include dynamic misperception, multiphasic diagnostics, health potentials, and scales of school and family environments.

D. Sinha founded the department at Allahabad and nourished it into the Centre for the Psychological Study of Social Changes and National Development. His team of teachers focused on applying theoretically sound social-psychological research to Indian problems. Intergeneration conflict, social deprivation, and cross-cultural dimensions were also studied under his leadership.

R. C. Tripathi is engaged in applied social psychological research. J. Pandey (1988) has recently published a three-volume review of current psychological work in India. Other teachers of this department are actively engaged in the broad area of social change and development.

R. Rath of Utkal University, like D. Sinha, founded a department that led to the establishment of a research institute, the Advanced Centre of Psychological Studies. Rath had primary interests in areas of educational psychology, but he encouraged investigation into physiological and social areas, too.

A. K. Singh of Ranchi University has been responsible for research on industrial psychology, modernity, and the psychology of prejudices.

L. B. Tripathi of Gorakhpur University has contributed significantly in the areas of social psychology (prolonged deprivation, religiosity, and "n" approval). His team of colleagues has focused on social areas.

Among the nonuniversity researchers, Udai Pareek is a distinguished scholar. He started as a lecturer in a teachers' training college but is recognized today as an outstanding management specialist. He has also worked on Rosenzweig's P. F. study on the Indian situation.

Delhi University has excellent researchers, but their interests are so varied that it is difficult to feel the impact of their contributions. A similar pattern is evident in most other university departments. A thematic cohesiveness and consistency of interests is generally missing, and as a result, a great deal of research work remains scattered.

S. Sharma, of Himachal Pradesh University, has done significant work in the areas of anxiety and stress. E. G. Parmeswaran, of Osmania University, initially conducted research in developmental psychology but has recently shifted to management. N. Y. Reddy and G. Reddy are other outstanding researchers from south India who are now concentrating in the area of managerial psychology.

M. C. Joshi has been interested in test development (cognitive, diagnostic, and projective) and personality characteristics in relation to childrearing practices across socioeconomic status and caste factors. Another area of investigation by him is TM vis-à-vis personality variables.

Current Trends

Since up-to-date data on all the publications from 1960 to 1987 could not be located despite considerable effort, the following sources were used to analyze current trends: PhD dissertations, periodic reviews of surveys of research in psychology sponsored by the Indian Council of Social Sciences (Mitra, 1972; Pareek, 1980), and Pandey's *Psychology in India* (1988).

The Association of Indian Universities (formerly the Inter-University Board of India) has published several volumes of bibliography of doctoral dissertations. Those dealing with social sciences are referred to here and cover the period from 1857 to 1984. The dissertation themes fall into 40 categories, listed in Table 20.1. The themes are reclassified under broad categories in Table 20.2.

Surveys of research in psychology have been sponsored by the Indian Council of Social Sciences Research (ICSSR) from time to time. The first was

TABLE 20.1
PhD Dissertation Theme Areas in India, 1960–84 (N = 754)

Area	%
Personality	15.65
Educational psychology	9.28
Child psychology	9.02
Clinical (diagnostic testing, disorders, mental deficiency, psycho-somatics, aggression, projective technique, behavior therapy)	8.89
Industrial & organizational behavior	7.03
Adolescent psychology	5.97
Sensory & perception	5.31
Intelligence & testing	4.51
Creativity	4.24
Abnormal (drug abuse & criminal behavior)	3.85
Emotions & feelings	3.45
Attitude measurement	3.05
Comparative psychology	2.25
Psychology of women	2.12
Social psychology	1.99
Interest testing	1.59
Memory	1.50
Adult psychology	1.46
Miscellaneous (environmental, subconscious, parareligiosity, palmistry, response set, evolutional)	1.46
Learning	1.33
Physiological	1.33
Aptitude	1.19
Motivation	1.19
Concept formation	0.93
Childrearing & personality	0.80
Cognition	0.66

edited by Mitra (1972), who analyzed the different areas of work from 1961 to 1970. There is a high degree of parallelism in the research output by area during the first 5 and last 5 years of the decade of the 1960s. A rho coefficient of 0.867 ($p<.01$) also attests to the consistency in the trend. It may be recalled that many new universities and hence departments of psychology were started during this decade and yet the earlier trends continued.

TABLE 20.2

Broad Areas of Psychological Research in India, 1960–84

Area	%
Personality correlates	15.65
Developmental	15.51
Measurement	10.48
Experimental	9.68
Educational	9.28
Clinical	8.89
Industrial & organizational behavior	7.03
Social	5.04
Creativity	4.24
Abnormal	3.85
Comparative	2.25
Psychology of women	2.12
Others	5.98

The survey of research in psychology between 1971 and 1976 has been edited by Pareek (1980) (Table 20.3). The 1980 survey provided a broader classification of the areas of research. It also identified newer areas of interest such as organizational variables, voting behavior, social change, population, family planning, poverty, inequality, and environmental psychology. However, when the whole analysis is condensed into broad specialties, it is revealed that (1) clinical and abnormal psychology contributed 27.6 percent; (2) social psychology (poverty, inequality, and change), 14.6 percent; (3) experimental psychology, 9.8 percent; (4) organizational psychology, 14.4 percent; (5) industrial psychology, 13.9 percent; (6) political process studies, 6.3 percent; (7) educational psychology, 4.2 percent; (8) developmental psychology, 4.0 percent; and (9) theory and methodology, 1.0 percent. Unfortunately, the survey data were found to suffer from a serious, unavoidable error: namely, the same study may be referred to in different areas. There are many such repeated uses of the same study in different contexts.

The earlier surveys adopted broad thematic units for their work. The latest one, sponsored by the same organization (ICSSR) under the editorship of Janak Pandey, resulted in a three-volume survey entitled *Psychology in India: The State of the Art* (Pandey, 1988). A "more focused treatment of certain selected areas of theoretical, conceptual, and methodological importance,

TABLE 20.3
Research in Psychology in India, 1971–76 (N = 1,784)

Area	%
Culture & personality	1.01
Developmental processes	4.02
Cognitive processes	3.03
Learning	2.30
Remembering, forgetting, & problem solving	4.43
Pathology & society	5.04
Psychoses & neuroses	5.16
Body-mind interaction (psychosomatic)	2.69
Mental retardation	2.07
Drug abuse	0.78
Criminal & delinquent behavior	1.23
Social aspects of illness	1.96
Emotional problems of children	1.07
Counseling & therapy	5.21
Behavior therapy	2.41
Assessment	3.03
Organizational structure, climate, & process	3.92
External environment	4.20
Organizational leadership	2.07
Intergroup and industrial relationships	1.12
Job satisfaction, productivity, & quality of working life	3.98
Organizational development	4.20
Work in educational settings	4.20
Work in industrial settings	8.80
Political process & behavior	0.90
Process of democratization	0.84
Voting behavior & campaigning	4.58
Environmental psychology	1.57
Psychology of inequality	4.48
Psychology of population and family planning	2.68
Social change (macrolevel)	4.32
Social change (microlevel)	1.87
Psychological intervention: theory & methodology	0.95

and of striking empirical topicality" is the frame of reference. It also attempts to evaluate "the extent to which psychology has been responsive to Indian sociocultural context and reality" (Pandey, 1988, p. 9). The three volumes have 1,188, 1,074, and 1,055 references, respectively, pertaining to the work of Indian psychologists during the 1977–86 period. As indicated, this survey concentrates on "selected areas" only. Table 20.4 presents a summary of the major areas of research covered.

Space limitations prevent a detailed analysis of the three volumes edited by Pandey. During the 1976–86 period Indian psychologists appear to have been more productive than before, with more departments coming into existence as well. The areas of interests have widened. The use of reformulated conceptual approaches to social problems is in evidence. The increasing search for newer conceptual approaches in Indian work in the West resulted in experimenting with attribution and cognitive psychology approaches. The impact of the community psychological approach has stimulated Indian psychologists to investigate the influence of family and community presses on various forms of psychopathology. Gender susceptibility to mental stress has also been investigated. Attempts at understanding stress in terms of the Hindu philosophy of Yoga, Gita, and Ayurveda (Hindu medical system) are also found during the 1980s. An extensive search for the parameters of social, religious, and caste prejudices has been undertaken, and the influence of age, education, and residential background has also been investigated. But few studies deal with interventions to ameliorate or remove prejudices.

Research in communication and influence processes has been attempted. Family planning, adopter's psychology, the characteristics of farmers adopting innovative farming techniques, and psychological effects of crowding (Jain, 1987) have also been studied. With the establishment of an Advanced Centre for Psychological Study of Social Changes and National Development at the Allahabad University, concerted efforts are being made in this direction at both macro- and microlevels. Newer variables have attracted the attention of some researchers in practically all areas of psychology. But the bulk of research remains rooted in the pattern of Western studies, however cleverly one may try to remodel the analysis and terminology. In the 1977–86 selective survey only studies readily available to reviewers are mentioned. No attempts were made to collect information from all possible sources.

What is surprising is that work reported in earlier reviews enters into subsequent reviews also. That which was not included in the first and second reviews is excluded in the third review as well. The unpublished work of many institutions remains unrepresented because no attempts were made to obtain information widely. The state of the art appears to be promising, but abrupt grafting in social science research is not likely to lead to a healthy

TABLE 20.4

Major Areas of Psychological Research, 1977–86 (N = 3,317)

Area	%
Personality & Mental Processes	
Assessment	6.79
Developmental	7.54
Personality	3.92
Stress & anxiety	9.89
Perceptual & cognitive processes	3.14
Higher mental processes	4.55
Total	35.83
Basic & Applied Social Psychology	
Attitudes & social cognition	3.53
Social influence processes	3.71
Applied social psychology	7.99
Intragroup relations & social tensions	4.13
Dynamics of rural development	3.38
Social psychology of education	9.65
Total	32.39
Organizational Behavior & Mental Health	
Job attitudes	6.63
Organizational effectiveness	8.80
(a) Total	15.43
Mental health	7.54
Mental illness & treatment	8.83
(b) Total	16.37

Source. Data from *Psychology in India: The State of the Art*, 3 vols., edited by J. Pandey, 1988, New Delhi: Sage Publications.

self-sufficient growth of the discipline, particularly with respect to the choice of issues to be investigated.

Indian work shows a gradual trend toward the hypothesis testing level, although exploratory studies still persist in large numbers. Absence of professionalism has led to a wild growth of psychological research in India. In most universities there is no stability or consistency in interests in research problems. The absence of an external effective evaluative agency has also led many researchers to produce what appears to be spurious research. Lack of prompt communication has led to duplication of research within the country. Despite the fact that research methodology is a required course at the MA level, the basic principles of study design and appropriate application of statistics are usually overlooked. These problems require prompt resolution. Only then can a healthy, well-nourished, and socially sensitive discipline emerge; only then will it provide opportunities for the large number of psychologists who appear to be at the crossroads of confusion, ennui, expediency, and soaring individualistic aspirations. Only sheer philistinism can explain the absence of any meaningful effort to recover a psychological identity, without which it will not be possible to redeem the present and plan the future of psychology in India.

The present situation of cynicism is a projection of the wider political culture that has prevailed since 1960. Regional and local forces are employed to gain political and economic power. Even on the floor of the national parliament an M.P. of the ruling party declared, without reprimands, that everything is fair in politics. Similar winds have been blowing over the academic institutions. National professional bodies are for name's sake only. Regional societies are more active. All these sociopolitical cross-currents have led to deficiencies in the overall development of the field of psychology. However, many lamps of promise are visible in some institutions whose collective efforts may enlighten the discipline and guide its steady natural growth if they expand from self-centeredness to other-centeredness. Otherwise growth is likely to remain vertical and scattered in a few places only.

Original contributions can be made by Indian psychologists if they rediscover the rich Hindu philosophical literature and pick up the analysis of the theory of *karma* to explain motivation, the resolution of anxiety, and the necessity of acting in a desirable way to realize one's potential and thereby happiness in life on the basis of Gita. Potential topics include personality expansion on the basis of Yoga, Buddhism, and other philosophical approaches, as well as with TM; study of personality and constitution on the *trigunas* and *tridosh* of Ayurveda (Hindu medical system); the concepts of nonviolent and nonaggressive reactions to frustration; the Hindu way of life, universal citizenship, and the process of attaining psychological *nirvana*, to mention a few. It will be in the utmost interest of academic and applied research if explorations of personality of Indian people together with those of various subcultural milieus could be undertaken. This type of work would bring out the basic as well as the other clusters of personality patterns stemming from varying socialization practices. The collective cultural psyche of the Indian psychologist comprehends these concepts in their proper senses and hence he or she can initiate fruitful research by applying scientific methodology.

Bibliography

Association of Commonwealth Universities. (1986). *Commonwealth universities yearbook, 1986*. London: Author.

Association of Indian Universities. (1979). *Bibliography of doctoral dissertations: Social sciences, 1970–75*. New Delhi: Author.

Association of Indian Universities. (1982). *Bibliography of doctoral dissertations: Social sciences, 1976–80*. New Delhi: Author.

Association of Indian Universities. (1984). *Bibliography of doctoral dissertations: Social sciences, 1981–83*. New Delhi: Author.

Association of Indian Universities. (1985). *Universities handbook, 1985–86*. New Delhi: Author.

Association of Indian Universities. (1987). *Bibliography of doctoral dissertations: Social sciences, 1983–84*. New Delhi: Author.

Association of Indian Universities. (1988). *Bibliography of doctoral dissertations: Social sciences, 1984–85*. New Delhi: Author.

Inter-University Board of India. (1974). *Bibliography of doctoral dissertations: Social sciences, 1857–1970*. New Delhi: Author.

Jain, U. (1987). *The psychological consequences of crowding*. New Delhi: Sage Publications.

Mitra, S. K. (Ed.). (1972). *A survey of research in psychology*. Bombay: Popular Prakashan.

Pandey, J. (Ed.). (1988). *Psychology in India: The state of the art* (Vols. 1–3). New Delhi: Sage Publications.

Pareek, U. (Ed.). (1980). *A survey of researches in psychology, 1971–76* (Parts 1 & 2). Bombay: Popular Prakashan.

Sinha, D. (1986). *Psychology in a third world country: The Indian experience*. New Delhi: Sage Publications.

21 / Iran

IRAJ AYMAN & ROYA AYMAN

Iraj Ayman pursued his postgraduate studies at the Universities of Nottingham and Edinburgh in the UK and the University of Southern California, USA, where he received his PhD in personnel psychology. He later completed postdoctoral studies at Harvard University.

Ayman served as professor and head, Department of Psychology, and director of the Institute of Educational Research, National University of Teacher Education, as well as president of the National Institute of Psychology, Tehran, Iran. More recently he has been research associate at the University of Chicago; chief, Educational Management Service, UNESCO Regional Office for Asia and the Pacific; and chief, Section for Training of Educational Personnel, UNESCO, Paris, among other positions. He has published more than 40 articles and books and has developed and standardized nine psychological tests for use in Iran. His editorial positions include service on psychology journals in Iran, Pakistan, Japan, and Africa. Ayman is director of Academic Affairs, Landegg Academy, and director of the Institute of International Education and Development, Switzerland.

Roya Ayman received her PhD in social/organizational/cross-cultural psychology from the University of Utah in 1983. Her specialties include leadership, cross-cultural psychology and international management, organizational development, and program evaluation. Her publications and professional presentations cover a wide range but have focused mostly on issues of management. She has conducted numerous management training sessions in both the USA and Europe. While at the National Institute for Psychology in Tehran, she assisted in personnel selection, conducted validation studies, and developed personnel profiles. She has also translated several books into Persian. Ayman is associate professor of psychology at the Illinois Institute of Technology, Chicago, USA.

Historical Background

Psychology, in the classic literature of Persia, was known as the "science of the spirit" (*Ilmul-Rouh*) or the "knowledge of the mind" (*Ilmunnafs*). Though closely associated with philosophy and considered an essential and integral part of philosophical studies, it was recognized as an independent field of knowledge.

Pre-Islamic Persian literature contained ideas and references that suggest there was an interest in the study of the mind and its development. However, it is difficult to document a claim that any specific knowledge was classified as psychology before the 10th century, when references to a specific field dealing with the knowledge of the mind began to appear in Persian classics.

The Islamic era, which began in the 7th century A.D., witnessed more evidence of psychological thinking and studies. A series of world-famous scientists and philosophers appeared in Iran. They not only studied and commented on the works of such Greek philosophers as Plato and Aristotle, but enriched and expanded the available knowledge of the human mind and human conduct. The most prominent of these scholars was Avicenna (980–1037). His writings overshadowed all earlier works and heavily influenced writings up to the 18th century, not only in Iran and the Arab countries but in Europe as well (Ghani, 1935).

If we trace Iran's modern psychological literature to its roots, we can conclude that ancient Iranian scholars were concerned with psychology's theoretical and metaphysical framework as well as with its practical and applied aspects. Numerous writings describe how human behavior can be predicted and controlled. Such works as *Kalileh va Demneh* and *Siasatnameh* have gained international significance and reputation. These essays were based on observations of everyday human behavior and interpersonal interaction. It is interesting to note that the applied aspect of this literature was especially important to kings, princes, court ministers, and politicians in ancient Iran.

The practice of composing behavioral guidebooks for kings and rulers can be traced back to the common culture of the Aryans and the available classical works in Sanskrit. The famous book *Kalile va Demneh*, (produced in India about 600 B.C.; the present Persian text was prepared around A.D. 1143), an ancient metaphor depicting day-to-day human behavior, is based on some of the same assumptions and premises as 20th-century behavioral psychology. This philosophical treatment and standard-setting approach to the study of the human mind and action remained unchanged in Iran for many centuries. The experimental approach to the study of psychology, which in Europe was pioneered by Wundt and flourished in the opening decades of 20th century (Watson, 1971), did not penetrate Iran and was not introduced in the Iranian colleges and seminaries until the 1930s (Hushiyar, 1938).

Contemporary Psychology

At the beginning of the 20th century, and especially during the years before World War I, some Iranian students were sent to Europe for advanced studies. Most were sent to France and Germany to study education and teacher training. In the 1920s and 1930s, when they returned, some of these students were employed as faculty members in the first teacher training college in Iran (Daneshsaraye'Aali). This small group of professionals, with a few French professors, introduced psychology as an independent subject in the curriculum of the teacher training college. By World War II some books and articles published in Persian had introduced psychology as a new discipline in the departments of philosophy and education.

During the 1930s the National Teachers' College (Daneshsaraye'Aali) offered psychology courses and training for students in the Department of Sciences at the University of Tehran. These courses were taught by Iranian scholars trained in Europe and the United States. Special acknowledgment should be given to the pioneering work and efforts of Reza Zadeh Safaq, Assadullah Bijan, A. A. Siyassi, and M. B. Hushiyar. The first two (trained in Germany and the United States, respectively) introduced psychology courses at the National Teachers' College, but it was Siyassi and Hushiyar (trained in France and Germany, respectively) who formally established this discipline. It should also be noted that P. N. Khanlari, who later became a highly respected scholar in Persian literature, produced the first introductory text on psychology in the Persian language. The first standard college textbook was published by Siyassi (1936). Hushiyar (1938) established the first psychological laboratory and was the author of the first Iranian experimental psychology textbook.

Applied Psychology

The 1950s brought the first practice of applied psychology outside the activities of Iran's universities. In 1953 Iraj Ayman established the Testing and Vocational Guidance Unit at the U. S. Technical Operation Mission in Tehran, Iran. This unit introduced batteries of tests and other psychological services. By 1955 it was a full-fledged research and service operation called Personnel Management and Research Center (PMRC) and was affiliated with the University of Tehran.

This center successfully introduced psychological testing and measurement and also guidance services (PMRC, 1954–1959). In just 5 years PMRC carried out more than a thousand projects, developed many psychological tests, and produced Iran's first professional psychological publications. At the end of the 1950s applied psychology was established as a useful, much-needed activity (Ayman, 1963, 1977; PMRC, 1954–1959).

Training of Psychologists

In 1959 Iraj Ayman initiated formal training of psychologists when he established Iran's first psychology department at the National Teachers' College in Tehran. This independent program provided a BA degree in psychology and an MA degree in psychological measurement and educational guidance. In the next decade similar departments were created at other universities (Ayman, 1966, 1977).

By 1979 10 colleges and universities offered BA degrees in psychology and 5 of them offered MA degrees in various psychological specialties. Most of these university programs were oriented toward educational psychology, clinical psychology, and tests and measurement. Each had a psychology laboratory and a small faculty of psychologists trained in Europe and the United States (Ayman, 1966, 1977).

In the 1970s, in addition to special programs in psychology, the inclusion of psychology courses in different university curricula gained wider acceptance. Introductory courses were offered as part of general studies, and special courses were taught at medical schools, teachers' colleges, army training centers, and in such new programs as journalism and public communication.

The teaching of psychology was heavily influenced by its parent discipline, philosophy. Most of the teaching consisted of classroom lectures, reading assignments, papers, and essay-type examinations. Some programs included demonstrations of experiments, testing, interviewing, and field trips. Psychology's practical and experimental aspects received inadequate emphasis, largely because qualified staff and faculty were scarce. This limitation resulted in inadequate professional training for graduates. Beginning in the 1970s, because of the growing demand for applied psychologists, the practical orientation in psychology training started to gain attention.

Most psychology classes and training programs were conducted in Persian. Senior and graduate students were sometimes required to use foreign texts, but all their papers were written in Persian (Ayman, 1966, 1977). Among the specialized libraries devoted to psychology, those at the Institute of Psychology of the Faculty of Arts and Humanities of the University of Tehran and at the Pahlavi University of Shiraz were relatively well supplied with periodicals published in the West and adequately stocked with an appropriate selection of texts in foreign languages, especially English.

To educate Iranian psychologists effectively, Iran's schools needed psychological literature in the Persian language, but such literature was limited (Hashemi, 1971). Since 1979 some texts have been translated and published, enriching the body of literature available in Persian. Recently, Ahadi (1988) described 956 titles of published books in Persian on various areas of psychology. Most are directed translations or are based on Western publications, theories, and research. However, 7 of these books seem to be original works incorporating empirical research or essays on Iranians' behaviors or attitudes. Thus, more than 1,000 titles are now available in the Persian language, although they are not proportionately distributed among various fields of psychology. In addition, none of the aforementioned bibliographical works is a complete and comprehensive list of Persian publications covering the whole field of psychology.

Closely related to this limitation is the problem of the lack of Persian equivalents for many psychological terms. Various translators and authors have prepared lexicons as appendices to their works. In addition, a few authors have developed small dictionaries of psychological terms (see Ayman, 1958; Done et al., 1960; Ordobady, 1958; Shoarinejad, 1965; Bahrami et al., 1967; Sultanifar, 1977; Mansur, 1978; Tafazzuli, 1985; Ashuri and Shakibapour, no date; all cited in Ahadi, 1988). More recently, Shoarinejad (1986) has published a greatly expanded version of his dictionary, which includes 4,700 entries.

Psychological Research

A research program began in 1953 when the Vocational Guidance Testing Unit was established (Ayman, 1969). However, most research efforts were restricted to developing and conducting tests. The unit occasionally conducted survey-type research projects, but these were by-products of its main activities.

The surge of psychology research that started at the Personnel Management and Research Center (PMRC) was soon followed by research at the National Institute of Psychology (NIP) and the Institute for Educational Research and Studies (IERS). Iraj Ayman planned and established these institutes and served as executive director of NIP (1958–78) and director of IERS (1963–69). Psychology departments at various universities also carried out research. The Universities of Pahlavi and Tehran led the way in original and applied research.

Psychology researchers were active in both educational and noneducational settings. Education and psychology studies were carried out at the Institute of Educational Research at the National Teachers' College; the Institute of Psychology at the Faculty of Arts and Humanities of the University of Tehran; and the Department of Psychology, Human Behavior, and Education at the Universities of Shiraz, Ahvaz, Isfahan, Tabriz, and Mahshad. Until 1980 psychological research outside the universities was mainly conducted by the NIP in Tehran (established 1958), the first institution devoted to applied psychological services and research. It was confiscated and dissolved by the present regime in Iran in 1980. Many other institutions involved in social and psychology studies within or outside the universities have suffered similar treatment since 1980.

Before 1979 there were psychological testing centers in such governmental organizations as the Civil Service Organization, the armed forces, and the Ministries of Education and of Science and Higher Education (Ayman, 1969, 1977). At present the only active testing center is the one attached to the Ministry of Science and Culture, which conducts university entrance examinations.

Before the change of regime, professors engaged their students in surveys and governmental projects. The Tehran School of Social Work and Tehran Girls' College (now called Al-Zahra) were particularly successful in such projects.

In 1964 IERS started an experimental program in which psychologists received grants to conduct independent psychological research projects. This program was successful, and other institutions soon followed this practice. Various government agencies started awarding research grants for studies directly related to psychology and other disciplines. Between 1964 and 1968 IERS supported 20 psychological investigations. These projects included studies of television's impact on schoolchildren, the attitudes of males and females toward each other, the effect of education on the change of attitudes of Iranian youth, learning problems of children, vocational interests of high school students, and students' activities during summer vacation. In addition, IERS adapted and translated several tests into Persian.

It is difficult to obtain information on current psychological research in Iran. Moreover, there is no system to compile research information on Iranians conducted by scholars around the world. The following brief review is based on articles published in journals included in the American *Psychological Abstracts* between 1965 and 1988.

During this period research on Iran represented in these periodicals has increased in both number and scope. Using titles and abstracts, we identified 136 articles, the majority of which represent the two dominant research areas: clinical psychology ($N = 37$) and educational/developmental psychology ($N = 39$). Other empirical articles can be classified as psychometric ($N = 12$), cross-cultural studies ($N = 15$), family studies ($N = 9$), and research on work behavior ($N = 8$). There were also historical reviews on Iran and topics related to Islam and the 1979 revolution ($N = 6$). In addition, 5 general psychological review articles written by Iranian authors were published in these journals.[1]

Professional Psychology

Attempts to develop professional psychology paralleled the development of academic psychology. The first psychology services with professional standards were offered in the 1950s by the Testing and Vocational Guidance Unit and Research Center (Ayman, 1969, 1977). These services were mostly devoted to psychological testing to select and place students and personnel. In the 1960s and 1970s the NIP expanded this field by additionally offering services related to psychological guidance and counseling, public opinion studies, marketing research, and personnel and consulting psychology. The NIP completed about 3,000 such projects for both Iranian and international clients, including industries and universities in the United States and Europe.

These services were later offered by other centers. The Children's Protection Society organized centers similar to child guidance clinics. By 1979 some clinical psychologists either had private practices or cooperated with psychiatrists.

In the 1970s the Department of Exceptional Children at the Ministry of Education established schools for retarded and handicapped children. This ministry also started a countrywide program to provide vocational guidance services to all secondary schools. The Ministry of Labor and Social Welfare created a special fund for technical training, which included certain trade testing services. Some industrial organizations created their own personnel research and services units. However, professional psychology as a recognized field of study developed more slowly in Iran than academic psychology.

The Psychological Association of Iran, after many attempts, was established in 1968. It published a quarterly journal, the *Journal of Psychology*, and worked to encourage and protect the new science and profession. The association, largely made up of university professors, was chiefly concerned with psychology's academic aspects. This association, like many similar scientific and professional organizations, became inactive after the revolution. A new society of medical and clinical psychology, however, made up of psychologists working with the Ministry of Public Health and various medical schools, was established in 1979 and publishes a quarterly journal of medical psychology.

Conclusion

The introduction of modern psychology in Iran was slow and remained limited even after World War II. The return of young Iranian psychologists trained in Western universities in the 1950s and 1960s gradually accelerated its growth. We can conclude that psychology, as an independent discipline with some fields of specialization, is now established and recognized in Iran.

Many psychologists left Iran after the government changed in 1979, however. By the 1980s, with the dominant ideology under the new government and the limitations created by the prolonged war between Iran and Iraq (1980–88), behavioral sciences seemed to be developing at a slower pace than they had in the 1960s and 1970s.

Note

1. The complete list of research articles mentioned in this chapter may be obtained from Roya Ayman, Department of Psychology, Illinois Institute of Technology, Chicago, Illinois, 60616, USA.

Bibliography

Ahadi, H. (1988). *A descriptive bibliography of psychology* (in Persian). Mashad, Iran: Astane Qudse Rasavi Publications.

Ayman, I. (1966). *International opportunities for advanced training and research.* Paper presented at the annual conference of the American Psychological Association, Washington, DC.

Ayman, I. (1969). Educational testing in Iran. In K. Igenkamp (Ed.), *Developments in educational testing.* London: University of London Press.

Ayman, I. (1977). Industrial and organizational psychology in Iran. *American Psychologist, 32,* 905–909.

Ghani, Q. (1935). *Avecina* (in Persian). Tehran, Iran: Farhangestan Secretariat.

Hashemi, E. S. (1971). *A bibliography of Persian books in psychology and education* (in Persian). Tehran, Iran: Institute of Education Research and Studies, Daneshsaraye'Aali.

Hushiyar, M. B. (1938). *Experimental psychology* (in Persian). Tehran, Iran: Sherkate Matbuat.

National Institute of Psychology. (1959–). *Annual reports* (in Persian). Tehran, Iran.

Personnel Management and Research Center (PMRC). (1954–1959). *Monthly and annual reports* (in Persian). Tehran, Iran: University of Tehran.

Psychological Association of Iran. (no date). *Journal of Psychology* (quarterly publication, in Persian). Tehran, Iran.

Shoarinejad, A. A. (1986). *A dictionary of behavioral sciences* (in Persian). Tehran, Iran: Amirkabir.

Siyassi, A. A. (1936). *Science of mind or psychology from the standpoint of education* (in Persian). Tehran, Iran: Chape Rengin.

Watson, R. I. (1971). *The great psychologists* (3rd ed.). New York: Lippincott.

22 / Ireland

THÉRÈSE BRADY & JAMES MCLOONE

Thérèse Brady completed both her undergraduate and postgraduate studies at University College, Dublin. She established the first community-based child and family clinic in Ireland and has continued to introduce psychology into other clinical settings. A past president and founding member of the Psychological Society of Ireland, her special interests include bereavement, community psychology, and professional development. Since 1979 Brady has been director of the Master's Course in Clinical Psychology at University College, Dublin.

James McLoone is also a graduate of University College, Dublin, and a past president and founding member of the Psychological Society of Ireland. His main interests are mental handicap, bilingualism, and professional issues. As director of psychology at Woodlands Centre, Galway, McLoone led a team providing services for people with mental handicaps. He is former editor of the Irish Psychologist *and coordinating editor of the* Irish Journal of Psychology. *Currently, he is lecturer in psychology at University College, Galway.*

Ireland is a small island country whose 4.5 million people are divided politically into two administrations. In 1922 26 of the 32 counties of Ireland became an independent state, which declared itself a republic in 1948. The other 6 counties have remained under the jurisdiction of the British government and are now officially called "Northern Ireland." Psychologists on the two sides of the political border enjoy excellent relations and cooperate closely in academic and professional matters. This chapter focuses on the republic, which is referred to as "Ireland," the name by which the state is known in its constitution and in international organizations.

Although psychology has only recently become an independent field of study in Ireland, scholarship in the subject can be traced back to the early Christian era when philosophical studies flourished in Irish centers of learning. One early contributor to psychological thought was John, the Irishman (Johannus Eriugena, or Scottus), who, in the 9th century, was regarded as the leading scholar of his day. In the 17th century Robert Boyle was engaged in investigations that, according to Boring (1950), could be regarded as the earliest recorded experiments in psychology. Somewhat later, in 1709, George Berkeley, who at the time was on the staff of Trinity College, Dublin, published *An Essay Towards a New Theory of Vision*, regarded by some as the first psychological monograph. In 1890 the first edition of Michael Maher's *Psychology: Empirical and Rational* was published (Maher, 1890). In spite of these and other distinguished but isolated contributions to psychological thought (e.g., Brooks, 1973, 1983), psychology as we now know it was relatively late in coming to Ireland.

Psychology in the Universities

In Irish universities, as in universities in Britain and elsewhere in Europe, psychology was seen as a philosophical discipline for many years. The word "psychology" first appeared in the title of an Irish academic post in 1909, when a chair of logic and psychology was instituted in the Dublin College of the newly founded National University of Ireland. Somewhat later psychology's practical applications justified its inclusion in programs of teacher education. For one such course, a Gaelic-language psychology textbook entitled *Aigneolaíocht* was published in 1928 (Máire, 1928). In the late 1940s psychology emerged as an independent, empirical discipline in Ireland.

Psychology's practical value was first realized in the field of education. Under the aegis of the Department of Education at the Queen's University of Belfast, George Seth introduced Northern Ireland's first professional psychology course in 1947. Significantly, in 1958, when E. F. O'Doherty of University College, Dublin, was planning the Republic of Ireland's first professional course in psychology, the INTO (primary school teachers' union) provided a grant in support of the venture. That course, leading to a diploma in psychology, was an important milestone, not only because it marked the emergence of psychology as an independent discipline in Ireland, but also because so many of its graduates became pioneers in applying psychology in different service areas throughout the country. The course itself was a 2-year, full-time one, modeled on master's courses in North American graduate schools. In addition to meeting the minimum entry requirement of an honors university degree, most entrants had several years of professional experience in areas such as education, medicine, and the social services. Since it was anticipated that graduates from the course would be involved in initiating psychological services throughout the country, the selection of mature, professionally experienced candidates showed prudent foresight.

University College, Dublin, has the country's largest department of psychology. It introduced a first degree in psychology in 1967. At the postgraduate level it offers two 1-year courses and is the only department in the country offering a 2-year professional course. Its students are pursuing a wide variety of research topics, including stress in organizations and the effects of brain injury on memory. The theoretical orientation of the department tends to be cognitive and philosophical. The students, assisted by the staff, edit and publish an occasional publication called the *Thornfield Journal*.

Peter Dempsey established the first honors degree course at University College, Cork, in 1964. The theoretical orientation of the department is reflected in its title, Department of Applied Psychology, and in some of its research output, which includes information technology, coping with stress, and forensic psychology. However, significant work is also being done in cognitive processes and child development.

Ireland's oldest university, Trinity College, Dublin, introduced a 4-year honors degree course in psychology in 1964. Under the leadership of Derek Forrest, its department of psychology has a tradition of catering to students who are above the usual university admission age. The theoretical orientation of the department is eclectic. Its research output has included studies in driver behavior, political psychology, behavior analysis, and depression.

In 1972 Martin McHugh established the country's youngest department of psychology at University College, Galway. The Galway department is eclectic in theoretical orientation. The significant research areas are the development of gender identity, reading skills, mental handicap, mental illness, alcoholism, and suicide (Curtis & McHugh, 1986).

University education in Ireland is funded by the state; only a small portion of university income comes from the fees paid by students. In psychology, as in other areas, university practice follows the British model. First-degree courses in psychology vary somewhat in structure, duration, and content. The typical curriculum is a 3-year BA course. Some students combine psychology with another scientific discipline in a 4-year BSc course. Variations in the content of courses in the different colleges reflect differences in tradition and resources. All courses are similar enough, however, to enable their graduates to claim a broadly based training in psychology and to qualify them to apply for graduate membership in both the Psychology Society of Ireland and the British Psychological Society. First-degree courses cover a wide range of areas, including cognitive psychology, experimental psychology, psychophysiology, personality theory, developmental and educational psychology, clinical psychology, and social psychology, as well as research methods and statistics. Students must demonstrate their ability to carry out research by completing a small-scale empirical study.

Those obtaining an honors degree or diploma in psychology may go on to take a master's degree by thesis, by examination, or by coursework and professional training. The PhD is a research degree that involves the presentation of a major research thesis completed under supervision over a period of 3 or more years. A significant number of psychology graduates from Ireland go abroad for postgraduate study, mainly to Britain and North America.

Precise statistics are not available about the number of psychologists in Ireland. The number of honors graduates in psychology from Ireland's four university colleges in 1987 was 153. Our best estimate of the total number employed as psychologists is 550; about 55 percent of them are women. A further 150 psychology graduates have jobs in allied fields such as remedial education, career guidance, and personnel work. About 20 percent of Irish psychologists have doctorates, and a further 30 percent have master's-level training.

The Development of Professional Psychology

While psychologists in Ireland work in a wide variety of fields, by far the greatest number are employed in health and educational services operated by public and voluntary organizations. Voluntary organizations have played a special role in the development of health, social, and educational services in general and of psychological services in particular. Hospitals in the modern sense were first established in Ireland by philanthropic individuals and groups of doctors in the mid-18th century. Since then many hospitals, schools, and services for people with sensory, physical, and mental handicap have been developed by religious orders, parent groups, and voluntary bodies. Although increasingly dependent on state funding and thus no longer voluntary in the original sense, these organizations have retained a certain independence that has enabled them to continue to initiate and develop a variety of services. Professional psychology in Ireland has greatly benefited from these initiatives, especially in the areas of child guidance and mental handicap.

The Health Services

The first psychological service was established in 1955 under the directorship of John McKenna at Ireland's first child guidance clinic, which was opened in that year by the Brothers of St. John of God. Later, psychologists were appointed to other child guidance clinics, pediatric hospitals, and services for the mentally handicapped. The Department of Education's requirement that children be psychologically assessed before placement in special education led to a demand for psychologists throughout the country. The emphasis in the early years was on psychological assessment. Psychological services for adults were slower to develop. First appointments were in psychiatric hospitals, where the main demand initially was for assessment and diagnostic work.

The number of psychologists employed in the health services has increased rapidly from fewer than 20 in 1970 to about 270 today. Their role has also expanded. Psychologists are now involved in a wide variety of assessment and therapeutic procedures. They work with the full age range from infancy to old age; with individuals, families, groups, and organizations; and in various settings, including general and psychiatric hospitals, specialist centers, and community facilities. There is an increasing emphasis on prevention and on providing consulting services to other professionals and to various health agencies. Research constitutes a small but expanding part of their work. Although the level of autonomy enjoyed by clinical psychologists varies with their employment setting, in general they are gaining greater freedom as their profession develops. Few psychologists in Ireland work in independent private practice.

The first formal postgraduate course in clinical psychology was established at University College, Dublin, in 1977. It is a 2-year, full-time course leading to a master of psychological science degree. In 1978 a 3-year, inservice training course leading to the diploma in clinical psychology of the British Psychological Society was established by the Eastern Health Board in association with Trinity College, Dublin. Both courses are recognized by the Psychological Society of Ireland and accredited by the British Psychological Society. In accord with the scientist-practitioner model, students are required to follow an intensive course of academic study, to gain a broad range of supervised clinical experience, and to present a dissertation on a clinically relevant research topic. At present, not more than 14 students are in training at any one time.

Before the establishment of these courses, some psychologists obtained professional training outside Ireland. Many were able to attend courses in Britain through funding from the Irish Health Boards. A small number of Irish psychologists continue to acquire professional training abroad. The demand for places in postgraduate courses in clinical psychology as well as for graduates from these courses far exceeds the supply. Two courses in psychotherapy leading to a master's degree are provided in Dublin; one has a psychoanalytic emphasis, while the other is more eclectic in orientation. Training in family therapy and in the use of projective techniques is also available.

There is a need for expansion of services in many areas. Such expansion is dependent on available financial and personnel resources. The relatively rapid growth of psychological services and of psychologists in the 1970s has been followed in the 1980s by a slower rate of progress. In the next few years little increase in the number of psychologists or of services can be expected because of the current recession and recent government policy involving major cutbacks in health service expenditure.

Services for Persons with Mental Handicap

Since 1960 Ireland's mental handicap services have developed rapidly and have now achieved a very high standard. Most of these services are conducted by state-supported voluntary organizations. They have used their relative freedom from bureaucratic constraints to be innovative in developing new services and in reorganizing existing institutions, thus enhancing the quality of life enjoyed by their clients. In developing their services, voluntary agencies have relied heavily on the expertise of psychologists from both educational and clinical backgrounds. The psychologists involved are organized into an effective professional group that arranges regular meetings and an annual conference to help develop its members' professional and research skills. The group makes presentations to public bodies and has published some policy documents, including *A Place to Live* (1982) and *The Challenge of Disturbed Behaviour in Mental Handicap* (1987).

Educational Services

Although the first educational psychologist was appointed as early as 1960, the Department of Education's Psychological Service, in which most of the 36 Irish educational psychologists currently work, was not initiated until 1965. Educational psychologists work mainly in postprimary schools, while services to primary schools continue to be provided principally by psychologists employed in the health services. Educational psychologists have been responsible for developing pupil guidance and remedial education services in second-level schools. They provide a consultancy service to schools, working with teachers and guidance counselors as well as with individual students. They offer in-service training for teachers, are actively involved in research and development, and are also responsible for advising the Minister for Education on policy matters. Some psychology graduates are also employed in schools as remedial teachers and as guidance counselors. Others hold positions as school principals.

At present no formal postgraduate training for educational psychologists is available in Ireland. Candidates for positions as educational psychologists are usually required to have an honors degree in psychology and, in addition, a few years of experience in teaching or in psychology. The majority of educational psychologists are, in fact, qualified teachers.

Teaching and Research

The third major group of psychologists lecture in universities and in other third-level colleges. These lecturers work not only in departments of psychology, but also in other academic areas such as education, medicine, business studies, and remedial linguistics.

As in other countries, in Ireland research forms an essential component of all courses leading to a degree or diploma in psychology and is claimed as a special skill of the psychologist. Since funding is limited, research is not the most developed part of Irish psychology. The research efforts of psychologists are concentrated mainly in the universities and in certain state-funded and voluntary research centers. Candidates for research degrees must present a major thesis. Abstracts of the theses presented are published regularly by the *Irish Journal of Psychology*. Though no clear pattern in research areas is discernible, cognitive psychology and aspects of health and education are popular topics of investigation. The number of candidates taking research degrees increased dramatically in the 1980s. Currently, 123 postgraduate students are registered for higher degrees in Ireland's four University Colleges.

Among the state-funded agencies outside the universities, two deserve special mention. Since its establishment in 1966, the Educational Research Centre, in Dublin under the direction of Thomas Kellaghan, has clearly demonstrated the value of systematic research in Irish education. Its research program has included evaluations of educational programs and of school effectiveness, and studies of participation rates in education and of the scholastic development of pupils. The center has also provided a range of widely used standardized achievement tests for Irish schools. Researchers based at the Economic and Social Research Institute in Dublin have published valuable research reports on issues such as juvenile delinquency, job satisfaction, and attitudes toward politically motivated violence.

St. Michael's House, a voluntary organization providing services for people with mental handicaps, has had an active research department headed by Roy McConkey since 1977. McConkey and his colleagues have an impressive record in applied research in the field of mental handicap. Other voluntary organizations catering to the mentally and physically handicapped have also sponsored applied research projects.

Psychologists are also involved in collaborative research with colleagues from other disciplines, in hospitals, in the prison service, and in business and management organizations. Unfortunately, more generous funding has not accompanied the growing awareness of the need for more basic and applied research. Nevertheless, the existence of excellent library facilities, the expansion in the range and sophistication of computer resources, and the availability of more skilled researchers should facilitate an increased output of psychological research.

Developing Areas of Employment

A small but growing number of psychologists are employed in government departments other than health and education and in various areas outside public service, including commercial and manufacturing businesses and trade unions. While some are employed as organizational or occupational psychologists, the majority are not so designated but are engaged in management consulting, personnel work, or industrial relations. A master's degree in social and organizational psychology is now available at University College, Dublin.

Organizations

The Psychological Society of Ireland (PSI), the representative body of Irish psychologists, was founded in 1970 and became a member of the International Union of Psychological Science in 1974. Since its foundation, PSI has made a major contribution to the development of both scientific and professional psychology in Ireland, not the least of which has been to provide psychologists from different backgrounds a common identity and professional loyalty. The society organizes a 4-day annual conference at which members report on advances in research and practice. An Annual Society Lecture is given by a distinguished Irish psychologist, and many other scientific and professional meetings are held. Conscious of the need to develop a positive attitude toward psychology, PSI has organized many lectures and other activities for the general public. PSI has several subgroups that are active both in the professional development of their members and in promoting appreciation of psychology among the public. The society has published several policy documents, including two major statements on the role of psychologists in the education and health services. PSI publishes two periodicals: the *Irish Journal of Psychology*, founded in 1971 and issued in an annual volume of two numbers, and the *Irish Psychologist*, a monthly bulletin introduced in 1974. The society adopted a code of professional ethics in 1979 and has since established procedures for handling complaints of alleged professional misconduct by members.

Many psychologists in Ireland are members of the British Psychological Society. Meetings organized jointly by PSI and the Northern Ireland Branch of the British Psychological Society are held regularly. An agreement between PSI and the American Psychological Association (APA) enables Irish psychologists to become foreign affiliates of the APA. Irish psychologists have close links with British and international colleagues through societies such as the International Association of Applied Psychology.

Psychology in Context

Although a small island, Ireland has escaped the dangers of excessive insularity because of its easy communication and historical links with Britain to the east and North America to the west. In Britain, Canada, and the USA millions of people are Irish by birth or claim Irish ancestry. Traditional links with continental Europe, originally forged by Irish scholars who contributed to the religious and cultural life of many lands during the so-called Dark Ages, have recently been renewed by Ireland's membership in the European Economic Community.

It is not surprising, therefore, that the main influences on psychology in Ireland came from Britain, North America, and continental Europe. All departments of psychology in Ireland were established by psychologists who received a substantial part of their professional education in either Britain or North America, and all maintain close links with colleagues abroad. Although Irish psychology inherited from Britain a high regard for cognitive and experimental work, the papers presented at the PSI annual conferences suggest a primary interest in community needs among Irish psychologists (Kirakowski & Delafield, 1982). Organizational and clinical psychology in Ireland owe much to North America. Psychologists such as Pavlov, Luria, Freud, and Piaget from continental Europe have had considerable influence. Libraries in Ireland subscribe to all the major periodicals published in English. There is a growing awareness of the psychological literature from continental Europe, including Eastern Europe, and from countries such as Japan and Israel, where significant advances are being made.

Future Directions

Much has been achieved by Irish psychologists since the 1960s. Their numbers and the variety of roles they occupy have grown considerably. Although the current economic recession will undoubtedly slow down the development of psychology, the momentum gained is likely to continue. Many other areas of Irish life would benefit from the application of psychological knowledge and skills. These include the traditional areas of health and education, as well as administration, information technology, and the media. Already there is a welcome trend to involve psychologists in the development and evaluation of public policy. It is hoped that the profession will retain the youthful enthusiasm and concern with human well-being that has characterized its early development, along with the positive public attitude that psychologists now enjoy.

In the 1990s psychology in Ireland is likely to become a registered profession and will probably be influenced by a proposed European Economic Community directive, "A General System for the Recognition of Higher Education Diplomas," currently being considered by the EEC Council of Ministers. Being free to work anywhere within the EEC's domain of 321 million people is a challenge to all European psychologists, but particularly to Irish psychologists, coming as they do from a country with a population of only about 4 million. On the basis of past achievement and respect for both local genius and influences from without, Ireland's psychologists look to the future with confidence.

Bibliography

Boring, E. G. (1950). *A history of experimental psychology* (2nd ed.). New York: Appleton, Century & Crofts.

Brady, T. (Ed.). (1982). Psychology in Ireland [Special issue]. *Irish Psychologist, 8,* 48–58.

Brooks, G. P. (1973). The use of psychological concepts in the writings of an Irish psychiatrist of the nineteenth century. *Irish Journal of Psychology, 2,* 102–112.

Brooks, G. P. (1983). Francis Hutcheson: An important Irish contributor to eighteenth-century psychological thought. *Irish Journal of Psychology, 6,* 54–68.

Curtis, R., & McHugh, M. (1986). *Time present and time past: A retrospection on the Department of Psychology, University College, Galway (1971–1986).* Galway: University College.

Kirakowski, J., & Delafield, G. (1982). The Department of Applied Psychology in University College, Cork. *Thornfield Journal, 10,* 38–54.

Maher, M. (1890). *Psychology: Empirical and rational* (1st ed.). London: Longmans, Green.

Máire, An tSr. (1928). *Aigneolaíocht*. Dublin: Browne & Nolan.

McHugh, M., & McLoone, J. (1980). The roots that clutch: The origins and growth of PSI. *Irish Psychologist, 6*, 1–8.

23 / Israel

YEHUDA AMIR & RACHEL BEN ARI

Yehuda Amir (born 1926) received his PhD from New York University in 1959. A specialist in social psychology, he has authored more than 60 regular journal articles, 25 more for Israel Army publications, and several books. Amir has served on the editorial board of the Journal of Cross-Cultural Psychology *and the* International Journal of Intercultural Relations, *and he has held offices in the Israel Psychological Association, the Israel Association for the Study of Labor Relations, and the International Association of Applied Psychology. He was the chairman of the 21st International Congress of Applied Psychology in 1986 and the scientific chairman of the 2nd European Regional Congress of Labor Relations. He is professor in the Department of Psychology at Bar-Ilan University.*

Rachel Ben Ari (born 1946) received her PhD from Bar-Ilan University with a specialty in social psychology. Among her published works are two coedited books, School Desegregation: Cross-cultural Perspectives *and* Integration in Education; *a coauthored book,* Being Together; *13 book chapters; and more than 20 journal articles. She is assistant professor in the Department of Psychology at Bar-Ilan University.*

Compared to other professions, psychology in Israel is flourishing. Growing in numbers as well as scope, it ranks high in social status, its services are viewed positively by all levels of the population, and its university departments are among the most desirable in terms of student demand. It is worth noting that Israel appears to have the highest rate of psychologists per capita in the world (Rosenzweig, 1982).

Much of this development may be traced to the unique characteristics of Israel as an immigrant society. Most of its inhabitants arrived in the late 1940s and early 1950s, either as refugees from the Nazi concentration camps or from neighboring Arab countries. This mass immigration produced major problems of personal adjustment that, in turn, pointed to the need for trained

The data for this chapter were derived from interviews with prominent psychologists in Israel, from information received from the Israel Psychological Association, from research centers and universities, and from previously published articles (see bibliography).

professional personnel and the development of psychological services. Indeed, the need still exists today.

Education and Background

To practice as a psychologist in any field in Israel, one is required by law to have an MA degree. An additional 2 years of training, minimum, is required for practice in the applied fields of clinical, educational (school), or industrial (vocational) psychology. On average, then, the typical certified psychologist spends 8 to 10 years in training: 3 years for the BA, 3 to 5 years for the MA, and 2 years on the job under direct supervision. To obtain a PhD degree in Israel generally requires an additional 5 years of study.

Most of the young psychologists have been trained in Israel. However, some psychologists studied in their native countries before emigrating, chiefly the United States and South America, and some young Israeli psychologists chose to study abroad. Of psychologists aged 50 or more, most studied in the United States during the 1950s when advanced degrees in psychology were not yet available from Israeli universities. The percentage who received their graduate degrees abroad, primarily from the United States, is greatest among university teachers of psychology, for whom a PhD degree is required.

Since the early 1960s the total number of psychologists has multiplied more than 10 times, to a current total of almost 2,500. There are twice as many female psychologists as male, though the ratio varies depending on occupational setting. Thus, for instance, males tend to dominate in university settings. Among university students, females outnumber males, but the ratio seems about even among PhD students.

Specialization and Work Settings

Clinical psychologists and school psychologists are about equal in number and, combined, make up two thirds of all psychologists. Clinical psychologists work primarily in hospitals and mental health clinics; school or educational psychologists work in guidance centers. The remaining third may be found in a variety of specialties including vocational guidance, industrial psychology, rehabilitation psychology, and the military.

Clinical psychologists may be employed by public organizations, including the military, university student-counseling centers, some of the municipalities, the Youth Immigration Department of the Jewish Agency, and various ministries. The largest employers, however, are two national institutions that operate most general and psychiatric hospitals, mental health clinics, and child guidance centers. These institutions are the Ministry of Health and the Labor Union's Sick Fund. Psychologists who conduct private practices generally do so in addition to their regular jobs.

The orientation of clinical psychologists is varied from both a theoretical and a practical point of view. Well represented are the classic psychoanalytical and neo-Freudian approaches, as well as biofeedback techniques, behavior therapy, Gestalt therapy, and individual and family therapy. Two general trends are seen, the first emphasizing individual treatment, the second emphasizing the community approach and including preventive psychopathology and multidisciplinary teamwork.

Educational and school psychologists work in child guidance centers under the jurisdiction of the local government. There are about 130 such centers, each serving schools in its locality, thereby providing services to practically every school in the country. The Ministry of Education and Culture coordinates these centers and provides them with special professional services.

Among school psychologists, as with clinicians, a change in orientation can be found over the years, from individual treatment to a community and social orientation. Services have been enlarged to include work with teachers and administrative staff, prevention techniques, implementing ethnic integration, assisting children from disadvantaged backgrounds, crisis intervention for students as well as family and community, and the promotion of special programs and teaching techniques for gifted children.

Industrial psychologists are viewed in a positive light by the general population and, in particular, by the managers of industrial concerns. Part of this esteem is no doubt due to the managers' university training, in which the general attitude toward the use of psychology in work settings is favorable. The primary tasks of the industrial psychologist are to establish training procedures and criteria for selection and assessment. Sometimes this work also includes human relations, organizational development, and management counseling. In the larger companies in industry and transportation, and in government, industrial psychologists are part of the organization. In smaller companies these services may be hired on a part-time basis.

Vocational guidance is, to a limited degree, provided by school psychologists within their special field. Two public institutes, however—the Center for Vocational Counseling and Information and the Hadassah Vocational Guidance Institute—also offer major services to the public. Along with some smaller private institutes, they provide guidance in occupational choice based on personality, interests, and ability. Evaluations are typically available before high school entrance and may determine the course of study.

Military psychology is composed of two units. One focuses on the mental health of soldiers; the other is concerned with organizational problems. From the beginning the Israel Defense Force (IDF) has emphasized areas requiring the services of professional psychologists. In addition, in part because of the multiethnic population, psychological services were needed for special problems associated with selection, training, discipline, morale, and prejudice. Thus, guidance from psychologists has proved to be a critical factor in the IDF complex and is both respected and used.

Rehabilitation psychology was developed to offer psychological support and guidance services to the physically handicapped, including amputees, burn victims, the brain-damaged, and those otherwise disfigured. Many recipients of these services are direct victims of the frequent military activity. Sex therapy, vocational guidance, and retraining may all form a part of this specialty.

Licensing

A law regulating the profession of psychology was first passed in 1977, largely as a result of lobbying by the Israel Psychological Association (IPA). Before 1977 licensing was carried out by the IPA, although it had no legal basis for doing so, nor any power of enforcement. Still, it was largely accepted by professionals and the public. The new Law of Psychologists has made the public more aware that psychological work should be done by psychologists. Its main purpose is to protect the public from inappropriate psychological practice. The law clarified eligibility for the practice of psychology and the qualifications for various psychological services. Increasingly, clients inquire about credentials before entering into a therapeutic relationship.

Administrative responsibility for the Law of Psychologists is held by the minister (secretary) of health, who appoints members of the Council of Psychologists to enforce the law. The council, which meets four or five times a year, is composed almost entirely of psychologists and represents all major organizations where psychologists are employed, such as university departments of psychology, governmental departments, and the IPA. In addition, subcommittees are established to deal with current issues.

The Universities

Bachelor's degrees in psychology are given by the six major universities in Israel. Doctoral and master's degrees are available from Bar-Ilan, Haifa, Tel-Aviv, and the Hebrew University. Be'er Sheva offers an MA, and Technion in Haifa awards a master's in industrial psychology. Psychology courses are also taught in other disciplines, including sociology, education, medicine, and business.

Up to 100 students are accepted annually for study as psychology majors at the BA level in each university. Tel-Aviv and Bar-Ilan accept about 60 master's applicants each. The Hebrew University accepts 30, with another 15 in school psychology in a joint program of the School of Education and the Department of Psychology. Haifa University accepts 20. About 20 students are carefully selected each year for the PhD programs.

Completion of a BA in psychology requires a minimum of 3 years and 60 credits in psychology. MA degrees require about 40 to 50 graduate credits, plus a specialty examination and the submission of a research thesis. The average time from university entrance to MA status is 7 to 8 years. About one third of graduate students specialize in clinical psychology, one third in school or educational psychology, and one sixth in social psychology, with the remainder in other areas. Doctoral studies require 5 or 6 years in the PhD program, on average, with most of the time devoted to the research dissertation.

All graduate training emphasizes theory, research, and application. Field placements are arranged for student apprenticeships for one full day a week over a period of 2 years, thus smoothing the path for entry into the work force. All universities offer specialties in clinical, school, social, and experimental psychology. In addition, Bar-Ilan offers rehabilitation and industrial psychology, and Tel-Aviv offers vocational psychology.

Each university has a special psychology library, in addition to general facilities, which includes all major journals, books, and tests in psychology published in English and in Hebrew. It is understood that completing the MA degree requires mastery of the professional literature in English. Psychology departments have laboratories for experimental research and training, as well as facilities for designing the necessary instrumentation. Computer facilities include interuniversity and intercontinental communication networks, such as the BITNET system.

The Israel Psychological Association

The Israel Psychological Association was organized in 1950, when there were only a few psychologists in the country. Today there are more than 2,300 members, representing over 90 percent of all psychologists in Israel. This high membership rate is not accidental. Virtually all psychologists in Israel are salaried, and their salary is closely linked to professional status. Membership in the IPA, though voluntary, is seen as one clear measure of professional status. In the 1960s the Union of Psychologists was created. Often viewed as a subsidiary of the IPA (the membership of the two groups is virtually identical), the newer group fulfills the specific functions of a union.

The IPA is divided into six professional sections: clinical, educational (i.e., school), social and vocational (including industrial), rehabilitation, developmental, and health psychology. Some sections include special interest groups. The sections of the IPA have two major functions: (a) the organization and promotion of professional training and experience, including nationwide meetings of selected interest groups and special seminars, and (b) accreditation of psychologists as "expert" or "supervisor," the two levels of professional status of the IPA.

In addition, the IPA organizes and sponsors national conventions and international congresses; publishes a directory of psychologists; serves as a source for the representation of psychologists in various governmental, civil, and international organizations; organizes postgraduate courses; and is responsible for the implementation of professional ethics, among other activities.

Recently, the IPA became involved in the issue of human experimentation. Some members of the Knesset, Israel's national representative body, considered passing a law on human experimentation resembling that of the Helsinki Convention. With the close participation of the IPA, as well as universities, departments of psychology, and individual psychologists, the decision was made not to pass formal legislation. Instead, the IPA and the universities undertook the responsibility for the ethical conduct of their researchers. Rules and regulations were established concerning human experimentation which were generally adopted by the universities and their psychology departments.

Finally, the IPA has begun to publish a scientific journal (in Hebrew), the *Israel Quarterly of Psychology*, which at the beginning of 1988 became a regular publication. Although there are several scientific journals in Hebrew— and one in English—that include psychology as a major component, none of them deals exclusively with psychology. Among these journals, the following should be noted: *Megamot* (Trends), which includes articles on psychology and other social sciences, especially education and sociology; *Iyunim Bechinuch* (Studies in education), education and psychology; *Israel Annals of Psychiatry and Related Disciplines* (in English), psychiatry and clinical psychology; and *Psychology and Counseling in Education*.

Research

All psychological research is supported with public funds in one way or another. The bulk of research is conducted at universities, although some, usually with an applied orientation, is undertaken at other institutions. The topics of investigation are diverse and represent the variety and level found throughout the international community in psychology.

Most research is conducted by single staff members, sometimes with the assistance of a graduate student or two. Where a special institute exists, its researchers generally work on different topics, and the institute serves only as an organizational or fundraising entity. One of the few exceptions to this rule is the Institute for the Advancement of Social Integration in the Schools at Bar-Ilan University. The researchers at this institute, almost all of whom are social psychologists, are engaged in the study of ethnicity, particularly ethnic relations and integration in the schools. Interestingly, Israeli psychologists have produced a large volume of cross-cultural research, second only to the United States in number of studies, and first, when the number of psychologists in the two countries is taken into consideration (Lonner, 1980).

Although much research deals with basic or theoretical issues, there is an emphasis on applied and socially meaningful aspects. Basic questions to be answered through the research are: What use can be made of this research? How can psychologists, policy makers, and the general public use this information? For instance, on the topic of ethnic integration the questions asked are: How do people of different ethnic groups interact? Under what conditions? With what results? Though these may be regarded as general questions, almost all research in this area finds direct application in situations such as ethnic integration in the schools, Arab-Jewish relations, and the relation of religious and nonreligious Jews. Other topics of special social relevance in Israel include the psychological aftermath of the Holocaust, intergroup relations, childrearing techniques and the kibbutz, cultural variations, and special intervention techniques with disadvantaged groups.

Nonuniversity Research Settings

There are six major institutes of research outside the university setting, each of them with a special research emphasis. (1) The Israel Institute for Applied Social Research in Jerusalem was established and directed by Louis Guttman. It conducts various research projects in the social sciences, including psychology, sociology, and social work. (2) The Henrietta Szold Institute in Jerusalem focuses on research in the behavioral sciences with a special emphasis on education and educational psychology. (3) The Hadassah Vocational Guidance Institute in Jerusalem devotes part of its activities to research and occupational information retrieval. (4) The Center for Vocational Counseling and Information has a research division devoted to exploring various aspects of vocational counseling. (5) The Institute for the Study of Education in the Kibbutz and the newly established Institute for Research of the Kibbutz at Haifa University explore a wide array of the social and psychological aspects of life in the kibbutz. (6) Finally, the Psychological Research Division of the Social Science Department of the IDF conducts research on psychological aspects of the military and has done so from the time of the establishment of the state of Israel.

Scientific Contributions

Any number of measures may be employed to evaluate the general quality of scientific contributions. Two of the more common indices include the total number of published papers and the number of citations for those papers. The latter is frequently considered the best indication of scientific quality, impact, and utility. However, cross-cultural studies of scientific contributions and citations in psychology are almost nonexistent.

Two studies include data for Israel. Corrigan and Narin (1982) compared 22 countries and geographic regions on various citation indices. The comparisons were made in nine scientific fields—one of which was psychology—based on publication data for the 1970s, generated from the Science Citation Index (SCI). The analyses revealed that in terms of number of papers, Israel ranked 10th. If the rankings had been adjusted for population size or ratio of psychologists, the ranking would have been either 3rd or 4th out of 22. Qualitative rankings are even more provocative. The average quality rating across the 10 indices developed for the study was 5th. On the measure of the top 1 percent of cited papers, however, Israel was 1st (Table 10, p. 57). In their summary the authors note that two countries were of particular interest when their papers were compared on quantitative versus qualitative aspects:

Sweden and Israel. Both countries rank in the average range in number of papers but in the high range in their overall quality.

One final item on the contribution of Israeli psychology to cross-cultural research is available. Lonner (1980) analyzed the authors who published papers in the *Journal of Cross-Cultural Psychology* from 1970 to 1979. He found that the number of contributions by Israeli psychologists ranked 2nd, preceded only by the United States and followed closely by Canada. Clearly, the contribution of Israeli psychology to the advancement of knowledge in this area is impressive.

Bibliography

Amir, Y., & Ben-Ari, R. (1981). Psychology and society in Israel. *International Journal of Psychology, 16*, 239–247.

Ben-Ari, R., & Amir, Y. (1986). Psychology in a developing society: The case of Israel. *Annual Review of Psychology, 37*, 17–41.

Corrigan, J. G.. & Narin, F. (1982). *Relationships between national publication rates and participation in highly cited papers within fields and within countries.* Cherry Hill, NJ: Computer Horizons.

Greenbaum, C. W., & Kugelmass, S. (1980). Human development and socialization in cross-cultural perspective: Issues arising from research in Israel. In N. Warren (Ed.), *Studies in cross-cultural psychology* (Vol. 2). London: Academic Press.

Greenbaum, C. W., & Norman, J. (1966). Israel. In S. Ross (Ed.), *International opportunities for advanced training and research in psychology* (pp. 160–166). Washington, DC: American Psychological Association.

Kugelmass, S. (1976). Israel. In V. S. Sexton & H. Misiak (Eds.), *Psychology around the world* (pp. 219–227). Monterey, CA: Brooks/Cole.

Lonner, W. J. (1980). A decade of cross-cultural psychology: JCCP, 1970–1979. *Journal of Cross-Cultural Psychology, 11*, 7–34.

Raviv, A. (1984). Psychology in Israel. In R. S. Corsini (Ed.), *Wiley encyclopedia of psychology* (Vol. 3, pp. 135–138). New York: Wiley.

Rosenzweig, M. R. (1982). Trends in development and status of psychology: An international perspective. *International Journal of Psychology, 17*, 117–140.

Sanua, V. D. (1971). Psychology programs and psychological research in Israel. *American Psychologist, 26*, 602–605.

Winnik, H. Z. (1977). Milestones in the development of psychoanalysis in Israel. *Israel Annals of Psychiatry and Related Disciplines, 15*, 85–91.

24 / Italy

ANNA LAURA COMUNIAN

Anna Laura Comunian (born 1940) is a specialist in the theoretical and technical aspects of personality assessment. Her research has employed both qualitative and quantitative methodology. Her publications include studies of children's drawing, interpersonal distance, anxiety measures, anger scales, and coping styles. She is associated with the General Psychology Department of the University of Padua.

Educational Background of Psychology Students

Reform in the curriculum for psychology students was enacted in Italy by a state law in 1985 instituting a more elaborate, up-to-date program, extending the period for obtaining a degree to 5 years. This period of study is divided into two subgroups: a first term of 2-year courses and a second term of 3-year courses.

The first term focuses primarily on basic knowledge of psychology. All students take nine mandatory courses and three optional ones. On completion of these courses, they take compulsory examinations in the following subjects: general psychology, psychodynamics, theories of personality and individual differences, child development, physiological psychology, social psychology, general biology, basic anatomy and physiology, and psychometric statistics.

The remaining exams, which are required for completion of the first 2-year term, can be chosen from anthropology, ethnology, human genetics, methodology of behavioral sciences, general education, sociology, contemporary philosophy, and the history of psychology. An English-language examination is also required of all students for enrollment in the second term.

The courses of the 3-year term provide professional preparation. They include general and experimental studies, developmental and educational psychology, clinical and community psychology, and psychology of labor and industrial organization. At the end of the 3-year term each student must have passed eight mandatory exams and five optional ones. Only then can application be made for a degree, which is awarded after completion of the final thesis. This thesis must be prepared during the final year in collaboration with a faculty professor. Most of the faculty professors are in the Department of General Development and Social Learning.

Characteristics of the Psychologist

The number of psychologists in Italy is about 20,000. Sixty percent are women and 40 percent are men. The preponderance of women is seen in the mental hygiene and psychomedical centers. In teaching and school advising, the presence of the two sexes is almost equal, while in other sectors men seem to prevail. In market organizations and industrial areas, more men are found, mostly because of Italy's traditional sociocultural background. In the educational area, many psychologists have a degree in literature and philosophy, while in the area of mental hygiene, there are many physicians.

In medical psychoteaching, a large number of psychologists have a degree in teaching methods. Many psychologists from law and political science departments can be found in the industrial, marketing, and social sectors. In private practice, a degree in medicine is preferable for work in psychotherapy.

Psychologists with a degree in literature and philosophy are more numerous in academic and research areas. Younger psychologists, up to 32 years of age, constitute the highest percentage. In other sectors the average age ranges from 33 to 42. The industrial and free-lance sectors absorb most young graduates. In clinical psychology, the free-lance profession could become one of the most attractive careers for young people. Public and local administrations encourage health centers to hire young psychologists for the valuable services they can provide in the community, such as advising, testing, and social assistance to the needy.

Until 1975 Italian psychologists held many different degrees. They trained especially in departments of medical research and medicine or in professional specialization courses, or they were self-trained. Their professional preparation, before entering the field of psychology, was usually rather long.

Since 1973 there has been a significant increase of work for psychologists, mostly in teaching and research. Workers in both fields are often poorly paid. Furthermore, in other areas such as training and free-lance work, psychologists operate in unstable conditions because they are not officially recognized by the State Educational Department.

In the psychotherapy sector, there is a multitude of different schools with different orientations. Though such schools are popular, qualifications are sometimes questionable and not at all standardized. Despite these difficulties, in 1989 legal recognition for Italian psychologists was achieved.

Programs and Specialties

Since 1971 the degree in psychology has been available in Padua and Rome. In 1987 a new course of study was instituted in Palermo (Sicily), in Turin, and in Trieste. Though Padua and Rome admit the highest number of undergraduates, psychology courses are also offered in other universities such as Bari, Bologna, Cagliari, Ferrara, Florence, Genoa, L'Aquila, Milan, Salerno, Sassari, Turin, Trento, Trieste, Urbino, Verona, and Venice. Additional courses are scheduled to open in Naples, Florence, Bologna, and Milan. In 1988 new postdegree specializations became available in various universities. This academic growth in psychology is also reflected in the increased number of psychological specialties.

From 1979 to 1984 psychoanalytic therapy was the most popular therapeutic approach. Recently, interest in this approach has declined because of the many other emerging methods, such as behavior therapy, hypnotism, and bioenergetics, all of which are becoming increasingly popular.

The psychologist's practical training takes place in private clinics or hospitals. Recent progress in mental health has increased the prevention of mental illness, mainly because of research that has helped develop modern methods and refined technology. The Centro Nazionale di Ricerche (National Institute for Research, CNR) in the field of psychology functions at the same level as the university institute. Furthermore, many research centers operate in Milan, Rome, Turin, Padua, Siena, and Bologna, together with therapeutic centers.

Health and community psychology are important areas to which psychologists are dedicated. Industrial organization, environmental psychology, ecological psychology, social development, and other applied fields fall under this category. In this area one finds support for the handicapped, pain control, family planning, bereavement counseling, hygiene services, and the like.

Journals, Societies, Textbooks, Laboratory Instruments, and Facilities

The rising interest in psychology is reflected in the recent establishment of several scientific journals, such as *Psicologia Italiana* (1979) and *Rivista di Psicologia* (1983), the official publication of the Società Italiana di Psicologia (Italian Psychological Society) (SIPS). *Psicoanalisi* (1955), *Psiche* (1964), and *Rivista di Psicologia Analitica* (1970) are edited by members of the psychoanalytic movement.

Other journals focusing on experimental and applied psychological research are *Bolletino di Psicologia Applicata* (Florence, 1954), *Rivista di Psicologia Sociale* (Turin, 1954), *Rassegne di Psicologia Generale e Clinica* (Palermo, 1956), *Annali di Psicologia* (Milan, 1968), *Infanzia* (Florence, 1973), *Rivista di Psicologia del Lavoro* (Milan, 1974), *Giornale Italiano di Psicologia* (Bologna, 1974), *Neuropsichiatria Infantile* (Rome, 1975), *Ricerche di Psicologia* (Milan, 1977), *Psicologia e Società* (Florence, 1977), *A. P. Rivista di Applicazioni Psicologiche* (Milan, 1979), *Giornale Italiano di Analisi e Modificazione del Comportamento* (Rome, 1979), and *Età Evolutiva* (Florence, 1981). Space limitations preclude a complete listing.

As in other countries, in Italy one finds many centers of research, encompassing almost all experimental trends of contemporary psychology. These trends are apparent on inspection of journals and publications of national congresses and indicate some distinct lines of research.

Apart from SIPS, there are many other psychological associations. The most influential are the Società Italiana di Neuropsichiatria Infantile, Associazione Psicologica Italiana del Lavoro, Associazione Italiana di Orientamento Scolastico e Professionale, Associazione Italiana di Psicologia dello Sport, Società Italiana di Medicina Psicosomatica, Società Italiana Rorschach, Società Italiana di Psicologia Individuale, Società Italiana di Psicoterapia di Gruppo, Società Italiana di Psicomotricità, Società Italiana di Psicologia Analitica, Società Italiana di Neurologia, Società Italiana di Logica e Filosofia delle Scienze, Gruppo di Psicologia Religiosa, Associazione Consulenti e Psicologi del Ministero di Grazia e Giustizia, Associazione Italiana Scuola di Marketing, Associazione Medica Italiana per lo Studio dell' Ipnosi, Centri Salesiani Orientamento Scolastico Professionale Educazione Sociale, and Centro Studi di Terapie Relazionali e Familiari.

Textbooks and psychometric instruments are supplied by Organizzazioni Speciale (Florence) according to the following specifications. (1) Psychological tests are sold exclusively to psychologists. (2) It is necessary to demonstrate professional qualifications or membership in SIPS, with a registration number. This requirement will hold until the psychological profession is further recognized. (3) For those having a psychology degree, a copy of the degree is acceptable. All those who do not meet the above requirements, including students, may have the tests only if a psychologist certifies that the applicant will use the material under direct supervision. (4) The user agrees to abide by the specifications ordained by the supplier of the material.

Laboratory instruments and computers are fairly well distributed and facilities are generally available, although naturally within the limits of government funding. Library facilities are available, especially in Padua and Rome, with a wide range of foreign publications.

Regarding computer facilities, Organizzazioni Speciali employs a system that offers psychologists and researchers computerized psychological diagnosis and other assistance. This project consists of (1) standardized procedures, and general programs for recording and establishing individual records; (2) programs for administering and scoring psychological tests, including the psychological tests most frequently used in Italy; (3) under special procedures, a program allowing access to the various test results for statistical elaboration; (4) a program for the use of optic readers and computers for automatic reading and scoring; and (5) special programs for special applications.

Unfortunately, in Italy, governmental financial support for psychology (as for all the faculties) is limited. Thus requests for funding are not always honored. This situation is in marked contrast to the great public interest in psychology, which is evident in the increasing number of requests for *Psicologia Contemporanea*, the first psychological magazine readily intelligible to the general public.

Current Status of Psychology

Italian psychology has again lapsed into a dialogue between the representatives of epistemological trends and those of a naturalistic orientation. Strong criticism in both fields has resulted in many differences in conceptual approaches. As is true in other countries, however, a changing structural and functional point of view toward more scientific approaches seems to be developing. The successful use of scientific procedures justifies an optimistic outlook for the future development of Italian psychology.

These methods must be used in all areas, but particularly in psychotherapy, where there are so many different points of view. All these differences seem to divide Italian psychologists, especially academics working in laboratories and professionals practicing in the community. But all are guided by a main purpose—namely, to transform and study psychology as an applied science.

Recently, laws to promote reform in psychology were enacted. They were primarily aimed at achieving more mature and competent work and at solving the complex problem of regulating the profession. To produce more qualified and professional workers, a modern department of human sciences is being planned, which will provide better research procedures and increased availability of practical experience in specific specialties.

Professional Congresses and Symposia

SIPS organized seven meetings from 1965 to 1987. The XV Assembly in Rome in January 1969 ended in a protest and the dissolution of the society, with all operations coming to a halt. This event played a central role at all psychological institutes, where lengthy discussions on vital issues were often held. Thereafter, SIPS became a private association, open only to members and special guests.

After several controversies the society reopened with a new set of regulations and a more democratic approach. These modifications were approved in a general assembly held in Rome in December 1971. In 1973 a new committee was elected, with L. Meschieri as chairman, followed by V. Spaltro, G. Fumai, and M. Bertini, who is the current chairman.

It is noteworthy that during the SIPS crisis researchers had no meeting place. However, they started to meet twice a year in Trieste in an informal atmosphere. These meetings provided them with a rich opportunity to discuss and compare information and to become familiar with up-to-date research on important topics such as learning, memory, and language.

The congress in Viareggio and the General Congress of 1979 highlighted new scientific trends in the study of perception, memory, social learning, social psychology, personality and cultural groups, psychotherapy, methodology, and psychological research. Later, in Urbino (1981), Bergamo (1984), and Venice (1987), special symposia were organized to discuss relevant psychological issues and to try to solve various political problems.

At the Bergamo congress some of the main fields of research were psychology faced with the data elaboration revolution (O. Andreani), new psychological problems in a postindustrial society (E. Calvi), the human as a biological and sociocultural organism (M. Cesa-Bianchi), the family in the future (A. Quadrio), projects for action in the clinical field (R. Canestrari), psychological projects for the civil approach (G. Trentini), and psychoeducational input for the development of personal and professional identity (M. Groppo).

New scientific nonclinical specialties were established, such as sports psychology, and schools for particular theoretical frameworks. Furthermore, in agreement with the World Health Organization, health psychology was organized. Finally, impetus was given to research and activity in new areas such as the armed forces, marketing, advertising, tourism, art, fashion, music, journalism, cinema, and television.

The 1983 Assembly of Professional Psychology in Rome introduced a definite change of approach, focusing on stress, health, and environmentally caused illnesses. Areas of attention were the relationship between normal and deviant behavior, and strengthening the scientific basis and the professional impact of psychology. More attention was also directed to institutions and their administration, particularly as they increase employment opportunities for young psychologists.

In Venice the theme of the congress was the laboratory and the city. The congress was an exchange between researchers and professional psychologists, with all the activities aimed at solving personal developmental problems and maintaining well-being. The input of Italian psychology to improve work and community life has shown signs of progress, even though many contradictions and complications remain.

Although it is obvious that empirically based studies are essential for understanding complex social behavior, most investigators feel that epistemological studies are also necessary to achieve a more mature theoretical base and to improve the efficiency of the methods of the specific schools. The value of a psychological theory must be judged not only by how well it explains laboratory findings, but also by the efficiency of the behavioral changes it produces.

Significant Areas of Current Research

Beginning in 1968 psychology in Italy was subjected to severe criticism, which became significant for the future of research. Interests were widened and new theoretical studies were undertaken, more in line with other European and American movements. Noteworthy investigations were conducted on hemispheric differences, mental elaboration processing, and visual space analysis, as well as perception, language, and thought and memory (largely in the cognitive theoretical framework).

A new generation of researchers emerged who worked in collaboration with other countries, such as the USA, the UK, and the Netherlands. New approaches were developed and adopted in child development, social psychology, language and communications, and group relationships. In child development, after a period of enthusiasm for Bernstein's models and Piaget's research (G. Petter), interest moved toward language and the social learning model. Social psychology covers various fields such as intergroup comparisons, verbal communication, and social and cognitive behavior. Experimental studies to assess the structure of personality have also been undertaken.

C. Musatti's published works mainly focus on Freud's psychoanalysis, but always with particular regard to different social and cultural backgrounds. F. Fornari's psychoanalytic publications of the Coinemi Theory and his definition of the discipline have been an important contribution to today's psychoanalytic knowledge in Italy. J. Ancona and E. Servadio overcame the opposition of professional psychologists from SIPS and the academic psychologists, with a discussion linking psychoanalysis and the world of human sciences, including critical remarks on existential psychotherapy.

F. Metelli's scientific work on perception, such as the revelation of figural and chromatic conditions that govern the perception of a transparent object, has been important. Metelli developed a model that describes perceptive transparency by means of algebraic equations. Perception psychologists all over the world acclaimed the usefulness of this model, which was also published in *Scientific American*. In 1967 Metelli was elected a fellow of the American Psychological Association.

Other researchers continue investigating movement, hearing, and tactile perception (P. Bozzi). Also outstanding is the work of G. Vicario, a former student of G. Kanizsa, on acoustic and visual perception, temporal phenomena, and the perception of successive visual stimuli displayed in overprinting.

Visual perception, harmony of colors, perceptual transparency with chromatic hues, and the perceptual phenomenon of fog have been studied by Da Pos. Art psychology is studied by Samerin. Bonaiuto studies perception, perceptual incongruence, the psychology of art, fashion trends, and creativity, for which he has devised a measure. Bartoli studies the psychoanalytic approach to visual art. In Padua, optical illusions are studied by Roncato; visual perception and learning in animals, by Zanforlin; psychophysical investigation on transparency, by Masin; memory, by Cornoldi; and the field of neuropsychology by Marzi, Stegagmo, and Semenza. In Rome, Bertini studies sleep and dreams; Pizzamiglio, balance and aftereffects of brain lesions.

In psychosociology, an ongoing study on the quality of life in postindustrial society is being conducted, particularly regarding the problems of the young (Harrison). The sociopsychology of interpersonal and intergroup relations and comparisons is also being studied. Capozza has adopted mathematical models in sociopsychology, while various other methods are being used by Burigana, Cristante, Lucca, and Renzi in Rome.

Majer and Novaga lead research on psychology in the industrial world. In Rome, De Grada studies social stereotypes, and Ponzo studies child stereotypes in adults. Studies on theoretical and empirical assessment of personality are performed by Rubini and Comunian; investigations of psychodiagnostic techniques, by Passi and Cattonaro. Rational dynamics for solving marital conflicts have been developed by Cusinato (Padua). In Rome, Caprara studies aggressiveness and personality theories, and Laicardi studies aging. Psychiatry, psychoanalysis, mental health, and prevention are also active areas of research.

An important cultural link was made in the history of psychology by Brozek and Ross. This was facilitated by the widespread interest shown in the history of psychology when it was introduced in Italy as an epistemological trend by N. Dazzi, of the Centro Nazionale di Ricerche (Rome), G. Mucciarelli and Caramelli (Bologna), and Marhaba (Padua).

Generally, it can be said that the 1980s witnessed a growing interest in studies in all areas of psychology. This trend is caused by the expansion of the universities and the resulting increase in the number of positions, but mostly by the restructuring of the courses necessary to obtain a degree in psychology.

Issues that are still open and currently being discussed are offering courses in psychology in other Italian universities, improvement in the quality of the courses, more specific orientation for students after graduation, and development of the most valid techniques of psychotherapy to be applied in the community and private practice. The solution to these problems represents a real challenge to Italian psychology. The psychologists committed to their science and profession have started to look to the future. Out of this state of affairs has come international cooperation, already begun, with other European universities.

Bibliography

AA. VV. (1976). Gli psicologi interrogano se stessi. *Psicologia Contemporanea, 3,* 14–18.

Brozek, J., & Pongratz, L. J. (1980). *Historiography of modern psychology.* Toronto: Hogrefe.

Brozek, J., & Pongratz, L. J. (1980). *Storiografia della psicologia moderna.* Centro Scientifico Torinese.

Lazzerani, V. (1972). La psicologia scientifica in Italia. In L. Ancona (Ed.), *Nuove questioni di psicologia* (pp. 75–119). Brescia: La Scuola.

Lo Verso, G., et al. (1987). *Viaggio attraverso l'acipelago: Una ricerca sulla psicologia clinica e psicoterapia in Italia.* Milan: Franco Angeli.

Luccio, R. (1984). Quindici anni di psicologia in Italia [Special issues]. *Psicologia Contemporanea, 60, 61, 62.*

Marhaba, S. (1981). *Lineamenti della psicologia Italiana (1870–1945).* Florence: Giunti.

Marzi, A., & Chiari, S. (1976). Italy. In V. S. Sexton & H. Misiak (Eds.), *Psychology around the world* (pp. 228–241). Monterey, CA: Brooks/Cole.

Minguzzi, Gian Franco. (1974). Lo psicologo alla ricerca del suo sè. *Psicologia Contemporanea, 5, 7–11.*

Trentini, G., et al. (1977). *La professione dello psicologo in Italia.* Milan: Istituto Editoriale Internazionale, ISEDI.

Vegetti Finzi, S. (1986). *Storia della psicoanalisi.* Milan: Mondadori.

25 / Japan

SEISOH SUKEMUNE

Seisoh Sukemune (born 1929) received a PhD from Hiroshima University in 1977. A specialist in child development, he has published more than 160 articles and books on prosocial behavior, concept attainment, observational learning, and related topics. He serves on the editorial review board of three Japanese journals of psychology and is a board member of the Japanese Psychological Association. He is professor of psychology in both the Research Institute of Early Childhood and the Graduate School of Hiroshima University.

Psychology was first taught in Japan at Tokyo University and Kyoto University in the early part of this century. The pioneers were Yujiro Motora (1858–1912) and Matataro Matsumoto (1865–1943). Matsumoto studied under Scripture at Yale University in the USA and under Wundt at Leipzig University in Germany. Before World War II, there were a limited number of colleges and universities under the old school system, although psychology was taught at several major institutions. The most important fields of psychology in those days were perception and learning. After studying in Germany or the United States, most psychologists became teachers.

After World War II several colleges and universities were created as part of the new school system. Many psychologists studied in the United States rather than in Germany, and new fields such as developmental, educational, social, clinical, industrial, and physiological psychology were born. In 1972 the 20th Congress of the International Union of Psychological Science (IUPsyS) was held in Tokyo; the 22nd International Congress of Applied Psychology was held in Kyoto in 1990. The 48th Annual Convention of the International Council of Psychologists was held in Tokyo in 1990; the 9th Biennial Convention of the International Society for the Study of Behavioral Development (ISSBD) was held in Tokyo in 1987. There are about 4,400 psychologists in Japan at the present time.

I wish to thank Toshiyuki Shiraiski, a graduate student of Hiroshima University, for his assistance in collecting materials for this chapter.

Education and Training

Educational system

The modern school system in Japan was formally inaugurated in 1872 after the Meiji Restoration. In 1947, after World War II, the school Education Law was enacted which greatly modified the old system. The new law established the principle of equality of educational opportunity, as required by the United States Educational Mission, as the basis for Japanese education.

Under the new school system, all children who have completed the elementary school course proceed to the junior high school course, thus extending the compulsory education period from 6 to 9 years. A senior high school course, which was started in 1948, consists of full-time, part-time, and correspondence courses. Colleges and universities began operation under the new school system in 1949. A senior college system started operation in 1950 and was legally established in 1964; a technical college system began in 1962; a new graduate school system started in 1953. Figure 25.1 is a sketch of the present school system in Japan.

There are schools for the deaf, schools for the blind, and schools for other physically and mentally handicapped people. Attendance at the schools for the deaf and the blind has been compulsory since 1948, but attendance at the schools for other handicapped people became mandatory only in 1979. Kindergartens, special training schools, and other miscellaneous schools are also provided. There is a 6-year medical school system corresponding to both the undergraduate course and the graduate school master's course, as seen in Figure 25.1. There is also the University of the Air, founded in 1983. All the aforementioned schools are under the jurisdiction of the Ministry of Education, Science, and Culture. The day nursery system for preschool

Nursery School	Kindergarten	Elementary School	Junior High School	Senior High School		University	Graduate School Master Course	Graduate School Doctor Course
					Medical School			
					Junior College			
				Technical College				

| 1 | 2 | 3 | 4 | 5 | 6 | 7 | 8 | 9 | 10 | 11 | 12 | 13 | 14 | 15 | 16 | 17 | 18 | 19 | 20 | 21 | Grade |
| 0 | 1 | 2 | 3 | 4 | 5 | 6 | 7 | 8 | 9 | 10 | 11 | 12 | 13 | 14 | 15 | 16 | 17 | 18 | 19 | 20 | 21 | 22 | 23 | 24 | 25 | 26 | 27 | Age |

FIGURE 25.1. *Japan's school system.*

TABLE 25.1
Higher Education in Japan: Number of Schools, by Sponsor (as of 1988)

Classification	National	Local Government	Private	University of the Air	Total
Technical college	54	4	4		62
Junior college	40	54	477		571
University	95[a]	38[b]	357	1	491
Graduate school	93	23	178		294

a 95,481 freshmen as of 1989.
b 11,694 freshmen as of 1989.

children (ages 0–5) is under the jurisdiction of the Ministry of Welfare (see Figure 25.1).

The percentages of students at each level attending the various levels of schools are kindergarten, 33.6 percent; day nursery, 25.5 percent; elementary school, 99.9 percent; junior high school, 99.9 percent; senior high school, 94.2 percent; junior college, college, and university, 37.4 percent; and graduate school, 4 percent (Ministry of Education, Science, and Culture, 1980, 1981, 1982; Nihon kyouiku Nenkan Publishing Committee, 1985).

Training Instruction and Curricula

In Japan there are 1,348 institutions of higher education available for the population of 118 million (Ministry of Education, Science, and Culture, 1980, 1981, 1982; Nihon kyouiku Nenkan Publishing Committee, 1985) (Table 25.1). The major universities having doctoral programs in psychology are shown in Table 25.2. Table 25.3 lists the courses provided for undergraduate students majoring in psychology at Hiroshima University. This program is fairly typical of students in other programs. Table 25.4 shows the courses for experimental psychology, educational psychology, and child psychology at the Hiroshima University graduate school.

The entrance examination for most graduate schools in psychology in Japan consists of major subject tests and one or two foreign-language tests. Students generally take English, German, or French, but some students take Chinese or Russian. There are more male graduate students than female, but the number of the latter is increasing gradually.

Students studying for master's degrees are required to write theses. Stu-

TABLE 25.2

Main Japanese Universities with Doctoral Programs in Psychology, as of 1988

National Government	Private	Local
Kyushu University (Fukuoka)	Doshisha University (Kyoto)	Tokyo Metropolitan University (Tokyo)
Hiroshima University (Hiroshima)	Kwansei Gakuin University (Nishinomiya)	Osaka City University (Osaka)
Osaka University (Osaka)	Chukyo University (Nagoya)	
Kyoto University (Kyoto)	Keio University (Tokyo)	
Nagoya University (Nagoya)	Waseda University (Tokyo)	
Tokyo University (Tokyo)	Rikkyo University (Tokyo)	
Tsukuba University (Ibaragi)	Aoyama Gakuin University (Tokyo)	
Tohoku University (Sendai)	Nihon University (Tokyo)	
Hokkaido University (Sapporo)	Komazawa University (Tokyo)	
	Hiroshima Shudo University (Hiroshima)	
	Meisei University (Tokyo)	
	Konan Women's University (Kobe)	
	Gakushuin University (Tokyo)	
	Aichigakuin University (Aichi)	

dents who wish to study for doctoral degrees, after obtaining their master's degrees, must take another entrance examination. Usually, it is difficult for Japanese graduate students to obtain PhDs. Generally speaking, Japanese PhD students in psychology spend quite a few years working on their dissertations after having completed their graduate courses. The number of PhDs is much fewer than that of non-PhDs who complete their graduate coursework. However, the number of PhD dissertations has been increasing recently. Those who submit their dissertations are usually required to take two foreign-language examinations. The Japanese higher educational system is basically similar to the American system, with some differences. Figure 25.2 shows the total number of PhDs in psychology.

An assistant in Japanese colleges and universities is not a graduate student but a staff member. Graduates of graduate schools can be given this job. This

TABLE 25.3 *Courses for Undergraduate Students Majoring in Psychology (Hiroshima University)*

Experimental Psychology (lec., sem.)
Perceptual Psychology
Research Methods in Psychology
Computer Practice in Psychology (sem.)
Introductory Laboratory Projects I, II (sem.)
Advanced Laboratory Projects I, II (sem.)
Learning Psychology (lec., sem.)
Psychology of Thinking
Animal Psychology (lec.)
Statistical Methods in Psychology I, II (lec.)
Educational Measurement and Evaluation
Introduction to Physiology
Social Psychology (lec., sem.)
Group Dynamics
Introduction to Industrial Psychology
Introduction to Culture Psychology

Introduction to Social Welfare for the Handicapped
Research Methods in Social Surveying
Educational Psychology (lec., sem.)
Introduction to Clinical Psychology (lec., sem.)
Theories of Personality
Introduction to Psychological Testing I, II (lec., sem.)
Advanced Psychological Testing (lec., sem.)
Developmental Psychology (lec., sem.)
Early Childhood Psychology
Psychology of Adolescence
Life-Span Developmental Psychology
Introduction to Psychology of the Handicapped
Pathology of the Handicapped
Introduction to Psychiatry
Guidance Counseling for the Handicapped

Note. lec. = lecture; sem. = seminar.

differs from the assistant system in the USA. With regard to staff positions in Japanese colleges and universities, there are four levels: professor, assistant professor, lecturer, and assistant. The Japanese assistant professor is approximately equivalent to the associate professor in the United States; a Japanese lecturer is approximately equivalent to an American assistant professor.

Eligible graduate students are given scholarship loans from the Japan Scholarship Foundation. The amount for a master's course student is 69,000 yen per month, and 80,000 yen for a doctoral course student. However, students do not have to repay the loans if they are employed in higher educational institutions as part of the teaching staffs.

TABLE 25.4
Courses for Experimental Psychology, Educational Psychology, and Child Study (Hiroshima University Graduate School)

Experimental Psychology Major

Experimental Psychology (lec., sem., directed study)

Perceptual Psychology (lec., sem.)

Group Psychology (lec., sem., directed study)

Social Psychology (lec., sem.)

Educational Psychology Major

Educational Psychology (lec., sem., directed study)

Psychology of Personality (lec.)

Clinical Psychology (sem.)

Psychology of the Handicapped (lec., sem., directed study)

Developmental Psychology (lec., sem., directed study)

Environmental Cognition (sem.)

Learning Psychology (lec., sem., directed study)

Foundation of Behavior (lec.)

Child Study Major

Child Health (lec., sem., directed study, clinical work)

Child Psychiatry (special lec.)

Comprehensive Pediatrics (sem.)

Early Childhood Education (lec., sem., directed study, special lec., fieldwork)

Sociology of Early Childhood Education (sem.)

Theories of Curriculum in Early Childhood Education (special lec.)

Child Psychology (lec., sem., directed study, special lec., fieldwork)

Psychology of Early Childhood and Care (special lec.)

Methods of Measurement in Child Development (sem.)

History of Early Childhood Education (special lec.)

Child Development Theory (special lec.)

Note. lec. = lecture; sem. = seminar.

The Practice of Psychology and Current Research

Psychology graduates have made great contributions to Japanese society, and many hold important positions in schools, boards of education, educational and corrective institutions, companies, and governmental organizations. Table 25.5 lists their main professional jobs.

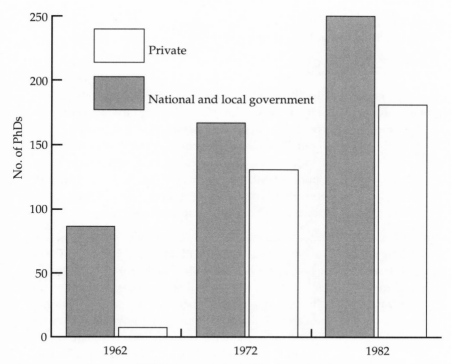

FIGURE 25.2. *Number of PhDs in psychology (data from* A Fifty-Year History of the Japanese Psychological Association, *Vol. 2, by the Japanese Psychological Association, 1987, Tokyo: Kaneko Shobou).*

The two major psychological associations are the Japanese Psychological Association (JPA) and the Japanese Association of Educational Psychology (JAEP). Figure 25.3 shows the total number of paper presentations at JPA from 1974 through 1988. Currently, more than 800 individual papers are presented each year. Figure 25.4 shows the mean number of paper presentations in each field at JPA from 1980 through 1988. The two major fields are: (1) sensation, perception, and cognition, and (2) learning, memory, language, thinking, and behavior. Figure 25.5 shows the total number of paper presentations at JAEP from 1968 through 1988. Over the past several years, about 500 individual papers were read at JAEP each year. The mean number of paper presentations in each field at the JAEP, 1980 through 1988, is shown in Figure 25.6. About half of the presentations are in the field of development.

A license system for clinical and counseling psychologists has not been established yet, although this problem has been discussed for some time. Nevertheless, psychology graduates work at the Child Guidance Center, the

TABLE 25.5

Main Employers of Psychologists in Japan

Employer	Affiliations and Status
Schools and boards of education	Teaching staffs: elementary schools, junior high schools, senior high schools, technical colleges, junior colleges, colleges and universities, schools for the mentally retarded, schools for the physically handicapped, schools for the deaf, schools for the blind, schools for the health-impaired, etc. Teacher consultants and superintendents: municipal and prefectural boards of education, etc.
Education and corrective institutions, governmental organizations	Educational testing and classification specialists: juvenile classification and detention homes, juvenile schools for boys, juvenile schools for girls, child guidance centers, consultation rooms for family and children, detention homes, scientific investigation research laboratories, prefectural police headquarters, corrective headquarters, prisons, etc. Probation Officers: Family Court. Governmental officials: Ministry of Education, Science, and Culture, Ministry of Labor, Ministry of Welfare, etc.
Companies	Correspondents: public broadcasting, private broadcasting, newspapers, etc. Editors: publishing companies. Office workers: trading companies, insurance companies, manufacturing companies, etc.
Hospitals	Psychometrists: hospitals, etc.

Juvenile Detention and Classification Home, and the Boys' and Girls' Reform and Training schools. There is an ad hoc committee on licensing for clinical and counseling psychologists in the Japanese Psychological Association. A system of licensing should emerge soon.

Studies unique to Japan and the Japanese people are not often done by young Japanese psychologists, but rather are carried out by a few elderly psychologists. For instance, Ryo Kuroda did work in the 1930s on *kan*, which means "hunch" relating to oriental ideas such as *satori*, which means "spiritual awakening," and Zen. Akishige did work on *chosin* and *chosoku*, associated with Zen and self-control. The Morita therapy is a unique therapeutic

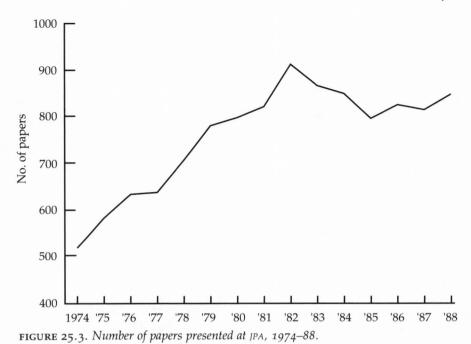

FIGURE 25.3. *Number of papers presented at* JPA, *1974–88.*

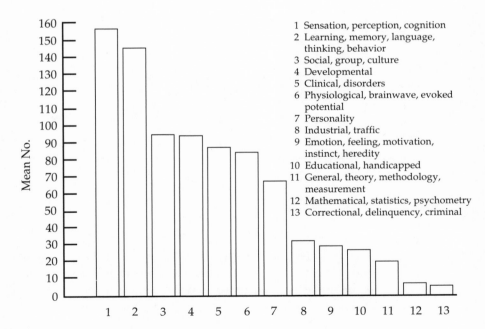

1 Sensation, perception, cognition
2 Learning, memory, language, thinking, behavior
3 Social, group, culture
4 Developmental
5 Clinical, disorders
6 Physiological, brainwave, evoked potential
7 Personality
8 Industrial, traffic
9 Emotion, feeling, motivation, instinct, heredity
10 Educational, handicapped
11 General, theory, methodology, measurement
12 Mathematical, statistics, psychometry
13 Correctional, delinquency, criminal

FIGURE 25.4. *Mean number of papers presented in each field at* JPA, *1980–88.*

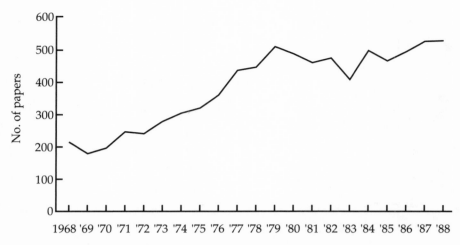

FIGURE 25.5. *Number of papers presented at JAEP, 1968–88.*

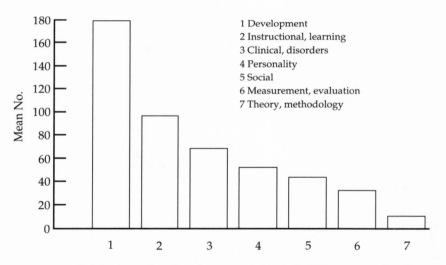

FIGURE 25.6. *Mean number of papers presented in each field at JAEP, 1980–88.*

technique for neuroses developed by Morita. Ichiro Koura has been working on the phenomenon of *iki ga au*, which means "interpersonal breath harmonization" between two persons such as guitar players or Japanese fencers, with the goal of understanding personality and interpersonal relations. Several psychologists are doing research on *amae*, which means "dependency, passivity, interdependence, intersubjectivity, or symbiosis." Generally speaking, most studies by Japanese psychologists are closely concerned

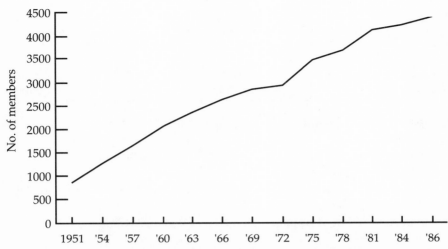

FIGURE 25.7. *Number of* JPA *members, 1951–86 (data from* A Fifty-Year History of the Japanese Psychological Association, *Vol. 2, by the Japanese Psychological Association, 1987, Tokyo: Kaneko Shobou).*

with basic and fundamental areas, even though clinical and educational psychologists have started to enter applied fields (Sukemune, 1983).

Psychological Associations

Figure 25.7 shows the number of members of JPA, 1951–86. The proportion of female members has been rising slowly, from 7 percent in 1952 to 20 percent in 1982. There are 15 major psychological associations in Japan, shown in Table 25.6.

National Journals

The main national journals for psychology in Japan are the *Japanese Journal of Psychology* (editor: Takayoshi Kaneko; published in Japanese with English abstracts); *Japanese Psychology Research* (editor: Takayoshi Kaneko; published in English); the *Japanese Journal of Educational Psychology* (chief editors: Tamotsu Fujinaga and Giyoo Hatano; published in Japanese with English abstracts); the *Annual Report of Educational Psychology in Japan* (editors: S. Hanazawa and others; published in Japanese with English abstracts).

TABLE 25.6

Major Psychological Associations in Japan

Name	Founding Date	Current President	No. of Members
Japanese Psychological Association	1927	Hiroshi Motoaki	4,400
Japanese Association of Educational Psychology	1959	Chitoshi Tatsuno	3,800
Association of Japanese Clinical Psychologists	1982	Hayao Kawai	3,600
Japan Association of Applied Psychology	1931	Toshio Akiyama	850
Japanese Clinical Psychological Association	1964	Mutsuharu Shinohara	500
Japanese Association of Criminal Psychology	1963	Fumio Mugishima	820
Japanese Society of Social Psychology	1960	Tomio Kinoshita	900
Japanese Group Dynamics Association	1949	Jyuji Misumi	600
Japanese Society for Animal Psychology	1933	Yoshitaka Umeoka	450
Japanese Association of Humanistic Psychology	1982	Tetsuo Okado	350
Japanese Association of Theoretical Psychology	1960	Taijiro Hayasaka	90
Japanese Society for Physiological Psychology and Psychophysiology	1983	Yo Miyata	420
Japanese Psychonomic Society	1983	Takashi Ogawa	440
Man Environment Research Association	1982	Yasumi Yoshitake	160
Japanese Association of Health Psychology	1988	Tadashi Oda	200

Bibliography

Hidano, T. (Ed.). (1980). *The trends of modern psychology: 1946–1980* (in Japanese). Tokyo: Kawashima Shoten.

Hoshino, M., & Umemoto, T. (1987). Japanese psychology: Historical review and recent trends. In G. H. Blowers & A. M. Turtle (Eds.), *Psychology moving East: The status of Western psychology in Asia and Oceania* (pp. 183–196). Boulder, CO: Westview Press.

Iwahara, S. (1976). Japan. In V. S. Sexton & H. Misiak (Eds.), *Psychology around the world* (pp. 242–258). Monterey, CA: Brooks/Cole.

Japanese Psychological Association. (1980). *A fifty-year history of the Japanese Psychological Association* (in Japanese) (Vol. 1). Tokyo: Kaneko Shobou.

Japanese Psychological Association. (1986). *Psychological institutions in Japan.* Tokyo: Kenkyusha.

Japanese Psychological Association. (1987). *A fifty-year history of the Japanese Psychological Association* (in Japanese) (Vol. 2). Tokyo: Kaneko Shobou.

Kaneko, T. (1987). Development and present status of psychology in Japan. In A. R. Gilgen & C. K. Gilgen (Eds.), *International handbook of psychology* (pp. 274–296). New York: Greenwood Press.

Kodama, S. (1984). Historiography of psychology in Japan (1). In H. Carpintero (Ed.), *La Psicología en su contexto histórico: Ensayos en honor del Prof. Joseph Brozek* (pp. 187–192). Monografías de la Revista de Historia de la Psicología. Valencia, Spain: University of Valencia.

Ministry of Education, Science, and Culture. (1980). *Mombusho* (in Japanese). Printing of the Bureau of Ministry of Finance.

Ministry of Education, Science, and Culture. (1981). *Mombusho* (in Japanese). Printing of the Bureau of Ministry of Finance.

Ministry of Education, Science, and Culture. (1982). *Gakko kihon tokei* (in Japanese). Printing of the Bureau of Ministry of Finance.

Ministry of Welfare. (1982). *Shakai fukushi shisetsu chosa hokoku* (in Japanese). Printing of the Bureau of Ministry of Finance.

Nihon kyouiku Nenkan Publishing Committee. (1985). *Nihon kyouiku nenkan* (in Japanese). Tokyo: Gyosei.

Omura, A. (1988). *A status report on psychology in Japan.* Bangkok: UNESCO Regional Office for Education on Asia and the Pacific.

Sukemune, S. (1983). Japan, Japanese children and adults, and Japanese psychology today. *International Psychologist, 24,* (2), 16–18.

Sukemune, S. (1987). Psychology in Japan. In S. R. Perls (Ed.), *Psychology: An international perspective* (pp. 62–80). Albuquerque, NM: Professional Seminar Consultants.

Tsukada, T. (1977). Educational psychology in Japan. In A. Yoda (Ed.), *New dictionary of educational psychology* (pp. 621–622). Tokyo: Kaneko Shobou.

Umeoka, Y. (Ed.). (1986). *The trends of modern psychology: 1981–1985* (in Japanese). Tokyo: Jitsugyo Kyouiku Shuppan.

Yoshida, M. (1971). The state of research of psychology in Japan. In T. Suenaga (Ed.), *Psychology: Vol. 1. History and trends* (pp. 275–291; in Japanese). Tokyo: University of Tokyo Press.

26 / Korea

GENE YOON

Gene Yoon (born 1945) received BA and MA degrees from Seoul National University and the PhD in social psychology from St. Louis University in the USA. Before returning to Korea, he taught at the University of Wisconsin-Manitowoc and worked as a postgraduate fellow at the Andrus Gerontology Center at the University of Southern California.

His major interest areas are life-span developmental psychology, social psychology, and adjustment. He has published more than 20 articles and a book, Psychology of Adulthood and Aging *(in Korean), and has translated two books into Korean, Aronson's* The Social Animal *(2nd ed.) and Seligman's* Helplessness. *In 1987–88 Yoon was secretary-general of the Korean Psychological Association. He is professor at Yonsei University.*

Status of Psychology

With the economy and industry booming since the late 1960s, Korea has been prospering in every respect: political, economic, social, cultural, technological, and academic. Psychology is no exception. In fact, it is one of the areas to derive the greatest benefit from the social and economic development. For example, since the first psychology major graduated from Keijo University (the former main body of the current Seoul National University) in 1930, up until 1977, Korea had only five psychology departments (Seoul National University, Korea University, Chung-ang University, Ewha Women's University, and SungKyunKwan University). There are now 25 colleges and universities with psychology departments. Many more colleges have departments of education and child studies that offer courses in educational psychology, human development, personality, psychological testing, and mental health. The trend of expansion in psychology departments is particularly noteworthy since 1977, and the psychological sciences have become one of the key areas of the social and basic sciences.

Until 1945, when the Second World War ended, Korea had only six BA degree holders in psychology. In 1954 two MA degrees were bestowed for the first time. The Korean Psychological Association was begun by seven first-generation psychologists in February 1946. Recently, its membership has grown to 314. The number of full-time faculty members rose from 28 to approximately 143 (in 1987). The number of undergraduate majors increased from 582 in 1976 to more than 3,096 in 1983. Finally, the number of graduate students grew from 53 in 1976 to 199 in 1983 (149 in the MA programs and 50 in the doctoral programs) (Cha, 1987).

Korean Psychological Association

The Korean Psychological Association (KPA) is the only comprehensive academic organization for psychology in Korea. Its membership stood at 314 (212 males and 102 females) in 1987. A master's degree in psychology is the minimum requirement for full membership. However, some other degree holders who have demonstrated extraordinary performance and experience in teaching or in research can become members in accordance with the review processes of the KPA.

The KPA has six divisions. Their names and membership size in 1987 are as follows: Experimental and Cognitive Psychology ($N = 45$), Social Psychology ($N = 50$), Developmental Psychology ($N = 30$), Industrial and Organizational Psychology ($N = 50$), Clinical Psychology ($N = 65$), Counseling and Psychotherapy ($N = 56$).

The KPA holds an annual convention in October and a Spring Symposium of Psychology each year. Whereas the annual convention focuses on academic activities and the presentation of research articles, the Spring Symposium Program emphasizes the application of psychological knowledge to the real world. Since 1981 the association has also sponsored Winter Workshops, a series of lectures to introduce new developments in research methodology and recent trends in different areas of psychology to members and graduate students.

The *Korean Journal of Psychology*, the only official, academic journal in Korea, was launched in 1968 and is published twice a year with articles in Korean and English. Its English abstracts are carried by *Psychological Abstracts*, a publication of the American Psychological Association. Another official publication of the KPA is the *KPA Newsletter*, published bimonthly. Although not official journals of the KPA, the *Journal of Clinical Psychology* (Clinical Psychology Division) and *Studies in Social Psychology* (Social Psychology Division) are published annually. Other divisions were also preparing to create divisional journals in 1988.

Currently, the KPA and two of its divisions, Clinical Psychology and Counseling and Psychotherapy, are jointly operating licensing examination systems under which qualified clinical and counseling psychologists are licensed. As of 1987, 30 clinical psychologists and 15 counseling psychologists were licensed under this system. They work in hospital settings (more than 10 of them hold faculty positions in the departments of neuropsychiatry of medical colleges) and college counseling centers. The KPA is affiliated with the International Union of Psychological Science and is a member of the Korean Social Science Research Council.

The occupational breakdown of the 298 KPA members in 1983 shows the largest single occupational group to be full-time college professors (152), followed by employees of mental hospitals (20), part-time college instructors (16), full-time researchers in the institutes (16), government officials (including military officers) (6), and miscellaneous (38) (Cha, 1987).

Of the total of 71 doctorates, 36 came from departments of psychology (as contrasted with departments of education, educational psychology, and others). Half of the 36 psychology degrees came from Korean universities, and another 18 came from foreign universities: 11 from the USA, 5 from West Germany, 1 from France, and 1 from Canada. Of the other 35 doctoral degree holders from nonpsychology departments, 11 came from Korea, 23 from the USA, and 1 from Japan. Relatively large numbers of doctorates are represented in counseling, educational, social, developmental, and experimental psychology.

Education and Professional Activities

Traditionally, psychology has been taught at the college level as a course in general studies or the humanities. After 1990, however, psychology will be taught as an elective course at the senior high school level.

The universities that offer undergraduate courses and MA and PhD graduate training are as follows: (1) Eight universities have all three (undergraduate, master's, and doctoral) degree programs: Chung-ang U., Ewha Women's U., Korea U., Kyungpuk National U., Seoul National U., Seoul Women's U., SungKyunKwan U., and Yonsei U. (2) Ten universities have only undergraduate and master's degree programs: Chonnam National U., Chonpuk National U., Choongnam National U., Choongpuk National U., Daegu U., Hyosung Women's U., Kyemyung U., Pusan National U., Sookmyung Women's U., and Yeungnam U. (3) Seven universities have only undergraduate programs: Aju U., Dueksung Women's U., Kangwon National U., Kyungnam U., Kyungsang National U., Sacred Heart Women's U., and Sungshin Women's U. Of these 25 universities, SungKyun-

Kwan U. has a Department of Industrial Psychology, and three women's universities (Ewha, Sookmyung, and Seoul) have a Department of Educational Psychology.

The departmental enrollment quota for each college is regulated by the Ministry of Education. The total number of freshmen majoring in psychology is approximately 1,000; the total enrollment for undergraduates in psychology is around 4,000. The master's and doctoral programs are separate. Each program applicant takes a separate entrance examination (psychology, English, and one other foreign language—typically, French or German in most graduate psychology programs).

Psychology instruction depends mainly on lectures in college, and the major textbooks in Korean and English are used. Since the late 1970s, 40 or more basic textbooks have been published in Korea. Some of them were written originally by Korean psychologists, and others were translated from foreign textbooks and references.

Several psychological tests and appraisal instruments are used in Korea. For example, the Wechsler Adult Intelligence Scale (WAIS) (renamed the KWIS, Korea Wechsler Intelligence Scale), the WISC, the MMPI, the TAT, the Rorschach, and the Bender-Gestalt Test are all popular in the clinical settings, as are the Draw-a-Person Test and the Draw-a-Tree Test.

Most psychology departments have psychology laboratories for basic experimental research and demonstration. Their facilities include personal computers and basic equipment for perception, cognitive, and memory studies. Korea University and Yeungnam University have a physiological psychology laboratory with facilities for animal research and psychopharmacology. Yonsei University and Seoul National University take pride in their laboratory facilities for perception and cognitive science research.

Training for the clinical and counseling psychologist is somewhat different from the regular graduate programs. The KPA Division of Clinical Psychology requires the MA degree in clinical psychology and 3 years' practicum for the license. Therefore, there are several hospital settings that supervise the clinical psychologists' practice. For example, Seoul National University, Department of Neuropsychiatry, has a 3-year residency program for clinical psychology. Hanyang University and Wonkwang University hospitals have similar residency programs for young psychologists.

Most student guidance centers, affiliated with all colleges and universities under governmental policy, provide the opportunity for both counseling and psychological testing practica during the MA course and the post–MA course period.

The major research grants come from several funding sources: the Ministry of Education; the A-san Foundation for Social Welfare, affiliated with the Hyundai Business Group; the Daewoo Foundation, sponsored by the Daewoo Corporation Group; and other, small-scale funding agencies. College faculty members can receive some grants from their own college funds. Foundations and the Ministry of Education partly support the publication of the official journal, the *Korean Journal of Psychology*.

In Korea there are several private institutes for applied research and psychological services. The Korean Institute for Research in Behavioral Sciences (KIRBS) is the representative institute in the country for the study of behavioral sciences, psychology, education, sociology, anthropology, and management sciences. It was founded by Bum Mo Chung and his colleagues, supported by the Ministry of Education in 1967, and its purposes are the development of social sciences and the dissemination of research results. The Institute of Human Development and Welfare (established by Bong Yon Suh in 1979) has several programs for child care, including a special class for autistic children, and publishes a series of developmental psychology books. The Institute for Psychological Counseling (created by In Za Kim, of Seogang Jesuit University, in 1986) is actively providing counseling and psychological services for the public. Its programs include sensitivity training, group counseling, special mental health services for young workers in an industrial complex, and some unique workshops for the clergy.

Leading Psychologists and Their Contributions

The prevailing trend in scientific psychology is the cognitive or behavioral approach, similar to that in much of the Western world, including the USA. Korean psychology has had a tradition of experimental psychology since the early 1930s, and most of the pioneers and the first-generation psychologists worked in experimental and empirical research. However, counseling and clinical psychologists take diverse theoretical approaches, including traditional psychoanalysis, behavior modification, and client-centered (Rogerian) therapy. Recently, for example, Tong-Shik Lee (a psychiatrist), Ho Kyun Yun (a psychologist), and their colleagues started a new counseling and psychotherapy method based on Buddhism and Zen.

The leading scholars and instructors of psychology include Euichul Lee, Yang-Eun Chung, Yong-shin Joen, Sung-Tae Kim, Ki-Suk Kim, Bum Mo Chung, Wonshik Chung, Jae-Ho Cha, Chunghoon Choy, and Bong-Yon Suh. Four on this list belong to Seoul National University, which has the longest history and the largest psychology faculty (11). Euichul Lee, a professor emeritus, taught many prominent young psychologists throughout his life of 75 years. Yang-Eun Chung, who has been teaching for more than 30 years, set the cornerstone of experimental social psychology and created the journal *Studies in Social Psychology*. Jae-Ho Cha, who holds the PhD in social psychology from the University of California, Los Angeles, has conducted several research projects on value systems and on attitude and attributional processes. Bong-Yon Suh, a female psychologist, has completed several important studies in child development, ego identity development, and the training of autistic children.

At Korea University there are three leading psychologists. Yong-Shin Joen, a professor emeritus, developed the Korean Wechsler Intelligence Scale, the Korea University-Binet Intelligence Test, and Rorschach Scoring Manual. Sung-Tae Kim, a widely known personality developmental psychologist, has published numerous articles and two books, *Sung-Sook-In-Gyunk-Ron* (The mature personality) and *Kyung-Kwa-Jui* (Kyung thought and attention). Ki-Suk Kim is a mentor of physiological psychology in Korea. In the 1960s and early 1970s he taught Rogerian counseling and led the counseling movement in Korea, and then returned to his original academic interest, physiological psychology. At Yonsei University, Chunghoon Choy, a counseling psychologist who had studied at Stanford and the University of Northern Colorado, introduced humanistic approaches.

Two more persons should be mentioned. Bum Mo Chung, a former professor of educational psychology at Seoul National University, who studied at the University of Chicago in the 1950s, established the psychometry and educational psychology laboratory at the Department of Education, Seoul National University. Many prominent educational psychologists in the country were his students. He also established the Korean Institute for Research in Behavioral Sciences and contributed to the application of the behavioral sciences to the real world. Wonshik Chung, of the Education Department at Seoul National University, a counseling and educational psychologist, has written several basic books and developed psychological tests for high school and college students.

There are several newly emerging areas. First of all, the fields of clinical and counseling psychology are prosperous, consistent with the economic development of the country and the social welfare policy of the government. More jobs have been created for mental health professionals. Second, the education and care of autistic children and children with learning disabilities are growing areas. Many psychologists and special education specialists are interested in these fields. Third, the subjects of adulthood and aging are gaining widespread attention. Some young psychologists trained in the USA have returned to Korea and are offering courses and working on aging problems and on the well-being of the middle-aged and elderly. Basic experimental psychology currently focuses on laboratory technology and computer use for primary areas such as perception, cognition, memory, and physiological psychology.

Bibliography

Cha, Jae-Ho. (1978). Korean psychology: A study of science and profession (in English). *Social Science Journal* (Korean Social Science Research Council), 5, 142–184.

Cha, Jae-Ho. (1987). Psychology in Korea. In G. H. Blowers & A. M. Turtle (Eds.), *Psychology moving East: The status of Western psychology in Asia and Oceania* (Chap. 11). Boulder, CO: Westview Press.

Chang, Hyun-Kab. (1984). *Ko-rip Sung-chang Kwa Haeng-dong Chang-ae*. Gyongsan: Yeungnam University Press.

Hahn, Duck-Woong. (1985). *Jo-Jik Hang-dong Eui Dong-gi E-ron* (2nd ed.). Seoul: Bummunsa.

Kim, Jai-Eun. (1974). *Han-kook Ka-jok Eui Shim-ni*. Seoul: Ewha Women's University Press.

Kim, Sung-Tae. (1976). *Sung-Sook-In-Gyunk-Ron*. Seoul: Korea University Press.

Kim, Sung-Tae. (1982). *Kyung-Kwa-Jui*. Seoul: Korea University Press.

Yoon, Gene. (1985). *Sung-In Noh-In Shim-ni-hak*. Seoul: Jung-Ang Chuksung Chulpansa.

Yoon, Tae-Rim. (1966). *Han-kook-in Eui Sung-Gyuk*. Seoul: Hyundai Kyoyuk Chongseo Chulpansa.

Zoh, Myung-Han. (1982). *Han-kook Ah-dong Eui Eun-Er Hyek-Duk Yon-Gu*. Seoul: National University Press.

27 / Mexico

ROLANDO DIAZ-LOVING &

PABLO VALDERRAMA ITURBE

Rolando Diaz-Loving (born 1954) received a PhD from the University of Texas at Austin in 1982. A specialist in social psychology and cross-cultural psychology, he is the author of more than 30 scientific articles and the textbook Introducción a la psicología. *Diaz-Loving is past president of the Mexican Association of Social Psychology and editor of* Revista de Psicología Social y Personalidad. *He is currently chair of the Graduate School of Psychology of the National University of Mexico (UNAM).*

Pablo Valderrama Iturbe (born 1959) received a licenciate from the National University of Mexico in 1984. His major areas of interest are the history of Mexican psychology and sport psychology. He is the author of scientific articles and editor of the Information Bulletin of the Latin American Society of the History of Science and Technology. *He is currently technical secretary to the Area of Services at the Faculty of Psychology of the National University of Mexico.*

Contemporary Mexican psychology can be traced from pre-Colombian antecedents of modern-day clinical practice (Leon-Sanchez & Patiño-Muñoz, 1984), through colonial ethnographic descriptions considered to be precursors of contemporary social psychological, ethnographic, and epidemiological research (Diaz-Loving & Medina-Liberty, 1987), to relevant psycophysiological and sociocultural studies conducted during the present century (Valderrama & Rivero del Pozo, 1983). However, the cornerstone for the current development, image, and practice of psychology was the installation in 1973 of the Faculty of Psychology at the Universidad Nacional Autónoma de México (UNAM) (National University of Mexico). Before this event only a few universities had psychology departments, and they were embedded within philosophy faculties. Moreover, most educational institutions did not include psychology courses in their curricula.

With the founding of the Faculty of Psychology in 1973, an already growing interest in the field crystallized into the creation of psychology faculties, schools, and departments around the country. (Faculties are formed in Mexican universities when a school or department grows to include a large

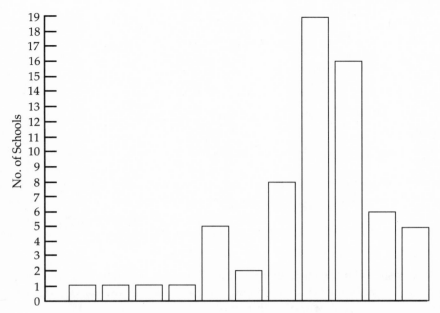

FIGURE 27.1. *Number of psychology schools created in Mexico, 1950–85 (data from* Un análisis curricular de la enseñanza de la psicologiá en México *by M. L. Morales, M. López, P. Parra, & J. Guadarrama, 1980, Mexico City: ANUIES, SEP, CENEIP).*

number of professors and students and offers both professional [licenciates] and graduate degrees) (Figure 27.1). The proliferation of psychology programs coincided with an overwhelming enrollment of students in the area (Table 27.1).

Educational Background, Training, and Certification

Currently, to practice as a psychologist, students must first complete a high school education with a major degree in the chemical-biological sciences. They then enter a university, where after nine semesters of psychology courses, one semester of social work, and a written thesis, they obtain a professional degree in psychology (licenciate). The training includes six semesters of basic and general psychological and methodological knowledge and three semesters in a specific area (social, clinical, educational, experimental, industrial-organizational, or physiological). In the specialty,

TABLE 27.1

Number of Students Enrolled in Mexico's Professional Psychology Schools, 1956–83

	1956	1970	1976–77	1977–78	1978–79	1979–80	1981–83
No. of students	200	2,300	15,188	19,310	22,645	25,698	40,000

Source. Data from "Un decada en la psicología experimental" by F. Cabrer, A. Herrera, L. Rodríguez, & E. Díaz, in *Una decada de la Facultad de Psicología, 1973–1983*, edited by F. García, & J. Molina, 1983, Mexico City: UNAM; "Contemporary Psychology in Mexico" by R. Díaz-Guerrero, 1984, *Annual Review of Psychology, 35,* 83–112.

courses should integrate both applied and research materials. All university curricula, professors' credentials and student theses are reviewed and sanctioned by either UNAM or officials of the Secretaría de Educación Pública (SEP) (Ministry of Public Education).

Once students complete a university program of study, they present their degree to the SEP and obtain a professional certificate (*cédula profesional*), which enables them to practice as psychologists in their area of specialization. However, the certification process is not strictly controlled. Consequently, it is virtually impossible to estimate accurately the number of active psychologists in the country.

Characteristics of the Psychologist

A review of 10 studies conducted from 1964 to 1984 (Lavalle, 1987) shows a predominance of female psychology students and professionals (between 63 percent and 78 percent of the psychologist population). The pattern of percentages for each sex across time does not show a clear trend, and hence predictions for the future are not possible.

The orientation of psychology in Mexico is predominantly clinical and/or applied. This emphasis is evident both in the school curricula and in the activities undertaken by professionals in the field. The basic degree constitutes a formal authorization to practice psychology. A very high percentage of the 64 schools that offer psychology as a career stress applied and/or clinical specializations. Thus, 60 percent of the universities have clinical, educational, and organizational-labor-industrial programs, and 30 percent give general

TABLE 27.2

Number of Students at the Faculty of Psychology, UNAM, by Area, 1972–82

Area	1972	1973	1974	1975	1976	1977	1978	1979	1980	1981	1982
Clinical	316	232	335	423	551	847	895	877	854	834	820
Educational	171	199	367	394	403	472	452	389	326	210	186
Experimental			48	126	148	186	139	98	58	56	35
Psycho-physiology		6	8	19	15	24	48	51	29	24	35
Social	112	170	153	196	200	167	341	295	255	163	128
Industrial		226	302	323	499	471	465	475	465	498	470

Source. Data from Planning and Evaluation Department of the Faculty of Psychology, UNAM.

psychology degrees with an emphasis on the clinical approach. By contrast, only 37 percent offer social psychology and, even then, with a strong community orientation; 12 percent have experimental programs stressing behavior modification. Only two schools offer degrees in psychophysiology.

The numbers of programs offered in specific areas are a reasonable reflection of the numbers of students enrolled in each area at a specific institution. An average of more than 50 percent of the students enroll in clinical psychology, followed by industrial, educational, and social. Very few students are enrolled in the experimental and psychophysiology areas (Table 27.2).

The workplace and the activities in which psychologists are involved also reflect an applied orientation. In general, the greatest demand is for industrial psychologists, who are hired by private companies to work in personnel selection and, more recently, to conduct training programs. The two other areas of demand are in the clinical and educational fields; these psychologists usually work for the government. Educational psychologists are hired by the SEP to conduct vocational and school guidance, special education, and general educational programing and evaluation. Clinical psychologists work mainly in health institutions, coordinated by the Secretaría de Salud (Ministry of Health) or by decentralized federal government agencies such as the Social Security System or the Centers for Juvenile Attention. In these facilities they conduct clinical evaluation and psychodiagnosis through interviews, clinical histories, and psychological testing. Although psychotherapy is becoming more common, it has been generally carried out by psychiatrists.

The opportunities in social, experimental, and physiological psychology are much more limited, since they focus primarily on research, and few institutions foster this activity. These psychologists are found largely in state universities and research institutes. However, recent trends in applied social psychology are creating a demand for the services of such professionals in community work, communication and marketing, as well as in the development and evaluation of public programs.

The orientation toward applied work is so prevalent that it even shows up in the type of research conducted by the Psychology Faculty at UNAM. (University and government officials estimate that more than 70 percent of the research in Mexico is done at UNAM.) In an analysis of the research conducted between 1977 and 1980, Urbina, Mercado, Colotla, Sanchez-Bedolla, and Aguilar (1982) report that of 613 research projects, 409 could be classified as applied research and 204 as basic. The explanation for the higher amount of applied work is twofold. First, there is a firm belief that the social sciences should be dedicated to assisting the public. In addition, as a developing country, Mexico has many social and economic problems to be solved, and the meager resources available are allocated to applied work.

Interestingly enough, in a survey conducted by Macotela (1979) on the public image of psychologists in Mexico, most people identified the psychologists' field of action as clinical; the reason given for soliciting their services was fundamentally to solve emotional problems. A large proportion of those interviewed believed that further participation of psychologists in the community was needed.

Universities Offering Studies in Psychology

As indicated earlier, 64 universities in Mexico offer degrees in psychology. These degrees range from the professional licenciate (a 5-year program) to master's degrees (2 to 3 years beyond the licenciate) and doctoral degrees (an additional 2 years). Graduate degrees require courses in theoretical subjects and methodological issues, research seminars, and a dissertation. The master's program was designed to prepare teachers of psychology, while the doctoral program prepares its graduates to do research in their field of interest.

The specialization at each level can be in psychophysiology or experimental, industrial, clinical, educational, or social psychology. There are some differences, but they are mostly variations on the basic programs. For example, human or animal experimental psychology or behavior analysis or modification could be emphasized within an experimental program. Universities with larger programs and their areas of specialization are presented in Table 27.3.

National Journals

The history of Mexican psychology journals dates back to 1874, when the first issue of *El Craneoscopio: Periódico Frenológico y Científico* (The skullscope: Journal of phrenology and science) was published. During the present century, as early as 1921, Pablo Border, a student of Wundt, published the first issue of the *Boletín Psicotécnico* (Psychotechnique bulletin) in which the new scientific methodologies of psychometric testing were presented.

By the late 1940s the first journals, published and sponsored by scientific and professional associations, had appeared. Examples are *Psiquis*, first published in 1947 by the Mexican League for Mental Health; the *Revista de Psicología* (1956–57), published only for a 2-year period; *Este Mes* (This month), which appeared from 1962 to 1967 under the auspices of the University Society for Scientific Psychology; and the *Revista Mexicana de la Investigación Psicológica* (Mexican journal of psychological research), published for several years in the late 1960s by the Sociedad Mexicana de Psicología (Mexican Psychology Society).

Most of the journals published before 1975 have been discontinued. According to Diaz-Guerrero (1984), most of these journals depended solely on the economic resources and efforts of their editors. Fortunately, and probably because of the growth of psychology after 1973, several journals initiated in the late 1970s have been systematically published into the 1980s. This is the case for *Enseñanza e Investigación en Psicología* (Teaching and research in psychology), published since 1975 by the National Council of Teaching and Research in Psychology (currently edited by Alberto Perez Cota at the Psychology Department of the Universidad de las Americas in Puebla), and the *Revista Mexicana de Análisis de la Conducta* (Mexican journal of behavioral analysis) which was started in 1975 by the Sociedad Mexicana de Análisis de la Conducta (Mexican Society of Behavioral Analysis) (currently edited by Francisco Cabrer of the Faculty of Psychology of UNAM in Mexico City).

In the 1980s there was a consolidation in the quality, quantity, and continuity of the journals. In addition to those listed above, there are two other examples of the current trend: the *Revista Mexicana de Psicología* (Mexican journal of psychology), sponsored by the Mexican Psychology Society since 1984 and edited by Juan Lafarga, who is at the Psychology Department of

TABLE 27.3

Universities Offering Studies of Psychology in Mexico

University	Areas of Specialization	Degree Offered
Universidad Autónoma del Edo. de Morelos	Social Clinical Educational Industrial	L
Universidad Autónoma de Guadalajara	Social Clinical Educational Industrial	L
Universidad de Guadalajara	Social Clinical Educational Industrial	L
Instituto Tecnológico de Estudios Superiores de Occidente	Social Clinical Educational Industrial	L
Universidad Veracruzana	Social Clinical Educational Experimental Industrial	L
Universidad Anahuac	Clinical Educational Industrial Psychophysiology	L
Universidad Autónoma Metropolitana Iztapalapa	Social	L
Universidad Autónoma Metropolitana Xochimilco	Social Educational	L

TABLE 27.3
(*Continued*)

University	Areas of Specialization	Degree Offered
Universidad Nacional Autónoma de México (UNAM)	Social Clinical Industrial Educational Experimental Psychophysiology	L, M, D
UNAM, Escuela Nacional de Estudios Profesio-nales, Iztacala	Social Clinical Experimental Behavior modification Behavior pharmacology	L, M
UNAM, Escuela Nacional de Estudios Profesio-nales, Zaragoza	Social Clinical Educational	L
Universidad Femenina de México	Clinical Industrial	L
Universidad Iberoamericana	Clinical Educational Industrial	L, M, D
Universidad Intercontinental	Social Clinical Educational Industrial	L
Universidad Autónoma de Nuevo León	Social Clinical Industrial Human development Analysis of behavior	L, M
Universidad Regiomontana	General Industrial	L

TABLE 27.3
(*Continued*)

University	Areas of Specialization	Degree Offered
Universidad de Monterrey	Social Clinical Educational Industrial Analysis of behavior	L
Instituto Tecnológico de Sonora	Social Clinical Educational Industrial	L
Universidad de las Americas	Social Clinical Educational Experimental	L, M
Universidad Autónoma de Puebla	Social Clinical Educational Experimental	L
Universidad Autónoma de Querétaro	Social Clinical Educational Industrial	L, M
Universidad Autónoma de Coahuila	Social Clinical Educational Industrial	L
Universidad Autónoma del Noroeste	General	L
Universidad del Noroeste	Clinical Educational Industrial	L

TABLE 27.3
(*Continued*)

University	Areas of Specialization	Degree Offered
Universidad Autónoma del Edo. de México	Social Clinical Educational	L
Universidad Autónoma de Yucatán	Educational	L, M

Note. L = licentiate, M = master's, D = doctorate.
Source. Data from "Mexico" by R. Díaz-Loving & A. Medina Liberty in *International Handbook of Psychology,* edited by A. Gilgen & C. Gilgen, 1987, New York: Greenwood Press.

the Universidad Iberoamericana in Mexico City, and the *Revista de Psicología Social y Personalidad* (Journal of social psychology and personality), published by the Asociación Mexicana de Psicología Social (Mexican Association of Social Psychology) since 1984 and edited by a council of the association.

Professional Societies and Organizations

In 1951 the Mexican Psychology Society was founded as a branch of the Interamerican Society of Psychology. Its first president was Manuel Falcon Guerrero, who was followed by Guillermo Davila, Rafael Nuñez, Rogelio Diaz-Guerrero, Angel San Roman, Mario Cicero, and Victor Colotla, who is the current president. This society officially represents Mexican psychologists and is a member of the International Union of Psychological Science. Other organizations and societies representing particular interests and/or approaches in psychology have also been formed. The most important organizations and societies are (1) the Mexican Society of Behavior Analysis, which, as already mentioned, publishes a journal. It holds an annual congress, and its current president is Arturo Bouzas. (2) The Mexican Association of Social Psychology publishes a journal (noted earlier) and holds a biannual congress. Patricia Andrade-Palos is president. (3) The Asociación Psicoanalítica Mexicana (Mexican Psychoanalytic Association) holds an annual congress and publishes the *Revista de Psicoanálisis, Psiquiatría y*

Psicología (Journal of psychoanalysis, psychiatry, and psychology). Its current president is José Camacho. (4) The Instituto Mexicano de Investigación en Familia y Población (IMIFAP) (Mexican Institute of Family and Population Research) carries out social psychology research, the development of applied programs, and program evaluation. Susan Pick de Weiss is the current president. (5) The Instituto Nacional de Ciencias del Comportamiento y la Actitud Pública, A.C. (INCCAPAC) (National Institute of Behavioral Science and Public Opinion), whose president is Rogelio Diaz-Guerrero, is involved in basic culture and personality research and applied educational and attitude research. (6) The Instituto Mexicano de Psiquiatría (Mexican Institute of Psychiatry) conducts epidemiological and clinical research and applications. Its current president is Ramón de la Fuente.

Current Status of Psychology

In the 1950s Mexican psychology was primarily dominated by psychiatrists and philosophers with either Frommian or Freudian psychoanalytic orientations. During that decade the only systematic psychological research was conducted by Rogelio Diaz-Guerrero on culture and personality, Erich Fromm on the Mexican agricultural worker, and Raul Hernandez-Peon in the area of psychophysiology. By the early 1960s the work of Diaz-Guerrero and several of his students (among them Serafin Mercado, Luis Lara Tapia, and Hector Capello), together with a vigorous academic exchange program (especially with the Departments of Psychology and Educational Psychology of the University of Texas at Austin), had instituted an experimentalist-behaviorist position as an alternative to the traditional and well-established psychoanalytic approach. Research during the 1960s centered primarily on the work of Hernandez-Peon and his collaborators, who conducted neurophysiological studies on sleep and dreaming, sensory-evoked potentials, and wakefulness and attention; and on the investigations of Diaz-Guerrero and his group at INCCAPAC on cross-cultural aspects of child development, coping styles, and affective meaning, among other topics.

During the late 1960s and early 1970s, once psychology as an area of study became more accepted, the behaviorist approach retreated, allowing for a more eclectic orientation that included the humanistic, cognitive, psychodynamic, behavioral, and social psychological positions. During the 1970s Emilio Ribes, Arturo Bouzas, Florente Lopez, Gustavo Fernandez, Vicente Garcia, Jorge Molina, and Hector Ayala conducted extensive experimental analyses of behavior, investigating response patterns, concurrent schedules, contingency of reinforcement, and, in general, observing the relationship among behavior theory, experimental research, and behavior modification techniques and applications. In the area of educational psychology, Ely Rayek, Fernando García, Juan Jose Sanchez-Sosa, Javier Aguilar, and others were concerned with the development and evaluation of educational programs and materials. Psychophysiological research conducted by Victor Colotla, Victor Alcaraz, Maria Corsi-Cabrera, and others continued Hernandez-Peon's tradition in this area, especially in studies of the psychophysiology of dreams and biofeedback. In the field of clinical psychology, research emphasized the diverse therapeutic orientations that became prevalent in Mexico. From a client-centered perspective, Juan Lafarga was absorbed in the study of the development and growth of human potential; Jose Cuelli and his colleagues developed a psychoanalytic model of community psychology; Santiago Ramirez incorporated a historical and cultural approach into psychoanalytic theory.

The emancipation and consolidation of the field of psychology through the late 1970s into the 1980s is best represented by the area of personality and social psychology. Research on culture, personality, attitudes, and applied psychology conducted during the 1970s by Rogelio Diaz-Guerrero, Isabel Reyes, Maria Luisa Morales, and Lucy Reidl, among others, established the relevance of psychology to the understanding of educational, political, and social issues, as well as its ability to find effective solutions to various social problems.

Following in this tradition, during the 1980s Eduardo Almeida and an interdisciplinary group immersed in a rural area of Puebla have contributed a substantial amount of ethnographic data and growth to the community through participant observation and action research. Another group, formed by faculty and students of the social graduate program at UNAM (Susan Pick de Weiss, Patricia Andrade-Palos, Rolando Diaz-Loving, and other collaborators) has developed and validated more than 20 multidimensional personality and social interaction inventories used in both basic and applied research. The extent and volume of information gathered about the Mexican people in the research conducted by these groups, as well as many others (for a review of Mexican psychological research during the 1980s, see Diaz-Guerrero, 1984; Pick de Weiss and Diaz-Loving, 1986; Diaz-Loving and Medina-Liberty, 1987), led Diaz-Guerrero (1986) to celebrate the emergence of a Mexican ethnopsychology. In fact, a graduate program on Mexican ethnopsychology directed by him is scheduled to open in 1990 at the State University of Morelos.

Other interesting developments in the 1980s were the creation of the first environmental psychology master's program, headed by Serafin Mercado and collaborators (1987), and the formation in 1988 of a master's program in health psychology, headed by Graciela Rodriguez. Both programs are offered at UNAM.

Bibliography

Cabrer, F., Herrera, A., Rodriguez, L., & Diaz, E. (1983). Una decada en la psicología experimental. In F. Garcia & J. Molina (Eds.), *Una decada de la Facultad de Psicología, 1973–1983*. Mexico City: UNAM.

Diaz-Guerrero, R. (1984). Contemporary psychology in Mexico. *Annual Review of Psychology, 35*, 83–112.

Diaz-Guerrero, R. (1986). Una etnopsicología mexicana. *Revista de Psicología Social y Personalidad, 2* (2), 1–22.

Diaz-Loving, R., & Medina-Liberty, A. (1987). Mexico. In A. R. Gilgen & C. K. Gilgen (Eds.), *International handbook of psychology* (pp. 297–323). New York: Greenwood Press.

Iturbe, P. V., & Rivero del Pozo, F. (1983). *Ensayos de historia de la psicología en México*. Unpublished professional thesis, UNAM, Mexico City.

Lavalle, I. (1987). *El perfil del psicólogo en México*. Unpublished professional thesis, UNAM, Mexico City.

Leon-Sanchez, R., & Patiño-Muñoz, G. (1984). *Historia de la psicología en México: La época prehispanica*. Unpublished professional thesis, UNAM, Mexico City.

Macotela, S. (1979). *Estudio sobre la imagen del psicólogo en el sector público*. Mexico City: Facultad de Psicología, UNAM.

Morales, M. L., Lopez, M., Parra, P., & Guadarrama, J. (1980). *Un análisis curricular de la enseñanza de la psicología en México*. Mexico City: ANUIES, SEP, CENEIP.

Pick de Weiss, S., & Diaz-Loving, R. (1986). Applied psychology in Mexico. *International Review of Applied Psychology, 35*, 577–598.

Urbina, J., Mercado, S., Colotla, V., Sanchez-Bedolla, G., & Aguilar, J. (1982). La investigación en la Facultad de Psicología, UNAM: Un análisis cuantitativo. *Tercer Congreso Mexicano de Psicología. Resumenes de las Sesiones Temáticas*. Mexico City: Sociedad Mexicana de Psicología.

28 / The Netherlands

HENK M. VAN DER PLOEG

Henk M. van der Ploeg (born 1944) received his PhD from the University of Amsterdam in 1980. His specialties include clinical and personality psychology, health psychology, and psychotherapy. He is the author of Persoonlijkheid en Medische consumptie *(Personality and medical consumption) and* Late gevolgen van gijzelingen *(Long-term aftereffects of hostage taking), as well as more than 100 journal articles, book chapters, and other publications. He has edited a number of Dutch-language books, served as editor or coeditor for six volumes of* Advances in Test Anxiety Research, *and continues as coeditor of* Anxiety Research: An International Journal.

A director-at-large for the International Council of Psychologists (ICP) (1986–89), president of ICP (1992–93), and secretary-treasurer for the Society of Test Anxiety Research (1980–90), van der Ploeg is head of the Division of Medical Psychology, head of the Stress Research Group, professor of medical psychology, and professor of psychotraumatic stress at the University of Leiden.

Work Settings and Education

The Netherlands, a constitutional monarchy with a parliamentary system, is located in the northwestern part of Europe. Within a 300-mile (500-km) radius of Amsterdam, the Dutch capital, are London, Paris, Bonn, Brussels, Copenhagen, and Luxembourg. The Netherlands has a total population of 14,700,000; about 13,000 persons are trained psychologists.

Approximately 5,500 Dutch psychologists are members of the Nederlands Instituut van Psychologen (NIP) (Dutch Psychological Association). Forty-five percent of these members are female, a ratio that also seems to apply to the total group of Dutch psychologists.

Of the membership of the Dutch Psychological Association, about 54 percent are employed in clinical settings (including counseling and guidance) or engaged in personality psychology; 23 percent are developmental psychologists (child/adolescence psychology, gerontology). The remainder are

The office of the Dutch Psychological Association was most helpful in providing statistical material about psychologists and psychology in the Netherlands.

employed in industrial and personnel settings (8 percent), social psychology (6 percent), and experimental psychology, physiological psychology, psychometrics, and other specializations (9 percent).

Within the Dutch Psychological Association are various divisions, sections, and working groups, of which the group of developmental psychologists seems to be the largest (25 percent of those in divisions are listed in this group). About 15 percent are listed in the division of industrial and organizational psychology, and 6 percent are in the group of vocational guidance or career personalization psychologists. Educational psychology (8 per cent) and teaching of psychology (2 percent) include a somewhat smaller group of psychologists. About 6 percent have their main interest in the psychology of aging. Clinical psychology (outpatient mental health care) includes about 13 percent of the psychologists of the association, and about the same number (13 percent) are engaged in psychology related to general health care. As a result of the organization of the Dutch health care system, most of these psychologists work in independent practice. Some 6 percent are psychologists in psychiatric hospitals, 3 percent work mainly with patients in general hospitals, and 2 percent work in institutions for mentally retarded or deficient individuals. These last three groups of psychologists also have a common interest in health psychology, consulting psychology, clinical and counseling psychology, and psychotherapy.

It should be clear from this description that the divisional structure of the Dutch Psychological Association is different from the organization of the American Psychological Association, that is, some working groups are relatively small. These include psychology and hearing deficits (80 members), psychology and automation (73 members), psychology and special education (48 members), and psychology and social relief work (46 members).

In order to study psychology in the Netherlands, one must complete secondary school and attend a university. Secondary school takes about 6 years to finish; the final years include about seven subjects in which one has to take examinations. Among these subjects are the Dutch language and English. To study psychology, one must take mathematics (including some basic statistics). The university study of psychology takes, according to the official programs, 1 year to finish the propaedeutical examination and another 3 years to complete the doctoral examination. Most students require more than 4 years to finish their university training. For example, at the national level, while 75 percent of the students complete work for their propaedeutical examination within 2 years, only 33 percent complete this part within the 1 year stated in most programs.

The first year at the university is an introductory year. Courses include general psychology and an introduction to the fundamental areas of psychology such as personality, developmental, experimental, social, and theoretical psychology, and also some physiological psychology and statistics. Furthermore, there are courses in communication skills training, psychometrics, sociology, and philosophy. Students must finish this "introductory year" within 2 years after the start of study or, according to government regulations, they will not be allowed to complete their studies.

Generally, the second year is more specific yet still includes a rather general introduction to the various branches of psychology. Besides different working groups, there are training programs, such as communication skills training, testing, experimental and methodological psychology, and statistics. The final 2 years of the curriculum focus mainly on a specialty. The student selects a certain area and takes a substantial number of courses (basic and applied) in that area. Students also must work for a certain amount of time in an applied setting with a trained psychologist. In addition, they must write some essays, including a literature review and a report on a minor research project. Both tasks have to be completed before the final doctoral examination. In some cases the final research project and its accompanying report can be considered a PhD dissertation.

After obtaining the MA degree (in Dutch, *doctorandus*, or *Drs.*), one may continue work on the PhD dissertation in order to obtain the Dutch title of *doctor* (*Dr.*). The completion of the PhD dissertation takes about 4 years, although only a few candidates finish in less than 4 years, and others take much longer. A Dutch PhD dissertation usually includes experimental work, a detailed literature review, a thorough analysis of the data, and a thoughtful discussion section. These dissertations are usually published as books and can be found in libraries and academic bookshops.

In the future, Dutch students shall have to take additional career training after the doctoral examination in the area of (a) teaching, (b) applied psychology, or (c) experimental/research psychology. This means that most students who complete university study in psychology will require additional training in the applied professions. A smaller group of somewhat more gifted students will be allowed to enter (the sometimes paid) experimental/research training at a university. Members of this latter group will automatically work on their PhD dissertations during their training as fully licensed experimental psychologists. However, the programs for this professional career training are still in development.

Although there is ample opportunity to study psychology in neighboring countries, nearly all Dutch psychologists are trained at Dutch universities. The reasons include the language barrier and the full opportunities to study in The Netherlands itself. There are hardly any limitations to entering psychological or social faculties at Dutch universities (other than easy-to-fulfill entrance regulations and the payment of fees).

After completion of university study in psychology, one is allowed to use the title "psychologist" and the degree *Drs.* (*doctorandus*). Persons using the title "psychologist" without proper qualifications can be penalized. Regardless of the area of specialization, all psychology graduates become "psychologists" without identifying their specialties. However, the Dutch Psychological Association maintains some committees with special registers for (a) clinical psychologists and (b) psychologists-psychotherapists. One has to fulfill certain qualifications, including additional training and some years of practical experience and employment under supervision, before one can apply for registration. Employers usually require these special licenses or certificates for certain jobs. The Dutch government has recently created a registration system of all fully licensed psychotherapists. Almost automatically, all registered psychologist-psychotherapists have been accepted by the government as fully licensed psychotherapists and have been included in the Dutch governmental system of psychotherapists.

Finally, the Dutch Psychological Association has an ethical code, which guides all the professional activities of its members. The organization has an Inspection Committee, with whom one can file a complaint about a psychologist who is a member of the Dutch Psychological Association, as well as a Committee of Appeal. These committees have the power to act against members who do not behave in accordance with the ethical guidelines. For example, in the early 1970s the rule was adopted that a client has the right to read the written report after having been tested. A psychologist must write this report in order to allow inspection by the client. Also, the interests of human rights committees about human psychological research projects have been included in these guidelines. Unfortunately, psychologists who are not members of the Dutch Psychological Association are not bound by these ethical rules, and in their case, there are no sanctions for unethical behavior. Of course, all clients have access to the judicial system, but professional misconduct by psychologists is not easy to prove under Dutch law (see also Roe, 1984).

Universities, Sources, and Instruments

Psychology can be studied at seven universities in the Netherlands: the University of Amsterdam, the Free University of Amsterdam, the State University of Leiden, the State University of Utrecht, the State University of Groningen, the Catholic University of Nijmegen, and the University of Brabant (Tilburg), which is also a Catholic institution. All these universities offer undergraduate and graduate training. Nearly every area of psychology can be studied at each of these seven universities, and all have adopted the same Dutch university system of 1 general introductory year and 3 years of doctoral training. Local preferences, the attractiveness of a certain location for study, and choice of specialty may influence a student's entrance to one university instead of another.

Postgraduate courses are also available to psychologists. Every year, training possibilities, courses, and workshops are organized by the universities, although there is not yet an official need for psychologists to engage in continuing education, even for license renewal. There are also ample opportunities to attend national conferences, conventions, meetings, and seminars, where one may learn about recent developments and ongoing research and attend presentations about the state of the art. Because of the easy access to many different countries, a large number of psychologists attend international conferences to present their research to an international forum and to learn from their colleagues abroad.

About a dozen Dutch journals publish Dutch psychological articles. Among them, the *Nederlands Tijdschrift voor de Psychologie en haar grensgebieden* (Dutch journal of psychology) is the oldest, with its first volume dating back to 1933. Other general psychology journals are *Gedrag en Gezondheid* (Behavior and health), *De Psycholoog* (The psychologist), the monthly publication of the Dutch Psychological Association, and *Psychologie* (the Dutch adaptation of *Psychology Today*). Other journals are related to certain specialized fields, such as the *Journal of Psychotherapy, Monthly of Mental Health, Child and Adolescence, Journal of Gerontology*, and journals related to industrial and organizational psychology.

Besides these Dutch journals, Dutch psychologists, especially those with easy access to libraries, read many English-language and American psychology journals. For example, references in the *Dutch Journal of Psychology* for the year 1985 were 30 percent to Dutch articles, 2 percent to German articles, and 69 percent to English-language articles.

As mentioned above, many Dutch psychologists are members of the Dutch Psychological Association, which was established in 1938. Psychology at Dutch universities actually dates back to 1892. In that year Gerard Heymans established the first Dutch psychological laboratory and institute in Groningen. In 1921 psychology could be studied as a major at the doctoral level in philosophy. Thereafter, psychology advanced to become an independent subject at the doctoral level. In 1927 a national organization related to psychology was founded to further the development and growth of

psychology. The Dutch Psychological Association is today the major professional organization of psychologists in the Netherlands. For psychologists-
psychotherapists, there is the major Dutch Association of Psychotherapy,
besides a large number of smaller associations for various specialties in
psychotherapy, such as the Dutch Associations of Behavior Therapy, of
Psychoanalysis, of Rogerian Psychotherapy, of Group Therapy, of Youth
Psychotherapy, and others. Additional professional organizations and societies are available as well. In fact, nearly every large group of professionals
has its own organizational structure to discuss matters of mutual interest.

All Dutch universities have large libraries with a substantial number of
psychological textbooks and journal subscriptions. Psychological institutes
and university departments usually have their own smaller libraries. Sometimes one has to consult the Royal Library in the Hague to determine where
in the Netherlands a certain book or journal is available. This library has
a catalog system that lists all books and journals available in the Netherlands. Even books and journals with a limited circulation usually can be
traced.

Psychometric instruments and tests are published (in Dutch) by several
firms, which provide catalogs listing the various instruments. The Dutch
Psychological Association has its own committee for tests and the use of
tests. This committee provides guidelines by which tests and test manuals
are screened and evaluated. In fact, all published Dutch tests with manuals
are evaluated according to certain criteria, including test construction theory,
quality of manual and test material, norms, and reliability and validity of
data. Psychological tests may be used only by qualified professionals. Unqualified persons usually are not allowed to buy these tests, inventories,
and questionnaires. Recently, a demand has grown for more openness about
psychological tests (e.g., by consumer organizations), and discussions have
been held about the use, proper instruction, and administering of tests as
selection and screening instruments.

Large computers with statistical packages (such as SPSS and many others)
are available at all universities and university mathematical/computer centers. The Dutch university computer centers are also linked to BITNET and
EARN, which allow Dutch scholars to communicate as easily and rapidly
as possible with colleagues from all over the world. Computer facilities for
psychologists include the availability of a growing body of Dutch-language
psychological software. English-language software is widely available but
difficult to use with some clients. Another problem is that English-language
tests cannot be administered with the use of computer facilities because of
the unavailability of norms and reliability and validity data. Personal computers with statistical packages for the social sciences are widely available

for psychologists (especially at universities). The number of psychologists with word processors is growing, and all psychology students are trained to use personal computers.

Psychological research equipment can be found in many research institutes, either at universities or at government-sponsored research settings. Even in clinical settings and in hospitals, laboratory research is done. Limitations on the use of equipment are mainly of a financial kind. The Netherlands has many opportunities to import whatever is needed if the necessary equipment is not constructed in the country itself.

Financially, the government is a major employer of psychologists. The Dutch government supports the universities and the postgraduate training of psychologists to a large extent, although budget cuts have limited the number of possibilities and reduced the number of university departments where one can study a certain area of psychology. In the various work settings of applied psychologists, the government is a major employer, directly or indirectly, too. For example, institutes of mental health, hospitals, and clinics in the field of somatic health care are largely funded by the government. Educational psychologists are paid by national, regional, or local authorities. Psychologists in the criminal justice system also obtain their income from the government, as do psychologists working at the ministries (national level) and at the regional and local administrative levels. Actually, only a few psychologists are employed in industrial, business, or trade settings that are not governmentally supported, and some have private practices (full-time or part-time). So, in general, the Dutch government can be regarded as the major financial support system for Dutch psychologists and psychology.

The Dutch Psychological Association is an independent professional organization without governmental support. Annual membership fees and additional income amount to about 2 million Dutch guilders a year (about 1 million USA dollars).

In 1988 the Dutch Psychological Association celebrated its 50th anniversary. One of the larger Dutch news agencies provided newspapers with a text entitled, "Psychology Penetrates Society to a Larger Extent." The article opened, "The haze of secrecy and mystery around psychology has largely disappeared. Psychological concepts, such as feelings of insufficiency and stress, are common knowledge." Psychological services are widely available. For example, psychologists are involved in testing and screening at elementary and secondary schools. Psychologists carry out personnel selection procedures and are widely employed in mental and somatic health settings. Psychologists with private practices are listed in the yellow pages of the phone book, and persons with minor psychological problems prefer to consult a psychologist rather than a psychiatrist.

The professional status of a psychologist is evaluated as reasonably high, somewhat lower than that of a physician, lawyer, or public notary, but higher than that of a sociologist or a teacher. Women and younger people seem to rank psychology higher; those with a lower educational level rank psychology, on the average, somewhat higher (see also Veldkamp & van Drunen, 1988).

Current Status of Psychology

The number of psychologists in the Netherlands has grown substantially since the 1940s. The Dutch Psychological Association had about 100 members in 1950, about 500 in 1960, about 1,500 in 1970, more than 3,000 in 1980, and about 5,500 in 1988. At the end of the 1960s most psychologists were still members of the association. In 1980 just over 3,000 were members, while the total number of psychologists approached 8,000.

On the one hand, the substantial growth in the number of professionals and areas of specialization shows the increasing status and esteem of psychology in the Netherlands. On the other hand, it is almost impossible today to summarize the significant research areas and research centers. There are many nationally and internationally recognized psychologists in the Netherlands. Nearly every type of psychology is studied. In the seven universities where one can study psychology, and in the numerous research centers, many projects have been done and are being conducted. Because of their multilingual education, Dutch psychologists have the opportunity to publish in Dutch, English, French, and German, and many of them publish regularly in international journals and books. Furthermore, the opportunity for many psychologists to travel all over the world to attend international meetings and to present their work to an international audience makes it much more difficult to delineate current and emerging trends and specialty areas in Dutch psychology. To mention some names, centers, and projects would not do justice to the many projects of high quality being conducted. On the whole it is no longer possible to keep fully abreast of the growing body of varied psychological advances.

To conclude, according to van Strien (1988), Dutch psychology can be described in relation to international psychology. By studying the number of citations, one may be able to evaluate the importance of Dutch psychologists in Dutch psychology. It has been said (without a detailed count of citations) that Dutch psychology was greatly influenced by German psychology until World War II. Then French influences became apparent, especially in phenomenology. Finally, American psychology became the most influential.

However, when the citations in the general *Dutch Journal of Psychology* are actually counted, as was done by van Strien (1988), the picture seems more complicated. Also, in the various fields of Dutch psychology, the pattern is not identical. References to German publications were most common before 1950 (over 50 percent of all citations were German). French citations (about 10 to 20 percent) were found in the years 1947–52. And in the years 1968–88 French references are practically nonexistent. In recent years German citations vary between 1 and 5 percent. English citations actually increased after 1950 (in 1950 the figure was 20 percent, and it reached its highest point in 1975 at 81 percent). Thereafter a slight drop in English citations can be observed (1980: 74 percent; 1985: 69 percent). The remaining references are to Dutch sources, which have increased since the 1960s (from 20 to 30 percent). In this context it should be made clear that the high percentage of English citations does not automatically mean American citations. The English language is more and more *the* language of the scientific community (like Latin in earlier times). Dutch training in psychology is mostly done with English-language textbooks. Some articles in Dutch psychology journals are written in English, and some Dutch PhD dissertations are completely written in English. In 1985 16 percent of the English-language citations in the *Dutch Journal of Psychology* were references to English-language publications of Dutch psychologists. So the development of Dutch psychology is not exclusively in an American direction, but in an international direction.

Besides this international orientation, one might also look at Dutch psychology as becoming part of a European tradition. European organizations, journals, and conferences have become more common in recent years. The clearest example was the scheduling of the First European Congress of Psychology in Amsterdam (Netherlands) in 1989. At that meeting almost 2,000 psychologists, the majority of whom came from West and East European countries, gathered in Amsterdam. A great number of distinguished speakers presented major addresses, related symposia were organized, and hundreds of papers and posters were presented. The various contributions were categorized under the following headings: theoretical, psychometrics, personality, developmental and educational, cognitive, gerontological, clinical and health, stress and anxiety, neuropsychology, psychophysiology, work and organizational, social and economic, and cross-cultural. Finally, three volumes were published (Drenth, Sergeant & Takens, 1990). In these volumes some Dutch recognized experts in their fields presented their views, among them De Groot, "Unifying Psychology: A European View" (theoretical); Koops, "A Viable Developmental Psychology in the Nineties by Way of Renewed Respect for Tradition" (developmental); Diekstra, "Public Health Psychology: On the Role of Psychology in Health and Health Care in the 21st

Century," (clinical); Sergeant, "Clinical Decision Making: The Role of Controlled and Automatic Information Processing" (clinical); Maes, "Theories and Principles of Health Behavior Change" (health); van der Ploeg, "Anxiety Research in Europe" (stress and anxiety); Drenth, "Industrial Democracy in Europe: Cross National Comparisons" (work and organizational); Rijsman, "How European is Social Psychology in Europe?" (social and economic); and Poortinga, "Differences between Psychological Domains in the Range of Cross-Cultural Variation" (cross-cultural). English is the language employed at such meetings and in such journals, sometimes with French and German summaries or partial translations. Although the majority of all psychologists live in the USA, European psychology cannot be neglected. In the international arena, European and Dutch psychology have some influence. Future developments may see a greater impact of the Dutch on international psychology.

Bibliography

Drenth, P. J. D., Sergeant, J. A., & Takens, R. J. (Eds.). (1990). *European perspectives in psychology* (Vols. 1–3). Chichester, England: Wiley.

Roe, R. A. (Ed). (1984). *Wat doet de psycholoog?* Assen, Netherlands: Van Gorcum.

Strien, P. J. van. (1988). De Nederlandse psychologie in het internationale krachtenveld. *De Psycholoog 23*, 575–585.

Veldkamp, T. A., & Drunen, P. van. (1988). *Psychologie als professie.* Assen, Netherlands: Van Gorcum.

29 / New Zealand

GEORGE SHOUKSMITH

George Shouksmith (born 1931) received his PhD from Queen's University, Northern Ireland, in 1967. A specialist in applied psychology, he has written 4 books and more than 60 articles, with particular emphasis on occupational psychology and the application of psychology to everyday life. His most recent book is Stress and Life in New Zealand.

Shouksmith developed the first professional program in clinical psychology in New Zealand and has served as president of the New Zealand Psychological Society and chairman of the Psychologists Board for New Zealand. He is professor and head of the Department of Psychology at Massey University.

Historical Beginnings

Two traditions provide the stems for New Zealand psychology. The primary tradition was pure, bedded in philosophy and the new experimental approaches of the early 20th century. The undoubted "father" of psychology in New Zealand was T. A. (later Sir Thomas) Hunter, who became lecturer in mental and moral philosophy at the Victoria University College of Wellington in 1904 and assumed the multidisciplinary chair in 1907. Hunter, whom today we might call a creative thinker, visited Titchener at Cornell in 1906, returned to found the first psychological laboratory in the Southern Hemisphere in 1908, and persuaded the college in 1909 to change his title to "professor of philosophy and psychology." In those days the University of New Zealand was a federal university consisting of four colleges teaching a common syllabus, in which psychology was linked with philosophy as a major component.

The next significant development came in 1930, when Henry Ferguson arrived at the University of Dunedin and became the first to hold the title of "lecturer in experimental psychology." Ferguson came from the Scottish tradition as befitted New Zealand's Scottish settlement of Otago and, as well as bringing with him a large range of brass instruments, proceeded to broaden the approach of psychology with an examination of such obviously applied topics as the effect of fluorescent lighting on factory workers and a study of ways of improving wool sorting. Unfortunately, Ferguson departed, and after its promising start, psychology languished at Otago.

Meanwhile, the applied tradition had been established elsewhere and in a different way. In the 1920s departments of education were established at each of the university's constituent colleges. At Canterbury in 1927 James Shelley, the professor of education, encouraged a local graduate to take a joint position with philosophy as "director of the Psychological and Educational Laboratories." This was C. E. Beeby, who moved on to become first director of the New Zealand Council for Educational Research and later the director of education for all New Zealand. This appointment and Beeby's remarkable character and dynamism meant that applied psychology became a central force in education in New Zealand. It also meant that other aspects of applied psychology were given less emphasis and that the discipline as a whole developed in the educational, as opposed to the experimental, setting. The impetus for applied psychology remained with education as Ralph Winterbourne joined the staff of Canterbury College in the 1930s, organizing and promoting vocational and other guidance services (Winterbourne, 1944).

Industrial psychology, in contrast, had a false and somewhat belated start. Only the pressures of war led to the 1942 government sponsorship of an Industrial Psychology Division (IPD) of the Department of Scientific and Industrial Research. Leslie Hearnshaw, who had "served his time" at the National Institute of Industrial Psychology in England, was advanced from his post at Victoria University to be its director (Hearnshaw, 1948) and for some 5 years fostered excellent practical research into the application of psychological ideas and findings in small production units, of which most of New Zealand's industry was composed. Unfortunately, Hearnshaw's departure to take up the chair at Liverpool and political maneuvering among government departments led to the demise of the IPD, and apart from its application to education, psychology relapsed into a "pure" condition.

The more fundamental research approaches were not languishing, however. Indeed, at the end of World War II psychology was at the point of blossoming into a full-blown discipline. Ivan Sutherland and Ernest Beaglehole, at Canterbury and Victoria, respectively, were beginning for the first time to develop a true "New Zealand psychology," combining anthropological and psychological approaches to cross-cultural studies. This new-look psychology was both empirical and reflective, neither neglecting nor yet solely tied to experimental psychology. As Ritchie, Beaglehole's student and biographer, remarks, it led to "breadth, a firm foundation in history, philosophy, empirical enquiry and social relevance." This social relevance was seen not least in the studies of the Rakau Maoris which Ritchie (1963) himself, prompted by Beaglehole, was to undertake. These may well be the first empirical studies of an indigenous tribal group made from a psychological viewpoint.

By the late 1950s the old University of New Zealand had been replaced by four separate universities. Psychology had become a separate department at Victoria in 1951 and at Canterbury in 1953. Beaglehole continued to foster sociocultural psychology at Victoria, while at Canterbury the superb academic politician Alan Crowther, a Cambridge PhD and one of Bartlett's students, built up an eclectic and powerful department. The impetus, in fact, could be said to have moved once more to Canterbury. First Leslie Reed, then Barney Sampson, established a firm, modern, experimental tradition. Reed introduced Skinnerian behaviorism to New Zealand, and Sampson, a McGill graduate, brought Hebb's broader experimental approaches. Sampson was enticed to New Zealand by Harry Scott, a New Zealander, who completed his PhD with Hebb and was associated with the McGill work on perceptual isolation. On his return, Scott left Canterbury to establish a separate department at the University of Auckland but 4 years later was tragically killed in a mountaineering accident. Sampson followed him to Auckland to take up the newly established chair, and so the firm foundation was set in that university for a sound North American–oriented experimental tradition. Back in Canterbury, I had arrived from Edinburgh with a brief to develop applied, and particularly occupational, aspects of psychology, by introducing in 1961 the first professional training programs in clinical psychology and developing separate occupational (industrial and organizational) studies at the graduate level.

Psychology in New Zealand had come of age. In 1964 Otago reestablished its psychology department under Stephen Griew, and the new universities of Massey and Waikato both established chairs, their first incumbents being Laurie Brown and Jim Ritchie, respectively.

Current University Programs

New Zealand has six major universities, each offering full programs in psychology with similar patterns of study. Universities are divided into groups of departments, called faculties, on the British model, and psychology appears interchangeably in both Arts and Science. The degree structur varies to some extent among institutions but is essentially that of a general 3-year bachelor's program in which psychology may be taken as a major subject, covering about four tenths to a half of the required study. Students intending to become professional psychologists then take either a fourth "honors" year or a 2-year master's program, which contains a strong independent research component, as well as further study and teaching in selected areas. Professional programs follow the graduate degree study, or are integrated with it, to form a professional training program of 6 years. Doctoral studies, leading to the PhD degree, take the form of supervised research, again on the British, rather than the North American, model.

Educational psychology programs, which qualify graduates for positions in the State Department of Education Psychological Services, remain separate from those in general psychology, following the historical schism noted earlier. These programs are at the graduate level for students in any discipline area. These students must also have teaching qualifications (and usually experience) as well as a qualifying degree. In addition, they are required to have 2 complete years of study in general psychology (two thirds of a major) before being accepted for entry into these programs, which are offered only at the universities of Auckland and Otago.

University of Auckland

At the University of Auckland the department retains the laboratory experimental emphasis given it by Scott and Sampson and continues to strengthen its contributions to this field, in which it has a justifiable international reputation. Particular areas of research in the 1980s were information processing, memory, and bilateral transfer (under M. Corballis); sensory processes, specifically psychoacoustics (R. J. Irwin); and operant learning studies and the experimental analysis of behavior (I. Beale and M. Davison). The present head of department, Graeme Vaughan, is, perhaps surprisingly, a social psychologist, though his interests are also in experimental social psychology, where he has been endeavoring to promote the newer European approaches in this field. The Auckland department's main base is the Science Faculty; even its clinical psychology program is biased toward clinical neuropsychology. It has been a matter of regret to some observers that in New Zealand's major industrial and manufacturing city, the Department of Psychology has remained so firmly oriented toward pure research. Following a recent departmental review, however, some movement has been made to extend its applied offerings, and through the personal interest of Barry Kirkwood, a course in ergonomics is being introduced into the undergraduate syllabus.

University of Canterbury

The early experimental tradition and strong concerns in animal psychology going beyond operant studies have continued (under J. Pollard and R. Hughes) to dominate the Canterbury department, as has the clinical program on the applied side. The latter, under W. Black, remains one of the strongest in the country. More recently, Bruce Jamieson has persuaded the university to extend the offerings at the graduate level in industrial and organizational psychology, and in 1986 the department offered for the first time a professional diploma in this second applied area. Notwithstanding these graduate offerings, the main emphasis of the department remains general and experimental, with a growing concern for cognitive psychology, strengthened by the arrival of the present head of department, K. Strongman.

Undergraduate programs fit this model, offering a general, laboratory-based course, with little or no choice, thereby providing basic training before any specialization is allowed. Students may take any combination of masters' papers, since the general nature of undergraduate study provides the necessary base. Currently, graduate papers are offered in behavior modification, clinical, cognitive, comparative, developmental, emotion, experimental analysis of behavior, industrial and organizational, mathematical, perceptual processes, personality, personnel, physiological, social, and statistics and measurement.

Although psychology and sociology are now taught as separate disciplines, Canterbury's department can claim to have initiated the formal teaching of the latter in New Zealand. Richard Thomson, then teaching social psychology in the department and actively involved in promoting social change in race relations in New Zealand, was persuaded to offer initially a first-year course and later advanced papers in theoretical and applied psychology.

Massey University

One of the new universities established in the 1960s from an amalgamation of both agricultural and liberal arts colleges, Massey University has a different approach, fostering greater interdisciplinary involvement and a strong applied orientation.

As at Canterbury, sociology at Massey University was first developed within the Department of Psychology. Later, in a separate department, a professional social work degree was developed to which psychology contributes. The department at Massey also fostered the first New Zealand university programs in nursing studies, appointing Nan Kinross to form what is now a full department, with its own programs to which psychology contributes core papers. Cross-faculty teaching and research led to the appointment of D. Clarke of the psychology department as New Zealand's representative to the 19th International Dairy Congress—an unusual assignment for a psychologist! Recently, the department has developed both certificate degree and advanced diploma programs in rehabilitation (under R. Gregory and P. Disler), with the Royal New Zealand Foundation for the Blind sponsoring teaching and research programs for orientation and mobility in the visually impaired (S. La Grow). Currently, a graduate diploma in ergonomics is being developed on a cross-faculty and cross-discipline basis, under a separate Board of Studies, of which the head of the Department of Psychology is chairperson. Finally, within the Business Studies Faculty, majors in human resource management contain set papers taught by the Department of Psychology. Research interests follow these applied and cross-disciplinary foci, with teams from the department having held research contracts to investigate a wide variety of applied topics, including stress in prison officers and in nursing, work loads and system capacity of air traffic controllers, job satisfaction parameters of health professionals, and a psychoeconomic justification for the rebuilding of a rural road bridge. An Applied Psychology Centre, sponsoring research, teaching, and consultancies in applied areas, has recently been established under the directorship of N. Long.

Massey University has the responsibility for extramural teaching (off-campus distance teaching through correspondence, audiovisual aids, together with short, intensive, on-campus programs) throughout New Zealand, and for this reason, the department's undergraduate programs must offer a sound general approach to meet the needs of students who may wish to transfer at an advanced stage to other universities. In addition to this general base, however, undergraduates may take some special applied papers, in industrial organizational psychology and vocational guidance, for example. At the graduate level, post-master's professional diplomas are offered both in clinical psychology (Malcolm Johnson) and in occupational psychology (M. Smith and J. Brook).

University of Otago

Psychology in Otago in recent years has had two major foci. Throughout the 1970s, under P. McKeller, the department developed an eclectic, applied orientation, while retaining a strong operant and radical behavioral core to its teaching. McKeller, himself a phenomenologist with sympathy for the psychodynamic approach, encouraged his staff to broaden the teaching base and expand not only into applied areas, but also into others then regarded as "on the fringe." In clinical psychology, the testing and assessment model of psychologists working in hospitals was exchanged for an "interventionist" model with a broad approach. R. Kamman looked at general models of well-being and corresponding environmental issues, while D. Marks and others investigated the effect of drugs and alcohol on ordinary everyday behaviors like car driving and "party going." Further out on the fringe, Marks moved beyond imagery (Marks, 1986) and objective experience to take a skeptical look at ESP and other parapsychological phenomena. Even in the behavioral areas, nonstandard studies were emerging, such as L. Leland's investigation of paint colors for litter bins, which reinforced their use.

In 1981 G. Goddard (1986) brought a new approach, with strong support from the Otago Medical School, centering the department's focus on neuropsychology. His untimely death has left the department in a state of flux between traditions and the need to rebuild.

Otago differs from the other universities in having a 4-year honors program within each specific discipline, including psychology. Its professional program in clinical psychology thus consists of a further 2 years of integrated study and practice, to make up the student's 6-year training. The acting head of department is G. White.

Victoria University of Wellington

Victoria University adopts the North American model of separating the professional chairs in the subject from the role of chairman of department. The Department of Psychology has two full professors, A. R. Forbes and A. J. W. Taylor, neither of whom is chairman of the department, a role now held by M. J. White. The previous head was N. Adcock, widow of one of the department's distinguished earlier members, C. J. Adcock, who both brought factor analysis to New Zealand and was responsible for one of only two general introductory texts published in this country (Adcock, 1964), the other coming later from myself (Shouksmith, 1988). The two current professors have distinctly different approaches. Forbes is concerned with work on human factors and has contributed significantly to research on accidents and safety. Taylor, both a clinical and a forensic psychologist (Taylor, 1977), has recently produced a series of research studies examining various facets of exposure to adverse climatic conditions, and resultant stress, taking advantage of New Zealand's involvement in Antarctica for the necessary field studies. Other research interests in recent years have been those of F. Walkey in methodology and a strongly developing yet diverse set of experimental studies covering discrimination learning in animals and humans (G. White, now at Otago), memory and cognition (M. White), and psychophysics and physiological psychology (S. Slater and J. Whitmore).

It is interesting to note that the content of papers, both at undergraduate and graduate levels, apart from those specifically in clinical psychology, reflect these experimental concerns to a greater extent than the applied ones of the two senior professors. Like Otago, Victoria offers a 4-year integrated honors program, which has a laboratory experimental bias. Applied teaching is in a separate, 2-year program, stretching beyond the honors degree, leading to what is called an MA (Applied).

The University of the Waikato

The second "new" university, Waikato, also offered a new look to its programs. Schools of studies with broader emphases, rather than narrow departments, were established, and the degrees offered in psychology were a bachelor's and master's in social science, all of which eminently suited Waikato's first professor, J. Ritchie. The second professor, D. Thomas, also comes from the Beaglehole tradition of Victoria, continuing the strong emphasis on social psychology. Special features of the Waikato program and of the department's research include women's studies (Jane Ritchie), child and adolescent development (Ritchie & Ritchie, 1984), and a generally cross-cultural approach taken by the majority of staff. Thomas was responsible for introducing a strong emphasis on community psychology, this department being the only one offering a separate diploma in the field, distinct from the clinical offerings. The community psychology program combines interventionist approaches with concerns for social policy and social change, planning, and community development. Somewhat surprisingly, against this general background, clinical psychology under B. Parsonson, who is now also head of department, takes a more strictly behavioral approach.

In its general teaching the department of the University of the Waikato offers a broader selection of papers than is the case for any other New Zealand university. As well as the mainstream papers, students at the undergraduate level may select as topics "self-awareness and interpersonal relations," "psychology and women," "growing up in New Zealand," or "cross-cultural studies." At the graduate level the choice includes "conflict in a multicultural society," "transpersonal psychology," "race relations," "violence in family and society," and "the psychology of sex roles."

Psychological Practice

A registration act for psychologists has been in operation since the mid-1980s. Only registered psychologists may be employed in government and as psychologists in specified educational and health-related positions. Others are free to practice as "psychologists," providing they do not state or imply that they are "registered psychologists." By March 1987 some 815 psychologists had registered, 348 (43 percent) of whom were females. At the same time, there were only 776 full members of the New Zealand Psychological Society. Given the fact that academic staff members were not required to register, this suggests that registration has, in spite of its noncompulsory nature, become accepted as a mark of a professional psychologist in New Zealand.

The major single area of psychological practice is institutionally based clinical psychology, mainly in hospital clinics or psychiatric services. Because of the tradition of state-funded medical care, private practice and private clinics have been slow to develop, though they are now being established in the major cities. Behavioral approaches on British and European models have predominated. More recently, however, and related to the increase in non-institutionally based intervention, broader perspectives have emerged, particularly in the area of family therapy, where the group dynamics of complete and incomplete families have formed the basis for interventions. Developing concerns for community psychology have broadened the interventionist approach even further, taking psychologists into government departments concerned with social policy and welfare and into city and regional planning offices.

A second major area of involvement for practicing psychologists is educational psychology. Employment is in the State Education Department, and service is concerned with individual casework on behavior problems, learning disabilities, and other remedial issues. A smaller group of psychologists works in the Department of Justice, both in research on forensic and organizational issues and in providing counseling services in prisons. A growing area, which links both these fields and also includes psychologists in private practice, involves work for the family court system.

Personnel psychology has for some years had its main practical work outlet in the triservices Defense Psychology Corps, whose members have mainly been involved in military selection and training studies. However, staff has been leaving the corps, which has provided the stimulus for a more recent increase in consulting practices operating in industrial and organizational psychology. New Zealand's slow growth in this area is probably due mainly to the relatively small size of industrial organizations in the country and the lack of competitiveness (until recently, local industry was largely a protected one). New economic policies have spurred the extension of practical psychology to fostering more effective organizational functioning in both government and private sectors.

The Nature of Psychology

In the early years Sutherland and Beaglehole emphasized distinct local cultural problems, albeit from different sociophilosophical bases, giving New Zealand the foundations for a unique "native" psychology. The expansion of the 1960s and 1970s, however, found New Zealand–based psychologists concerned more with establishing a worldwide acceptability for

New Zealand psychology than with fostering investigations of local needs. The dominant academics in this period were, and still are, international in outlook and focus, as attested by their publication records. In this context, it is interesting to note that the *New Zealand Journal of Psychology*, in its 16 years of publication, has never contained an article written by any one of those psychologists who are fellows of the New Zealand Royal Society!

At that time of expansion in New Zealand, it may well be argued, as did one distinguished psychologist in discussions with the author, that world psychology had, for the most part, "lost interest in each individual's own symbolic world." He and others pointed to the general concern of New Zealand's psychology more with methodological than philosophical concerns, a second senior psychologist adding the comment that local psychology had overemphasized statistical analysis and design, to which "understanding of human behavior has had to take second place." Other reviewers were kind enough to say that only Massey University and the University of the Waikato went different ways, but for Massey at least, I would have to state that the difference was more in practical focus than in establishing any "New Zealand" theoretical positions.

One area that did flourish in this developmental phase of New Zealand psychology was that of operant behaviorism, but in the eyes of at least one indigenous psychologist, it adopted a "midseventies" guise, "which the rest of the world has given away." Such was the domination of behaviorism, even if it was, as another colleague remarked, "a behavioral blind alley that had run its course" and had become for New Zealand a philosophical system "amounting to a religious dogma and theology."

The predominance of behaviorism, together with the emphasis on methodology, as opposed to either theory or the presenting problem, has also prevented New Zealand's psychology from developing its own identity. Even in the early 1990s, when the country is faced with rapid social change, unprecedented unemployment, and community problems of race relations and vandalism, the emerging concerns of psychologists, with few exceptions, are still international and often laboratory bound.

Bibliography

Adcock, C. J. (1964). *Fundamentals of psychology* (rev. ed.). London: Penguin Books.

Goddard, J. V. (1986). Learning: A step nearer a neural substrata. *Nature, 319,* 721–722.

Hearnshaw, L. (1948). Industrial psychology in New Zealand. *Occupational Psychology, 6,* 1–6.

Marks, D. (Ed.). (1986). *Theories of image formation.* New York: Brandon House.

Ritchie, J. A. (1963). *The making of a Maori: A case study of a changing country*. Wellington, NZ: Reed.

Ritchie, Jane, & Ritchie, J. A. (1984). *The dangerous age: Surviving adolescence in New Zealand*. Auckland, NZ: Allen & Unwin.

Shouksmith, G. (1988). *Becoming ourselves: The psychology of human relations* (2nd rev. ed.). Auckland, NZ: Longman Paul.

Taylor, A. J. W. (1977). Forensic psychology: Principles, practice and training. *New Zealand Psychologist, 6*, 97–108.

Winterbourne, R. (1944). *Educating backward children in New Zealand*. Wellington, NZ: New Zealand Council for Educational Research.

30 / Norway

HALLGRIM KLØVE

Hallgrim Kløve (born 1927) received the candidatus degree in psychology from the University of Oslo in 1952. A frequent contributor to various scientific journals, Kløve has also served as consulting editor to Epilepsia, the Journal of Clinical and Experimental Neuropsychology, Clinical Neuropsychologist, the Journal of Learning Disability, Cephalgia, and Neuropsychology.

A specialist in neuropsychology, he has been president of the International Neuropsychological Society, chairman of the Professional Ethics Committee of the Norwegian Psychological Association (1974–84), member of the Board of Governors of the International Neuropsychological Society (1974–79), and committee chair on Clinical Neuropsychology of the Norwegian Psychological Association (since 1988). Kløve is professor of clinical neuropsychology at the University of Bergen.

In Norway psychology is taught at several institutions of higher learning, but only two universities, the University of Oslo and the University of Bergen, grant degrees leading to licensing as a psychologist by the Department of Health and Social Affairs. The other universities, the University of Trondheim and the University of Tromso, offer psychology courses at various levels but not for the career of a professional psychologist.

The educational system in Norway does not grant the doctorate as a professional degree. The system is the same for all major professions, such as medicine, dentistry, law, and psychology. The professional degrees are candidatus degrees, which constitute the basis for licensing. The educational system also grants doctoral degrees, but they are strictly research degrees without any direct relevance for professional practice. In Norway a doctoral degree alone is not sufficient for granting a license as a professional practitioner.

Doctoral training in Norway is of two basic types. The *dr. philos.* degree is based on a scientific dissertation. There are few formal requirements, but the thesis must be approved by a committee appointed by a university. Two public lectures and a public defense of the dissertation are required. This degree system is old and is considered the traditional doctoral degree in Norway. However, during the last several years a new degree system has evolved. In psychology this degree is called *dr. psychol.* In addition to a dissertation, more explicit research training is mandatory. The doctoral candidate is required to attend a certain number of lectures and courses pertaining to scientific techniques, methods, and procedures. It is also a requirement to write one popular article and to document teaching experience. The requirements pertaining to public lectures and defense of the dissertation remain the same for the *dr. psychol.* degree as for the *dr. philos.* degree. Other professional fields have a similar profession-specific degree system.

In psychology it is estimated that 10 to 15 percent of those graduating from the professional programs each year will go on to obtain a doctorate, but this goal will probably not be achieved until the mid- or late 1990s. The doctoral degree is considered to be a prerequisite for teaching positions at the universities, and it will probably also become an informal requirement for leading positions such as chief psychologist in larger institutions and organizations.

Characteristics of the Psychologist

In February 1988 it was estimated that there were 2,160 psychologists in Norway. A psychologist, for the purpose of this article, is defined as a licensed psychologist. In this connection it should be emphasized that graduates of programs in school psychology, special education, or general education are not licensed and thus are not defined as psychologists.

A recent major survey of Norwegian psychologists (Engevik, Myklebust, & Ommundsen, 1987) indicated that 38 percent are women. During the period from 1972 to 1982 there was little change in the ratio between male and female psychologists. However, future changes are expected since, during the 1980s, women constituted between 55 and 60 percent of the students admitted to the professional programs. The trend for an increasing percentage of women is also evident in other professions in Norway such as medicine, dentistry, law, and engineering.

Work Settings

Psychologists in Norway work in a wide variety of settings (Table 30.1), which may be divided into nine categories. (1) Public health system: here psychologists work mainly in adult psychiatric outpatient clinics, adult psychiatric hospitals, child and adolescent psychiatric institutions, institutions for the mentally retarded, somatic hospitals; in other institutions within the Public Health System such as specialized hospitals for alcohol and drug abuse; and in private practice. (2) Family counseling: psychologists are usually employed by outpatient clinics, most often financed by the Pub-

TABLE 30.1

Where Psychologists Work (in Percent)

Category	1973 (N = 663)	1976 (N = 880)	1979 (N = 1,142)	1982 (N = 1,606)
Public health system	33.8	35.7	37.3	40.1
Family counseling	1.1	1.6	2.9	2.9
School system	27.0	28.6	28.4	27.3
Social services	0.8	0.8	1.3	2.7
Research and higher education	24.1	21.0	18.5	16.0
Public administration	2.7	2.5	2.5	2.1
Defense	2.4	1.9	1.7	1.4
Vocational psychology	3.9	3.0	3.7	2.8
Private business	3.5	2.5	2.1	1.8
Other	0.8	1.6	1.8	2.8
Total	100	100	100	100

lic Health System. (3) The school system: most psychologists are employed in guidance offices attached to the various local school systems. (4) Social services: psychologists are employed in the various service divisions of the social service system. (5) Research and higher education: this category includes academic positions at the universities and other institutions of higher learning and positions for psychologists in various independent research institutions. (6) Public administration: psychologists are employed in various positions in both central and local government. (7) Defense: Norwegian psychology has been an essential part of the mental health care and the personnel selection procedures in the Norwegian armed forces since the end of World War II. (8) Vocational psychology: psychologists are employed in vocational guidance offices and in rehabilitation facilities outside the Public Health System. (9) Private business: psychologists are working in organizational psychology, personnel psychology, advertising, and similar areas.

Licensure

A psychology licensing law was adopted by the Parliament in 1973 (*Norges Lover*, 1984). The main provision of the law is that only those who have been granted a degree in professional psychology (cand. psychol.) may use the title "psychologist." Another important feature is that the licensing board may authorize psychologists under the law if they have a level of training in psychology comparable to the Norwegian professional degree. Thus, only training in psychology constitutes the basis for granting a license as a psychologist. The law has some other provisions. It authorizes the establishment of a licensing board, it mandates rules in regard to record keeping, and it demands observance of confidentiality by psychologists and their assistants. The law also makes it possible to recall a license for behavior incongruent with the responsible practice of psychology. Fines or imprisonment are authorized for breaking the law.

When this law was adopted by the Parliament, several other laws were also modified. Psychologists were included in the list of professionals subject to penalties for breach of professional confidentiality. Legislation regulating the practice of medicine and dentistry was also amended so that psychologists were excluded from the regulations pertaining to quacks and charlatans. The law relating to the use of hypnosis was amended so that only psychologists and physicians are allowed to use hypnosis in the treatment of illnesses.

All graduates of the professional programs (the University of Oslo and the University of Bergen) are automatically licensed on application. Graduates of PhD programs approved by the American Psychological Association are also automatically licensed on application, provided that certain language requirements are satisfied. Credentials in professional psychology from other countries are subject to individual evaluation. Individuals holding a master's degree are not eligible for licensing. In general, degrees in professional psychology from the other Scandinavian countries are acceptable for licensing in Norway.

Characteristics of Psychology

As mentioned initially, of the four universities in Norway, only two offer degrees qualifying for licensing. The University of Trondheim offers a degree in psychology with an emphasis on research methodology. The graduates of this program may obtain positions in work settings where the professional practice of psychology is not required. The University of Tromso offers introductory programs, and some of the regional colleges of higher education also offer introductory psychology.

The Norwegian Psychological Association
The Norsk Psykologforening (Norwegian Psychological Association) is the professional society for psychologists in Norway. The association was

founded in 1934. Its membership was approximately 1,900 in February 1988. In comparing this figure with the estimated number of psychologists in Norway one can conclude that approximately 90 percent of Norwegian psychologists are members of the association. Only licensed psychologists can be members.

The *Tidsskrift for Norsk Psykologforening* (Journal of the Norwegian Psychological Association) is a prominent responsibility of the association. There are 12 issues a year. The content of the journal relates to scientific and professional matters and includes communications from the association to the membership. A large section is also available for advertising positions in Norwegian psychology. There is no doubt that the "Vacant Positions" section is the main marketplace for Norwegian psychologists.

The Norwegian Psychological Association maintains a large number of permanent committees. One committee is particularly concerned with salary and reimbursement issues. A general professional committee coordinates the activities of the various specialties, and numerous committees are related to each of these specialties. In addition, there is a committee for professional ethics, a committee for international relations, and an advisory committee that cooperates with the Public Health System to fill positions in the system. The association is decentralized in the sense that there are 19 regional psychological associations that focus on local issues.

The Training of Psychologists

The training of psychologists in both Oslo and Bergen has an international scope. Although the early development of Norwegian psychology was heavily influenced by European psychology, after World War II North American psychology had a major impact. This influence is reflected in all aspects of the profession. While there has been considerable interest in East European psychology, the most influential educational and research efforts have clearly been inspired by West European and North American psychology.

Psychology as a profession in Norway has developed in part from education, in part from physiology and philosophy, and in part from medicine and psychiatry. The establishment of professional psychology developed rapidly after World War II with the creation of a program at the University of Oslo which was explicitly aimed at applied psychology rather than the more traditional academic psychology.

Public Opinion of Psychologists

Bjoern Christiansen (1986) has recently published the results of a survey based on a representative sample of approximately 100 Norwegians in regard to their perceptions of psychology in Norway. With the impressive increase of psychologists in Norway from approximately 100 in 1952 to more than 3,000 estimated by the year 2000, it is natural to examine the attitudes of the Norwegian population toward psychologists. Two surveys were conducted for this project, one in 1969 and one in 1984. A comparison of the results indicates that psychology in Norway has become more visible. Professional psychology is viewed as a unitary profession with a large degree of homogeneity with respect to professional competence.

Psychologists are perceived as health professionals, and approximately half the population knows the difference between a psychologist and a psychiatrist. Approximately 60 percent of the population have a clearly positive attitude toward psychologists, approximately 15 percent have a negative attitude, and about 25 percent are uncertain. The survey indicated that there are at least four persons who are strongly positive in their attitude toward psychologists for every one person who is strongly negative. There is also a clear correlation between a positive attitude toward psychologists and a feeling that psychologists should be more accessible. The general recognition of professional psychology improved during the period from 1969 to 1984. Other conclusions from the survey are that psychologists are the most knowledgeable about human nature, are the preferred professionals to ask for help in cases of depression and nervousness, and are most likely to provide better service to many people currently being cared for by physicians, ministers, and social workers. This survey clearly indicates that psychology as a profession has improved its status in Norwegian society.

Economic Reimbursement of Psychological Services

The year 1966 was important for professional psychology in Norway. The Parliament adopted the National Health Insurance Law (*Norges Lover*, 1984), which provided that examination and therapy by a psychologist be paid for by the National Health Insurance System. As a direct consequence of this law, the public health authorities had a legitimate need for a definition of "psychologist." The adoption of this law represented an important event, which together with some other circumstances led to the "Psychology Law" adopted in 1973. A rather comprehensive set of regulations details the circumstances under which a psychologist may be reimbursed by the National Health Insurance System. Before 1966 psychologists had been reimbursed by the system on an ad hoc basis, usually related to a referral by a neurologist or a psychiatrist claiming that assessment or treatment by a psychologist was essential to the management of the patient. In the 1966 law some changes were introduced. First, it was required that a psychologist eligible for reimbursement by the National Health System should be certified as a specialist in clinical psychology by the Norwegian Psychological Association. A psychologist's services were free of charge in public health institutions such as hospitals and outpatient clinics when the psychologist was a directly salaried employee. However, it was possible to establish a private practice, providing the psychologist was a certified specialist. The National Health Insurance would reimburse the psychologist according to a fee schedule established through an agreement between the National Health Insurance System and the Norwegian Psychological Association. Relatively few clinical psychologists engaged in private practice in the beginning, mainly because of a general shortage of clinical psychologists, who at that time seemed to prefer positions in the National Health System. During the 1980s, however, several events changed this situation.

First, there has been a substantial increase in the number of certified specialists in clinical psychology. Second, in April 1984 the reimbursement system underwent a change. New regulations provided for a sharing of the health cost between the National Health Insurance System and regional government units. To meet the public need for budget control, it was necessary for psychologists to negotiate a reimbursement contract with the regional government to provide services that private practice had furnished up to that time. All psychologists in full-time private practice at that time were granted such a contract. Other psychologists who wanted to establish private practice had two possibilities. They could be granted a contract, as mentioned previously, whereby the local government would pay 60 percent of the fee and the National Health Insurance would pay 40 percent, or they could establish a private practice without a contract. All certified specialists are reimbursed 40 percent of the fee by the National Health Insurance System. Thus, the establishment of a private practice without a contract implies that the remainder of the fee, namely, 60 percent, has to be collected from the patients. Statistics are unreliable at the present time, but a relatively large number of psychologists who are certified in clinical psychology have established themselves in private practice without a government contract. Thus, there are two models of private practice in clinical psychology in Norway, one in which the economic basis for the practice is a contract between the psychologist and the regional health authorities, and another in which the patients have to pay a substantial part of the fee themselves.

Specialties

The first formalized specialty in clinical psychology was established by the Norwegian Psychological Association in 1950. Considerable development has occurred since that time. There are now three main group of specialties: clinical psychology, industrial and organizational psychology, and general psychology. The regulations pertaining to the requirements and procedures for certification as a specialist are available in the *Norsk Psykologforenings ABC* (the Norwegian Psychological Association's handbook for psychologists [1987]).

The specialty of clinical psychology is divided into several subspecialties, each with a common core of requirements. The subspecialties are (a) psychotherapy, (b) adult clinical psychology, (c) child clinical psychology, (d) clinical neuropsychology, (e) the clinical psychology of intoxicating agents and dependency problems, (f) the clinical psychology of mental retardation, and (g) the clinical psychology of the school systems. In the specialty of industrial and organizational psychology, it is also possible to subspecialize in various related areas, such as industrial psychology or organizational psychology separately. The specialty of applied general psychology has just been adopted by the Norwegian Psychological Association, and its implementation is underway. The general idea has been to create a specialty in which both clinical and social psychology are essential parts. Community psychology, health psychology, social service psychology, and primary community services are typical areas in which this competence is relevant.

Several requirements must be met in order to be a specialist certified by the Norwegian Psychological Association. They include 5 years of experience within the field, varied experience within the area, and some requirements with regard to supervision. Further, an applicant must participate in courses and workshops. Some of these courses are elective, while others are mandatory. There must be a major mandatory course in the area of the chosen subspecialty. Mandatory courses exist for all specialties in such areas as administration, office management, and professional and ethical issues. With regard to supervision, a separate set of requirements is being developed.

There is also a regulation requiring a written thesis. The intent of this requirement is for an applicant to demonstrate ability to present a clinical issue, a literature survey, or some related topic in written form. The requirement of this written thesis is not meant to be so overwhelming that it in itself is a barrier to obtaining certification.

The Norwegian Psychological Association has the responsibility of maintaining the professional level of the practice of psychology by administration of the certification procedure. This arrangement is arrived at on the basis of an agreement with the Department of Health and Social Affairs and follows in general a model that is also employed with regard to other professions such as odontology and medicine.

Research

Funding

Funding of psychological research is available from various sources. The Norwegian Research Council for Science and the Humanities has been the main source of extramural funding for psychology. The Norwegian Council for Research in Technology and Science has also funded behavioral research. In addition, funds and foundations, some private and some public, are available for research support. Some of these funds are administered by the universities, while others are independent foundations. The research councils maintain a formalized procedure for evaluation of applications for research funds based on professional peer review. The research foundations at the Universities of Oslo and Bergen are also important sources for funding research and travel in the behavioral sciences.

It is difficult to estimate what percentage of total research money in Norway is allocated to the behavioral sciences. The main problem is that much research in psychology is interdisciplinary, particularly in the areas of social sciences, medicine, and odontology. It is, however, safe to state that applications for research assistance which satisfy the quality criteria are far in excess of the available funds. Partly through the efforts of the Council for Social Science Research, a subdivision of the Norwegian Research Council for Science and Humanities, the quality of research proposals in Norwegian psychology have greatly improved in recent years. Most sources for research funding also allocate money for scientific travel to attend conventions or to visit relevant research institutions abroad. The opportunity for international travel, particularly for psychologists working at the universities, has been an important factor in the development of high-quality research in Norway. The universities themselves, through state appropriations, also allocate funds for research.

Research Institutions

The four universities conduct research programs in psychology, but the scope is naturally dependent on the size of the institution. Some regional colleges also maintain research programs in psychology. In addition, there are independent state-funded research institutions, such as the National Institute for Alcohol Research, the National Institute for Gerontological Research, and the National Institute for Research in Social Science. These institutions are funded directly by the state and are viewed as important providers of information essential to public policy-making decisions.

Areas of Research

The areas of psychological research in Norway cover most topics common to Western psychology. While clinical psychology in Norway has a fairly strong standing as a professional discipline, it is probably biological psychology that has been the main focus of Norwegian research. However, the National Research Council for Social Science made a special effort during the period 1977–86 to improve the quality of research in clinical psychology. A comprehensive program for research in clinical psychology was established at the universities in Oslo and Bergen. Fellowships and a system of guidance were funded to improve the quality of research in clinical psychology in Norway. During the life of the program the equivalent of approximately 75 man-years was expended. The program also provided for operating funds and professional travel. Ursin (1987) has recently written a comprehensive review of psychological research in Norway.

Those institutions of higher learning that teach psychology, in particular those that grant advanced degrees in psychology, all combine research and teaching. Thus psychological research in Norway is comprehensive and covers a wide range. Interdisciplinary research is, as mentioned earlier, increasing rapidly.

Bibliography

Christiansen, B. (1986). Hva bestemmer befolkningens syn på psykologer? *Tidsskrift for Norsk Psykologforening, 23*, 691–707.

Engevik, H., Myklebust, J. P., & Ommundsen, R. (1987). *Undersøkelse av psykologer, 1983: Teknisk rapport, Frekvensfordeling, Tabeller, Dokumentasjon.* Oslo: Norwegian Psychological Association.

Holte, P. A., Magnussen, S., & Sandsby, S. (1984). *Norsk psykologi i 50 år: Norsk Psykologforening, 1934–1984.* Oslo: Universitetsforlaget.

Norges Lover. (1984). Pp. 1958–1988. Oslo: Grondahl & Son Forlag A/S.

Norges Lover. (1984). Pp. 2239–2240. Oslo: Grondahl & Son Forlag A/S.

Norsk Psykologforening's ABC. (1987). Oslo: Norwegian Psychological Association.

Ursin, H. (1987). Psychology in Norway. In A. R. Gilgen & C. K. Gilgen (Eds.), *International handbook of psychology* (pp. 347–367). New York: Greenwood Press.

31 / Pakistan

ZAFAR AFAQ ANSARI

Zafar Afaq Ansari (born 1937) received his MA from Karachi University and his PhD from the University of Glasgow. He is the chief editor of the Pakistan Journal of Psychological Research *and president of the Pakistan Psychological Association. Ansari has published numerous research articles in areas such as educational testing, personality assessment, and creativity. He taught at Karachi and Peshawar universities before joining the National Institute of Psychology in Islamabad, where he has been professor and director since 1981.*

Characteristics of the Pakistani Psychologist

Psychologists in Pakistan usually start their professional careers after 16 years of education with a master's degree. At present two types of institutions offer psychology programs. Some institutions are located in colleges that mainly offer undergraduate teaching programs leading to BA/BSc degrees, but in some areas they offer MA/MSc programs also. Other institutions are general universities that offer MA/MSc and higher programs in a large number of areas and are usually much better equipped in terms of staff, laboratories, and libraries. The opportunities for higher education in the country are limited, although they seem to be increasing. Most people who have obtained the PhD have done so from universities in the UK or the USA. Until the late 1960s most students went to British universities, but there is an increasing tendency now to go to the USA. The total number of psychologists with a PhD is not more than 40 (from the UK, 15; USA, 12; Pakistan, 8; others, 5).

The exact figures regarding the number of psychologists in various specialties are not available. The *Directory of Psychologists* published by the Pakistan Psychological Association is under revision. However, the approximate number of psychologists engaged in psychological professions is 600. Psychology is a popular subject among females; the male:female ratio among students of psychology is about 1:5.

Nevertheless, women constitute only a little more than half of the work force of psychology. Many women graduates become full-time homemakers instead of following a career. Some areas (such as the armed forces) are not fully open to women psychologists.

By far the largest number of psychologists are engaged in undergraduate teaching in colleges. Psychology is a popular subject at the undergraduate level. Therefore, most colleges have a department of psychology. Universities and postgraduate colleges are the second largest employers. At present there are 10 departments of psychology that offer MA/MSc programs. To be employed by them, one must have a good academic background. Since the chances of employment in higher education, and for promotion, are better in these institutions, a teaching position there is considered attractive. The armed forces and the Federal and Provincial Public Service Commissions carry out assessment and selection work in the public sector. These organizations also develop tests and conduct research. They offer good employment opportunities for psychologists.

Clinical work is a field that is rapidly expanding. With the recent establishment of two institutes of clinical psychology, many psychologists receive training and, later, employment in government hospitals. Some clinical psychologists also practice privately. A fifth field in which some psychologists are employed is research. At present the National Institute of Psychology is the only organization that has been created specifically for research. However, some other organizations have psychologists as researchers. Other areas in which psychologists have been employed in small numbers are special education, police work, and jails. An approximate distribution of psychologists in various occupations is as follows: undergraduate teaching, 60 percent; graduate teaching, 15 percent; assessment and selection, 7 percent; clinical work, 7 percent; research, 4 percent; and other, 4 percent.

Licensure

There are no official or formal requirements for the practice of psychotherapy or related services in Pakistan, and some people who offer such services are not qualified psychologists. The result is that, at times, people claiming to provide psychotherapy are actually dealing in the occult, palmistry, and exorcism. Additionally, some private psychological institutions make exaggerated claims regarding the effectiveness of their psychotherapy.

The Pakistan Psychological Association (PPA) took notice of this situation, appointed a committee to develop standards for the practice of psychotherapy, and recently published a report (PPA, 1987). The committee has tried to establish minimum qualifications, including clinical experience, that would make a person eligible to practice psychology. The recommendations do not have any legal standing at present but are likely to serve as guidelines.

The use of psychological tests in Pakistan is not widespread, yet many tests are being misused. People unqualified to use or interpret tests are administering and interpreting them. Many tests for which there is no evidence of validity, at least in Pakistan, are being interpreted as valid tests. Similarly, the possibility and extent of error in psychological tests is not fully conveyed to the client. The PPA has appointed a committee to look into the ethical and professional aspects of this problem.

Teaching of Psychology

The teaching of psychology as a discipline begins at grade 11. It is available as an optional subject to students in the humanities and sciences. The curricula are not exactly the same everywhere, but they usually include a course in general psychology and another in experimental, social, or developmental psychology. Elementary experiments in learning, memory, and perception are also taught, along with some statistics.

At present 10 institutions offer master's-level education: the Departments of Psychology in the Universities of Karachi, Sind, and Peshawar; the Department of Applied Psychology of Punjab University; and 6 postgraduate colleges (two of them in Lahore and one each in Sialkot, Jhang, Gujranwala, and Rawalpindi). The details of master's programs vary a great deal, but they usually cover the traditional areas of history, methodology and testing, and developmental, social, experimental, and clinical psychology. There has always been a good deal of emphasis on clinical psychology in Pakistan. Recently, two Institutions of Clinical Psychology have been established, one in Karachi and the other in Lahore. These institutions offer postgraduate training in clinical psychology.

Some Pakistani universities have MPhil and PhD programs, but they are still not very productive. Peshawar University was the first to organize a regular program for PhD students. PhD programs are being offered by the universities of Punjab, Karachi, and Peshawar, as well as the National Institute of Psychology in Islamabad. An MPhil program is being organized by some of these institutions and by the University of Sind.

Journals

There were no professional journals of psychology in Pakistan until 1965. Psychologists published their research in journals of education or philosophy. Some science journals also published psychological papers. In 1965 the first professional journal, the *Pakistan Journal of Psychology*, appeared. This journal has been published more or less regularly since then. The Department of Psychology, Government College, Lahore, publishes the *Psychology Quarterly*, and the Department of Psychology at Peshawar University has started the publication of *Pakistan Psychological Studies*. Neither of these journals has appeared regularly. Recently, the National Institute of Psychology started publishing the *Pakistan Journal of Psychological Research* twice a year.

A shortage of funds is one major problem of these journals. Another problem is an insufficient supply of good research papers. Most of the articles published in these journals, at least between 1965 and 1980, were theoretical rather than research-based. Since editors do not have sufficient time or resources for technical editing, many papers that could be improved with rewriting are left unrevised. The *Pakistan Journal of Psychological Research* introduced the system of blind review in Pakistan. It is expected that this practice will lead to improvement in the quality of research.

Professional Organization

There is only one national-level organization of psychologists: the Pakistan Psychological Association. The association held its first meeting in Dhaka in 1968 (Ali, 1968). It has held a total of six such conventions, usually one every 2 or 3 years. Some proceedings of the conventions have been published (see, for instance, Ali, 1968; Ansari, Tariq, Zaman, Chowdhri, & Watanabe, 1986; Rashid, 1979). The conventions have been very useful in developing contacts among psychologists in the country and enhancing the level of research. The conventions have also been occasions to highlight the activities of psychologists and their potential for contributions in various areas.

Other activities of PPA include publication of a directory of Pakistani psychologists and publication of a newsletter, which, although it appears irregularly, has been a significant source of contact among psychologists of the country. PPA has been working to establish itself as an effective academic organization concerned with promotion of the discipline. In recent years it has organized seminars and workshops throughout the country to

focus attention on selected issues. As noted earlier, it is also trying to develop standards for psychotherapy and guidelines for test administration
and interpretation.

Books and Other Resources

Textbooks up to grade 12 are locally written and are readily available. Some books are also available for the BA/BSc level. Textbooks used
for the master's level and higher are exclusively foreign, however, and their
availability is limited because of their high cost. Library facilities are also
rather poor. Only two departments of psychology have well-established
laboratories. Psychometric instruments are generally available and are used
in some establishments, but their applicability is questionable on cultural and
linguistic grounds. Three out of 10 postgraduate establishments have some
computing facilities, although they are not being widely used. The National
Institute of Psychology has a strong computing section and uses computers
for data processing as well as desktop publishing.

Financial support from the government has recently increased but is still
quite limited. The total allocations for education and research and development activities are quite small, and the major share of these funds goes to
science and the technology sector. Psychology, like other social sciences, gets
but a small share of these funds. Two programs, however, received considerable financial support in the 1980s. They are training programs for clinical
psychology and special education.

Image of Psychology

A few decades ago psychology was viewed with much hostility
and suspicion. This was so because most psychologists were analytically oriented, and psychology was regarded as synonymous with psychoanalysis
and as being somewhat contrary to theology and morality. This attitude has
changed considerably, but psychology is still widely seen to focus on abnormal behavior only. The relevance of psychology to other areas of human
behavior has not been fully realized.

Psychology has remained an alien discipline in other ways also. Most
textbooks used for higher levels of education are written in the USA. The
contents of these books bear little relevance to the realities of life in Pakistan.
The problems that beset Pakistani society, such as illiteracy, poverty, overpopulation, and corruption, find no mention in these books. Pakistan, like

many other Third World countries, is struggling to develop a sense of nation-hood in its people, to reduce social tensions, and to develop economically. Neither the textbooks published in the West nor the locally produced text-books, which borrow most of their contents from foreign publications, seem to reflect these aspects of national life. Psychological research in Pakistan is improving (Ansari, 1987), but it still needs to reorient its priorities.

Trends

As Zaidi (1976) noted in the earlier edition of this book, Paki-stani psychology inherited the traditions of Indian psychology, which was essentially philosophically oriented. Another major influence on early Paki-stani psychology was that of analytic psychology. During the early 1960s when the first group of foreign-trained psychologists took over from the old guard, there was an attempt to reorient completely and thereby to establish a more behavioristic, quantitative-psychometric psychology. It was during this period that early laboratories, including animal laboratories, were estab-lished. However, the behavioristic psychology proved to be too sterile to survive in Pakistan. The only advantage of this period was the development of a large number of psychometric devices, including the translation and adaptation of the Differential Aptitude Test, the MMPI, the TAT, and many others.

During the same period another major development, curiously, was a movement aimed at developing an indigenous psychology. This movement started with an interest in the Islamic heritage, particularly the writings of Muslim mystics. Later an attempt was made to understand human nature and to develop a system of psychotherapy based on Islamic teachings. This movement was headed by Ajmal (1969). The same period saw the develop-ment of social psychological research. Zaidi (1975) and some of his associates started working on problems of social change, modernization, the status of women, and stereotypes. Moghni (1969) initiated studies on motivation.

The late 1970s saw major changes in psychological research and practice. The establishment of the National Institute of Psychology by the Federal Ministry of Education to carry out psychological research brought about important qualitative changes in research. The institute began to carry out large-scale research projects in areas such as cognitive development, crime, mass media, psychological testing, guidance and counseling, school drop-outs, and women's studies. The institute also initiated studies that are policy-oriented, cover the entire country, and include the neglected majority, such as primary schoolchildren and the rural population. Other significant areas of research in Pakistan are the effects of television on children, creativity (Peshawar University), Islamic traditions in psychotherapy (Government College, Lahore), aptitude testing (Punjab University), cross-cultural psychology (Sind University), and clinical psychology (Karachi University).

The applications of psychology are extremely limited at present. They are largely confined to assessment, selection, and psychotherapy. In recent years some progress has been made in applying psychological knowledge to education, particularly curriculum development, guidance and counseling, and special education. But other areas, such as industry, media, and agriculture, have not been opened up for psychologists. The future of psychology in Pakistan ultimately depends on whether psychologists remain confined to academic institutions or begin to serve the needs of the whole society.

Bibliography

Ajmal, M. (1969). Muslim traditions in psychotherapy. *Pakistan Psychological Studies, 1*, 57–63.

Ali, M. R. (Ed.). (1968). *Proceedings of the First Annual Conference of Pakistan Psychological Association*. Dhaka: PPA.

Ansari, Z. A. (1987). *Teaching and research in psychology in Pakistan: A country report.* (Contract No. 381.070.6[86/84][86]). Bangkok: UNESCO.

Ansari, Z. A., Tariq, P. N., Zaman, R., Chowdhri, S., & Watanabe, S. (Eds.). (1986). *New directions in Pakistani psychology*. Islamabad: PPA.

Moghni, S. M. (1969). Development of a questionnaire for achievement-related attitudes. *Pakistan Psychological Studies, 1*, 80–91.

Pakistan Psychological Association. (1987, April). Standards for practicing psychology. *Newsletter of the Pakistan Psychological Association*.

Rashid, N. (Ed.). (1979). *Proceedings of the Fourth Session of PPA*. Karachi: PPA.

Zaidi, S. M. H. (1976). Pakistan. In V. S. Sexton & H. Misiak (Eds.), *Psychology around the world* (pp. 329–340). Monterey, CA: Brooks/Cole.

Zaidi, S. M. H. (Ed.). (1975). *Frontiers of psychological research in Pakistan*. Karachi: Department of Psychology, Karachi University.

32 / Philippines

ESTEFANIA ALDABA-LIM

Estefania Aldaba-Lim (born 1917) received her PhD from the University of Michigan in 1942. A specialist in clinical psychology, counseling, and population issues, she has served as president of the World Federation for Mental Health, the Philippine Association of Psychologists, and the Philippine Mental Health Association. In addition, she has been chair of the UNESCO International Commission for Peace and vice-chair of the UNESCO Executive Board and the United Nations University Council. In 1978 she received the UNESCO Medal for Distinguished Service, and in 1979, the UN Peace Medal. Currently, Aldaba-Lim holds an executive position in the Philippine Psychological Corporation. She is on the Executive Board of the International Social Science Council, UNESCO, Paris, and chairs the Executive Committee of PATH (Program for Adaptation of Technology in Health), based in Seattle, Washington, USA.

Psychology in the Philippines has evolved from the founding fifties to the scientific sixties, to the relevant seventies and eighties, when interest in the larger social issues, the dynamics of community development, and the nationalist aspirations of the Filipino psyche was developed. The Filipino pioneers in the field had two things in common: first, all except one came from fields other than psychology, the most common of which, understandably, were philosophy and education; second, all received their advanced psychology training (PhD) in the USA. The founders of the discipline of psychology in the Philippines are Agustin Alonzo, Isidro Panlasigui, Sinforoso Padilla, Jesus Perpinan, Elias Bumatay, Alfredo Lagmay, Mariano Obias, Jaime Bulatao and Estefania Aldaba-Lim.

Characteristics of the Psychologist

It is estimated that at present 70 percent of Filipino psychologists have master's degrees, 20 percent have doctoral degrees, and 10 percent have bachelor's degrees. Increasingly, the holder of a bachelor's degree is not really considered a psychologist. Employment and workload, financial difficulties, and social pressures are the constraints to the pursuit of graduate degrees. Research—a professional function—is infrequently undertaken because of lack of funds, time, and personnel.

From the handful of schools offering degrees in psychology in the 1950s and early 1960s, academic programs in psychology have mushroomed. From a total of 44 schools all over the country, there are now 24 schools offering an AB in Psychology, 15 a BS in psychology, and 5 an AB in the behavioral sciences or in guidance and psychology. From the same list of 44 schools, 25 offer MA/MS degrees in psychology, while 7 schools offer MA programs in education, with a major in psychology, and guidance and counseling.

PhD programs are few. Only four universities offer a PhD in psychology; three other colleges offer a PhD in guidance and counseling or educational psychology, or an education major in psychology.

The existence of these PhD programs, along with the drying up of grants for graduate study abroad, have decreased the proportion of psychologists trained abroad and increased the number of locally trained PhDs. Local PhD programs have also changed the profile of the typical PhD student in psychology. Compared to the psychologists who received their PhDs in the 1960s and early 1970s abroad, the more recent crop of local PhDs tend to be in their mid- to late 30s, have been in the field longer, and were more experienced when they were going through their PhD programs. Because they went through Philippine programs and were immersed in Philippine psychology before and even during their PhD training, these PhDs of the 1980s are better prepared for work in the Philippine setting.

It is estimated that the number of psychologists in the Philippines is close to 500. This figure does not include guidance counselors and personnel managers, many of whom consider themselves psychologists but are allowed only affiliate status in the Psychological Association of the Philippines because their degrees are in education, business, or social studies. If these people were included, the number would be about 2,500.

The Psychological Association of the Philippines (PAP), founded in 1962, counts among its members 43 PhDs, 25 of whom are fellows, and 125 associates, 86 of whom possess MAs. An AB degree holder may become an associate after practicing as a psychologist for at least 10 years.

Filipino practitioners in psychology are predominantly young women who have not yet earned graduate degrees in psychology, are working as full-time permanent employees with fixed hours in various work settings, and have varying numbers of years of work experience. They assume the functions of testing, interviewing, counseling, research, and psychotherapy. Among PAP membership, the sex ratio is five females to one male. It is believed that a significant number of male psychologists do not join the PAP because of nonconformity or because most male practitioners in business and industry do not have their degrees in psychology. PAP membership is composed mostly of educators and government-employed psychologists. A great number of educators are practitioners part-time.

There is a growing number of psychologists in government service. The original psychologists in government were those employed in hospital settings and practicing in the areas of testing and general psychology. Psychologists at the National Mental Hospital are the prime example.

The National Bureau of Investigation (NBI) also employs psychologists, whose main tasks involve aspects of legal, clinical, and investigative functions. Although the hospitals and the NBI were the first groups in government to hire psychologists, a rapidly increasing number of psychologists are employed in such government agencies as the National Economic and Development Authority, Development Academy of the Philippines, National Housing Authority, Ministry of Human Settlements, and National Irrigation Administration. Those in this new group do not fall under the traditional category of psychologist but may be classified as rural sociologists, community development organizers, researchers, or training specialists. Psychologists in government will probably be a new force in applied psychology.

To help meet the need to insure and protect the competent practice of psychology in the Philippines, the Psychology Act, a bill to professionalize and license psychologists, has been submitted to the new Congress.

Status of Psychology

A cursory examination of the undergraduate psychology programs of the University of the Philippines, the Philippine Women's University, St. Louis University in Baguio, the University of San Carlos in Cebu City, and De La Salle University shows that the most common basic courses are general psychology, statistics, social psychology, experimental psychology, personality theories, psychological testing, and practicum. Not all psychology subjects offered in academe have maximal applicability to actual work settings. Highly specialized clinical psychology subjects such as psychotherapy, Rorschach technique, and counseling are more appropriate for the graduate level. The distinction between AB and BS pychology programs of study is unclear. AB and BS programs differ from one educational institution to another, as indicated by (a) variety of subjects offered, (b) differences in sequential arrangement of subjects in the program, (c) nonuniformity of credits given to some subjects (particularly experimental psychology), (d) total number of units in psychology subjects, and (e) total number of units required for graduation.

Inadequacies of trainee performance in practicum facilities are due largely to deficiency in communications skills, limited clinical background and training, and poor evaluation of test results via reliance on Western standards. It has been suggested that universities and colleges stress the development of verbal and communication skills, human relations, and psychological testing and evaluation, giving allowance to cultural factors and research methods and techniques.

The PAP, universities, and other agencies are encouraged to continue sponsoring a regular program for continuing education for practitioners, and agencies are urged to offer scholarships to deserving practitioners for graduate education. The possibility of giving grants to practitioners who are engaged in thesis writing should also be studied. To facilitate this grant, it would be helpful if agency-related problems were investigated in the thesis.

Practice

In the area of psychology practice, the first mental health clinic in the country, the Institute of Human Relations, was established at the Philippine Women's University in 1948. Its major objective was to help every student achieve the highest possible degree of maturity, not only intellectually but also emotionally. The clinic was directed by a clinical psychologist, and the staff included a guidance counselor (who was also the chief of the student counseling center), a remedial reading specialist, two junior-level psychologists in charge of testing, and a consulting psychiatrist (part-time). In 1950, in response to public demand, the institute extended its services to other schools and to the community at large, offering diagnostic services and training programs for guidance counselors of the public school system. It pioneered in the teaching of human relations for secondary schools, a psychodynamic approach to self-understanding for adolescents. The institute also undertook an experimental pilot program for educable mentally retarded children which led to the founding of two notable institutions for retarded children.

In 1962 the Institute for Human Relations became public and evolved into the present-day Philippine Psychological Corporation (PhilPsyCor), with the majority of stock owned by the Ayala Group of Companies. PhilPsyCor holds the franchise for the sale of various psychological tests and instruments, mainly those from abroad and particularly those marketed by the Psychological Corporation in the USA. PhilPsyCor was the first institution to carry out industrial testing and consultation, training seminars and workshops for organizational development, job evaluation, and morale surveys.

In the government sector, Jaime Zaguirre, noted psychiatrist and instructor of clinical psychology at the University of the Philippines (1948–57), established the first neuropsychological services unit at the V. Luna General Hospital in October 1947. At this unit, psychiatrists, psychologists, and social workers made up the therapeutic team. Their clients were mainly military personnel and their families.

Among the early applied psychological services was Ateneo University's Central Guidance Bureau (CGB), established in 1960 by Rev. James Culligan. In its first year of existence CGB assisted students from the Ateneo campus, as well as from other schools and from religious orders, and referral cases from parents or agencies. The psychological services offered in its early days were counseling, testing for employment and placement, and surveys for business firms.

From these pioneering beginnings, there have developed quite a number of psychological institutions. It was not possible to arrive at a definite figure, but Philippine Psychological Corporation files show 27 psychology organizations, mainly involved in testing. From the Psychological Association of the Philippines roster of members, 16 more names of applied psychology organizations turned up. A look at the directory of the Philippine Society for Training and Development revealed 9 names of psychology organizations providing services in training and human resource management. The clients of these applied psychology groups vary; they may include children and adults with emotional or family problems or those working to apply for local or overseas employment. The reason for the marked increase in the number of applied psychology offices is the volume of workers leaving for overseas jobs who have to be tested. It is precisely because of the increase in potential business that some abuses have surfaced.

Organizations, Facilities, and Public Exposure

As previously mentioned, the main professional organization is the Psychological Association of the Philippines (PAP), which marked its 25th year in 1987. It publishes the annual proceedings of its convention as well as the *Philippine Journal of Psychology*, also once a year. The journal provides the medium for sharing the best of studies, researches, and graduate theses in the profession. The Pambansang Samahan ng Sikolohiyang Pilipino (Association of Filipino Psychologists, PSSP), founded by Virgilio Enriquez, is primarily composed of academic psychologists but is open to any person interested in Filipino psychology or the Filipino psyche; hence, anthropologists, poets, and choreographers are among its members. The Personnel

Managers Association of the Philippines also has numerous psychologists on its roster.

Today there are 14 general psychology textbooks authored by Filipinos, but there are only 2 or 3 higher-level texts. The major USA texts in introductory psychology, testing, social psychology, personality, clinical, and experimental psychology have been reprinted locally—about 3 texts in each of these areas. Otherwise, they are not affordable for Filipino students.

Library facilities are generally poor. The State University of the Philippines once had a good collection of foreign journals but has discontinued purchases because of inadequate resources.

Laboratory instrumentation is close to nonexistent. Psychometric instruments are the domain of PhilPsyCor. The psychometric instruments used in practice are almost exclusively American, with little work done to test their local validity.

Computer facilities constitute the one bright spot in the practice of psychology in the Philippines. With desktop computers becoming more popular, multiple regression and complex analyses of variance are now within psychologists' capabilities, and factor analysis should follow soon, as computers become more affordable.

The following are the leading research centers and their respective research areas: (1) Philippine Psychological Corporation: human resource development and management; (2) Human Research Center: community psychology; (3) Psychology House: Filipino indigenous psychology; (4) Silliman University: research on farming attitudes and practices; (5) La Salle Social Research Center: family relationships; (6) Greenhills Creative Child Center: autism; (7) Ateneo University: altered states of consciousness; and (8) University of the Philippines at Los Banos: farmers' decision making, psychology, and nutrition. Some government support exists in the form of research grants; beyond that, there is very little.

The greatest exposure of the general public to psychology is through overseas employment. Thousands of applicants for overseas employment have to undergo "psychological testing." It is questionable whether those who administer the tests are qualified.

Another area of exposure is through the National College Entrance Examinations, which all graduating high school students planning to pursue university studies must take. Though a psychometric instrument developed under the supervision of the Fund for Assistance to Private Education (FAPE), it may be viewed simply as an educational test. Some locally developed tests are used as professional entrance examinations to colleges, such as medical college admission tests, nursing tests, business management tests, and the like.

Trends

General trends reveal that the bulk of research was undertaken in the decade of the seventies. In the sixties the dominant interests were in the areas of testing and measurement and personality variables. Child development and behavior modification and therapy were also among the more common research areas. Personality variables included intelligence, anxiety, creativity, self-concept, coping patterns, and emotional adjustment. Child development papers covered such areas as childrearing practices and cognitive and personality development, particularly in relation to school adjustment and family.

Then came the clamor for relevance. There was a cry for a psychology that addressed real issues and real people. There was a demand for a Filipino psychology. It was also during this period that practitioners wanted equal time. Discussions focused more and more on national development, and papers were written in Filipino. Psychology moved away from the laboratory and away from the factorial designs. It was during the seventies that the Pambansang Samahan ng Sikolohivang Pilipino was formed, the objective of which was the understanding of Filipino behavior in terms of Philippine history, culture, and language.

In general, the late 1960s and early 1970s were characterized by the experimental laboratory approach. Scientific rigor rather than relevance was the main concern. The late 1970s and the 1980s saw more interest in the resolution of problems and social issues facing a country struggling to free itself from an authoritarian regime, in the dynamics of Filipino communities, in the intricacies of the Filipino psyche, and in the use of Filipino as the language of research. In methodology, there was a veering away from the experimental approach, with more emphasis on phenomenological field approaches.

The changes in type of content as well as methodology may be due partly to personal change and personal growth and partly to the pressures from the changing political climate in the country, which made a difference in the spirit and consciousness of the times.

We are now more self-assuredly Filipino. Gone is the dependence on the West and on Western models and methods. Also gone is the counterdependence on the self-conscious avoidance of anything that might be interpreted as Western. In many circles there is a genuine and spontaneous awakening of Filipino consciousness that finds expression in our work as psychologists. People now work in many low-income communities; many clinical psychologists are involved with groups other than those belonging to the middle class, and they use techniques that do not cater only to the literate population.

Although there is a small core of very solid and involved social psychologists, there is also a marked and growing interest in clinical psychology, and locally trained PhDs are helping to develop indigenous therapies.

A wide range of opportunities for psychology practice exist in the Philippines today. The psychologist can perform the traditional tasks of teaching, research, testing, and therapy. In addition, the psychologist can work in such areas as training, organizational development, community organizing, program planning, implementation and evaluation, as well as academia, the clinic, industry, government, and the community.

Bibliography

Aldaba-Lim, E. (1955, September). *A brief history of the part psychiatry and psychology are playing in the Philippine campuses*. Paper presented at the WFMH Princeton Conference on Student Mental Health, Princeton University.

Aldaba-Lim, E. (1959). Reeducating the emotions. *WCTOP, 1,* 3. Geneva.

Aldaba-Lim, E. (1966). *The role of the psychologist in manpower development*. Manila: PMAP Publication, Personnel File.

Catalan, N., Dayan, N., & Tehs, L. (1983, August). *The psychologist as a practicing social scientist and professional: Manpower and training survey*. Paper presented at the 20th Annual Convention of the Psychological Association of the Philippines, Manila.

Licuanan, P. (1983, August). *History and current developments in Philippine psychology*. Paper presented at the 20th Annual Convention of the Psychological Association of the Philippines, Manila.

Montes, L., & Ilaya, G. (Eds.). (1983, August). *Developments in Philippine psychology*. Papers presented at the 20th Annual Convention of the Psychological Association of the Philippines, Manila.

Padilla, S., & Aldaba-Lim, E. (1961, November). *States and trends in psychology in the Philippines*. Manila: Science Review.

33 / Poland

ZDZISŁAW CHLEWIŃSKI

Zdzisław Chlewiński (born 1929) received his PhD and habilitation degrees from the Catholic University of Lublin in 1963 and 1972, respectively. His areas of special interest are cognitive processes, concept identification, and cognitive skills.

Chlewiński has published more than 175 research articles and several books, including Concept Identification, Attitudes and Personality Traits, *and* The Formation of Cognitive Skills. *An active editor of several journals, he was also cofounder of the Polish Ergonomic Association in 1977. He is professor of experimental psychology at the Catholic University of Lublin.*

Poland, with 37 million inhabitants, has about 6,000 psychologists, approximately 75 percent of whom are women. The majority of psychologists work in educational-professional guidance centers, which deal with educational and school problems and offer professional guidance. About 30 percent of psychologists work in health service—that is, in psychiatric hospitals and mental health centers—as clinical psychologists. In the health service they cooperate with physicians, deal with diagnostics, and conduct individual and group psychotherapy. Clinical psychologists are well respected, and their skills seem to be increasingly acknowledged. In Poland the entire health service is socialized and free of charge. As a result, many people consult psychologists. Children and young people are also directed to the educational-professional guidance centers by their schools.

Some psychologists (about 25 percent) work in personnel/industrial/organizational psychology. They not only carry out diagnostic studies, such as examinations of driver skills, but also concentrate on conditions related to work adjustment. Others work on the adaptation of these conditions to the needs and capacities of workers (e.g., distribution of rest periods, microclimate, lighting).

The development of Polish psychology is best reflected in scientific and professional periodicals. At present, four psychological periodicals are published in Poland, including *Psychologia Wychowawcza* (Educational psychology), *Studia Psychologiczne* (Psychological studies), and *Przegłąd Psychologiczny* (Psychological review), all of which contain summaries in English.

The *Polish Psychological Bulletin* is published solely in English. Polish psychologists also publish their papers in periodicals dealing with the physiology of the nervous system, pedagogics, and praxiology. In addition to these periodicals, one of the volumes of *Roczniki Filozoficzne* (Philosophical yearbook) is devoted completely to psychological problems.

The Polish Psychological Society has a membership exceeding 4,000. Every 3 years a convention of psychologists is held. Thus far, 26 such conventions have taken place.

The characteristic feature of Polish psychology is that it is based on the output of both Russian psychology and that of Western Europe and the USA. Poland provides a place for communication between different cultures, a bridge between the East and the West. Consequently, different influences overlap. As a result, it is difficult to determine precisely what is truly "Polish" and what is inspired by Polish psychology.

From a Polish viewpoint the psychology of English-speaking countries is characterized by a highly specialized approach, with detailed and discriminating "technical-quantitative" analyses. Similar tendencies can be seen in Polish psychology, though to a lesser extent. Research in Poland is more general and somewhat less "technically" advanced. There exists a tendency for various metareflections, both in the approach to the solution of problems and in the solutions themselves. This tendency is in agreement with Polish scientific tradition and interest in philosophy and goes hand in hand with the tendency to ask questions concerning the identity of psychology.

In Polish psychology great importance is placed on the search for assumptions that frequently go unquestioned. Often people are simply unaware of the existence of the assumptions. Usually, one becomes aware of them only after they are questioned. In principle, that is not possible until some alternative assumptions are formulated. That is why, in Polish psychology, the assumptions to be accepted are reviewed, and the methodology of logical empiricism is often questioned (see the work of E. Paszkiewicz).

Recent Developments

Since the late 1960s considerable progress has been made in several different areas of Polish psychology. This progress has been particularly evident in the area of research, where the topics have broadened, the number of researchers and research centers has increased, and the quality of research has improved. In this period psychology has become a more mature science, both in its essence and in its methodology. Of course, the output of Polish psychology in recent years has been, to a large extent, determined by the world level of the discipline. The dynamic flow of information (e.g., access to literature, personal contacts, exchange of scientists), the standard of technical equipment in laboratories (e.g., computers), the number of people engaged in research, and the level of psychological knowledge worldwide have all had an impact.

Among the achievements of Polish psychological thought in this period is "regulatory activity theory," characterized by a high degree of generality of great heuristic value. In the 1960s and 1970s T. Tomaszewski developed the paradigm that assumes activity to be a complex, directed set of processes; the structure changes in response to various conditions, leading to a complex result.

In this conception, the functional viewpoint is clearly emphasized. External behavior and mental processes are regarded as different forms of regulation of the relation between a person and the environment. The emphasis is on characterizing these activities as processes, that is, as behavior with an organized and directed course. A cybernetic-systemic viewpoint is often stressed (in which a human being can be regarded as a particular kind of self-controlled system) which operates on the principle of reception and transformation of information.

Under the influence of this regulational-functional conception, studies on the structure and function of personality have been conducted. Particular emphasis has been placed on cognitive factors, cognitive motivation, and value systems. Cognitive conceptions, concerned not only with behavior but also with what people think of themselves and of the world, have become popular in psychology. The conceptions of personality created in Poland by such authors as W. Lukaszewski, K. Obuchowski, and J. Reykowski are of particular importance. The common feature of these conceptions is that human activity, considered from the point of view of its function in regulating the relation between a person and the environment, is the starting point. The person chooses the goals of his or her own development and the realization of these goals. This conception is similar to the American conception of setting aims. In European psychology there exist similar ideas (for example, those of J. Nuttin, in Belgium), expressed in slightly different terms. The standards determined by an individual need not be of a biological character; they may be purely cognitive. The individual aims that a person sets have important motivational functions (Z. Zaleski).

Areas of Research Interest

While behaviorism was dominant in the USA, Polish psychology had, in principle, a cognitive character. In spite of accepting numerous behavioristic research techniques, its major thrust remained cognitive. This climate of Polish psychology has, since the late 1960s, spread all over the world. J. Kozielecki developed the original theory of self-recognition, as well as transgression theory, in this cognitive spirit. Studies on cognitive processes, particularly on the formation of concepts, reasoning, cognitive structures, and schemes and cognitive styles, are being carried out by psychologists such as A. Biela, Z. Chlewiński, A. Falkowski, M. Goszczynska, J. Kozielecki, M. Lewicka, T. Maruszewski, M. Materska, Cz. Nosal, J. Trzebinski, and B. Wojciszk.

The original psychology of individual differences and especially the regulational theory of temperament (in the tradition of Pavlov) were developed in Poland (J. Strelau, A. Eliasz). Studies on the origin and conditioning of prosocial and antisocial attitudes (J. Reykowski, A. Fraczek, M. Jarymowicz) have also attracted interest.

Many centers of psychological research in Poland attempt to combine the latest achievements of world psychology with their own experimental ideas. A brief survey of the major research areas follows.

The psychological theory of decision was developed largely by J. Kozielecki, with various applications for the interpretation of information processes (A. Biela, M. Goszczynska, T. Tyszka). These include the analysis of individual and group decisions in laboratory and real situations (Z. Chlewiński), and game theory applied to the analysis of conflict situations (J. Grzelak, T. Tyszka) and to risk-taking behavior (Cz. Wałęsa).

Research in general and developmental psycholinguistics has developed since the late 1960s. These studies are closely connected with worldwide trends in this field. However, they also have some native features, particularly in the area of developmental studies (M. Przetacznik-Gierowska). I. Kurcz supervises the group that deals with general psycholinguistics, neurolinguistics, and developmental psycholinguistics. These studies are based on the principle that human mind structures and the knowledge of a language (internal vocabulary and the rules for using it) all overlap (I. Kurcz, G. W. Shugar, D. Kadzielawa).

There has been a remarkable increase in social psychology research, including studies of conflict, attitudes, social perception, sense of justice, and optimism, and work employing attribution theory (J. Czapinski, J. Grzelak, S. Mika, K. Skarzynska). More recently, investigations concerning ecology have been undertaken (A. Biela).

The psychology of religion is being developed by H. Srzymala-Moszczynska, J. Krol, and W. Prezyna. Its method, in general, is similar to the methodology of social psychology and the psychology of personality. The studies are concerned with various attitudes toward religion, the relation of these attitudes to different features of personality, and the function of mature and immature religiousness in a person. Studies in thanatology are also being conducted (J. Makselon).

Profound and extensive studies are being carried out regarding the theory of development. Such work is being conducted on the development of the entire life span, especially with respect to aging and the aged and early conditioning in the development of childhood disturbances (Z. Babska, A. Brzezinska, A. Jurkowski, A. Niemczynski, M. Przetacznik-Gierowska, M. Tyszkowa, Cz. Wałęsa).

The output in the areas of learning and memory is also considerable (W. Buduhaska, W. Szewczuk, Z. Wlodarski). Among the various aspects of memory and learning, the organization of content and information processing is being studied. My own research deals with the formation of cognitive skills and the function of attention in the formation of these skills.

The closest relation to East European psychology exists in the field of physiological psychology, particularly for psychologists at the M. Nencki Institute of Experimental Biology in Warsaw, who continue the work of J. Konorski, an early student of Pavlov. Three other prominent physiological psychologists are J. Kaiser, T. Marek, and J. Matysiak.

Polish psychological research has long neglected the human emotional-motivational sphere. Recently, however, Polish psychologists have begun studying the influence of the emotions on information processing and are identifying the close relationships between the system of subjective meaning and emotions—both of which play a major role in the formation of the human system of values (G. Kochanska, M. Lewicka). Articles concerning the psychology of emotion have been published, and studies are also being carried out concerning stress and psychological resistance to stress (M. Kofta, Z. Zaleski).

The development of methods of measurement and the use of various mathematical models have become very popular in Polish psychology. This field includes both theoretical publications and papers concerned with psychometric tools (J. Brzezinski, R. Drwal, T. Marek, M. Nowakowska, R. Stachowski).

Applied Research

Considerable research, both by university centers and by various research institutes, concentrates on applied disciplines, such as educational psychology, clinical psychology, and the psychology of labor.

Research in education is carried out primarily by psychologists and concentrates on relevant psychological mechanisms and on the effectiveness of education. Psychologists have developed theories regarding the psychological fundamentals of education and have undertaken studies on educational procedures (A. Gurycka). A specific feature of Polish educational psychology is the personal approach toward the tutor-pupil relationship, that is, it emphasizes that subjective educational relations are specific and are different from all other social relations. Another specific feature is the emphasis on the systemic character of educational interaction in the system. Not only is there tutor influence, but there is pupil influence as well. The importance of the system of moral values in education is emphasized. Studies concerned with aspects of family education on the effectiveness of the school educational system are also carried out. Here the structure and function of a family, attitudes of parents, and educational influence are of particular concern. The systemic character of a family, the individual characteristics of family members, and the creative character of their relations are all emphasized. Great emphasis is placed on proper prophylactics, that is, preparation for marriage and family life, rather than on family therapy, generally a more difficult process (M. Braun-Galkowska, J. Rembowski). Studies on the psychological fundamentals of teaching and on the effectiveness of this process are also proving beneficial, as are some studies concerned with school maturity (M. Przetacznik-Gierowska, Z. Wlodarski).

Research carried out within the broadly defined field of clinical psychology is distinctive, in terms of both the problems undertaken and the techniques of research. It has long been characteristic of Polish clinical psychology that two different approaches have existed that nevertheless have many common points. The first goes back to the conception of the regulatory function of the psyche and to neuropsychological analyses; the second is based on psychometric techniques. Many papers concerning psychological conditioning and the effects of mental and psychosomatic diseases have been published. Research on selected problems of defectology, psychopathology, neuropsychology, and medical and forensic psychology are also being carried out. Polish research psychologists who have worked in these and related fields include T. Galkowski, I. Heszen, M. Klimkowski, J. Kostrzewski, S. Kowalik, I. Obuchowska, Z. Pluzek, and H. Sekowa.

An attempt to consider the problems of mental health within a broader theoretical context has also been undertaken. Among the numerous approaches, humanistic psychology is a reference base for many clinical psychologists. The methods of group dynamics, individual and group psychotherapy (including psychotherapy with entire families) (S. Leder, J. Melibruda, J. Strojnowski), guidance concerned with mental health, and studies on communication skills (L. Grzesiuk) are all being developed in Poland.

Research on the psychological determinants of addiction (Cz. Cekiera) has also been conducted.

The 1980s were characterized by considerable progress in the psychology of labor organizations (X. Gliszczynska, Z. Ratajczak) and in engineering psychology (L. Paluszkiewicz). Particularly important in these disciplines are studies on psychological costs and merits in the course of work, mental overload (threat, difficult conditions), grave responsibility in work, selection for executive positions, psychological conditioning and effectiveness in work, and preparation and selection for professions.

Certain achievements have been noted in other branches of applied psychology, such as the psychology of sport (e.g., studies of the influence of personality and psychophysical features on sports activity and its effectiveness), military psychology (studies on the psychological foundations of the human-machine system and on the personality characteristics of a commander), and the psychology of art (original studies on psychological aspects of musical education and on the selection of musically gifted pupils—e.g., M. Manturzewska).

The Current State of Psychology

Psychology as a science is being developed in nine Polish universities and in two Research Institutes of Psychology of the Polish Academy of Sciences (in Warsaw and in Poznan). About 800 psychologists are engaged in research work.

After 5 years of university studies in psychology, graduates obtain the degree of master of psychology, entitling them to engage in the profession of psychologist. Postgraduate studies for a doctorate require 3 to 4 additional years. In principle, the program of study is similar in all universities, although there are some differences. The content of major psychological courses is similar to that offered in the USA. The only difference is a greater emphasis on psychological and methodological problems. In the early phase, students follow an almost identical curriculum. A certain degree of specialization takes place only during the last 2 years. Students use handbooks and monographs written by Polish psychologists as well as translations of foreign authors. About 10 to 15 translations of foreign books are published every year. In some libraries important foreign periodicals are available, such as *Acta Psichologica, Cognition, Cognitive Psychology, Contemporary Psychology, Journal of Experimental Psychology, Journal of Personality and Social Psychology, Psychological Review*, and a Russian journal, *Voprosy Psichologii. Current Contents*, published in the USA, is particularly useful, as it furnishes the titles and addresses of authors of interest. Most research workers in psychology have had some research experience abroad, mainly in Western Europe and the USA.

In general, the 1970s and 1980s witnessed an increased sophistication in the methodology of many Polish studies. Polish psychology, however, continues to face serious challenges. They include the use of more advanced methods of gathering and analyzing data and the problem of coordinating studies of various laboratories, both national and foreign.

Bibliography

Brzezinski, J. (Ed.). (1984). *Consciousness: Methodological and psychological approaches.* Amsterdam: Rodopi.

Chlewiński, Z. (1976). Poland. In V. S. Sexton & H. Misiak (Eds.), *Psychology around the world* (pp. 341–356). Monterey, CA: Brooks/Cole.

Grzesiuk, L. (1987). Poland. In A. R. Gilgen & C. K. Gilgen (Eds.), *International handbook of psychology* (pp. 368–391). New York: Greenwood Press.

Kozielecki, J. (1987). *Koncepcja transgresyjna czlowieka.* Warsaw: PWN.

Obuchowski, K. (1985). *Adaptacja tworcza.* Warsaw: KIW.

Paszkiewicz, E. (1983). *Struktura teorii psychologicznych: Behawioryzm, psychoanaliza, humanistic psychology.* Warsaw: PWN.

Ratajczak, Z. (1985). Psychology of work in Poland: Theoretical and current trends in research. *Polish Psychological Bulletin, 16*(3), 211–220.

Reykowski, J. (1982). Social motivation. *Annual Review of Psychology, 33,* 123–154.

Reykowski, J. (1986). *Motywacja, postawy prospoleczne a osobowosc.* Warsaw: PWN.

Strelau, J. (1983). *Temperament, personality, activity.* London: Academic Press.

Tyszka, T. (1986). *Analiza decyzyjna i psychologia decyzji.* Warsaw: PWN.

34 / Romania

MARIA GRIGOROIU-SERBĂNESCU

Maria Grigoroiu-Serbănescu (born 1950) studied psychology at the University of Bucharest, where she obtained both her licentiate (1973) and her PhD degree (1979). A specialist in child psychology and psychopathology, she has conducted research in various areas, including the psychometric properties of several assessment devices, children at risk, depressive disorders in children and adolescents, and the psychological development of premature children. She is a member of the editorial board of the Romanian Journal of Medicine: Neurology and Psychiatry *and was awarded the Gh. Marinescu Prize of the Romanian Academy for studies of children at risk. She is a researcher at the Institute of Neurology and Psychiatry, Bucharest.*

Romania is one of the East European countries in which psychology has developed both theoretically and experimentally since the end of the 19th century. The first courses in experimental psychology were given at the Universities of Iassy and Bucharest in 1893 by E. Gruber, in 1895 by A. Binet, and in 1897 by C. Radulescu-Motru. The first laboratories of experimental psychology were established at the University of Iassy in 1893 and at the University of Bucharest in 1906. At the beginning of the 20th century, research performed by Romanian psychologists in physiological psychology (Gruber, Vaschide, Nădejde) was published in German and French journals of psychology. Psychology in Romania has continued to develop over time and remains sensitive to international influences.

Educational Background and Work Settings

Two universities in the largest cities of the country (Bucharest and Cluj) provide full training in psychology in independent departments, while the University of Iassy offers a mixed training in psychology and sociology. Before 1972 5 years of training were required for the degree of psychologist, and 4 years of postgraduate study were required for the PhD degree. Since 1973 university study has been reduced for all sciences, including psychology, to 4 years, and the PhD stage has been maintained at 4 years. After completing 4 years of university study, psychologists work in applied fields such as medicine, industry, or education. After 3 years of practical work in a special field, a certification examination must be passed, whether or not the respective psychologist plans to go on to the PhD postgraduate stage.

The Universities of Bucharest and Cluj have a common training program, including basic courses in general and experimental psychology, child psychology, psychopathology and clinical psychology, psychological testing, statistics, psychophysiology, psychology and the education of handicapped children, school and vocational guidance, educational psychology, industrial psychology, and social psychology.

The content of the programs taught at the universities has been based on results of both domestic and foreign research. After 1968 scientific communication with European countries and the USA increased considerably, so that foreign psychology (especially French, German, Swiss, English, and American) has had a strong influence on training and research in Romanian psychology.

Work settings for psychologists include both practical and research institutions in child and adult psychiatry and in the safety of public transportation (railroad, motor, and air), as well as the network of personnel selection centers of the Ministry of Electric Energy, forensic institutions, foster-care centers, special schools, and factories.

Professional Organization

The professional organization of Romanian psychologists is the Association of Romanian Psychologists, founded in 1964. It is affiliated with the International Union of Psychological Science. The number of psychologists registered by the association is 720, but the actual number of psychologists is somewhat higher. The male:female ratio cannot be estimated exactly, but there is a clear prevalence of females among psychologists in all fields (clinical, industrial, educational).

Journals of Psychology

The Publishing House of the Romanian Academy publishes two psychology journals. One, the *Revista de Psichologie*, publishes papers in the Romanian language. It was founded by Florian Stefănescu-Goangă in 1938.

The other, in spite of its French title, *Revue Roumaine des Sciences Sociales—Série de Psychologie,* a holdover from its founding in 1964, publishes papers in English. It is sent to 45 countries.

Research in Psychology (1960–87)

Psychological research has been developed in several universities and research institutes since 1960 (the Universities of Bucharest, Cluj, and Iassy; the Institute of Psychology and the Institute of Neurology and Psychiatry in Bucharest; the Institute of Hygiene in Bucharest and its division in Cluj; and research institutes sponsored by different industrial ministries).

Child Psychology and Psychopathology

For many years child psychology has focused on cognitive development as related to learning activity. Piaget's genetic theory has also strongly influenced the research preoccupations of Romanian child psychologists. In this area, many works have been published by Ursula Schiopu (1963, 1966, 1967), Valentina Radu (1973), E. Fishbein, Ileana Pampu, and I. Minzat (1970–78). Child psychologists have also worked on adapting foreign psychodiagnostic tools to the peculiarities of the Romanian child population and on producing native tools. The effect of pollution on the neuropsychological development of children growing up in industrial centers has been studied by mixed teams of physicians and psychologists at the Institutes of Hygiene in Bucharest and Cluj.

Beginning in the late 1970s an interest in the development of children at risk has emerged. This type of research has been conducted by younger psychologists working in medical research institutes. For example, I have studied the intellectual, emotional, and psychomotor development in pre-term children from 1 to 7 years of age (Grigoroiu-Serbănescu, 1981, 1984). I have also investigated the psychopathology and psychological development in children aged 10 to 17, of bipolar and unipolar depressive parents, compared to that of children of psychologically normal parents.

Between 1981 and 1984 the first nationwide epidemiological study of psychological disorders in children aged 1 to 16 years was conducted in Romania using the DSM-III diagnostic criteria. The study was coordinated by two researchers from the Institute of Neurology and Psychiatry of Bucharest (Dan Christodorescu and myself) and was completed with the participation of 19 teams of child psychiatrists and psychologists throughout the country.

Psychophysiology and Learning Psychology
These branches of psychology have been represented by several researchers, among whom a remarkable contribution was made by Gheorghe Zapan
(1897–1976), professor at the University of Bucharest. For his extension of the
Weber-Fechner Law to the extreme values of stimulus intensity, published in
the German *Zeitschrift für Psychologie* (1963), he was elected to membership in
the American Academy of Sciences. Another important contribution to the
psychophysiology of memory was made by I. Ciofu (Institute of Psychology
in Bucharest), whose works were published between 1960 and 1980.

Psycholinguistics
This specialty has been represented by an outstanding psychologist,
Tatiana Slama-Cazacu, who has benefited from international recognition of
her research developed at the Psycholinguistics Laboratory of the University
of Bucharest from 1957 until the present. Several of her books have been
translated in different countries: the Netherlands (1961, 1973), Czechoslovakia (1966), France (1972), and Spain (1976). She is a member of the editorial
board of the international journal *Language*.

General Psychology
This broad area deals primarily with the analysis of thinking, language,
creativity, and problem-solving processes. Prominent researchers include
P. Popescu-Neveanu, B. Zörgö, Al. Rosca, and M. Bejat.

Industrial Psychology
This specialty has been concerned with the psychological peculiarities
of, and training in, different professions, as well as with personnel selection and counseling. Among its prominent researchers are C. Botez, I. Iosif,
V. Ceausu, and Z. Bogaty. Their research has found wide application.

Art Psychology
Research in art psychology has been conducted by S. Marcus and his co-
workers at the Institute of Psychology of Bucharest since the late 1960s. Their
results have been published in several books by the Publishing House of the
Romanian Academy (1971, 1980, 1987).

Clinical Adult Psychology
Though practiced in Romania for a long time, adult clinical psychology
has generated little research and few publications. Among the exceptions
are studies concerned with personality in major affective disorders performed at the Institute of Neurology and Psychiatry of Bucharest by Cristina

Popescu since 1982. Psychological approaches to different disorders have been presented at various domestic psychiatry and psychology conferences and meetings.

Results of 20 years of research in Romanian psychology were presented in a four-volume work, *Contemporary Psychology Syntheses*, published by the Romanian Academy Publishing House between 1980 and 1985. It covered the major fields of psychology: general and experimental, industrial, developmental, and educational and clinical. The coordinators for this project were B. Zörgö, P. Popescu-Neveanu, Al. Rosca, I. Iosif, C. Botez, U. Schiopu, M. Bejat, and V. Pavelcu.

Addendum

The Institute of Psychology of Bucharest and the official teaching of psychology were abolished in Romania by order of the former dictator N. Ceausescu between 1980 and 1989. Psychological research and teaching were performed in a very few medical and industrial institutes, their nature masked by the apparent specificity of those institutions.

Bibliography

Bejat, M. (Coord.). (1981). *Creativity in science, technique, and education*. Bucharest: Pedagogical Publishing House.

Grigoroiu-Serbănescu, M. (1981). Intellectual and emotional development in premature children from 1 to 5 years. *International Journal of Behavioral Development, 4*, 183–199.

Grigoroiu-Serbănescu, M. (1984). Intellectual and emotional development and school adjustment in preterm children at 6 and 7 years of age. Continuation of a follow-up study. *International Journal of Behavioral Development, 7*, 307–320.

Grigoroiu-Serbănescu, M. (1986). Factor structures and validation of the Junior Eysenck Personality Questionnaire based on a Romanian sample. *International Journal of Psychology, 21*, 141–151.

Grigoroiu-Serbănescu, M., Christodorescu, D., Jipescu, I., Totoescu, A., Marinescu, E., & Ardelean, V. (1989). Psychopathology in children aged 10–17 of bipolar parents: Psychopathology rate and correlates of the severity of the psychopathology. *Journal of Affective Disorders, 16*, 167–179.

Grigoroiu-Serbănescu, M., Christodorescu, D., Magureanu, S., Jipescu, I., Totoescu, A., Marinescu, E., & Ardelean, V. (in press). Adolescent offspring of endogenous unipolar depressive parents. *Journal of Affective Disorders*.

Grigoroiu-Serbănescu, M., Christodorescu, D., Totoescu, A., Jipescu, I., Marinescu, E., & Ardelean, V. (1990). Depressive disorders and depressive personality
traits in offspring aged 10–17 of bipolar and normal parents. *Journal of Youth and
Adolescence, 19*, 6.

Marcus, S. (1971). *Empathy: Experimental studies*. Bucharest: Publishing House of the
Romanian Academy.

Popescu, C. A., Totoescu, A., Christodorescu, D., & Ionescu, R. (1985). Personality
attributes in unipolar and bipolar affective disorders. *Romanian Journal of Medicine:
Neurology and Psychiatry, 23*(4), 231–242.

Popescu-Neveanu, P., & Golu, M. (1970). *The sensibility*. Bucharest: Scientific Publishing House.

Rosca, Al. (1973). Current state of psychology in Romania. *Romanian Journal of Social
Sciences: Psychology, 1*.

Rosca, Al., & Bejat, M. (1976). *History of sciences in Romania: Psychology*. Bucharest:
Publishing House of the Romanian Academy.

Schiopu, U. (1987). *Developmental psychology*. Bucharest: Publishing House of the
Romanian Academy.

Slama-Cazacu, T. (1968). *Introduction to psycholinguistics*. Bucharest: Scientific Publishing House.

Zörgö, B., Iosif, I., & Schiopu, U. (Coord.). (1980, 1981, 1983, 1985). *Contemporary
psychology syntheses*. Bucharest: Publishing House of the Romanian Academy.

35 / South Africa

JOHANN LOUW

Johann Louw (born 1951) was educated in both South Africa and the Netherlands, where he received a drs. psych. degree from the University of Leiden in 1977 and a PhD from the University of Amsterdam in 1986. A specialist in the history of psychology, he has published in various journals, including the Journal of the History of the Behavioral Sciences, Professional Psychology: Research and Practice, *and the* Journal of Cross-Cultural Psychology. *He is senior lecturer in the Department of Psychology at the University of Cape Town.*

Psychology in contemporary South Africa presents a contradictory image even to the most casual observer: on the one had, it is a highly popular academic discipline, whose professional expertise is accepted by various sectors of the economy and the lay public; on the other hand, it is a discipline absorbed in introspective self-criticism and plagued by self-doubts about the progress it has made. The more optimistic interpretation of psychology's position is based on its strong position at the universities and its achievements in different sections of South African society. The less optimistic view takes into account the "crises" in psychology worldwide and, more important, the teaching and practice of the discipline in a country torn apart by violent political conflict. This chapter reveals aspects of both images of South African psychology.

Characteristics of the Psychologist

The title of "psychologist" is protected by the Medical, Dental, and Supplementary Health Service Professions Act, No. 56, of 1974, which established a Professional Board for Psychology, subordinate to the South African Medical and Dental Council. The board keeps a professional register of all psychologists, and only those registered may call themselves psychologists and perform certain activities.

The Professional Board allows for three levels of registration: psychologist, psychometrist, and psychotechnician. For registration as a psychologist, a master's degree in psychology, industrial psychology, or educational psychology is required, plus completion of a 12-month internship at an approved institution. Registration as a psychometrist requires an honors degree plus 6 months of practical training. To register as a psychotechnician, a candidate must have a bachelor's degree in psychology and must have completed a 6-month practical training course. In 1978 727 psychologists, 13 psychometrists, and 488 psychotechnicians were registered. In 1982 these numbers had increased to 1,340 psychologists, 300 psychometrists, and 500 psychotechnicians, and by 1986 to 1,938, 908, and 524, respectively. (The actual number of psychologists may be slightly higher, as some academics see no need to register with the board.)

The 1980s were a period of rapid growth for psychology, as the number of psychologists in South Africa nearly trebled. These figures imply that there are approximately 7 psychologists per 100,000 inhabitants in South Africa (compared to more than 40 for the USA, the Netherlands, and the Scandinavian countries, and 21 for Spain).

Psychologists can register in one or more of five categories: clinical, counseling, industrial, educational, or research and academic psychology. The last category of registration is probably unique to South Africa and reflects the dominance of a professional model in South African psychology. Numerically, clinical psychology is the strongest category. Ebersohn (1983) found that, of all registered psychologists, 44 percent were clinical; 23 percent, counseling; 20 percent, industrial; and 12 percent, research psychologists. When one examines the figures for trainees (i.e., intern psychologists), the trend becomes even more pronounced: 63 percent were registered as intern clinical psychologists; 23 percent, counseling; 11 per cent, industrial; and 3 percent, research psychologists. Educational psychologists work mostly in clinics and schools, mainly in child guidance. Industrial psychologists are typically employed in personnel sections of industry or engaged in staff selection, recruitment, and management development. Academic and research psychologists work in universities and research organizations.

Most psychologists are "white." Ebersohn (1983), for example, found that 97 percent of his group of respondents were whites. (Whites form only 15 percent of the South African population.) In 1987 the Institute for Counselling Psychology of the Psychological Association of South Africa indicated that there were only 15 black counseling psychologists out of a total of 317. Graduation data reflected the same picture; in 1984 only about 5 percent of all master's degrees in psychology were awarded to black students. South African psychologists also tend to be relatively young; numerous surveys found a large majority to be younger than 40, with most in the 30-to-39-year cohort.

Men outnumber women in the discipline; of Ebersohn's sample, 64 percent

were men and 36 percent were women. Furthermore, at university departments of psychology and industrial psychology, the male:female ratio is 3:1.
In 1982 men still dominated the number of master's degrees awarded by
about 3:2. In 1984, however, women outnumbered men for the first time (55
percent to 45 percent).

Leading Universities

As an academic discipline, psychology enjoys immense popularity. Between 1979 and 1983 psychology was by far the most popular major
subject in the arts and social sciences, while industrial psychology was the
fourth most popular subject in the area of commerce. When one examines
the number of master's degrees awarded in the 5 years since 1980, a steady
growth is also discernible. In 1980, 98 master's degrees in psychology were
awarded; in 1982, 118; and in 1984, 131. A survey conducted among South
African universities for the purpose of this chapter revealed that there were
approximately 45,000 undergraduate students at departments of psychology
and industrial psychology in South Africa and about 2,000 postgraduate students. At a rough estimate, it means that 20 percent of all students at South
African universities enroll for a course in psychology. At some universities
the growth was so dramatic that restrictions had to be placed on the intake
of students into the first-year course.

Postgraduate training in educational psychology is traditionally offered in
faculties of education. Virtually all departments of psychology offer training
that leads to professional registration in clinical psychology. Nearly 80 percent of the universities offer similar education in industrial psychology, often
in separate departments, and about 50 percent of them also train counseling
psychologists. Several universities have introduced training programs for
research students similar to the ones for the professional areas. The professional training courses have become increasingly popular and the traditional
master's degree by research and thesis less so. In 1987 there were approximately 80 clinical students in training at the master's level, 40 counseling, 34
research, and 90 industrial psychology students.

The competition for places in postgraduate psychology is keen. In 1985, at
the University of Cape Town, for example, 60 people applied for six places
in the master's clinical psychology program. When all universities are considered, about 20 percent of all applicants for clinical training are accepted,
30 percent for counseling, and 75 percent for industrial. For students wish-
ing to do a master's degree by research, the acceptance rate is considerably
higher, ranging from 40 to 100 percent.

The areas of psychology most often taught at the undergraduate level are (in decreasing order of frequency) developmental psychology, research methodology, psychopathology, social psychology, personality theory, psychotherapy, psychometrics, counseling, cognition, and neuro- and physiological psychology. For industrial psychology departments, the most frequently taught courses are personnel psychology, organizational psychology, psychometrics and measurement, occupational psychology, and consumer behavior.

Approximately 340 academics are affiliated with departments of psychology and industrial psychology at South African universities. About 16 percent of them received some overseas training; most were trained in the USA ($N = 25$), followed by the UK ($N = 12$) and the Netherlands ($N = 7$). The most popular specialty areas among academic psychologists are clinical ($N = 68$), counseling ($N = 38$), research methodology ($N = 31$), psychometrics ($N = 26$), developmental psychology ($N = 24$), and social psychology ($N = 21$). Among industrial psychologists at universities, popular choices are personnel psychology ($N = 13$), organizational psychology ($N = 13$), research methodology ($N = 12$), consumer behavior ($N = 8$), and occupational psychology ($N = 8$).

Most textbooks used at universities are published overseas—fewer than 10 percent of the prescribed books are produced locally. Traditionally, South African psychologists were not prolific publishers. Since the 1980s, however, there has been a change. One reason is the increasing cost of imported textbooks, and in some cases the threat of textbooks being withdrawn from the country. Another is a new government subsidy formula, which rewards universities financially for books and articles published by their staff members. Since 1982 for example, four introductory psychology textbooks have been published: one in Afrikaans, two in English, and one with both an Afrikaans and English version. Increasingly, locally written and produced textbooks are becoming available in environmental psychology, personality theory, industrial psychology, industrial relations, and so-called black advancement. Three more specialized books deserve special mention: a bibliography on studies of black people of Africa, south of the Sahara, by Andor (1983); a book by Biesheuvel (1984) on work motivation and compensation; and a book of readings on organizational behavior and industrial psychology in the South African context, edited by Barling (1983).

Professional Associations

For many years two psychological associations existed in South Africa: the South African Psychological Association and the Psychological Institute of the Republic of South Africa. These two associations went their separate ways in 1962, when a group of psychologists decided to form the Psychological Institute, which admitted only white South African psychologists to membership. In 1983 the two associations amalgamated to form the Psychological Association of South Africa (PASA), which opened membership to all psychologists. Thereafter, PASA's membership gradually increased, with 1,000 members in 1983, 1,146 in 1984–85, 1,338 in 1986, and 1,442 in 1987.

PASA consists of five institutes representing five subdisciplines: clinical psychology, counseling psychology, industrial psychology, educational psychology, and academic and research psychology. The official journal of the association is the *South African Journal of Psychology*, by far the most significant local psychology publication. Published four times a year, it contains mostly articles by South African psychologists.

The political crisis in South Africa manifests itself in the organizational domain, as many psychologists question their role in current and future South Africa. A growing number of psychologists feel that social service workers ought to be cooperating with progressive organizations, rather than the state, to provide for the mental health and social welfare of all South Africa's people. The organizational outcome was the formation of the Organization for Appropriate Social Services in South Africa (OASSSA) in 1983. One of OASSSA's aims is to "examine and research the causes of social and personal problems," and the group stresses that "apartheid and economic exploitation provide the base for poor living conditions, work alienation, and race and sex discrimination, which are antithetical to mental health." Another manifestation of dissent is the publication *Psychology in Society*, a journal that "aims to critically explore and present ideas on the nature of psychology in apartheid and capitalist society." It is produced by psychologists at the Universities of Cape Town, Natal, and the Witwatersrand.

Support for Psychology

Psychology enjoys considerable support and recognition from many sectors of South African society. Raubenheimer (1981) wrote: "Psychology in South Africa has never before flourished as at present"; "the psychologist has gained recognition far beyond what was envisaged"; and "psychologists in South Africa have succeeded in attracting the attention of the public at large. The demand for their services is certain, they are increasingly acquiring esteem and respect, and have secured a particular status in society" (pp. 2–3).

Evidence of government support for psychology is seen in the role of the Human Sciences Research Council, discussed below. Further evidence can be found in the use of psychological services in at least two government departments. One is the Department of Manpower, which has a Department of Vocational Services, employing mainly counseling psychologists. Psychologists are also very active in the South Africa Defense Force, whose Military Psychological Institute has existed for many years. It performs numerous industrial, clinical, and counseling services for the army, air force, and navy. Many of the activities of the institute deal with personnel selection of officers, navigators, pilots, computer programmers, artisans, divers, submariners, and so on.

One area of limited acceptance of psychology is in medical schools. Schlebusch (1985) observed that only three out of seven (43 percent) of the medical schools have at least two clinical psychologists working on a full-time basis, compared to 98 percent of medical schools in the USA. The small beginning that has recently been made with medically applied psychology could fill this gap. The few clinical psychologists currently in medical psychology specialize in neuropsychology, stress and hypertension, pain, surgery, obstetrics and gynecology, cardiovascular disorders, pediatrics, and psychonephrology. Psychiatry departments, with one exception, constitute the base for medical psychologists.

A serious shortcoming is that psychologists work mostly with educated, white, middle-class people in urban areas. Unfortunately, people in the black townships generally have limited contact with, and knowledge of, psychologists. The consequence for psychology could be serious, calling into question the status of psychology and the contribution it can make. It also implies that training in psychology will increasingly be seen as irrelevant by black psychologists.

Major Philosophical and Theoretical Influences

In a survey done for this chapter, most academic psychologists indicated that they were eclectic in their theoretical orientation. The theoretical influences mentioned most often were the behavioral, humanistic, psychodynamic, phenomenological, and systems approaches. Systems theory seems especially to have gained a strong foothold at some universities beginning in the mid-1980s. A Rogerian therapeutic approach was indicated by at least two departments of psychology, and one specified a strong and explicit phenomenological orientation. Surveys of clinical psychologists (e.g., by Manganyi & Louw, 1986) revealed a similar picture; the majority indicated an eclectic orientation, followed by a psychoanalytic, Rogerian, and behavioral orientation.

Leading Native Psychologists

South African psychologists are generally not well known overseas, but a few are acknowledged in their own areas of interest. The doyen of South African psychologists is still Simon Biesheuvel, a prominent industrial psychologist, now in semiretirement, who has published widely on African intelligence, cross-cultural research, industrial and organizational psychology, and motivation. Dreyer Kruger, also in semiretirement, is well known for his books and articles on phenomenological psychology. One of the leading fully active psychologists is Chabani Manganyi, whose work spans the area between literature, biography, and psychology. He is currently working on aspects of clinical psychology in South Africa. John Verster is well known for his work on cognitive competence and assessment, with particular reference to cross-cultural studies. Finally, Don Foster has conducted research on intergroup relations and has published on psychological aspects of detention, policing, and repression.

Research Centers

Three research institutes form the nexus of institutional support for psychological research outside the universities: the National Institute for Personnel Research (NIPR), the Human Sciences Research Council (HSRC), and the Human Resources Laboratory. Since 1984 the NIPR has been incorporated into the HSRC, but because it was an independent institute for a major part of the period under review, it is mentioned separately. At present it defines its task as undertaking, promoting, and coordinating industrial psychological research to improve the efficiency, productivity, and quality of life in the work environment. Its research ranges from investigations into the improvement of personnel assessment, training, and career development, to research on broader issues such as human adaptation, management development and organizational structure, labor relations, and the relationship between brain function and behavior. The NIPR currently employs 65 people with psychological training (total number of staff = 150), most of whom are registered as industrial psychologists.

The HSRC Institute for Educational Research conducts studies on the treatment of learning problems and of gifted children. The Institute for Manpower Research does research on power motivation and aptitude and vocational choice. The Institute for Psychological and Edumetric Research is responsible for developing a large number of psychological measurement techniques, including personality, career choice, intelligence, aptitude, and scholastic achievement tests. It also conducts research on personnel selection and placement, mental health, environmental psychology, and human factors in road safety. The current trend in psychological research at the Institute for Sociological and Demographic Research deals with studies of criminal offenders, such as the psychological and criminological assessment of prison inmates.

In the 1980s, the HSRC has initiated numerous large-scale research projects. For example, the Investigation into Intergroup Relations occupied more than 200 researchers for 4 years, with psychologists playing an important role. A second project was the Educational Research Program, which studied all aspects of South African education for the South African government. A third is the Investigation into Research Methodology, which by 1985 had involved more than 70 researchers, in 18 human science disciplines, working on 30 projects.

The HSRC also offers support services to researchers, including research information, library services, an opinion survey facility, and a center that makes computer-readable survey data available. It also furnishes more general services, such as the training of intern psychologists, test distribution, vocational counseling, EEG examinations, and neuropsychological assessments. It employed 929 people in 1986, inclusive of technical and secretarial staff, of whom 266 had psychological training. These are primarily research psychologists, but industrial, educational, and counseling psychology are also well represented.

The Human Resources Laboratory is part of the Research Organization of the Chamber of Mines of South Africa and is financed by the South African gold mining industry. It has a staff of 40, including 25 professional researchers, of whom about a third are psychologists and industrial psychologists. It conducts research on problems pertaining to the human resources of the gold mining industry, focusing on the following major research areas: workpower supply and demand, communication, work performance, quality of working life and behavior of people at work, management of industrial conflict and change, selection and testing, and health and safety. Since 1986 its objectives have focused increasingly on the handling of industrial relations issues and the management of conflict and change in the industry.

Another research institute, the Institute for Behavioral Sciences, is affiliated with the University of South Africa. It investigates black infant development (including studies of electrocortical functioning, psychomotor abilities, and cognitive abilities), malnutrition and its psychosocial causes and effects, and the development of interaction between mothers and their infants, focusing on black mothers and children.

Current and Emerging Trends

First, all commentators on South African psychology agree that an extraordinary emphasis has been placed on psychological testing. Raubenheimer (1981) calculated that nearly 20 percent of all theses and dissertations in the country dealt with topics such as test construction, refinement of measurement procedures, and so on. Psychological tests are used extensively at child guidance clinics, in schools, at university guidance bureaus, in commerce and industry, and in the Defense Force. Tests are standardized for at least 11 different language groups (e.g., Afrikaans, English, Tswana, Xhosa, and Zulu) and are available for age groups ranging from preschool children to adults. The HSRC Institutes for Psychological and Edumetric Research and for Personnel Research remain the two main test publishers (see Prinsloo, 1984, for examples of tests developed in South Africa). The Test Commission of the Republic of South Africa is prominent in the control and use of psychological tests.

Second, in recent years a more tolerant attitude has developed toward the practitioners of traditional or indigenous healing methods, including diviners, herbalists, and *sangomas*. Evidence of this trend is seen in the official cooperation between the Department of Psychiatry at the Medical University of South Africa and traditional healers. The Department of Psychology at the University of Zululand also conducts research on diagnosis and treatment rendered by these indigenous healers.

Third, a growing number of South African psychologists see community psychology as an alternative to a psychology that is rooted in Western culture and is insensitive to the sociopolitical context. When asked by Lazarus (1985) what issues should be addressed in South Africa, the majority indicated political problems, including racial/sex/class oppression, intergroup conflict, and discrimination.

Finally, it appears that psychologists are also being drawn into the growing conflict in South Africa. Responses differ, of course, but a sizable number of psychologists define their role in increasingly political ways (e.g., OASSSA). The Institute for Clinical Psychology of PASA adopted a policy statement at the 1987 national congress which called on the government to note the psychological consequences of apartheid, violence, indefinite detention without trial, detention of children, media restrictions, and the state of emergency. The HSRC reported in 1986 that the country's unrest and the state of emergency proclaimed by the government severely handicapped research on different population groups. In addition, it complained that ulterior motives were often attributed to its research on topical issues.

In conclusion, I borrow a metaphor that Mauer (1987) derived from Mozart's *Don Giovanni* to address the issue of psychology's relevance in South Africa. In the final scene of the opera, the statue of the Commendatore (which may be symbolic of past injustices, missed opportunities, and ultimate retribution) demands repentance from the nobleman. The reactions of Don Giovanni and Leporello, his servant, to the request may symbolize the broad options available to psychologists in South Africa. Don Giovanni remains unrepentant and intransigent, and that is his ultimate undoing. Leporello adopts an attitude of repentance when he realizes that things have gone too far, and by doing so, he seems to be able to make a new, dramatically chastened, start.

Bibliography

Andor, L. E. (1983). *Psychological and sociological studies of the black people of Africa, south of the Sahara, 1960–1975: An annotated select bibliography.* Johannesburg: National Institute for Personnel Research.

Barling, J. (Ed.). (1983). *Behavior in organizations: South African perspectives.* Johannesburg: McGraw-Hill.

Biesheuvel, S. (1984). *Work motivation and compensation* (Vols. 1 and 2). Johannesburg: McGraw-Hill.

Ebersohn, D. (1983). *Die sielkundiges van die RSA.* Pretoria: Human Sciences Research Council.

Lazarus, S. (1985). *The role and responsibilities of the psychologist in the South African social context: Survey of psychologists' opinions.* Paper presented at the Third National Congress of the Psychological Association of South Africa, Pretoria.

Manganyi, N. C., & Louw, J. (1986). Clinical psychology in South Africa: A comparative study of emerging professional trends. *Professional Psychology: Research and Practice, 17,* 171–178.

Mauer, K. F. (1987). Leporello is on his knees: In search of relevance in South African psychology. *South African Journal of Psychology, 17,* 83–92.

Prinsloo, R. J. (1984). Test practices and the legal control of psychological tests in the Republic of South Africa. *Bulletin of the International Test Commission,* Supplement to *Revue de Psychologie Appliquée, 34,* 39–53.

Raubenheimer, I. van W. (1981). Psychology in South Africa: Development, trends and future perspectives. *South African Journal of Psychology, 11,* 1–5.

Schlebusch, L. (1985). *The development of medical psychology and the employment of clinical psychologists in the faculties of medicine in South Africa.* Paper presented at the Third National Congress of the Psychological Association of South Africa, Pretoria.

36 / Spain

HELIODORO CARPINTERO

Heliodoro Carpintero (born 1939) received his PhD from the University Complutense, Madrid, in 1969. He is the author of more than 100 papers and several books, including General Psychology, History of Psychology, *and* Freud in Spain.

Carpintero founded the Revista de Historia de la Psicología *in 1980 and continues as its director. He also serves as an editorial consultant to* Revista de Psicología General y Aplicada, Análisis y Modificación de Conducta, *and* Teorie e Modelli. *In 1984 Carpintero was the chairman of the 1st International Congress on Psychology and Traffic Safety, held in Valencia. Currently, he is professor of psychology and dean of the Faculty of Psychology at the University of Valencia.*

Background and Training

Psychological studies in Spain have been established in the universities only in recent years. In general, the master's degree is necessary for applied work in psychology, while the doctoral degree is required for an academic career.

The Professional School for Psychology and Psychotechnology was established at the University of Madrid in 1953 as a postgraduate school that granted a "certificate" (diploma) for professional work. A similar center was opened at the University of Barcelona. The curriculum covered the main psychological topics, distributed over 3 years. A master's degree (most frequently in education, philosophy, or medicine) was required in order to enroll. Thus the training in psychology provided a complementary qualification.

In 1968 these studies became a specialty within the area of the humanities (Filosofía y Letras). But this arrangement did not prove to be the correct solution. Psychology was seen by the students more as a literary field than a scientific one. Later an independent curriculum was established for psychologists, and some faculties of psychology (1980) and psychology departments were created. That is the present situation, and the career of psychologist has received the same academic status as scientific studies.

Today students interested in a psychology degree must satisfactorily complete a high school course oriented toward the sciences or humanities. Students are usually 18 years old when they enter the university. Once there, they are required to take a certain number of specialized courses, selected according to their preferences and distributed over 5 years, resulting in a master's degree. Two more years, mainly oriented to methodological questions and highly specialized topics, and including a thesis, are required to receive the PhD.

The current training program has generated much interest among young people. Previously, the old schools issued diplomas to some 3,000 or 4,000 people. In recent years universities have given licenses to more than 30,000 persons. Now Spain appears to be in the top rank of countries according to the ratio of psychologists per million people (528). Requirements for the license have yet to be clearly established.

According to recent information, most licensed psychologists are women (63 percent), graduates of a university (91 percent), under 30 years of age, and with psychology as a second title or degree (40 percent).

The largest number of psychologists work in school psychology or in an educational setting (41 percent). The next largest group are clinical psychologists (30 percent), followed by psychologists working with disabled persons (18 percent) and those specializing in industrial psychology, organizational problems, and delinquency (less than 10 percent) (Hernandez, 1984).

Many psychologists are self-employed or work in private centers. Others are employed in institutions receiving governmental or local support, such as schools and welfare centers. Psychologists work in hospitals and health care centers, mental health programs, drug addiction prevention and treatment programs, welfare programs, and in the areas of family protection, delinquency, and sexual, family, and vocational counseling.

Although there are no detailed statistics related to the employment of psychologists, only about half of the persons with psychology degrees have registered with the Colegio Oficial de Psicólogos (Professional Union of Psychologists), in existence since 1980. The largest group of persons registered in the union are currently working (50 percent), others have part-time employment, and a significant number are without jobs (25 percent) (Hernandez, 1984). The difficulties in getting jobs have not had any visible influence on the student population.

The Universities

As previously noted, a career in psychology in Spain requires the master's degree. It is possible to receive the degree in several public universities (most of the universities in Spain are public) and also in a few private ones.

There is a faculty of psychology in each of the following universities: the University of Barcelona, the Autonomous University of Madrid, the Complutense University of Madrid, the University of Valencia, and the UNED (or National University at a Distance). There are also departments of psychology within faculties of philosophy and humanities, offering professional training in psychology with curricula similar to those existing in the faculties of psychology. This is true of the Autonomous University of Barcelona and the Universities of Granada, La Laguna (Tenerife), Malaga, Murcia, Oviedo, País Vasco (San Sebastián), Palma de Mallorca, Salamanca, Santiago, and Sevilla. It is also possible to study psychology at two private universities, the Pontifical Catholic University (Salamanca) and the University of Comillas (established by the Jesuits).

Valid diplomas or degrees in psychology are usually obtained after 5 years of academic study. New proposals are under consideration which would open the possibility for degrees requiring only 3 years of study, oriented toward practical work, and complementing work done by licensed psychologists.

The universities offer curricula that include some degree of specialization, but there is a large common core of subjects. At present, the academic field of psychology has been organized into six specialty areas: basic psychology, social psychology, developmental and educational psychology, psychobiology, personality-evaluation-treatment, and methodology for the behavioral sciences. Each area organizes the teaching of its own topics and promotes contacts and discussions dealing with the priorities of research and teaching throughout the country.

Psychological Journals

Although psychological articles have been published in a variety of journals, in recent years an increasing number of journals have been dedicated specifically to psychological themes. In fact, the evolution of Spanish psychological journals may be seen as a barometer of changes and influences acting on the science in the country.

The first journal to publish research papers in psychology was the *Archi-*

vos de Neurobiología, founded in 1920 by two psychiatrists, G. R. Lafora and J. M. Sacristan, and a philosopher, J. Ortega y Gasset. Other journals began to appear in the early 1930s.

Additional journals mainly oriented to psychopathological and psychiatric problems were founded in the 1940s and 1950s. In 1946 the *Revista de Psicología General y Aplicado* was established under the direction of J. Germain. It is the oldest existing journal in psychology in Spain. It became the organ of the Spanish Society of Psychology, and it covers a large variety of themes, including methodology, industrial psychology, general psychology, clinical problems, and personality. In recent years it has stressed the experimental approach.

In the 1970s the number of specialized journals in psychology increased as a consequence of the establishment of psychology as a new profession and university area. Some of these new journals are oriented toward general psychology, such as the *Anuario de Psicología, Estudios de Psicología, Psicologica, Quaderno de Psicología*, and *Revista de Psicología y Pedagogía Aplicada*. Other journals are focused on specialized areas, such as *Análisis y Modificación de Conducta, Revista Española de Terapía del Comportamiento, Revista de Psicología del Trabajo y de las Organizaciones, Infancia y Aprendizaje, Revista de Análisis Transaccional y Psicología Humanista, Revista de Psiquiatría y Psicología Humanista, Boletín de Psicología, Evaluación Psicólogica*, and *Revista de Historia de la Psicología*. Some of them bridge the psychological and the psychiatric areas, such as *Archivos de Neurobiología* (reappeared in 1954) and *Revista de Psiquiatría y Psicología Médica de Europa y América Latina*.

The professional journals include *Papeles del Colegio* and *Informació Psicológica*, published by different sections of the Professional Union of Psychologists. International and foreign publications are available in university libraries. The publications of the USA are among the most commonly read, and the British and French journals are also well known and appreciated. Some Latin American journals, such as the *Revista Latinoamericana de Psicología*, are highly valued, too.

Professional Societies and Organizations

The Sociedad Española de Psicología (Spanish Society of Psychology) is the largest and oldest psychological society. Founded in 1952 by J. Germain, the society has about 2,000 members today. Four divisions have been established: theoretical-experimental, clinical, educational, and organizational. Each year, the society organizes special annual meetings. Every 4 years, beginning in 1963, there has been a national congress, now attended by thousands of people. The society has been accepted as a member of the International Union of Psychological Science and has a federal structure with regional sections in Galicia, Catalonia, and Valencia. The headquarters are in Madrid.

In recent years new scientific societies have been founded, such as the Spanish Society of Psychological Assessment and the Spanish Society of Behavior Modification. Other groups deal with psychodrama, Rorschach techniques, treatment of autism, and so on. The Professional Union of Psychologists, already mentioned, is concerned with professional and labor problems. It was established in 1980 as an independent entity and now has about 15,000 members distributed in various regional divisions. Its main target is the consolidation of the psychologist's role in society. Its first congress took place in 1984 in Madrid.

Facilities and Research Support

Psychologists in Spain have at their disposal a large variety of library resources. Many modern handbooks have been translated into Spanish in recent years (e.g., those of Hilgard, Wolman, Lindsay-Norman, Whittaker, Hebb, Richelle-Droz, Delay-Pichot, Fraisse-Piaget, Osgood, Boring, Anastasi, Reuchlin, and Zazzó), along with the main works of well-known psychologists from all over the world (such as Eysenck, Skinner, Luria, Vigotsky, Piaget, Bandura, and many others) and classical works of Freud, James, Pavlov, Wundt, and Dilthey. A large number of those translations have appeared in Latin American countries, to be added to those published in Spain.

A growing number of textbooks are written by Spanish professors and are well adapted to the educational background of the students. Those prepared for the courses offered by the open university (UNED) provide a portrait of the entire field of psychology. The contemporary psychological literature is well known by the academic and research groups, but complete collections of scientific journals are rare. Frequently, there are serious problems in gathering all information relevant for a research project.

For psychological assessment, various tests have been translated into Spanish and adapted to the Spanish population. The first sophisticated adaptation of a test (the Stanford-Binet) was made by J. Germain and M. Rodrigo in 1930. Many other translations have followed (Wechsler's WISC and WAIS, Eysenck's EPI, Bender, Luria, Rosenzweig, the MMPI, and many others). Some publishers have specialized in the publication of tests, such as Paidos, TEA (Técnicos Especialistas Asociados), MEPSA, and CIOS, among others. One original Spanish contribution has been Mira's Myokinetic Psychodiagnosis (or PMK). Created by Emilio Mira-López in 1939, it is a personality test based on the analysis of expressive movements. It was intended as a diagnostic instrument, but certain difficulties in its application and the quantification of its results have limited its use.

Scientific research in psychology has received some support from governmental agencies for science, although the amount is far below the levels of funding provided to other natural sciences. As a new science, psychology suffers from some limitations, including its capacity for application as a social tool.

Psychologists are beginning to play a greater role in Spain, a role that now includes dealing with child learning problems, family and marriage counseling, clinical treatment of neurosis and depression, organizational design, personnel selection, mass communication, and disability, among others. Psychologists increasingly appear as professional persons capable of helping people to solve personal and social problems. Psychology has been required in the programs of study for criminologists, nurses, social workers, and advertising personnel, among others.

Contemporary Psychology

The development of Spanish scientific psychology, rooted in the last decades of the 19th century, was dramatically interrupted by the civil war (1936–39) and its political consequences. A slow process of recovery took place after the late 1940s, based on the efforts of a small group of persons headed by J. Germain in Madrid.

Germain (1898–1986), a psychiatrist, had been interested in psychological questions early on, first as a student of S. Ramón y Cajal and G. Rodriguez Lafora and later working with F. C. Bartlett at Cambridge. In the early 1930s he sought to apply psychology to mental health problems. Demoted after the war because of his connections with such liberal figures as Lafora and Ortega y Gasset, he patiently began to reestablish the old tradition of scientific research. He organized a small center for research in the newly created Consejo Superior de Investigaciones Científicas (Higher Council for Scientific Research, Madrid) (1948); founded a journal, Revista de Psicología General y Aplicada (1946); established the Spanish Society of Psychology (1952); and promoted the first Professional School of Psychology (Madrid, 1952). He was able to gather around him a group of people who eventually became the first psychology professors when departments of psychology were founded at the universities in the following years.

One of Germain's students was Mariano Yela (Madrid, 1921), one of Spain's leading psychologists, who received postdoctoral training in the USA with Thurstone and also worked with Michotte in Louvain. He promoted the development of mathematical psychology, including a factorial approach to intelligence and verbal behavior. He also had firsthand knowledge of applied psychology and testing.

José Luis Pinillos (Bilbao, 1919), another leading figure, did postdoctoral work with Behn and Rothacker in Germany and with Eysenck in Great Britain. He studied religious and political attitudes of youth during the years of Franco's authoritarian regime but was not allowed to publish his results, which showed a growing rejection of the then-dominant reactionary mentality. In recent years he analyzed the psychological characteristics of urban life and wrote a highly influential textbook, *Principios de psicología* (1975), integrating ideas from experimental research with conscious and purposive aspects of human personality.

Another of Germain's students, Miguel Siguán (Barcelona, 1918), after receiving special training in the Institute of Industrial Psychology in London, did work on projective techniques (TAT), human relations in industry, social migrations in Spain, and bilingualism. He founded the Professional School of Psychology at the University of Barcelona, and since 1969 he has been the editor of *Anuario de Psicología* while heading a group exploring Piagetian theory and cognitive development.

Other students of Germain worked in developmental psychology (F. Secadas, García Yagüe), clinical psychology (J. Pertejo, Alvarez-Villar), and psychophysiology (Ubeda). They have been joined by Miguel Cruz, a specialist in Islamic thought; Maria E. Romano, an expert in Rorschach techniques; and J. Forteza, who is interested in the application of differential psychology to industry and organizations.

The "second generation" of Germain's students continues his tradition, conducting research projects, teaching, editing journals, and further organizing and developing the field. Communication with foreign colleagues and centers is increasing, and Spanish psychology is becoming more similar to that of many Western countries.

A well-organized group is working in mathematical psychology and simulation processes (Jañez, Ponsoda, Sierra, Arnau), while many others are oriented toward methodological questions (Amón, Martinez-Arias, Domenech, Santisteban, Anguera). In psychobiology, there has been research on aggression (Simón), sexual differences (Guillamón), psychophysiology (Pérez, Puerto, Sanchez-Turet), and ethology (Sabater Pi).

Many groups are working in personality theory. The problems of assessment have been studied by R. Fernandez-Ballesteros and F. Silva, among others. Behavior analysis and modification has received attention from Pelechano, the founder and editor of *Análisis y Modificación de Conducta*. Psychopathological problems, mainly related to depression, have been studied by Polaino, Domenech, Belloch, and Monedero. Bermudez, Blanco, Ibañez, and Vila are more oriented toward the study of psychosocial correlates of illness and to biofeedback. Tous is interested in experimental approaches to personality, and Forteza and Canovas in differential psychology.

Social psychology is receiving increasing attention. The task of theoretical delimitation of the field has been carried out by Jimenez-Burillo, Torregrosa, and Morales; organizational problems and role theory are the main topics of research for Peiró and Rodriguez-Marin. Community and political psychology has been the central subject in the works of Blanco, Barriga, Seoane, and Serrano.

The field of developmental and educational psychology has a large group centered on cognitive human development, including Aragó, Coll, Díaz-Aguado, Dosil, Barnusell, Hernandez, Muntané, Palacios, Serra, del Val, and Vega. Methodological and instructional problems have been the concern of Beltrón, García-Alcañiz, and Rivas; Marchesi has focused on educational problems of handicapped children; Genovard is oriented toward the training of gifted children.

Various groups working on the history of psychology may be included in the area of basic psychology: Caparrós (paradigms and technological aspects of psychology), H. Carpintero (bibliometric analysis of scientific literature in psychology, and evolution of Spanish psychology), and Gondra (historical archival sources for modern psychology). Some other groups are engaged in experimental research on cognitive theory—for example, those headed by Carretero and de M. Vega. Work on attention and unconscious information processing is led by Tudela. A more instrumental approach to learning has been proposed by Bayés, who also did much to disseminate Skinnerian ideas in Spain; Fernandez-Trespalacios is working on perceptual problems; Mayor, Miralles, and Serra, on psycholinguistics; Freijo, on dynamic processes; and Ferrandiz, on animal learning. Some well-known researchers working in foreign centers and universities should not be omitted, such as Pascual-Leone, a leading neo-Piagetian theorist, and Poyatos, who works on nonverbal communication processes (both in Canada).

The current topics of research in Spain are the same as those studied by psychologists all over the world. Cognitive as well as behavioral approaches are well represented. A certain unity seems to dominate these developments, unity due partly to the tradition rooted in the seminal achievements of Germain's "invisible college" decades ago.

Bibliography

Buendía, J., et al. (1985). *El ejercicio profesional del psicólogo: Un análisis empírico de la situación actual en la Región de Murcia.* Murcia: Colegio Oficial de Psicólogos.

Carpintero, H. (1980). La psicología española: Pasado, presente, futuro. *Revista de Historia de la Psicología, 1,* 33–58.

Carpintero, H. (1982). The introduction of scientific psychology in Spain, 1875–1900. In W. Woodward & M. G. Ash (Eds.), *The problematic science: Psychology in nineteenth-century thought* (pp. 255–275). New York: Praeger.

Fernandez Seara, J. L., et al. (1983). *Status de la psicología en la universidad española.* Salamanca: Facultad de Filosofía y CC. Educación, Universidad de Salamanca.

Hernandez, A. (1984). La psicología como profesión. *Papeles del Colegio, 16–17,* 61–63.

León, R., & Brozek, J. (1980). Historiography of psychology in Spain: Bibliography with comment. In J. Brozek & L. Pongratz (Eds.), *Historiography of modern psychology* (pp. 141–151). Toronto: Hogrefe.

Peiró, J. M., & Carpintero, H. (1983). History of psychology in Spain through its journals. In G. Eckardt & L. Sprung (Eds.), *Advances in historiography of psychology* (pp. 229–240). Berlin: VEB Deutscher Verlag der Wissenschaften.

Siguán, M. (1977). La psicología en España. *Anuario de Psicología, 16,* 7–21.

Siguán, M. (1981). *La psicología a Catalunya.* Barcelona: Ediciónes 62.

Yela, M. (1976). La psicología española: Ayer, hoy y mañana. *Revista Psicología General y Aplicada, 141–142,* 585–590.

37 / Switzerland

RUTH BURCKHARDT & RÉMY DROZ

Ruth Burckhardt (born 1932) received her licentiate degree from the University of Geneva in 1968 and her PhD from the University of Lausanne in 1983. A specialist in psychopharmacology, learning, and methodology, she has published extensively on mechanisms of thirst induction and related behaviors. A past president of the Swiss Society of Psychology, president of the Federation of Swiss Psychologists, and vice-president of the European Professional Psychologists Association, Burckhardt is a lecturer at the University of Lausanne.

Rémy Droz (born 1940) received both his licentiate and his PhD in psychology from the University of Geneva. A specialist in genetic psychology, epistemology, and educational psychology, Droz is the author of Lire Piaget *(Read Piaget) (with M. Rahmy), coeditor of* Manual de psychologie *(with M. Richelle), and the author of more than 60 journal articles. He is a past president of the Swiss Society of Psychology and a member of the editorial board of* Archives de Psychologie, *Geneva, and of* Psychologie, *Berne.*

By its topographical, linguistic, and political characteristics, Switzerland appears to many as a sort of European microcosm. The diverse attitudes, cultural contacts, beliefs, and opinions are faithfully reflected in the multiplicity of educational systems currently in use in Switzerland. There are, for instance, about 28 different laws concerning primary education in a country of about 6 million inhabitants (roughly 25 percent of whom are foreigners residing in the country permanently or temporarily). Switzerland has four national languages, and its polyglot character is enhanced by the fact that Schwyzerdütsch (the Swiss German dialect) is actually an impressive collection of local subdialects that are tied not to social origins, as they are in many other countries, but to geographical regions. This conglomeration of dialects makes it necessary to teach High German in the German-speaking parts of Switzerland almost as if it were a foreign language. In recent years the use of dialect has shown a significant increase, and interlingual communication difficulties have become a much-debated political and journalistic theme.

Mostly as a function of linguistic affinities, the cultural, scientific, and intellectual exchanges between Switzerland and neighboring countries (Germany and Austria; Italy; France) are at least as intensive as those within the country. It would be, therefore, quite misleading to think about Swiss psychology in terms of a more or less unified approach, just as it would be inappropriate to think, as many Europeans do, of one "American" psychology.

Characteristics of the Psychologist

Most psychologists in Switzerland have a complete university training of 4 years or longer. This training is considered the minimum necessary for a qualified psychologist. Earned degrees are licenses (after about 4 years), diplomas (1 additional year), or doctorates (at least 2 more years). University training is characterized by an important proportion of psychology courses and seminars, as well as practical work, sometimes including clinical and similar activities. Usually, specific training is completed by studies in related disciplines (education, sociology, biology, or philosophy, for example). A prerequisite to university training is a state-recognized matriculation certificate that is obtained after 12 years of education and that is considered to be approximately equivalent to the level attained after 2 years of college training in the USA.

A diminishing proportion of psychologists receive basic training in private-application institutions delivering locally recognized, but nationally rejected, titles. In some cases, university and private training are combined to demonstrate the real or imaginary advantages of academe and reality. Finally, it is unfortunate that some persons get a thoroughly unqualified training in psychology or psychotherapy by correspondence courses and by 1-day or weekend seminars.

The number of psychologists in Switzerland is somewhere between 2,000 and 5,000. Estimates vary for three main reasons. First, an unknown but probably significant number of qualified psychologists hold part-time positions or work in informal settings. This seems to be especially true for young married women and for young couples who share responsibility for householding and childrearing. Second, estimates are a function of the level of qualification. There is an important gap between the number of working and the number of actually qualified psychologists. It is mainly due to the rapid development of psychology as a profession and the changing profile of required, necessary, and sufficient qualifications. Third, a growing number of charlatans are offering their help through the application of cartomancy, chirology, and similar methods. Qualified psychologists tend, obviously, to ignore this phenomenon, but objective proof exists that (sometimes quite effective) help is given by these "borderline" specialists.

The male:female ratio of psychologists varies strongly as a function of the professional group under consideration. Since the mid-1960s a constant majority (from 60 percent to 80 percent) of psychology students have been women. Within the professional field and in professional associations, however, the proportion is nearer a 1:1 ratio. Universities are outstandingly conservative: on the professorial level more than 90 percent of the psychologists are men.

If we start from very global estimations, the structure of professional fields and professional specializations appears as follows: 30 percent clinical psychology and psychotherapy; 25 percent research and teaching of psychology; 20 percent counseling, vocational and school guidance, and educational psychology; 13 percent business and industry, including personnel; and 12 percent private practice. Employers are mostly public administrations on the local and on the state (canton) level. Incomes are roughly comparable to those of teachers at the secondary (ages 12 to 18) level.

Specialties are neither offered by all universities nor required in most settings. Some employers, though, have traditions, theoretical beliefs, or practical requirements that constitute indirectly informal areas of specialization. Vocational counselors, psychotherapists according to their theoretical orientations, speech therapists, and some similar groups have constituted small pressure groups of specialists, either locally or on a national level.

On a national level there exists no protection either for psychologists and their titles or for the legitimate interests of a sometimes ill-informed or just naive public. Several cantons have recently issued certification laws that regulate the basic and advanced, theoretical and practical training of practicing psychologists, especially of psychotherapists.

University Programs

All universities in Switzerland have professorial chairs in the field of psychology. All except St. Gall (comparable to a complete business school offering specific courses in psychology) and the Ecole Polytechnique Fédérale of Lausanne (an engineering school with a chair in psychology and in didactics of university teaching, which is unique in Switzerland) offer complete study courses with psychology as the main field (Table 37.1).

Specific doctoral programs and postgraduate training opportunities are not highly developed to date, although adequate offerings are underway

TABLE 37.1.
Comparative Presentation of the Psychology Departments of Swiss Universities

	Lausanne	Zurich								
	EPF	ETH	Zurich	St. Gall	Neuchâtel	Lausanne	Geneva	Fribourg	Berne	Basel
No. of students with psychology as main field		50	1,000		30	100	700	200	300	100
No. of professors in psychology	<5	<5	<10	<5	<5	<10	<20	<5	<10	<5
No. of lecturers in psychology (excluding assistants)	<5	<10	<30	<5	<5	<10	<30	<20	<20	<10
AVAILABILITY OF DEGREE PROGRAMS										
License		S	N		S	S, N	N	S	N	N
Diploma		X			X	X	X	X		
Doctorate	X	X	X	X	X	X	X	X	X	X
Working language	F	G	G	G	F	F	F	G, F	G	G

FIELDS OF INTEREST, RESEARCH, AND TEACHING IN PSYCHOLOGY

Field	1	2	3	4	5	6	7	8
General methods		X	X	X	X	X	X	X
Social		X		X	X	X	X	X
Clinical		X		X	X	X	X	X
Experimental	X	X		X	X	X	X	X
Industry, labor	X	X	X	X	X	X	X	
Counseling, vocational, and school guidance		X		X	X			
Applied		X		X	X	X		X
Philosophical		X			X			X
Biological	X	X		X	X			
Educational	X	X	X	X	X	X	X	X
Neuro- and physiological	X	X		X	X	X	X	X
Environmental	X						X	

Note. All numbers are approximate. ETH and EPF = Federal Institutes of Technology, N = nonspecialized degree, S = specialized degrees, F = French, G = German.

in most universities or among several universities. Professional associations and scientific societies partly compensate for this obvious deficiency by offering, on a regular basis, the needed training programs, sometimes in close cooperation with universities.

Journals, Associations, Equipment, and Funding

Quite a number of journals and newsletters concerned with psychology are published and edited in Switzerland or on an international level with the participation of Swiss psychologists. Noteworthy scientific journals include, in particular, *Psychologie* (*Schweizerische Zeitschrift für Psychologie und ihre Anwendungen; Revue Suisse de Psychologie Pure et Appliquée;* founded in 1942, edited by the Swiss Society of Psychology, and published by H. Huber & Co., Berne), and the *Archives de Psychologie* (founded in 1901 by Th. Flournoy and E. Claparéde, currently edited by the Faculté de Psy-' chologie et des Sciences de l'Éducation, Section de Psychologie, University of Geneva, and published by Ed. Médecine et Hygiéne, Geneva). The *BSP* (*Bulletin der Schweizer Psychologen; Bulletin Suisse des Psychologues; Bollettino Svizzero degli Psicologi;* founded in 1960, edited by the Swiss Society of Psychology, and published by H. Huber & Co., Berne) is an information- and discussion-oriented professional journal.

Most foreign journals in many different languages are available in university libraries, which tend to specialize in certain fields. An active and well-working national and international exchange service of journals guarantees the availability in Switzerland of all major and many minor publications.

An incomplete but representative *BSP* (1985) analysis of existing professional associations of psychologists lists 14 regional or local associations and 27 scientific or professional societies of local or national importance. In 1987 more than 20 of these societies and associations joined together to create the Federation of Swiss Psychologists (FSP).

All research laboratories and psychological institutes in universities and elsewhere are usually well equipped with the needed instruments, including tests, books, and library and computer facilities. All internationally available equipment is theoretically and practically within reach. Biases in choice are based on personal or team preferences and not on formal or ideological limitations. Working languages always include English, usually two national languages, and quite often additional languages.

All Swiss universities are state universities and are funded by public finances. Teaching and research in psychology benefit from the usual support but are not particularly preferred. Many psychologists work in settings that are supported by public administrations. The Fonds National Suisse de la Recherche Scientifique (Swiss National Fund for Scientific Research) subsidizes an important part of psychological research through grants for material, personnel, and equipment, usually limited in time but renewable.

An increasing number of foreign (often American) universities that own small campuses in Switzerland are not subsidized by public means and rarely benefit from the available facilities. Exchanges between foreign universities of this type and Swiss universities are not customary.

The Schweizerische Akademie der Geisteswissenschaften (Swiss Academy of Human and Social Sciences) is a government-funded independent association coordinating several scientific disciplines and supporting scientific publications (books and journals) and international exchanges through the Swiss Society of Psychology.

Public Acceptance

Psychologists are fairly well accepted, though they are sometimes the subject of good-natured teasing by the general public. Their services are sought and accepted, but usually not with the limitless credit and enthusiasm psychologists like to dream about. In the same way, the suspicion many psychologists apparently expect to find in the public does not really exist anymore; relations are neutral but friendly. Yet quite often psychologists expend considerable energy to find out how they are accepted, instead of spending the same energy to act in a way to make themselves acceptable and to be accepted. To ponder these questions is perhaps symptomatic; some psychologists have a problem with their self-image, and that is perhaps what they should reflect on.

Status of Psychology

Just as in all European countries, psychology in Switzerland has been uncomfortably located from the beginning, when the first chairs of psychology were created in the late 19th century, in the interfaces between philosophy, biology, medicine, linguistics, mathematics, education, and so on. Psychological research and theorizing are strongly influenced by these varying affiliations, which are quite often caused by the administrative attachment of psychology departments to different faculties (philological, scientific, economic, and social, for example). This diversity has probably greatly affected the behavior and thinking of psychologists. To be in daily contact with historians, for example, does not have the same effect as daily contact with biologists or engineers. Effective interdisciplinary cooperation is currently fashionable but nevertheless hard to implement.

On more specific levels, some classical forces are still present. In Zurich there is a strong interest in psychoanalytical thought, and postgraduate training programs with specific theoretical emphasis are available in many private institutions, the best known being the C. G. Jung Institute. In Geneva the work of the late Jean Piaget has led to extensive original theorizing concerning different aspects of development which is clearly neo-Piagetian, either by direct influence or by comprehensible reaction formations. Globally speaking, the impression dominates that psychological thought, research, and theory are problem-centered rather than method-centered. The era of the grand old men is dead.

With generous governmental help, many younger people have had the opportunity to confront their initial training and beliefs with the work of psychologists in other countries by studying, doing research, or teaching abroad (mainly in the USA, Great Britain, France, or Germany). Scientific recognition is no longer sought regionally or nationally, but rather is found within an international peer group organized around specific problems, groups of subjects, scientific subdisciplines, or schools of thought.

Significant Areas of Research

The Swiss federal government has initiated several national research programs on various themes, some of them involving the central or marginal participation of psychologists. Areas studied include transitions from school to active life, vocational choice and adaptation processes in apprenticeship, feminine value systems, active participation in democratic communities, present and future structure of work and leisure, and human relations in various settings.

The psychology departments of the universities of the French-speaking part of Switzerland are coordinated into a sort of "pool," students being allowed to change universities during their studies as a function of their professional projects and interests. Each university offers at least one field of specialization besides the general areas. The University of Geneva maintains its interests in developmental processes with a range of themes and approaches including social development, motor development, and the development of creative thought. Lausanne mainly focuses on vocational and school guidance and counseling, including learning disabilities. Neuchátel, finally, concentrates on personnel management and organizational and industrial psychology.

Other domains of specialization, as well as the range of available approaches, can be seen in Table 37.1. The Eidgenossische Technische Hochschule (Federal Institute of Technology, Zurich) has a leading position in psychological studies concerning problems of labor and industry, such as the analysis and engineering of human-machine interaction in computerized environments. Several research institutions are located outside of universities, notably the C. G. Jung Institute (in Kusnacht, near Zurich) and the Archives Jean Piaget recently created in Geneva.

Emerging Trends

To learn about emerging trends and their impact and probable significance, we conducted a small, informal, and nonrepresentative survey by interviewing about 60 leaders in the field of psychology in Switzerland. The results were, not unexpectedly, quite disappointing. Like similar surveys conducted in the USA or France, for instance, our investigation showed that psychologists are characterized not by innovative thoughts or scientific imagination, but rather by an egocentric and somewhat petit bourgeois reference system, in which the future is essentially seen as the consolidation and development of present personal interests and privileges. Typically, psychologists seem to lack a global view, a (self-)critical approach, or adventure-oriented thinking. They tend to defend acquired positions rather than to accept challenge and questioning, and they seem afraid of enterprising action. In the area of education, most psychologists think that professional training needs to become more complete and more effective and that available methods should be of better quality.

The most interesting future research fields emerging from responses to the questionnaires or from interviews were environmental psychology, health psychology (in particular, as related to lifestyles and well-being), psychological aspects of AIDS, conflict and peace analysis, human-computer interactions, and coping with anxieties and fears related to change processes and the insecurity of the future, including death. It also seems important to translate psychological and scientific knowledge into "consumer-ready" products and to teach psychology to nonpsychologists. Many psychologists think that skills related to interdisciplinary exchange and to cooperation in professional situations must be better conceived and taught and should be emphasized throughout the university years.

Bibliography

Grunding der Föderation der Schweizer Psychologen. (1987). *BSP (Bulletin der Schweizer Psychologen)*, 10, 361–386.

Psychologenvereinigungen in der Schweiz. (1985). *BSP (Bulletin der Schweizer Psychologen)*, 10, 323–328.

Psychologie in der Schweiz: Studium und Beruf. (1986). *BSP (Bulletin der Schweizer Psychologen)*, 2, 51–54.

38 / Turkey

GÜNDÜZ Y. H. VASSAF

Gündüz Y. H. Vassaf (born 1946) received his PhD from Hacettepe University in 1977. A specialist in community psychology, clinical psychology, and migration studies, he has published more than 30 articles in North American, European, and Turkish journals. His books and monographs include Wir Haben Unsere Stimme Noch Nicht Laut Gemacht: Turkische Arbeiterkinder in Europa, Mental Testing: What It Is and Isn't, *and* Primary Mental Abilities.

The recipient of a UNESCO *grant in 1981, Vassaf has served as associate editor of* School Psychology International, *a founding member of the Turkish Psychological Association, on the Board of Directors of the International Council of Psychologists, on the Commission for Peace of the International Union of Psychological Science, and as the regional coordinator for Europe and the Middle East for the* APA *Division of Community Psychology.*

Formerly of Bogazici University, Istanbul, he resigned, along with more than 1,500 other academicians, in protest of the 1982 Turkish University Law abrogating all academic autonomy and freedom. Vassaf is a nonresident fellow at the Centre for Developing Studies at McGill University, Montreal, Canada.

You are on a public bus, getting a haircut, or standing in line at a bank in Istanbul, and the person next to you finds out that you are a psychologist. How does he react? Until recent years the typical reaction was, "Oh, I must watch out what I'm saying," accompanied by a sense of intrigue, fear, and curiosity. These days people immediately state a problem.

The first McDonald's Restaurant opened in Istanbul in 1986. The first annual Turkish Congress of Psychology was held in 1983. Fast food and pop(ular) psychology have come of age in Istanbul. Newspapers have regular columns written by psychologists. The national radio network has a resident psychologist who addresses 30 problems in just as many minutes; and most recently the following advertisement popped up in my mailbox:

With this letter we would like to introduce our psychological counseling, education, and orientation center. . . . Our areas of service:

- Effective youth
- Pregnancy education
- Family efficiency
- Adjustment to Turkey
- Effective behavior
- Effective leadership

•Coping with stress • Individual counseling
•The language of art • Training for specialists.

Some categories mean as little to me as they might to you. I have no doubt, however, that the newly founded center will turn a quick profit and lead to many similar ventures in both the fashionable and popular districts of Istanbul.

Who are Turkish psychologists and how did we get here?

The Early Years

The beginning of modern psychology (in contrast to classical Greek and Islamic) is almost contemporary with that of USA psychology. The first translation of the Stanford-Binet appeared in Turkey only a few years after the USA edition was published. It was, however, used for educational purposes rather than in clinical practice. By the 1920s the University of Istanbul had a psychology program within the Department of Philosophy. It was headed by Sekip Tunc, who had studied under Ribot in Switzerland. The department emphasized structuralism in its approach. My mother, who received her BA from this department and went on to Smith, Radcliffe, and Columbia for graduate work in the 1930s, was surprised to find that Piaget was still unheard-of in North America.

The classic Swiss-French introspective tradition in Turkish psychology did not continue. In 1936 Wilhelm Peters, fleeing from fascist Germany along with other academicians, came to Istanbul and founded the first department of psychology in Turkey, the *Journal of Experimental Psychology*, and a psychology laboratory.

The experimental approach of the German school did not establish roots. With the death of Peters, the implementation of the Truman Doctrine, and the Turkish entry into NATO, American pragmatic psychology, in the form of counseling and intelligence tests, came to Turkey in the mid-1950s. Since then, the development, or rather the imitation, of psychology has been under USA influence.

The changing dependency of Turkish psychology from one Western country to another has meant that the discipline has not established its own independent tradition. Instead, an export-import relationship has prevailed, with Turkey importing concepts and instruments, not on the basis of its needs or intellectual tradition, but rather on the basis of what is readily available from the West. Furthermore, what is to be imported has been determined not by conscious scientific choice, but by the particular political alliance of the country at the time.

An examination of the card catalog at the psychology library of Istanbul University is one specific illustration of this point. Between 1920 and 1950 approximately 80 percent of the books at the library came from either Germany or France. Turkey's abandonment of a neutral foreign policy in favor of a pro-American policy after 1947, and emerging American world dominance, is also clearly reflected in the psychology books acquired after that period. Since then, publications have come mainly from the USA. The library has now approximately 1,300 books. The intellectual tradition based on a closeness to France, Switzerland, and Germany was abruptly cut off and replaced by American dominance.

Training of Academicians

The same situation is reflected in the background and training of academicians. The continuation of dependency on Western psychology is provided by succeeding generations who go abroad to study. However, because of changing historical conditions in both Turkish and international politics, each generation comes back with the perspective of a different Western country. That, too, partially explains the influence on Turkish psychology of French, German, and eventually USA psychology. These dependency shifts also make it impossible for any particular relationship to have continuity, thereby preventing the formation of an intellectual tradition. At one time it was thought that PhD programs at Turkish universities would eventually allow for a new generation of psychologists raised and trained in Turkey. Indeed, in 1965 a psychology department was founded at Hacettepe University in Ankara with this goal in mind. Although the department became the largest of its kind in Turkey and was at one time a showcase for psychology, 14 years after it was founded, "out of eleven faculty members who had PhDs, all but two had received their PhDs either in England or the USA" (LeCompte, 1980, p. 796). In every psychology department throughout the country the textbooks are by American authors. In all this time not one textbook has been written in Turkish. Furthermore, psychological concepts, many of questionable applicability and validity to Western culture, are discussed and used in research without consideration of their relevance for Turkish culture and society.

Professional Associations

The two psychological associations in Turkey have not yet reached the point of development where they are able to give direction to the growth of psychology or to set professional standards. With respect to other activities such as publications and meetings, however, they have been consistent and productive. Of the two associations, Türk Psikoloji Dernegi (Turkish Psychologists' Association), founded more than 30 years ago in Istanbul, has a membership of approximately 200. It officially represents Turkey at the meetings of the International Union of Psychological Science. The more recent Psikologlar Dernegi (Psychologists' Association) has approximately 500 members. Since its founding in 1976 it has been publishing the quarterly *Psikologlar Dernegi Dergisi* (Psychologists' association journal) with a circulation of about 750. Another journal, *Tecrübi Psikoloji Calismalari* (Studies in experimental psychology), has been published by Istanbul University since 1936.

The Universities

There are at present 27 universities in Turkey, of which 5 have graduate departments, all in clinical psychology. Each year approximately 200 students graduate with BAs in psychology. About 70 percent are females, more than 50 percent of whom do not work or do not have the opportunity to work. For those men and women who do go on to work in psychology, there are no licensing requirements and almost all find jobs as clinical psychologists—mostly in psychiatric hospitals and more and more in private practice. Needless to say, they are all unqualified for the work that they do, having received, at the most, a one-semester course in psychological testing and theories of personality.

Psychological Testing

To make matters worse, the psychometric instruments in use are all invalid. The most widely used intelligence tests are the Wechsler series and the Stanford-Binet. Raven's Progressive Matrices and the Porteus are also popular. The Rorschach and TAT lead the personality tests. None has been standardized for use in Turkey. There are no comprehensive validity and reliability studies. Testing conditions, especially at the Ministry of Education's Guidance and Research Centers and the psychiatric hospitals where they are most widely used, are substandard. This situation—unqualified psychologists, unstandardized tests, poor testing conditions—readily leads to misuse and unethical practices. Literally thousands of Turkish schoolchildren have been "diagnosed" as retarded and placed in special classes. There is no end in sight; the situation continues unabated.

Psychologists who would, on ethical and scientific grounds, be expected to object to such misuse of testing remain silent. Instead, they passively collaborate with the system by translating and teaching the use of tests to those who will, because of conditions, misuse them. Professional psychological associations on the national level also keep silent and prevent open discussions on the grounds that, because psychologists are associated with tests, the young profession will be blemished in the eyes of the public. Those who object are immediately ostracized. Many educators and psychologists fail to raise objections because they derive their income from tests. The people, many of whom are critically affected as their children are unjustly labeled mentally retarded, do not protest because they have respect for science and scientists. In this context, Fulbright exchange professors come to Turkey and lecture at Turkish universities on the finer points of testing, and the Psychological Corporation continues to sell newer and more expensive editions of its tests. Thus, the system perpetuates itself, with those who have the greatest knowledge and the greatest power to stop the misuse keeping silent (Vassaf, 1982).

Government Influences

The military regime of the 1980s is another negative influence on the development of the sciences in general and psychology in particular. The new university law (YOK), enacted by the military government, eradicated university autonomy and academic freedom. In the space of a few years nearly 1,500 academicians were either summarily dismissed from the university or resigned in protest. All research became subject to the permission of the military authorities. More than 8 years after the coup, a state of emergency still exists in Istanbul, in which even scientific meetings require the permission of the police.

Suppression of freedom of thought throughout the history of the Turkish Republic has led to a stifling of research and a subsequent brain drain. Thus, Turkey's foremost psychologist, Muzafer Sherif, went to the USA, where he radically influenced the development of social psychology, only after he had been imprisoned in Turkey. His research with Turkish peasants disturbed the authoritarian regime of the time. It was this research that was to be the basis of his classic work, *The Outline of Social Psychology*. Almost 50 years later books by Turkish psychologists about Turkish workers and peasants are still a rare phenomenon. The only recent exceptions are by Gitmez (1979), Kağitçibaşi (1981), and Vassaf (1985).

Current Perspectives

Most research in Turkey has dealt with mere applications of intelligence tests from the USA. This lack of originality and avoidance of issues pertinent to Turkey are clearly reflected in the dissertations of university students. In the period between 1934 and 1972 there were 450 such works. Nearly half reported the results of the administration of tests to Turkish students. During the 1962–72 period 163 works dealt with the administration of tests and only 85 with other topics. Faculty members openly encourage such studies (Canitez & Togrol, 1983).

On the positive side, the current list of psychology books available at bookstores in Turkish offers an exciting variety. Works by Freud, Fromm, Reich, Foucault, Lacan, Adler, Jung, and Piaget are widely read. The names of such psychologists, however, are more frequently heard at coffeehouses frequented by students and intellectuals than at universities.

The universities' lack of autonomy and appeal has inadvertently led to the raising of professional standards and the quality of private practice. Many who would normally have concentrated on academic work have become practicing psychologists. They meet regularly to exchange information, to supervise peers, and to hold therapeutic groups. The founding of the Bilar Science Center in 1986 by former academicians forced out of the universities by the military has also furthered the development of psychological studies. Many multidisciplinary courses concerning culture and behavior have found wide appeal among the public and students.

As in other Third World countries, the development of science in general and psychology in particular must go hand in hand with both the preservation of freedom of thought and the availability of material resources. Solidarity and sensitivity to each other's needs among members of the international academic community are critically important in achieving this goal.

Bibliography

Canitez, E., & Togrol, B. (1983). Findings about some tests used in Turkey (in Turkish). In N. Bilgin (Ed.), *Proceedings of the First National Congress of Psychology*. Izmir: Aegean University Faculty of Literature Publications, No. 1987.

Gitmez, A. (1979). *The story of migration* (in Turkish). Ankara: Maya.

Kağitçibaşi, C. (1981). *Values of children: Values and fertility in Turkey*. Istanbul: Bogazici University Press.

LeCompte, A. (1980). Some recent trends in Turkish psychology. *American Psychologist, 8*, 745–749.

Vassaf, G. (1982). Mental massacre: The use of psychological tests in the Third World. *School Psychology International, 2*, 43–48.

Vassaf, G. (1985). *Wir haben unsere Stimme noch nicht laut gemacht: Türkische Arbeitskinder in Europa*. Felsberg: Res Publicae. (Original work published in Turkish in 1983)

39 / Union of Soviet Socialist Republics

ALEX KOZULIN

Alex Kozulin (born 1949) received his MD *degree from the Moscow Institute of Medicine in 1972 and his PhD (equivalent) from the Moscow Institute of Psychology in 1978. His special interests are history and systems, social factors, cognitive development, and the psychopathology of language and thought. His writings include the book* Psychology in Utopia: Toward a Social History of Soviet Psychology. *In addition, he has served in several editorial positions and in 1987 was awarded a research fellowship at the Russian Research Center of Harvard University. Kozulin holds a joint appointment in Boston University's School of Medicine and Department of Psychology.*

For a better comprehension of the current situation in Soviet psychology, one should take a quick look at its historical past. The study of human behavior was traditionally carried out in Russia in two different settings: in somewhat more philosophically oriented departments and institutes of psychology and in psychophysiological laboratories affiliated with departments of biology or medicine. The historically significant embodiment of the former tradition is the Moscow Institute of Psychology, founded in 1912 by Wundt's student, Gregory Chelpanov. The second trend has its origin in the laboratories of famous Russian reflexologists Ivan Sechenov and Ivan Pavlov and continues to flourish in the Institute of Higher Nervous Activity of the Academy of Sciences. An attempt to create a school that would encompass scientific, clinical, and humanistic approaches to human behavior was made by Vladimir Bekhterev, who founded the Psychoneurological Institute in St. Petersburg in 1907. Although intellectually influential, that attempt was not successful in the long run.

After a brief period of hectic activity in the 1920s, when psychologists worked on the creation of a "new Soviet man," psychological studies suffered a major setback under Stalin and held relatively low priority in the

Research for this chapter was supported in part by a fellowship from the Russian Research Center at Harvard University.

Soviet academic hierarchy. Graduate training was available only in Moscow, Leningrad, and Tbilisi; the psychology faculty was integrated into either departments of philosophy or departments of pedagogics; existent research facilities were used almost exclusively for studies focusing on child welfare and educational psychology. Psychology as a mental health profession was nonexistent for all practical purposes. Finally, an aggressive attack of some Pavlovian reflexologists on "mentalistic" psychologists launched in the late 1940s further weakened psychology's position (for a historical review, see Kozulin, 1984).

The true revival came only in the mid-1960s. Independent departments of psychology were established at Moscow and Leningrad universities. In 1971 a new, research-oriented Institute of Psychology of the prestigious Academy of Sciences was opened in Moscow. The importance of psychology started to be recognized not only in such traditional areas as education and child welfare, but also by the air force and in the space program. Industrial psychology and human-machine interaction became fashionable topics of research. A department of psychology was even opened in the police academy. By the mid-1970s programs in psychology existed in 11 universities: Moscow, Leningrad, Yaroslavl, Saratov, Rostov/Don, Kiev and Kharkov (Ukraine), Tbilisi (Georgia), Tartu (Estonia), Vilnius (Lithuania), and Tashkent (Uzbekistan). In spite of this spectacular growth, psychology as a profession still remained underdeveloped both in comparison with other popular professions, such as medicine or engineering, and relative to the number of psychologists in Western countries. In 1984 there were only 5,000 members of the Soviet Psychological Association, slightly more than 20 per million (compared with 219 per million in the USA and 83 per million in Hungary).

Education and Degrees

To understand the system of psychological training, one must take into account that, unlike in the USA, higher education in the USSR does not place a college of arts and sciences at the center of its system; one may say that there is no equivalent of liberal arts education in the Soviet Union at all. High school graduates are supposed to be well prepared in terms of the core curriculum of language, literature, mathematics, and sciences. In this respect the Soviet high school curriculum resembles those of European gymnasiums. The university is the place for *specialized* professional and academic training, with the field of concentration selected from the very beginning. There are entrance exams, which in the case of psychology programs include language/literature, mathematics, and biology. An applicant may send documents and sit for exams in one university only. This rule preselects stronger applicants for the leading universities.

Education is free, and some students receive stipends depending on their academic achievements and financial status. These stipends, however, barely provide more than half the minimal survival income, so it is expected that students will receive help from their families. Dormitory housing is provided for out-of-town students only; local residents continue to live with their parents.

Although the universities differ in quality, the curriculum itself is highly uniform and must be approved by the Ministry of Higher Education. As one example, the psychology curriculum at Moscow University includes required courses in mathematics, physiology, foreign language, Marxist philosophy, and social sciences. Required courses in the psychology core curriculum include general, developmental, educational, social, engineering, and industrial psychology, psychophysiology, psychopathology, neuropsychology, and five semesters of psychological practicum. Elective courses vary, depending on the field of specialization. In Moscow University psychology students may specialize in general and experimental, developmental and educational, clinical (psychopathology and neuropsychology), or social and engineering psychology.

The course of study takes 5 to 6 years and leads to the degree called *diploma*, which is comparable to the *Diplom-Psychologie* of German universities. Each student must conduct graduate research culminating in a thesis, which must then be defended before a graduate committee. Graduates are perceived as specialists fully trained to take a junior teaching position of lecturer, to engage in research at the junior researcher level, or to perform psychological evaluations in a child welfare or mental health setting as a psychologist. There is no separate licensing procedure, since all psychology programs have basically the same curriculum and the same diploma requirements.

Those seeking the advanced academic degree may, on receiving the diploma, apply for a PhD program called *aspirantura*. This program is found in such leading universities as Moscow and Leningrad, as well as in some academic research institutes such as the Institute of Psychology, the Institute of General and Educational Psychology, and the Institute of Psychology of the Georgian Academy of Science. There are two forms of *aspirantura:* full-time and "night time." A full-time aspirant receives a stipend for 3 years, comparable to the salary of a junior researcher. Night-time aspirants usually work elsewhere and attend research institutes or universities for lectures and consultations with a dissertation adviser. Degree requirements include a foreign language, Marxist philosophy, and a field of concentration. All other seminars, internships, and consultations are individually chosen by the aspirant and the adviser. The role and choice of adviser is of paramount importance; most aspirants select an adviser before applying to the program.

The focal point of *aspirantura* is not coursework, for the aspirant is expected to be well educated. Rather, the focus is on the preparation of an independent research project, which should be designed, conducted, and written as a dissertation. The aspirant is expected to publish at least two research papers and to present the research material at scientific meetings. Once the research has been completed and a draft of the dissertation has been discussed in the department and approved by the adviser, the aspirant prepares a final version, usually about 200 typewritten pages with a 25-page summary. The full text of the dissertation is then sent to another psychological research institute or university department for review. In addition, two outside reviewers are selected to write an opinion. A summary of the dissertation is printed and distributed to psychologists around the country, and copies are deposited in leading libraries. The next step is the oral defense. The aspirant presents the dissertation to the Academic Council, which includes senior researchers and professors of the institute. Two reviewers read their opinions, and members of the council ask questions and voice their views, after which they vote by secret ballot. If the vote is favorable, the aspirant becomes a PhD (*Kandidat Psikhologicheskikh Nauk*). However, granting of the degree must be confirmed, and the actual certificate can be issued only by the National Higher Certification Commission (VAK). In the past, VAK commonly sent dissertations for additional review when they were controversial or when the aspirant was suspected of being ideologically "unreliable."

Psychologists who earn a PhD may advance only to the level of senior researcher or associate professor. To become a full professor or head of department, one needs yet another degree, that of doctor of science. It has no equivalent in the USA but bears a certain similarity to the "habilitation" procedure of German universities. Those seeking this degree must present a monograph that "opens a new direction in psychological research," contributes to fundamental knowledge, and is extensively backed up by publications. In reality, this type of monograph is very often the product of a collective effort of an entire research group directed by the "author."

Academic and Professional Psychology

Although recent developments reveal a growing professionalization of Soviet psychology, it still remains predominantly an academic discipline with a strong emphasis on fundamental research in such areas as

TABLE 39.1

Soviet PhD Degrees Awarded in Psychology (1976–84)

Field	%
Developmental and educational	38.8
General and experimental	24.5
Social	10.7
Engineering	10.2
Clinical	6.0
Psychophysiology	4.0
Psychology and law, forensic psychology	0.7
Other (sport psychology, psychology of handicapped, zoopsychology, etc.)	5.1

Source. Data adapted from *Voprosy Psikhologii,* No. 3 (1982) and No. 2 (1985).

cognitive, developmental, and educational psychology. An overview of the structure of psychological scholarship in the USSR between 1976 and 1984 can be seen in Table 39.1. The total number of PhD degrees awarded is about 1,090.

The predominance of developmental and educational psychology is not surprising since the Department of Education and the Academy of Pedagogical Sciences remain the major employers of psychologists. The preeminent role here is played by the research centers of the Academy of Pedagogical Sciences. Among the best known of these are the Institute of General and Educational Psychology, the Institute of Pre-School Education, and the Institute of Handicapped Children (Defectology). One should also note that the greater concentration of teaching jobs is in schools of education, where the emphasis is on child psychology and educational problems.

Currently, the number of PhDs in engineering psychology is growing, reflecting an increasing concern with the human factor in human-machine interaction and with the behavior of operators under stress. Although exact figures are unavailable, it seems likely that the air force and space programs are among the major benefactors of engineering psychology. At the same time, some of the best research in the field is done in such an unlikely place as the Institute of Technical Design.

Social psychology—for a long time a neglected area—seems to be gaining in popularity in connection with a growing concern over such problems as the high rate of divorce, alcoholism, and labor conflicts. For example,

Moscow City Hall (Mossoviet), established a committee on social problems of the family which includes 26 psychologists. Large industrial plants have established their own social-psychological services to assess and provide counseling in such areas as labor conflicts, family problems, and asocial behavior.

The service aspect of psychology has always been underestimated in the USSR. In part that could be a result of an early optimism of Soviet authorities who regarded the socialist mental environment as inherently "therapeutic." This attitude may also account for the nonexistence of the profession of social work in the USSR. The only clinical area where psychologists felt welcome and well established was clinical neuropsychology. The situation started to change in the mid-1970s, when the Department of Health decided in favor of staff psychologists in outpatient mental health clinics. The question of the future development of psychology as a profession was raised at the First National Meeting on the Problem of Psychological Services held in 1984. Certain areas considered "nonexistent" before were recognized as legitimate concerns of psychological service, among them counseling and psychotherapy of university students. If psychological service programs are implemented, their primary professional beneficiaries will be clinical and medical psychologists. In spite of current optimism, however, their position remains precarious. Neither their legal status vis-à-vis psychiatrists nor their professional responsibility—for example, assessment versus therapy— has been clearly delineated. It is also worth noting that until the mid-1980s Soviet psychologists were not allowed to practice privately. This situation has been somewhat remedied recently by the availability of psychological help through the system of so-called psychological cooperatives. In 1989 a new Association of Psychologist Practitioners was established as a professional organization of service-oriented psychologists. Another important recently formed professional organization is the independent Psychiatric Association, which serves as an alternative to the much-compromised Soviet Psychiatric Association.

Three major psychological journals published in Russian are *Voprosy Psikhologii* (Problems of psychology), six issues per year; *Psikhologicheskii Zhurnal* (Psychological journal), six issues per year; and a quarterly, *Vestnik Moskovskogo Universiteta: Psikhologiia* (The herald of Moscow University: Psychology). Selected articles from these journals are translated into English and published in a quarterly, *Soviet Psychology*, by M. E. Sharpe, Armonk, NY. Editors exercise a tight control over the content of papers published in their journals. They also require a guarantee that papers submitted do not dissent significantly from the main line of research carried out in the respective institutions. The authors are required to have their manuscripts "endorsed by the head of the department or laboratory, and to be accompanied by a letter of recommendation from the institution where the research was undertaken" (*Voprosy Psikhologii* [1986], No. 6, p. 180). This strict control over publications is spontaneously "balanced" by official and semiofficial seminars and colloquia in which the authors may express less orthodox and more original views and ideas.

Although in the past Soviet psychology suffered from a lack of up-to-date textbooks, by the 1980s this problem was largely overcome for such fields as experimental, developmental, and social psychology, but it still exists for clinical psychology and personality theory. A fair number of Western studies are translated into Russian and published by academic publishers, but the same cannot be said about test materials. While some tests such as the MMPI are widely used, there is no commercial publisher from whom test materials can be ordered, so tests and questionnaires are simply copied again and again. This creates a paradoxical situation in which, for example, students who have a special seminar on the Rorschach assessment cannot acquire their own sets of the test.

Psychologists in Moscow and Leningrad have the advantage of access to well-stocked national libraries that receive all major foreign psychological periodicals. Their colleagues in the provinces do not have such an opportunity, and their university libraries are rather poor. At the same time, there is a well-organized system of reviewing and abstracting foreign works. A Soviet equivalent of *Psychological Abstracts* is published as a section of *Biological Abstracts* by the National Institute of Scientific Information.

The quality of laboratory equipment and its availability vary considerably from one research center to another, but even in the leading centers there is a lack of modern electronic equipment, personal computers, and software packages.

Although there is an apparent public interest in psychology, the Soviet book market does not reflect this fact. Only a handful of titles in popular psychology are published, and all of these are sold out immediately. This shortage is somewhat alleviated by the existence of a psychology section in the popular family magazine *Sem'ia i Shkola* (Family and school) and by the sporadic publication of psychology-related articles in other magazines.

The Soviet Psychological Association was established in 1957. Its primary role is to organize national meetings and to sponsor professional and academic conferences.

Current Trends

Theory

Soviet psychologists have always paid more attention to theoretical and philosophical issues than their colleagues in the English-speaking countries. This characteristic trait may have been learned from German mentors and later reinforced by the pressure to measure psychological findings by the yardstick of Marxist philosophy. Theoretical problems formulated in the 1930s by Lev Vygotsky, Sergei Rubinstein, and Alexei N. Leontiev remain a standard reference point in contemporary debates (Kozulin, 1984). The 1970s and the 1980s witnessed renewed discussion of what should be considered a proper subject of psychological inquiry and what kind of research epistemology (*metodologiia*) befits a modern psychologist. This preoccupation with theoretical issues was, in part, provoked by what some psychologists perceived as an illegitimate encroachment of neuroscience, sociobiology, and computer science on the subject of psychological inquiry. Others called for a more harmonious coexistence of all of the aforementioned approaches. The relationship between Marxist philosophy and psychology has changed considerably since the 1950s, when it was common advice for psychologists to derive their theories directly from the works of Marx and Lenin. In the 1980s these relations resembled more of a dialogue and led to a substantive discussion about similarities and differences in philosophical versus psychological interpretation of the socially active human subject.

One important factor contributing to theoretical debate was the "discovery" in the 1970s of the works of such distinguished scholars as Vygotsky, Luria, and Bakhtin, written in the 1920s but never published. The publication of Vygotsky's *Historical Meaning of the Crisis in Psychology* (written in 1927, published in 1984) helped to bring recognition to him as an original philosopher of science who foretold much of what became associated with Thomas Kuhn's concept of "scientific revolution" (see Kozulin, 1986). The publication of Luria's cross-cultural study undertaken in the early 1930s added fuel to the discussion about culturally and historically specific forms of cognition and the relationship between literacy and cognitive development (Wertsch, 1985; Valsiner, 1987). Publication of these works prompted reconsideration of Alexei Leontiev's theory of psychological activity, which in the 1960s became *the* official Soviet psychological doctrine (for discussion, see Kozulin, 1986).

In the 1970s psychologists also discovered the theoretical legacy of the original thinker and literary scholar Mikhail Bakhtin. His theory of "life as authoring" and the concept of "dialogical speech" foretold some of the contemporary Western deconstructionist ideas and offered an interesting parallel to Vygotsky's study of inner speech (see Wertsch, 1985). What is probably more important is that Bakhtin's works, which incorporate linguistic, literary, and philosophical arguments, furnish new inspiration for those who are seeking a foundation for a humanistically oriented psychology.

Child Development and Education

The interest in theoretical issues has a direct bearing on recent discussions in child and educational psychology. At the heart of these discussions lies a fundamental question: What type of learning process is preferable in a classroom, empirical or theoretical? An "empiricist" position that adheres to the rule "from empirical example to abstract principle," "from elements to whole," and "from historical precedents to logical schemas" seemed to be a grass-roots philosophy of Soviet education for a long time. This position was vigorously attacked by a group of Moscow psychologists led by Vasili Davydov who argued in favor of theoretical learning. "Theoreticians" emphasized that a theoretical rather than an empirical approach to learning material makes a schoolchild into a real thinker, capable of discerning essential properties of objects and processes from accidental properties. They also claimed that theoretical learning is a special form of activity that does not coincide in either structure or dynamics with those forms of activity and learning that are spontaneously acquired by a child. Theoretical learning is not an amplification of natural learning skills, but a process of acquiring an entirely new world view based on scientific rather than everyday types of concepts. In this respect "theoreticians" opposed child-centered, Piagetian, as well as Soviet formalistic, approaches to child learning. In the highly centralized system of Soviet education, this psychological argument had the potential for serious consequences, since all Soviet schools use the same curriculum, the same textbooks, and similar teachers' manuals.

Implementation of the theoretical learning program has led to substantial rewriting of primary school textbooks and teachers' manuals. The authors of the program admitted, however, that the dynamics of a child's cognitive development cannot be directly derived from the logic of the development of learning activity (Davydov & Markova, 1983). The focus of the program, therefore, shifted from the battle with "empiricists" and the design of a comprehensive system of theoretical learning to a more detailed investigation of the motivational aspects and personalization of learning activity.

These changing priorities in the psychology of learning highlighted research in adult-child interaction and its influence on cognitive development. It was shown that sustained interaction with an adult during problem-solving activity helps a child to establish an emotional attitude toward the problem at hand. Recently, this line of research was extended to cover the problem of how differently children act on the human versus the inanimate component of situations, and how this difference translates into verbal versus manipulative types of problem solving (Valsiner, 1987).

Social Psychology

An area that was hardly discernible in the past but is now a focus of interest is social psychology. In a certain sense the state of social psychology is a mirror of Soviet psychology in general, because its inquiry reaches deeply into the specific problems of a socialist society that claims to create radically new conditions for individuals living in organized social groups, or collectives. Historical records show, however, that in the past the socialist state was more reluctant to enlist psychologists to solve its social problems, relying instead on party cadre and propaganda apparatus. Change in this attitude became visible only in the 1960s when the first social psychological laboratories were opened in Leningrad and Moscow. The precise reason for this change of heart on the part of authorities is not clear. Nevertheless, it is an empirical fact that by 1980 social psychology had firmly established itself as a specific field of study.

Because of its late arrival on the scene, social psychology still struggles with the problem of identity, devoting considerable effort to ascertaining the proper subject and adequate methodology for social psychological research (see the discussion in Strickland, 1979). The first task was to catch up with Western studies and methodologies and to decide what is adaptable and what is not. The second task was to identify the main targets of inquiry. One target was defined by the chair of social psychology of Moscow University, Galina Andreeva, as "the investigation of cognitive processes in the context of real social groups united by joint group activity" (Strickland, 1984, p. 72). This target may have been dictated by the state's concern with the influence of different types of social interaction on workers' productivity. The other target is the long-neglected problem of marital relationships. Moscow University was among the first places in the USSR to establish, on an experimental basis, family counseling services. On the academic side, it produced studies on empathy and attraction and contributed to better understanding of the phenomenon of *obschenie*, that is, meaningful social interaction (Strickland, 1979, p. 62).

Finally, some Soviet psychologists, notably Artur Petrovsky, suggested that the main target of inquiry should be an organized group of people carrying out some socially meaningful activity, that is, a socialist collective. It was further claimed that many processes observed in ordinary small groups assume an entirely different form in a collective (Strickland, 1984, pp. 99–112). Instead of group pressure and conformism, Petrovsky talks about collectivist self-determination. The main problem with such an approach is that the conclusions reached by Petrovsky and his colleagues are difficult to evaluate in the absence of a truly open discussion about social pressure existing in Soviet society. For example, what appears as a collectivist self-determination may actually reflect a conformism toward a superordinate reference group or a simple fear of retribution from the authorities. As a footnote to the issue of openness, it seems appropriate to mention that in 1984 the first paper in 50 years was published on the topic of rumors as social-psychological phenomena. The authors frankly admit that it is not Western propaganda but an unsatisfied public interest and a deficit of information that are the real causes of various rumors circulating in Soviet society (*Psikhologicheskii Zhurnal*, No. 5, 1984).

The Unconscious

Another recently legitimized trend is the study of the unconscious. The legitimization of this field was neither easy nor painless after decades of ideological attacks on psychoanalysis. The first attempt to approach the issue academically rather than ideologically was undertaken by Philip Bassin in his monograph *The Problem of the Unconscious* (1968). Bassin's major goal was to prove that the problem is much wider than its psychoanalytic interpretation and that Soviet psychologists can therefore approach it without being compromised by a liaison with Freud's doctrine. Since then, numerous approaches have been developed, including clinical analysis of so-called significant experiences (P. Bassin); experimental analysis of dreams and their relation to stress reduction and coping (V. Rotenberg); further development of the ideas of the late Georgian psychologist Dmitri Uznadze concerning psychological "set" phenomena; a model of unconscious processes based on the principles of mathematical statistics (V. Nalimov); and some others. This period of growth culminated in the International Symposium on the Unconscious held in Tbilisi, Georgia, in 1979. For the first time, Soviet psychologists confronted some Western approaches, including the Lacanian version of psychoanalysis, Louis Althusser's synthesis of Marx and Freud, and Gunter Ammon's concept of social energy. Soviet participants also used the occasion to compare theoretical preferences. One of the focal points of these discussions happened to be the relationship of Uznadze's theory of "set," Freudian interpretation of the unconscious, and the theory of psychological activity advanced by the students of Alexei N. Leontiev. Materials of the symposium, published in four volumes, include representative papers of all of the aforementioned authors and provide a unique source of information on current research in this field (Prangishvili, Sherozia, & Bassin, 1978–85).

The status of psychodynamic training and therapy remains precarious, or at least unusual, by Western standards. Although some training in clinical psychodynamics is provided at the Moscow Institute for Advanced Medical Studies, it does not compensate for the lack of a strong psychodynamic clinical tradition and for the absence of a professional forum to discuss the issues. Freud's books, translated in the 1920s, became priceless rarities long ago. Current psychoanalytic literature, although available in leading professional libraries, has never been translated. What is probably more important, the status of the psychotherapist remains poorly defined, especially regarding those trained at departments of psychology rather than psychiatry (Miller, 1985).

Perspectives

The trends mentioned above certainly do not exhaust the richness of contemporary Soviet psychology, but rather highlight some of the focal points of development occurring in the 1970s and 1980s. The future of Soviet psychology strongly depends on changing social circumstances and continued self-reflection on the part of the psychological community. The current attempt at social-economic restructuring of Soviet society may bring greater and more versatile functions for psychologists and may enhance professional psychology. Soviet psychologists will probably continue to struggle with the problem of "self-identification," that is, they will be searching for a unique formula for Soviet psychology. Such a formula must take into account the European roots of their discipline but also uphold a strong, specifically Russian cultural tradition that has always provided a broader context for social and behavioral sciences. Theoretical scholarship and a humanistic orientation will most likely remain a strong point of Soviet psychology. At the same time, this type of scholarship must be reconciled with the tasks imposed by the socialist form of government. The originality of Soviet psychology, which revealed itself in the 1920s, may once again appear in the form of a "creative conflict" between culturally informed theory and pragmatic socialist tasks set up by the government.

Bibliography

Bassin, P. (1968), *The problem of the unconscious*. Moscow: Medicine.

Davydov, V., & Markova, A. (1983). A concept of educational activity for school children. *Soviet Psychology, 21*, 50–76.

Kozulin, A. (1984). *Psychology in utopia: Toward a social history of Soviet psychology*. Cambridge, MA: MIT Press.

Kozulin, A. (1986). Vygotsky in context. In L. Vygotsky, *Thought and language* (rev. ed.). Cambridge, MA: MIT Press.

Miller, M. (1985). The theory and practice of psychiatry in the Soviet Union. *Psychiatry, 48,* 13–24.

Prangishvili, A. S., Sherozia, A. E., & Bassin, P. V. (1978–85). *The unconscious* (Vols. 1–4). (In Russian, English, German, and French). Tbilisi: Mecniereba.

Strickland, L. (Ed.). (1979). *Soviet and Western perspectives in social psychology.* New York: Pergamon Press.

Strickland, L. (Ed.). (1984). *Directions in Soviet social psychology.* New York: Springer.

Valsiner, J. (1987). *Developmental psychology in the Soviet Union.* Brighton: Harvester Press.

Wertsch, J. (1985). *L. S. Vygotsky and the social formation of mind.* Cambridge, MA: Harvard University Press.

40 / United Kingdom

LUDWIG F. LOWENSTEIN

Ludwig F. Lowenstein (born 1928), an American citizen of German origin, has been living in Great Britain since 1958. He received his undergraduate degree from the University of Western Australia and his advanced degrees, including a diploma in clinical educational psychology and the PhD in psychology, from the University of London (1966). His primary interests are the diagnosis and treatment of children and adolescents.

The author of more than 150 articles, several chapters, and 10 books, in-cluding The Gifted Child *(with Frieda Painter), he was the first to conduct a national survey on violence and disruptive behavior in British schools. He founded* School Psychology International *in 1979 and was its editor-in-chief until 1985. Lowenstein has also been chairman of the Hampshire Branch of the Association for Gifted Children, secretary of the International School Psychology Association, a member of the editorial board of the* International Journal of Group Tensions, *and visiting professor and lecturer in the Sudan, the UK, the USA, and Switzerland. He is director of the Lowenstein Therapeutic Community, the Allington Manor School.*

Psychology in the United Kingdom has moved from a close re-lationship with philosophy to a gradual disentanglement from it. It is now becoming slowly involved with the sciences, especially biology, zoology, physics, and mathematics, a trend not welcomed by everyone. There has also been a drift away from a close association with classical psychoanalytic psychology toward behavioristic and other approaches. At present there is a tendency to fashion psychology into a predictive science, based on the outcome of certain hypotheses.

There is still a shortage of useful information readily available to practition-ers in clinical, educational, and occupational psychology. The trend toward specialties within psychology, in part because of the richness of information in these areas, makes it difficult to be a "general psychologist" now. Some

Many people contributed to this chapter. Perhaps the individual who helped most to make it as current as possible is Colin V. Newman, executive secretary of the British Psychological Society.

feel that the overall role of psychologists is to combine knowledge in many areas and to use it eclectically in problem solving.

Educational Background

Initially, psychology was offered at the university level. Since the early 1960s, however, psychology has been studied at the secondary school level and is one of the examination areas for the advanced level (considered equal to the first years of university in the usa) and also at the ordinary level (equal to the final year of high school in the usa).

Though a university education in psychology is considered preferable, an increasing number of other institutions, such as polytechnics, provide degrees in psychology. There is also the Open University, to which any person with relevant qualifications and ability may apply. The tutoring of the Open University is conducted by radio and television and is supplemented by written materials and assignments. Psychology is taught in teacher training colleges and institutes of education. There are also part-time psychology courses offered in the evenings through the Workers Education Association (wea).

Psychology has recently become a popular subject for study in Great Britain. There has been no increase in psychology students, however, partly because of education cutbacks at the university level and elsewhere.

Most students interested in studying psychology enroll at a university or polytechnic. At present, the ratio is three times higher for universities than for polytechnics, probably because there are more universities in Great Britain. There are more female students—with a ratio to males of more than 2:1. Table 40.1 is based on students in 1986 who were committed to psychology as a subject, from both universities and polytechnics, and gives the actual destination of 174 students who graduated from three universities and three polytechnics in that year.

For one to be called a psychologist in Great Britain, the minimum qualification is a degree, either a BA or BSc, or a higher qualification in psychology. Many graduates continue their study toward the MA, MSc, or PhD in particular areas.

Postgraduate courses are of two types: first, professional training programs in clinical, educational, and occupational psychology. These courses normally lead to a master's degree, which is the usual qualification for work as a fully qualified, autonomous, professional applied psychologist in the United Kingdom. The first degree in the uk is far more specialized than its usa counterpart. A student on a BSc or BA course at a university may well

TABLE 40.1

What Do Graduates Do? Destinations of 174 psychology students who graduated from three universities and three polytechnics in 1986

Further Full-Time Study:
38 graduates

17 higher degrees
10 Postgraduate Certificate in Education
1 Common Professional Exam (Law Society)
2 Diploma in Secretarial Studies
1 Teaching English as a Foreign Language preparatory certificate
1 Diploma in Marketing
1 Diploma in Personnel Management
1 Diploma in Advertising
1 Diploma in Information Administration
1 Diploma in Health Education
1 Diploma in Clothing Technology
1 course in French, Sorbonne

Permanent Employment:
65 graduates

6 research assistants: Hull University (2); Humberside CHE; Sheffield Health Authority; Airedale Hospital; Peterborough Community Health Association
6 psychology technicians: Hull Health Authority (2); Dudley Health Authority; East Berkshire Health Authority; Leeds Health Authority
6 retail management graduate trainees: Mothercare (2); B & Q;

E. H. Booth, British Home Stores; Jaeger
5 working overseas: kibbutz; teaching English in Spain; campsite manager in France; unspecified work in Belgium; au pair in USA
4 student nurses: various health authorities
4 trainee chartered accountants: Arthur Young; Pole Arnold; Robson Rhodes; Stoy Hayward
3 houseparents: children's home (2); Aycliffe School
3 trainee account executives: Chapter One Direct; Rex Stuart; Lansdowne Recruitment
2 research psychologists: Royal Air Force; Yorkshire Regional Health Authority
2 trainee personnel officers: Ford; unspecified health authority
2 trainee recruitment consultants: Inverdata; Lansdowne Appointments
2 community workers
2 care assistants
2 executive officers: Home-Office; Medical Research Council
2 graduate trainee administrators: regional health authority; Oxfordshire County Council
1 occupational psychologist: Advanced Personnel Technology
1 quality circles facilitator: Marconi Instruments

TABLE 40.1
(*Continued*)

1 personal development consultant: Development Training Ltd.	1 marketing administrator: W. N. Sharpe Ltd.
1 community development worker: Council for Voluntary Service, Hull	1 distribution management trainee: Marks & Spencer
1 industrial relations trainee: Ford	1 graduate management trainee: British Road Services
1 trainee computer programmer: CAP	1 sports manager: Reflex Gym, Rugby
1 trainee accountant: International Leisure Group	
1 graduate insurance trainee	Plus: 9 not available for employment; 14 in short-term employment; 27 no information; 21 unemployed six months after graduating
1 graduate marketing trainee: Kodak	

Source. From *What Do Graduates Do?* by Alun R. Jones, 1984–85, Cambridge: Hobsons Publishing Co. Copyright 1984–85 by Hobsons Publishing Co. and Alun R. Jones.

spend 80 percent or even more of his or her time reading psychology with only little time devoted to minor subjects. The final examination will probably relate only to the major topic: psychology. Following this specialized degree, only a further 2 or 3 years spent working for a university master's degree, or the British Psychological Society's diploma in clinical psychology, are required to become a fully trained professional psychologist. A doctorate qualification is therefore not held by many professional psychologists.

The second type of postgraduate qualification is the doctoral degree, either a PhD or a DPhil (considered synonymous). In the United Kingdom the doctorate degree is usually a qualification awarded on the basis of a thesis submitted after a period of independent research. A doctoral student normally takes few, if any, taught courses, and the final degree does not normally require the candidate to sit for any written examination papers in addition to the thesis or dissertation, which forms the basis of an oral examination.

Status and Certification

The general criteria for inclusion in the Register of the British Psychological Society (BPS) are (1) passing the qualifying examinations set by the society and (2) a first degree conferred by a university or the Council for National Academic Award for which psychology was taken as a main subject. Graduates not covered under these two criteria may qualify by virtue of experience or postgraduate qualifications in psychology.

Under the terms of its charter and statutes, members of the society whose names appear in the register, except those who have conditional registration, are entitled to use the designation "chartered psychologist," and the abbreviation "C. Psychol" after their names. F. B.Ps.S. means Fellow of the British Psychological Society; A. F. B.Ps.S. means Associate Fellow of the British Psychological Society.

There is no legal requirement to join the register in order to work as a psychologist in the United Kingdom, although employers may require it as a condition of employment. Some qualified psychologists have not obtained, nor do they want to obtain, this qualification. In these cases the National Health Service and local education authorities are responsible for setting standards of appointment and practices for their employees. For psychologists from overseas, additional qualifications, such as postgraduate professional qualifications and training courses suggested by the society, may be required. The BPS has an accreditation program for training courses in applied professional psychology similar to that of the American Psychological Association.

Normally, chartered psychologists are required to hold practice certificates, which the society issues annually on payment of a fee. At the discretion of the BPS Council, however, permission may be granted to certain chartered psychologists to remain on the register without holding a practice certificate. Such permission is granted only to psychologists who satisfy either of the following conditions: (1) psychologists who have previously held practice certificates but are currently not resident in the United Kingdom or are not employed; or (2) teachers, students, or research workers, in educational or research establishments noted by the Council, who give assurance that they will not (a) in their work as psychologists carry out psychological techniques, investigations, or interventions (apart from teaching and publishing) that are held out in advance as being of direct personal benefit or as having a direct influence on the people on whom they are carried out; or (b) seek to compete commercially for financial gain, either for themselves or for their employing bodies or institutions with other chartered psychologists.

At present the society has five divisions to which a chartered psychologist may belong as a fully qualified member: (1) DCLP, Division of Criminological and Legal Psychology; (2) DCP, Division of Clinical Psychology; (3) DECP, Division of Educational and Child Psychology; (4) DOP, Division of Occupational Psychology; and (5) SDECP, Scottish Division of Educational and Child Psychology.

Number of Psychologists

The total membership of the British Psychological Society was 13,131 as of December 1987, including 11,175 voting members (graduate members, associate fellows, and fellows) (Newman, 1988). The remaining 1,946 members were "contributors" (student subscribers, foreign affiliates, and affiliates).

Male:Female Ratio

Within the society's membership there is almost an equal number of men and women, and it seems reasonable to conclude that the male:female ratio in the profession is currently 50:50. If one looks at undergraduate admissions, however, women now outnumber men by 2:1. It is likely in the future that the ratio of women to men will rise, resulting in a preponderance of women in psychology, a reversal of the past when the field was almost totally dominated by men.

Employment

Only a small percentage of psychology graduates become professional psychologists. Others go into applied work such as social work and counseling. Still others join the police and armed forces or enter advertising, banking, management, accounting, personnel work, and market research.

The careers of professional psychologists fall predominantly into five areas. (1) Clinical psychologists, who work in hospitals and community settings with the mentally ill, mentally handicapped, young children, and other clients. (2) Educational psychologists, who work with school-age children who have behavioral or emotional problems, and their parents and teachers. Their main role is testing children's intelligence, recommending special educational methods for slow learners, and helping teachers deal with children who are disruptive in the classroom. (3) Occupational psychologists, who are concerned with the world of work. They advise people as to jobs for which they are most suited, they conduct research to discover optimum working environments, they suggest the best methods of communication between workers and managers, and so on. (4) Prison psychologists, who work with prisoners and staff in prisons and borstals. They help prisoners cope with various problems and teach prison officers how to deal with withdrawn, apathetic, or aggressive prisoners. (5) Psychologists who teach and/ or do research in their area of expertise.

The necessary qualifications for a clinical psychologist are an upper second class degree in psychology; postgraduate professional training (which may be for 2 or 3 years at a university or polytechnic leading to an MSc or MPhil); or in-service training for 3 years as a probationer in a training program leading to the British Psychological Society's diploma in clinical psychology. Most clinical psychologists work in the National Health Service.

Educational psychologists are mainly employed by the psychological service of local education authorities. They also work in assessment centers, community schools, and children's hospitals. Some educational psychologists teach courses in universities and polytechnics. Others train teachers in colleges of higher education. Some also work in multidisciplinary teams with psychiatrists, social workers, and teachers. The necessary qualifications for educational psychologists are an honor's degree in psychology, a teaching qualification, and (usually) 2 years of teaching experience and professional training in educational psychology.

Occupational psychologists work in companies, both private and public; in government and public services; in colleges of technology and management; in training centers; and in private consulting firms. They also work in multidisciplinary teams of managers, trade unionists, training officers, and engineers. Necessary qualifications for occupational psychologists are a first degree in psychology and a degree course offering occupational psychology options. There are opportunities to enter trainee-level posts directly, but increasingly, either full-time or part-time postgraduate study is required. Many occupational psychologists work in the Civil Service or public corporations.

Prison psychologists train and treat prisoners and educate and work with prison staff. They train prison officers and work with prisoners likely to become aggressive or suicidal. They work in Home Office prison departments, including borstals, which deal with 17–21-year-olds, as well as remand centers and different types of prisons. Psychologists also conduct a Research and Evaluation Unit and are on the staff of the Prison Service College and Officers' Training Schools. The minimum and necessary qualification for prison psychologists is a second class honor's degree in psychology. There is a well-defined promotion structure within the Civil Service for prison psychologists.

Many research psychologists are employed in the Civil Service, trade unions, commercial and voluntary organizations, and various research institutes. A necessary qualification for the research psychologist is a first degree in psychology and work toward a postgraduate research degree, such as an MSc or PhD.

Another branch of psychology is the teaching of psychology. Currently, in Great Britain psychology is taught at levels from 16+ to the postgraduate degree, from schools to universities. There are many adult education courses taught by psychology lecturers, such as WEA and extramural courses. Psychologists are also involved in teacher training and specialize in child development and the psychology of education. Psychologists train nurses, paramedical therapists, doctors, and managers.

Psychology teachers and lecturers work in universities; polytechnics; colleges of art, technology, and higher education; adult education colleges; further education colleges; and schools. Students range in age from 15 to 80 years. A necessary qualification for teachers is a first degree in psychology, followed by a postgraduate research degree, for example, the PhD. About 2,000 psychology graduates are currently employed in higher education: 1,200 at universities, 300 in polytechnics, and 450–500 in college sectors. Clinical and educational psychology employ more than 1,000 psychologists each; the Civil Service employs more than 200.

Recently, other areas of psychological competence have been emphasized, including counseling, cognitive psychology, developmental psychology, the role of psychology in education, health, philosophy, mathematics, statistics and computing, psychotherapy, and psychobiology.

Counseling psychology is not a well-developed specialty in the United Kingdom, and much that counseling psychologists do in the USA is routinely performed by educational and clinical psychologists in the UK. Most psychologists in the UK work for large corporate employers and often national or local government agencies. Therefore, private practice, particularly in clinical or educational psychology, is relatively uncommon.

British Psychological Society

The British Psychological Society was founded in 1901 and was incorporated under the Companies Act in 1941. It was subsequently incorporated by Royal Charter in 1965. Its principal aims are to advance the study of psychology and its application and to maintain high standards of professional education and conduct.

In 1987 the society's royal charter was amended to require the society to "maintain a code of conduct for the guidance of Members and Contributors, and to compel the observance of strict rules of professional conduct as a condition of membership," and "to maintain, with such particulars as the

Council shall decide, a Register of Chartered Psychologists, consisting of those Members of society who have applied for and been granted admittance to the Register."

The BPS is the only national organization of psychologists within the United Kingdom to which all psychology graduates can belong. There is no comparable organization representing all aspects of psychology and all subspecialties within psychology. All members of the British Psychological Society have agreed to abide by its code of conduct. Failure to abide by the code of conduct results in penalties, which include the removal of chartered psychologists' names from the register. Other organizations cater to educational psychologists (the Association of Educational Psychologists) and to occupational psychologists.

The BPS plays an important role in disseminating information concerning conferences and other events. The Scientific Affairs Board deals with standards of psychological research and teaching, and animal research. The Membership and Qualifications Board is involved with the Board of Examiners and is concerned with the qualifying examinations in psychology and the diploma in clinical psychology. The Professional Affairs Board deals with test standards, handicap, and equal opportunities for professionals. There is also a Standing Committee on Publications and a committee working with the press.

The society's main divisions are education and child psychology, clinical psychology, occupational psychology, and criminological or legal psychology. Subdivisions are concerned with education; mathematics, statistics, and computing; medical psychology; and psychotherapy. There are sections on occupational psychology, developmental psychology, social psychology, cognitive psychology, history and philosophy of psychology, counseling psychology, psychobiology, and health psychology.

Currently, branches of the society exist in the north of England, Northern Ireland, Scotland, Wales, Wessex Isle, and the Isle of Wight. All sections offer training courses both in the university and through the BPS conferences and training courses.

On December 18, 1987, a new section of the BPS was established. Entitled the Psychology of Women, it is the 12th section of the society and the 5th to be formed since 1980. It was established in response to the growing realization that the study of the psychology of women "should be encouraged in its own right and not merely comparatively in terms of gender differences." It was noted that both sexes could join this group. There has also gradually been an elimination of sexist language based on the guidelines established by the American Psychological Association.

Progress has been made also on the establishment of the British National

Committee for Psychological Science. This follows the agreement by the International Council of Scientific Unions to admit the International Union of Psychological Science in membership. Psychology must now be seen in the United Kingdom as a mature profession. It is a full member of the scientific consortium of disciplines that comes under the aegis of the country's superordinate national academy of sciences, the Royal Society.

In the spring of 1987 the British Psychological Society's Board approved proposals to simplify the process for foreign psychologists seeking assessment of their credentials in clinical psychology. There is now an overseas clinical qualifications committee. The committee advises on whether or not candidates should be regarded as eligible to be exempt from the diploma in clinical psychology because they have comparable qualifications and experience elsewhere. They are then given a "statement of equivalents" that is accepted by the Whitley Council representing clinical psychologists in Great Britain.

Journals

The chief and most prestigious national journals of Great Britain are (1) *British Journal of Psychology*, (2) *British Journal of Mathematical and Statistical Psychology*, (3) *British Journal of Social Psychology*, (4) *Journal of Occupational Psychology*, (5) *British Journal of Clinical Psychology*, (6) *British Journal of Medical Psychology*, (7) *British Journal of Developmental Psychology*, and (8) *British Journal of Educational Psychology*. *The Psychologist*, the monthly bulletin of the British Psychological Society, carries a calendar of future events within the United Kingdom. Conferences, scientific meetings, and similar activities organized under the auspices of the society are announced in *The Psychologist* as soon as final details are available. The BPS library, located at Senate House, University of London, has the largest collection of psychology journals in the United Kingdom and is said to have the second largest collection in any one place in the world.

Research and Its Support

Psychological research is conducted in diverse areas. In particular, British psychologists have contributed considerably to cognitive psychology, child development, and personality. There are many leading native psychologists in Great Britain, and it would be presumptuous and prejudicial to name any number of them here, meaning that consequently many others would not appear. There is still strong commitment to the importance of learning theory and behavior therapy. Somewhat less interest is directed to the psychoanalytic approach through assessment and treatment. Interest in the role of psychology in business and industry has increased over the past few years. Among the current emergent trends is a greater interest in psychology outside Great Britain and the desire of psychologists to associate themselves with an international organization, such as the International Council of Psychologists and the International School Psychology Association.

Financial support in Great Britain comes from the Science Research Council (SRC), the Social Science Research Council (SSRC), and the Medical Research Council (MRC). The Department of Education and Science (DES) conducts some research principally relating to education rather than to general psychology. The MRC also supports research at the Applied Psychology Unit (Cambridge). This research is government financed but also receives funding from both industry and business. Several government departments, such as the Department of Health, have their own means of funding research. Centers such as the Hester Adrian Research Centre and the Thomas Coram Research Centre are funded by the Department of Health. Charitable organizations such as the National Association of Mental Health and the Spastics Society conduct research in their specialties.

Attitudes toward Psychology

The ordinary British citizen views psychology with suspicion and even concern, although less so now than in the 1950s to 1970s. Psychology is seen as having certain esoteric associations. Confusion between psychiatry and psychology is rampant. However, the general public increasingly employs psychological services, although there is much variation among individual psychologists. Psychology has not yet attained the respect accorded such sciences as physiology, zoology, and medicine. The role of psychologists is frequently dismissed because of their lack of medical training, although sometimes psychological information is considered relevant. For example, in court, psychiatric opinion is usually sought, but in the educational sphere, psychologists, especially educational psychologists, are more likely to be called on than psychiatrists. Psychology has drifted closer to science and away from philosophy, the occult, and what was formerly termed "parapsychology." The emphasis is increasingly on obtaining and conveying objective scientific information effectively.

Bibliography

British Psychological Society. (1988). *Annual Report.*

Foss, B. M. (1969). Psychology in Great Britain. *Bulletin of the British Psychological Society*, Supplement, p. 48.

Lowenstein, L. F. (1976). *School psychology service in Britain.* In C. D. Catterall (Ed.), *Psychology in the schools in international perspective.* Vol. 1. Columbus, OH: International School Psychology Steering Committee.

Lowenstein, L. F. (1984). School psychology in Great Britain. *Contemporary Educational Psychology, 9* (3), 275–285.

Newman, C. V. (1988). *Answers to questions asked by psychologists.* Leaflet issued by the British Psychological Society.

Williams, M., North, P., Riddick, E., & Wilson, R. (1986). *Opportunities for psychologists.* Manchester, UK: Careers Services Trust.

41 / United States

JOHN D. HOGAN & VIRGINIA S. SEXTON

John D. Hogan (born 1939) received his PhD from Ohio State University in 1970. A specialist in developmental psychology, he has published articles and chapters in various areas, including creativity, Piagetian theory, adult development, retardation, humor, hyperactivity, death anxiety, reading, and professional issues. He has been president of the Academic Division of the New York State Psychological Association (NYSPA) (1985–86), president of the Division of Adult Development and Aging of NYSPA (1990–91), and vice-president of Psi Chi (1986–87). Hogan is academic division editor of the New York State Psychologist *and consulting editor to the* Journal of Genetic Psychology *and to* Genetic, Social, and General Psychology Monographs. *He is associate professor of psychology at St. John's University, NY.*

Virginia Staudt Sexton (born 1916) received her PhD from Fordham University in 1946. She has been president of the New York State Psychological Association (1982–83), the Eastern Psychological Association (1983–84), the International Council of Psychologists (1981–82), Psi Chi (1986–87), and five divisions of the American Psychological Association. She is consulting editor to the Journal of Mind and Behavior, Humanistic Psychologist, *and* Professional Psychology: Research and Practice *and has published extensively on the history of psychology, professional issues, and international psychology. Sexton is the author of more than 100 articles and six books, including (with H. Misiak)* History of Psychology: An Overview; Phenomenological, Existential, and Humanistic Psychologies; Catholics in Psychology; *and* Psychology Around the World. *She is distinguished professor of psychology at St. John's University, NY.*

History

Beginnings: The 1800s

Psychology was taught in American colleges and preparatory schools in the early 1800s. However, it was taught as moral or mental philosophy and mainly by theologians. With the emergence of a more vigorous psychology in the latter half of the 19th century, scientific psychology began to emerge as a distinct discipline.

American scientific psychology depended on Germany for training. Most early USA leaders studied in Germany, although they modified their approaches to suit the national climate. Wundt's influence on Americans who studied with him, though it appeared strong, was largely confined to methodology. A greater influence on content and spirit, not immediately recognized, was that of Galton.

The rise of scientific psychology in the USA was remarkable. Introduced during a time of reform in American higher education, it was quickly accepted. Moreover, the association with Johns Hopkins University, where G. Stanley Hall developed the first American psychological laboratory (1883), gave prestige to the discipline. Among American universities, Johns Hopkins had attained fame for its leadership in graduate education.

While William James was the foremost thinker in the beginning period of the new psychology in America, his student, G. Stanley Hall, was its principal organizer and promoter. Hall founded several psychology periodicals, including the first American psychology journal, the *American Journal of Psychology* (1887), still in existence. In addition, he founded the American Psychological Association (1892), of which he was twice president, counted several outstanding psychologists among his students, and literally introduced psychoanalysis to America by inviting Freud, Jung, and several psychoanalytic associates to present a symposium at the 20th anniversary of the founding of Clark University (1909).

By the turn of the century American psychology was making rapid strides as a science. Instead of traveling to Europe, most students studied at universities in the USA.

Early 20th-Century Trends

Between 1900 and 1915 psychology laboratories almost doubled in number, seven or more psychology-related journals started publication, and clearly defined schools of psychology began to arise.

The functional psychology begun by John Dewey and James Angell at the University of Chicago found expression in the work of Hall and Cattell. Wundt's elementism, in the form developed by Titchener (called structuralism), was under considerable attack. Then, in 1913, John B. Watson introduced his new system of behaviorism. Along with the appearance of Freud's psychoanalysis, American psychology was developing influences that would last for decades.

Psychology in the USA soon broke loose from its European moorings and acquired its own distinctive character. A significant impetus was given by America's entry into World War I, which created an opportunity for psychology to demonstrate its usefulness. In the military, psychologists developed

instruments to classify and test recruits. The efficient selection and allocation of manpower generated a postwar demand for personnel selection and
testing in education and industry.

Between 1920 and 1940 American psychology expanded in different directions. There were increases in the number of psychologists, departments
of psychology, publications, and the amount and variety of research. Public interest in applied psychology grew because of psychology's wartime
accomplishments and contributions. Advances were made in clinical psychology, vocational guidance, and industrial psychology. At the same time,
the number of individuals interested in pure experimental psychology decreased, especially in formerly popular topics such as sensation, perception,
and aesthetics. An important factor stimulating psychology's postwar expansion was the renewal of the controversy among competing schools of
psychology.

The 1940s and Beyond

With the entry of the United States into World War II in 1941, a new era of
modern American psychology began. Although the war curtailed academic
research, it provided new service and research opportunities in military,
clinical, and industrial psychology. Psychology had a new confidence and
prestige, amply illustrated by success in the areas of selection, training,
morale, instrument design, psychological diagnosis, and psychotherapy.

The postwar years brought an unprecedented demand for psychological
services. Large numbers of students enrolled in graduate and undergraduate
programs. Old curricula were revised, and new curricula were developed.
Government and foundation support became available for research, and
grants became available for students. Psychologists now collaborated with
other scientists on interdisciplinary projects. All these developments opened
new horizons for American psychology in the 1950s and 1960s. Postwar
America unmistakably supported psychology; the *Zeitgeist* clearly favored
behavioral sciences. Thereafter, psychology made rapid progress both as a
science and as a profession.

Education and Training

Secondary Schools

The first exposure to formal psychology for many students in the
USA today occurs in the secondary schools, and the trend is growing. In
1951 only nine states certified high school psychology teachers. By 1981 only
three states did not have some legal provision for teaching psychology in

the secondary school. There is still considerable variation among the states, however, and it is possible to teach psychology in secondary schools without ever having taken a psychology course.

The course offering on the secondary level is often a general one, stressing personality and developmental issues. No enrollment figures are available, but it is reasonable to estimate that millions of students are first exposed to formal psychology in the high schools. The American Psychological Association (APA) has shown its concern with the impact of psychology at this level and has issued guidelines for specialty training and certification of secondary school teachers of psychology, as well as ethical guidelines.

Undergraduate Education

At the undergraduate college level, both 2-year and 4-year institutions ordinarily offer courses in psychology, and a large percentage of both require a psychology course to fulfill graduation requirements. The number of students graduating with a major in psychology from the 4-year institutions in the mid-1980s has been estimated at 40,000 per year, a drop of more than 10,000 from the previous decade. Currently, about 6 percent of these graduates are expected to continue and complete the doctoral degree in psychology. Psychology majors account for two thirds of all doctoral students in psychology. Another third of those entering doctoral programs in psychology have undergraduate degrees in areas other than psychology.

Graduate Education

An annual publication of the APA, *Graduate Study in Psychology and Associated Fields*, lists more than 700 departments and schools of psychology. Approximately 300 offer the doctoral degree. The number of doctoral degrees awarded annually in psychology is slightly more than 3,000; master's degrees number more than 8,000. The APA considers the doctoral degree in psychology (PhD, EdD, or PsyD) as the necessary degree for the independent delivery of services. The master's degree, in the APA's view, is appropriate for the supervised delivery of services.

A large university may contain several specialized psychology departments, each offering its own advanced degree. Additional departments and schools offer advanced degrees in psychology, or closely related specialties, but reside in settings without "psychology" in the title.

Unlike many other doctoral training programs that began to decline in the 1970s, psychology has continued to grow, although at a slower rate than before. Its vitality is such that of all doctoral degrees granted in the United States in 1984, 10 percent, or 3,223, were awarded in psychology. In 1987

3,100 doctoral degrees were granted in psychology, approximately 20 percent of all doctorates in science in the USA.

Accreditation

In 1947 the APA began a process of accreditation for doctoral programs in professional psychology, which currently includes programs in clinical, counseling, and school psychology (or an appropriate combination). Internship training in these areas is accredited as well. Participation in the process is voluntary, and accreditation status is subject to periodic review. By the end of 1988 246 doctoral programs and 347 internship sites had been accredited. Of the doctoral programs, 155 were in clinical, 51 were in counseling, 37 were in school, and 3 were in combined programs (Nelson, 1989). According to one proposal, graduation from an APA-accredited program could be a condition for licensure by 1995. The APA Council of Representatives has endorsed in principle a policy by which new programs, beyond those currently accredited by APA, could be accommodated.

Models of Training

The issue of training for the psychologist, and particularly the psychology practitioner, has been a matter of debate for more than 50 years. In 1937 James McKeen Cattell was among the first to propose the establishment of professional schools of psychology. In 1938 Poffenberger proposed the establishment of a professional training program as an alternative to the PhD programs then in existence. In 1949 a conference on graduate education in clinical psychology was held in Boulder, Colorado. The Boulder Model, formulated at this conference, became the prototype for most clinical programs. This model emphasized the role of the clinician as a scientist-practitioner and endorsed the proposal that training for such professionals be located in academic departments. Conferences on graduate education which followed were largely in support of that model, and for many years the Boulder Model remained the norm. There was, in fact, only one program in the country devoted mainly to the education of practitioners in psychology, namely, the program at Adelphi University in New York, begun in 1951.

The situation was soon to change. In 1965 a practitioner program was established at the Fuller Graduate School of Psychology, and 2 years later another program began in Illinois, granting the doctor of psychology degree, or PsyD. By 1982 there were 44 practitioner programs in operation, with almost 5,000 students enrolled. Of those 44 programs, 20 were in universities and 24 were in freestanding professional schools. Twenty-seven programs led to the PsyD degree and 17 to the PhD. This new model received support from a conference on graduate education held in 1973, the Vail Conference. Because both models, to meet the standards of APA accreditation, must subscribe to certain courses and criteria, their differences are not as great as might be expected.

At the 1987 conference on graduate education, sponsored by the APA Board of Directors, some elements of both the Boulder and Vail conferences were present. While affirming that research and scientific inquiry are an essential part of every psychologist's background, even for practitioners receiving the PsyD degree, the participants agreed that the accreditation arm of the APA should recognize that programs differ in their emphasis on training and research, that there is no single standard, and that the accreditation process should reflect those differences.

Licensing and Certification

Passage by the States

Although some interest in obtaining legal safeguards for the definition and practice of psychology had been expressed before World War II, there was no legal regulation of the title "psychologist" or any laws regarding practice. In 1945 Connecticut became the first state to approve a law regulating the practice of psychology. Virginia and Kentucky soon followed with their own legislation in 1946 and 1948, respectively. By 1977, with the approval of legislation in Missouri, all 50 states and the District of Columbia had passed some form of legislation regulating the practice of psychology.

Requirements

Although requirements vary from state to state, in general, certification laws regulate the use of the title "psychologist." Licensing laws also regulate the use of the title, but in addition, they specify those activities that constitute the practice of psychology for which the license is required.

Usually, the candidate for the license or certificate must possess the doctoral degree from an accredited institution, in a program that is primarily psychological in content, and must have a background of 1 or 2 years of supervised experience. In addition, most state boards require the candidate to pass a standardized multiple-choice examination, called the *Examination for Professional Practice in Psychology* (EPPP), which may be supplemented with oral and essay questions. However, some states have more than one level of professional practice, which may include subdoctoral credentials and, therefore, different practice requirements.

Limitations

Licensure or certification is frequently generic, that is, it does not indicate area of specialty. However, adherence to the ethical principles of psychologists, developed by the APA (1953) and used in some form by most states, requires psychologists to limit their practice to areas in which they are competent by virtue of training and experience. The association has further specified minimally acceptable levels of performance for service providers.

There are some exceptions to the typical profile. Since the purpose of licensure or certification is to regulate psychologists who offer direct services to the public for a fee, laboratory researchers and college and university faculty are typically exempt from the requirements. Even school psychologists in certain states are certified at different levels. Those certified to deliver services within an educational setting may not be authorized to deliver such services in an unsupervised, private practice. Some states also make use of a dual standard for employment. State mental health workers may be called "psychologists" without having to meet the standards in force in the private sector. To further complicate the issue, some states require evidence of continuing education for renewal of the license or certificate.

Twenty-one states have passed additional legislation, beyond their initial approval, to upgrade, clarify, or otherwise modify existing statutes. Ethical codes and certification and licensing regulations, like training programs, are subject to change as needs, circumstances of society, and the profession demand.

The Model Licensure Act

In February 1987 the APA Council of Representatives unanimously approved a Model Act for State Licensure of Psychologists. This is the fourth set of APA guidelines for state legislation regulating the practice of psychology, but the first in 20 years. The model act represents a standard against which individual psychologists and state associations can evaluate the need for revision of legislation in their own states.

Diplomate Status

In addition to licensure, experienced psychologists may, on a voluntary basis, apply for the ABPP diploma issued by the American Board of Professional Psychology. Diplomate status is regarded as the highest standard of professional practice available and has been expanded to include six areas: clinical psychology, clinical neuropsychology, counseling psychology, forensic psychology, industrial/organizational psychology, and school psychology.

Work Force and Specialization

Personnel Census

In 1983 the APA conducted a census of all psychological person-nel residing in the United States. "Psychological personnel" included all those who have a doctoral or master's degree in psychology or who are cur-rently working in psychology. It was the first national census of psychology personnel since 1972 that surveyed more than 62,000 people. In the most recent survey (Stapp, Tucker, & VandenBos, 1985) the authors concluded that, as of mid-1983, the population of psychological personnel in the USA was slightly over 102,000. Breaking this population down into overlapping subsets, the authors estimated (in round figures), the following personnel numbers: 43,000 involved in research; 68,000 involved in education; 45,000 doctoral individuals who provide or administer mental health services; and 24,000 nondoctoral individuals who do so. (It seems clear from the data that most psychological personnel engage in more than one activity.)

Comparisons of these data with APA membership data lead the authors to conclude that the APA membership is representative of doctoral psycholo-gists in the USA. APA membership is not representative for master's-level individuals, however, who are more likely to be employed in 2-year colleges and school settings.

Another survey of psychologists employed in the United States (National Science Foundation, 1988), using more flexible criteria, estimated the total number of psychologists at 254,000 in 1986, more than double the number of a decade before. This same survey placed psychology third in growth among science fields, after computer science and the mathematical sciences.

Specialties

In the APA survey the largest number of respondents reported their spe-cialty to be clinical psychology, followed by school psychology and counsel-ing psychology, but the proportions varied considerably by highest earned degree. For those at the doctoral level, the most frequently reported specialty was clinical psychology (44 percent), followed by counseling psychology (11 percent), educational psychology (6 percent), industrial/organizational psy-chology (5.5 percent), school psychology (5 per cent), and developmental psychology (4 percent). By contrast, for those at the master's level, the most frequently reported specialty was school psychology (29 percent), followed by clinical psychology (26.5 percent), counseling psychology (13 percent), and educational psychology (7 percent).

Of the 3,223 new doctorates granted in psychology in 1984, the top six specialties (in the groupings available) were clinical, counseling, and school psychology, 53 percent; experimental, comparative, and physiological, 8 percent; educational psychology, 6.5 percent; developmental psychology, 6 percent; personality/social psychology, 6 percent; and industrial/organizational psychology, 3 percent. The remainder, 17 percent, fall into the "other" category.

Professional Organizations: The APA

The American Psychological Association is the largest professional psychological association in the world, as well as the major organization of psychologists in the United States. This is true whether one looks at size, influence, or resources. For the year 1983, it was estimated that 73 percent of all doctoral level psychologists in the USA belonged to APA. It is also worth noting that the annual operating budget of APA in 1990 was more than $40 million.

With its stated goals to "advance psychology as a science and a profession, and as a means of promoting human welfare," the organization is necessarily a diverse one. Nowhere is this more evident than in its divisional structure. Beginning with 18 divisions at the major restructuring that took place in the mid-1940s, the organization currently has 47 divisions. There is no limit on the number of divisions a member may join.

The central office structure of the association reflects this diversity as well. In its latest configuration, in 1987, three directorates were created under the executive officer: the science directorate, the practice directorate, and the public interest directorate, reflecting very clearly the tripartite goals of the organization. A fourth directorate, education, was later added.

Forces for Reorganization

In 1988 the membership voted against a long-debated plan for restructuring. The plan was proposed in response to some separate difficulties, including problems of increased size, cumbersome governance structures, dissatisfaction from specialty groups, and purported nonrepresentative leadership. The organization, once largely scientific, has become increasingly practitioner-oriented and has not been able to adjust to the relatively sudden transition. Alternative psychology organizations have been proposed, and discussions will undoubtedly continue for many years to come. As the debate goes on, the history of the organization is invoked to point out that APA has a rather vibrant background of such battles. Indeed, that history represents a partial history of the development of psychology in the USA during that period.

Threats to the Unity of the APA

Virtually from the beginning of the organization in 1892 there was dissatisfaction expressed from some quarter. Within a decade of the founding, for instance, one group of members withdrew to found the American Philosophical Association. In that same period E. B. Titchener attempted to form a competing organization and, failing that, met informally with a group that eventually became the Society of Experimental Psychologists. Clinical psychologists defected from the APA on two early occasions. In 1917 the American Association of Clinical Psychologists was formed, but it was soon absorbed into APA as the Section of Clinical Psychology, thereby maintaining organizational unity. By 1921 standards for admission to APA had changed so that published scientific research of a certain quality was required, and the applied psychologists, with less opportunity for research, felt they were being discriminated against. The problem was solved by instituting two classes of membership.

Another serious challenge to APA unity also began in 1921, with the formation of the Association of Consulting Psychologists. That organization focused on professional issues and was the first psychological organization in the USA to adopt a code of ethics for the practitioner. When the American Association of Applied Psychologists (AAAP) was formed in 1937, the Association of Consulting Psychologists was replaced by the newer organization and turned its property over to it, including its journal. This new organization, though never approaching APA in total membership, had a power beyond numbers.

With the coming of World War II, a greater need and respect for applied psychology emerged, and in fact, some cooperative efforts had already been made between the APA and the AAAP in anticipation of the war. The impending war established a climate of cooperation among different psychological organizations. In 1943 an Intersociety Constitutional Convention of Psychologists was held in New York City and the decision was made to retain the APA as the parent organization, although a dramatic change in the by-laws was required. The present divisional structure was instituted then, approved by all participating groups. Delayed by the war, the first APA convention under the new by-laws was held in 1946, with 18 divisions, 5 of which had been sections of the AAAP.

In 1959 Clifford Morgan organized the Psychonomic Society, an effort to form a group with clear scientific/research goals as opposed to the mixed scientific and professional goals of the APA. Though many members of this organization retain their APA membership, the group nonetheless has drawn some of the scientific members from APA, skewing its already skewed membership. Finally, in 1988 the American Psychological Society was formed, also as an alternative to the increasingly professionally oriented APA. Though it is a new organization whose influence is still unclear, it boasts many distinguished psychologists among its founding members.

Other Professional Organizations

Despite the primacy of the APA, many psychologists belong to other organizations, whether international, regional, state, or specialty associations, whose goals may be different from but not necessarily in direct competition with those of the APA. These groups may provide a more intimate gathering than is possible for a large national organization, a greater specificity for research interests or professional concerns, or simply a geographic convenience.

To give only a brief list: each of the 50 states has a psychological association, there are seven regional associations, and there are numerous specialty groups, such as the National Association of School Psychologists, the Association of Women in Psychology, the Association for the Advancement of Behavior Therapy, the Psychonomic Society, the Human Factors Society, the Gerontological Society, the Society of Experimental Social Psychologists, the Association of Gay Psychologists, the Behavior Pharmacology Society, the Society of Experimental Psychologists, the Association of Black Psychologists, and many more. In short, an organization is available for psychologists of virtually any interest and description.

Women in Psychology

In the late 19th century, and for several decades thereafter, opportunities for higher education for women were severely limited. Because most psychologists then were college and university professors, women had little chance to obtain the credentials necessary to become a psychologist. Even if a woman were to complete graduate school successfully, few universities and colleges would be willing to hire her.

Despite discrimination and limited opportunities, women made contributions to psychology from the beginning, and a few were able to reach an unusually high level of accomplishment. Mary Whiton Calkins, for example, who was denied a PhD from Harvard University because of her gender, became a distinguished scholar and, in 1905, the first woman president of APA. Two other women pioneers were Christine Ladd-Franklin, probably best known for her theory of color vision, and Margaret Floy Washburn, the first female PhD in psychology and an active researcher who, in 1921, became the second woman president of APA. No woman would be elected to that position again for 50 years.

In the early part of the 20th century the number of women in psychology increased, though for women the master's degree was more likely to be terminal (Sexton, 1974). Women were also more likely to be employed in service positions rather than in universities. Yet a substantial number of women made significant contributions, particularly in the areas of mental testing, developmental psychology, educational psychology, and clinical psychology.

During the 1950s and early 1960s women still were not elected to office in professional organizations nor were they appointed to relevant boards and executive committees in proportion to their numbers, although in the later 1960s some distinguished women scientists (e.g., Nancy Bayley, Eleanor Gibson, Anne Roe) were honored by several organizations. Nonetheless, representation among APA fellows, journal editors, and similar positions remained low. Only as secretaries to professional organizations were women serving in proportion to their membership (Sexton, 1974).

Although some symposia on the status of women psychologists had been held in the 1960s, it was not until the emergence of the national women's movement that changes were felt in the APA. In 1970 the APA Council of Representatives established the Task Force on the Status of Women in Psychology, and for the first time the female membership of the APA was surveyed and described, and recommendations made.

By 1984 the proportion of doctorates granted to men and women had become approximately equal, although significant differences in specialties continued to exist. Almost 70 percent of new doctorates in developmental psychology in 1987 were granted to women, for instance, but women accounted for only 33 percent of those in psychometrics. In the two specialties in which the most degrees were awarded in 1987, women were granted 54 percent of the PhDs in clinical psychology and 52 percent of the degrees in counseling psychology. Because of the rapid changes taking place in the discipline, however, recent figures may be misleading. For instance, though the percentage of women receiving PhDs in industrial/organizational psychology in 1987 was at a new high of 47, for the period 1960–87 the figure stood at 19 (Committee on Women in Psychology, 1988).

In 1988 women made up 37 percent of the total membership of the APA, including only 18 percent of the fellows but 51 percent of the associate members (Committee on Women in Psychology, 1988). The higher figure for associates is due largely to the greater number of women holding only the master's degree. The number of women receiving doctoral degrees continues to increase, however, and is consistent with increased doctoral production among women in other areas. This increase has been accompanied by a decline in male recipients of PhDs in psychology and has raised questions regarding the female dominance of American psychology in the future. Some projections suggest that psychology doctorate production will strongly favor women in the 1990s.

One of several groups promoting equality of women in the psychological community has been the Committee on Women in Psychology, established by the Board of Directors of APA in 1973. Among the issues the committee has addressed have been guidelines for diagnosis and therapy with women, sexism in graduate education, sexist language in APA publications, underrepresentation, and continuing education. It also recommended the creation of the Division of the Psychology of Women (Division 35) of APA, formed in 1973, a group that promotes research on women and its applications. The committee has set as a current priority an increase in the visibility and participation of ethnic minority women and has published directories to assist in that effort.

Gavin (1987) conducted a peer rating of the leading English-speaking women in psychology. From a sample of approximately 600 individuals, her raters generated a list including the following top 10 (actually, 11, because of a tie): (1) Anne Anastasi, (2) Leona Tyler, (3) Janet T. Spence, (4) Anne Roe, (5) Nancy Bayley, (6) Florence Denmark, (7) Molly Harrower, (8) Edna Heidbreder, (9) Eleanor Maccoby, and (10) Tamara Dembo and Eleanor Gibson.

Journals

The tally of journals published in the USA in psychology numbers in the hundreds. The APA alone publishes 24 journals, as well as the monthly newspaper, the *APA Monitor*. Additional journals are published by 13 of the APA divisions, making the association "the world's largest publisher of scientific journals" (Fowler, 1989). Virtually every specialty has a print vehicle to carry its research or its message. When journals published in related areas such as psychiatry, education, and sociology are added to the list, the catalog becomes enormous. The typical psychologist complains that it is impossible to read all the new material, even within one's specialty.

With such a large and variegated publication system, there is, necessarily, a range in quality. However, no assessment of journal quality can be totally satisfying. The premier journal of one specialty may never be read by members of another specialty. Even within specialties there may be a hierarchy of excellence based on subspecialty interests. The APA journals are often identified as the leaders in their subfields—and they frequently are. They are not only the most widely circulated psychology journals in the USA overall, but they are also the most frequently cited. For many psychologists, it is a mark of particular distinction to publish in an APA journal.

The APA began its alliance with professional journals in the 1920s, when it acquired several already existing journals. In 1927 it began publishing *Psychological Abstracts*, the first journal that it also initiated. By the early 1930s the APA was publishing 40 percent of journals viewed as core to the field (Eichorn & VandenBos, 1985). (This percentage was to change with the explosion of new, non-APA journals in the ensuing decades.)

When the APA was reorganized in the 1940s, the *American Psychologist* became its official organ and remains so to this day. In 1985 the journal program and related information services cost $9.5 million, or 45 percent of the total APA budget. In that year the APA published more than 16,000 pages in its primary journals, 2,400 pages in the *American Psychologist* and *Contemporary Psychology*, and more than 7,000 pages in *Psychological Abstracts* and related materials (Eichorn & VanderBos, 1985).

There are exceptions to APA journal dominance, however. According to citation counts in subsequent research, non-APA journals were leaders in both experimental psychology and developmental psychology (Feingold, 1989). The overall leaders, however, were not specialty journals, although they were APA journals. Most often cited were the APA general journals of psychology: *Psychological Review*, *Psychological Bulletin*, and the *American Psychologist*.

Among the leading journals in psychology identified by Feingold (1989), using citation counts, were the following: in applied psychology, *Journal of Applied Psychology*; in clinical/abnormal, *Journal of Consulting and Clinical Psychology*, and *Journal of Abnormal Psychology* (tied); in developmental, *Child Development*; in experimental/learning and memory, *Journal of Memory and Language*; in experimental/perception, *JEP: Human Perception and Performance*, *JEP: General*, and *Perception and Psychophysics* (tied); in personality, *Journal of Personality and Social Psychology*; in quantitative, *Psychological Bulletin*; and in social, *Journal of Personality and Social Psychology*. This selection of journals was highly correlated with earlier studies using reputational indices.

Research Support

There is an extensive network of funding sources available from both government and private sources for the social and behavioral sciences.

The APA has compiled a list of these sources in a volume called *Guide to Research Support* (Dusek et al., 1984; Herring, 1987).

The scope and amount of federal funding varies, depending on appropriations by Congress. Organized psychology has become increasingly sensitive to the need for educating those who dispense the funds, and it now engages in extensive lobbying through such groups as the APA and the Association for the Advancement of Psychology. The APA provides further information on working with Congress through the association's Research Support Network. Attempts at education extend to the personnel who decide on the grant requests within a particular agency. These scientists are not always psychologists.

Major sources of federal funding for psychology include the National Science Foundation; the National Institutes of Health; the Department of Education; the Alcohol, Drug Abuse and Mental Health Administration; and the Department of Defense. In 1983 these five sources supplied 92 percent of the federal support to psychology. According to a report by the National Science Foundation (quoted in Dusek, 1984), the federal government spent nearly $258 million for basic and applied research in psychology in 1983. This figure represents less than 1 percent of the total research and development funding available that year. The budget for basic research, approximately $100 million, represents a decrease in real dollars since 1972 of almost 34 percent. The ratio between basic and applied research, 39 percent versus 61 percent, has varied no more than two percentage points in the 1980s.

Federal research funds are awarded on the basis of proposals submitted by institutions for scientists who intend to conduct the research. Although the general form for submission is similar, some variation is seen among agencies. The quality and importance of the research is typically determined by peer review. Approximately 25 percent of the proposals are funded.

The number of private foundations and corporations that give grants has been estimated at more than 22,000 (Dusek et al., 1984). Although most are small, some have assets of almost $1 billion or more (e.g., the Ford Foundation, the Rockefeller Foundation, the MacArthur Foundation). The chief beneficiaries tend to be educational institutions. Less than 10 percent of the private sector grants are estimated to support research activities. Less than 3 percent of the total grants are given to mental health and to the social sciences combined.

Public Image

The public image of psychology continues to be a source of great concern among psychologists, and with good reason. A positive image may create opportunities for support, both from government and the private sector. Although there has been no adequate sample of public opinion, a frequently stated impression is that a large proportion of the population in the USA does not fully understand the discipline, particularly in its scientific aspects.

The earliest notions of psychology were often closely linked to magic and the occult. Now, though such misconceptions are rare, there is concern that new misunderstandings may replace them. The mass media, with their proliferation of psychology-based programming, constitute a powerful tool to aid in understanding the discipline, and professional groups have been formed to try to channel those opportunities. Nonetheless, many misunderstandings still exist. For example, members of the general public often do not know, or care, about the credentials of the individual offering advice on radio or television.

Most surveys suggest that the public has some knowledge of the background and work of the psychologist. However, only the most informed segments of the population are able to describe the role of the psychologist with a suitable degree of sophistication, and few of these individuals are aware of licensing and title-protection laws that offer the major safeguards to the public. If any positive changes are taking place, they are due in part to the tremendous number of students who have taken psychology courses over the years and to the efforts of various psychological organizations to educate the public. Between 1983 and 1988, for example, the APA published, at considerable expense, the journal *Psychology Today*, so that it might have a means to present the discipline to the public.

Benjamin (1986) points out that although psychology has been concerned with its image virtually from the beginning of its organization in the USA, the impact of an image problem could still be seen in substantial ways in the 1980s. Among the specific areas he lists are curtailed government funding for research and for clinical training, the picketing of professional meetings by animal activists, public ridicule through the use of a sardonic research "award" sometimes bestowed on psychology, and statements from biomedical colleagues who remain unclear as to the value of animal research in psychology.

Benjamin (1986) also presents a history of the public image of psychology, beginning with the display of apparatus and photographs to the public at the Chicago Exposition in 1893 and the presentation of an illustrious group of psychologists as speakers at the St. Louis Exposition in 1904. (Even today the APA sponsors public lectures by distinguished psychologists at its annual convention.) No direct information is available on the attitude of the public to psychology early in the century, but the writings of several psychologists suggest a lack of public understanding even then.

World War I contributed to the public awareness of psychology, particularly in an applied way, though some of the claims for psychology may have aroused unrealistic expectations. After a decline in public interest during the depression, World War II brought renewed life to psychology, as immense psychological resources were put into service for the war effort. With the end of the war came the emergence of professional psychology, an event that led to the changed character of psychology in the USA today. The end of the war also signaled the beginning of a reorganized APA (1946), which, despite attempts to usurp it, continues to serve as the strongest voice for the entire discipline.

Wood, Jones, and Benjamin (1986) reviewed surveys conducted on the public image of psychology beginning in 1948. They found a generally favorable attitude toward psychology, although on a concrete level the attitude is less favorable (e.g., Should your child choose psychology as a profession?). In their own survey, they found that most of those questioned believed psychology is a science (84 percent), but also that day-to-day life provides training in psychology (83 percent), that psychology is incompatible with their religious beliefs (60 percent), and that psychology has supported liberal political positions (67 percent). Direct comparisons among the surveys over the years were not possible because of differences in samples and areas sampled, although there was some evidence that a more positive attitude toward psychology was associated with a satisfying exposure to the discipline.

Marsten and Takooshian (1987) found attitudes toward psychologists less positive than previous findings (e.g., Woods et al.). Twenty percent of their sample spontaneously asked for the distinction between a psychologist and a psychiatrist. Their sample also viewed psychologists as more likely to be wise and influential but less likely to be scientific and mentally healthy.

Leading Native Psychologists

The size and diversity of psychology in the USA makes it difficult to identify contemporary leaders whose designation would go unchallenged. Psychologists of different theoretical orientations, specialties, and even subspecialties have their favorite candidates. Moreover, among the younger contributors, it is puzzling to know whose work will be meaningful even a decade from now. Although there are certain guides that could be used, they tend to be geared toward older, more established psychologists, and each has particular problems associated with it.

One measure of eminence is election to the office of president of the American Psychological Association. In recent years the office has become increasingly political and subject to all the excesses such a change implies. But for many years the office was awarded to important contributors to the science of psychology and, more recently, to the practice of psychology. It is worthwhile noting that even in "older, less political" times, B. F. Skinner was never elected APA president, although his contribution to psychology in the USA and worldwide is generally acknowledged to be immense.

The following is a list of presidents of the APA since 1960, the date that commences the major focus of this report. The year of the APA presidency follows the psychologist's name. In a curious happenstance, the first name listed is not that of a psychologist from the USA, but rather an eminent Canadian, and the last received his PhD from the University of London. The psychologists are D. O. Hebb (1960), Neal E. Miller (1961), Paul E. Meehl (1962), Charles E. Osgood (1963), Quinn McNemar (1964), Jerome S. Bruner (1965), Nicholas Hobbs (1966), Gardner Lindzey (1967), A. H. Maslow (1968), George A. Miller (1969), George W. Albee (1970), Kenneth B. Clark (1971), Anne Anastasi (1972), Leona E. Tyler (1973), Albert Bandura (1974), Donald T. Campbell (1975), Wilbert J. McKeachie (1976), Theodore H. Blau (1977), M. Brewster Smith (1978), Nicholas A. Cummings (1979), Florence L. Denmark (1980), John J. Conger (1981), William Bevan (1982), Max Siegel (1983), Janet T. Spence (1984), Robert Perloff (1985), Logan Wright (1986), Bonnie R. Strickland (1987), Raymond D. Fowler (1988), Joseph D. Matarazzo (1989), Stanley R. Graham (1990), Charles D. Spielberger (1991), Jack G. Wiggins (1992), and Frank H. Farley (1993).

In addition to the APA presidency, individuals serve in many other offices, both elected and appointed, associated with the organization. These include the APA Board of Directors, the Council of Representatives, and various committee and division offices. Other organizations, such as the newly formed American Psychological Society, boast executive committees whose names are also well known among psychologists in the USA. In short, activity and visibility in major psychological organizations is a handy, though incomplete, guide to significant contributors to psychology in the USA.

Gilgen and Hultman (1979) surveyed the *Annual Review of Psychology* from 1950 through 1974 to identify those individuals with the most citation counts. It has been argued that citation count is a stronger indicator of contribution to the discipline than actual number of contributions. The 10 individuals with the highest number of total citations for the years 1950 to 1974 (the number of citations is in parentheses) were R. B. Cattell (133), N. E. Miller (121), K. W. Spence (90), H. J. Eysenck (77), H. F. Harlow (62), P. Suppes (61), L. Postman (59), S. S. Stevens (59), S. Messick (54), and J. S. Bruner (53).

Gilgen (1982) also surveyed several groups to identify the "most important people in American psychology during the post–World War II period." The 679 members of the APA who responded gave the following top 10 rankings: (1) B. F. Skinner, (2) S. Freud, (3) J. Piaget, (4) C. Rogers, (5) E. Erikson, (6) D. Wechsler, (7) H. Harlow, (8) K. Lewin, (9) C. Jung, and (10) C. Hull. The "13 recognized experts on the history of psychology" whom he surveyed gave slightly different results, including among their top 10, W. Köhler, E. Tolman, and R. Woodworth. The number of psychologists on these lists who were born outside of the USA should not go unnoticed. In all, respondents rated 286 individuals.

In another measure of eminence, in 1956 the APA instituted an award for distinguished scientific contributions. The first awardees were Wolfgang Köhler, Carl R. Rogers, and Kenneth W. Spence. Each year since then, a minimum of three awards have been given. Other categories of awards followed. Since 1972 the APA has presented awards for distinguished professional contributions to those whose contributions have advanced psychology in the area of knowledge, public service, and professional practice. The first two recipients were Carl R. Rogers (1972) and David Wechsler (1973).

The distinguished scientific award for the application of psychology, begun in 1973, has been conferred on an individual who has made important theoretical or empirical advances related to practical problems. The first recipients were Conrad L. Kraft (1973) and Gerald S. Lesser and Edward L. Palmer (1974). Awards for distinguished contributions to psychology in the public interest were begun in 1978, with Kenneth B. Clark receiving the first award and Marie Jahoda and Otto Klineberg receiving the second (1979). Education and Training Board awards were given for the first time in 1987, with Wilbert J. McKeachie as the first recipient.

The APA began giving early career awards in 1974 to those recipients who have not held the PhD for more than 9 years. All the awards, with appropriate explanations and biographical statements, are listed in annual issues of the *American Psychologist* (e.g., *American Psychologist*, April 1992). The American Psychological Foundation (APF) also presents awards, in this case to psychologists 65 years of age or older who are residents of North America, for lifetime achievements and enduring contributions to advancing psychology. In addition, the foundation presents awards in teaching and to the media.

Finally, some psychologists are members of the prestigious National Academy of Science, begun in 1863, whose charter was signed by President

Abraham Lincoln. The Section of Psychology is one of 25 sections in the academy, whose total membership (in July 1989) was 1,563 active members and 77 emeritus members. The Section of Psychology has 58 active members and 3 emeritus members.

Future Directions

The discipline of psychology is continuously redefining itself. Although it took applied psychology painstaking years to break free from the university and establish its own legitimacy, now new areas of psychological activity emerge in what seems to be a breathlessly short period. Some areas are short-lived and capture little interest beyond their initial flurry. Other areas appear to have the potential for dramatically changing the discipline.

Gilgen (1982) surveyed three groups of psychologists to identify the most important events and influences in psychology in the USA since World War II. A sample of several hundred members of the APA produced a list that includes the following leading 10 events or influences: (1) Skinner's contributions, (2) behavior modification, (3) the growth of applied psychology, (4) the growth of behavioral psychology, (5) government funding of psychology, (6) the general growth of psychology, (7) the impact of World War II, (8) the growth of clinical psychology, (9) the impact of Piaget, and (10) the information explosion.

A second group of psychologists, a sample from the Division of History of the APA, chose 8 from the above list but included 2 other items to complete their top 10: the increasing influence of cognitive theory and the increased interest in complex psychological processes. A final group surveyed, consisting of 13 recognized experts in the history of psychology, chose 7 from the lists above but added 3 others to complete their top 10: the growth of psycholinguistics, Harlow's primate research, and the return of mind and consciousness to psychology.

The evolution of psychology continues. The sources of the most recent areas of interest and emphasis are varied. Some have grown out of the larger social climate, such as the empowerment of women and minorities. Others have followed sources of funding and general utility. Still others seem to have responded to the intrinsic versatility of the discipline itself. The rare combination of rigorous scientific education and practical application, which is the backbone of training for most new psychologists in the USA, seems ideally suited to the fast-moving and rapidly changing culture of recent years.

One indication of emerging interest areas can be seen in the establishment of new divisions of the APA. When the APA was reorganized in 1946, it instituted a system of interest groups, formally called divisions, to satisfy the diversity within the organization at that time. Additional divisions have been added, with the approval of the APA governance, as sufficient concern has been substantiated. In 1959 there were 22 divisions. Since then the number has more than doubled.

The divisions added to the APA since 1960 (with the year of initiation in parentheses) are as follows: Consumer Psychology (1960), Theoretical and Philosophical Psychology (1962), Experimental Analysis of Behavior (1965), History of Psychology (1966), Community Psychology (1967), Psychopharmacology (1967), Psychotherapy (1968), Psychological Hypnosis (1969), State Psychological Association Affairs (1969), Humanistic Psychology (1972), Mental Retardation (1973), Population and Environmental Psychology (1974), Psychology of Women (1974), Psychologists Interested in Religious Issues (1976), Child, Youth, and Family Services (1978), Health Psychology (1979), Psychoanalysis (1980), Clinical Neuropsychology (1980), Psychology-Law Society (1981), Psychologists in Independent Practice (1982), Family Psychology (1985), Society for the Psychological Study of Lesbian and Gay Issues (1985), Society for the Psychological Study of Minority Issues (1986), Sport and Exercise Psychology (1986), Media Psychology (1986), and Peace Psychology (1989).

The preceding list is perhaps as succinct a summary of recent developments in USA psychology as it is possible to generate. Though some of the content areas have a long-standing history (e.g., mental retardation, psychotherapy), their appearance as divisions attests to renewed visions and organizational interests. Some divisions (e.g., history, and theoretical and philosophical psychology) represent demands that contemporary psychology recognize the underpinnings to the discipline. Other divisions (e.g., health psychology, clinical neuropsychology, psychology and law) represent innovative developments and, potentially, major new directions for the discipline. It is worth noting that some of the emerging areas (e.g., sport and exercise psychology) did not originate in the USA.

Another way to explore new directions in USA psychology is through an examination of the *Annual Review of Psychology*. This volume, which periodically reviews new research and thought in traditional areas in psychology, such as sensation and perception, is also a sensitive indicator of emerging areas in the discipline. A survey of the table of contents over the years can be used as a broad indicator to identify some of these trends.

Among the chapters appearing in the *Annual Review* since 1960 which suggest a less-than-traditional scope or emphasis (with the year of the chapter appearing in parentheses) are the following: Computer Simulation and Artificial Intelligence (1968), Geropsychology (1970), Behavior Therapy (1971),

Psychology of Women (1975), Psychology and the Law (1976, 1982), Environmental Psychology (1978, 1982), Nutrition and Behavior (1978), Biofeedback (1978), Attribution Theory and Research (1980, 1984), Behavioral Medicine (1983), Sport Psychology (1984), Health Psychology (1985, 1989), Political Psychology (1987), Contributions of Women to Psychology (1987), and Psychology of Religion (1988).

The *Annual Review* also periodically summarizes the development of psychology in other countries. Since 1960 these summaries have included psychology in the USSR (1962, 1964), Japan (1966, 1972), France (1976), the German Democratic Republic (1980), Latin America (1982), Mexico (1984), Israel (1986), and Australia (1988). This suggests at least a modest interest in international psychology on the part of USA psychologists, rather than the extreme national focus that characterized USA psychology in its "middle years."

Bibliography

Aiken, L. H., Somers, S. A., & Shore, M. F. (1986). Private foundations in health affairs. *American Psychologist, 41*, 1290–1295.

American Association of State Psychology Boards. *Entry requirements for professional practice of psychology: A guide for students and faculty.* Montgomery, AL: Author.

American Psychological Association. (1986, February). *Background: The practice of psychology* (rev. ed). Washington, DC: Author.

Benjamin, L. T. (1986). Why don't they understand us? *American Psychologist, 41*, 941–946.

Committee on Women in Psychology. (1988). *Women in the American Psychological Association.* Washington, DC: American Psychological Association.

Dusek, E. R., Holt, V. E., Burke, M. E., & Kraut, A. G. (Eds.). (1984). *Guide to research support* (2nd ed.). Washington, DC: American Psychological Association.

Eichorn, D. H., & VandenBos, G. R. (1985). Dissemination of scientific and professional knowledge: Journal publication within the APA. *American Psychologist, 40*, 1309–1316.

Fagen, J. W. (1984, April). Research grants in psychology: An overview. *New York State Psychologist, 35*, 19–20.

Feingold, A. (1989). Assessment of journals in social science psychology [Comment]. *American Psychologist, 44*, 961–964.

Fowler, R. D. (1989, Fall). Open letter to the scientific community. *Science Agenda*, p. 14.

Gavin, E. A. (1987). Prominent women in psychology, determined by ratings of distinguished peers. *Psychotherapy in Private Practice, 5*, 53–68.

Gilgen, A. R. (1982). *American psychology since World War II*. Westport, CT: Greenwood Press.

Gilgen, A. R., & Hultman, S. K. (1979). Authorities and subject matter emphasized in the *Annual Review of Psychology, 1950–1974*. *Psychological Reports, 44*, 1255–1262.

Graduate study in psychology and associated fields. (1986). Washington, DC: American Psychological Association.

Herring, K. L. (Ed.). (1987). *Guide to research support* (3rd ed.). Washington, DC: American Psychological Association.

Hilgard, E. R. (1987). *Psychology in America: A historical survey*. San Diego, CA: Harcourt, Brace.

Howard, A., et al. (1986). The changing face of American psychology. *American Psychologist, 41*, 1311–1327.

Marsten, H. P., & Takooshian, H. (1987, August). *A profile of public opinion toward psychology*. Paper presented at the annual meeting of the International Council of Psychologists, New York.

Misiak, H., & Sexton, V. S. (1966). *History of psychology: An overview*. New York: Grune & Stratton.

National Science Foundation. (1988). *Profiles—Psychology: Human resources and funding* (NSF 88–235). Washington, DC: U. S. Government Printing Office.

Nelson, P. (1989, September). Accreditation grows, but values remain same. *APA Monitor*, p. 29.

Nelson, S. D., & Stapp, J. (1983). Research activities in psychology: An update. *American Psychologist, 38*, 1321–1329.

Pryzwansky, W. B., & Wendt, R. N. (1987). *Psychology as a profession*. New York: Pergamon Press.

Russo, N. F., et al. (1981). Women and minorities in psychology. *American Psychologist, 36*, 1315–1363.

Scheirer, C. J., & Rogers, A. M. (1985). *The undergraduate psychology curriculum: 1984*. Washington, DC: American Psychological Association.

Sexton, V. S. (1974). Women in American psychology: An overview. *International Understanding, 9/10*, 66–77.

Stapp, J., Tucker, A. M., & VandenBos, G. R. (1985). Census of psychological personnel: 1983. *American Psychologist, 40*, 1317–1351.

Wood, W., Jones, M., & Benjamin, L. T. (1986). Surveying psychology's public image. *American Psychologist, 41*, 947–953.

42 / Uruguay

JULIETA LAGOMARSINO GIURIA

Julieta Lagomarsino Giuria (born 1934) was educated in Uruguay at the University of the Republic, where she received the licenciada *degree from the Department of Science and Humanities in 1956 and the* téchnico en psicología *degree from the Department of Medicine in 1958. Her specialties include clinical and occupational psychology. Her publications have focused on clinical issues, including treatment of the borderline personality, and various testing instruments, particularly projectives. She has also published articles on psychology in Uruguay, Argentina, and Mexico.*

Giuria was president of the Latin American Rorschach Association, serves on the Board of Directors of the Uruguay Psychological Society, and is a former vice-president of the International Rorschach Association. In addition to her work as a clinical psychologist and psychotherapist, she is a member of the Advisory Council of the Institute of Psychology at the University of the Republic.

Because of exceptional cultural and socioeconomic conditions, the development of sciences (including psychology) in the Republic of Uruguay, a small Latin American country situated between Argentina and Brazil, almost matched that of the United States and European countries. Beginning in 1933 a series of events signaled the evolution of psychology as a science; if they were not recorded in this chapter, full comprehension would be impossible.

In 1933 the Laboratory of Psychology of the Normal School (Primary School Teachers' Training Institute) was founded, an institutional response to the first autodidactic efforts taking place in the country. Under the direction and guidance of Sebastian Morey Otero, a Cuban-Spanish psychologist, an important line of technical development and research was initiated. Morey Otero also promoted psychological testing and favored a psychosomatic understanding of medicine. In 1937 a medical and pedagogical department was established within the Universidad del Trabajo del Uruguay (School of Technology of Uruguay, an institution officially training students in all branches of technical education), which was the beginning of the later Laboratory of Biotypology and an antecedent of the Servicio de Orientación (Counseling Service). This service continued to 1976, a model of its kind that gave advice to students on nurturing their own mental and physical health as well as on how to make the most of their aptitudes.

The clinical line began with the founding by Julio Marcos of the Medical and Psychological Clinic within the Dr. Pedro Visca Children's Hospital, whose goal was to ensure psychological study and full care for the patients of the hospital. In 1948 a course in child psychology was created in the clinic which in 1950 became a regular course for training medical assistants in child psychology within the Faculty of Medicine.

During the 1940s Valentín Pérez Pastorini introduced psychoanalysis as a theory and technique, and in 1955 a group of specialists drawn by the increasing respect inspired by psychoanalysis created the Asociación Psicoanalítica del Uruguay (Uruguayan Psychoanalytic Association), which had its own vocational training institute, thanks to the collaboration of psychologists.

In 1949 the Faculty of Humanities and Sciences and Horacio Rimoldi, an Argentine living in Princeton, signed a contract by which Rimoldi undertook to plan the course of studies of the *licenciatura de psicología* (master's degree in psychology), which was to begin in 1956. In December 1953 the Sociedad de Psicología del Uruguay (Uruguayan Psychological Society) was created. It was a pioneer institution in bringing Uruguayan psychologists together and defending their profession.

Psychology Training (1960–87)

The curriculum for medical assistants in child psychology was created in the Faculty of Medicine in 1950, and the curriculum corresponding to a master's degree in psychology began in the Faculty of Humanities and Sciences in 1956. Both faculties are part of the Universidad de la República (University of the Republic), the only university officially providing vocational training at the highest level in Uruguay.

In addition, there is a Catholic university that gives vocational training in psychology. Students graduating from this university are recognized as having a status identical to that of graduates of the University of the Republic. However, this view was not shared by the psychologists' union.

In 1975, under a dictatorial government, the executive power closed the courses leading to a master's degree in psychology by means of a decree and created the Escuela Universitaria de Psicología (School of Psychology). For psychologists, this action meant the loss of important attainments regarding their status and professional level—for example, their access to chairs in the Faculty of Medicine, university extension services, and psychological assistance in district centers. These achievements were lost for quite a few years, as the School of Psychology was created on the basis of a rather jumbled course of study that did not give the students the required proficiency.

In 1984, with the restoration of democracy, psychologists, as well as other university professionals, began to regain their former positions. For example, during 1988 a center was created which is now the only institution officially in charge of university education in psychology: the IPUR, the Instituto de Psicología de la Universidad de la República (Institute of Psychology of the University of the Republic). Uruguay is in the process of recovering its high level of psychology training, particularly through the implementation of a new course of study intended to equip professional psychologists to meet the realistic demands of the country, both theoretically and practically.

The prerequisite to enter the IPUR is the completion of a course of basic and higher secondary education (6 years) in any of its sections (i.e., the humanistic, biological, or scientific). The duration of undergraduate courses is 5 years, after which students obtain their degrees, and four postgraduate courses of specialization are projected: educational psychology, clinical psychology, social psychology, and occupational psychology.

Psychology training by the IPUR is the only program officially recognized. Vocational training in private colleges is rather alien to Uruguayan tradition, and except for the Catholic university, there are no other such institutions providing it. Since the state undertakes to give free university education in all its branches, it also supports the budget of each one of the faculties within the University of the Republic. The university celebrated 150 years of existence in 1988—in a country with only 158 years of independent life.

The new curriculum for psychology students emphasizes participation in the community through early practical training experiences in different centers, including hospitals, district polyclinics, educational institutions, and factories.

Psychologists and Psychology Today

Before the creation of the IPUR a professional psychologist in Uruguay graduated from one of the following institutions: the Escuela de Tecnología Médica (School of Medical Technology) of the Faculty of Medicine, the Faculty of Humanities with a *licenciatura de psicología* (master's degree in psychology), the Escuela Universitaria de Psicología (School of Psychology); or the Universidad Católica del Uruguay (Catholic University of Uruguay).

The register of the Coordinadora de Psicólogos del Uruguay (Federative Psychologists' Union) includes approximately 1,200 members. A nonevaluated minority of psychologists—which, in any case, does not exceed 5 percent—is not affiliated with this organization. In a population of less than 3 million, the number of graduates in psychology has risen markedly during recent years. A survey made at the School of Psychology which studied the reasons leading to the student's vocational choice showed that the latent fantasy of the cure and prevention of mental disease at a personal or family level was a prevailing motive. Relative to the small area of the country, a great number of psychologists practice in Uruguay, either in the capital (Montevideo) or in the provinces. Although the exact number is not available, it is estimated that only 105 psychologists live permanently in the provinces, and few of those who come to the capital to study return to their original towns or villages to stay.

Most psychologists in Uruguay are women. That is probably due to the fact that, as already noted, interest in psychology came first from the field of education, and most teachers are women.

Fields of Study

A Uruguayan psychologist's field of activity is limited by the needs to be met and the institutions and technicians connected with these needs. Psychologists can specialize in research, teaching, or applied areas, but there are no places institutionally prepared to conduct research, except for the one projected by the IPUR. Regular research was formerly done, however, in the Instituto de Psicología (Department of Psychology) of the Faculty of Humanities, the School of Technology, and the Department of Psychology run by the Primary Education Council. Research usually relies on each psychologist's initiative and is sporadic; it tends either to be done following techniques devised in other countries or to be of a clinical nature. As for teaching, those who give courses in psychology have not necessarily been trained as teachers. Sometimes a university degree is presumed to involve appropriate training and teaching aptitudes.

Consulting rooms are the privileged workplace of clinical psychologists, but usually they also work in hospitals, polyclinics, and different institutions devoted to the prevention and care of mental disease. Psychologists who work at private and state hospitals, as well as at the care centers of mutual benefit societies, are mainly engaged in psychodiagnostics and individual and family advising. They also take part in joint research when it proves necessary for the different services.

According to the traditional link between psychology and education at its different levels (primary, secondary, and technical school), teams of psychologists care for students and advise on such matters as academic performance, behavior problems, vocational guidance, and neurological disorders. Work is usually approached from a multidisciplinary point of view and in teams that include psychologists, medical doctors, and social workers. A student requiring psychological services may be directed, after a review of the case, to the person in the team best qualified professionally to help him or her. There are also private educational institutions that have their own carefully organized psychological services and that serve students during the whole cycle of academic studies. In Uruguay, schooling begins at age 4 or 5, when a child begins preschool, and continues to age 17 or 18, when a young person can enter the university. Within the framework of the IPUR, an advisory service is projected to assist psychology students during the whole course of studies. This function is similar to that of the already well-known "counseling" departments.

Those psychologists who have chosen occupational psychology as a specialty are gradually being absorbed by state and private organizations as people's awareness of the need for this kind of assistance increases. The municipality of Montevideo, for instance, employs psychologists to test applicants for driving licenses. Other state services hire psychologists to evaluate personnel aptitudes and the difficulties workers may find in fulfilling their duties.

Technological development involves adapting workers to changing conditions. As many employers in Uruguay are becoming aware of this reality, they are beginning to rely on either psychologists or consultants. Sometimes they organize their own specialized departments to meet the needs of their companies.

Social psychologists take part in community experiences and give advice on individual, family, and school problems to the members of housing cooperatives, rural associations, and the like.

Public Perception of the Psychologist

The previous comments regarding the place of psychologists in the community are also a clue to the average citizen's views of the profession and its tendency to be increasingly accepted and appreciated. The deeply rooted prejudice that links psychology to madness is gradually disappearing. People think of the psychologist as an important person whose advice may be needed to deal with personal, family, or social problems. A psychologist is seen as a person who administers tests, who is a scientist, and who studies other people's personalities. His or her knowledge is compared to that of the physician, the teacher, the judge, and the confessor.

Sometimes the psychologist's role is confused with that of the psychiatrist or the psychoanalyst, but it is generally connected with mental health and diseases, or with intellectual, emotional, or relational difficulties.

Psychological services are sought by people coming from all social groups. However, only an elite can afford long psychoanalytic treatment. Although some people may still hold the view that psychologists are suspicious persons, this remains a personal limitation and is not, in any case, a widespread prejudice.

Professional Associations

The Coordinadora de Psicólogos del Uruguay includes all the psychologists who were formerly members of the Sociedad de Psicología del Uruguay (Uruguayan Society of Psychology), the Asociación de Psicólogos Universitarios (University Psychologists' Association), and the associations of graduates from the School of Medical Technology, the School of Psychology, and the Catholic University of Uruguay. There are also associations of professional psychologists based on their theoretical inclinations: Asociación Psicoanalítica del Uruguay (Uruguayan Psychoanalytic Association, APU), Asociación Uruguaya de Psicoterapia Psicoanalítica (Uruguayan Association of Psychoanalytic Psychotherapy, AU de PP), Centro Integral de Formación y Asistencia Dr. Enrique Pichon Riviere (Dr. Enrique Pichon Riviere Training and Care Center, CIFA), Sociedad Uruguaya de Terapia Familiar (Uruguayan Society of Family Therapy, SUTeFa), Asociación de Psicoterapia y Psicopatología de la Infancia y la Adolescencia (Association for the Study of Psychotherapy and Psychopathology of Childhood and Adolescence, APPIA), and other professional associations such as those connected with dynamic and expressive therapy, psychodrama, and Jungian psychology. All of them organize training courses, seminars, and congresses. The associations also publish books, magazines, and journals. A monthly magazine called *Relaciones* usually deals with people and their nature and contains a considerable number of specialized articles on psychology. Books and other publications from Argentina and other parts of the world can be bought at specialized bookshops. Although they are easily available, they are expensive, as are psychometric tests and instruments.

The Biblioteca Nacional (National Library) and the libraries of the IPUR and the University of the Republic are open to the public. Members of the different associations also have access to their respective libraries.

Computers are not widely used in connection with psychological work. They are beginning to be adopted, however, in private projects, institutions providing assistance for research, and as part of extension services, such as the assistance that the Faculty of Engineering may give to the IPUR.

The theoretical orientation exerting the deepest influence is that of psychoanalysis, in its Freudian, Kleinian, and Lacanian versions (in that precise order). Interest in the Chicago School and in self-psychology has been increasing in recent years. There are also smaller groups that conduct their own training centers within the framework of Gestalt psychology, behaviorism, transactional analysis, and psychodrama.

To mention leaders among psychologists would involve not only extending this chapter beyond the desired limits, but also probably omitting some important names. I shall state only that there is a prominent role being played by Uruguayan psychologists in national and international congresses of applied psychology, experimental psychology, and clinical research.

Conclusion

After 12 years of dictatorial government, during which, as is usual in these cases, the successive rulers vented their anger on liberal professions —particularly on those contributing to full human development—Uruguay is still trying to regain and improve what had formerly been achieved.

Economic difficulties are serious. The share of the national budget allocated to the university is not enough for vocational training. The budget of the Ministry of Health is inadequate not only to satisfy the wishes of the psychologists working for national projects related to mental health, but also to meet basic needs. Salaries paid to psychologists working in government institutions do not cover their personal expenses. They are forced to work, in addition, for other institutions (frequently private institutions) as a means of balancing their accounts. Workplaces do not have many basic materials, and most of these materials must be provided by the psychologists themselves.

In spite of the difficulties arising from underdevelopment in Latin American countries, there is an awareness of the need to extend the application of psychology within the community and a willingness to contribute to that extension. This will become apparent in the claims for legal recognition of the profession and for more and better paid positions, the inclusion of psychological services in a national health insurance system, psychohygiene schemes, the promotion of health within the community through the creation of new clinics, the establishment of psychopedagogic assistance services in educational centers, and the inclusion of psychotherapeutic care within mutual benefit societies and government care centers.

Bibliography

Documentos de la Coordinadora de Psicólogos del Uruguay. (1981). *Revista Uruguaya de Psicología*, 2 (3–4), 78–91.

Korovsky, Edgardo. (1985). El psicoanálisis en el Río de la Plata. *Revista de la Asociación Uruguaya de Psicoterapia Psicoanalítica*, 1 (4).

Liberman, José. (1980). Campos de actividad del psicólogo. *Revista Uruguaya de Psicología*, 1 (4), 28–32.

Origen, estructura y funcionamiento del departamento de orientación. (1966). Publicación informativa No. 14 de la Universidad del Trabajo del Uruguay.

La psicología en el Uruguay de hoy (informe). (1982). *Revista Uruguaya de Psicología*, 2 (1–2).

Sobrado, Enrique. (1983). *Rol del psicólogo*. Montevideo: Imago.

Universidad de la República. (1987). *Anteproyecto de plan de estudios*.

Universidad de la República. (1988). *Anteproyecto de estructura del Instituto de Psicología de la Universidad de la República*.

43 / Venezuela

JOSÉ MIGUEL SALAZAR

José Miguel Salazar (born 1931) received his PhD in 1957 from the University of London. A specialist in social psychology, he has published extensively on social and cross-cultural issues, including cross-national perceptions and attitudes. Of his three books, the most recent is Supra-nacionalismo y regionalismo (1986).

Salazar serves on the editorial committees of Revista Interamericana de Psicología, *the* Journal of Cross-Cultural Psychology, *and* Applied Social Psychology Annual *and is currently editor of the* International Journal of Psychology. *He served as president of the Interamerican Society of Psychology (1987–89) and is coordinator of the Post-Graduate Program in Social Psychology, Universidad Central de Venezuela, Caracas.*

Characteristics of the Psychologist

The first psychologists in Venezuela included psychiatrists who became interested in psychology, Spanish emigrés from the Civil War, and some native professionals who had been trained in the USA, England, or France. In 1950 the Instituto de Psicología (Institute of Psychology) of the Universidad Central de Venezuela (Central University of Venezuela) was established to help organize psychology studies in the country and to work on the problem of vocational guidance. Nevertheless, it was only in 1960 that the first group of locally trained psychology students graduated.

To become a psychologist in Venezuela, a high school graduate must complete 5 years of university training and must present a thesis, after which the degree of *licenciado en psicología* is granted. It is also possible to obtain magister and specialization degrees in several fields of psychology in Venezuela. Although a relatively small percentage of psychology graduates pursue postgraduate work, the number is increasing. Some, particularly those working in the academic field, have gone abroad to obtain higher degrees.

A doctoral program in psychology was begun at the Universidad Central de Venezuela in 1989. The program is centered on the development of a dissertation related to one of the research programs of the Institute of Psychological Research. It requires a minimum of 3 years of work, and the candidates should preferably hold a master's degree. The number of psychologists may be estimated at around 3,500, with more women than men in the profession. Although no exact statistics are available, the proportion is approximately 3:1. Since psychology training in Venezuela started in 1956 and the boom of the profession was perceptible only in the 1970s, the average psychologist is relatively young. There is no overproduction of psychologists, as only three universities grant degrees, and the supply is in keeping with the demand.

The largest number of psychologists are clinicians, either in institutions or in private practice. They work individually or in mental health teams, both in assessment and in treatment. The second largest number of psychologists work in industry, personnel recruitment and selection, industrial relations, and personnel evaluation and training. Some have established their own consulting firms.

Schools, both public and private, employ psychologists for psychological assessment, treatment of learning disabilities, teacher training, and course evaluation. Counseling in secondary schools and in student services at universities and colleges also engages some psychologists. In addition, psychologists work within the penal system, either in retention centers or as parole officers, and in therapeutic communities. Some work in advertising and in the mass media, and some do community work. Finally, a certain number teach in secondary schools, colleges, and universities.

In 1978 the Law of Psychological Practice was approved by the National Congress, stating that only those holding the degree of *licenciado en psicología* may practice psychology. Psychologists with foreign degrees must submit to a cumbersome process of revalidation to demonstrate that their degrees are equivalent to the local *licenciado* degree. Usually, only university courses that require 5 years and the presentation of a thesis are considered; other training may be used as credit toward the degree.

Characteristics of Psychology

Training

There are only three degree-granting bodies in psychology in the country: Universidad Central de Venezuela (UCV), which is a public university; Universidad Católica Andrés Bello (UCAB), and Universidad Rafael Urdaneta (URU), both of which are private. Undergraduate training extends over 5 years or 10 semesters, with somewhat different curricula. At UCV there is a 3-year common-core training, followed by an optional 2-year period of prespecialization in clinical (behavioral), clinical (psychoanalytic), educational, industrial, counseling, or social psychology. At the other universities certain electives are taken during the last years, but the student obtains a general training.

Graduate programs exist at ucv (magister in behavioral analysis, social psychology, instructional psychology, and human development; specialist in group dynamics; doctorate in psychology); ucab (magister in both organizational development and cognitive psychology); and Universidad Simón Bolivar (usb) (magister and specialization in behavioral technology; counseling, and human development; individual, group, and culture).

Publications

Three journals related to psychology are currently published in Venezuela: *Niños*, the publication of the Instituto Nacional de Psiquiatría Pedagógica (National Institute of Child Psychiatry); *Psicología*, a publication of the Escuela de Psicología de ucv (School of Psychology of ucv), and *Boletín de AVEPSO*, the publication of the Asociación Venezolana de Psicología Social (Venezuelan Association of Social Psychology, avepso). The Centro de Investigaciones Psicológicas (Center for Psychological Research) (formerly the Laboratorio de Psicología [Laboratory of Psychology]) of the Universidad de los Andes (University of the Andes, ula) publishes research reports under the general name of *Monografías*, and avepso publishes a series of *Fascículos* of similar character.

Extensive use is made of American and European journals, and conicit (Consejo Nacional de Investigaciones Científicas y Tecnológicas, National Council for Scientific and Technological Research) is connected to the most important psychological information data bases. The university libraries have reasonably good collections of foreign journals, and the Library of the School of Psychology at ucv has an outstanding collection of psychological journals dating to the early 1980s. At that time the sudden drop in the rate of exchange made these purchases too expensive and forced a reduction in the number of titles acquired. There is growing interest in making use of Latin American journals, and to this end a Center of Latin American Psychological Information (cipla) has been organized at the Institute of Psychology of ucv.

Recently, more psychology books have been published in Venezuela, as local psychologists have become more productive and foreign books have become expensive, especially those coming from the usa and Europe. Nevertheless, a good number of titles published in Mexico, Spain, and Argentina are widely available.

Some firms specialize in the distribution of psychometric tests and laboratory instruments. Hence it is possible to have access to this material currently in the market, even though an unreasonably long time must be allowed for shipment and delivery.

Organizations

After the law of Psychological Practice was passed by the National Congress (1978), a federation of psychologists was established. La Federación Venezolana de Psicólogos is legally recognized by the government, and all practicing psychologists must hold membership in one of the *colegios* that form part of it and that correspond to each one of the states of the country. The *colegios* and the federation have as their main objectives the defense of the profession and the improvement of the working conditions of members of the profession. At the same time, they aim to keep unqualified people from working in the field.

In a parallel organizational structure there are scientific societies that maintain a loose relationship with the federation. These are the Asociación Venezolana de Psicología Social (AVEPSO), the Sociedad Venezolana de Psicología Escolar (SOVEPSE), the Sociedad Venezolana de Psicología del Deporte, and the Sociedad Venezolana de Psicología Humanistica. The first two have held several biennial scientific meetings. No national congress of psychology has taken place, although several international psychological events have been organized in the country, such as the 20th Interamerican Congress of Psychology, held in 1987.

Funding

Government funding for the discipline has been channeled mostly through the universities, which support training and research programs. The government-sponsored scholarship program, FUNDAYACUCHO, placed psychology among its priority areas in 1980. Since then many students have traveled to the USA and Europe for postgraduate training. More recently, financial support has been given to local postgraduate programs, such as scholarships to students and funds to bring staff from abroad for brief sojourns.

For research, the main funding source is CONICIT, with nationwide coverage, and the Council for Scientific and Humanistic Development (CDCH), within each of the universities. Some private foundations also provide funds for research projects.

Social Status

Psychology is a very popular subject among high school students. In the universities the ratio of applicants to available places is one of the highest among university options, sometimes surpassing medicine. Psychologists have attained many high positions in Venezuela: at least two have become ministers in the national cabinet and several have been or are members of the National Congress, presidents of national universities and deans of faculties.

Although psychological services are not evenly distributed and most psychologists work in the larger cities, there has been an increase in the number of psychologists working in smaller localities, often in government agencies, in the Ministries of Education, Family, or Justice. The psychologist is no longer a mysterious character, as in the 1950s. Even people in the provinces have come to appreciate the role of the psychologist, at least in relation to behavioral and school problems. And psychologists have even been cast as heroes and/or villains in locally produced television serials.

Evolution of Psychology

In Venezuela the discipline started in the late 1950s and early 1960s under eclectic influences. In the late 1960s psychology came increasingly under the influence of behaviorism, both in its radical (Skinnerian) version and in its cognitive-social modality. The influence of the experimental analysis of behavior became particularly important in the Department of Clinical Psychology and in the Laboratory of the Institute of Psychology of UCV. In addition, it became important in the Department of Behavioral Technology of USB and, for a period, also at UCAB. Social psychology, as an area of study and a theoretical orientation, with emphasis on cognitive aspects, also acquired importance from the 1970s onward, particularly in the UCV but at USB as well. Psychoanalysis, which after a period of influence was abandoned at the universities, has had a comeback in some academic circles in the 1980s, and psychologists with that orientation have also become organized and active.

As far as connections with the power structure of government are concerned, the most successful group has been the developmental psychologists. Coming from a strong Piagetian orientation, they acquired significant positions in the Ministry of Intelligence during the 1979–84 period. Their project was an ambitious attempt to stimulate cognitive development nationwide through diverse projects directed at different age levels. After the governmental change in 1984, some of these projects disappeared, some were incorporated into the Ministry of Education, and still others were taken over, although with a less ambitious scope, by private organizations.

Among the leading native psychologists deserving mention, together with their field specialties or outstanding achievements, are the following: Julia Becerra de Penfold (experimental analysis of behavior), Eric Becker (founder of the Federation of Psychologists), María J. Bustamante (groups), José María Cadenas (developmental and social psychology), Henry Casalta (experimental analysis of behavior), Max Contasti (measurement), Edmundo Chirinos (president of UCV), Miriam Dembo (experimental analysis of behavior), Yolanda de Venanzi (social psychology), Senta Essenfeld (guidance), Nusia Feldman (educational psychology), Josefina Fierro de Ascanio (educational psychology), Elena Granell (experimental analysis of behavior), Elisa Jiminez (sexual behavior), Felicitas Kort (clinical), Aline Lampe (president of two national universities), María Luisa Lodo-Platone (group dynamics), Beatriz Manrique (developmental psychology), Andrés Minarro (electoral behavior), Maritza Montero (social psychology), Juan B. Moretti (industrial psychology), Carlos Muñoz (social psychology), Carlos Noguera (developmental psychology), Alfonso Orantes (instructional psychology), Miguel Padrón (general psychology), Guillermo Pérez Enciso (founder of the School of Psychology, UCV), Carlos Pittaluga (experimental analysis of behavior), Mercedes Pulido (exminister for women), Oswaldo Romero-García (social-educational psychology), Ileana Recagno-Puente (developmental-social), Roberto Ruiz (experimental analysis of behavior), José Miguel Salazar (social psychology), Euclides Sánchez (social psychology), Ligia Sánchez (general psychology), Eduardo Santoro (social psychology), and Milena Sardi (exminister for the family).

Research in Venezuela is conducted mainly at the universities. It is most frequent at UCV, where an Institute of Psychology has been functioning since 1950, and at ULA, which has a Center for Psychological Research.

Among the main areas of research being conducted in the country are the following: (1) theoretical and empirical work to establish continuity between operant and classical conditioning (UCV), (2) early stimulation and ecological factors and their effect on child development (UCV), (3) effects of mass media, particularly television, on the formation of stereotypes in children (UCV), (4) nationalism, national identity, and the ideology of dependence (UCV), (5) sociopsychological factors affecting academic achievement (including locus of control, motivation, language) (ULA), (6) instructional psychology (UCV), (7) environmental psychology and community participation (UCV), (8) cognitive development in youth (UCV), (9) human resources optimization (USB), (10) family integration (UCAB-UCV), and (11) development of intelligence (Ministry of Education and several private enterprises organized by former members of the Ministry of Intelligence).

Bibliography

Del Olmo, F., & Salazar, J. M. (1981). 30 años de Instituto de Psicología. In Instituto de Psicología, *Contribuciones recientes a la psicología en Venezuela*. Caracas: UCV.

Escuela de Psicología, UCAB. (1984). *Catálogo de investigaciones*. Caracas: UCAB.

Salazar, J. M., & Rodríguez, P. (1986). 10 años de investigacíon psicologíca en Venezuela. In Instituto de Psicología, *Contribuciones a la psicología en Venezuela: Vol. 2*. Caracas: UCV.

Salazar, J. M., & Sánchez, L. (1987). Psychology in Venezuela. In A. R. Gilgen & C. K. Gilgen, (Eds.), *International handbook of psychology* (pp. 557–573). New York: Greenwood Press.

Sánchez, E., Weisenfeld, E., & Cronick, K. (1983). Environmental psychology in Venezuela. *Journal of Environmental Psychology, 3*, 161–172.

44 / Yugoslavia

VID PEČJAK

Vid Pečjak (born 1929) received his PhD from the University of Ljubljana in 1966 and continued with postgraduate work at the University of Illinois in 1977–78. A specialist in cognition, psycholinguistics, theory in psychology, and the history of psychology, he has published three books: Psychology of Cognition, Psychology in the Making, *and* Distinguished Psychologists. *Pečjak has served as consulting editor for the journal* Anthropos *and as foreign editor for the* Encyclopedia of Psychology. *A recipient of a British Council Fellowship, a Ford Foundation Fellowship, and a National Science Foundation Fellowship, he has been a visiting professor in both the United States and Australia. He is professor of psychology at the University Edvard Kardelj of Ljubljana.*

To a large extent, psychology in Yugoslavia has been determined by its national, cultural, economic, historical, and even geographical characteristics. Yugoslavia became an independent country only after 1918. Before that time some parts had belonged to neighboring countries, while other parts had been independent. In 1945 it became a socialist federal republic consisting of six federal units, which are named republics: Socialist Republic (SR) Serbia, SR Croatia, SR Slovenia, SR Macedonia, SR Montenegro, and SR Bosnia and Herzegovina. After World War II it underwent rapid industrial development with a marked change in the educational level of the population. Yet three republics, Slovenia, Croatia, and (partially) Serbia, are still more highly developed than the rest.

Psychological Practice and Work Settings

Although the origins of Yugoslav psychology go back to the Renaissance and to the Enlightenment period of the 18th century, psychology became an empirical science only after World War I. At that time approximately 20 psychologists were engaged in the field. After World War II development became more rapid. Now there are about 4,500 psychologists in the country, the majority in the three more developed republics. Nearly three quarters of them are employed as applied psychologists, most of them in clinical, educational, or industrial psychology.

Because of the rapid industrialization of the country, industrial psychology developed swiftly after World War II, but in recent years the economic recession has slowed its growth. Yet it is still one of the most diversified psychological disciplines. These psychologists are involved in such areas as job analysis, professional education, advertising, and marketing. Many of them work in industry and some in special employment agencies, management institutions, and centers for marketing.

About 25 percent of psychologists work in the field of educational and school psychology. They are mostly employed by schools, but some of them work in special educational institutions. Most work as counselors, but some also as teachers in the high schools having psychology as a course. Some 30 percent of elementary schools in Slovenia, Croatia, and Serbia employ a psychologist. This percentage is much smaller in the other republics.

Clinical psychology is among the most prominent fields of applied psychology, particularly in the three developed republics, and employs more than 25 percent of psychologists. Clinical psychologists work in hospitals, medical and counseling centers, centers for social work, and prisons. Most of them work with physicians, especially psychiatrists. Sometimes disagreement arises between them, though generally they cooperate well, and some psychologists hold significant positions in medical institutions. Clinical psychologists are involved in diagnostic as well as therapeutic work, though more often in the former. They use a variety of clinical methods deriving from different orientations, such as psychoanalysis, client-centered therapy, behavior therapy, transactional analysis, and Gestalt and radex therapy.

Besides the classical applied disciplines, others have developed as well, especially traffic psychology, sport psychology, forensic psychology, military psychology, ecological psychology, and economic psychology. It is said that only space psychology is not included in Yugoslav applied psychology.

About 15 percent of psychologists work in the academic field, mostly at universities, colleges, and research institutes. Quite a few psychologists work in other professions that are close to psychology—for example, as educators, reporters, and politicians. In big cities, especially the capitals of the more developed republics, some psychologists are unemployed. Unemployment is not severe, but it is on the rise.

Applied psychology is more a female than a male profession. The general ratio is 4:1, yet in some fields, such as industrial psychology, the ratio is more in favor of men. Academic staff is mostly male. In the 1950s the general ratio was almost 1:1.

Education

Every psychologist must have a diploma, which may be obtained after 4 years of study at a department of psychology. To obtain the diploma, one must pass more psychological courses than are required for the bachelor's degree in the USA. In addition, one must pass a final exam requiring an integrated knowledge of psychology. A written paper of some length, often empirical, must also be submitted. The diploma makes one eligible to work as a professional psychologist and to become a member of a psychological society.

About 15 percent of students continue with postgraduate studies, which last 2 more years, resulting in a master's degree. The students are obliged to pass certain courses and a final exam, but the emphasis is on the master's thesis, which is usually empirical and quite elaborate. Another 5 percent of the students go on to defend a doctoral dissertation, a comprehensive research project requiring independent thought. Students having an MA degree, or a certain number of published scientific papers, are accepted as PhD candidates.

The majority of psychologists study psychology in their own republics (except when their universities have no department of psychology). Only rarely do they study abroad, and as a rule only for the MD or PhD degree. About 20 Yugoslav psychologists work permanently abroad, mostly at universities in America and Australia.

Study in psychology is offered at eight Yugoslav universities, located in Zagreb (since 1920), Belgrade (since 1928), Ljubljana (since 1950), Nis (since 1971), Skopje (since 1975), Rijeka (since 1978), Zadar (since 1979), and Novi Sad (since 1982). All of them, except the department in Nis, offer both graduate and undergraduate training. The departments all offer the basic courses in theoretical and applied psychology, which are mandatory. These are general psychology (perception, learning), personality, developmental psychology, social psychology, psychometrics, statistics, psychophysiology, psychopathology, industrial psychology, educational psychology, and clinical psychology. These courses may be labeled differently in some departments. Some other courses differ in content from university to university. A few courses may be found only at certain universities, such as traffic psychology, ecological psychology, or the history of psychology. Many of these are optional. The length of some courses varies from university to university as well. A two-term course at one university may take four terms at another.

At most universities students attend lectures but also undergo some practical training in laboratories and institutions, such as schools or clinics. Term papers are also important. Each student must submit several papers during the 4 to 6 years of study.

Journals and Societies

In Yugoslavia five psychological journals are currently published: *Acta Instituti Psychologici Universitatis Zagrabiensis* (since 1932), published sporadically by the Psychological Institute at the University of Zagreb; *Revija za Psihologiju* (Psychological journal, since 1970), published twice a year by the Association of Yugoslav Psychological Societies; *Psihologija* (Psychology, since 1967), published quarterly by the Psychological Society of Serbia; *Primenjena Psihologija* (Applied psychology, since 1980), published quarterly by the Psychological Society of Croatia; *Anthropos* (since 1968), published six times yearly by the Psychological Society of Slovenia and some other professional societies of this republic. These journals are general in subject matter and publish a variety of papers, though *Acta Instituti* publishes mostly experimental reports and *Applied Psychology* gives priority to applied psychology. In addition, special newsletters publishing information about psychology in the country and abroad are issued by the psychological societies of Croatia, Serbia, and Slovenia. Reports from national congresses and conferences are usually published in special books.

In 1950 the Psychological Association of Yugoslavia was founded, together with Psychological Societies of Croatia, Serbia, and Slovenia. In the 1960s and 1970s the Psychological Societies of Macedonia, Bosnia and Herzegovina, and Montenegro were also established. Recently, the association changed its name to the Association of Psychological Societies of Yugoslavia. The societies work quite independently, organizing meetings, courses, and lectures and publishing psychological literature. The association is supervised by a committee, which has mostly a coordinative role. Every 3 years the republic from which the president is appointed is rotated. At the same time the residence of the committee is changed as well; for example, during the 1984–86 period the residence was in Zagreb, and beginning in 1987 it was in Belgrade.

Every third or fourth year a congress of Yugoslav psychology is organized. All told, there have been seven psychological congresses, the last five, respectively, in Skopje in 1974, in Sarajevo in 1977, in Zagreb in 1980, in Herceg Novi in 1984, and in Belgrade in 1988, each organized by the society from another republic. Yugoslav psychologists also organized the 15th International Congress of Applied Psychology in Ljubljana in 1964. The number of papers presented at congresses has rapidly grown, forming a kind of positively accelerated curve. Now the growth is diminishing, and the curve is reaching a plateau.

Facilities and Support

Working places of psychologists used to be sufficiently equipped with tests, instruments, and literature decades ago, but since the economic crisis the situation has grown worse. Even departments of psychology at the universities cannot provide enough literature and the most necessary equipment. Yet most of them have at their disposal university computer facilities. It is not likely that the situation will improve in the near future.

Psychological research is sponsored either directly by various institutions, such as factories and hospitals, or more often by special self-governmental committees, similar to foundations, which are typical of the Yugoslav social system. The budgetary contracts for scientific projects are based on agreement between the representatives of various branches of economy and science. Psychology used to receive much support for its research, but in the 1980s the sources grew smaller.

Educational work at schools and departments is supported by similar foundations. Financial support for education, laboratory equipment, and library facilities is not sufficient, and the situation is becoming worse.

In the past the ordinary citizen viewed psychology quite favorably. Its services were offered to every citizen regardless of sex, social status, age, or other social factors. In recent years public opinion about psychology has been less favorable, a change that is at least partially due to the field's relative inefficiency. In Yugoslavia psychology is a young science, and it seems that expectations were too high. Much of its inefficiency is caused by the unfavorable economic situation. The reputation of a psychologist is also very dependent on the quality of his or her individual work and personality.

Approaches in Psychology

Yugoslav theoretical psychology is a mixture of various opinions, theories, systems, and ideological approaches. Generally speaking, it is quite eclectic, though it has followed different individual orientations at different historical periods. The following orientations have been the most influential.

(1) *Marxism and Marxist psychology.* Immediately after World War II Yugoslav psychology was under pressure to conform to the Soviet version of Marxism, though it lasted only a short period and was never fully ac-

cepted by the leading Yugoslav psychologists. After this period Yugoslav philosophers, aided by some psychologists, tried to create a kind of Marxism based on "real" and "original Marx," "young Marx," and especially the Frankfurt school of Marxism. Today Marxism is less likely to be included in psychological theory. Yet it is still important and is based mostly on the Frankfurt school. Other influences include German critical psychology, the Yugoslav self-governmental theory and practice, and even existentialism, the Reichian movement, antipsychiatry, and Lacanian structural psychoanalysis, a coexistence of quite diverse orientations. Orthodox Marxism is much less popular, though it is still strong in official ideology.

(2) *Positivism.* This approach has been active since the foundation of the first psychological laboratory in Zagreb in 1920. The psychologists following this line of thinking emphasize experimentation, psychometric foundations, measurement of psychological phenomena, and validation. The orientation is especially influential at departments of psychology and psychological institutes, but most of all at the University of Zagreb. Because of this orientation much of Yugoslav psychology has rid itself of speculation and metaphysics.

(3) *The physiological and psychophysical orientation.* Croatian psychology has been oriented toward the study of physiological psychology and sensory processes from its beginning. These processes were in the forefront of investigation in the first laboratory in Zagreb. This line was later resumed under the guidance of Z. Bujas, who had been educated in Paris (French psychology has always been physiologically oriented). The school conducted extensive experimentation resulting in many original findings. To some extent it influenced other psychological centers in Yugoslavia.

(4) *Behaviorism and Pavlovian psychology.* Although there is no psychology in Yugoslavia calling itself behavioristic psychology, the orientation has had some influence on Yugoslav academic and applied psychology. The processes of learning are studied, and behavior therapy is practiced at some clinical institutions.

(5) *Psychoanalysis.* Although the tradition goes back to the period before World War II, when many of Freud's books were translated into the Serbocroatian language, psychoanalysis in its original form was spread more among psychiatrists than psychologists. The latter have been influenced by some neoanalytic ideas (e.g., by Schultz-Hencke), the neo-Reichian movement, and recently, by a small but very active group of Lacanian structural psychoanalysts. Psychoanalytical ideas are generally more typical of clinical psychology than academic psychology.

(6) *Humanistic psychology and related ideas.* This movement is relatively new and has spread among all kinds of psychologists, though nowhere

is it dominant. Such movements as psychodynamics, Gestalt therapy, and transactional therapy are comparatively strong, particularly among young psychologists.

(7) *Cognitive psychology* is tied especially to academic psychology. Piaget is much appreciated, and a group from Belgrade has further developed his ideas. In Ljubljana computer simulation of human behavior is practiced by some scientists who are not psychologists.

Current Research

Yugoslav theoretical psychology has not been very original. At best, it tried to modify some paradigms or to adjust them to its findings. Yugoslav empirical psychology, however, has been more fruitful. One of its main and most successful fields is psychophysics, together with sensory processes, both of which have yielded some original observations and ideas.

One of the primary tasks of Yugoslav psychophysics has been to modify present methods and devise new ones to reduce such shortcomings as excessive variability of results, unsuitability of scales for precise judgment, incongruity of units, or the effect of nonsensory factors. A group of scientists (S. Szabo, A. Rohacek, Z. Vukosav) guided by Z. Bujas devised some effective new psychophysical methods—for example, the method of perception of stimulus increments, the confidence rating method, and the method of minimal and maximal judgments. In addition, many other psychophysical problems have been studied, such as the influence of context on judgments (S. Szabo, A. Kolesaric, J. Gregorac, K. Brenk) and the effect of training on the capacity of sensory channels (A. Fulgosi, B. Zaja, D. Bacun). Bujas and Ostojcic discovered that adaptation is not a unitary process that could be defined as general diminution of sensory sensitivity. Another important discovery was made by A. Trstenjak concerning reaction times for colors, found to depend on wavelength.

Many Yugoslav psychologists have been engaged in devising new tests or adapting foreign tests (B. Stevanovic, Z. Bujas, I. Tolicic, V. Smiljanic, R. Kvascev, I. Stajnberger, T. Lamovec) and in subjecting them to factor analysis (K. Momirovic, M. Bogdanovic, A. Fulgosi). The Binet-Simon test was standardized in 1934 (Stevanovic); psychomotor abilities (M. Cuk, K. Momirovic) and creativity (R. Kvascev, I. Dizdarevic, D. Zagar, A. Fulgosi) have been studied for a long time.

Psycholinguistics has long been one of the interests of Yugoslav experimental psychology (S. Savic, G. Opacic, A. Fulgosi, O. Glamus, V. Pečjak, I. Ivic, J. Musek, I. Todorova-Cvejic, P. Ognjenovic). The Yugoslav psycholinguists investigate all kinds of problems, from the origin of language to the question of function and structure of language, and physiology of speech. Every year since 1985 they have organized a conference on their research.

Nowadays there is hardly an important academic field that has not been investigated by Yugoslav psychologists. The following are especially notable: detection of signals (I. Stajnberger, B. Sverko), personality traits (J. Musek, A. Fulgosi, B. Popovic), values (J. Musek), learning (S. Radonjic, A. Fulgosi), human symbols (V. Pečjak, J. Musek, M. Polic), and ecology (M. Polic).

Yugoslav developmental psychology has an old tradition, and the first such studies were initiated at the beginning of the century (B. Stevanovic). Today research is related to the problem of readiness for school (I. Tolicic, V. Smiljanic), cognitive development (I. Ivic, L. Horvat, L. Umek), gifted children (J. Makarovic, Z. Ivezic, N. Jausovec), and the process of aging (P. Turcinovic, V. Smiljanic).

Yugoslav social psychologists primarily investigate problems related to the Yugoslav social, political, and national system, such as political attitudes (I. Sibar, J. Obradovic, R. Supek, R. Bojanovic), national belonging (N. Rot, J. Lazaroski, N. Havelka), and self-management of workers (N. Rot, M. Zvonarevic, N. Havelka, J. Obradovic, B. Kuzmanovic), but also social perception (N. Havelka, P. Turcinovic), psychology of women and sexes (V. Smiljanic), and family psychology (N. Kapor Stanulovic, G. Cacinovic).

Industrial psychologists have done considerable experimentation on fatigue (Z. Bujas, B. Petz, V. Kolesaric). Now research is focused on work accidents (B. Petz, D. Stary), ergonomics (B. Sverko, L. Sebek, D. Taborsak, S. Milosevic), and motivation for work (E. Konrad). School psychologists investigate primarily the process of teaching (B. Marentic, R. Kvascev) and factors influencing school success (L. Zorman, I. Tolicic, L. Vucic). Clinical psychology is mostly an applied discipline, but some studies are performed here, too—for instance, on legastenia (B. Sali), psychosomatics (B. Sali, M. Pajntar), and epilepsy (J. Turdui-Simunec, J. Rojsek).

The main centers of research are departments of psychology at the universities and the institutes of psychology. At present there are two research institutes of psychology in Yugoslavia: at the University of Belgrade (since 1961) and the University of Zagreb (since 1929). Research is also done at other institutes where psychologists are employed, especially at institutes of sociology and of education, and some at institutes of criminology, economy, medical research, experimental phonetics and speech pathology, which are located in the capitals of some republics.

The differences among the main centers are considerable. In Zagreb, the capital of Croatia, the academic, "hard," experimental, positivistic, psychometric, and physiological psychology prevails, though some other branches, such as social psychology, are also stressed. In Belgrade, the capital of Serbia and Yugoslavia, clinical, social, educational, and developmental psychology are the most developed, though research on some other problems, such as signal detection, is prominent. Psychology in Belgrade is relatively "soft" and heterogeneous. In Ljubljana, the capital of Slovenia, psychology is heterogeneous, too, with an emphasis on personality, cognition, developmental processes, and applied disciplines. Other centers are younger and less structured. At the University of Skopje and the University of Novi Sad psycholinguistics is a favored research topic.

Yugoslav psychology was stagnant in the 1980s. The number of investigations and books on psychology is smaller, and unemployment among psychologists is on the rise; there is little growth in job opportunities. This situation is probably due to the extensive growth of psychology in the recent past and to the present economic recession. It is not likely that the situation will change much in this century.

Bibliography

Brozek, J. (1972). Quantitative explorations in the history of psychology in Yugoslavia. *Psychological Reports, 31*, 397–398.

Bujas, Z. (1972). Psihofizika nekad i danas. In *Psiholoske razprave* (pp. 16–19). Ljubljana: Drustvo psihologa Slovenije.

Pečjak, V. (1981). Kratki prikaz razvoja psihologije u Jugoslaviji. *Primenjena Psihologija, 2*, 77–91, 191–199, 205–216.

Pečjak, V. (1984). *Nastajanje psihologije*. Sarajevo: Univerzum.

Stary, D. (1975). Publicirani radovi jugoslovenskih psihologa. *Revija za Psihologiju, 5*, 129–135.

Zvonarevic, M. (1964). A review of the development of psychology in Yugoslavia. *Bulletin de l'Association Internationale de Psychologie Appliquée, 13*, 3–8.

45 / Zimbabwe

JOSEPHINE JORDAN

Josephine Jordan (born 1957) specializes in psychometrics, occupational psychology, and cross-cultural psychology. As a lecturer in the Department of Psychology, University of Zimbabwe, she is responsible for professional postgraduate training in occupational psychology. She received her academic training at the University of Zimbabwe and her professional training with Human Resources (Pvt) Ltd, Harare. Jordan was president of the Zimbabwe Psychological Association from 1985 to 1987.

Characteristics of the Psychologist

Licensing

Psychological practice in Zimbabwe is governed by the Psychological Practices Act of 1971. All practicing psychologists are required to be registered with the Health Professions Council. The council maintains a single register of practicing psychologists, not distinguishing among sub-disciplines. Subsidiary legislation requires practicing psychologists to limit themselves to those activities for which they have been adequately trained. In early 1988 the register contained 51 names, of which 28 were women. Of those psychologists currently registered, 44 registered for the first time after national independence in 1980.

Training

Psychologists are registered as practitioners in Zimbabwe if they hold a 3-year honors degree in psychology, or the equivalent, and either a recognized postgraduate qualification or a 3-year internship supervised by a registered psychologist. The University of Zimbabwe offers a 3-year honors program and four alternative postgraduate programs.

Students enter the honors program with British "O" and "A" levels, or the equivalent, and are required to select 80 percent of their courses from the Psychology Department. After graduation, students are able to apply for one of the four postgraduate programs. A 2-year MSc (clinical psychology) program is provided by the Department of Educational Foundations. Entry qualifications to this program, in addition to the honors degree, are 2 years of teaching experience or 1 year of experience in the School Psychological Services of the Ministry of Education. Students are also required to be suitably employed for the duration of the program. Finally, students may read for a research degree, the MPhil, for which they must conduct a major piece of research under the supervision of an academic staff member.

Employment

The two major employers of psychologists in Zimbabwe are the School Psychological Services in the Ministry of Education and the University of Zimbabwe. The Ministry of Education has posts for 37 psychologists and trainees, and the university has posts for 12 lecturers and 3 teaching assistants, with unlimited possibilities for research scholars, assistants, and fellows. The Ministry of Health will, in time, become a major employer. A variety of other ministries and work organizations employ psychologists. A new graduate has no difficulty in finding a post in which to complete his or her professional training and be paid for the duration of the postgraduate degree.

Professional Society

Professional psychology began in Zimbabwe with the promulgation of the Psychological Practices Act of 1971. At that time psychology was already being taught in the Department of Sociology at the University of Zimbabwe, and some foreign-trained psychologists were already practicing.

As a consequence of the Psychological Practices Act, psychologists in Zimbabwe formed the Zimbabwe Psychological Association. The professional society has the dual function of promoting and controlling professional activity. To coordinate control, the Health Professions Council has a subcommittee, the Psychological Practices Advisory Committee, made up of five members representing clinical psychologists, educational psychologists, occupational psychologists, government psychologists, and academics. The academic member is the chairperson of the Department of Psychology at the University of Zimbabwe. The remaining members are elected by the full members of the association, who choose a convenor from among themselves. The Psychological Practices Advisory Committee is charged with all matters dealing with regulations, misconduct, and related issues. The convenor is an ex officio member of the council, which has powers of veto in professional affairs, but not rights of initiation.

The Health Professions Council has six other officers who are elected to their specific positions of president, vice-president, secretary, treasurer, seminar convenor, and *Feedback* editor. The seminar convenor is responsible for organizing seminars and symposia, usually in Harare, on a monthly basis. *Feedback* is the association's newsletter/bulletin, which is published twice yearly, running approximately 30 pages per issue. *Feedback* has a sub-editor who assists with the acquisition of copy.

Scientific Infrastructure

Numerous academic journals in the southern Africa region are suitable for psychological publications. Three of the main Zimbabwean journals are *Zambezia*, *Zimbabwe Journal of Educational Research*, and *Central African Journal of Medicine*.

The University of Zimbabwe and the Ministry of Education have access to large computer installations with numerical analysis packages, including applied statistics. The Department of Psychology also has microcomputers suitable for experimental psychology, a well-equipped laboratory, and a library of foreign tests. The University of Zimbabwe Library is known for its excellent stock and effective management. It is currently reorganizing its journal system to include more journals from the Third World which are generally acquired through interuniversity exchange agreements. Funds for research are made available from the state, through the university, and are allocated by the University of Zimbabwe Research Board.

Relationship of Psychology to Other Professions and the Public

The Psychological Practices Act established psychology as a profession and limits those activities commonly associated with psychology to registered psychologists. Consequently, there is a boundary, which is not always free from conflict, between psychology and the professions of personnel management, clinical social work, medicine, and the church.

A second relevant act of parliament, promulgated since national independence in 1980, is the Traditional Medical Practitioners Act of 1981. This act governs the practice of traditional healing, which exists in parallel with "modern" psychology and medicine. Relations between the Zimbabwe Psychological Association and the Zimbabwe National Traditional Healers Association are patchy; they exist (to the extent that they do) only because the president of the Traditional Healers Association is also a professor in the Department of Sociology of the University of Zimbabwe. On the whole, services provided by members of the Zimbabwe Psychological Association are available in urban areas, to clients who are able to pay, and to institutions such as teacher training colleges. The traditional healers provide psychological care for the bulk of the population.

Current Status of Psychology

Psychology in the University of Zimbabwe has been dominated by the cross-cultural paradigm. Research began as early as 1963 in the Faculty of Education, by Sidney Irvine, now of Plymouth Polytechnic, England. Irvine's work initiated a strong tradition of both psychometric competence and caution in the use of psychometrics. The origins of the Department of Psychology in the Department of Sociology left a further imprint. Psychologists were engaged to teach applied psychology, and the department has retained this orientation.

Since national independence in 1980, the Department of Psychology has seen both the return of Zimbabwean psychologists from abroad and the employment of domestically trained psychologists. It is difficult in the span of 8 years to isolate those contributions that are more important than others. The focus of Zimbabwean psychology since 1980 has been to establish the trio of professional training programs and to supply adequate numbers of professionally trained psychologists for public service. The figures quoted earlier indicate how successful this venture has been. The credit goes as much to individuals as to the capacity of Zimbabwean psychologists to pull together.

Bibliography

Each career academic employed in the Department of Psychology at the University of Zimbabwe was asked to volunteer one representative publication for inclusion in this bibliography.

Jordan, J. (in press). Resurrection of the education-psychological testing controversy in Zimbabwe. *Zambezia*.

McMaster, J. M. (1985). Reasons black African adults use to explain their acceptance of sex-role reversals. *Sex Roles, 13,* 393–403.

Mundy-Castle, A., & Bundy, R. O. (in press). Morality in Nigeria. *African Journal of Psychology*.

Myambo, K. (1985). Re-entry: A case study of returning exiles in Zimbabwe. In I. R.

Lagunes, I. R., & Y. H. Poortinga (Eds.), *From a different perspective: Studies of behaviour across cultures* (pp. 49–52). Lisse: Swets & Zeitlinger.

Nyandiya-Bundy, S. (1986). *Child abuse and neglect in Zimbabwe: The initiation of a study.* Paper presented at the First African Network on the Prevention of and Protection against Child Abuse and Neglect (ANPPCAN) International Workshop, Enugu, Nigeria.

Wilson, D. J., & Wilson, C. (in press). Knowledge of AIDS among Zimbabwean teacher-trainees before the public awareness campaign. *Central Africa Journal of Medicine.*

Epilogue

Fifty-five authors representing 45 countries and geographic areas have described the discipline of psychology as it exists in their respective locales. The variation among their descriptions is substantial, but that was expected. Some nations were among the leaders when modern psychology first emerged as a discipline; others are still trying to define themselves professionally, legally, and ideologically. None is a complete newcomer to psychology, however, and almost all have sufficient development in the discipline to be accepted as members in the International Union of Psychological Science.

An overview of the chapters prompts some questions: Are there different definitions of "psychologist" among countries? What characteristics do psychologists have in common? Is there a core of psychology that is crossnational? What is the future of psychology around the world?

The observations that follow discuss these issues, among several others, and are based largely, although not entirely, on the material contained in the preceding chapters.

Who Is a Psychologist?

Each nation has developed its own definition of a psychologist. It is not surprising to find, therefore, that the definitions vary. The diversity in the discipline can be easily demonstrated by using a single criterion: educational background.

In some countries the bachelor's degree may be sufficient for practice, for others the master's degree is the necessary prerequisite, and for still others the doctorate is required. Within these broad categories, there is further variation. In South America and Central America, for example, many universities offer a 4- or 5-year program leading to the *licenciado* degree. This is a professional degree with no precise counterpart in most other countries. Moreover, even within Latin America there is not total uniformity. In some countries (e.g., Uruguay) much emphasis is placed on acquiring the doctoral degree. By way of contrast, in the USSR the degree approximately equivalent to the PhD is labeled "candidate of psychological sciences." A further degree, the "doctor of psychological sciences," is a more advanced degree and is obtained by only a small percentage of psychologists.

The USA also displays a considerable amount of diversity. Although the

American Psychological Association considers the doctoral degree a requirement for the independent practice of psychology, many people function as
psychologists in schools, state hospitals, and even in private practice without the doctorate. In fact, in most countries the doctoral degree is not required for the practice of psychology. The modal degree for the international
psychologist is the master's degree or its equivalent. In the academic and
scientific areas of psychology, however, the doctorate is more likely to be the
preferred degree.

The Growth and Impact of Psychology

The record of growth in psychology over the last several decades has been phenomenal. The activity in the USA is one clear example. It
took from 1892 to 1929 for the American Psychological Association to grow
to 1,000 members. Since then, however, the growth has been exponential
(Hilgard, 1987), such that by the mid-1980s the APA had more than 60,000
members. In recent years the growth rate has leveled off, but as the rate
in the United States began to wane, rates in many other parts of the world
began to explode.

Among the countries showing particularly rapid growth are Israel, where
since the early 1960s the total number of psychologists has increased more
than 10 times (to almost 2,500), and South Africa, where the number of psychologists tripled during the 1980s alone. However, numbers themselves do
not tell the whole story. In Brazil, for instance, psychology is very popular
(with more than 60,000 psychologists) and there is fierce competition for
entry into graduate programs, but psychologists are poorly paid and the majority of them do not work full-time in the profession. In Spain, with 30,000
psychologists graduated in "recent years," 25 percent of those registered are
unemployed. The lesson is clear. The number and growth of psychologists
in a country is a useful but incomplete measure of the state of the discipline
in that country.

Density of Psychologists

Using estimates of the ratio of psychologists in the general population, we see that in several countries the density of psychologists equals or
exceeds that of the United States. Rosenzweig (1984) identified five (Israel,
Denmark, Sweden, Finland, and Norway), but he noted that the figures
were based on membership in a national society, the percentage of member-

ship in which was variable. He specifically mentioned Brazil as an example in which the total pool of psychologists was large but membership in the national organization was small.

The data reported here may reasonably be compared to that of Rosenzweig, at least in a broad sense. Although they are derived from different sources, both sets of data represent gross estimates of the same phenomenon. Though there is no information on Denmark or Sweden, densities were estimated for 42 countries. It must be emphasized that these figures are only approximations; the actual number of psychologists in most countries is an estimate. The value for the USA was obtained by using an estimate of 125,000 psychologists for the 1988–89 period, a figure that is probably on the low side but is based on several calculations: the last census by the APA in 1983, the rate of new MAs and PhDs, and considerable guesswork. Using a population value of 240 million, we project the USA density of psychologists at 521 per million.

Some countries are estimated to have densities greater than, or approximately equal to, that of the United States. All 42 countries, with their estimated densities, are listed in the appendix. These figures are consistent with Rosenzweig's in showing a great density of psychologists in western Europe, the Scandinavian countries, and Israel. Also of note is the prominence of several South American countries on the list. Considerably lower densities tend to be found in Africa and Third World countries.

The Ratio of Males and Females in the Discipline

Psychology around the world tends to be a female occupation, in some cases dramatically so. For example, in the Dominican Republic 95 percent of the new psychologists are female. In the Philippines the ratio of female to male psychologists is 5:1, in Yugoslavia and Argentina it is 4:1, in Venezuela and Poland 3:1, in Israel 2:1, and so on.

Of all the countries that reported the male/female ratio in the discipline, the number of male psychologists exceeded that of the females only in Australia, Canada, Egypt, Japan, Korea, the Netherlands, New Zealand, Norway, South Africa, and the USA. In most countries, including those in which there are currently more male psychologists, female students are in the majority, suggesting changes for the future. However, there are also countries where females predominate among students but do not go on to work in the same numbers (e.g., Pakistan, Turkey, India). And there is at least one country where the number of males in the profession seems to be on the increase (Colombia).

There is a tendency for subfield differences to exist between the sexes. Where these differences occur, women are more likely to be involved in certain applied settings, including general clinical work, school psychology, and teaching at the college level or below. As a group, women are less likely to be involved in research, industrial psychology, or teaching at a university.

When male/female ratios are compared in various areas of the world, clear differences can be found. For example, among the European countries 53 per cent of all psychologists are women. In South American and Caribbean countries, 70 percent are women. In Asian countries 25 percent are women, with only Hong Kong having a greater number of female psychologists (Ribarich & Sexton, 1987). All of these data suggest highly variable opportunities for women throughout the world in psychology, both educationally and occupationally.

The Status of Licensure and Certification

Some countries have strict licensing laws; others have no form of licensure at all. In between, there are countries with licensing laws pending, other countries with some form of licensing that is not strictly enforced or not clearly defined, and still other countries with a licensing system that is voluntary and implies no legal requirements.

In comparing those countries with clear licensing laws to those with more ambiguous laws or no laws at all, we see some trends. Among western European countries, only 2 of the 13 countries included have no form of licensing and none pending (Ireland and Finland). In both of these countries some form of registration has been projected for the near future. In Belgium licensing laws are pending, while in France a law was passed in 1985 but only implemented in 1990. In the United Kingdom psychologists register with the British Psychological Society, although there is no legal requirement that they do so. In Switzerland no legal protection exists on a national level, but there is some regional regulation. In Italy laws and decrees regulating the practice of psychology were passed in 1989. In Spain licenses are granted by the universities, but the requirements for licensure are not clearly established. In each of the remaining western European countries there is some form of licensure, certification, or registration for psychologists which gives them legal status.

Among eastern European countries, only Hungary reported clear legal regulation of the profession. In Romania there is a certification exam, and in Greece a certification exam was passed in 1979 but has never been implemented. Czechoslovakia has no form of licensing. The remaining eastern European nations did not report on licensing.

In Australia five out of the six states require registration in order to practice. The law in New Zealand is less strict. Psychologists must register only for government positions and for specified education- and health-related jobs.

In the three African countries included in this book, licensure is a legal requirement. South Africa and Zimbabwe have mandatory registration, and Egypt has had a law since 1956 that regulates the clinical practice of psychologists.

In North America both the USA and Canada have some form of legal recognition of the discipline. In the USA regulation of the practice of psychology is the responsibility of each state, and each state has some form of regulation. In Canada regulation of practice is the responsibility of each province, and certification is currently required in all but 1 of the 10 provinces. In Mexico a system of certification exists, but it is not strictly controlled.

In South America there are strict licensing laws in Argentina, Brazil, and Colombia. In Uruguay and Venezuela there is no formal licensing system, but only those with specified degrees or training are recognized as practitioners.

Each of the Third World countries included in this volume has made some attempt to develop regulation, although none has a strictly enforced system. In Cuba the degree is said to be equal to a license. In the Dominican Republic permission by the government is supposed to be necessary to practice, although this policy is not enforced. In the Philippines there is a law pending.

Finally, Asia appears to have the fewest licensing requirements. Korea is the only country reported with licensing. In Japan and Pakistan committees within their respective psychological associations are developing standards. In the remaining two countries, India and Hong Kong, there is no form of licensing.

Despite the variation among countries, the worldwide trend for psychology is to have achieved some degree of legal recognition or to be working toward it. As the record shows, only a few of the countries included have made no effort in that direction.

Science Versus Practice

The general picture of psychology around the world is that of a discipline dominated by practice and much less involved in science. For some countries, such a result is obvious. The demands of the economy, including lack of funding for research, require that all efforts be directed to practical issues. In effect, these countries cannot afford the luxury of research. However, even in those parts of the world long-established in psychology—for example, Western Europe and the United States—an increasing number of psychologists are moving into the practice arena.

In some countries science still predominates and there is little or no practice. India, Romania, and the USSR are three examples where the scientific/research emphasis continues. At least in the case of the USSR, however, there is considerable nonclinical application in the schools, armed forces, and industry.

In some countries psychologists are employed primarily in educational settings: Australia, Egypt, Korea, Pakistan, and Zimbabwe. Other countries, such as Norway and Switzerland, consider themselves about equally balanced between science and practice. In Finland, while practice dominates, there has been a recent effort to emphasize the more scientific aspects of psychology, with government grants for research being doubled for the period 1987–91. The report from Italy indicates that since 1973 there has been a large increase in the number of teaching and research positions in psychology. An example of the opposite trend, a strong practitioner orientation, is that of Turkey, where there are five graduate departments of psychology, all in clinical psychology. Other strongly practice-oriented countries include Argentina, Austria, Brazil, Cuba, the Dominican Republic, Greece, Hong Kong, Hungary, Ireland, Israel, Mexico, the Philippines, Poland, South Africa, Uruguay, Venezuela, and Yugoslavia. The United States, although becoming increasingly practice-oriented, remains a leader in psychological research, in part because of the sheer size of its psychological community.

Public Image

The image of psychology among most nations is a positive one. In some cases, the discipline has had to battle back from being associated with charlatans and magicians; in other cases, such confusion still exists. However, the general public has become increasingly aware of the role of the psychologist, and in many countries that is translated into prestige and economic benefit, although neither of these items is universal. There is much less attention paid to the scientific basis for psychology, but that is consistent with the state of the discipline in many countries.

Some countries do not fit the general picture. In India the ordinary citizen is totally unaware of psychology, while in Zimbabwe most "psychological services" are provided to the public by traditional healers. Psychology was synonymous with psychoanalysis for many years in Pakistan, which caused conflict with moral and religious beliefs. In addition, most of the psychology is taught from Western textbooks, distancing it from the realities of life in Pakistan—poverty, overpopulation, corruption, illiteracy—and thereby causing it to remain an alien discipline. Some countries report that psychologists are still confused with psychiatrists (for example, Australia and Uruguay) or that the image of psychologists has suffered for their lack of medical training (France and the United Kingdom).

Major Influences

Although the influence of the usa is considerable, it is far from the only one. Only a few nations acknowledge the usa as their single major influence. Some nations consider their own historical influences to be the greatest force in their psychology (e.g., France, Hungary, New Zealand, the ussr). Others acknowledge the contributions of western Europe, Great Britain, and the United States combined (e.g., Brazil, Ireland, Norway, Romania). Still others list a more complicated set of forces governing their discipline, including a mixture of Eastern and Western thought (e.g., Hong Kong, Japan). It may be worth noting that the discipline of psychology has not emerged from a single source, with minor variations along the way. The history of international psychology reflects multiple sources resulting in divergent paths with several fundamental differences.

National Emphases

Certain nations have shown themselves to be leaders in particular subfields of psychology. A few of those specialty areas and the countries that are active in their development follow. The list is not meant to be exhaustive.

(1) *Developmental psychology*. West Germany has been strongly committed to developmental psychology, particularly to the study of social and emotional development, and has conducted a considerable amount of funda-

mental research in the area. Great Britain and Norway have made a great investment in the longitudinal study of birth cohorts, an area that does not receive a significant degree of support in the USA.

(2) *Neuropsychology*. The USSR appears to be most advanced in neuropsychological diagnostics and the etiology of neuropsychological deficits. West Germany has been particularly adept at integrating neuropsychological knowledge with allied fields. The USA is strong in some aspects of neuropsychology, including conditioning.

(3) *Social psychology*. The European emphasis on the social psychology of groups and on intergroup conflict and mediation is significant. The emphasis on group psychology in the USA is comparatively weak.

(4) *Sports psychology*. The USSR and some other European countries (e.g., German Democratic Republic, Hungary) have cultivated the area of sports psychology. The USA is only beginning to do so. Basic research in sports psychology focuses on control of autonomic processes and sequences of motor behavior, and covert stimulation. This knowledge has direct application to situations in which effective performance and decision making are critical.

(5) *Cognitive psychology*. While the USA remains a leader in cognitive psychology, other countries have considerable strength in this area. For instance, the United Kingdom is strong in studies of cognitive processes linked to language ability, the interrelationship of cognition and emotion, and temporal orientation of goal-directed problem solving. The USA is relatively weak in cross-cultural studies of cognition, particularly in those related to non-Western cultures that have strategic importance, such as the Middle East and South America.

(6) *Industrial/organizational psychology*. Overall, the United States maintains a leading role in industrial/organizational psychology, especially in studies fostering work productivity and in decision making for personnel selection and training programs. Other countries, however, such as Sweden and Great Britain, are leaders in the study of group behavior, in the identification of stressors in the work environment and their physiological and mental health correlates, and in the investigation of effects of work schedules on job satisfaction. Western European countries, particularly the United Kingdom, have made significant advances in understanding the interrelationship of biological, organizational, and environmental influences on human performance, including the interaction of personality and stress. In contrast, the United States has made its mark in the cognitive realm, specifically human information processing.

(7) *Behavioral research with animals*. The USA is preeminent in laboratory studies of primate behavior, particularly in the psychobiological area. It is also a leader in the study of social behavior of primates in seminaturalistic

settings and is well represented in naturalistic, ethological studies of primates. However, both the United Kingdom and Japan have made significant contributions in behavioral research with primates.

Future Directions

Since this volume was begun, remarkable political turmoil has erupted in several parts of the world, including in some participating countries. Such events underline the need for caution in attempting to describe the future of international psychology. Nonetheless, several trends, mentioned earlier, appear to be of obvious importance to the near future. Other trends, some of which are less clear, also need to be noted.

Current Trends

Among the current trends, three are bound to have repercussions in the future: (1) the rapid growth of psychology throughout the world, including Third World nations and nations that are new to psychology; (2) the disproportionate increase in the number of female psychologists; and (3) the increasing emphasis on practice aspects of the discipline and the decline of the scientific.

As Rosenzweig (1984) has noted, as "psychology spreads to ever more countries and as it continues to grow more rapidly in many other countries than in the United States, American psychology will become a steadily smaller proportion of the world psychological community" (p. 880). This trend will inevitably result in a loss of power in the discipline for the USA. What will be the final result? At least two scenarios present themselves. The USA could continue its relative isolation from psychology in other parts of the world, and an increased fragmentation of psychology could result. More likely, psychology in the USA will respond to modern thought and modern technology; communication between countries has never been more convenient. As convenience is coupled with need—the need to incorporate the most up-to-date and innovative ideas into each psychologist's individual work—a genuine international psychology may emerge, one independent of national boundaries and linguistic barriers and powered principally by the desire to advance the discipline. This is an idealistic notion but certainly a possible one.

The increase in females entering the field is a more complicated issue. Among other items, the increase in women in the discipline is inconsistent among countries. In some countries women have always dominated the field, so that no genuine change has been occurring in recent years. In many other countries the change is authentic, however. In the United States, for example, although the ratio of male to female PhD psychologists is approximately 2:1, those figures are rapidly changing. In 1984, for the first time, the number of females in the USA obtaining doctorates in psychology exceeded the number of males receiving the degree, and the proportion continues to rise. Projections to the turn of the century suggest that the number of women in the discipline will begin to equal the number of men. Will that shift bring problems? According to Denmark (1979), female-typed occupations are devalued cross-culturally, and when women enter previously male-dominated fields, the prestige of the field often drops. Whether such a judgment will remain valid for the next century remains to be seen. If the public image is positive and stable, presumably this tendency could be offset.

The shift from psychology as a scientific discipline to one dominated by practice has been occurring for decades. Nonetheless, the dramatic changes of recent years have the potential for drastically altering the discipline. A unique feature of psychology, even as an applied specialty, has been its research base. Few applied disciplines can claim the rigorous scientific training that was, and perhaps still is, the hallmark of the PhD-trained psychologist. Even though the usual goal of the individual student may be to engage in private practice only, that student is still likely to have extensive training in research methodology and statistics. But there are decreasing numbers of psychologists with the interest and special background to provide such training. If too few psychologist-researchers exist to replenish that base, the training will eventually erode and, with it, the special strength of the psychologist-practitioner will likewise diminish. The result, inevitably, would be a psychology without a science.

Other Possible Trends

Various other trends and observations gleaned from the foregoing chapters need to be commented on. They are less dramatic and, perhaps, not entirely true. But a reading of the chapters suggests their presence if not their importance or undisputed universality. They are mentioned briefly here and in no particular order.

(1) Worldwide psychology continues to undergo a "cognitive" revolution, perhaps in response to its long domination by behaviorism. (2) The public need for a "popularized" psychology is expanding, resulting in publications and other activities that are sometimes speculative and often not supported by research. (3) The influence of psychoanalytic thought has diminished, even in countries where it was the dominant psychological theory. (4) The discipline of psychology continues to expand into new areas, a source of con-

stant replenishment. (5) International psychology has itself become a subject of greater awareness and activity. (6) There has been and continues to be a proliferation of specialty organizations within psychology. (7) Financial support for psychology in recent years has shown no great gain. Finances are either holding constant or decreasing. (8) Computers are almost everywhere, at least for word processing and simple statistics. (9) Increasingly, countries are able to offer adequate preparation and their own degrees, including the PhD, in psychology. There is much less need for going outside of one's country for an education in psychology. (10) Large pockets of unemployment exist for psychologists in diverse countries. Lack of legal recognition is one source. (11) Subdoctoral education for psychologists is the norm for most countries. (12) Females are still not much in evidence in academic positions despite their numbers in the general population of psychologists. (13) Psychology has a surprisingly short history in many countries. Consequently, psychologists around the world tend to be relatively young. (14) The two "modern" names most mentioned in psychology around the world are Skinner and Piaget. (15) Professional journals continue to grow in number, and English seems to be their common language. (16) Animal research is mentioned very sparingly among the countries represented. (17) Although the private practice of psychology is a vital and basic activity among some nations, it is not the modal activity for psychologists around the world. (18) One of the areas in which psychology has found increasing application and acceptance has been in the workplace. (19) Clinical psychology is the dominant specialty around the world, but there is little discussion of humanistic or existential approaches in its practice.

Bibliography

Denmark, F. (1979, July). *The status of women in psychology in the Americas.* Paper presented at the 17th Interamerican Congress of Psychology, Lima, Peru.

Hilgard, E. (1987). *Psychology in America: A historical survey.* San Diego, CA: Harcourt Brace Jovanovich.

Marin, G., Kennedy, S., & Boyce, B. C. (1987). *Latin American psychology: A guide to research and training.* Washington, DC: American Psychological Association.

Ribarich, M. T., & Sexton, V. S. (1987). The status of women psychologists around the world: Report of a survey. *International Psychologist, 29* (3), 22–24.

Rosenzweig, M. R. (1984). U. S. psychology and world psychology. *American Psychologist, 39*, 877–884.

Appendix

Density of Psychologists around the World

Country	Psychologists/ Million Population
The Netherlands	884
Belgium	606
Israel	568
Finland	540
Switzerland	531[a]
Spain	528
United States of America	521
Norway	514
Federal Republic of Germany	490[b]
Brazil	433
Uruguay	387
Italy	348
Australia	342[a]
Argentina	323
France	322
Canada	313
New Zealand	247
United Kingdom	244
Czechoslovakia	226
Venezuela	202
Yugoslavia	192
Cuba	186
Austria	178
Poland	159
Ireland	157
German Democratic Republic	151
Colombia	143[c]
Dominican Republic	134
Hungary	113
South Africa	83
Greece	60
Hong Kong	36

Country	Psychologists/ Million Population
Japan	36
Romania	32
Armenia	29
Union of Soviet Socialist Republics	18
Turkey	14
The Philippines	9
India	7
Korea	7
Pakistan	6
Zimbabwe	6

a For these countries, the density was estimated using the mean of the range given for the number of psychologists.

b Although there were 490 psychologists/million in the FRG, only 261/million were active psychologists.

c The number of students of psychology in Colombia is double that of the number of psychologists currently active.

Name Index

Subject Index